The contemporary history handbook

This volume is dedicated, with gratitude, to two of the leading contemporary historians in the UK: Professor Peter Hennessy and Dr John Ramsden of the Department of History, Queen Mary and Westfield College

The contemporary history handbook

edited by

Brian Brivati,
Julia Buxton and
Anthony Seldon

Manchester University Press

Manchester and New York

distributed exclusively in the USA and Canada by St. Martin's Press

Published by Manchester University Press
Oxford Road, Manchester M13 9BR, UK
and Room 400, 175 Fifth Avenue,
New York, NY 10010, USA

Distributed exclusively in the USA and Canada
by St. Martin's Press, Inc.,
175 Fifth Avenue, New York, NY 10010, USA

British Library Cataloguing-in-Publication Data
A catalogue record for this book is available from the British Library

Library of Congress Cataloging-in-Publication Data
The contemporary history handbook / edited by Brian Brivati, Julia Buxton
   and Anthony Seldon.
        p.   cm.
    Includes bibliographical references.
    ISBN 0–7190–4835–4 — ISBN 0–7190–4836–2 (pbk.)
    1. History, Modern—1945–   I. Brivati, Brian.   II. Buxton, Julia.
III. Seldon, Anthony.
D842.C65   1996
909.82—dc20   95–50535

ISBN 0 7190 4835 4 hardback
ISBN 0 7190 4836 2 paperback

First published in 1996

00 99 98 97 96   10 9 8 7 6 5 4 3 2 1

Typeset in Great Britain
by Northern Phototypesetting Co Ltd, Bolton

Printed in Great Britain
by Bell and Bain Ltd, Glasgow

Contents

Contents

Acknowledgements

My first debt must go to my fellow editors. Anthony Seldon, who edited the first version of this book – and has been the single most important inspiration behind the ICBH – was a constant help. Julia Buxton was instrumental in putting the international section together. In editing a volume with such a wide range of contributors and subjects the greatest debt must be to the writers who have taken time out of their busy schedules to address their topics in ways that – for many of them – were new and distinct from their own research agendas. In these days of the RAE this was a particularly important sacrifice of precious research time and I am deeply grateful. I must particularly thank Tom Nossiter, who, having submitted his chapter on opinion polls, was prevailed upon to write the chapter on India at very short notice, and John Erickson, who, because of my mistake, was also given very short notice of the final deadline – I am grateful to both. I would also like to thank Virginia Preston at the ICBH, Jane Thorniley-Walker, the former, and Vanessa Graham, the present – patient and professional – history editor at MUP, and Mridul for tolerating the intrusion of a forty-chapter book into our lives and home.

Brian Brivati
Stoke Newington, 1995

List of contributors

Gerard Alexander is completing his Ph.D. in political science at Columbia University, New York.

Joe Bailey is a professor of sociology at Kingston University.

Philip Boobbyer is a lecturer in Modern European History at the University of Kent at Canterbury.

Brian Brivati is a lecturer in modern British history at Kingston University.

Julia Buxton is a senior research student at the London School of Economics and is a lecturer in Soviet and East European politics at Kingston University.

Richard Cockett is a lecturer in history at Royal Holloway and Bedford New College, University of London.

Nicholas Cox has been Director of Modern Records at the Public Record Office since 1993.

Dermot Engelfield is a former librarian of the House of Commons.

John Erickson is a professor of history at the University of Edinburgh and director of the Centre for Defence Studies.

Anthony Gorst is a senior lecturer in history at the University of Westminster.

Andrew Graham is a fellow and tutor in economics at Balliol College, Oxford.

Brian Harrison is a reader in modern British history at the University of Oxford.

Edward Higgs is a Wellcome research fellow at the University of Oxford.

Eric Hobsbawm is Emeritus Professor of History at Birkbeck College, University of London.

Chris Hughes teaches international relations at the University of Birmingham and the London School of Economics.

Lorna Hughes is director of the humanities computing facility at Arizona State University.

Harriet Jones is a senior lecturer in contemporary British history at the University of Luton.

Michael Kandiah is a fellow of the Institute of Contemporary British History.

Chandrika Kaul is a research student at Nuffield College, Oxford.

Ian Neary is professor and director of the Contemporary Japan Centre at the University of Essex.

Sian Nicholas is a lecturer in history at the University of Wales, Aberystwyth.

Tom Nossiter is a former professor of government at the London School of Economics.

Lucy Noakes is a part-time tutor in history, women's studies and cultural studies at the University of Sussex.

Elizabeth Meehan is Jean Monnet Professor of Politics at the Queen's University of Belfast.

George Philip is a reader in comparative and Latin American politics at the London School of Economics.

Jeffrey Richards is professor of cultural history at the University of Lancaster.

Michael Roper is a lecturer in the department of sociology at the University of Essex.

Seamus Ross is assistant secretary for information technology at the British Academy and visiting fellow in humanities computing at London Guildhall.

Angela Raspin is an archivist at the British Library of Political and Economic Science, London School of Economics.

Shamit Saggar is a senior lecturer in the department of government at Queen Mary and Westfield College, University of London.

Margaret Scammell is a lecturer in the department of politics and communication studies at the University of Liverpool.

Anthony Seldon is founding director of the Institute of Contemporary British History.

Bradley Smith, formerly of Cabrillo College, Aptos, California, is a historian specialising in intelligence history.

Howard Smith is a senior lecturer in broadcasting at the Institute of Communications Studies, University of Leeds.

Philip Taylor is reader in international communications at the University of Leeds.

Michael Twaddle is based at the Institute of Commowealth Studies, specialising in the recent history and politics of Africa and the Caribbean.

Karen Wells is a research student in international relations at the London School of Economics.

John Young is professor of politics at the University of Leicester.

Preface

The British have never regarded the study of contemporary history very highly. When history became established as a firm subject in schools and universities towards the end of the nineteenth century, periods beyond the Napoleonic Wars were seldom studied.[1] Llewellyn Woodward reminds us that the *English Historical Review* from its first number in 1886 until after 1918 did not print a single article on English domestic history after 1852.[2] He notes further that the syllabus of the Modern History School at Oxford in 1914 excluded English political history after 1837.

The First World War provided a major boost, spawning an unprecedented burst of literature, and flooding the library of the Imperial War Museum in London within ten years of the armistice with over 13,000 books and pamphlets on the war. The war also precipitated a novel release of government papers by the Soviet Union from 1917, and by Germany from 1918.[3] In Britain the government decided that it too should be releasing documents on the war, and from 1930 started to publish a massive series.[4] The Royal Institute of International Affairs was founded in 1920 in the wake of the war, providing a further stimulus. But were these developments enough to ensure that students in the 1930s would learn about the origins and course of the war that had so affected their lives? 'I deplore,' wrote Sir Charles Oman angrily in 1939, 'the present trend away from the preliminary centuries towards the very last periods that are permissible. ... Someone lately called the curriculum "the School of *Very* Modern History".'[5] One might be forgiven for assuming that the history frontier had at last indeed crept forward to the verge of the new war. Not so. Even in 1946 the Oxford modern history degree terminated at 1878.[6]

The post-war period has seen conservatism again triumph, at least as regards syllabuses. The predictable flood of literature followed the Second World War, outstanding early examples being Lewis Namier's *Diplomatic Prelude 1938–39*, Chester Wilmot's *The Struggle for Europe* and Hugh Trevor-Roper's *The Last Days of Hitler*.[7] Looking back on his work nearly forty years after the events described, Trevor-Roper (Lord Dacre of Glanton) wrote, 'My evidence was largely "contemporary oral evidence"; even my documents were, in large part, contemporary oral evidence written down. What makes them more accurate, in some respects, than later reconstructions is this contemporaneity: the evidence was given when it was fresh.'[8] Not even the imprimatur of such a distinguished historian flexing his muscles on recent history, however, nor the legions of good and great historians who came to work on the massive official history of the war and its origins,[9] were sufficient to convince others that the diplomatic history of the 1930s and the events leading up to the war were subjects worthy of study, not at least until a number of years after 1945.

Major events were meanwhile occurring in the history world which should have made the study of contemporary history more attractive. The most notable of these was the Public Records Act of 1958. In the 1940s the latest documents available for consultation at the Public Record Office were dated 1885, and for most of the 1950s the terminal date was 1902. The new Act ensured that year by year, without the need to lobby, most documents fifty years old would become available for inspection. The procedures for selecting documents for preservation were also standardised and improved.[10] In 1967, after a prolonged campaign, the Labour government of Harold Wilson was persuaded to pass a new Public Records Act reducing the period after which documents became available from fifty years to thirty, issuing forth a rich harvest of documents on the inter-war years. Historians were not slow to capitalise on the cornucopia, one of the first fruits being Keith Middlemas and John Barnes's *Baldwin* (1969).[11] Other events, such as the transmutation of the Wiener Library into the Institute of Contemporary History in 1965, and the establishment of the Social Science Research Council in 1966, served to boost the cause of contemporary history, though in later years the SSRC, or ESRC as renamed by Mrs Thatcher, has often failed to give adequate support to contemporary history.

The 1980s saw a significant expansion in the study of contemporary, which increasingly meant post-war, British history. Universities, through a variety of approaches and departments – international history and relations, economic and social history, media and cultural studies, history of science and technology, history and political science – have offered an exciting and broad range of topics and courses. By the 1990s, despite squeezes on funding for research, it is likely that more original work is taking place in British universities on the period since 1945 than on 1900–45.

In schools, however, post-war British history remains a cinderella subject.[12] While components in the National Curriculum touch on Britain since 1945, there is no systematic treatment. Thus episodes such as the end of empire, the birth of the welfare state, the emergence of Britain as a nuclear power, and British accession to the European Economic Community, against a background of a generally declining economy and the attempts of successive Labour and Conservative administrations to find a role for Britain in a changing world, get overlooked. The inattention to such momentous developments indeed appears puzzling.

The Institute of Contemporary British History, founded in 1986, has given a boost to the study of post-war British history at several levels.[13] Its journal, *Contemporary Record*, founded in 1987, publishes research articles on a wide variety of branches of history, including economic, political, social, international, cultural and scientific. The Institute also spawned two other academic journals, Twentieth Century British History in 1990 and *Contemporary European History* in 1992. The Institute initiated research projects in a wide variety of areas, from the decline of religion to the decline of British industry.

Over thirty-five conferences were organised by the Institute in its first ten years. The largest, held at Queen Mary and Westfield College in London in July 1995 to mark fifty years since the end of the Second World War, attracted 150 papers and commentaries. In the 1990s the Institute increasingly organised events on post-war history for government and for private-sector companies. The aim has always been to show the importance of an understanding of recent history as a key ingredient in improving contemporary, and future, decision-making.

A wide variety of initiatives has also been aimed at giving the study of post-war history a boost in schools and colleges. The popular quarterly journal *Modern History Review* contains regular articles on the period, and other publications such as the extended series *Making Contemporary Britain* or the documentary readers are designed to enhance the accessibility of teaching and study materials.

It is doubtful, however, whether the ICBH has fostered a distinctively British *school* of contemporary history. It has certainly encouraged the development of certain techniques, such as 'witness seminars' (gathering together and taping the discussions of key parties in certain episodes or institutions). The Institute has also sought to combat the compartmentalisation of history into different branches – economic, political, international, and so on. It has sought to encourage research into and study of *all* principal aspects of post-war British history, and where possible to blend them. Yet this tendency falls far short of the total history espoused by the French 'Annales' school.

So contemporary history as studied in Britain has become a pluralistic, almost chaotic pursuit, not just produced by conventional academics in universities, but with some of the best products coming from television and radio producers and writers, from journalists, schoolteachers and professional authors, and indeed from the general public. This book sets out to reflect and indeed to encourage that diversity, which is likely only to increase in the future.

Notes

1 See E. A. Fulton's paper presented to the London Branch of the Historical Association in 1913, reprinted as 'The teaching of contemporary history', *History*, 26, June 1941, pp. 51–5.

2 Llewellyn Woodward, 'The study of contemporary history', *Journal of Contemporary History*, 1 (1), 1966, pp. 1–13.

3 F. W. Pick, 'Contemporary history: method and man', *History*, 31, March 1946, pp. 31–2.

4 Gavin Henderson, 'A plea for the study of contemporary history', *History*, June 1941.

5 Sir Charles Oman, *On the Writing of History* (1939), p. 255, quoted by Pick, 'Contemporary history', p. 29.

6 Pick, 'Contemporary history', p. 29.

7 L. A. Namier, *Diplomatic Prelude, 1938–39* (1948); Chester Wilmot, *The Struggle for Europe* (1952); H. R. Trevor-Roper, *The Last Days of Hitler* (1947).

8 Letter, Lord Dacre of Glanton to authors, 8 April 1982, quoted in Anthony Seldon and Joanna Pappworth, *By Word of Mouth* (1983), p. 171.

9 The Foreign Office authorised the publication in the 1950s of the eleven-volume series *British Documents on the Origins of the War*, ed. G. P. Gooch and Harold Temperley.

10 The message of the 1958 and 1967 Acts is discussed in Donald C. Watt's article 'Contemporary history: problems and perspectives', *Bulletin of the Society of Archivists*, III (10), 1968.

11 Keith Middlemas and John Barnes, *Baldwin* (1969).

12 Anthony Seldon and Stephen Howarth, 'Plugging the gap', *Times Educational Supplement*, 29 May 1987. See also Seldon and Howarth, *Teaching Postwar British History at A Level* (1990).

13 The origin of the ICBH can be traced to a leader in *The Times*, 20 August 1984.

Introduction

Brian Brivati

Historians in Britain have spent decades ... justifying their discipline: it teaches such skills as detection, synthesis, organisation, it empathetically recreates past worlds and reminds us of our human condition; it illuminates the context within which changes in art, music, economics take place. Unwilling to ape the social sciences' assertion of being 'relevant', however, we have contented ourselves with advancing only those indirect claims to utility – and paid a high price in consequence. Barraclough would have none of that. History indeed contained those other values, he felt; but the subject, especially contemporary history, possessed an even greater importance, in fact a fundamental relevance, because only by understanding the broad forces for global change over the past century would people – not just academics, but politicians, publics, scientists – have a chance of comprehending our present complexities and of peering, however dimly, into the future. Is it not time to reassert that claim?[1]

The purpose of this book is to lend a helping hand to those who wish to respond to the clarion call contained in Paul Kennedy's words about the impact of Geoffrey Barraclough's *Contemporary History*. The claim, that we may learn from the past, does not just apply to high-level diplomatic history – such as that contained in Kennedy's works – but also to the study of individual governments, individual people and all the rich tapestry of enquiry and analysis that makes the study of the contemporary period so fertile.

This volume combines a series of essays making interventions in established academic debates with essays attempting to push the terms of debate further; it features essays summarising the state of the literature on particular subjects or particular countries or regions; essays which advocate changes in policy on archives and essays which guide the student, the researcher or the academic in good practice in contemporary history. It is both a textbook in the conventional sense in that many of the chapters will lend themselves to teaching in seminar formats and an essay collection because many of the others will be a useful summary or intervention into existing debates. I hope the mix proves useful in itself and reflects the diversity of the field.

It has been clearly established over the last decade, in the United Kingdom by the ICBH and in other countries by similar organisations or by the simple passage of events, that the study of contemporary history is necessary – in some cases essential. Those critics of contemporary history who used to question whether such a thing could exist have, in the UK at least, been silenced. A combination of the quality of professional research in contemporary history, and the postmodern assault on the objectivity of the historian's project, have had a considerable equalising effect. In this country some once smug critiques of the 'present minded history' have been put politely but firmly in their place by the volume and the quality of contemporary British history. More widely, history itself has kicked out so strikingly in the last decade that few can ignore or fail to appreciate the need for an historical context to contemporary events.

The working definition for the ICBH – somewhat arbitrarily arrived at – of the contemporary period is the period since 1945. This was a practical and empirical decision which identified the point at which many school and university history courses used to end. Even today some courses trail off after 1945 with a cursory or survey lecture on the period after the war. Another kind of definition is related to sources and argues that the contemporary period is that for which there are living witnesses who can provide oral evidence of events – thus dating the period from perhaps the First World War. Another kind again would be to talk about the dominant modes or systems in whatever your specialism happens to be: for political economy the contemporary period starts with the intervention of the wartime economy; if you are a military historian it makes sense to date things in terms of conflicts; if you are a social historian you may have much more trouble with the 1945 date and look to the social changes of the late 1950s and early 1960s as your cut-off; if a constitutional historian you may look to the British joining the European Community as the end of Gaitskell's thousand years of history and the beginning of something new. Any – and all – of these definitions are operating in the literature in differing ways and I could go on and list more. In terms of convergence across a number of different subjects, and thinking simply in terms of Britain, one could do worse than move the beginning of the contemporary period up to 1956 and its aftermath: the combination of Suez, Eden's expression of the lessons as being the need to move Britain towards the European Community, the beginning of the social changes that were to have such an impact, the real feeling that the post-war period had ended, the beginnings of the impact of television and communications on the political process, and so on. The root, if you like, of many of the things that were to make the period of the 1960s, 1970s and 1980s different from what had gone before. Of course it is not as neat as the peace, but it serves better to mark the period as being different. Therefore the emphasis of the bulk of this book, with important exceptions in the source chapters, is on this 'later' contemporary period.

In taking this later period as the central, though not exclusive, concern the book reflects the maturity of contemporary history as an academic discipline. It is particularly concerned with the diversity of the subject in two respects. First, that the basic nature of what constitutes 'history' has been revolutionised under the influence of the new social history of the 1960s – gender history and the developing question of national and racial narratives within historical traditions. Second, that the pace of technological advance threatens to outpace the intellectual frameworks we have for understanding this advance as an historical process. Both these newer areas of enquiry run parallel to – and do not replace – the traditional concerns and traditional approaches to contemporary history. The emphasis on debates that may challenge the traditional ways of doing history are balanced by a strong emphasis on the need to keep the quality of archive – based research high – there is no substitute for solid empirical work – but there is also no reason why these techniques should not be applied to a broader range of questions.

Thus this book combines a reference work for the contemporary historian who wishes to explore the recent past in conventional terms with some aids to those who are pushing at the boundaries and expanding the definitions of what constitutes contemporary history. At times the chapters on sources might just as easily have been placed in the debates section, and by organising the material into sections and by combining reference-style essays with more analytical essays we have tried to reflect the sheer breadth of issues involved in the field.

We have tried to avoid overemphasis on Europe,[2] and rather have attempted to present snapshots of the state of contemporary history around the world. Barraclough, writing his classic study of contemporary history in 1960, concluded:

> The European Age – the age which extended from 1498 to 1947 – is over, and with it the predominance of the old European scale of values. Literature, like politics, has broken through its European bonds, and the civilisation of the future, whose genesis I have tried in the preceding pages to trace, is taking shape as a world civilization in which all the continents will play their part.[3]

The key to understanding this process of change is to understand that the definition of a period in terms like these – the European Age – the American Age, is itself now redundant. The point, as in the second part of the quotation from Barraclough, is that all the continents of the globe are experiencing change and development at a varying pace and in varying ways, as well as change and development continuing in Europe and America. Indeed, it is now commonplace to argue that there has been a shift to the Pacific away from the Atlantic. This highlights a debate touched on in the international perspectives sections – the conflict between the impact of the globalisation of economies and communications and the resilience of national histories and cultures.

Two other things permeate these essays: the ending of the Cold War and the resurgence of market economics. In drawing out the implications of these developments a range of often conflicting opinions are expressed and some of the competing conclusions are contained here. For some, the initial euphoria of the fall of the Berlin Wall has given way to profound uncertainty about the efficacy of market solutions to the reconstruction of the former communist countries. This scepticism is reflected in some of the reflections on the role of the market in modernising the developing world. In contrast, other writers argue for an optimistic view of the ability of the market to deliver economic growth in developing countries and the general prospects for democracy. The extent to which the debate is within the terms of reference of the market and not within the terms of reference of collectivism is striking.

There are other kinds of problems which are often seen as being unique to the contemporary period. Donald Watt clearly articulated the vibrant nature of contemporary records:

> Every day the record of yesterday in the newspapers of today is the first step in the creation of history, a version of the immediate past that enters into a process of continuous examination and re-examination, becoming in the process encrusted with mythology, overlaid with misrepresentation, distorted by selective memory, perverted by systematic and deliberate propagation of versions useful and favourable to the dominant orthodoxies of the present.

Each part of this judgement can be extended to all evidence, of any historical epoch. The idea that because one is writing about and working on the twentieth century one is more prey to the manipulation of evidence is a dangerous one which is indicative of complacency. Moreover, the process of invention, the process of influencing and distorting the meaning of the record, does not magically stop when one moves back beyond living memory. All evidence is tainted so why should one assume that twentieth-century evidence is more tainted than eighteenth-century or that historians working on the twentieth century are any more able to step outside their personality and socialisation than those working on the eighteenth century? One of the major problems for the contemporary historian that is unique is that often we have too much information. Not enough recognition is given to this fact.

> We know a thousand times more about the collapse of France [in 1940] than we know about the collapse of Carthage. We know a thousand times more

about the evacuation of Dunkirk than we know about the Battle of Hastings. We can meet and discuss matters, any day we like, with men who were at Dunkirk. Would not not a true medievalist give up his whole life's research for the sake of one interview with one Saxon who fought beside Harold at Hastings?[4]

The Contemporary History Handbook is divided into three sections: debates, international perspectives and sources. The third section is in turn divided into general archives and debates, printed sources, oral/audio sources, visual sources and electronic sources. There is an appendix to the international section which lists bibliographical sources for Africa, Latin America, Russia and Eastern Europe and China. (Further information on Chinese sources is contained at the end of chapter 15.) Chapters 2, 3, 7, 8, 11, 13, 14, 15, 16, 17, 18, 21, 24, 29, 33, 34, 36 and 37 contain guides to further reading and sources of information. These are arranged as parts of chapters rather than in a separate reference section for ease of use. Within the text of each of the source chapters there are useful pieces of information and, in some cases, addresses. All addresses and some additional ones are summarised in the appendix to the sources section.

The collapse of the Soviet Empire has presented a series of political challenges to the European Union but has also forced the rewriting of the world strategic rule book. This volume opens with the text of a lecture delivered by Eric Hobsbawm in 1993 which considers the role of the historian amidst the rebirth of European war and the renewal of nationalisms, 'for history is the raw material for nationalist or ethnic or fundamentalist ideologies, as poppies are the raw material for heroin addiction'. The key security debates – also coming out of the collapse of the Berlin Wall – are explored by John Erickson's essay on world security in which he surveys the end of the Cold War and sketches the shape of some of the on-going strategic problems provoked by nuclear proliferation, new challenges of uncertainty and new forms of threat to world peace.

The ending of the Cold War forms a part of the series of intellectual and sociological challenges to our understanding of contemporary society. The diverse aspects, responses and disputes about the meaning of these changes are considered by Richard Cockett on the 'end of history' debate and by Joe Bailey in his consideration of postmodernism. Harriet Jones looks at more conventional historiographical debates in a challenging new light in her essay on the consensus debate in the UK and summarises the emerging revisionist work which questions some of the assumptions that have underpinned general British political history since the war and particularly the work influenced by the Thatcherite agenda of the 1980s. Taking this revisionist theme further is Shamit Saggar, who critically assesses the arguments for a multicultural history and raises important questions about the 'Whose history?' debate.

As mentioned above, the reasonance of the market is felt heavily in this volume and the alternatives and challenges to the economic orthodoxy of our time are considered by Andrew Graham in his essay on debates in political economy. He places the debate in a European and global context and tellingly concludes that the simple importation of models from other countries may not be the answer.

> The difficulty with institutional political economy is that even if we know that a good outcome in, say, Germany is the result of German 'habits and practices' we do not know how to bring about such habits and practices. The experience of the 1980s has given plenty of examples of institutions being destroyed. There is still much to be learnt about how useful institutions can be created.

The historical pedigree of such importation is described by Hobsbawm:

> After 1918, when most of the successor countries were new, the model was Western democracy and economic liberalism ... was the region's patron saint, except for the Bolsheviks, who went their own way. (Actually, they too had foreign models: Rathenau and Henry Ford.) This did not work. The model broke down politically and economically in the 1920s and 1930s. The Great Depression eventually broke the multinational democracy even of Czechoslovakia.
>
> A number of these countries then briefly tried or flirted with the fascist model, which looked like the economic and political success story of the 1930s. (We are inclined to forget that Nazi Germany was remarkably successful in overcoming the Great Depression.) Integration in a Greater German economic system did not work either. Germany was defeated. After 1945 most of them chose, or found themselves being forced to choose, the Bolshevik model, which was essentially a model for modernising backward agrarian economies by planned industrial revolution.

It is a theme repeated and questioned by Karen Wells when considering the use of the market and structural adjustment in Ethiopia in Chapter 12, by Michael Twaddle in his general consideration of Africa in Chapter 11 and by George Philip in his analysis of democratisation and economic change in Latin America in Chapter 13. The model, in the contemporary as in the inter-war period, is Western democracy and economic liberalism.

A separate, but related, set of concerns that have increasingly influenced historical writing since the 1960s have been the issues of gender and citizenship. They are related by the concept of identity and by the way in which they have expanded the scope of what previously constituted historical analysis. Lucy Noakes argues that contemporary history is far too often and too simply equated with political history and concludes that 'If contemporary historians of British society are to develop a full and clear analysis of Britain since 1945 [attention] needs to be paid to the construction of gender roles in this period. Gender and women's history need to move from the margins of contemporary history into the centre.' Similarly Elizabeth Meehan argues that there are many identities for the individual and the too easy dismissal of 'European' identity ignores a rich area of debate. Both essays echo the concern expressed by Joe Bailey that the idea of a single 'identity' in the contemporary period is increasingly problematic. An attempt to synthesise the conventional historiography and the newer agendas is made in the final essay in the section.

While no single conclusion can be drawn from the range of issues touched on in this section, it is clear that traditional debates about political ideology and political economy are enjoying a period of vibrant controversy and that newer debates on gender, race and identity are developing to complement and expand the field. This new diversity is in the context of an uncertain international situation and the ever increasing politicisation of the past.

As mentioned above, the second section, international perspectives, begins with three chapters considering the impact of the political economy of market liberalism and Western democracy on the developing world. Japan is the core of this new global centre, and the speed of change – economic, social and political – in such countries is breathtaking. As Ian Neary concludes in his chapter on Japan and the Pacific, 'The role of the contemporary historian in explaining the position of these countries in the world will become increasingly important to those societies; and it is important that their non-Asian colleagues keep abreast of these developments.' A feeling echoed by Christopher Hughes. In Chapter 15 he chronicles the contemporary debate on Chinese national identity. This form of academic analysis has been made possible by the liberalisation of access to China and Chinese resources. China remains a vast and relatively understudied field with an as yet underdeveloped historiography in English, a situation that must change, for, as Andrew Graham argues, the entry of China into the world economy is 'the equivalent of starting world trade afresh'.

Philip Boobbyer and Julia Buxton consider the political and economic impact of the fall of the Berlin Wall on Russia and the eastern European states. In 'Forward into history' Julia Buxton argues that the attempt to impose a democratic civic society and market economy on the newly liberated states fundamentally underestimated the importance of historical evolution in creating sustainable state formations. She concludes, 'The overriding lesson of the East European experience is that domestic history and not international pressure has the greatest role in shaping the final contours.' A similar point is made by Philip Boobbyer – it will take time for the culture and society of Russia to catchup with the models of democracy. 'The Russians have two words for freedom: volia and swoboda. The first of them implies anarchic freedom; the second assumes that freedom goes with duties and responsibilities. To know this balance between freedom and responsibility is the sign, surely, of a healthy mind. It is this balance which Russia most needs.'

The retreat from the initial surge of enthusiasm for the unbridled market in many of the new democracies has of course been echoed in many of the older democracies in the 1990s. Nevertheless, philosophically the market still strides – wounded but not defeated – forward from the gains of the 1980s and collectivism seems cowed – though the wealth of alternative policy positions is explored in Andrew Graham's chapter on political economy. Intellectually market or conservative viewpoints have been underrepresented. Gerard Alexander argues that this has impoverished historical writing in the United States and that, while in Europe we enjoyed engaging debates between clearly differentiated positions, historical work in the United States has for too long been dominated by a 'liberal establishment'. This feeling of being an embattled minority has, paradoxically, probably been shared by Eric Hobsbawm for much of his career. What both writers agree on is the reasonance of the historical method for the exploration of evidence and the reconstruction of events or personalities.

But any historian, Marxist or conservative, is only as good as her or his sources. Therefore the concluding section of the handbook contains a series of guides to dealing with the vast range of source material available to the contemporary historian. The first section deals with general archive holdings in private papers, parliamentary sources, and national archives in the United States. Each chapter is designed to give practical advice as well as some indication of the range of the holdings. More information on specific archives can be gleaned from the archive reports which regularly appear in the journals *Contemporary Record*, published by Frank Cass, and *Twentieth Century British History*, published by Oxford University Press. The section concludes with two discursive essays which overview areas of debate and which would provide a basis for interesting seminar debates. The case study of the Waldegrave initiative questions the extent to which freedom of information legislation would serve the interests of the historian, and the overall importance of understanding and preserving the media as a source is passionately advocated by Philip Taylor in Chapter 26.

The media are perhaps the most expanded source for the contemporary historian. Chandrika Kaul looks at the print media, Tom Nossiter the specialised part of the media that so often reflects and influences the political process – opinion polls; the sheer volume of written material is explored by Michael Kandiah and three case studies – for use in teaching situations – of problems with these contemporary written sources are provided in Chapter 27.

The use of living witnesses of the contemporary period and the problems and amazing possibilities it poses are explored by Michael Roper in the chapter on general oral history sources and by Anthony Seldon in a consideration of the art of elite interviewing in Chapter 32. Sian Nicholas examines the relatively neglected use of radio as a source and argues that it provides one of the most interesting and stimulating contemporary sources.

There is perhaps more recognition of the importance of visual images in historical research, but still, relative to the written word, images are a poor second. The chapters contained here – Brian Harrison on the use of still images and Jeffrey Richards, Margaret Scammell and Howard Smith on the use of different kinds of moving image – make the case for the equality of images with words as a way of understanding the past. Margaret Scammell's chapter also chimes with the arguments put forward in Chapter 26 – that we need to understand and use the medium of television much more systematically as a way of understanding the contemporary world. In turn these practical guides to the new sources of the last fifty years complement the theoretical arguments in Chapter 3 and Chapter 4 about the possibility that we have lived through a profound shift in the nature of the world we inhabit.

One of the main characters in this postulated shift is information technology and the explosion it has produced in communication. This 'information overload' is increasing steadily and the use of personal computers in government, business and the home has created a completely new set of historical documents. Government's use of information technology and its consequences for the historian are considered by Edward Higgs, the general implications are considered by Seamus Ross and the specialised form of multimedia by Lorna Hughes. Many questions and crucial assessments are made in each of these chapters and a further set of problems are aired by Brian Brivati in his consideration of the CD-ROM.

If by the end of this book you still need to be convinced of the importance of contemporary history then visit Berlin. Drive through Checkpoint Charlie. Have dinner in the Café Oren, next to the restored synagogue, with an armed policeman standing outside. Walk around the quiet streets of the east. Stroll through the opulence of the west. Smell history in the breeze, touch history in the buildings. They do not question the need to understand the events of the last decade, and we should not. Understanding, as Eric Hobsbawm argues in this volume, is too important to leave to the merely partisan. I hope that the mixture of essays presented here will help you in trying to understand 'our age'.

Notes

1 Paul Kennedy, *Times Higher Education Supplement*, 17 December 1993.
2 For a full set of essays on the development of the European Union and Britain's relationship with integration see Brian Brivati and Harriet Jones (eds), *From Reconstruction to Integration: Britain and Europe since 1945* (1993) especially Anne Deighton, 'Britain and the Cold War, 1945-55: an overview', pp. 7–17; John W. Young, 'Britain and the EEC, 1956-73: an overview', pp. 103–13 and

Stephen George, 'The awkward partner 1973–92: an overview', pp. 179–90. For two short examinations of the European debate in the main political parties in the United Kingdom see Andrew Geddes, 'Labour and the European Community, 1973–93: pro-Europeanism, "Europeanisation" and their implications', and Wolfram Kaiser, 'Using Europe and abusing Europeans: the Conservatives and the European Community, 1957–94', *Contemporary Record*, 8 (2), 1994, pp 370–99.

3 Geoffrey Barraclough, *An Introduction to Contemporary History* (Penguin, 1984), p. 268.

4 G. B. Henderson, 'A plea for the study of contemporary history', *History*, 26, June 1941, pp. 51–5.

Part I
Debates

Chapter 1

The new threat to history

Eric Hobsbawm

This chapter is based on a lecture given at the beginning of the academic year 1993-94 to the Central European University in Budapest.

Although I am a second-generation English-born British citizen, I am also a Central European. Indeed, as a Jew I am a characteristic member of the Central European diaspora of peoples. My grandfather came to London from Warsaw. My mother was Viennese, and so is my wife, though she now speaks better Italian than German. My wife's mother still spoke Hungarian as a little girl and her parents, at one stage of their lives in the old monarchy, had a store in Herzegovina. My wife and I once went to Mostar to trace it, in the days when there was still peace in that unhappy part of the Balkans. I want to say three things.

The first concerns central and eastern Europe. Anyone who comes from there is a citizen of a country whose status is doubly uncertain. I am not claiming that uncertainty is a monopoly of Central and East Europeans. It is probably more universal today than ever. Nevertheless, their horizon is particularly cloudy. In my own lifetime every country in that part of Europe has been overrun by war, conquered, occupied, liberated and reoccupied. Every state in it has a different shape from the one it had. Only six of the twenty-three states which now fill the map between Trieste and the Urals were in existence at the time of my birth, or would have been if they had not been occupied by some army: Russia, Rumania, Bulgaria, Albania, Greece and Turkey, for neither post-1918 Austria nor post-1918 Hungary is really comparable to Habsburg Hungary and Cisleithania. Several came into existence after World War I, others since 1989. They include several countries which have never in history had the status of independent statehood in the modern sense, or countries which had it briefly – for a year or two, for a decade or two – then lost it, though some have since regained it: the three little Baltic states, Belarus, Ukraine, Slovakia, Moldova, Slovenia, Croatia, Macedonia, not to go farther eastward. Some were born and have died in my lifetime, like Yugoslavia and Czechoslovakia.

It is perfectly common for the elder inhabitants of some central European city to have identity documents of three successive states. A person of my age from Lemberg or Czernowitz has lived under four states, not counting wartime occupation; a man from Munkacs may well have lived under five, if we count the momentary autonomy of Podkarpatska Rus in 1938. In more civilised times, as in 1919, he or she might have been given the option of which new citizenship to choose, but since the Second World War he or she is more likely to have been either forcibly expelled or forcibly integrated into the new state. Where does a Central or Eastern European belong? Who is he or she? The question has been a real one for a great number of people, and it still is. In some countries it is a question of life and death, in almost all it affects and sometimes determines their legal status and life chances.

However, there is another and more collective uncertainty. Most of central and eastern Europe belong to that part of the world for which diplomats and United Nations experts since 1945 have tried to devise polite euphemisms: 'underdeveloped' or ' developing' – that is to say, relatively or absolutely poor and backward. In some respects there is a slope to the east and to the west of what we might call the main mountain range or crest of European economic and cultural dynamism, which ran from northern Italy across the Alps to northern France and the Low Countries, and extended across the Channel into England. It can be traced in the medieval trade routes and the distribution map of Gothic architecture, as well as in the figures for regional GDP within the European Union. In fact today the region is still the backbone of the European Unity.

However, in so far as there is a historical line separating 'advanced' from 'backward' Europe, it ran, roughly, through the middle of the Habsburg empire. I know that people are sensitive about these matters. Ljubjana thinks of itself as a great deal nearer the centre of civilisation than, say, Skopje, and Budapest than Belgrade, and the present government in Prague does not even wish to be called 'central European' for fear of being contaminated by contact with the east. It insists that it belongs exclusively to the West. However, my point is that no country or region in central and eastern Europe thought of itself as being at that centre. All looked elsewhere for a model of how to be really advanced and modern – even, I suspect, the educated middle class of Vienna, Budapest and Prague. They looked to Paris and London, just as the intellectuals of Belgrade and Elias Canetti's Ruse in Bulgaria looked to Vienna. And this even though by most accepted standards the present Czech Republic and parts of the present Austria certainly formed part of the advanced industrial heart of Europe, and culturally Vienna, Budapest and Prague had no reason at all to feel inferior to anywhere else.

The history of backward countries in the nineteenth and twentieth centuries is the history of trying to catch up with the more advanced world by imitating it. The nineteenth-century Japanese took Europe as their model, the West Europeans after World War II imitated the American economy. The story of central and eastern Europe in the twentieth century is broadly that of trying to catch up by following several models one after the other and failing. After 1918, when most of the successor countries were new, the model was Western democracy and economic liberalism. President Wilson – is the main station in Prague named after him again? – was the region's patron saint, except for the Bolsheviks, who went their own way. (Actually, they too had foreign models: Rathenau and Henry Ford.) It did not work. The model broke down politically and economically in the 1920s and 1930s. The Great Depression eventually broke the multinational democracy even of Czechoslovakia.

A number of these countries then briefly tried or flirted with the fascist model, which looked like the economic and political success story of the 1930s. (We are inclined to forget that Nazi Germany was remarkably successful in overcoming the Great Depression.) Integration in a Greater German economic system did not work either. Germany was defeated. After 1945 most of them chose, or found themselves being forced to choose, the Bolshevik model, which was essentially a model for modernising backward agrarian economies by planned industrial revolution. It was therefore never relevant to what is now the Czech Republic or to what was until 1989 the German Democratic Republic, but it was relevant to most of the region, including the USSR.

There is no need to dwell upon the economic deficiencies and flaws of the system, which eventually led to its breakdown, and still less upon the intolerable, the increasingly intolerable political systems it imposed on central and eastern Europe. Still less do I need to remind anyone of the incredible suffering it imposed on the peoples of the former USSR, particularly in the iron age of Joseph Stalin. And yet I must say, although many will not welcome my saying so, that up to a point it worked better than anything since the break-up of the monarchies in 1918. For most of the common citizens of the more backward countries in the region – say Slovakia and much of the Balkan peninsula – it was probably the best period in their history. The system broke down because economically it had become increasingly rigid and unworkable, and especially because it proved virtually incapable of generating or making economic use of innovation, quite apart from stifling intellectual originality. Moreover, it became impossible to hide from the local populations the fact that other countries had made far more material progress than the socialist ones. To put it another way, it broke down because ordinary citizens were indifferent or hostile, and because the regimes themselves had lost faith in what they were pretending to do. Still, however you look at it, it failed in the most spectacular manner between 1989 and 1991.

And now? There is another model which everyone rushes to follow, parliamentary democracy in politics and the extremes of free-market capitalism in economics. In the present form it is not really a model but chiefly a reaction against what has gone before. It may settle down to become something more workable – if it is allowed to settle down. However, even if it were to do so, in the light of history since 1918 there is not much likelihood that this region, possibly with marginal exceptions, will succeed in joining the club of the 'really' advanced and up-to-date countries. The results of imitating President Reagan and Mrs Thatcher have proved disappointing even in countries which have not been laid waste by civil war, chaos and anarchy. I should add that the results of following the Reagan-Thatcher model in the countries of its origin have not been brilliantly successful either, if I may be permited a British understatement.

So, on the whole, the peoples of central and eastern Europe will go on living in countries disappointed in their past, probably largely disappointed with their present, and uncertain about their future. This is a dangerous situation. People will look for someone to blame for their failures and insecurities. The movements and ideologies most likely to benefit from that mood are not, at least in the present generation, those which want a return to some version of the days before 1989. They are more likely to be movements inspired by xenophobic nationalism and intolerance. The easiest thing is always to blame strangers.

This brings me to my second and main point, which is much more directly relevant to the work of a university. Or at least to that part of the work which concerns me as a historian and a university teacher. For history is the raw material of nationalist or ethnic or fundamentalist ideologies, as poppies are the raw material of heroin addiction. The past is an essential element, perhaps the essential element in these ideologies. If there is no suitable past it can always be invented. Indeed, in the nature of things there is usually no entirely suitable past, because the phenomenon these ideologies claim to justify is not ancient or eternal but historically novel. This applies both to religious fundamentalism in it its current versions – Ayatollah Khomeini's version of an Islamic state is no older than the early 1970s – and to contemporary nationalisms. The past legitimises. The past gives a more glorious background to a present that has not much to say for itself. I recall seeing somewhere a study of the ancient civilisation of the cities of the Indus valley with the title *5000 Years of Pakistan*. Pakistan was not even thought of before 1932–33, when the name was invented by some student militants. It did not become a serious political aspiration until 1940. As a state it has existed since 1947. There is no more evidence of any connection between the civilisation of Mohenjo Daro and the current rulers of Islamabad than there is of a connection between the Trojan War and the government of Ankara, which is at present claiming the return, if only for public exhibition, of Schliemann's treasure of King Priam of Troy. But 5,000 years of Pakistan somehow sounds better than forty-six years of Pakistan.

In this situation historians find themselves in the unexpected role of political actors. I used to think that the profession of history, unlike that of, say, nuclear physics, could at least do no harm. Now I know it can. Our studies can turn into bomb factories like the workshops in which the IRA learned to transform chemical fertiliser into an explosive. This state of affairs affects us in two ways. We have a responsibility to historical facts in general, and for criticising the politico-ideological abuse of history in particular.

I need say little about the first of these responsibilities. I would not have to say anything but for two developments. One is the current fashion for novelists to base their plots on recorded reality rather than inventing them, thus fudging the border between historical fact and fiction. The other is the rise of 'postmodernist' intellectual fashions in Western universities, particularly in departments of literature and anthropology, which imply that all 'facts' claiming objective existence are simply intellectual constructions. In short, that there is no clear difference between fact and fiction. But there is, and for historians, even the most militantly anti-positivist ones, the ability to distinguish between the two is absolutely fundamental. We cannot invent facts. Either Elvis Presley is dead or he isn't. The question can be answered unambiguously on the basis of evidence, in so far as reliable evidence is available, which is sometimes the case. Either the present Turkish government, which denies the attempted genocide of the Armenians in 1915, is right or it is not. Most of us would dismiss any denial of that massacre from serious historical discourse, although there is no equally unambiguous way to choose between different ways of interpreting the phenomenon or fitting it into the wider context of history. Recently Hindu zealots destroyed a mosque in Ayodhya, ostensibly on the grounds that the mosque had been imposed by the Muslim Moghul conqueror Babur on the Hindus in a particularly sacred location which marked the birthplace of the god Rama. My colleagues and friends in the Indian universities published a study showing (1) that nobody until the nineteenth century had suggested that Ayodhya was the birthplace of Rama and (2) that the mosque was almost certainly not built in the time of Babur. I wish I could say that this has had much effect on the rise of the Hindu party which provoked the incident, but at least they did their duty as historians, for the benefit of those who can read and are exposed to the propaganda of intolerance now and in the future. Let us do ours.

Few of the ideologies of intolerance are based on simple lies or fictions for which no evidence exists. After all, there was a battle of Kosovo in 1389; Serb warriors and their allies were defeated by the Turks, and that did leave deep scars on the popular memory of the Serbs, although it does not follow that it justifies the oppression of the Albanians, who now form 90 per cent of the region's population, or the Serb claim that the land is essentially theirs. Denmark does not claim the large part of eastern England which was settled and ruled by the Danes before the eleventh century, which continued to be known as the Danelaw and whose village names are still philologically Danish.

The most usual ideological abuse of history is based on anachronism rather than lies. Greek nationalism refuses Macedonia even the right to its name on the grounds that all Macedonia is essentially Greek and part of a Greek nation state, presumably ever since the father of Alexander the Great, king of Macedonia, became the ruler of the Greek lands on the Balkan peninsula. Like everything about Macedonia, this is far from a purely academic matter, but it takes a lot of courage for a Greek intellectual to say that, historically speaking, it is nonsense. There was no Greek nation state or any other single political entity for the Greeks in the fourth century BC; the Macedonian empire was nothing like the Greek or any other modern nation state, and in any case it is highly probable that ancient Greeks regarded the Macedonian rulers, as they did their later Roman rulers, as barbarians and not as Greeks, though they were doubtless too polite or cautious to say so.

Moreover, Macedonia is historically such an inextricable mixture of ethnicities – not for nothing has it given its name to French mixed fruit salad (*macédoine*) – that no attempt to identify it with a single nationality can be correct. In fairness, the extremes of emigrant Macedonian nationalism should also be dismissed for the same reason, as should all the publications in Croatia which somehow try to turn Zvonimir the Great into the ancestor of President Tudjman. But it is difficult to stand up against the inventors of a national schoolbook history, although some historians in Zagreb University, whom I am proud to count as friends, have the courage to do so.

These and many other attempts to replace history by myth and invention are not merely bad intellectual jokes. After all, they can determine what goes into school books, as the Japanese authorities knew when they insisted on a sanitised version of the Japanese war on China for use in Japanese classrooms. Myth and invention are essential to the politics of identity by which groups of people today, defining themselves by ethnicity, religion or the past or present borders of States, try to find some certainty in an uncertain and shaking world by saying, 'We are different from and better than the Others.' They are our concern in the universities because the people who formulate those myths and inventions are educated people, schoolteachers lay and clerical, professors (not many, I hope), journalists, television and radio producers. Today most of them will have gone to some university. Make no mistake about it. History is not ancestral memory or collective tradition. It is what people learned from priests, schoolmasters, the writers of history books, and the compilers of magazine articles and television programmes. It is important for historians to remember their responsibility, which is, above all, to stand aside from the passions of identity politics – even if they also feel them. After all, we are human beings too.

How serious a matter this may be is shown in an article by the Israeli writer Amos Elon about the way in which the genocide of the Jews by Hitler has been turned into a legitimising myth for the existence of the state of Israel.[1] More than that: in the years of right-wing government it was turned into a sort of national ritual assertion of Israeli state identity and superiority and a central item of the official system of national beliefs, alongside God. Elon, who traces the evolution of this transformation of the 'Holocaust', argues, following the recent Minister of Education in the new Israeli government, that history must now be separated from national myth, ritual and politics. As a non-Israeli, though a Jew, I express no views about this. However, as a historian I sadly note one observation by Elon. It is that the leading contributions to the scholarly historiography of the genocide, whether by Jews or non-Jews, were either not translated into Hebrew, like Hilberg's great work, or were translated only after considerable delay and then sometimes with editorial disclaimers. The serious historiography of the genocide has not made it any less of an unspeakable tragedy. It was merely at variance with the legitimising myth.

Yet this very story gives us grounds for hope. For here we have mythological or nationalist history being criticised from within. I note that the history of the establishment of Israel ceased to be written in Israel essentially as national or Zionist polemic about forty years after the state came into being. I have noticed the same in Irish history. About half a century after most of Ireland won its independence, Irish historians no longer write the history of their island in terms of the mythology of the national liberation movement. Irish history, both in the Republic and in the North, is producing brilliant work because it has succeeded in so liberating itself. This is still a matter that has political implications and risks. The history that is written today breaks with the old tradition which stretches from the Fenians to the IRA. But the fact that a new generation has grown up which can stand back from the passions of the great traumatic and formative moments of their country's history is a sign of hope for historians.

However, we cannot wait for the generations to pass. We must resist the *formation* of national, ethnic and other myths as they are being formed. It will not make us popular. Thomas Masaryk, founder of the Czechoslovak republic, was not popular when he entered politics as the man who proved, with regret but without hesitation, that the medieval manuscripts on which much of the Czech national myth was based were fakes. But it has to be done, and I hope those of you who are historians will do it.

That is all I want to say about the duty of historians. However, before I close, I want to say one other thing. University students, are privileged people. The odds are that they will attain a good status in society, have a better career and earn more than other people, though not as much as successful businessmen. I want to remind them of something I was told when I began to teach in a university. ' The people for whom you are there,' said my own teacher, 'are not the brilliant students like yourself. They are the average students with boring minds who get uninteresting degrees in the lower range of the second class, and whose examination scripts all read the same. The first-class people will look after themselves, though you will enjoy teaching them. The others are the ones who need you.'

That applies not only to the university but to the world. Governments, the economy, schools, everything in society, are not for the benefit of the privileged minorities. They can look after themselves. They are for the benefit of the ordinary run of people, who are not particularly clever or interesting (unless, of course, we fall in love with one of them), nor highly educated, nor successful, or destined for success – in fact, nothing very special. It is for the people who, throughout history, have entered history outside their neighbourhoods as individuals only in the records of their births, marriages and deaths. Any society worth living in is one designed for them, not for the rich, the clever, the exceptional, although any society worth living in must provide scope for such minorities. But the world is not made for anyone's personal benefit. A world that claims that as its purpose is not a good world, and ought not to be a lasting on.

Notes

1   See 'The politics of memory', *New York Review*, 7 October 1993.

Chapter 2

World security after the Cold War

John Erickson

In a world muddled, muddied and increasingly bloodied it is not surprising that a certain nostalgia for the supposed certainties of the Cold War has developed recently. The 'New World Order' which US President George Bush was so eager to proclaim in the aftermath of the Cold War and triumph over Iraq in Desert Storm has signally failed to materialise, for nothing appreciably new in the way of institutional innovation seems to have emerged to cope with changing circumstances, and 'world order' appears to be more a matter of disarray, confusion and in many regions wild, unmanageable disorder. Little or no preparation had been made for a world which became with astonishing swiftness 'depolarised'. The structures which had sustained the Cold War cracked and the regimes which had accompanied it over several decades in a number of instances began to disintegrate. Systems designed to confront or contain 'the threat', as it was variously perceived, were deprived of their main purpose yet lacked any mechanism to adapt to a rapidly changing world.[1]

'Depolarisation', clumsy though the term is, does encompass the nature of the process which has occurred since the Cold War was terminated. Removing the psychological and military straitjacket of the Cold War, 'forty-five years of ossified terror' have revealed features which are ascribed as 'new' in terms of conflict but which, in fact, existed over the last few decades. There was a pattern of warfare and conflict which existed outside the framework of the Cold War, 145 such wars waged since 1945 claiming millions of lives. The roots of 'new' conflict in many instances are more complex than the consequence of an end to the Cold War. The security problem is to determine what is so 'new' as to require radically new policies and the reorganisation of institutions which may have passed their prime.

It is generally agreed and it appears eminently plausible that classic 'great power war' is an unlikely eventuality, least of all a global nuclear clash between 'super-powers'. Whatever the uncertainties of the Cold War period,

---

11

the dreaded nuclear apocalypse never materialised, even as confrontation was spread globally and pursued in unrestrained ideological terms. The 'certainties' were not entirely illusory. It is also arguable that 'nuclear strategic doctrine and concepts' developed during the Cold War have not lost all their relevance, though they will require amendment and rethinking.

That may well apply to Eurasia, to 'mature nuclear powers', but radically new approaches will be called for in dealing with other regimes acquiring nuclear weapons. Nuclear deterrence as part of the system may not yet be wholly past its 'sell by' date. The prevention of the proliferation of nuclear weapons and the stabilisation of conflict may be its future form: deterrence in a conventional mode. Nevertheless, the degree of collaboration between 'mature' and 'immature' nuclear powers will assume growing, critical importance.[2]

What have to be distinguished across the whole spectrum of developments in global security are those circumstances which are directly attributable to the disappearance of the Cold War and those which have evolved or continue to evolve outside that particular geopolitical framework. The immediate consequence of the ending of the Cold War was the dismemberment of empires, specifically the former Soviet empire, accompanied by the actual dissolution or the diminished relevance of alliance systems. That applies to the Warsaw Pact and NATO respectively. The 'proxy wars' waged on behalf of the super-powers throughout the Cold War period may have ceased but a consequence of super-power disengagement has been to leave specific countries and areas, Afghanistan serving as a particular example, without any residual political structure.

Areas which were formerly of strategic importance, some little more than enlarged dots on the map, artificially supported and sustained, have been abruptly abandoned, left as geostrategic orphans. With the visible collapse of the predominance of the global super-powers during the Cold War, regional power centres have begun to exercise their own kind of power. There are those aligned with the United States, Japan, Germany and post-Soviet Russia. They are complex associations, their relations a mixture of competition and co-operation. The result is an uneasy balance, with one unfortunate consequence in the development of expanded and intensified regional arms races.[3]

It would be easy enough to ascribe the present turbulence and widespread conflict to the destabilisation produced by the ending of the Cold War, the world seemingly plunged abruptly into disorder and lawlessness. That, however, would be an over-simplification. The majority of recent and current conflicts were either unconnected with the Cold War or the circumstances of its ending. The exceptions lie on the continent of Europe, with armed conflict in the former Yugoslavia, Georgia, Azerbaidzhan and with one unambiguous example in Asia: Afghanistan.[4]

Inter-state warfare has been a most uncommon event, the armed clash between the United Kingdom and Argentina over the sovereignty of the Falklands (Malvinas) untypical, the coalition effort of Desert Storm directed against Iraq possibly unique. The prevalence – indeed, the profusion – of internal conflict, while variously induced, is evidence of a trend which has become more pronounced over the past two decades. Another feature is the visible decline in the power of the traditional nation state, coupled with multiple examples of the collapse or the disintegration of states.

The diffusion of political power, the increased number of international 'actors', the globalisation of economic institutions and the active dissent of populations, deprived of economic well-being or unfulfilled in their ethnic or cultural claims, have put the traditional nation state under great pressure. These phenomena hazard the integrity of the multinational state, whether China or Indonesia, even Canada. What is involved here, on a global scale, is a major shift in yet another balance of forces: that which had previously existed between 'state authority and populist elements'. It is the latter which are becoming increasingly predominant.[5] What has been described as 'state entropy' has resulted from the pressures exerted by supranational capitalism, the 'global economy', population growth and environmental degradation. All these have diminished state authority and undermined political legitimacy. The consequences have been political turbulence and social unrest born of impoverishment. Those who talk cosily about the 'global village' need to remember that for many it is a pestilential place, environmentally at risk, riven with violence and marred by gross inequalities in representation, wealth, access to markets and personal opportunity.

The security system which has evolved over the past half-century – nuclear deterrence, strategic alliances and regional security pacts, a form of international policing and peacekeeping, whether exercised by the two former super-powers themselves or through the United Nations – is now under the most severe strain, largely because of its irrelevance to or its remoteness from current problems. Some see its limited capability as suited only to maintaining elements of a precarious *status quo*, while the objective should be progress to a post-nuclear world.

The ending of the Cold War has by no means signalled an end to the nuclear nightmare, save perhaps in one respect, the improbability of all-out global nuclear war between two massively armed powers. A certain consensus has emerged between American and Russian senior military men that there is diminishing utility in nuclear weapons, General Charles A. Horner going as far to say that such weapons are 'obsolete and unusable'. On the other hand, in September 1994 the US Secretary of Defence, William Perry, defending the *US Nuclear Posture Review* argued against a further reduction in American strategic nuclear forces because of the uncertainties posed by the rapidity of change, political and economic, in the former Soviet Union.

The demise of the Soviet Union left nuclear weapons in the possession of four republics: Russia, Ukraine, Belarus and Kazakhstan. In Belarus all tactical weapons had been removed by May 1992 and all strategic nuclear weapons placed under Russian control, the non-nuclear status of Belarus confirmed by official military doctrine; in February 1993 Belarus ratified START I and the Non-proliferation Treaty. On 2 July Kazakhstan also signed up to the START I treaty and was looking favourably at the Non-proliferation Treaty.

Ukraine's 'nuclear legacy' from the Soviet Union amounted to some 1,600 warheads, 1,240 of them on ICBMs, intercontinental ballistic missiles, making Ukraine technically the third most powerful nuclear state in the world.[6] On 2 July 1993 the Ukrainian government announced its full ownership of all nuclear assets on Ukrainian territory, though the operational control of strategic forces remains, on paper at least, in dual Russian–Ukrainian hands. However, Ukraine declared its intention of becoming a 'nuclear-free state' once all nuclear weapons had been removed in accordance with the provisions of the START I (Strategic Arms Reduction Talks I) treaty. But what may best be called 'nuclear landlordism' appeared to hold a certain attraction for Ukraine, sufficient to delay Ukrainian ratification of START I. That transpired only on 18 November 1993 and was subject to ten reservations, among them the requirement of security guarantees once Ukraine was denuclearised, financial aid to meet the cost of dismantling nuclear weapons, and compensation for the fissile material so recovered. Once international financial assistance and technical aid were duly forthcoming the government of Ukraine agreed that 36 per cent of 176 of strategic missiles and 42 per cent of the warheads should be destroyed forthwith.

It remained to confirm provisional agreements with formal undertakings. On 14 January 1994 a trilateral treaty concluded between Russia, Ukraine and the United States established that Ukraine would become a nuclear-free state within seven years, an agreement which facilitated Ukrainian acceptance of the START I treaty, *de facto* ratification, though deferring as yet a decision to sign the Non-proliferation Treaty.

On 4 November 1992 the Russian parliament ratified the START I treaty but with the reservation that the other three republics must sign also and adhere to the Non-proliferation Treaty. The Russian position was that only Russia could exercise effective command and control as well as facilities for dismantling weapons. Without adherence to the Non-proliferation Treaty potential nuclear powers on Russia's borders – Iraq, Pakistan, Israel, North Korea – would be encouraged. It could also complicate control over fissile materials in particular and nuclear technology in general. Not much later, on 3 January 1993, Russia and the United States signed the START II treaty with its provision for reducing the existing level of deployed nuclear warheads, some 17,070 (9,300 Russian, 7,770 American) to a ceiling of

7,000 by the year 2003. Russia and the United States would each keep 3,500.[7]

In an increasingly strained atmosphere in Russian–American relations, bedeviled by Russian military operations in Chechnya and Russian plans to sell a nuclear reactor to Iran, START II faces escalating Russian opposition. Russian critics see in START II nothing less than the beheading of the Russian strategic missile forces with the elimination of the multi-warheaded SS-18 ICBM, a drastic reduction in Russian strategic power in itself and magnified if the United States should deploy a limited form of anti-missile defence. Russian insistence on the absolute integrity of the 1972 Anti-ballistic Missile Treaty has scarcely abated, with proposals by the Yeltsin government to collaborate with the United States in the area of anti-missile defence severely criticised by Russian politicians and scientists alike.

America proposes to convert what remains of the programme for space-based defence into an operational system of theatre missile defence (TMD) and national missile defence (NMD), the latter designed to protect the United States from limited ballistic missile attack, whether deliberate, accidental or unauthorised.[8] Russia objects to this and also to the expense involved in any restructuring of strategic forces following deep reductions in the ICBM component, while those same reductions, with further cuts envisaged, would mean that Russia as a diminished strategic power would be comparable in numbers to other nuclear states, a weakening of Russian defence potential against other powers, not least China. Nevertheless, shortage of money is likely to bring about a substantial reduction in the Russian strategic nuclear arsenal, bringing force levels significantly below the START II ceiling, one estimate of figures for the total Russian nuclear arsenal over time varying between 1,300 and 2,650.[9]

On 11 May 1995 the extension without time limit of the Nuclear Non-proliferation Treaty by the review conference, a mandatory assembly after the passage of twenty-five years stipulated by Article X of the original 1970 treaty, signalled the affirmation of the global nuclear *status quo*: nuclear 'haves' and nuclear 'have-nots'.[10] The nuclear status of the established 'nuclear powers', America, Britain, China, France and Russia, was confirmed, subject to an undertaking to work for nuclear disarmament, the offer of nuclear aid for peaceful purposes and a vague formula covering nuclear intimidation. Though no comprehensive test ban treaty has yet been accepted, an end to the production of fissile material on the part of some of the 'nuclear powers' has been agreed.

Nevertheless, military stocks of fissile material are gross: of the order of 1,500 tons, with 900 tons from civilian nuclear reactor programmes.[11] In the absence of any enforcement mechanism available to the Non-proliferation Treaty regime, signatories to the treaty – Iraq, Iran, North Korea – have been at liberty to work on nuclear weapons. Those not signatories to the treaty – India, Pakistan and Israel – pursue their own weapons programmes, with Arab and Muslim countries failing to force Israel to abandon its 'nuclear ambiguity'. Israel was not named specifically in a resolution which proposed a 'Middle East zone free of nuclear as well as other weapons of mass destruction'. As part of the 'nuclear bargain' nuclear-weapon states are urged to complete negotiations for a comprehensive nuclear test ban and an 'early conclusion' of talks designed to end the production of fissile materials for weapon manufacture.

At present the Nuclear Suppliers Group, the 'London Club', co-ordinates export controls on nuclear materials and associated technologies, but there is the growing problem of 'nuclear smuggling', 'nuclear leakage', not least from the former Soviet Union. Recent over-dramatisation of one case does not invalidate the argument that security procedures in former Soviet nuclear installations, in Russia, Ukraine and Kazakhstan, are in need of major overhaul, a state of affairs which has been openly and officially admitted. Measures are needed to improve and expand the safeguards programme of the International Atomic Energy Authority (IAEA), to detect undeclared and illegal activities. One relevant step would be to increase the IAEA safeguards budget, which has remained unchanged at $65 million for eight years even as the calls upon the agency have grown, extending into Argentina, Brazil, Iraq and North Korea.[12]

The 'post-nuclear world' would appear to be a distant prospect, with a North–South 'nuclear divide' taking the place of what had been previously a predominantly East-West confrontational division. It can be argued, however, that an overall international non-proliferation regime is clearly taking shape, for all its imperfections, as one important step towards the formation of what has been termed a 'global civil society'. A positive signal was sent out by the fact that the Nuclear Non-proliferation Review Conference took place, was attended by 170 nations and was successful. This should encourage further work to pursue that elusive comprehensive test ban, fissile materials cut-off, ratification of the Chemical Weapons Convention and the measures needed to strengthen the Biological Weapons Convention.

The real nightmare is the spread of weaponry, specifically missile technology and agents of mass destruction, combined with regional conflicts. When infused with any mix of ethnic, nationalist or even religious passions such conflicts show extremist features, exacerbated in turn by the military arsenals increasingly available. In almost Cold War copy-cat style several nations are seeking ballistic missiles and associated mass destruction agents in an effort to build a 'deterrent' force, supposedly, reportedly, a counterbalance to 'Western aggression'. Ballistic missiles in the Third World with a range of 1,000 km (625 miles) are multiplying, with ranges steadily expanding to reach 3,000 km, and including the possibility of delivering with nuclear, chemical or biological weapons.[13]

The span of this development is wide, embracing as many as twenty-five countries. Many of those states possessing, producing or purchasing ballistic missiles are also suspected of developing associated programmes of weapons of mass destruction. The attractiveness of the ballistic missile as a weapons system is undeniable, primarily its speed in reaching a target, its range, and in its mobile configuration it is difficult to detect and destroy. Even when the coalition forces in the Gulf War attained complete air superiority Iraq continued to launch modified SCUD-B missiles until the very end of the war.

What began as a mere dribble in the 1960s, with the delivery to client states and quasi-allies of the Soviet road-mobile SCUD-B with a range of the order of 280 km, supplied to Egypt and Syria, has turned into a virtual flood, with more such missiles going to Afghanistan, Libya and Yemen. Syria proceeded to take delivery of the Soviet SS-21, for which it may have worked on developing chemical warheads with North Korean assistance. The modified SCUD then made its appearance in other countries, including Iran and North Korea. It was the latter which delivered SCUD-MOD Bs to Iran for use in the Iran–Iraq war, also arranging for Iranian purchase of SCUD-MoD Cs in 1991, the same models delivered to Syria. Additionally, from models first acquired from Egypt, North Korea not only developed the SCUD-MoD C but also engineered an indigenous ballistic missile, the No-dong 1, with a range in excess of 1,000 km. North Korean missile/weapons developments have generated a very considerable literature.[14]

Missile technology also went to Israel, not always legally, to assist in the production of the JERICHO II missile, a road-mobile weapon, while the Pakistan HATF 1 missile was derived from French sounding rockets. Prominent among the 'suppliers' has been China, which in 1988 concluded the sale of medium-range CSS-2s to Saudi Arabia and is developing mobile solid-fuel short–medium-range missiles, the M-9 and M-11 models, designed for markets in south Asia and the Middle East. Manufacturing technologies for both of these missiles were passed to Pakistan and Iran. The technology transfer to Pakistan in 1993 was in breach of the Missile Technology Control Regime (MTCR), prompting the United States to retaliate with trade sanctions against China. China reaffirmed its adherence to the MTCR, insisting that the M-11 was outside those constraints, but declined to sign up to the revised MTCR regime promulgated in 1993.

Independent production of ballistic missiles is becoming more common, confined to those states with adequate resources, whether financial or technological. Argentina, Brazil, India, South Africa and Taiwan would fall into that category, India presenting a particular prominent example. Indian designers and engineers have developed the two-stage AGNI ballistic missile with a range up to 2,500 km, and a tactical missile, the PRITHVI, which may be nuclear-armed. Ballistic missiles developed indigenously are clearly immune from the effects of controls on trade, while the proliferation of technology is equally difficult to check.[15] A case in point is the reported development of a North Korean ICBM, the No-dong X, with Chinese and possibly Russian assistance, while efforts continue to 'leapfrog'the No-dong series with multi-stage missiles, Chinese–Korean hybrids, bringing all north-east and south-east Asia within range, even Russia, while any transfer of that capability to the Middle East would directly threaten Europe.

Inevitably North Korea's ballistic missile programme and its interest in mass destruction weapons, plus an anti-ship cruise missile programme, have shaken Japan's nerve and given rise to concern that the effort to contain proliferation may conceivably fail in north-east Asia. That prospect would require a major revision of Japan's security policy, hints of which have already been discreetly voiced in public. North Korean missiles able to strike at Japan, a limited North Korean nuclear arsenal, cruise missiles variously armed, chemical and biological programmes, all pose an undoubted threat which may be only partly deterred and not wholly deflected by the American 'nuclear umbrella' extended to Japan.

What is more alarming is that this form of proliferation may produce 'counter-proliferation' on the part of both South Korea and Japan, namely the rapid production of nuclear weapons, what has been termed 'virtual weaponization': secret research into key elements of nuclear weapons capability, not expressly outlawed by the Non-proliferation Treaty. Details have been disclosed of a secret Swedish nuclear weapons programme, literally buried for some thirty years in the underground AGESTA 65 MW reactor.[16] Current Swedish research is attributed to the requirements of defence, safety and counter-terrorism.

The Gulf War may have ushered in a new phase of ballistic missile proliferation, advertising the attractiveness of such systems, coupled with significant changes in 'the market' – more suppliers, more demand, with indigenous manufacture turning out more 'hybrids' and expanding areas of shared technology. If there is profit, which there certainly is, there is also saving, for example in research and development, assisted in the first instance by external funding, as in the Libyan–North Korean arrangement and a cost subsequently passed on to the buyer.

The profusion and diversification of such systems clearly have a major impact on regional security arrangements on the one hand and on potential regional conflict on the other. Adding fuel to a potential fire is an additive which can scarcely be ignored, the volume of conventional arms transfers to the Third World involving not merely numbers but quality, the latter increasing the sophistication of the weaponry available.[17]

Ironically, the five permanent members of the UN Security Council, together with Germany, are responsible for more than 85 per cent of global arms sales. Increasingly clients in the global 'arms bazaar' demand not merely the various systems themselves but also technology transfer and local manufacture, thereby helping to widen the pool of supplies and suppliers.

While it would be an exaggeration to say that the world is awash with weapons, the proliferation of ballistic missiles, weapons of mass destruction and advanced conventional weapons has the potential to produce unprecedented levels of violent regional conflict, or at best intensive regional arms races. In Asia, for example, competition will intensify not only owing to the transfer of high-technology weaponry from Russia, North America and Europe but also on account of the increased capabilities of the indigenous industrial base, of which China, Japan, India and Singapore are prime examples.

China's fighter modernization programme is evidently based on planned co-production involving the Russian Su-27 and its engine, manufacturing several hundred modern aircraft to replace 4,000 or more ageing machines. Should Russia not agree to co-production, with possible help from Israel the Chinese would attempt reverse engineering of the SU-27's Lyulka AL-31F turbofan, thus providing the power-plant for China's own F-10 multi-role fighter. A long-range fighter could patrol the South China Sea and keep watch over the fiercely disputed Spratly Islands. Such a modern aircraft could also counter Taiwan's F-16s and Mirage 2000-5s, as well as stimulating the Chinese aerospace industry which could find a ready market in Pakistan, Iran and possibly Iraq, which are not supplied by Western firms.[18] Within the next decade China will not only have ballistic missile submarines but also an improved, modernized strategic nuclear force with both mobile launchers and hardened silos, the ICBMs capable of targeting Asia, western Russia and America's east.[19] This scale and sophistication of weaponry, with states endowed with the capability to build a further generation of weapons themselves, renders the term 'regional' somewhat misleading. 'Regional conflict' must inevitably involve very large theatres of war, missiles in offence and defence, land, sea and air capabilities. Most would start from force levels not appreciably constrained by regional arms control agreements, without effective conflict control mechanisms to limit either ends or means, a situation possibly ignited but inevitably further inflamed by 'ethno-nationalism'.

Deterrence might be neither persuasive nor effective. Threaten the use of nuclear weapons? Intervention on the model of the Gulf War could be too costly in men and machines in view of the growing complexity and sophistication of the advanced conventional weaponry on the other side, the threat of the use of weapons of mass destruction, improved command and control facilities, early warning systems, anti-missile defences.[20] The initial American enthusiasm for what was termed 'second-generation peace operations', associated with 'assertive multilateralism', has steadily waned. The rules of international intervention will have to be radically reviewed in order to arrive at some consensus on what constitutes 'peacekeeping'. Hitherto it has been somewhat narrowly defined. The role, possibly the structure of the United Nations, or both, may have to be redefined and reorganised, with Germany and Japan admitted as permanent members to the Security Council, possible alteration of the composition of the Security Council having already come to the notice of the Commission on Global Governance. In 1992 the newly elected UN Secretary General produced his famous 'Agenda' with its proposal to create 'peace enforcement units', an ambitious plan, but, chastened by experience and a growing number of dangerous deployments, the January 1995 *Supplement* to the earlier Agenda draws back from the ambitious plans conceived three years ago. There is much confusion over the relationship between traditional peacekeeping and enforcement, confusion compounded by the using the same term, 'peace-keeping', for the two different functions.[21]

There are suggestions that we are on the verge of seeing a 'three-tier world'. The first formed by the developed, stable states of North America, western Europe and Asia. A second, less determinate in nature, formed of states which veer between stability and periodic crisis-induced internal dissent. The third, visibly expanding, an agglomeration of states run to or running to ruin – Afghanistan, Bosnia, Liberia, Mozambique, Somalia, the periphery of the former Soviet Union – with central government in full retreat and power passed to groups or enclaves ethnically, tribally or religiously defined and determined.[22]

Where the nation state has collapsed completely power is passing or has passed to non-state groups, criminal organisations with their own well-equipped forces, militias, warlord armies, revolutionary movements turning to large-scale crime to finance their movements. The defensive response to such a combination of threats, backed in some cases by access to weapons of mass destruction (Sarin, nerve gas, was recently unleashed in the Tokyo Underground by a cult with organised research and production facilities, steadily 'militarising' itself), will require immigration controls, counter-terrorism, military protection for humanitarian missions, intelligence and support for ecological agencies, provision against the possible use of weapons of mass destruction. A new term has come into the vocabulary to describe the threats, both real and potential, from non-state actors, 'grey-area phenomena' (GAP) – terrorism, ethnic discord, transnational crime, threats to security and dangers to stability which encompass both western and eastern Europe.[23]

While the bickering continues about the expansion of NATO, 'European security', in the widest sense, requires that a European regime should be developed to provide legislative and enforcement measures to deal with transnational problems. Europe's problems in the post-Cold War era are an image of global problems, the need to provide new institutional and organisational instruments to cope with a transition phase which may last a decade or more, threats to security and stability which fall short of all-out war but which involve spasms of conventional warfare, low-intensity conflict, 'grey-area phenomena' destabilisation and the crises brought on by environmental and ecological degradation. The 'global civil society' has yet to emerge. Until such time as it does, the task of institutions and organisations is to ward off global civil war.

Notes

1 See a general survey in Michael T. Klare, 'The new challenges to global security', *Current History*, 92 (57) April 1993, pp. 155-61. Michael Klare is also the author of *World Security: Trends and Challenges at Century's End*, second edition (1993).

2 Discussed in Stephen J. Cimbala, 'Nuclear weapons in the new world order', *Journal of Strategic Studies*, 16 (2), June 1993, pp. 173–99, also his monograph *US Military Strategy and the Cold War Endgame* (1995). On deterrence at large, also J. C. Garnett, 'Deterrence – Dead but it won't lie down', University of Manitoba Occasional Paper (1995).

3 A global review is presented in the authoritative *Strategic Survey 1994–95* (1995). Also the introductory essay by Lawrence Freedman, 'The future of conflict', in *The World in Conflict 1994–95, Jane's Intelligence Review Yearbook* (1995), pp. 5–7.

4 One conflict also unconnected with the Cold War and which requires mention is Northern Ireland. Conflicts in Colombia, Guatemala and Peru in Latin America are similarly wholly isolated from the circumstances of the Cold War.

5 Discussed in Michael Klare, 'The new challenges to global security' *Current History*, 92 (573), April 1993, pp. 155–61, where he argues that the nation state is 'caught between ever more powerful supranational capitalism ... and restive populations' (p. 157), a problem compounded by rapid population growth and environmental decline.

6 The report by Robert Banks, 'Nuclear Weapons in the Former Soviet Union', Scientific and Technical Committee of the North Atlantic Assembly, (1993), pp. 2–14, covers treaty commitments, proliferation threats, nuclear smuggling, transfers of personnel. On the movement and storage of Russian nuclear weapons see Anton Surikov and Igor Sutyagin, 'The movement and storage of Russian nuclear weapons', *Jane's Intelligence Review* 6 (5), May 1994, pp. 202–3.

7 For detailed figures see Stephen J. Cimbala, 'From deterrence to denuclearization: US and Russian nuclear force reductions', *Journal of Slavic Military Studies*, 7, (3), September 1994, pp. 421–42.

8 Tom Lewis, *Missile Defence Technology*, Scientific and Technical Committee Report, North Atlantic Assembly (November 1992), p. 12, concluded that 'a new era in the nuclear age, and therefore, in world history' had begun with the combination of the 'fall of the Soviet Union and the proliferation of ballistic missile threats', hence the growing importance of 'missile defence technology'.

9 See Joshua Handler, 'The future of Russian strategic forces', *Jane's Intelligence Review*, 7, (4) April 1995, pp. 162–5, with tables of production rates: also on the road-mobile TOPOL SS-25 ICBM, 'the [Russian] missile for the twenty-first century', and silo-based TOPOL-M see Stephen J. Zaloga, *Jane's Intelligence Review*, 7, (5), May 1995, pp. 195–200, with technical data.

10 On nuclear proliferation and the non-proliferation regime see Sir Peter Emery, *Nuclear Proliferation Report*, Scientific and Technical Committee, North Atlantic Assembly (October 1993).

11 See Joseph Cirincione, 'The Non-proliferation Treaty and the nuclear balance', *Current History*, 94 (592), May 1995, pp. 201–6.

12 See Patricia Lewis, 'Strengthening Safeguards', Verification Matters Briefing Paper 95/2, March 1995, on strengthening IAEA, VERTIC, Verification Technology Information Centre, London.

13 Data in Keith Payne, 'Ballistic missile proliferation – an audit', *The World in Conflict 1994/95, Jane's Intelligence Review Yearbook* (1995), pp. 20–4.

14 For data see Joseph S. Bermudez Jr, 'North Korea's chemical and biological warfare arsenal', *Jane's Intelligence Review* 5 (5) May 1993, pp. 225–8, with map of chemical and biological warfare related locations; also 'North Korea: a potential time bomb', *Jane's Intelligence Review*, Special Report No. 2, Ballistic Missile Programme, pp. 11–15, tables, maps; also the latest study by Greg Gerardi and Joseph Bermudez Jr, 'An analysis of North Korean ballistic missile testing', *Jane's Intelligence Review* 7 (4) April 1995, pp. 184–90, tables, maps. On Iran see a detailed study countering much alarmism, James W. Moore, 'An assessment of the Iranian military rearmament program', *Comparative Strategy*, 13 (4), pp. 371–89, graphs, tables.

15 See Tom Lewis, *Ballistic Missile Proliferation*, Scientific and Technical Committee, North Atlantic Assembly (October 1993). Part IV 'Proliferation Countermeasures', Missile technology control regime (MTCR): also Jing-dong Yuan, *Non-proliferation Export Controls in the 1990s*, Martello Papers 7 (1994), pp. 5–47.

16 'Sweden's quiet quest: nuclear arms option', *International Herald Tribune*, 16 November 1994. See also Andrei Shoumikhin, 'Russian approach to advanced weapons proliferation: change and continuity', *Comparative Strategy*, 13 (4), Octtober–December 1994, pp. 447–53.

17 Mr. Sherwood L. Boehlert, *Conventional Arms Transfers*, Interim Report, Subcommittee on the Proliferation of Military Technology, Scientific and Technical Committee, North Atlantic Assembly (November 1994); also John Sislin and David Mussington, 'Destabilising arms acquisitions', *Jane's Intelligence Review*, 7 (2), February 1995, pp. 88–90.

18 Details in 'China pursuing two-fighter plan', *Aviation Week and Space Technology*, 27 March 1995, pp. 44–5.

19 In *Comparative Strategy* 14 (2), May–June 1995, special issue, *Regional Conflicts and Co-operation*, see John Arquilla, 'Bound to fail: regional deterrence after the Cold War', pp. 123–35.

20 See Paul Dibb, 'The future military capabilities of Asia's great powers', *Jane's Intelligence Review*, 7 (5), May 1995, pp 229–33, with table of projections of military capacity to 2010 (China, Japan, India, Pacific Russia and the Pacific United States) minus strategic nuclear forces.

21 Boutros Boutros-Ghali, *An Agenda for Peace*, (1992); for 'Peacekeeping and the new international environment' see Henk Vos and James Bilbray, *NATO, the UN and Peacekeeping: New Context, New Challenges*, Defence and Security Committee, North Atlantic Assembly (November 1994), pp. 3–17.

22 See, *Military Review*, LXXV (1), December 1994–January/February 1995, spe-

cial issue, *Controlling Chaos*, especially Steven Metz, 'A strategic context for Third Tier conflict', pp. 4–14, also articles on European terrorism, ethno-nationalist conflicts, 'non-traditional threats'.

23 On ethnic conflict, Ted Robert Gurr, *Minorities at Risk: a Global View of Eth-nopolitical Conflicts* (1993), also Gurr, 'Communal conflicts and global security', *Current History*, 94 (592), May 1995, pp. 212–17; also Daniel Livermore, *Ethnic Conflict in the New Europe*, Martello Papers 7 (1994). See also Donald E. J. McNamara and Philip John Sted, *New Dimensions in Transnational Crime* (1982). For narcotics trafficking and terrorism see the journal *Low Intensity Conflict and Law Enforcement*.

Further reading

Akbar Ahmed and Hasting Donnan (eds), *Islam, Globalization and Postmodernity* (1993).

Asian Security, 1994–95 (1994).

Hans Binnendijk (ed.), *Strategic Assessment, 1995: US Security Challenges in Transi-tion* (1995).

Canada Bibliography on Arms Control Verification, Fourth Update (October 1995).

Andrew Cottey, *East Central Europe after the Cold War: Poland, the Czech Republic, Slovakia and Hungary in Search of Security* (1995).

Joan DeBardeleben and John Hannigan (eds), *Environmental Security and Quality after Communism: Eastern Europe and the Soviet Successor States* (1995).

Stuart E. Johnson and William H. Lewis (eds), *Weapons of Mass Destruction: New Per-spectives on Counterproliferation* (1995).

John Keep, *Last of the Empires: a History of the Soviet Union, 1945–91* (1995).

Keith Krause, *Arms and the State: Patterns of Military Production and Trade*(1992).

Michael J. Mazarr and Alexander T. Lennon, *Toward a Nuclear Peace* (1994).

R. S. Norris, A. S. Burrows and R. W. Fieldhouse, *British, French and Chinese Nuclear Weapons: Nuclear Weapons Databook* (1994).

Wayne Sandholz, *The Highest Stakes: the Economic Foundations of the next Security System* (1992).

Strategic survey, 1994–95 (1995).

Maxwell Taylor and Ethel Quayle, *Terrorist Lives* (1994).

Trevor Taylor and Seizaburo Sato (eds), *Future sources of Global Conflict* (1995).

Trust and Verify. Bulletin of the Verification Technology Information Centre, London.

Chapter 3

Postmodernism and postmodernity: a user's guide

Joe Bailey

The excited rhetoric about postmodernism and postmodernity should not be allowed to hide the usefulness of these terms to the historian. Much of the theorising – and the agonising and the sheer display – has become rococo and tedious. But there is a basic sense in the warning voiced by writers on postmodernism: the contemporary world in which historians work has changed in the most dramatic ways and these changes affect the meaning of what historians write.

That world is one in which social events and their underlying social processes, all of which have an historical dimension, are given significance by those who comment upon them. Historians and social scientists are themselves caught up in this world and in turn cannot avoid descriptively creating it. Postmodernism and postmodernity are attempts to grasp that the present times are different in some very important sense from the past in both their social forms (embracing the economic, political and technological) and in their cultural and intellectual practices.

Social change

Our attempts to make sense of social change as some sort of sequence can be seen as describing a pattern to history. This may be proposed as a particular direction, for instance as evolutionary or as cyclical in form, or as the continuous functioning of a dominant and determinant mechanism, such as technology or production. The apparent need for the former – for a sense of direction – and its political use, and, perhaps, even its psychological relevance, go some way to explain the immense power of the idea of progress.

Seeing social change as involving betterment, improvement or advance in some way, as being, in a deep sense, the pattern of history, has been the dominant assumption for understanding the direction of social change.

Modernity

Labelling periods within the sequence of social change is a consequence of this patterning. Labels are devices imposed by the historian and, of course, justified by an appeal to evidence. Modernity is seen as the period beginning in post-feudal Europe (one such label) and emerging strongly from the eighteenth-century Enlightenment. Our social institutions and organisations, our economic and political life are self-consciously modern and still share, publicly, the belief in progress as the extension of reason, knowledge, freedom, justice and order. We are moderns. Our age is the age of modernity. We still believe the 'grand narratives' of progress and our recent experience of the problems of the world does not seriously qualify or undermine this. Or does it?

A break

The concern with postmodernism and postmodernity is essentially an attempt to describe the apparent ending of this long period of modernity and poses a variety of possibilities for what is coming next. The two parts are separable. What comes next does not necessarily or simply entail the ending of what we now have, and it is useful to concentrate on both the ending, and the sense of the ending, of modernity. One of the exasperating characteristics of the more flamboyant postmodernists is their tendency to treat the characteristics of the ending of modernism as themselves the shape of the future.

The idea of a break, a rupture or a discontinuity is uncomfortable. It discomfits the sense of connection which understanding the pattern of history requires of us. But that is what is being proposed in a variety of ways. Put very boldly, the fundamental energies and even the goals of modernity are now exhausted and ripe for abandonment. Scientific rationality, moral progress, justice, freedoms (both to and from) and the intelligibility and potential control of the natural and the social worlds can no longer be believed in as the foundations of our collective lives. And, more materially, the spatial and temporal conditions of our societies have now changed – they have become simultaneously globalised and individualised – and such irrevocable shifts are relatively recent and profoundly disruptive. These propositions about the end of modernity and its culture are drenched in a sense of anxiety, uncertainty and loss: a fear of what will or could happen.

The doubts and apprehensions which have accompanied the possible end of modernity are readily understandable. They reflect the failure of modernity to deliver progress in its own terms, and the existence of a wholly new range of intractable and potentially terminal social problems. On the one hand we know more than we have ever known – that is we understand history. We know that we know more, that is, we are exceptionally 'reflex-

25

ive'. And we know that all this knowledge does not seem to generate genuine progress. Knowledge is seriously in doubt for the first time. On the other hand modernity itself has given us a world of more extensive communal conflict, seemingly unstoppable abuses of nature and the apparent dissolution of hitherto basic social structures such as employment, social control and identity.

The transformative capacity of modernity which has given us huge increases in economic productivity and wealth, and such a variety of pleasures, seems unable also to require us to use the wealth wisely and safely or to prevent the pleasures from becoming our pains.

Postmodernism and postmodernity

An extensive debate about these issues has been going on in all the social science and humanities disciplines. It has been fed by other traditions of writing and thinking in the arts and aesthetic commentary, in literary criticism, in psychoanalysis and even in some of the physical sciences. This debate is highly self-conscious, often abstractly theoretical and increasingly self-referential. But it is an importantly alerting one. Postmodern*ism* is, loosely, the term we give to this debate. Postmodern*ity* is the social, political, cultural and historical condition which this debate takes to be its object. The historian of ideas may be able to concentrate on postmodernism alone but, generally speaking, the two should be seen as a unity for the historian interested in a past seen and read by an audience now in our 'new times'.

Society

Historians always make indirect sense of their own society, whatever period they examine. But the historical investigation of the contemporary world, in particular, requires a sense of society seen as a connected set of social structures, institutions, organisations and social practices.

Sociologists attempt to catalogue and order these social forms, and much of their debate concerns the priority and relative significance of these seen over chronological time. However, an understanding of the sheer complexity of contemporary society is all we really need to see the importance, though not necessarily the truth, of postmodernity. The massive and accelerating transformations in all sectors of society can be investigated and mapped. There are different 'levels' to these sectors. For instance, institutions such as the family or social stratification are primary and spontaneous social groupings which 'contain' organisations. The latter are more deliberately created devices, such as households and businesses, and thus more easily changeable. At whatever level we look, however, the extent, speed and uncontrolled nature of some changes are what strikes us, combined with lack of change and persistence where we did not expect it. No part of contemporary society, at any level, seems stable or predictable. The question is, do these changes in the parts of society warrant us talking of such a dramatic shift as postmodernism proposes in the whole?

An examination of the parts themselves cannot answer this. We would need to move from the evidence of discrete changes in institutions and organisations to a willingness to see them in the context of some particular social whole, for reasons that go beyond that evidence and which are concerned with theory and philosophy, to respond to this question. An additive approach which tries to make overall sense of the diverse movements by the sheer weight of evidence will not lead to a conclusion that there has been a shift to a postmodern world. For that we need an overall model which is, naturally, nourished by that evidence. The point of this is that postmodernism and postmodernity are heuristically valuable models in providing a context for historical research. This is the weakest case that can be made for it.

Dimensions of change

Consider the very significant changes we have experienced as modernity has aged or, perhaps, come to an end. Four dimensions will serve to illustrate the penetrating and ramified nature of the social shifts we are living with.

Identity

The sense of social location and the sense of identity – of who one is – are plainly socially relative. The contemporary breaking up (or breaking down) of the traditional sources of the sense of self, position, sharedness and community, can be seen in the increasing variety of possible identifications which people can adopt – gender, religion, nation, 'race' or, even, individuality itself.

The 'death of the subject' proposed by postmodernists, especially in the humanities, is an extreme way of recasting this visible confusion or, at least, pluralism. It proposes eliminating the stable, thinking, feeling, intending and socially connected man or woman as the prime focus of our understanding of the experience of history and culture. It can be replaced with 'desubjectified' language, or text or 'discourse' as alternative and privileged concepts to understand history. What this does is to put into highly abstract terms the plain facts of a collapse of certainty about identity.

The increasing pluralism of culture in general, the florid growth of youth and mass culture as a range of consumable and transitory styles, the availability of new (and the resurgence of old) understandings of gender, race and nation and the proliferation of radically different forms of religion (and their denial) all point to a great change from the relatively simple sources of available identity we are used to in modernity. Relatively fixed experiences of class, nation, locality, gender and religious denomination provided, until recently, the available sources of subjective identity. Now all is flux and change and the individual experiences this potentially flexible and multiple array as both an opportunity for expressive choice and a source of social and political problems.

The turn to the private, to giving new importance to the very plastic 'inner' self and the personal, as the area we look to for a sense of a satisfying identity is one recent example of this collapse of the stability of the old bases of our sense of belonging. Individualism is an important dimension of the fragmentation of identity because its materialist dimensions, seen in consumerism, mean that the stabilising demands of culture and social obligation, to, for instance, the family, the community or the formal requirements of religion are undermined. This has profound impacts upon politics itself.

Employment and marginalisation

De-industrialisation has led to a huge dislocation of social experience. The post-industrial shift in the old advanced economies of the world has removed from governments, and from social and personal experience itself, much of the sense of security and control which increasingly characterised modernity. Severe manufacturing job loss since the 1960s and its only partial compensation by the service industries have not led to an improvement in the quality of life but rather to massive and continuing unemployment. Combined with the dominance of the market as a mode of distributing the social product, this has resulted in a combination of the destruction of local communities (and the sense of community) and the marginalisation of sections of the population of all societies. The dominant experience is of increasing insecurity and this appears to be deeply structural and unchangeable.

These changes have had the effect of altering the character, and our treatment, of social stratification and, particularly, of the economically disadvantaged groups in our societies. The changing employment structure, combined with racism, has led to the pushing of particular groups to the margins of society, in a way that was thought to be over for ever. Loose notions of an 'underclass' of deprived, threatening people with little stake as citizens in a society which gives them only permanent insecurity and poverty can be attached to a view of the state (and hitherto a welfare state) which is unable to manage economic stability, let alone improvement. There is even a sense, in some writers, of a neo-medieval reversion to tyranny and terror at local levels to fill the power vacuum and in which these marginal groups can become politically volatile and significant. A concern with physical security and protection in the face of apparently increasing tensions and conflicts is connected with these changes, which, we can see, are a linked series stretching from transformations in the global economy to the personal sense of social membership.

Postmodernists speak of the relinquishing of the political projects of modernity, of the end, or the impossibility, of social emancipation through any 'grand narrative' of politics. The alternatives suggested are cynicism, playfulness or, less extremely, the reinvention of an alternative politics based upon a variety of 'new' political movements. Whether passively denying the possibility of any solutions or proposing the complete reconstruction of what we should mean by politics, these positions are a reflection of the profound difficulties of generating and distributing social wealth in the way modernity had suggested. These real changes can be seen to be the social condition of the theoretical positions now advocated by postmodernists.

Information and technology

In some sense we live in an 'information society' rather than an 'industrial society'. Telecommunications and computers have changed the very basis upon which our economic and social exchanges take place at an organisational level, and have increased the potential for the surveillance and control of everyday life by central political bodies. The new forms of the effective administration of our social lives and the largely unforeseen and, perhaps, unforeseeable changes in cultural life through the extension of particular kinds of communications, especially television, have had a deep impact.

The power of the image, especially the screened image, is seen by some postmodernists as radically transforming the nature of social experience itself. It dissolves traditional forms of signification and meaning. Images, codes and 'simulacra' become detached from their 'real' referents. They are the reality and impose a deep form of meaning both on what is experienced through them directly and on other forms of experience which come to be significant only in so far as they can be judged through them. Such a view is plainly extreme, and has led to some absurd pronouncements, such as that the Gulf War did not 'really' take place. However, these abstractions reflect the new power of telecommunications to transform daily, lived experience and the nature of contemporary politics as an extended form of advertising.

Although there is still uncertainty about the real impact of information technology there is little doubt that there are new perils which it is hard to control, in contrast to the optimistic modernist views of a decade ago that information technology meant progress. It has come to mean dehumanisation, vulnerability and secrecy as well. The most startling example of these effects concerns globalisation or the transsocietal nature of social change. The huge acceleration in the turnover times of capital through the electronic markets has decoupled economies from the nation state. The world has become a single unified place in economic, political and military terms and subsequently in cultural forms. The world is woven together in real time as far as economies, weaponry and mass culture are concerned. What one writer refers to as 'space–time compression' articulates everything in the world and thus puts genuine cultural diversity at risk and at a premium, to be fought for with only the most brutal weapons available. The growth of 'nationalist' conflicts can be seen, partly, in this light.

Consumption and consumerism

The transformation of everything into a commodity to be bought, sold and consumed is the striking feature of our mundane lives now. The market penetrates everything. Age, gender, ethnicity, religion, science and even truth itself come to have the status of a consumable. Consumption is our new social condition. It dominates people's lives. It defines their status and their social connection with each other. It becomes the social bond which knits society together and replaces conviction, duty, obligation, habit or compliance with authority. It dissolves other, more profound, foundations of social significance. Consumption is our new social condition.

One does not have to have been a Marxist to understand that production, and one's social connection with the social organisation of production, was the axis around which societies were structured. The economic and cultural means to live came from employment in production. Daily life was dominated by the social construction of employment; its routines, returns, costs, pleasures and the human and social reactions to it. All this has been replaced by consumption and the commodification of everything.

More significantly, consumption itself has become the prime value in society now, the standard by which social significance is judged. This is important because the depthlessness and necessary superficiality of consumption (what is consumed must, after all, be used up) is an extremely fragile foundation on which to base social and personal arrangements which must, by their nature, continue over a long period of time. Political choice, family organisation, education and health have dimensions beyond their status as comsumables.

The fear of a dominant consumerism is more than just a complaint about the market as the best method of distribution in society. It is an anxiety about the dilution of complexity in social affairs at all levels. The pleasures of rootless, free-floating and ever-ambitious consumption carry with them an attached 'thinning' of the sense of the intricacy and interconnection of social life as well as the loss of overarching and non-material values. The fear (and for some the pleasure) is of the trivialisation of social and natural life and the loss of a political attention to match the apparent dangers which surround us. The implications for the kind of ethics upon which the modernist project was founded are obvious.

These markers of social change are by no means exhaustive or exclusive.

They are intended to serve only as indications of the real alterations in our society. They serve to warn historians and others that there is evidence which should provoke attention to the possibility that we may indeed be shifting into a drastically different world: that there are grounds for considering that postmodernity may, indeed, be a valuable model for making sense of these unavoidable transformations.

A useful model

Recognition of the radical and dramatic nature of recent social change may be enough to characterise it as postmodern. Some writers see our current condition as a part of late modernity, as continuous with earlier experiences and involving no distinct break with the past or epochal shift. Nonetheless they see the new times as a distinctive, novel and remarkable social, cultural and political constellation. It is not necessary to hold the more extreme view, which would see some sort of rupture occurring. The issue concerns whether it is useful to label our current situation as postmodern.

The main obstacle for many social analysts to doing this concerns the very drastic implications of swallowing the immoderate methodological claims of some postmodernist writers to have dispensed with criteria of truth itself and thus to render all analysis, writing and, indeed, purposive social action null and void. What we might call 'extreme' postmodernism incorporates the prognosis of radical uncertainty, which we can see in the description of postmodernity, into its own view of what can now be said by social scientists – indeed, by anybody. That is, the death of the subject and the end of all motivating grand narratives in a world characterised by fragmentation, disintegration and potentially terminal danger lead to versions of nihilism as the only form of writing and speaking; to 'endism' and extreme pessimism.

Such a position is justifiably criticised. It means the end of disciplined critical thought and the collapse of the distinctions between illusion and reality and between accuracy and falsehood. It means the end of history as a practice as well as a process and the abandonment of judgement and the use of evidence. But we do not have to accept all this. We can still see the value of viewing our society as characterised by postmodernity and continue the quest for systematic social investigation.

We can characterise the intertwined contemporary social condition and cultural experience as postmodern. It is a useful warning device which alerts us to what are unprecedented changes in our society and the terrible dangers they have brought. It does not require us to become complete intellectual relativists and abandon all notions of progress simply because those of modernity have been shown to have failed – so far.

There are two senses in which the term 'postmodernism' is used here.

One is as a paralysing critique of the character and purposes of all social and historical analysis. Postmodernism means, here, the rejection of all conventional approaches to knowledge, truth and objectivity, and the abandonment of trying to attach knowledge to progress. The other tries to describe the latest stage of development of our society and its potentially radical new form. Postmodernism here draws attention to the profundity of recent historical change. The two conceptions are linked. But the paralysis of the former does not necessarily entail the use of the latter.

Further reading

Introduction to postmodernism

D. Lyon, *Postmodernity* (1994), is an excellent, concise, jargon-free and stimulating first port of call.

P. Rosenau, *Postmodernism and the Social Sciences: insights, inroads and intrusions* (1992), is a detailed account of nearly all the significant debates summarised in terms of 'skeptical' and 'affirmative' postmodernists and with a specific section on history.

B. Smart, *Postmodernity* (1993), is a clear, quite short and specifically sociological introduction with an extensive range of references.

Modernity, progress and social change

A. Giddens, *The Consequences of Modernity* (1990), is an important account of late modernity and its social formation from a writer who has gone on to look at the implications of our current society for the sense of self and identity.

K. Kumar, *Prophecy and Progress: the sociology of industrial and post-industrial society* (1978), is still the best account of the concept of progress in an empirical, historical context, and it summarises a great deal of other material.

P. Wagner, *A Sociology of Modernity: liberty and discipline* (1994), is a stimulating consideration of the whole issue of modernity and its various transitions, seeing postmodernity debates as one response.

Conceptions and histories of postmodernism and postmodernity

R. Boyne and A. Rattansi (eds), *Postmodernism and Society* (1990), provides useful sections on most of the major positions without guying their complexity or overwhelming the reader with jargon.

D. Harvey, *The Condition of Postmodernity* (1989), describes in detail the significance of postmodern changes, from aesthetics to the production and consumption processes, focusing on 'space–time' compression.

J-F. Lyotard, *The Postmodern Condition: a report on knowledge* (1986), started the ball rolling in the latest phase of the social science debate and stimulated much of the later discussion.

B. Smart, *Modern Conditions, Postmodern Controversies* (1992), a very clear and thorough account of the range of philosophical and sociological positions within the debate on postmodernism and postmodernity.

B. Turner (ed.), *Theories of Modernity and Postmodernity* (1990), helps to clarify the variety of positions and provides an account of the historical development of the concepts.

Critics

A. Callinicos, *Against Postmodernism: a Marxist critique* (1989), is a vigorous denial of the usefulness and viability of postmodernism as a social science perspective.

E. Gellner, *Postmodernism, Reason and Religion* (1992), is an acerbic and stimulating attack on postmodernism from a modified Enlightenment rationalist perspective.

J. O'Neill, *The Poverty of Postmodernism* (1995), is a defence of reason and democracy against a view of postmodernism as a threat to common sense and truth.

Chapter 4

The 'end of history' debate revisited

Richard Cockett

My purpose is not to offer yet another critique of Francis Fukuyama's thesis on 'the end of history', but rather to address the subsidary, but no less interesting question as to whether the debate provoked by Fukuyama's work can be of any use to contemporary historians. Fukuyama writes in a distinct tradition of 'universal history' that has usually been the preserve of philosophers and political activists, or even State Department officials, rather than practising historians and it could be argued that the only reason why philosophers and the like have felt able to generalise about *all* history is that they have spared themselves first-hand acquaintance with the complexities of the subject. Hegel, the founder of the modern school of 'universal history', travelled famously light on actual historical events in his seminal 'Lectures on the Philosophy of History', just as Fukuyama prefers to give the reader a rigorous philosophical framework in which he can locate his own approach to 'universal history' rather than an analysis of actual events which might justify his conclusions about the triumph of liberal democracy. A cynic might even argue that ignorance is a prerequisite for the writing of universal history.

Furthermore, the history of 'universal history' itself is a story of hubris and nemesis, of high comedy as its practitioners pronounce loftily on 'the end of history', only to see that wretchedly unpredictable creature break off in fresh and unexpected directions. Fukuyama himself has considerable fun with one of his principal forebears, the Russian émigré philosopher Alexander Kojeve, the most important modern interpreter of Hegel. Kojeve taught a series of highly influential seminars at the Ecole Pratique des Hautes Études in the 1930s, shaping the minds of a generation of post-war French intellectuals such as Raymond Aron and George Bataille. Kojeve resurrected Hegel for modern consumption, agreeing with his German precursor that history as an idea had come to an end at the battle of Jena in 1806. History rode past Hegel on the eve of the battle on a white horse in the small but significant shape of the emperor Napoleon, as Hegel recounted breathlessly to his mentor: 'I saw the emperor, this world-soul, ride through the town on a reconnoitre. It is truly a wondrous experience to behold such an individual, concentrated at one point, sitting on a horse, spread over the world and assume mastery over it.'[1]

Kojeve picked up from where Hegel had left off, determined to find his own world-souls – in tanks. Like Hegel, and anticipating Fukuyama, Kojeve argued that nothing of importance had happened since the French revolution of 1789 and that subsequent events had merely been the working out of the ideas of the revolution; the revolution was the pebble lobbed into the middle of the lake, and all we have been doing since is watching the ripples slowly but inevitably spread out towards the shores. Fukuyama, in the style of a modern bureaucrat, models this effect with bar charts and graphs. Kojeve himself wrote:

> Observing what was taking place in the world since the battle of Jena, I understood that Hegel was right to see in this battle the end of history properly so-called. In and by this battle the vanguard of humanity virtually attained the limit and the aim, that is, the end, of man's historical evolution. What has happened since then was but an extension in space of the universal revolutionary force actualized in France by Robespierre–Napoleon.[2]

But quite where this 'universal revolutionary force' had finally come to rest in the modern era presented Kojeve with rather more problems. Observing the heroic defence of the Soviet Union in 1942, Kojeve reached the conclusion that the Soviet Union was the ultimate destination of the world-historical spirit, that this was the ultimate society that could not be improved upon, with no internal contradictions. However, only a few years later he had changed horses and now saw the revived democracies of western Europe as the perfect embodiment of the principles of the revolution and the European Community, with its material prosperity and political stability, became, in Fukuyama's words, '... an appropriate institutional embodiment of the end of history'.[3] Such confusion seems to have mattered little to Kojeve, although it must have required a fertile imagination to see the world-historical spirit fulfilled in both the Soviet Union and the European Community within a few years of each other. Kojeve himself ended his career, appropriately, as a bureaucrat in the post-war European Economic Community.

Other projects of 'universal history' have come to grief in an equally entertaining manner. In 1960 Daniel Bell's book *The End of Ideology* announced the end of serious political divisions in the West with the triumphal rise of the Keynesian, 'middle way' consumer society, antedating the ferocious and unprecedented split on this issue between economic liberals ('Thatcherites' or 'Reaganites') and collectivists by just fifteen years. Thomas Macaulay's *History of England*, celebrating the success of the first liberal revolution in England and of the 'Whig' notion of 'progress' as measured by the growth in material wealth, was published in 1848, the very year that Marx and Engels exposed the contradictions at the heart of Macaulay's bourgoise nirvana in *The Communist Manifesto*. Within two generations England had essentially turned its back on Macaulay's version of 'progress'. And Marx's own pretensions to a 'scientific' interpretation of history were exposed almost as soon as the *Communist Manifesto* was published, based as it was on empirical research into an industrial society that was already changing quickly enough to frustrate Marx's hopes of a proletarian revolution. In our own time, Paul Kennedy's attempt to elucidate the iron laws of international power and diplomacy in *The Rise and Fall of the Great Powers* proved to be an equally unreliable guide to the future. Writing in 1986, Kennedy attracted a lot of attention for his gloomy predictions about the imminent collapse of American power but rather less for his assertion that the USSR was *not* close to collapse.

So just a brief glance at the track record of 'universal history' would seem to demonstrate that its practitioners have never been very reliable guides to the past, let alone the future. Indeed, they have frequently done little more than strike the appropriate note of ideological triumphalism at the very moment when the era they were celebrating was, in fact, coming to a close. The more astute politicians have never been convinced, either. When Fukuyama's original article on 'the end of history' was published in the *National Interest* magazine in summer 1989 Mrs Thatcher's closest adviser, Charles Powell, slipped it into one of her red boxes. Although Mrs Thatcher was herself one of the major beneficiaries (and catalysts) of Fukuyama's universal liberal revolution – a Hegelian world-historical figure with a handbag – the Prime Minister was reportedly unimpressed by Fukuyama's complacent assertions that she had fulfilled her mission. Within a year she was out of office. Equally ironic from Fukuyama's point of view is the fact that he was asserting the hegemony of an ideology – economic liberalism/liberal democracy – which had always been suspicious of, if not downright hostile to, the idea of universal history as a methodological concept in itself. The most compelling critic of 'historical determinism' remains Karl Popper, who first read his paper on 'The Poverty of Historicism' to a private seminar in Brussels in 1936 before publishing it in three parts in *Economica* in 1944 and 1945, and whose principal villains in *The Open Society and its Enemies* were the universal historians Marx and Hegel. Popper argued persuasively that 'We must reject the possibility of a *theoretical history*; that is to say, of a historical social science that would correspond to *theoretical physics*. There can be no scientific theory of historical development serving as a basis for historical prediction.'[4] Popper conceded the 'emotional appeal' of historicism whilst demolishing its claims to methodological exactitude.

Popper's work was one of the sources for the neo-liberal revolution in Britain and America in the 1980s together with other liberals of continental birth such as Isaiah Berlin, another critic of universal history. The title of his last book of essays is taken from Immanuel Kant – 'Out of the crooked timber of humanity no straight thing was ever made'.[5] As Perry Anderson has written, 'Here, we are given to understand, is a signal expression of that rejection of all perfectionist utopias which defines a humane pluralism.'[6] And first and foremost amongst all those 'perfectionist utopias' is any idea of a universal history, of an all-embracing theory to explain every dimly lit corner of human experience. Indeed, the very essence of pluralistic liberal democracy is its insistence on diversity and preserving the differences between people, of allowing people to cultivate their own micro-utopias, rather than attempting to usher society in the direction of some historically determined single goal – whether that be reason, the classless society or economic liberalism.

Hayek, the principal intellectual source for the neo-liberal revival that, according to Fukuyama, is supposed to have swept all before it by 1989, was an equally determined opponent of universal laws of explanation, particularly in his own field of economics; it was primarily Popper's interest in this same field that brought Popper to Hayek's attention in the first place, and prompted Hayek to secure Popper his post at the London School of Economics in 1946. Hayek spent most of his life attacking 'macro-economics', the attempt, in his view, to construct laws of economic determinism out of totally random and arbitrary pieces of information which could then be used to predict economic growth, output, etc. Indeed, for Hayek the whole discipline of economics was a misnomer, designed as a theoretical tool of analysis to explain and predict what was inherently unpredictable, unquantifiable and too complex to be reduced to neat theoretical formulas – he preferred to use the word 'catallaxy' to describe his subject, rather than 'economics', with its pretensions to universality. What all these thinkers shared was an absolute distrust of grand theoretical projects such as universal history; for them liberal democracy could succeed only if such constrictive and reductionist projects were cast aside. Although the liberalism that Fukuyama proclaims as the 'end of history' owes much to the work of modern writers such as Berlin, Hayek and Popper, they would have recognised his work as just another teleological doctrine of the type which they had had to subvert in order to rescue liberalism from the intellectual disrepute into which it had fallen by the 1930s. Not surprisingly, none of the aforementioned are referred to by Fukuyama – for the modern progenitors of liberalism were the most scathing critics of universality, and of universal history in particular. And I suspect that most historians would still side with Popper rather than Fukuyama.

Just as Fukuyama ends up asserting that liberalism and markets are the 'end of history', using analytical methods that were rejected long ago by those who did most to rejuvenate and inspire the modern liberal tradition, so Fukuyama also bears a striking resemblance to those thinkers of the post-war left, particularly in France, who have approached the questions of modernity that Fukuyama poses from a completely different direction. Far from being 'universal' in the sense that it draws upon a wide range of analytical sources, Fukuyama's history in fact confines itself to a very Anglo-Saxon concept of the role of ideas in history; that ideas, or *ideals*, may still be intelligible to most people and that history can be understood only as a linear progression. Jean Baudrillard, by way of contrast, challenges the whole idea of an 'end' to history, arguing that it is but a fantasy of linear history in his book *The Illusion of the End*. In some ways Baudrillard sounds very much like Fukuyama when he writes that 'Deep down, one cannot even speak of the end of history here, since history will not have time to catch up with its own end. Its effects are accelerating, but its meaning is slowing inexorably.' But as a postmodernist Baudrillard also sees the idea of linear history, inevitably moving towards some final destination, as just another meta-narrative of modernism; he prefers to see history as an 'immense simulation model', constantly referring to itself in a vortex of media and 'news' reports. For Baudrillard, history is now little more than 'feedback'; at the close of the twentieth century he postulates a very different model of the 'end' from Fukuyama, using the analogy of music:

> We are still speaking of a point of disappearance, a vanishing point, but this time in music. I shall call this the stereophonic effect. We are all obsessed with high fidelity, with the quality of musical 'reproduction'. At the consoles of our stereos, armed with our tuners, amplifiers and speakers, we mix, adjust settings, multiply tracks in pursuit of a flawless sound. Is this still music? Where is the high fidelity threshold beyond which music disappears as such? It does not disappear for lack of music, but because it has passed this limit point; it disappears into the perfection of its materiality, into its own special effect. Beyond this point, there is neither judgement nor aesthetic pleasure. It is the ecstasy of musicality, and its end.
>
> The disappearance of history is of the same order; here again, we have passed that limit where, by dint of the sophistication of events and information, history ceases to exist as such. Immediate high-powered broadcasting, special effects, secondary effects, fading and that famous feedback effect which is produced in acoustics by a source and a receiver being too close together and thus interfering disastrously ... We shall never again know what the social or music were before being exacerbated into their present useless perfection. We shall never again know what history was before its exacerbation into the technical perfection of news; we shall never again know what anything was before disappearing into the fulfilment of its model.[7]

Is Fukuyama's thesis one of Baudrillard's models of 'useless perfection'? Baudrillard is setting a further set of questions to contemporary historians – is it even useful any more to try and distinguish between 'events', as they have normally been conceived, and their consequences, or have we reached a post-historical condition in which, with the deconstruction of our formerly safe historical formulas, history has now 'degenerated into a video archive of past forms and events' which console us for the loss of meaning in the world and in our own existence.[8] If history has no 'meaning', Fukuyama-style, then why should it be anything more than a random pastiche of previous images, peoples and news events? One solution to this impasse is suggested by the author of the previous quotation, Lutz Niethammer, whose book *Post-histoire: Has History come to an End?* came out just before Fukuyama's, but in German, so it was almost immediately swamped by the tides of Fukuyama-fever. Niethammer, however, puts forward the best synthesis of Baudrillard's hyperreality and Fukuyama's determinism, accepting many of Baudrillard's claims about the postmodernist 'aesthetic' view of history but rejecting the more nihilistic implications of that view, whilst taking issue with the 'universal historian's' calculus of inevitable outcomes. Thus on Baudrillard's model:

> The recipient [the consumer of history] really is posthistorical, in the sense that he is constantly faced with fragments of the past which alienate him from his own historical situation and subjectivity. They do not make him present to himself, but flood him with the past and thereby allow him to escape from his historical existence.

Niethammer suggests a 'critical alternative', which would

> have to begin by asking what kind of service historians, or people with an education in history, can perform to support the subjectivity of individuals in their historical perception of themselves. Such a perspective may take up the legacy of bourgeois individualism, but must dispense with its ideal of greatness and power in order to arrive at a realistic assessment of the space for action within and against the existing social structures. It may also draw upon material instincts and collective traditions, but if it is to find and use such a space, it must not hope that objective characteristics will suddenly be converted into actions. Such a perspective might also be described as 'history from below', because it places the traditional hierarchy of historical tasks 'right side up'. It does not seek to guarantee meaning through a philosophy of history aesthetically translated into structural edifices or narrative representations, in which the truth of great systems, events and personalities is proved and ultimately adapted for didactic purposes.[9]

Even if the debate on the use or meaning of history provoked by Fukuyama proves as inconclusive as previous bouts of historical theorising, it is nonetheless always a positive sign that historians are once again looking up from their footnotes and examining some of the wider issues provoked by the extraordinary sequence of events that brought about the collapse of communism in eastern Europe and beyond in the late 1980s. The 'end of history' debate perhaps suggests new intellectual avenues for historians to explore in the post-Cold War era, and presents a challenge to historians to break some of their conventions and patterns of thinking which hardened into orthodoxies at the same time as the Cold War seemed to freeze the world historical process in the post-war era. Will the restructuring of historical categories and political 'models' that accompanied the changes of 1989 preface a reciprocal change or development in the writing of history, allowing historians to enter into constructive debate with Fukuyama, Baudrillard *et al.?* May the *historian*, as well as the philosopher, venture into the realms of universal history – and with what sorts of result?

Already Theodore Zeldin, the historian of modern France, has entered the fray with *An Intimate History of Humanity*.[10] In this work, deploying a wide range of both archival and oral sources, Zeldin explores the hidden meanings of human relations and discourse, based on a broad consideration of the historical roots of his subject. To a certain extent, Zeldin takes on the philosophers at their own game, trying to tease out meaning from a 'universal history' from the 'bottom up' – using the methodology of the professional historian to enter the domain of universal history. Zeldin set himself a very ambitious goal, and the result is never less than provocative and stimulating, even if it has met with a rather less than enthusiastic reception in some academic quarters. Nonetheless, Zeldin shows what can be done when a historian tries to reclaim the domain of the philosophy of history, and his conclusion is markedly different from Fukuyama's, that history, far from 'coming to an end', is only beginning to resolve the tensions of a previous era. If the 'end of history' debate can inspire some historians to start reclaiming some of the ground conceded to the philosophers – or would-be philosophers – of history, then Fukuyama's musings will not have been entirely wasted on his over-sceptical academic audience.

Notes

1 Quoted by Lutz Niethammer, *Post-histoire: has history come to an end?* (1994), p. 63.
2 Niethammer, *Post-histoire*, p. 67.
3 Francis Fukuyama, *The End of History and the Last Man* (Penguin, 1994), pp. 206–7.
4 Karl Popper, *The Poverty of Historicism* (1991), p. vii.
5 Isaiah Berlin, *The Crooked Timber of Humanity* (1990).
6 Perry Anderson, *A Zone of Engagement* (1992), p. 233.
7 Jean Baudrillard, *The Illusion of the End* (1994), pp. 4–6.
8 Baudrillard, *The Illusion*, p. 8.
9 Neithammer, *Post-histoire*, p. 149.
10 Theodore Zeldin, *An Intimate History of Humanity* (1994).

Further reading

See Chapter 3

Chapter 5

The post-war consensus in Britain: thesis, antithesis, synthesis?

Harriet Jones

One of the great ironies of contemporary British history and historiography is that, although unlike many of its neighbours on the continent Britain survived the Second World War with comparatively few casualties and with her ruling institutions intact, memories of the war continue to grip the British to an extent untrue of any other nation. This can be explained by what has happened to the country after 1945. Since the war, there has been very little for the British to feel good about: the empire is gone, economic performance has been dire, and everybody knows that the 'special relationship' is really just a euphemism for US replacement of Britain's role in the world. The past fifty years have completed the slope of decline from world superpower status which began at the end of the last century. In that context, the importance of the war years becomes understandable. For Britain's victory over Hitler was rather like the last win of an ageing world heavyweight boxer, and embodies for its citizens a national effort which affords a continuing source of pride. The undeniably evil nature of the Nazi foe has, moreover, enabled the British role during the war to be presented in moral and triumphant terms. Shared memories and myths surrounding the war have thus played a crucial role in the definition of Britishness since 1945.

Examples of this abound in popular culture here, often to the bemusement of outsiders. A recent television advertisement for a new brand of beer, for example, depicts a British tourist hurling his beach towel from the balcony of his hotel window with such force and skill that it skims across the water of the pool like a bouncing bomb and lands on the choicest lounge chair just before the German tourists arrive. But serious historians of recent British history have also been influenced by this perspective. The closing words of Alan Taylor's *English History, 1914–45*, for instance, represent a classic piece of British self-evaluation:

The British were the only people who went through both world wars from

41

beginning to end. Yet they remained a peaceful and civilized people, tolerant, patient, and generous. Traditional values lost much of their force. Other values took their place. Imperial greatness was on the way out; the welfare state was on the way in. The British empire declined; the condition of the people improved. Few now sang 'Land of Hope and Glory'. Few even sang 'England, Arise'. England had risen all the same.[1]

The way in which the war has come to operate as a sort of social glue for British society has unquestionably played an important role in the adjustment to its diminished international status. But for historians the challenge has been to disentangle sentiment from fact, and this has led to some intriguing problems of interpretation. In particular, the notion that the war had a transforming effect on British society and political culture – or, as Taylor puts it, that 'other values' took the place of 'traditional values' – has until recently dominated the historiography of post-war Britain. The transformative interpretation of the war's impact reached its height in the 1970s and early 1980s with the vigorous assertion by a group of distinguished historians that the war had engendered a remarkable degree of consensus after 1945 around a set of shared policies and objectives: Keynesian demand management, a mixed economy, and a welfare state. Since that time a younger generation of historians, who themselves have no memories of the war or early post-war years, has begun to examine the archives, and a revisionist body of work has emerged which not only rejects the idea of an unusual consensus springing out of the Second World War but which also questions the nature and extent of its transformative impact.

The phrase 'post-war consensus' has characterised writing on contemporary British history for a relatively short period, and dates approximately from the time when Margaret Thatcher became leader of the Conservative Party in 1975. In the 1950s and 1960s more emphasis was placed on the social and functional effects of war on society. This was primarily thought of in terms of social policy and, to be even more specific, on the emergence of the 'welfare state' after 1945. Richard Titmuss, in his seminal official history of the wartime social services, set the groundwork in 1950 when he argued that the universal services which had emerged from 1944 had done so in response to common need during the war, 'the pooling of resources and the sharing of risks' regardless of class or occupation. Continued austerity after the war 'served only to reinforce the war-warmed impulse of people for a more generous society'.[2] Titmuss's explanation of the emergence of the welfare state was not without its critics, but his influence on historiography throughout the 1950s and 1960s was nevertheless considerable.[3] This picture began to change, however, from the mid-1970s, and seems to have been an historiographical response to the rising influence of New Right criticism of post-war British politics. Under the influence of the Centre for Policy Studies (CPS), Margaret Thatcher made a series of speeches which attempted to distinguish her 'new' brand of Conservatism from what had gone before. Thatcher laid the blame for Britain's post-war decline and slide into ungovernability squarely on 'what I shall term, for want of a better phrase, the "progressive consensus", the doctrine that the state should be active on many fronts in promoting equality; in the provision of social welfare and in the redistribution of wealth and incomes'.[4] Of course, it is crucial to remember that the New Right agenda was shaped at that time by disgust over the policy reversals of the 1970–74 Heath government. From the perspective of the CPS, the existence of a post-war consensus against the kind of policies being promoted by the CPS seemed obvious; moreover, it was critically important for Thatcher herself to distinguish her leadership of the party from that of her predecessor and to make her 'cure' for Britain's malaise appear to be a new departure. Thus from the mid-1970s the idea of a political consensus emerging out of the war, and primarily based upon the acceptance of Keynes and Beveridge, became the telescope through which the British began to peer back at their recent history, because the rhetoric used by the Thatcherites was beginning to define the focus of political debate. Argument would centre on whether the consensus had been good or bad for the country; but no one, and least of all the contemporary historians, questioned the existence of such a consensus at the time.

Amongst the historians, the genesis of this much-vaunted post-war consensus was first explored by Paul Addison. His political history of the war years, *The Road to 1945*, took the transformative arguments of earlier historians such as Titmuss a step further. Painstakingly researched and argued, *The Road to 1945* concluded that 'the national unity of the war years gave rise to a new consensus at the top which dominated Britain long after the last bomb had fallen'; that is, out of the war there emerged a new elite political consensus which would define the boundaries of policy-making for the following three decades.[5] The Attlee governments of 1945–51 simply 'completed and consolidated a social reform programme which was essentially the vision of the Coalition'.[6] It was through the process of co-operation and compromise which led to the publication of a series of wartime White Papers on post-war reconstruction that agreement was hammered out on a series of objectives: full employment, social security, a national health service, universal secondary education, and management of the economy. The war, in short, provided the crucible in which the consensus at an elite level passed from the era of Stanley Baldwin to that of Clement Attlee. Addison's interpretation of wartime politics has proved remarkably influential among his colleagues, in spite of several important studies which subsequently suggested that wartime and early post-war politics and society were characterised more by conflict than consensus.[7] As is often the case with works of such groundbreaking importance, however, post-Addison interpretations of Britain since the war often simplified and reduced his argument to such an extent that 'post-war consensus' became shorthand for the belief that post-war Britain, particularly until 1964, was characterised by an absence of serious policy debate in any significant area. Addison's explanation of the emergence of an Attlee consensus was transformed in the historiography of the 1980s into an historical phenomenon which was somehow unique; the post-war consensus had become interpreted to mean an historically unusual degree of agreement ... in the full range of social and economic policies by which post-war government sought to fulfil its positive commitment to promote the welfare of all its citizens'.[8] By 1987 Addison himself seemed slightly bewildered by the way in which the term 'consensus' had come to be used.[9]

Addison was right to acknowledge a growing sense of unease among political scientists and contemporary historians over the way in which consensus had come to define our understanding of the post-war period. Given the political bitterness of the Thatcher years during which this perspective emerged, the almost reverential interpretation of the Butskellite era as one relatively free of conflict becomes more understandable, but it still dominates textbook interpretations of contemporary Britain in 1995. The most widely used text for students of British politics, for example, takes the concept of a post-war consensus as the basic framework for understanding post-war politics between 1945 and the late 1970s:

> The 'post-war consensus' is a key concept in understanding the recent past. It describes the overlap between the economic, social and foreign policies of both Labour and Conservative governments throughout the post-war period until its breakdown in the 1970s ... It does not mean that there were not disagreements; there were many. But it does suggest that the differences in the policies practised when the parties were in office were relatively small rather than fundamental ... Most writers now accept that the term 'consensus' is a useful or adequate description of British politics from 1945 until the late 1970s, when it began to be attacked by the advent of the most ideological government since 1945.[10]

The most recent, and certainly the most nostalgic and impassioned defence of a war-inspired post-war consensus has been provided by Peter Hennessy, both in his best-selling history of the Attlee years, *Never Again*, and through his Channel 4 television series *What has Become of Us?*, first aired in the autumn of 1994. 'Postwar Britain,' he writes,

> cannot be understood at all without a proper appreciation of the great formative experience which shaped it and dominated its economics, its politics, and its ethos for at least three decades – the war itself ... Virtually every serious politician, certainly every senior one, acted and calculated within the boundaries of what became known as 'the post-war settlement' built around an understanding that Britain would remain a great power abroad while operat-

ing a mixed economy and building a welfare state at home, a presupposition that a change of government from Labour to Conservative in 1951 did little to alter.[11]

At the time of writing the idea of a post-war consensus thus remains largely unquestioned by undergraduate students of British politics and contemporary history, and indeed by the popular audience to which Hennessy's work has been largely addressed.

Meanwhile, however, the term has fallen increasingly out of favour among academic historians of post-war Britain. Doubts about its usefulness were first raised by Ben Pimlott in an essay originally published in 1988 entitled 'The myth of consensus'. Pimlott did not deny that the war years represented an important turning point in domestic policy, but, he argued, 'it is not necessary, however, to leap from an observation of important changes in opinion and practice, to a belief in the Shangri La of a lost "consensus": you can acknowledge the past as different, without assuming that it was less argumentative'.[12] Historians, he warned, had 'committed the error of anachronism' by taking for granted hard-won reforms and forgetting the bitterness of past debates; Pimlott was the first to suggest that the post-war consensus was likely to end up in 'the dustbin of historiography'.[13] He did so at a time when much solid research on the 1940s and 1950s was beginning to appear, for the thirty-year rule which governs the release of official records in Britain is generally followed by a swarm of young researchers. This new research has borne out Pimlott's suspicions, for it has prompted increasing scepticism about the value of consensus as a description of British political culture in the 1940s and 1950s. The orthodox understanding of a post-war consensus has been attacked by a number of historians, and, while analysis varies considerably, several underlying themes have emerged. A number of studies have concluded that consensus never existed, either at an elite or at a popular level. Deep ideological divisions remained both between and within the parties, and the policies which are most often associated with consensus politics were actually the product of conflict or, often, of lack of choice dictated by external factors. A variant on this theme is the argument that, while a consensus did emerge in the 1940s, and continue for two decades, it cannot be explained by wartime experiences. A variety of alternative explanations have been put forward to explain the apparent convergence of policies between the parties after the war, the most common of which have been the structure of the electoral system itself, and the domestic impact of the emerging Cold War.[14] What all these analyses share is a basic scepticism about the transformative nature of the war, and the cool – indeed, in cases hostile – reception which the revisionist interpretations initially received was largely a reflection of the sanctity with which the war years have been endowed.

Addison's picture of the Churchill coalition, which lies at the heart of the traditional interpretation, has been questioned in the work of several historians. Kevin Jefferys, for example, has portrayed the Coalition's work on domestic policy as a series of painful compromises, which only worked provided Conservative and Labour Ministers could agree to disagree, and at times threatened to collapse altogether. He sees the White Papers which did emerge during the war as representing the extremes to which the two sides were willing to stretch, and argues that the outcome in most cases was so vague as to be capable of multiple interpretation when policies were eventually implemented. 'The government, to a large extent, was incapable of proceeding beyond promises of reform,' and that is why, he argues, apart from the 1944 Education Act, no major piece of social legislation was enacted before the end of the war.[15] Jefferys's interpretation of the Coalition as conflict-ridden has been confirmed by research into wartime party policy-making. Both Stephen Brooke's work on the Labour Party, and my own on the Conservatives, has concluded that fundamental differences on social policy were wholly intractable and would have represented quite different roads from 1945. In education, there were sharp differences over the structure of secondary schools; on Beveridge, Labour was in favour of a minimum income whereas the bulk of the Conservative Party rejected the whole notion of social security; on health, Labour's vision of a wholly nationalised service staffed by full-time salaried doctors in local health centres was miles away from the Conservatives' commitment merely to extend the system of pre-war provision to the rest of the population.[16] Thus to conclude that simply because there was a general bipartisan agreement on the desirability of universal secondary education or a national health service there was a consensus is highly misleading. That the war had failed to produce a political consensus at an elite level was obvious, moreover, during the bitterly fought election of 1945. As new work on that campaign makes clear, the Conservative leadership was determined to stop wartime collectivism becoming peacetime collectivism, and stressed the need to return to a freedom and enterprise society in rhetoric heavily influenced by the neo-liberal economist Friedrich von Hayek.[17] Even the existence of a basic leftward shift in popular attitudes has been questioned; one new study has argued that most voters were motivated, as ever, by bread-and-butter issues rather than impelled by a new utopianism, and that the existence of a widespread collectivist impulse is largely mythical.[18]

Jefferys himself concluded that it was not the war which produced a political consensus so much as the shock of defeat for the Conservatives in 1945.[19] And yet much of the new research into the Attlee years and into the 1950s has cast doubt on the extent of policy agreement in the golden age of Butskellism. 1945 was most certainly a salutory lesson for the Conservative Party, but neither its leadership, nor its backbenchers, nor its membership was shifted leftwards as a result. Party rhetoric grew far more cautious, but the search which ensued was for ways to make Conservative policies electorally attractive.[20] A whole range of studies are now emerging which stress the differences and conflicts between and within the parties on issues ranging from rationing[21] to economic policy,[22] industrial relations[23] social policy[24] and ideology.[25] In the view of these historians it seems that Pimlott's hunch was correct, and that the years following the war were characterised by a degree of conflict and debate which is normal in peace-time society. There was no unusual degree of political or social consensus in post-war Britain. Rather, one suspects, there was an unusual degree of conflict and disagreement in the mid-1970s and 1980s which coloured the historiography of those years. From the perspective of the Major years of the mid-1990s early post-war Britain no longer seems remarkable. This leads to an important point which is really rather an obvious one, and that is that a broad consensus on the acceptable parameters of policy must always exist between the parties in any functioning democracy. In order to understand the political culture of any given period, the roots of its governing consensus must be thoroughly debated.

The sticking point of the whole debate, it seems, has been the question of the impact of the war. If historians can begin to accept that the Second World War had a much more limited or even a different kind of effect on post-war political culture than has previously been assumed, then they can begin to look in other places for an understanding of the parameters of debate in the 1950s. The first place to look is the Cold War itself, and its impact on domestic politics. Britain was by no means the only western European country to adopt a mixed economy and a welfare state at the end of the war, yet British historians have explained its development in terms of a war experience which was very different from that of its European neighbours. What the political elites in these countries did share, however, was a common enemy at the war's end. It is time to consider the extent to which the Cold War may have narrowed domestic debate, or exerted a unifying effect in the same way as other wars seem to have done in this century. Some of the most interesting analysis of the post-war period has seen Britain's development in terms of a growing reaction against collectivism. Helen Mercer, for example, has argued that a consensus did emerge in this period, but that it was the outcome of agreement between the owners of industry and the leadership of the labour movement over the preservation of capitalism.[26] Richard Cockett's history of the rise of neo-liberalism which culminated in the election of Margaret Thatcher in 1979, also places stress on the response to the threat of egalitarianism.[27] In these studies, which are written from entirely different political perspectives, the war did play a role in the values which came to define the following decades, but a very different one from that which has been traditionally argued. Far from forging a consensus around Keynes and Beveridge which carried over into peace-time, the collectivist values associated with the war economy, combined with the emergence of the Cold War, created a domestic climate in the post-war period which made the resolution of class conflict within a capitalist framework an overriding imperative of elite policy formulation. This is a very different proposition from that first put forward in *The Road to 1945*. Such alternatives to the consensus school of interpretation are only beginning to emerge.

Notes

1 A. J. P. Taylor, *English History, 1914–45* (1965), p. 600.
2 Richard Titmuss, *Problems of Social Policy* (1950), pp. 507–8.
3 Taylor, *English History*; Arthur Marwick, *Britain in the Century of Total War* (1968).
4 Margaret Thatcher, *Let our Children grow Tall: Selected Speeches, 1975–77* (1977), p. 1. The words are from an address to the Institute of Socio-economic Studies, New York, 15 September 1975. Ten years later Corelli Barnett attempted to provide an historical defence of this argument in his controversial book *The Audit of War: the Illusion and Reality of Britain as a Great Power* (1986).
5 Paul Addison, *The Road to 1945* (1975), p. 16.
6 Addison, *Road to 1945*, p. 14.
7 See, in particular, Charles Webster, *Problems of Health Care: the National Health Service before 1957* (1988); Harold L. Smith (ed.), *War and Social Change: British Society in the Second World War* (1986).
8 Rodney Lowe, 'The Second World War, consensus and the foundation of the welfare state', *Twentieth Century British History*, 1 (2), 1990, p. 157.
9 Paul Addison, 'The road from 1945', in Peter Hennessy and Anthony Seldon (eds.), *Ruling Performance: British Governments from Attlee to Thatcher* (1987), p. 5.
10 Bill Jones *et al.*, *Politics UK*, second edition (1994), p. 42; see also Dennis Kavanagh and Peter Morris, *Consensus Politics from Attlee to Thatcher* (1989).
11 Peter Hennessy, *Never Again: Britain, 1945–51* (1992), pp. 2–3.
12 Ben Pimlott, *Frustrate their Knavish Tricks: Writings on Biography, History and Politics* (1994), p. 233. 'The myth of consensus' was first published in Lesley M. Smith (ed.), *The Making of Britain: Echoes of Greatness* (1988).
13 Pimlott, *Knavish Tricks*, pp. 234–239.
14 Helen Mercer, 'The organisation and ownership of industry, 1945–51', in Harriet Jones and Michael David Kandiah (eds), *The Myth of Consensus? New Views on British History, 1945–64* (forthcoming).
15 Kevin Jefferys, *The Churchill Coalition and Wartime Politics, 1940–45* (1991), p. 5.
16 Stephen Brooke, *Labour's War: the Labour Party during the Second World War* (1992); Harriet Jones, 'The Conservative Party and the Welfare State, 1942–55', University of London thesis, 1992, (forthcoming).
17 Jones, 'Conservative Party'; Richard Cockett, *Thinking the Unthinkable: Think-tanks and the Economic Counter-revolution, 1931–83* (1994).
18 Steven Fielding, Peter Thompson and Nick Tiratsoo, *England Arise! The Labour Party and Popular Politics in the 1940s* (1995).
19 Jefferys, *Churchill Coalition*, p. 6.

20 Jones, 'Conservative Party', chapter 3; Michael David Kandiah, 'Lord Woolton's Chairmanship of the Conservative Party, 1946–55', Exeter University Thesis, 1993.

21 Ina Zweiniger-Bargielowska, 'Rationing, austerity and the Conservative Party recovery after 1945, *Historical Journal*, 37, 1994, pp. 173–97; 'Consensus and consumption: rationing, austerity and controls after the war', in Harriet Jones and Michael David Kandiah (eds), *The Myth of Consensus? New Views on British History, 1945–64* (forthcoming).

22 Neil Rollings, 'Poor Mr Butskell: a short life, wrecked by schizophrenia?' *Twentieth Century British History*, 5 (2), 1994, pp. 183–205; 'Butskellism, the post-war consensus and the managed economy', in Harriet Jones and Michael David Kandiah (eds), *The Myth of Consensus?* (forthcoming).

23 Noel Whiteside, 'Industrial relations and the politics of the "social wage", 1945–60', in Harriet Jones and Michael David Kandiah (eds), *The Myth of Consensus?* (forthcoming).

24 Martin Francis, 'Not reformed capitalism but ... democratic socialism: the ideology of the Labour Leadership, 1945–51', in Harriet Jones and Michael David Kandiah (eds), *The Myth of Consensus?* (forthcoming); Harriet Jones, 'New tricks for an old dog? The Conservatives and social policy, 1951–55', in Anthony Corst, Lewis Johnman and Scott Lucas (eds), *Contemporary British History, 1931–61* (1991); 'The Conservative Party'.

25 Nick Ellison, *Egalitarian Thought and Labour Politics: Retreating Visions* (1994); 'Consensus here, consensus there ... but not consensus everywhere: Labour and "equality" in the 1950s', in Harriet Jones and Michael David Kandiah (eds), *The Myth of Consensus?* (forthcoming).

26 Mercer, 'Organisation and ownership'.

27 Cockett, *Thinking the Unthinkable*.

Chapter 6

Whose history?
National narratives in
multiracial societies

Shamit Saggar

Introductory remarks

To pose the question 'Whose history?' may, at first glance, appear to be another restatement of currently popular drives to challenge dominant ideological perspectives towards culture, race and ethnicity. Indeed, a large slice of recent historical writing in the field of national identity and nation building has sought to argue that the issue of historical narrative can no longer be thought of as occupying a culturally neutral middle ground. This approach has been particularly strident among studies of the emergence of official multiculturalism in mature industrial democracies facing new and varied patterns of immigration.

The 'Whose history?' question therefore has a strong feel of familiarity about it. However, behind this lie two simple points concerning method and conceptualisation. First, if today's broad awareness of the multicultural nature of modern societies is the result of recent changes in intellectual understanding of social forces, then it should, in principle, be possible to isolate key methodological developments that have permitted this transformation to come about. It is by no means clear, however, that the process of change can be explained in these terms of causation. The choice appears to be between the argument that historical frameworks have undergone revision, thus rendering greater knowledge and acceptance of a variety of responses to the 'Whose history?' question, or the counter-argument that places emphasis on social change brought about through new immigration patterns eventually reflected in otherwise unchanged historical data-gathering exercises.

Second, by accepting that a changed awareness of the social and cultural fabric of a society must be reflected in the study of the past, the case can then be made to re-examine perspectives in relation to familiar historical episodes. To be sure, whilst much has been written about the historical impact of the immigration issue upon British society and politics between

1948 and 1981, comparatively little has been said about the experiences and perspective of the immigrants themselves. If 'their' history is to be included, is the documentation of this material to be regarded as fuel to challenge conventional understanding of this episode, or merely used to tell another story that has no bearing on how we explain the general British immigration experience? We shall return to both these points towards the end of this essay.

This chapter will trace the ways in which the challenges faced by immigrant receiving societies have been responded to, using a framework that seeks to open up the questions of belonging and aspirations to national identity. It will also examine the extent to which more recent moves to embrace multicultural thinking as official orthodoxy have fundamentally altered minority–majority relations, especially in relation to observable immigration related conflicts. Finally, the chapter will offer some discussion about the culturally specific methodological implications involved in posing the question 'Whose history?'

Belonging and related aspirations

At the heart of the politics of post-war non-white immigration in several mature industrial democracies has been the question of belonging. Faced with largely European and white immigrant influxes in earlier periods, many of these societies in the post-war era had little experience in mediating membership claims that transcended clear cultural and ethnic differences from a range of new immigrant groups. Furthermore, in about the same time frame, the circumstances of historically discriminated against and segregated populations such as blacks and native peoples in the United States came to the fore of political debates concerned with re-examining the terms upon which assertions about national belonging had been founded. Throughout, the task set by policy-makers has centred on developing a strategy that values ethnic and racial diversity whilst concomitantly underpinning loyalty to and identification with the modern nation state. In that sense, these efforts have been geared, in principle at least, to unlocking various historical claims that the nation has been the representation of any particular sectional group.

A number of modern industrial democracies have responded to this general task by a process that explicitly decouples the link between group and state, inasmuch as such a connection could have been said to have existed and acted as an exclusionary barrier to other groups.[1] This approach, familiar in North America, Britain and other parts of Europe, and in Australia and New Zealand, has also placed great weight on the notion that a multiplicity of ethnic groups and cultures hold equal value in the public domain. Multiculturalism (as this broad approach is often dubbed), however, divides into several varieties when the argument is taken a step further to (1) the breadth of cultural coverage that can reasonably be accommodated in the public domain, (2) whether the public domain has specific implications for public policy service delivery, and (3) claims that the unintended consequences of official recognition lead to disintegrative tendencies for national cohesion. Whilst all these points raise important dilemmas, it is the last that is of greatest concern to us.

Addressing this claim is fraught with difficulties, however. For one thing, the picture is blurred by apparently contradictory political messages about the nature and purpose of multicultural policy. It is certainly common to observe multiculturalists who highlight the dangers of inter-community tension and strife. To them, the worry stems from exclusionary attitudes and practices that prevent visible minorities from entering the mainstream; the outcome, unless checked by public policy, is the reinforcement of anti-mainstream belief systems which can only serve to destabilise minority attachment to the nation. In noting the very real opposition to the immigrant or 'other' presence, so the argument goes, the prospects of engendering any sense of belonging will be remote. Such voices usually end up concluding that multiculturalism must, in order to address these problems, go beyond a form of passive orthodoxy that celebrates symbolic diversity. It needs in addition to promote the value – economic, cultural, social – of the newcomers to the society by showing that mainstream society is not averse to ethnic heterogeneity. In the United States this line of argument has been extended a stage further by radical multiculturalists who have argued in favour of a 'fair shares' public policy doctrine, suggesting that a theory of historic compensatory rights is required to bolster the credibility of the public ethnic mosaic. Diversity, in other words, is not a sufficiently desirable goal in itself and must be accompanied by a measurable tip in the balance of policy outcomes.

At one and the same time, a counter-argument is discernable which appears to be equally couched in the public rhetoric of multiculturalism. This view is often caricatured as taking a more upbeat, optimistic line in stressing the liberal, principled basis upon which these societies have historically been willing to adapt to cultural change. That is to say, the willingness to respond to and embrace the new and the different is driven by a deep-seated set of values that cherish the ideals of tolerance, mutual understanding and respect, and, of course, the central liberal doctrine of cultural relativism. So, whilst day-to-day issues may be shaped by pragmatic responses, underlying these negotiations there exists an on-going collective view of the nation as welcoming and hospitable. In particular, this position is keen to reject the exaggerated and generalised criticisms of those who argue that these minorities necessarily constitute a threat to, say, national cohesiveness or prosperity (a point returned to specifically later in this chapter). An early illustration of such a line of argument was seen in the work of Myrdal, who argued the case for greater systematic inclusion of black people in US society on grounds couched in terms of the ideals of American liberalism and democracy.[2] The broad thrust of this approach suggests that it is political principle, rather than political expediency, that drives mature democracies to meet aspirations of belonging and identity within a culturally neutral (and therefore negotiable) framework. It has been an approach that has been particularly influential in guiding successive multicultural and race relations strategies for reform, most notably in Britain and the United States since the 1960s.[3]

These are of course rather general accounts that try to explain philosophical and political grounds upon which multicultural policy strategies have either been sponsored or discouraged by the state. Behind these generalisations lie more specific arguments regarding the efficacy and measurement of the success of such policies. These arguments are essentially a restatement of by now familiar positions taken by supporters and critics, and whose claims reveal a great deal about their contrasting conceptions of the nation and its constituents.

On one hand supporters have argued that the recent history of many of these countries has been indelibly marked by the experience of immigration-driven diversity. Official responses to these profound changes have, they add, been well guided and enlightened in, firstly, recognising their deep significance and, secondly, moving to embrace many aspects of change. Multiculturalism therefore represents an interesting and worthy end in itself but, crucially, it has been a desirable path to follow because it has enabled the politics of public resource allocation to be opened up to a range of new groups and interests. The demands of these groups now command legitimacy and, indeed, may from time to time be the subject of special state action justified on the grounds of historic compensation for past exclusion or discrimination. The state is therefore entirely justified in encouraging and helping to mobilise the idea of minority group rights, an idea which will not only amount to the same rights as other citizens but also the possibility of certain compensatory rights in addition. Advocates therefore are reasonably clear that multiculturalism as a cogent force of ideas is equally about establishing the means of transforming the putative character of a society. This rather wider objective is conceived of as almost the inevitable product of having accepted equal value and diversity as desirable objectives. In this model, one can imagine, supporters may be reluctant to draw out limits upon the actual content of cultural diversity for fear of national identity slipping into the hands of cultural domination. That said, this does not mean that the politics of constraint do not count, for quite plainly they do, and no less so for champions of the doctrine. The need to set limits on the range and content of diversity permissible is usually guided by related and equally important liberal concerns about, *inter alia*, individualism, mutuality, tolerance, free expression, judicial even-handedness and equality of treatment.

Critics have plainly been much less sanguine about the purpose and content of the multicultural project. Their main hesitation seems to stem from doubts as to whether politics and the policy process need to be more accountable to social pressures, including the demands of immigrants and minorities for greater inclusion. A broad line is maintained by critics who stand by the claim that colour-blindness guides public decision-making and that this is reason enough to avoid going down the road of trying to identify the alleged in-built structural deficiencies of political institutions. Such a search, so the argument runs, ultimately leads nowhere because it is based on the recent belief that more nominal diversity is necessarily better. This leads to a second claim which draws attention to the possibility that the push for greater openness and inclusiveness can lead to, at best, the politics of inter-group rivalry and the bitterness that goes with such delineation of ethnic identities, and, at worst, the enhanced risk of an overload of incompatible demands being placed on the state. It is this latter risk which critics of multiculturalism are at pains to warn can mean that drives for inclusiveness all too easily result in divisiveness. This weakness in the multiculturalist position is attributed to the failure to see the nation as anything other than a legal–technical entity shadowing the state. Rather, they contend, the historical development of modern nations indicates that it is something more important which cannot be easily relegated to the footnotes of the multicultural agenda.

Describing and explaining conflict

Perhaps one of the best illustrations of the kind of controversy associated with the 'Whose history?' theme can be seen in the development of immigration politics and policies in post-war Britain. There is widespread agreement that immigration from non-white New Commonwealth sources led to considerable tensions in British politics. Indeed, from the mid-1950s the question of how to define and best tackle grass-roots pressure hostile to immigrants is a theme that is initially grappled with in the closed quarters of Churchill's final administration,[4] and which later developed a momentum of its own following the 1958 'race riots' in west London and the East Midlands.[5] The experience of the 1960s and 1970s, ranging from the 1964 Smethwick episode and the intervention of Enoch Powell in 1968 to the rise of the far right in the mid-1970s, highlighted the enormous depth of passion felt on the issue.[6] The task for the historian and social commentator then is to put forward a framework within which to explain the phenomenon of social and political conflict arising from immigration.

Several historical, political and sociological accounts have emerged that purport to describe the process of this immigration as well as its social and political consequences. Holmes, for example, traces this story from the mid-Victorian era, and has drawn attention to the ways in which British society responded at various levels to the immigrants' new presence, arguing that these were complex and exhibited considerable evidence of ambiguity and variability.'⁷ A clear, constant dividing line between admiration and fear, tolerance and intolerance, was not always easily drawn,' he writes.⁸ He implies that is difficult to isolate a continuous and dominant line of anti-immigrant sentiment and to show that this amounted to a specifically British approach to the task of absorbing newcomers and outsiders. Furthermore, in terms of drawing well grounded lessons about the notion of tolerance, Holmes's analysis would seem to suggest that the spectacle of racism has been one of several ideological forces at work. It is therefore a perspective that is in obvious and sharp contrast to the argument advanced by those who see 'race' and racism as lying at the heart of the contemporary legacy of immigration. Gilroy, for instance, is at pains to point out that the logic of racial superiority and racial exclusion has been anything but the sole political property of extreme nationalists and xenophobes: '"Race" and racism [are] not fringe questions but ... a volatile presence at the very centre of British politics, actively shaping and determining the history not simply of blacks, but of the country as a whole at a crucial stage in its development.'⁹

The underlying theme, therefore, that unites the immigrant experience on one hand and the experience of immigration for British society on the other is the question of hostility and how this can be placed into a broader picture that unlocks the reasons for the tensions that have undoubtedly arisen. The choice for observers of this picture reflects not only varying degrees of pessimism or optimism on the part of researchers but also a variety of ways in which the relationship between immigrant minorities and established majorities has been conceptualised.

To begin with, there have been those who have taken a broadly economic-centred approach to describing hostility towards immigrants, typically focusing upon both new and familiar forms of competition in labour and housing markets. Various waves of Jewish settlers, for example, have attracted resentment from locals threatened by the real or perceived pressure for identifiable economic opportunities. However, such changes in labour or other markets are often insufficient forces to build a coherent set of ideas through which opposition or resentment can easily be transmitted. For this to be the case it has been necessary for the distinctiveness of the threat posed by the newcomers to be expressed in some cultural form. Jews thus became the object of resentment in terms that highlighted more than anything else their culture difference. To perceive and oppose the Jewish presence as an 'alien culture' has, to be sure, been a recurring and broadly legitimate argument in British society, a large slice of which has usually been taken to be an indirect reference to economic hostility.

Secondly, there has been the rather different approach of those who have attempted to put cultural dilemmas at the heart of their explanation for hostility. This perspective has arguably sought to work on a larger canvas in taking account of the interests of the receiving society in conjunction with the interests and behaviour of immigrants themselves. The result has been to focus on the complex two-way interplay that has emerged, in which various traditional understandings of identity and belonging have certainly been contested, if not satisfactorily revised. The question of hostility is therefore seen as the product of such an interplay of what are in effect perceived values and assumptions about receiving societies and their newcomers. Taking the hostility shown to immigrants as being the consequence of either successful or unsuccessful cultural contact, commentators are then faced with two related questions. First, is it reasonable to presume that such contact will lead to the process of cultural adjustment, and, second, upon what terms and conditions are two-way adjustments or settlements based? Conceding the need for adjustment as inferred in the former question has not necessarily given any legitimacy to the latter question, based as it is on the understanding that British identity is essentially negotiable and flexible. Indeed, a remarkably common feature of immigration debates have been claims about the willingness of British society to welcome newcomers in the context of a determination to reinforce unchanged and unnegotiable beliefs about what it is to 'be British'. Speaking to the Commons during the passage of the 1976 Race Relations Act, one notable Conservative voice sought from the front bench to pay 'tribute to the wonderful way in which the British people have accepted ... the very substantial influx of alien culture and alien race into their midst without open conflict or prejudice'.[10]

Plainly, it is the latter of these questions that poses the greatest difficulty. It embodies, to begin with, a very real problem in knowing whether, and to what extent, British national identity and indeed nationhood more broadly are understood in cultural terms. Suggesting that nationhood is culturally linked implies that it may also be culturally determined. This inference in itself may not throw up widespread controversy but disagreement is arguably unavoidable once the claim is made that there is a particular causal determinism at work which makes national identity unlikely to be shared by many first-generation immigrants. The nation – and what it means to be considered a member of the nation – then ends up being sufficiently culturally particularistic as to be, in effect, an exclusionary force. Such a position is most closely associated with those political voices whose aim would be to put a question mark against the proposition that birth place, residence or just environment are sufficient grounds for national membership. For the time being, it is important to remember that cultural conservatives have in recent times conceded ground to counter-arguments that have sought to emphasise – even celebrate – the cultural contribution of the 'new British'.

It should be remembered that this rival perspective has undoubtedly gained considerable influence in British political debate over the past thirty years. Multicultural enthusiasts have in this period gone to considerable lengths to stress their belief that liberal integration measures have been founded on a clear demarcation between nation and culture. There is no essential culture involved in defining national belonging and identity, so the argument runs, and indeed many multiculturalists have explicitly tried to incorporate various aspects of minority immigrant cultures into the new orthodoxy. In this sense it is meaningful for proponents of this perspective to claim that modern British history is the history of people who make up the British Isles, and that current and traditional experiences need not have any overt or identifiable meeting point. The validity of historical content from today or the recent past may or may not share traditional patterns. Some have gone further and contended that the British nation has always been a cultural hybrid comprising several discernible strands which have been fused, co-opted, grafted, assimilated and captured from one era to the next. With that in mind, present public debates over whether it will prove possible to find a workable compromise between immigrant and non-immigrant cultures are misleading, since the process of adaptation and change was under way long before the post-war influx. The immigration of the past fifty or so years, they would argue, has been just the latest chapter in a long history of cultural adjustment, though arguably one that has involved a more exotic and hitherto uncharted process of mutual adjustment. All that remains is to ensure that the national narrative in a multicultural setting is sufficiently and satisfactorily reflective of this context. The politics of multiculturalism – involving, typically, mobilising pressure and tackling skewed portrayals of national cultural norms – can then be seen to be the natural instrument of this goal.

Raising doubts about the 'Whose history?' question

A large slice of this chapter has been devoted to examining the case for reinterpreting the cultural and/or ethnic specificity of national narratives in contemporary history. This goal has been guided by the broad belief that historical commentary and interpretation have been shaped by dominant ethno-cultural perspectives. The values and assumptions caught up in such a dominant framework have implicitly or explicitly served to leave untold other equally valid narratives and may possibly have led us to view minorities and immigrants as mere subjects, rather than agents, of processes of historical formation. This line of argument, as we have already seen, is not without its opponents. In this final section, we shall consider the counter-claim that raising the 'Whose history?' question is a methodological absurdity as well as a barely legitimate, fashion-driven diversion.

The school that has advanced the case for greater inclusion of minority and/or immigrant perspectives has tended to base its arguments on the need for increased awareness of the multicultural and multiracial nature of society. Britain, for instance, is a society whose ethnic and cultural composition has changed enormously and fairly rapidly since 1948. A once overwhelmingly homogeneous ethno-racial population has shifted to become a society comprising several identifiable groups. In methodological terms, it is claimed, this vital transformation must be reflected in the study of the recent past. However, this conclusion can rest on either of two lines of thought, each leading to rather different responses and counter-arguments.

One line would be that, as the component members and groups in society have changed, this has meant that Britain is now made up of significantly different stakeholders purporting to shape social and political developments. In linguistic terms, for example, it is virtually impossible to chart recent changes in language policy and practice without taking account of the introduction of a whole host of new, non-European languages that certain immigrant groups have brought with them. Likewise, British dietary habits and policies cannot easily ignore the arrival of various new cuisines and palates that have served to shape wider societal consumption patterns.

Contemporary historians in this sense are well advised to revise and fine-tune their analytical instruments in line with these kinds of obvious socio-cultural changes. It is an argument in favour of greater sensitivity and awareness – that is to say, approaches to contemporary historical analysis that sit comfortably alongside wider arguments in favour of inclusiveness and cultural neutrality found within progressive historical method. Notwithstanding this association, it would be reasonable to say that any counter-arguments tend to be pitched at the level of placing identifiable and agreed constraints upon the sensitising and awareness process. In general, few conservatives have voiced any principled opposition to this trend, though many are unlikely to be caught up in what are sympathetically seen as modernising influences. Rather, the cut-off point for support is more likely to arise from attempts to introduce retrospective re-evaluation, or to push for an intellectual understanding of the recent past as knowledge and interpretation that have been ideologically and socially constructed.

The other line of thought is rather different and goes a vital stage further. It puts forward the case for a revision of existing intellectual frameworks which does not so much ignore or marginalise minority perspectives as fail to conceptualise the study of the recent past as anything other than the collection and interpretation of objective facts. The claims of minorities that seek to contest the basis of historical 'facts' and which challenge inherent, in-built prejudice against minority perspectives often go to the heart of this approach.

It is perhaps less clear to know what is to be done in response to the allegation of bias. It might be to revise the framework of 'Which issues, interests and events count?' and which do not, or at least not as much. However, conservatives remain highly sceptical about the prospect of reopening debate on the basis of skewed intellectual frameworks. For example, a conservative doubter may wonder what could be made of reinterpretation of an event such as the passage of the 1962 Commonwealth Immigration Act. To be sure, the vast bulk of our understanding of the process leading up this piece of legislation has been couched in terms of the growing impact of the immigration issue upon domestic British politics. The escalation of the issue and the then government's move to restrict non-white entry on a statutory basis are processes that are commonly understood from the perspective of white-dominated political institutions and electoral competition. It is not an event or process that has been well documented from the point of view of ethnic minorities settled or seeking to settle in Britain at the time. The briefest understanding of their perspective will reveal that the politics of the Act seemed to begin and end with a discriminatory position towards non-whites, and yet racial discrimination at the point of entry into British society could hardly be described as a key aspect of the elite and mass debates surrounding the legislation. In moving to shift the very framework through which an historical process or event is understood can, quite plainly, extend to the point of throwing out established understandings as little more than 'one side of the coin'. The question presumably is whether researchers are content to go that far and whether commentators are prepared to jettison received views.

Opponents are clearly not prepared to move so far. However, for many, the doubts they hold are based not on differences over the extent of the revision called for, but rather on of the tendency for such an approach to throw up fundamental questions about the ownership of frameworks of intellectual understanding. The question of 'Whose history?' represents the very kind of flaw that they are critical of and see as the thin end of a debate they feel cannot be resolved.

Notes

1 Augie Fleras and Jean Leonard Elliot, *Multiculturalism in Canada: the Challenge of Diversity* (1992), pp. 269–80.
2 Gunnar Myrdal, *An American Dilemma: the Negro Problem and Modern Democracy* (1944).
3 Michael Banton, *Promoting Racial Harmony* (1985).
4 Zig Layton Henry, *The Politics of Immigration* (1992), p. 31.
5 E. J. B. Rose *et al.*, *Colour and Citizenship* (1969).
6 The direct and indirect impact of the immigration issue upon Britain's party system is recounted and theorised using a model of rational party strategy by Anthony Messina, *Race and Party Competition* (1989).
7 Colin Holmes, *John Bull's Island: Immigration and British Society 1871–1971* (1988).
8 Holmes, *John Bull's Island*, p. 312

9   Paul Gilroy, 'The end of antiracism', in James Donald and Ali Rattansi (eds), *'Race', Culture and Difference* (1992), p. 51

10 *Parliamentary Debates, House of Commons*, Hansard, vol. 906, cols 1550–52, 4 March 1976.

Chapter 7

Debates in contemporary political economy

Andrew Graham

The new political economy

Writing at the end of the 1980s, I remarked that, compared with the number of books on applied economics, relatively little work was being conducted on comparative political economy. The position in the mid-1990s is quite different. Almost all of the major questions in political economy are now discussed within a comparative perspective and, as a result, there is much greater interest in the institutions of different countries.

The immediate cause of the new direction in political economy was the collapse of the Berlin Wall in 1989. What matters for the 1990s is not how capitalism compares with communism, but how one capitalist country compares with another. This is not, however, the only reason why debates in contemporary political economy now take a more comparative, institutional and international perspective. Four other more gradual, but cumulatively powerful, influences have been at work.

First, there has been an enormous growth in world financial markets and in international communications. Events in Singapore or Tokyo, in Berlin or Beijing, now reverberate around the world in a matter of seconds and countries appear more interdependent. Second, there has been a less rapid, but equally important, expansion of international trade. This has been a continuous process since the end of the Second World War, but recent developments have increased its contemporary significance: the result of the technological and information revolution is that distance from the market is no longer central (an insurance claim can be processed as easily in Delhi or Limerick as in Eastbourne) and China is so large that its recent entry into world trade is almost the equivalent of starting world trade afresh. Third, there has been growing awareness of common symptoms among the industrialised countries. Most countries experienced high inflation in the late 1970s and early 1980s, followed by high unemployment that has persisted into the 1990s. Last, but not least, there is the emergence of the European

Union. In the United Kingdom, in particular, most of the large questions in political economy now revolve around two interrelated issues: how closely is the United Kingdom to be integrated into Europe and what kind of Europe will it be?

One other development, part theoretical and part empirical, should be noted. The 1970s were perceived by many on the right to have been an era of 'government failure' and so in the 1980s policy swung towards far greater reliance on the market. Now in the 1990s the pendulum has gone the other way and there is renewed interest in 'market failure'.[1] This, too, has generated greater interest in how institutions work – why do markets work well in some cases, but not in others?[2]

Main questions

The new political economy raises two interrelated questions of great importance. Are all countries bound eventually to follow similar patterns of development or is there scope for national differences? And, if countries can diverge, what are the causes and what is the extent of such differences?

So far, modern literature suggests two sharply differing answers to these questions. Writers approaching from the perspective of trade and finance[3] emphasise how dominant international finance has become and how integrated the world economy now is.[4] They suggest that the scope for individual countries to buck the trend of the world economy has been greatly reduced in the 1990s, with power shifting to financial markets and multinational companies. A logical extension of this line of reasoning is that the nation state will disappear.

Others emphasise the diversity of capitalist experience. Albert, in particular, suggests that capitalist countries are of two broad types, with rivalry between them.[5] On the one hand are countries such as Germany and other countries bordering the Rhine (and thus called 'Rhenish' capitalism by Albert) in which capitalism's competitive forces are shaped by a powerful set of networks, institutions and long-term relationships. On the other hand are countries such as the United States and the United Kingdom where capitalism is more free-market. In a similar vein Soskice distinguishes between co-ordinated market economies on the one hand and unco-ordinated or liberal market economies on the other, maintaining that the former group manages to achieve lower levels of unemployment for a given rate of inflation.[6]

Albert and Soskice are, of course, standing on the shoulders of many earlier writers. Shonfield's classic work *Modern Capitalism*[7] gave birth to a series of studies emphasising differences in national attitudes and national policy. This was followed in the 1970s by emphasis on the centralisation, or otherwise, of wage bargaining arrangements as the main explanation of differences in the inflation–unemployment mix between countries. Contemporary work is a natural development of these concerns. However, the new approach is distinguished by being more quantitative and by extending the range of institutions covered. Modern studies include the relationship between finance and industry, the role of the state and the central bank, the internal organisation of the firm and, most recently and most generally, the links between the individual and society.

Before looking at these studies it is worth noting that debate is frequently occurring at two different levels. Most obviously there is disagreement about the relative merits of developing long-term relationships as compared with a more competitive view (for example, job security versus hire-and-fire), but at a deeper level there are unresolved questions about the relationship between individuals and institutions. A central question to which we shall return is whether institutions are merely the aggregate of individual actions or whether institutions have a life of their own and individuals are fully understandable only in the context of the institutions within which they are embedded.

Contemporary issues

Within the confines of a single chapter many contemporary issues are necessarily omitted. The four issues below, however, stand out. In addition, they have important counterparts within the debate about Europe that is considered below.

Inflation and unemployment

The inflation–unemployment relationship has long been central to the functioning of capitalist economies. In the 1930s capitalism faced collapse until Keynes and rearmament rescued it. In contrast, in the 1950s and 1960s governments believed they could guarantee full employment, and they appeared to be successful. However, by the 1970s and 1980s mainstream economic theory claimed that there was a unique level of unemployment at which the rate of inflation would be stable (the so-called non-accelerating inflation rate of unemployment, or NAIRU). No other level of unemployment was sustainable in the long run.[8] The difficulty with the concept of the NAIRU, however, was that, even if it existed, it appeared to be highly variable not only within the same country over short periods but also between countries.

Attempts to explain the variation in the United Kingdom have spawned a series of debates. Does the problem lie on the demand side, with high levels of actual unemployment dragging the NAIRU up through a process of hysteresis?[9] Or does it lie on the supply side? And, if the problem is supply, is that because UK labour markets are not sufficiently flexible (as the government has maintained) or because, on the contrary, labour markets have become too casualised, so undermining the incentive for firms to invest in training? Alternatively, is the rise in unemployment a more general problem facing less skilled workers in all the industrialised countries because of new competition from newly industrialising countries, as Wood has argued?[10]

The variation in the inflation–unemployment relationship between countries has also generated much discussion. Calmfors and Driffill, for example, argue that wage inflation will be relatively high whenever wage bargainers have power and believe that they can free-ride (i.e. that their wage claim will not be followed by everyone else).[11] In particular they suggest that wage inflation will be low both when bargaining is highly centralised (because free-riding will then seem impossible) and when bargaining is highly decentralised (because, with lots of competition, unions will have no power), but between these two extremes wage inflation will be high. They therefore postulate a 'hump-shaped' relationship between inflation and the centralisation of bargaining – a hypothesis their data appeared to confirm.

In reply, Soskice claims that Calmfors and Driffill's results are highly dependent on two countries, Japan and Switzerland.[12] He agrees that these two countries have relatively decentralised unions, but points out that they also have a strong set of networks between the various unions and firms throughout the economy. As a result, Soskice argues, firms and unions not only know what others are doing but can co-ordinate their actions. Low inflation in these two countries is therefore the result not of decentralisation but of a high level of co-ordination. More generally Soskice maintains that the relevant way of looking at countries is in terms not of whether their bargaining is centralised but of whether firms and unions can co-ordinate their actions.

The significance of this debate for policy towards the labour market is clear. Calmfors and Driffill's interpretation would support the Conservatives' approach, whereas Soskice's argument implies that attempts to decentralise the UK labour market would have made the United Kingdom's already poor inflation–unemployment performance even worse. It also has wider significance. Soskice is looking at the particular institutional context of individual countries, whereas Calmfors and Driffill are using the conventional measurement of market structure of economists. In addition, Soskice's explanation works only if the networks have been in existence for sufficiently long to influence behaviour and if that influence is important.

Finance and investment

The question of long-term relationships has also generated renewed interest in the debate about the financing of investment. It has long been observed that investment in the United Kingdom and the United States is low relative to Japan and Germany and that the financial systems are different: primarily retained profits and equity finance in the United Kingdom and the United States in contrast to long-term bank finance in Germany and Japan. This has led to the suggestion that bank finance is more conducive to long-term investment, to which the traditional reply was that the highly sophisticated stock markets of the United States and the United Kingdom are an advantage to UK and US firms. Equity finance is the most long-term of all finance, and the Anglo-American markets are the cheapest place to raise it. According to this latter view the cause of the low level of investment in the United Kingdom is the low level of profitability, rather than anything to do with the supply of finance.[13]

The new twist to this debate comes from the argument of Stiglitz and Weiss that capital markets can suffer from market failure.[14] If markets work well a riskier project pays a higher interest rate. However, this does not happen, because lenders in a capital market do not know enough about *each* project to set the relevant interest rate. As a result lenders are worried that anyone providing finance at a higher interest rate will pick up *more than their fair share* of the bad projects. Setting an even higher interest rate to compensate the lender for this risk merely compounds the problem. There is what is called 'asymmetrical information'. Managers are better informed about projects than are lenders, so lenders handle risk by seeking collateral as a substitute for information – but it is frequently not available. Mayer, in particular, argues that intense competition in capital markets can discourage capital formation and risk taking.[15] The solution suggested[16] is to replace the UK/US arm's-length relationship with much closer and longer-term relations as in Germany and Japan so that the lenders come to know and trust the borrowers – though whether institutions can be 'transplanted' from one country to another, and if so, how, is another matter.

Central bank independence

A very different institutional response can be seen in the debates about whether the central bank should be made independent. Those in favour[17] point to the correlation between high independence and low inflation and argue that this comes from two effects.[18] First, the independence of the central bank removes the ability of the government to generate the political business cycle that Alesina claims to have found.[19] Second, it provides a commitment to control inflation and thus has a beneficial effect on expectations. The obvious problem with this position is that the same arguments were put forward in favour of control of the money supply in the early 1980s and, when that had failed, for membership of the ERM in the early 1990s. Why, one asks, should independence of the Bank of England fare any differently?

One possible answer to this question is that what is being fixed on this occasion is the *objective* of low inflation rather than any particular means and that the policy to achieve this can be more flexible and more intelligent. However, this is only partly satisfactory. The credibility and the legitimacy of the Bank of England would still be on the line. A critical question therefore remains. Does the correlation of high independence with low inflation show that success in the battle against inflation comes from the independence of the central bank or does belief in the power of the independent central bank come from success in the battle against inflation? Hall, for example, argues persuasively that the success of the Bundesbank in controlling inflation is heavily dependent on the wider institutional structure (including the wage bargaining structure) within which it is embedded.[20]

Hall's work has been followed by that of Iversen, who combines the literature on wage bargaining with that on central bank independence.[21] Iverson restricts his interest to Soskice's co-ordinated economies and shows, both theoretically and empirically, that good outcomes for unemployment occur either when bargaining is highly centralised combined with low independence or when it is less centralised combined with high independence. The argument is straightforward. When bargaining is highly centralised there has to be something to bargain about and a truly independent central bank is not sufficiently flexible, whereas, when bargaining is less centralised, unions need to know that there are firm limits and so an independent central bank is helpful.

Inequality

A further issue of central concern is inequality, especially as economists have long argued that there is a trade-off between inequality and growth and yet in the United Kingdom inequality has risen steadily since 1977 while growth has fallen. Why has this happened? In a purely accounting sense, the rise in inequality can be decomposed into three elements: a larger spread between high-paid and low-paid jobs, a movement of labour from middle-paid jobs (especially in manufacturing) to high-paid and low-paid jobs in services and a change in the structure of taxes and benefits (with a lowering of direct rates of taxation offset by higher rates of indirect taxation plus cuts in entitlement to state benefits). Clearly the first of these is consistent with the government's goal of making the labour market more flexible and the last is the direct result of a policy designed to increase incentives and, so it was claimed, economic growth and the welfare of all, via 'trickle-down'.

Beyond this and the fact that 'trickle-down' never occurred, little is known with any certainty. Is the rise in the inequality of wage incomes primarily the consequence of external competition[23] and, in the face of such competition, has the greater dispersion of wages been necessary to stop unemployment rising even more, or has the rise in unemployment been a major factor creating wage inequality by lowering the bargaining power of the weakest? Similar questions can be asked about the relationship between inequality and growth. Did external pressures lower growth that the rise in inequality partially offset (through possible positive effects on material incentives) or has the rise in inequality generated such insecurity that it has reduced growth (either directly via loss of efficiency or via possible indirect adverse effects on morale, the breakdown of families, the increase in crime, etc.)? Research pinning down such indirect effects is notoriously difficult, but in a comparison across countries Wilkinson found that what matters for the level of health between countries was not the level of income but its distribution.[24] More generally a number of writers have commented on the diverse ways in which higher levels of inequality may undo the fabric of society,[25] and this has led to renewed interest in the relation between the individual and society.

European issues

Europe returns us to a question raised earlier – does the expansion of trade and finance combined with the footloose nature of new technology imply the demise of the nation state? The emergence of the European Union suggests both that the pressures in this direction are strong and yet that a half-way house – half-way in two senses – may be the answer. First, Europe is a regional, not a global, institution. Second, even the most federally minded of Europeans believe that only a limited range of issues need to be decided centrally – subsidiarity is also a real concern.

European issues are, of course, especially complicated for the United Kingdom. This is partly because of the current state of party politics, in which genuine debate is stifled, and partly because of history – the United Kingdom is the only major European nation with a period of uninterrupted democratic rule for more than three hundred years. Nevertheless there are three issues that can be disentangled analytically: the single currency, fiscal policy within a single currency and micro-economic issues.

The single currency

The economic case for the single currency is threefold. First, it would lead to a further integration of trade and to greater competition. Second, it would reduce transaction costs. Third, it would eliminate currency instability and the resources wasted in speculation. The political case for the single currency is that it would bind European countries closer together and thus strengthen Europe. Of course, the same argument is also the political case against the single currency – binding together is just what those who are sceptical about European integration do not want on the grounds (amongst others) that it would force countries and peoples together against their wishes and so weaken Europe.

There are also economic arguments the other way. Ideally, before regions have the same currency they should have integrated labour markets, but this is an extremely strong condition and one that probably does not apply even to Scotland and England. If this condition were not met, and if, as a result, one region became uncompetitive, then there would need to be compensating fiscal adjustments from one region to another (a condition met by Scotland and England, but not by the European Union – at least, not yet). However, such fiscal compensation might not be necessary if regions were competitive at the outset and maintained similar inflation rates thereafter. This is why so much importance is attached to initial convergence. Nevertheless, even if convergence had been achieved, it would still be important for a region to be able to correct for any subsequent shocks. In other words the 'region' would need its own fiscal policy.

Macro issues: fiscal policy

In the United Kingdom the question of whether a country contained within a single currency zone can run its own fiscal policy has generated more heat than light. Nevertheless, if a distinction is drawn between the *ability* to run an independent fiscal policy and the *effectiveness* of any such policy, the problem is not difficult to analyse clearly.

Consider first *effectiveness*: in normal circumstances, the smaller the country the more it will import. Thus, the smaller the country, the more will the effects of any given fiscal policy spill over elsewhere and the smaller, correspondingly, will be the domestic effect. Such spill-over effects loom large in discussion of European Monetary Union. As trade becomes ever more integrated, fiscal policy will have less of its effect on the country (or region) within which it originates and more elsewhere. This creates a strong *prima facie* case in favour of close co-ordination of fiscal policy at the European level.

Consider second the *ability* to run an independent fiscal policy. This depends almost entirely on the creditworthiness of the relevant authority.[26] If a government (international, national or local) is creditworthy it can issue bonds and finance a deficit, otherwise not.[27] The effects of monetary union are again important. In the absence of a single currency the ability of a national government to sell bonds internationally is constrained on two sides by currency risks. First, the government will be concerned that fiscal expansion will worsen the balance of payments, push down the exchange rate and so generate inflation. For this reason it may choose to limit the number of bonds it issues.

Second, potential buyers of the bonds, similarly aware of the effects on the exchange rate and on inflation, will require a risk premium, thus making the issue of bonds more expensive. However, once there is a single currency, the exchange rate risk disappears and the inflation risk is reduced (both because there is no exchange rate effect and because, for the reasons discussed above, more of any fiscal expansion spills abroad).

Two views have been taken of the relaxation of the constraints on fiscal policy that occurs under monetary union. One is that the market will still act as a sufficient restraint on a potentially profligate government, because if the debt appears large to the market the government will pay an interest rate premium – and the more excessive the debt the higher the premium. The only qualification to this argument is that the government must not be able to avoid this interest rate premium by buying its own bonds. In other words, there must be an independent central bank.

Others hold that, even with an independent central bank, the market will not act as an efficient restraint. Two interrelated arguments are adduced. One, drawn from economic history, emphasises the extent to which financial markets have taken too sanguine a view of creditworthiness, only to react extremely sharply late in the day (e.g. Mexico in 1982 or 1995). The other suggests that it is unrealistic to suppose that the European Union could allow one of its members to default. If so, creditworthiness, in the eyes of the market, is no longer relevant – indeed if the market also allows for this the problem is compounded because the government pays no premium.

The latter view was influential among the architects of the Maastricht Treaty and so a protocol to the treaty states that countries come under surveillance if they have a public deficit greater than 3 per cent of GDP or have accumulated debt greater than 60 per cent of GDP. It is, however, important that these numbers are in a protocol. They could therefore be changed without redoing the treaty. It is also important that they are not binding rules but trigger points for investigation. How they will operate in practice therefore remains uncertain. Hardly surprisingly, those who favour greater integration expect benign implementation, others the opposite. What is surprising, at least at first glance, is the political intensity of the debates on this issue – it is important, but it hardly seems large enough to tear a major political party apart. The answer is that the true fault line in the Conservative Party lies in the micro-economic issues.

Micro-economic issues

The fundamental problem for the Conservative Party is that ever since 1979 UK policy has been based on a set of strong free-market assumptions that are out of step with most of the rest of Europe. Low taxation, minimal business regulation, 'flexible' labour markets (i.e. no unions, no minimum wage and no security of employment) and, above all, the striving of competitive individuals rather than the co-operation of collective activity, have been the name of the game. In contrast other European countries have taken the 'social' part of the European Union to be as important as the economic aspect. All the earlier debates about the nature of wage bargaining and the links between industry and finance therefore reappear with particular sharpness in the European context. Has Europe been correct or incorrect to favour a more consultative and solidaristic approach to wage bargaining plus more committed shareholders and longer-term banking? Above all, what should the UK now do?

The group and the individual

Political economy is still grappling with these problems, and contemporary research has much to offer through its insights into market failure and into how institutions can 'solve' such failures. In particular, in the 1990s there is far greater awareness of two interrelated points: first, that capitalism is not the same as unbridled individualism (on the contrary, pure individualism promotes anarchy) and, second, that, as a result, the successful operation of capitalism requires solutions to a whole range of collective action problems. Examples are the need to share information, the need to trust others when outcomes are uncertain and/or difficult to monitor and the need for regulators to ensure secure financial institutions or the provision of clean water.[28]

Despite this progress, there remains a large question about which we still know extraordinarily little. The difficulty is that the new institutional political economy is operating at two different levels. One concerns the structure of the economy, for example financial structure, and it is clear in such cases how institutions affect behaviour – the finance director cannot just borrow long-term from banks if that is not on offer. The other concerns the relationship between the group and the individual, and here we are much more in the dark. There is much evidence that the values and behaviour of individuals are influenced by the institutions of which they are a part – civil servants have a public-sector ethos, doctors a code of professional conduct and in the money markets, apart from a few notorious exceptions, 'my word is my bond'. Yet there is no good theory of how this works, nor of how far it can be stretched, nor of how it interacts with material rewards. The problem is not that the world is composed partly of some individuals driven by the pursuit of material gain while others act altruistically/co-operatively and a third group is held in the grip of routine, but rather that each person is some complex mixture of all three. Moreover, this mixture is itself a complex combination of genetic inheritance, cultural context, personal volition and institutional influence.

The answer to this question is of great importance. Among the industrialised countries in the post-war period the economies that appear to have performed best, such as Japan and Germany, are those that seemed to take a long-term view and to have combined competition between firms with commitment to the firm, rather than those, such as the United States and the United Kingdom, which have emphasised hire-and-fire and short-term profit maximisation. But what does the future hold? Can these more institutionally based economies with committed resources continue to compete successfully with the new low-cost, unregulated firms of the newly industrialising countries? There may be a choice ahead for Europe, not just for the United Kingdom.

Conclusions

The distinctive contribution of modern political economy has been to lead us to a far more sophisticated understanding of the contributions of different institutions to the success, or otherwise, of particular economies. Nevertheless, fundamental theoretical and practical problems remain. The discovery that Germany has had a more co-ordinated structure of firms and unions or a more consultative system of industrial relations than the United Kingdom or that the British system of finance is inimical to long-term relationships is interesting, but it is not sufficient to tell us what to do. It does not follow that the German system will survive the shake-outs of the 1990s or the continuing internationalisation of capital markets. Nor does it follow that the German system can be or should be transplanted into the United Kingdom. Still less does it tell us how such a transplant could be achieved. The difficulty with institutional political economy is that even if we know that a good outcome in, say, Germany is the result of German 'habits and practices' we do not know how to bring about such habits and practices. The experience of the 1980s has given plenty of examples of institutions being destroyed. There is still much to be learnt about how useful institutions can be *created*. This is the fundamental challenge facing those who advocate the creation of a 'stake-holder economy'.

Notes

1 Many causes of market failure were set out long ago by A. C. Pigou, *The Economics of Welfare* (1917), reprinted 1932 and 1948, but policy in the 1980s was so concerned with government failure that market failure was largely ignored.

2 R. E. Lane, *The Market Experience* (1991), offers a more fundamental critique, asking whether markets help or hinder personal autonomy.

3 S. Strange, *States and Markets*, second edition (1988); P. G. Cerny (ed.), *Finance and World Politics: Markets, Regimes and States in the Post-hegemonic Era* (1993).

4 M. Kitson and J. Michie, *Managing the Global Economy* (1994), estimate that the world economy is by now 50 per cent more open than it was in the 1960s (a period they regard as open as the world economy before 1914).

5 M. Albert, *Capitalisme contre capitalisme* (1991); trans. *Capitalism against Capitalism* (1993).

6 D. Soskice, 'Wage determination: the changing role of institutions in advanced industrialised countries', *Oxford Review of Economic Policy*, 6 (4), 1990, pp. 36–61; 'The institutional infrastructure for international competitiveness: a comparative analysis of the UK and Germany', in A. B. Atkinson and R. Brunetta (eds), *The Economics of the new Europe* (1991).

7 A. Shonfield, *Modern Capitalism* (1964).

8 Empirical work focused on trying to establish at what level it occurred, but a deep divide on policy remained. On the one hand monetarists and rational expectations theorists argued that the economy would find that level of its own

accord and that the level was 'natural'. On the other, Keynesians maintained that the government could and should use the level of demand to control the level of unemployment.

9 'Hysteresis' is a term borrowed from physics to denote a situation in which something, when squeezed, does not return to its original shape.

10 A. Wood, *North–South Trade, Employment and Inequality* (1994).

11 L. Camfors and J. Driffill, 'Centralisation of wage bargaining', *Economic Policy*, 4, April 1988, pp. 161–91.

12 'Wage determination'.

13 F. Capie and M. Collins, *Have the Banks failed British Industry?* Hobart Paper 119 (1992).

14 J. Stiglitz and A. Weiss, 'Credit rationing in markets with imperfect information', *American Economic Review*, 71, 1981, pp. 393–411.

15 C. Mayer, 'New issues in corporate finance', *European Economic Review*, 32.

16 For example, D. Goodhart, *The Reshaping of the German Social Market* (1994).

17 W. Hutton, *The State we're in* (1995).

17 For example, Treasury and Civil Service Select Committee, *The Role of the Bank of England*, Committee Reports I–II, 8 December, 98–II (1993); C. Bean, 'The case for an independent Bank of England', *New Economy*, sample issue, autumn 1993, pp. 26–31.

18 A. Cukierman, *Central Bank Strategy, Credibility and Independence* (1992).

19 A. Alesina, 'Politics and business cycles in industrial democracies', *Economic Policy*, 5 April 1989, pp. 55–98.

20 P. A. Hall, 'Central bank independence and co-ordinated wage bargaining: their interaction in Germany and Europe', *German Politics and Society*, 31, spring 1994.

21 T. Iverson, 'Wage Bargaining, Monetary Regimes and Economic Performance in Organised Market Economies: Theory and Evidence', paper presented to the American Political Science Association, September 1994.

22 A. Goodman and S. Webb, 'For richer, for poorer: the changing distribution of income in the UK', *Fiscal Studies*, 15 (4), 1994, pp. 29–62; Joseph Rowntree Foundation, *Income and Wealth*, I–II (1995).

23 Wood, *North–South Trade*, again.

24 R. Wilkinson, 'Health, redistribution and growth', in A. Glyn and D. Miliband (eds), *Paying for Inequality: the Economic Cost of Social Injustice* (1994).

25 For example, J. Gray, *The Undoing of Conservatism* (1996); Hutton, *The State we're in*; A. Graham, 'Myths and realities of Conservative capitalism in the UK: 1979–1995', in C. Crouch and W. Streeck (eds), *Capitalisms in Europe* (1996).

26 The focus here is exclusively on the balance of taxation and expenditure. Effects via the structure of taxation or expenditure would need a separate analysis.

27 The ability of a government to monetise its debt via sales to the central bank can be ignored here, since such effects concern monetary policy rather than fiscal policy.

28 There is an excellent survey of these issues in 'Institutions of economic policy', *Oxford Review of Economic Policy*, 10 (3), autumn 1994.

Further reading

Readers who wish to pursue these topics should begin with Hutton, *The State we're in*. An opposite view is Sir Alan Walters, *Britain's Economic Renaissance: Margaret Thatcher's Economic Reforms, 1979–84* (1985). The two cover well many of the issues in this chapter. Beyond that, the discussion above, with the references given there, provide material on most of the points discussed. They may be supplemented by D. Helm (ed.), *The Economic Borders of the State* (1989), which contains useful articles on the role of the state in a modern capitalist economy. In addition Glyn and Miliband, *Paying for Inequality*, cover the inequality issue in detail. There is a useful discussion of the financing of industry in M. Prevezer, 'Capital and control: an overview of City–industry relations', in T. Buxton, P. Chapman and P. Temple (eds), *Britain's Economic Performance* (1994). Alternative views of the NAIRU and what determines it are to be found in P. Minford, *Unemployment: Cause and Cure* (1983), and in R. Layard, S. Nickell and R. Jackman, *Unemployment: Macroeconomic Performance and the Labour Market* (1991). The case against unbridled individualism is well put in D. Marquand, *The Unprincipled Society* (1988). Contrary positions on the independence of the central bank can be found in Bean, 'The case for an independent Bank' (in favour), G. Holtham, 'The war of independence', *New Economy*, 1 (1), spring 1994 (against), and C. Doyle and M. Weale, 'Do we really want an independent central bank?', *Oxford Review of Economic Policy*, 10 (3), 1994, pp. 61–77 (questioning). Finally, the role of institutions in economic performance is discussed by W. Streeck, *Social Institutions and Economic Performance* (1992).

Chapter 8

'Sexing the archive': gender in contemporary history

Lucy Noakes

The task of the historian attempting to study issues of gender in the contemporary period initially appears easier than that of the historian researching, for example, attitudes towards women in the early modern period.
Women, in the years during and since the Second World War, have become
increasingly visible, their movement out of the home, and their increased
involvement in the 'public' worlds of work and politics, meaning that they
are leaving more records and traces behind for the contemporary historian.[1]
Added to this increased visibility of women, a large body of research on
gender issues has emerged from the women's liberation movement, with
journals such as *Feminist Review* and *Gender and History* frequently covering issues of interest to the contemporary historian.[2] More recently, academics across various fields have started to address issues of masculinity,
following Michelle Barratt's 1980 assertion that a full knowledge of femininity could not be achieved without some study of its structural opposite,
masculinity.[3] Studying issues of gender, it appears, have never been easier.

However, issues of gender are still marginal to much that goes under the
title 'contemporary history'. Contemporary history all too often means political history in its narrowest sense: the study of institutions and individuals
in positions of power, rather than a more inclusive study of recent and contemporary society and culture.[4] As women are still underrepresented in
these positions, debates about gender tend to be largely absent from writings on contemporary history. Few contemporary historians, for example,
have engaged with gender issues arising from the sexual and social revolution at the end of the 1960s – a movement responsible for many of the
changing attitudes and opportunities, and emerging academic studies, outlined above. In a similar vein, few researchers have attempted to analyse
the post-war changes in women's lives – the rise in consumption changes
in family size and structure, and increased work and education opportunities – in any historically minded way.[5] Debates about gender within the field
of contemporary history are few and far between.

Indeed, the main debate about issues of gender within contemporary history has been about the argument about the position of women during the Second World War. That was a time when large numbers of women took up paid work outside the home, often in occupations which had previously been thought of as 'masculine'; a time of vast social change when gender relations, as well as many other social structures, were subject to public debate and scrutiny, and thus a period when material about gender roles is readily available.[6] The debate has focused upon the extent to which the Second World War can be seen as a modernising force, 'liberating' women from their pre-war restrictions. Women, it appears, tend to enter contemporary history only when they make large-scale forays into the 'male' worlds of work and politics.

Contemporary historians who *have* focused on gender issues have tended to come from areas of historical research which are still in many ways peripheral to the mainstream of the discipline: women's history and oral history. Both these practices emphasise the study of the lives of the powerless and the marginalised in society: women's history by focusing upon women's lives, oral history by recording the thoughts and memories of the working class, ethnic minorities and women.[7] Much of the existing material on gender in contemporary history has come from these two areas.[8] However, an understanding of issues of gender is necessary for the contemporary historian who wants to undertake any fruitful research into the changes in contemporary British society and culture. Post-war Britain must be understood as a multiracial and multicultural society. It also needs to be understood as a gendered society.

Women's lives have changed enormously in twentieth-century Britain. The winning of the vote in 1917; the introduction of female conscription during the Second World War; the women's liberation movement of the late 1960s and the subsequent development of feminism; and the passing of the Equal Opportunities Bill into law in 1975 – these are all major social and political changes which have touched the lives of virtually every woman in Britain. Women are also affected, often in a different way from men, by social, cultural, economic and political change which is not specifically and explicitly concerned with women as a separate group. To understand fully the nature of the changes seen in the contemporary period, historians need to develop a more sensitive approach to issues of gender, using more varied and imaginative research techniques, and widening the variety of material studied.

The contemporary historian interested in issues of gender, whether these be the changing role of women in the late twentieth century, the structural and structuring relationship between masculinity and femininity, or current debates about the nature of masculinity, often has to turn initially to other disciplines in order to pursue his or her research. Anthropology has given us a framework from which to study the meanings of everyday life:

the ways in which traditions, rituals and beliefs both shape and are shaped by, attitudes towards gender.[9] Cultural studies, with their emphasis upon understanding texts separate from those of the traditional literary and artistic 'canon', and their subsequent investigation of various sites of cultural production such as television, magazines and photographs, have produced some interesting and innovative work on the ways in which masculinity and femininity are represented in contemporary society, and the ways in which women and men think about themselves.[10] The social sciences have illustrated the importance of qualitative methods of research for discovering more about women's lives in the contemporary period.[11] These other disciplines can 'lend' the contemporary historian the theoretical tools necessary for any profitable study of issues of gender in the late twentieth century.

An important and on-going debate within contemporary history has been the extent to which Britain has changed and modernised in the years since the Second World War. The diverse social, cultural, economic and political changes which have taken place since 1945 have been widely explored, with 1945, and the landslide election of a Labour government, and 1979, with the election of a radical 'new right' government, being pointed to as key moments of change. The founding of the welfare state in the 1940s is seen as a time when the class and income-based inequalities of the preceding years were 'levelled out', with the introduction of decent, widely available council housing, health care and secondary education for all, and state provision of universal child benefit and pensions. 1979, conversely, has been recognised as the moment when a post-war consensus around the principles of the welfare state was finally eradicated, with the election of a privatising and individualist right-wing government which put its faith in market forces and spoke nostalgically of a return to 'Victorian values'. The period since the Second World War can thus be seen as a time of rapid and thoroughgoing change in society; a time when Britain moved from the hardships of the pre-war world through consensus politics and social stability to the revolutions of the 1960s and the present fears about social breakdown and economic decline. However, a brief survey of some of the research into women's lives since 1945 shows that many underlying attitudes and social expectations underwent relatively little structural change in this period.

Some feminist researchers have argued that the welfare state, far from releasing women from economic dependence on others, in fact often simply replaced economic dependence on a man with dependence upon a patriarchal state.[12] The welfare state, it is argued, has the ability to determine women's social and sexual behaviour through the rules governing eligibility for benefits. Indeed, the ruling that women cohabiting with a (male) sexual partner are ineligible for a whole range of state benefits embodies the principle that women should be economically dependent on men. Although it is now far more common than in the pre-war years for women to go out to work and to be economically and socially independent, this particular ruling appears to enshrine and legitimate earlier attitudes towards gender roles.

The continued existence of established attitudes about gender can be seen in the state's response to the growing number of families headed by a lone parent, the majority of whom are women. Although state provision for such families has helped to widen the choice of living patterns for women, the nuclear family is still regarded as the norm, and alternative family structures are increasingly seen as deviant. This emphasis upon the nuclear family as the ideal family form has been remarkably consistent in the post-war years. In the 1940s the family was a major site of post-war reconstruction, with fears about a falling birth rate in wartime giving rise to pro-natalist policies.[13] This belief in the nuclear family, which is based upon a sexual division of labour, with the man earning the bulk of the family income whilst the woman undertakes the bulk of unpaid household labour and child care, continues to shape attitudes today.[14]

However, whilst state policy is an important indicator of prevailing beliefs about gender, the contemporary historian also needs to examine other sources to discover how these beliefs are transmitted, and how widely they are held. In her study of women's magazines in the post-war years Janice Winship has illustrated how traditional attitudes towards gender became incorporated into the emergent welfare state.[15] A brief examination of *Woman*, the best-selling magazine of the period, illustrates not only the continued existence of these attitudes but also how women were encouraged to construct their own identities in the post-war world. *Woman*, despite its reiteration of feminist arguments about the continued need for public child care provision in peacetime as well as wartime, and despite arguing that husbands needed to change their attitudes towards housework by jettisoning 'the idea that one man's comfort is one woman's full-time job'[16] still predominantly represented women in the role of housewife and mother. Fiction was almost invariably a romantic narrative, in which the heroine discovered happiness and fulfilment through attachment to one man, and the magazine, although it featured a regular careers column, also ran numerous weekly articles on child care, beauty care, cookery and home issues. The incipient feminist voice of *Woman*, moreover, was little more than a whisper by the early 1950s, when the election of a Conservative government and the end of rationing and austerity, combined with the widening availability of 'white' household goods such as fridges, vacuum cleaners and washing machines, helped to strengthen the idea of woman as homemaker. In the formative years of the welfare state, it appears, traditional attitudes towards gender predominated.

What, though, of the sexual revolution of the 1960s, the period perhaps most often pointed to as seeing a vital shift in beliefs about gender roles, particularly the existence of a 'double standard' in sexual behaviour for women and men? The advent of the contraceptive pill, the Abortion Act of 1967, the Divorce Reform Act of 1969, the Matrimonial Property Act of 1970 and the ideas emerging from the women's liberation movement have all been perceived as key factors in a general process of liberalisation. However, some feminist researchers have questioned the extent to which the 'permissive moment' of the late 1960s was especially liberating for women. Germaine Greer has argued that the availability of oral contraception in fact strengthened the existing gender balance of sexual relationships, increasing women's responsibility for contraception, and pressuring women into conforming to new standards of sexual behaviour.[17] Greer's argument is, however, difficult to quantify, as there is little evidence for the historian to turn to in order to study women's attitudes and expectations of the 'sexual revolution' of the 1960s. A study of women's memories of the 1960s, perhaps using the interview technique of oral history, could give contemporary historians a more detailed picture of the period.

This lack of evidence brings us onto a more general problem encountered by those researching women's history and gender history: the problem of sources. The archives and documents most often used by contemporary historians – the materials held in the Public Record Office, records of parliamentary debates in Hansard, Cabinet papers, and ministerial diaries and autobiographies – often have little to say about attitudes towards gender, being largely concerned with affairs of state and high office. Discussions of gender tend to be absent from these sorts of sources except at times of crisis and moral panic – when, for instance, the rising number of lone-parent families is discussed. Women's voices, which could provide the researcher with a record of female thoughts about gender roles, are also largely absent from these sources, as women are still relatively scarce in positions of power. The contemporary historian has to learn to read between the lines, questioning the absence of material on gender, and searching for underlying assumptions which feed into policy-making decisions. The range of sources studied also has to be widened: women's magazines, diaries, letters and interviews with those *not* in positions of power are all useful sources for the researcher attempting to discover attitudes and assumptions about gender in the contemporary period. In order to 'sex the archive', we first have to broaden it.

One particularly useful source for the historian working on gender in the contemporary period is the material collected by Mass-Observation. Mass-Observation was founded in 1937 by a group of young male upper-class intellectuals with the purpose of creating what they called 'an anthropology of ourselves'. Operating until 1949, when it became a limited company specialising in market research, Mass-Observation collected material on the thoughts, habits and beliefs of 'ordinary people' throughout the late 1930s, during the Second World War and into the 1940s. This material was derived from two main sources: 'observation' by a small group of trained investigators who watched, interviewed and surveyed the population, and contributions from a volunteer 'panel' who 'observed themselves' by keeping diaries and responding to monthly open-ended 'directives', or themed questionnaires. By 1945 approximately 3,000 people had contributed to the project.

The Mass-Observation project began afresh in 1982 when people responded to advertisements in the national press for volunteer writers. Since 1982 over 3,000 people have written for the project, responding to 'directives' covering such diverse areas as the royal family, AIDS, ageing, the Falklands and Gulf war, personal hygiene and relations between women and men. Whilst only a few of the Mass-Observation 'directives' directly address issues of gender, the historical researcher working on the archive will quickly discover that it is nevertheless a particularly rich source for examining the extent to which gender shapes identity and opinion in the contemporary period.

For instance the Mass-Observation files on the Falklands War of 1982 and the Gulf War of 1991 show a highly gendered response to both events. Female respondents, many of whom had personal memories of the Second World War, a conflict which both wars were repeatedly compared to in the press and in Parliament, often used these memories to express fear or worry about war, such as the woman who wrote in 1982 that:

> I remember going into Coventry after the Blitz in November 1940 and nursed those casualties afterwards ... I remember people from what were then considered the slums of West Ham after land mines had been dropped in their district ... I nursed the men who came back from Dunkirk, many of whom had severe neuroses ... I remember watching ships and men leaving Portsmouth for D Day sailing into the sunset for France, and the ghastly weeks that followed.[18]

This woman draws on personal images of horror, death and suffering in warfare to express her fears about the Falklands War. Men writing for Mass-Observation during the Falklands and Gulf wars were much more likely to write about them in language which illustrates military or political knowledge. Whilst many of the older male writers again drew on their memories of the Second World War as a means of shaping their responses and justifying their views, these memories were often of their own time as combatants, one man writing in 1991 that:

> I know what fighting in the desert means. An armour-piercing shell exploding in a tank causes horrific mess. I know, I have seen it ... so I'm not exactly an armchair warrior ... [Saddam Hussein] must be dealt with, otherwise there will be no peace or stability in the Middle East.[19]

This respondent uses his personal memories of combat to legitimise his views on the Gulf War, his experience of fighting in the desert in the Second

World War being called upon to show that he is no 'armchair strategist' but speaks instead from a special position of knowledge and experience. These two Mass-Observation files show how attitudes to war are often shaped and moulded by gender, and open up questions for the contemporary historian about the nature of memory and national identity in contemporary Britain.[20]

Of course, Mass-Observation respondents cannot be treated as a representative sample of British society. The people who write for the project are self-selecting, and tend to be white, middle-aged or older and middle-class. For the historian interested in gender, however, they provide a rich and fascinating resource, as many women write for Mass-Observation, providing female voices and opinions which are often absent from other public sources, such as newspapers. Mass-Observation perhaps provides an outlet for many women who in other circumstances are made to feel that their opinions and views on major political and national events are of less worth than those of men. The gender balance of Mass-Observation illustrates the extent to which women are still excluded from the public stage in contemporary Britain.

In this brief discussion of issues of gender in contemporary history I have shown how awareness of gender issues can help historians to rethink their ideas about the contemporary period. The fairly static attitudes towards gender in post-war Britain illustrate that perhaps social and cultural change has not been as far-reaching as is sometimes suggested. The material in Mass-Observation opens up questions around gendered forms of identity and gendered forms of remembering and writing, and points towards the ways in which women's voices are often absent from more 'traditional' historical sources. Historians working on earlier periods of history have shown how an examination of issues of gender can help us to gain a wider understanding of the past. For instance, Leonore Davidoff's and Catherine Hall's book *Family Fortunes* showed how gender roles became an important means of structuring and defining the emergent Victorian middle class, and marking them out as separate from, and morally superior to, both the aristocracy and the working class.[21] If contemporary historians of British society are to develop a full and clear analysis of Britain since 1945, similar attention needs to be paid to the construction of gender roles in this period. Gender history and women's history need to move from the margins of contemporary history into the centre.

Notes

1 For surveys of women in post-war Britain see J. Lewis, *Women in Britain since 1945: Women, Family, Work and the State in the Post-war Years* (1992); E. Wilson, *Only Half-way to Paradise: Women in Post-war Britain, 1945–68* (1980).
2 For a discussion of the work on women's history within the women's liberation

movement see C. Hall, *White, Male and Middle Class: Explorations in Feminism and History* (1992), introductory chapter, *'Feminism and Feminist History'*.

3 M. Barratt, *Women's Oppression Today* (1980). For historically aware discussion of issues of masculinity see M. Roper and J. Tosh (eds), *Manful Assertions: Masculinities in Britain since 1800* (1991); L. Segal, *Slow Motion: Changing Masculinities, Changing Men* (1990). K. Thewelweit's two-volume *Male Fantasies* (1989), provides an interesting case study for historians of masculinity by examining the lives, diaries and fantasies of a group of proto-fascists in inter-war Germany. Similarly A. Thomson, *Anzac Memories: Living with the Legend* (1994), is an excellent oral history study of the lives and memories of a group of First World War veterans in Australia.

4 See, for example, A. Sked and C. Cook, *Post-war Britain: a Political History* (1979), reprinted three times and a standard text on many university courses on the post-war period. Some political histories of Britain since 1945 have opened out wider issues, e.g. K. O. Morgan, *The People's Peace: British History, 1945–89* (1990); P. Hennessy, *Never Again: Britain, 1945–1951* (1992). A good cultural survey of the period is A. Sinfield, *Literature, Politics and Culture in Post-war Britain* (1989).

5 Two contemporary historians who are the exception to this rule are Jane Lewis and Pat Thane. See Lewis, *Women in Britain*; P. Thane and G. Bock (eds), *Maternity and Gender Policies: Women and the Rise of the European Welfare States, 1880–1950* (1991).

6 The main protagonists in this debate have been A. Marwick, who did much to popularise the view that the Second World War was a levelling force, and P. Summerfield, who has argued that in fact women workers were caught between the needs of wartime production and those of patriarchy. A. Marwick, *Britain in the Century of Total War: Peace and Social Change, 1900–1967* (1968); *War and Social Change in the Twentieth Century* (1974); *The Home Front: the British and the Second World War* (1976). P. Summerfield, *Women Workers in the Second World War: Production and Patriarchy in Conflict* (1984). Also see D. Riley, *War in the Nursery: Theories of the Child and Mother* (1983).

7 Much of this work, the recovery of 'history from below', has been carried out in Britain by the Oral History Society, which publishes *Oral History*.

8 See, for example, A. Woodeson, 'Going back to the land: rhetoric and reality in Women's Land Army memories', *Oral History*, 21 (2), autumn 1993; E. Roberts, Hall Carpenter Archives, Lesbian Oral History Group, *Inventing Ourselves: Lesbian Life Stories* (1989); A. Wilson, *Finding a Voice: Asian Women in Britain* (1978).

9 An interesting example of this is Mary Douglas, *Purity and Danger: an Analysis of the Concepts of Pollution and Taboo* (1966). Douglas examines the ways in which ideas about dirt and pollution, common to many societies, are shaped by a variety of factors, gender being a recurrent structuring idea across many societies.

10 See, for example, Angela McRobbie, *Feminism and Youth Culture: from 'Jackie' to 'Just 17'* (1991); Janice Winship, *Inside Women's Magazines* (1987).

11 See M. Maynard and J. Purvis (eds), *Researching Women's Lives from a Feminist Perspective* (1994). Liz Stanley is one of the key researchers in the field of qualitative research into women's lives. Her recent publications include *Feminist*

Praxis: Research, Theory and Epistemology in Feminist Sociology (ed.) (1990), and *The Auto/Biographical I: the Theory and Practice of Feminist Auto/Biography* (1992).

12 This argument has been put forward by E. Wilson, in *Women and the Welfare State* (1977). Lewis, in *Women in Britain*, points out that for many women this is presumably preferable to economic dependence on a man (p. 112).

13 For discussion of this see Riley, *War in the Nursery*.

14 See A. Oakley, *The Sociology of Housework* (1974), for the classic analysis of the sexual division of labour in the home.

15 Winship, *Inside Women's Magazines* and 'Nation before family: *Woman, the National Home Weekly*, 1945–53', in *Formations of Nation and People* (1984).

16 *Woman*, 29 March 1947, cited in Winship, *Inside Women's Magazines*, p. 198.

17 G. Greer, *Sex and Destiny: the Politics of Human Fertility* (1985).

18 Mass-Observation Archive, University of Sussex, Falklands War file, 1982, respondent No. R462.

19 Mass-Observation, Gulf War file, 1991–92, respondent No. W1476.

20 For an interesting discussion of these issues see Thomson, *Anzac Memories*. This book uses oral history techniques to discuss the ways in which memories of the First World War have fed into ideas about nationhood in twentieth-century Australia.

21 L. Davidoff and C. Hall, *Family Fortunes: the Men and Women of the English Middle Class, 1780–1850* (1987).

Further reading

M. Barratt, *Women's Oppression Today* (1980).

R. Chapman and J. Rutherford (eds), *Male Order: Unwrapping Masculinity* (1988).

G. Greer, *Sex and Destiny: the Politics of Human Fertility* (1985).

C. Hall, *White, Male and Middle Class: Explorations in Feminism and History* (1992).

A. Holdsworth, *Out of the Doll's House: the Story of Women in the Twentieth Century* (1988).

M. Kennedy, C. Lubelska and V. Walsh, *Making Connections: Women's Studies, Women's Movements, Women's Lives* (1993).

J. Lewis (ed.), *Women's Welfare/Women's Rights* (1983).

J. Lewis, *Women in England, 1870–1950* (1984).

J. Lewis, *Women in Britain since 1945: Women, Family, Work and the State in the Post-war Years* (1992).

A. Marwick, *British Society since 1945* (1982).

M. Maynard and J. Purvis (ed.), *Researching Women's Lives from a Feminist Perspective* (1994).

K. O. Morgan, *The People's Peace: Britain 1945–89* (1990).

A. Oakley, *The Sociology of Housework* (1974).

S. Rowbotham, *The Past is before Us: Feminism in Action since the 1960s* (1989).

L. Segal, *Is the Future Female? Troubled Thoughts on Contemporary Feminism* (1987).

L. Segal, *Slow Motion: Changing Masculinities, Changing Men* (1990).

D. Sheridan (ed.), *Wartime Women: a Mass Observation Anthology: the Experiences of Women at War* (1990).

L. Stanley, *The Auto/Biographical I: the Theory and Practice of Feminist Auto/Biography* (1992).

M. Stuart, 'You're a big girl now: subjectivities, oral history and feminism', *Oral History Journal*, 22 (2), autumn 1994, pp. 55–63.

P. Summerfield, *Women Workers in the Second World War: Production and Patriarchy in Conflict* (1984).

A. Thomson, *Anzac Memories: Living with the Legend* (1994).

J. Tosh and M. Roper (ed.), *Manful Assertions: Masculinities in Britain since 1800* (1991).

J. Winship, *Inside Women's Magazines* (1987).

A. Woodeson, 'Going back to the land: rhetoric and reality in Women's Land Army memories', *Oral History Journal*, 21 (2), autumn 1993, pp. 65–72.

Chapter 9

Citizenship and the European Union

Elizabeth Meehan

Let me begin with something that I find very frustrating about many commentaries on citizenship and the European Union. It is the oversimplified way in which people often speak of identity. The so-called Euro-sceptics, for example, argue that there cannot be real European citizenship without a single European identity. This means that, since Europe is composed of many different national identities, European citizenship is either impossible or would have to come into existence on the basis of coerced homogeneity. I suggest that they are wrong on three main counts.

First, it is ahistorical to insist that citizenship is coterminus with legal national identity. Secondly, as I shall then argue, people are not defined merely by their legal nationality but have complex sets of interests some of which may be best pursued by stressing their national identity but others of which involve commonalities with people of different national identities and may best be pursued as a transnational common cause. And thirdly I suggest in a brief conclusion that it can be argued, and indeed has been argued, that the success of a federal or quasi-federal political system depends not on homogeneity or common identity but exactly on the opposite. That is, a federalism which protects rights can do so only where there is diversity and where institutions reflect that diversity.

Ahistorical and broader conceptions of citizenship

Twenty years ago the eminent French social theorist Raymond Aron,[1] argued that there was no such animal as a European citizen. There were only Germans or French or Italians, and so on. Seventeen years later Lord Jenkins, despite his own enthusiasm for European integration, told an audience at my university that he could not foresee the day when citizens of member states of the European Community would say when in Japan that they were Europeans instead of French, German or Italians, and so on. He contrasted this with the Texan, who, he said, would happily claim when in Europe to be American.

These kinds of views contrast strongly with the language that is present in EU policy and which is used by EU institutions. European Union language speaks of 'a people's Europe' and, since the development and ratification of the Maastricht Treaty, 'citizens of the Union'. If we look at the history of citizenship, it is possible to argue that the language of the European Union is more justified than the language of Aron or even Jenkins.

Aron's care rests on drawing a distinction between human rights and citizenship rights. He concedes that a single belief in the equality of human beings gives rise to beliefs both in human rights *and* in citizenship rights. But, using the Hegelian distinction between people who participate in economic life and people as members of political society, he argues that there is a categorical difference between the two sets of rights.

Citizens are identifiable by a status which is conferred upon them in the rules about the administration of justice and about political participation. Such status and rules, he argues, can be guaranteed only in the context of a state – sometimes a nation state, often a state of several nations which coexist, as in the United Kingdom, under the same legal nationality. In contrast, property rights in the eighteenth century and socio-economic rights in the twentieth century do not depend exclusively upon the existence of a state or a shared legal nationality in order to be guaranteed. And so, according to Aron, it is perfectly possible to envisage two different political authorities protecting those two different kinds of rights. The state will continue in the European Union to protect people's rights of citizenship, and the fact that the European Union regulates economic and social rights cannot be taken as an indication of some kind of embryonic European citizenship. But, as I argue here, both the nationality/state condition and the content of those rights that count as citizenship rights can be disputed.

At a superficial level Aron's position seems to be corroborated by another French scholar, Jean Leca – a political scientist.[2] Jean Leca also draws attention to strong connections between nationality, the nation state and citizenship. But he differs from Aron. Aron refers primarily to one document, the French Declaration of the Rights of Man (and, secondarily, to the UN Convention on Human Rights) and constructs a theory of citizenship, arising from that particular historical experience, which is accorded the status of universal truth. Conversely Leca argues that both nationality and citizenship are social constructs imbued with ideological values which must be explained by what they mean to real people in their real contexts throughout history. Thus the meanings of both citizenship and nationality will vary according to people's historical situation.

One example of what Leca is talking about is the idea that some communities see society as based on contracts and associations while others think of society as communitarian. In a contract-based society, both nationality and the consequent rights of citizenship can be acquired relatively easily by anyone meeting the criteria, whereas in a society which thinks of itself as communitarian it is much harder to acquire such rights because the condition of membership is blood ties.

Derek Heater[3] provides a much broader account than most of understandings of citizenship and, in doing so, he does what Leca asks us to do about looking at historical contexts. Heater's work on citizenship shows that citizenship is neither connected exclusively with the nation state nor confined to rights to equality in the administration of justice and political participation. From very early on, he argues, the term 'citizenship' contained a cluster of meanings related to a defined legal or social status, a means of political identity, a focus of loyalty, a requirement of duties, an expectation of rights and a yardstick of good social behaviour. The early history of citizenship, Heater argues, must lead us to question the modern assumption that the status necessarily adheres to membership of the sovereign nation state. The status of citizenship can be associated with any geographical unit, from a small town to the whole globe itself. The links between the so-called nation state, citizenship and nationality arise from relatively modern strategic imperatives. That is, the links lie in the need of new states, emerging in the eighteenth and nineteenth centuries, to maintain their security by consolidating their frontiers and controlling the people allowed to cross them.[4]

Moreover, Heater's 'cluster of meanings' also undermines Aron's insistence that citizenship is about the administration of justice and political participation exclusively. Notions of citizenship – for a very long time, before the rise of nation states, and continuing since their inception and consolidation – have included what Aron calls human rights. In the Greek city states, citizenship was about the construction of a common moral order characterised by conviviality and social justice.[5] Many centuries later, the ideas of the Greeks still inspired political thinkers. John Stuart Mill, as Heater points out, argued that workers' rights could be citizens' rights. This arose from his Aristotelian view that people were by nature political and fully human only when they took part in constructing their society. However, that political nature could not be expressed in the same way as in Greek city states by people who now lived in large, complex societies. Therefore giving people rights in the workplace would be an alternative means of fulfilling their human need of participation.

That classical idea of human nature being essentially political and, at the same time, embodying the need and ability to engage in the construction of 'the good society' still exists in the thinking of those who advocate social rights. While it is true that some social rights advocates are individualistic in their conception of human nature and in the justifications (based on self-interest and self-development) they advance for counting social rights as part of citizenship, others retain the collectivism of the classical idea of a common moral order.[6] And there are traces of the latter in the language of EU policy.

European Union social policies and proposals for policy include workers' rights and social security and assistance. Although these policies and proposals are about individual rights – that is, individuals who migrate should not lose personal legal entitlements – their language is also quite Aristotelian. On the one hand, the most ambitious of EU proposals for workers' rights (still not law because of disputes in the Council of Ministers) are about the need of workers to participate in the management of their enterprises and in the political future of EU institutions. On the other, the preambles to all EU social measures and proposals always talk about the need to construct a common moral order within the European Union, a common moral order in which there are common standards of living and common outlooks and common forms of loyalty.

Thus, it seems to me, on the basis of Heater's view of citizenship, instead of Aron's, the existence of some workers' rights whose standards are set by the European Union mean that it is reasonable to discern the embryo of a kind of European citizenship. And I think we can see the same thing if we look at what are more indisputably social rights – the right to income maintenance and social services.

Although Aron argued that in the eighteenth century people distinguished between the human right to own property and the political right to participate, our forbearers linked them in practice. The possession of property was taken as a demonstration that people were rational or disinterested enough to be allowed to take part in political decision-making. It was for that reason that the poor and women (also debarred for other reasons) were excluded from citizenship. In the twentieth century various political theorists have proposed that there could be another solution. If people cannot be rational or disinterested, because of the grinding need to fend for themselves, it is not necessary for them to be excluded. Instead, they can be given the basic, material means from which they can develop their rationality and, thus, behave as responsible political beings.

European Union social policies came about in a period when dominant political ideologies in the member states accepted, either for philosophical or for expedient reasons, the ethical justifications of the welfare state. Even though much EU activity is about co-ordinating different national policies, the idea that there is a common interest in co-ordination (with a moral as well as economic justification – see the reference above to preambles) again seems to indicate acceptance at the EU level of a concept of citizenship in which it is difficult to distinguish, as Aron does, between political rights and social provision. Such a view is reinforced by the arguments that lie behind the political rights in the Maastricht Treaty.

These arguments brought together the rationales that motivated the proposals for workers' right to contribute to the management of their enterprises and to the direction of EU institutions, the justification for the increasing importance of consultation with the 'social partners' (employers, trade unionists, the voluntary sector), the ideas behind the creation of EU symbols (such as the flag and the adoption of Beethoven's 'Ode to Joy' as its anthem), and the implications of the reasons for co-ordinated social policy. If the exercise of opportunities in a new and larger economic space would be hindered by the loss of social rights, how much more of a disincentive would be the loss of political rights? The political rights in the Maastricht Treaty are confined to local government, European elections, consular protection, the redress of grievances and the representation of regional interests. Their limitations have caused them sometimes to be regarded as trivial. But it must be remembered that all that I have referred to in this chapter has taken place in thirty to forty years, whereas the universalisation of citizenship rights as we have known them so far took centuries of struggle to become normal.

I am not necessarily saying that political rights in Europe will, therefore, come about similarly. But my intention in this section has been to argue that, at the present time, we can only say that it is impossible to speak of European citizenship if we insist that workers' rights and social rights are not part of citizenship in general. I turn now to the second part of my argument, which is that identities and interests are more complex than the Eurosceptics would have us believe.

Identities and channels for the expression of interests

In my book on European citizenship,[7] I have argued more extensively than here that an embryonic system of European citizenship coexists with national citizenship. But I do not argue that citizenship, as we have known it, is being transferred from, as it were, little states to a big new state. What I am suggesting is that something complex is emerging in which there is a new kind of citizenship which is neither national nor cosmopolitan. Instead, there is a kind of multiple citizenship, in which people are able to express their various identities in an increasingly complicated configuration of institutions. These institutions simultaneously involve the common institutions of the European Union, governments of the member states, provincial, regional and local authorities, interest groups, voluntary associations, and alliances of regions and non-governmental associations which may sometimes bypass the state.

This framework reflects the complexities of our interests and different aspects of our identities. Sometimes, it is true, our interests do coincide with our legal national identity. For example, if groups of people – perhaps employers and trade unionists normally having different interests – in northern Italy or the north of England share a desire to minimise risks to a traditional industry, then they may unite on the basis of their nationality.

Workers, employers, local authorities (which may be of a different political complexion from that of national government) may pursue their common cause upwards through their national government and expect their national government to defend them at the EU level. But sometimes interests are not like that; they can be more regionally distinctive or social and transnational.

The region of Northern Ireland speaks with a common voice, even though there is dissent over the constitutional question, when there is a sense that the British government has not understood the European policy needs of Northern Ireland, that it has failed to defend the Northern Irish interest, or has subordinated it to something defined as the national interest but which is perceived locally as the English interest. In such situations – to do with agriculture, tourism, regional redevelopment, and so on – Northern Irish politicians, however divided they are otherwise, and pressure groups co-operate extensively with each other and with counterparts elsewhere – in Ireland, Wales, France, Denmark, and all over the European Union. Though perhaps later to learn, Northern Irish citizens, like those in Ireland, Scotland and other regions on the periphery, are very good at transnational regional alliance-building in order to pursue their interests in rural development and urban renewal.

Another example which I found in my research was the co-operation between iron and steel workers in northern Italy and Germany in order to promote common European policies on health and safety. Though competitors as producers of steel, they saw themselves as having common interests in the conditions of employment – common interests best realised through the promotion of common policies at the EU level. And, in looking at the European Court of Justice, it is possible to see in all kinds of cases that come before it a vindication of my argument that we all have very many aspects to our identities and that it is not always our national identity that is the most important one. The cases in the Court of Justice involve people who have to care for dependent relatives, people who are drug addicts in search of rehabilitation, victims of crime seeking compensation, invalids, pensioners, people who want to protect the environment, people whose immediate interest lies in the fact that, as a sports trainer, architect, teacher, researcher, doctor, lawyer or nurse, they have been denied the right to practise their occupation in another member state.

These social dimensions of people's identities have been recognised not only by the Court of Justice but also by the European Commission, which has been instrumental in providing many channels for the exercise of secondary political rights. Both the Commission and the European Parliament are very open to receiving visitors. The Commission has a huge number of monitoring committees through which officials know about people who share social and economic interests across European countries. The principle of involving people with social interests is a central feature of the way in which the European Union makes policy. Earlier I referred to the 'social partners'. The policy-making principle of partnership requires governments to consult them and regional and local authorities, as well as negotiating with the Commission. Such consultation is supposed to take place during policy formulation, implementation, evaluation and review. Recently, the Commission carried out a very major exercise in public consultation with people defined by their social identities over the Green Paper on social policy, which is to set the tone for the next ten years or so.

Sometimes people think it implausible that ordinary citizens know or care about the European Union, especially those in small, peripheral regions. Research directed by the European University Institute shows that people have quite a sophisticated understanding of what constitutes a transnational issue, which kinds of issues seem to call for a common approach and which are more appropriate for national action. Smallness and peripherality have the opposite effect to that supposed by the sceptics. Perhaps precisely because of such characteristics, there is a higher degree of knowledge in Northern Ireland than in England about the identity of local MEPs and about EU policies, as was shown in the consultation process to which I have just referred.

Though I suggested in my book the emergence of a kind of multiple citizenship, it is not possible to predict what form it might take. It could turn out to be something like the kind of neo-imperial citizenship discussed by Heater. He illustrates this by reference to St Paul, who, when he was arrested in Jerusalem, stated that he was a citizen of Tarsus but also a Roman citizen and, as such, able to claim the right to a trial in Jerusalem under the Roman system of justice instead of the local one. And some people argue that it may be possible to see the European Union developing in a similarly pluralistic way. Others suggest that what may come about is simply a European citizenship which is really a continuation of national citizenship with a European dimension built in. This approach can be seen, perhaps, in some of the proposals for correcting the 'democratic deficits', that is, that common institutions, such as the Court and Parliament, should not be strengthened or democratised but that some existing common powers should be restored to domestic courts and parliaments. Thus we seem to be at a fork in a road where one route leads to something like the Roman system and the other to a more complicated national system of citizenship. What will happen will depend on how citizens exercise the rights they already have. One example is that of students whom I teach in the Law Faculty. Thirty-five of them are bringing a case against the Irish Attorney General because their qualifications from Northern Ireland are not recognised at the Irish bar. The initial defence put forward by the Irish Attorney General is that students in Northern Ireland have no case because, according to him, they are not European citizens. On the face of it, this seems wrong, though the reasoning behind it may involve the question of whether or not the status of European citizenship under the Maastricht Treaty has any material meaning yet in Irish law. Whatever the details, I am using the example to demonstrate the general point that rights stop being symbolic and begin to have tangible consequences only when citizens work to make it happen.

Conclusion: the necessity of diversity

In conclusion, I should like to return to the point I made at the beginning about my frustration with people who oversimplify questions of identity and citizenship. They often point to the United States, as though the mere mention made it self-evident that there could never be a federalist design for Europe or even a pluralist institutional framework of the neo-Roman type. What they have in mind is the contrast between what they see as the homogeneity of the United States and the diversity of European countries. Again, it seems to me, they are being ahistorical. It is, I think, a great mistake to equate the present European Union with the modern United States. If we must compare the two, it seems more sensible to consider the United States when it was in a period of similar indeterminacy about where it was going, that is, in the period leading up to the initiation of its constitution. And, if we do, we find quite a different picture.

Much of the literature on the eighteenth-century context of the American constitution points out that there was more diversity than is now remembered. The extent of individual diversity, and the focus of collective identification being the territory of each state, meant that it simply was not possible to talk then of an American national identity. Because of this, the Americans had their own equivalent of the European need to abandon the word 'federal'. In the American case it was the term 'national' that was too sensitive to be used as a synonym for 'central' powers. The solution was to refer to 'union powers'.

The argument is often put that the emergence of an American national identity was almost accidental, or, if not, was a consequence, not a condition, of the constitution. Many of the arguments for and against a constitution (in *The Federalist Papers* and the responses of *The Anti-Federalists*) were very similar to the arguments that we hear for and against a federal Europe today. Two important themes in the writings of the founding fathers that are relevant to current debates about Europe are sub-central institutions and socio-cultural diversity among individuals. Not only was it expected then that people would look more to their state and local government than to the centre (comparable to the version of 'subsidiarity' in Europe that is thought to protect the exclusive powers of national governments). There was also a belief in a kind of social subsidiary. That is, the founding fathers believed that the problem of how to reconcile the need for federal government with the protection of individual liberty could be overcome not by enforcing uniformity but precisely by allowing diversity to flourish. Freedom was best protected in a civil society that was composed of a myriad of associations responsible for a plethora of small concerns. That philosophy is rather similar to the European concept of partnership to which I referred earlier and consistent with those who see 'subsidiarity' not as a means of protecting state sovereignty but as device for increasing popular influence on public policy.

I do not want to end by seeming to imply that if we could look ahead for two hundred years the Treaty of Maastricht would turn out to have been like the American constitution – the basis from which would arise a European identity. All I have intended to do is to try and show that citizenship in the European Union is a lot more complex and a lot more exciting than is often acknowledged by those who persist in analysing it in categories which appear to explain familiar things but are inadequate for new or uncertain situations.

Notes

1 Raymond Aron, 'Is multinational citizenship possible?', *Social Research*, 41 (4), 1974, pp. 638–56.
2 Jean Leca, 'Immigration, Nationality and Citizenship in Western Europe', paper presented to a conference on Social Justice, Democratic Citizenship and Public Policy in the New Europe, ECPR/Erasmus University, Rotterdam, 1991.
3 Derek Heater, *Citizenship: The Civic Ideal in World History, Politics and Education* (1990).
4 As Leca and many others argue, the existence of borders and firm legal nationality reinforce the need that people seem to have to define 'themselves' and 'the other'. But, given the relative modernity of nation states, it would seem that drawing the distinction by this means is contingent rather than necessary or inevitable.
5 See also Bill Jordan, *The Common Good: Citizenship, Morality and Self-interest* (1989).
6 The difference is explained very clearly by Jordan, *Common Good*.
7 *Citizenship and the European Community* (1993).

Further reading

Citizenship

Citizenship was a topic virtually unspoken of when I started research for my book. Explanations for the silence of modern political science on the ethical dimension of the relationship between individuals and the state were provided by the following authors, who were virtually the only ones interested in citizenship at that time: Andrew Vincent and Raymond Plant, *Philosophy, Politics and Citizenship* (1984); H. van Gunsteren, 'Notes on a theory of citizenship, in P. Birnbaum, J. Lively, G. Parry (eds), *Democracy, Consensus and Social Contract* (1979). Social theorists, such as

Bryan Turner, Ralf Dahrendorf, Bill Jordan and J. M. Barbalet took up the topic in the second half of the 1980s, often revisiting T. H. Marshall's ideas on the social rights of citizenship. Derek Heater's book, the details of which are in note 3 above, was the first comprehensive account of the various understandings of citizenship from the classical beginnings to the twentieth century. As such it remains unmatched. Heater's book is more speculative than detailed about the possibilities of the European Union. Since the publication of his and my books others have appeared which deal with policies in European countries which are associated with social citizenship. Two others which are conceptual as well as empirical and deal with the European Union are Paul Close, *Citizenship, Europe and Change* (1995), and Maurice Roche, *Rethinking Citizenship: Welfare, Ideology and Change in Modern Society* (1992).

European integration

There is a huge literature on the numerous aspects of European integration. Those referred to here concentrate on the dynamics of change and on general institutions and policy structures. In the first category, one which is both quite recent and comprehensive in its historical sweep is Brigid Laffan, *Integration and Co-operation in Europe* (1992). One of the most stimulating 'think pieces' about visions of Europe in the past, present and future is Etienne Tassin, 'Europe: a political community?' in Chantal Mouffe (ed.), *Dimensions of Radical Democracy: Pluralism, Citizenship, Community* (1992). In the second category a book that could almost be described as the standard text is Neill Nugent, *The Government and Politics of the European Union*, third edition (1994). It now has a rival in Desmond Dinan, *Ever Closer Union: an Introduction to the European Community* (1994), which also deals with institutions and policy-making but which has a more extended historical overview than Nugent's. The possibilities for citizens to influence the European Union through voluntary associations, pressure groups and regional associations are dealt with in Sean Baine, John Benington and Jill Russell, *Changing Europe: Challenges facing the Voluntary and Community Sectors in the 1990s* (1992) and Sonia Mazey and Jeremy Richardson (eds), *Lobbying in the European Community* (1993).

Chapter 10

The hedgehog and the fox: the writing of contemporary British political history

Brian Brivati

There is much to celebrate in historical writing about the contemporary period in Britain. But there is also a slight feeling of unease that, while the rich tradition of contemporary British political history continues to produce well researched and well written studies, the real feel and experience of the past forty years have been somewhat different. Books such as Clive Ponting's study of the Labour government 1964–70[1] focus very securely on the centre, as indeed they set out to do, but give little sense of the experience of those years, their impact and ultimately their meaning. Perhaps the volume of information and the complexity are such that they preclude any one author providing such insight, or perhaps there are particular reasons for the apparent distance between academic writing on the contemporary period and the actual experience.

There have been very broadly three main influences on the way contemporary history is currently written that stem from the historical tradition, and various others, historical sociology for example, that come from other fields. For reasons of space this chapter will be confined to the way in which the three main historical schools have influenced the way the history of contemporary Britain is written at the moment: the legacy of social history; the legacy of the high politics and the legacy of the style, if not the content, of Whig history. These, in various guises, form the intellectual background to contemporary British history. One should not, however, exaggerate the extent to which there is one contemporary history – there are many. Part of the way universities have developed in the post-war period has been divison and isolation of historians in different departments – social and economic, history, geography or political science. In each department the practioners of different brands tend to huddle together for warmth and argue over problems within their own period, interest or methodological approach. But all the different variations owe debts to the three main schools described below.

The legacy of social history

Richard Brent has asserted, calling Bentley[2] and Clarke[3] in support, that British political history is in a state of confusion. The Whig interpretation was wounded but not killed off by Butterfield and Namier – it was marginalized and nearly eliminated by social history

> but [social history's] deleterious effect was to confine 'politics', as traditionally understood, to the status of peripheral activity or epiphenomenon. This second school of writing was equally linear in outlook, but instead of telling the story of the rise of political institutions [as the Whig interpretation had done], it told of the rise of classes or groups, of which political developments were simply a reflexion.[4]

It is said that this line reached an end with G. Stedman Jones's book *Languages of Class*, trying to explain political change in terms of the language and action of politics itself.[5] This idea falls prey to a great temptation: the idea that historical schools somehow supersede each other. In fact, as new areas of historical analysis develop they become additions to the existing body of work: a diversity and process of growth that should be the envy of every discipline. In the case of social history there has indeed been a linguistic turn, but this is, as Mayfield and Thorne have argued in *Social History*,[6] part of a series of new revisionist currents in the field that have altered the balance between society-based explanations and those that have reasserted the explanatory role of institutions, the state or language. Jones should be understood as one influential strand among many. These developments, Adrian Wilson maintains,[7] have left social history lacking a clear sense of direction or unifying purpose.

However, Keith Wrightson, in the same collection, sees the challenges as opportunities and possible sources of strength:

> Despite its manifest deficiencies, all of which are remediable, social history, broadly defined, remains our best hope of 'understanding ourselves in time'. In its English form it has proved an extraordinary melting pot of influences. The result is a somewhat unstable compound ... [but] ... an extraordinarily rich inheritance of empirical expertise and interpretative potential which can be put to work in new and unpredictable ways.[8]

The essays in the collection *Rethinking Social History* are more than sufficent testimony to the truth of his assertion. Those writing in this tradition on the contemporary period – Nick Tiratsoo and Steve Fielding, for example, in their new collection on the post-war period[9] – have been noticably less affected by the crisis of confidence than some of their colleagues working on other periods and the importance of the study of what we might call the 'conversation of the governed' is clearly established. It is also, as Tom

Nossiter argues in Chapter 30, very much in evidence in the work of political scientists.

The legacy of high politics

While social history was coming to prominence in the late 1960s and early 1970s a 'school of political historians flourished in an entrenched academic backwater in opposition to [what they saw as] the prevailing ethos'. Centred on Cambridge in the 1970s, one of the products of the high politics school was once condemned by Ross McKibbon as 'a rather large book' based 'almost exclusively on gossip'.[10]

The ideas of the high politics school, as viewed by critics like McKibbon, were summarised as: a rejection of the idea that politics was either about the triumph of liberalism or determined by socio-economic factors, a stress on ambition as the motive of political action and manoeuvre as the occupation of politicians and a belief that the activity of parliamentary politics was discrete, impervious to changes in the world outside Westminster and that politicians competed solely for office.

The critics' charge was that this approach amounted to a series of historical opinions about the nature of particular politicians which were based on arbitrary assumptions. Brent defends the high politics approach:

> The tenets attributed to this school of thought were not axioms but the falsifiable conclusions of its inquiries. 'High politics' as a treatment of a subject was not so much obsessed with ambition and manoeuvre, as human imperfectibility. In this regard it had a polemical intent. This was to rid the study of politics of the prevailing liberal highmindedness which was seen as its most characteristic element in the 1960s.

To do this a 'new sociology' of power was evoked; there was a visible world of institutions and an invisible world of power.

From this followed 'historically debatable conclusions' which made up the high politics approach: power rested with a few politicians and not with public opinion. 'Public opinion mattered, but it appeared on the political stage not as a directing agent, manipulating the actors, but as a piece of scenery or prop, at times useful to politicians, at others hindering their ability to move across the stage.'[12] The second insight was that Westminster was a closed world 'like Whitehall or the City' and not the top of a pyramid of power resting on the people. Third, in such a world politics was conducted as a private game 'in which the object was office and success, rather than some conception of the welfare of the nation'. Richard Brent clearly stated the partisan nature of the high politics school but maintained that it did not really matter that the school 'was as much in danger of constructing false idols and dogmatic history as its liberal rivals'. What mattered was 'their rejection of certain languages of explanation, rather than the substitution of one set of partisan historical conclusions by another. In particular this school was distinguished by its opposition to the possibility of a scientific (and it believed liberal) study of politics.[13] Further by its view that the academy had nothing to teach the politician.

> The only rational action, [wrote Cowling] to which scholars, as scholars, are committed, the only moral action to which they are commanded and the only 'social responsibility' to which their professional position compels them, is to use their energies in order to explain in its full diversity as much as they can of the nature of the world in which they live.

There is no consideration of what happens to this thinking and to what end this reflection might take place.

In conversation with the past the historian would discover some of the story of politics and it was therefore essential to search out as much of that conversation as possible: 'It was thought that only in the intimacy of politicians' diaries, personal correspondence and notes did the scholar have the faintest chance of engaging in a truthful colloquy on the art of the politician,[15] because, as Cowling wrote, 'Power is exercised and decisions are made not by vast movements of opinion but specifically by individual men.'[16] Politics in this way was not very different from any other walk of life. Moreover, there was no way the historian could ever recreate the past because the historian did not understand politics; historians could approximate the past but not give a full picture. The best way of getting close was to construct a strict chronology and a rigid narrative in which the different events and actions could be contextualised. 'The essence of high politics was thus this pessimistic scepticism, a sense of the imperfection of both the historian and the politician, and not the historical conclusions, which have made it notorious.'[17]

The basis of this attack on the science of politics was that there were no laws of politics that could be learnt and taught. Politics was a craft and not a science, therefore it could not be taught but only learnt: 'The only school of political practice is the conversation of those who govern'.[18] There is more than a hint in this approach that the personal is indeed political – a contention that most of the practitioners of high politics would deny. But if politics was a 'practical activity', if the motivation of politicians was primarily ambition and if the place to discover the secrets of political life were in private diaries and private correspondence, does that not suggest the operation of a public and a private world? That in order to understand the public utterances of political figures one must delve into their private thoughts? If so, is that not a vindication of the importance of the internal life; the importance of language and modes of expression and their relationship; the importance of psychological history – perhaps we should add Davenport-Hines's *Macmillans* to the list.[19] Paradoxically, can we not see in the high politics school much that was to be later applied by others in broadening the scope of historical studies and in challenging the primacy of the approach dominated by the 'conversation of those who govern'?

More conventionally understood echoes of this approach reasound in the work of many of the leading contemporary historians, not quite in the self-conscious way that Cowling *et al.* pursued the elites of the nineteenth century and buried for ever the Whig interpretation, but with many of the same prejudices and practices of Cowling and his coven. The reason high politics is only an echo is because large numbers of contemporary historians have been imbued with the lessons of the Nuffield school and enjoy the benefit of being able to hear the conversation of those who govern at first hand. In fact what has really happened is that some of the prejudices of the high politics school concerning sources and the location of real politics have been grafted on to the techniques of the Nuffield school – the use of oral and newspaper evidence – to produce a vibrant and productive style of contemporary political history, but one which adopts a scornful attitude to political science and theory, which tends to believe that politics is what happens at Westminster and Whitehall, and that it is in the doings of the great and the good, in the structures of the political parties, that the real exercise of political power can be understood.

Whig history

The legacy of Whig history is not one of approach but of style, as derived from Gibbon, Macaulay and Trevelyan. It is not that the idea of historical change as progress in Macaulay or Trevelyan still dominates British historiography, though one sees echoes of this sometimes, but rather that history should have the same values of expression as literature. The striking characteristic of contemporary authors, especially Ben Pimlott and Peter Hennessy, is the importance they place on the quality of writing and clarity of expression; it is no accident that they are both best-sellers. In this we can see the presence of those inert gases of past historical schools. John Clive once asked himself, 'Why read the great nineteenth-century historians?'.[20] His initial and most convincing answer was 'Because they wrote well' – and while he fished for many other reasons he kept returning to the power and skill of the narrative; the dull or complex questions made accessible by the clarity of the prose. One should not take this too far. As John Clive states in the same essay, 'The old battle against those who wished to make history a science has been fought and won. A new battle may be shaping up, against those who wish to make it into pure literature.'[21] However, there are differences. By advocating that good writers should focus on the problems of the contemporary condition I am not arguing that history is literature; rather I am talking about the ability of fine history to make the complex intelligible and to help our understanding of the difficult.

Many of the traditions of the Whig school live on in historians' ability to master and organise large amounts of often conflicting information; controlling the great stream of data into a flowing narrative is also taming a difficulty by making it intelligible. Many of the writers I have mentioned are more than capable of this when dealing with conventional areas of concern. Indeed, they often criticise political science for its lack of literary concern; that is what the injunctions against number-crunchers mean. Complex ideas need to be made intelligible, need to be explored by people who are trained in creating illumination from a difficult knot of facts and information. We must salvage the values of Macaulay even as we abandon the travesties of Cowling.

To summarise, the field of contemporary British history is dominated by what we may call three central concerns, sometimes conflicting with each other, sometimes working in conjunction. Historians analyse the conversation of those who are governed and the conversation of the governed – perhaps too much. They do so in ways influenced by Whig history in terms of style, by a marriage of high politics and Nuffield in terms of methodology, and a sub-set within the field continue the traditions of the new social history of the 1960s. Most place themselves in one particular group and ply their trade securely within that tradition. Still others, whom there is insufficient space to explore here, acknowledge the importance of the concerns of the first two groups but believe that the nature and the content of the conversation between the governed and the governing is of primary importance.

The influences of the three main schools are not even and other influences are often at work. However, in the body of work with which I am most concerned, that which dominates the undergraduate syllabus, the inert gases mentioned above are definitely at work. The emphasis on the conversation of the governed, coupled with traditions of historical works on the body politic derived from the Whig legacy with an awareness of the importance of mass society, discussed above, has produced an impressive body of substantial work. Perhaps the leading figures currently writing administrative, biographical and institutional history are Peter Hennessy (Whitehall, the Cabinet and the Prime Minister), Ben Pimlott (political biography), John Campbell (political biography), Keith Middlemas (the state and the body politic in general), Kathy Burke and Alex Cairncross (economic management and political economy), W. H. Greenleaf (the state from a conservative viewpoint), Lewis Minkin (political parties). Important contributions have been made by the authors of the ICBH Making of Contemporary Britain series, the essays in *Ruling Performance*, and many of the papers from the ICBH summer schools.[22]

Many would deny the Cowling inheritance; others, while not accepting the inheritance, would quite rightly defend the choice of subject matter and approach. But the focus is very much on the 'conversation of those who govern' and the analysis is couched in terms of the impact of that conversation on wider society and indeed on Britain's place in the world.

Learning from other fields

Whilst acknowledging the richness of the field, I think the problem of academic specialism and interdisciplinary rivalry sometimes gets in the way. The conflict between political science and contemporary history is particularly destructive in this respect. Political scientists like Patrick Dunleavy charge contemporary history with being too evidence-led, while historians like Peter Hennessy reply that political scientists are more concerned with modelling the past than with understanding it.

We need to cut through these disciplinary divides much more, particularly as contemporary history moves out of the 1940s towards the technological and geopolitical changes of the late 1950s and 1960s. But, more than that, there is the agenda of questions raised by postmodernism and postmodernity as described by Professor Bailey in Chapter 3 and some which one can add. The central question is whether or not there has been a combination of changes of sufficient significance to speak now of a new age; if there has been such a change, then the research agenda of contemporary historians should shift to acknowledge and explore the nature of that change. If the criticial postmodernists, like Joe Bailey, are correct, then we have lived through the most significant historical epoch since the Enlightenment. I will try and spell out the changes that are claimed, keeping in mind that it is the coincidence of change that is significant. I will try and avoid the 'superfluous technicalities, and obscure jargon' that have dominated so much writing in this vein. As Ankersmit sums up his defence against a blistering attack from Zagorin in *History and Theory*:

> In a metaphorical way, the story that in each fat man there is a thin man who wants to get out, is almost paradigmatically true of postmodernism. But I am convinced that underneath the postmodernist fat the thin man really is there and that we ought to listen to him since he can tell us a lot about the (historical) text that we do not yet know and that the modernist never bothered to tell us.[23]

The new times?

The last thirty years, culminating in the collapse of the Berlin Wall, have witnessed a gradual and now complete disillusionment with the central explanatory themes or 'meta-narratives' of modernism: liberalism and the idea of progress, socialism and the idea of equality and religion and the idea of redemption. On the indvidual level this disillusionment has left people lacking identities that help them through life and has alienated people from politics, with many and varied repercussions – from the development of a therapetic culture to the collapse of the long recognised divide between the public and the private.

Another root of disillusionment with the public world of politics has been the globalisation of movements of capital, which has tended to undermine the notion of sovereignty in the nation state. This free movement of capital has been made possible by advances in technology which in turn have created what some writers term a post-industrial or post-Fordist society in which the advanced Western economies, like Britain's, no longer derive their wealth predominantly from manufacturing but from information as a commodity. This breakdown of the economic base of traditional captialist urban manufacturing – when combined with the eclipse of religion and the liberalisation of sexuality – produces an assault on the traditionally understood notion of the family and the identity derived from that unit. This in turn has impacts on the individual and on the political process. Putting it very crudely, information requires many fewer people to produce than manufactured goods, therefore the affluence that modernism produced, and particularly the full employment of the mid-century period, has disappeared, perhaps for ever. Thus new generations no longer take it for granted that they will be materially better-off than their parents. In terms of politics, these new generations, lacking beliefs engendered by the now obsolete ideas of modernism, turn away from traditonal forms towards apathy or non-traditional forms of protest over new issues such as animal, sexual or environmental rights. In turn mainstream politics, a victim of the information revolution and the lack of coherent ideologocal identification, becomes increasingly concerned with image and marketing and devoted to constructing the barest minimum support necessary to control national parliaments.

All these changes are expressed in intellectual life by an acute awareness, bordering on self-consciousness, of the process of analysis of anything, be it a historical text, a painting or a television programme.

Finally this loss of personal identity, nation-state autonmony, political or religious conviction, genuine argument in politics and belief in the positive power of enquiry combines into a social, economic and political world dominated by consumption in all its diverse forms.

Without necessarily accepting that this constitutes a shift of equal importance to the Enlightenment and largely a reaction against it, although this is an interesting argument to have, these observations need to be addressed – if only to be dismissed. Is there a thin man in postmodernism that contemporary historians should be addressing?

If there is, the real challenge to the contemporary historian is to train the skill and style of communication, and the richness of approaches that have been developed, on to some of the theoretical problems that advances in other fields are putting forward. The task of the contemporary historian in meeting this challenge is to utilise the skills of the historian in analysing of what it is that makes the contemporary period different rather than continuing the cycle of anecdote and retelling of memoir; the process of piling up our knowledge of the balance and distribution of historical actors and who lunched with whom, when and where; and our reconstruction in ever more elaborate detail of the chronology of particular events, nights or meetings.

The kind of history that the ICBH has evolved and perfected has validity and should, of course, continue to be practised. But the very real virtues of clear expression and integrity in research that this school has promoted need to be focused on more diverse areas of concern. In the process we should rejoice in the richness of the history of history; the fact that each strand and change of direction has not resulted in some sort of finished and perfect scientific history which we call professional history and which we measure by the standards so dominant in our view of the physical sciences. One discourse comes along and replaces the other. In the process it attempts to invalidate the entire body of work represented in the previous discourse by proving that it was concerned with the wrong questions. Or it attempted to show that the older style of history, say the literary style of Macaulay – was invalid because it was not based on a sufficient corpus of empirical sources and that the valid history of high politics was history conducted on the model of Cowling – it was a closer approximation of the historical truth. Are these though the right kinds of question to be asking of past historical traditions and is this the right kind of way to be writing contemporary political history now? In changing direction, in reformulating the kinds of questions that we need to ask of the past, we should not set out to invalidate, for the sake of it, the historical processes of the past. If we simply dismiss what has gone before then we are guilty of the arrogance of the converted. The approach we need is subtler and more problematic than simply replacing one discourse with another – we need to apply this very diversity to the diverse times in which we live.

The fox and the hedgehog

The message this chapter is trying to convey is a call for openness in the exchange between different approaches. The key to this is the language used to communicate ideas and insights. We need to develop and learn from each other; we need to do so by expressing ourselves in accessible and not jargon-loaded terminology. But more than that we need to rid ourselves of the vice of defensiveness and insecurity that pollutes so much academic life and acknowledge that there is scope for a study of contemporary politics that looks beyond the body politic, that asks questions beyond those demanded by the creation of a chronology, and that activity seeks that which makes the contemporary period different, rather than trying to reduce the contemporary period to a modernised version of what has gone before. The world in our century is fundamentally different but also has strong continuities. If the period we study is indeed qualitively different, particularly in terms of the diversity of political and culture discourses that compete in the spaces in which there were formerly fewer and more universal discourses, so the tasks of historians demand more diversity and more layers of analysis.

In *The Hedgehog and the Fox* Isaiah Berlin interpreted the fragment from the Greek poem 'The fox knows many things, but the hedgehog knows one big thing' as:

> Taken figuratively, the words can be made to yield a sense in which they mark one of the deepest differences which divide writers and thinkers, and, it may be, human beings in general. For there exists a great chasm between those, on one side, who relate everything to a single central vision, one system, less or more coherent or articulate, in terms of which they understand, think and feel – a single, universal, organising principle in terms of which alone all that they are and say has significance – and, on the other side, those who pursue many ends, often unrelated and even contradictory, connected, if at all, only in some *de facto* way, for some psychological or physiological cause, related by no moral or aesthetic principle. These last lead lives, perform acts and entertain ideas that are centrifugal rather than centripetal; their thought is scattered or diffused, moving on many levels, seizing upon the essence of a vast variety of experiences and objects for what they are in themselves, without, consciously or unconsciously, seeking to fit them into, or exclude them from, any one unchanging, at times fanatical, unitary inner vision. The first kind of intellectual and artistic personality belongs to the hedgehogs, the second to the foxes.[24]

Is there not also a clue here as to what it is that makes the contemporary different? We live in an age in which the movements of what we understand to be the main currents of history – society, economy, technology – are moving in centrifugal ways, our ability to predict their movements increasingly undermined as they in turn behaviour in ways which take our explanations further and further away from the centres of understanding which have held for centuries. But, rather than abandoning the process of trying to understand, should we not attempt to adopt centrifugal modes of thought and analysis, should we not try and become more foxlike in our approach to contemporary history?

There are three kinds of particular and complex change that Zygmunt Bauman[25] has summed up as central to the contemporary world: the first is the new world disorder, the second is the eclipse and fracturing of community in what he calls the postmodern city and the third is the implication of a political economy based on universal deregulation. Postmodernists spend a great deal of time debating the extent to which we are in the throes of what they call 'late capitalism'; they debate the changes as though the world began when the Wall came down and the net was turned on. The world did not become complex in 1989 because a bipolarity fractured. Much of the complexity and diversity of the current phase of capitalism began in the last 1950s. Historians, armed with the legacy of the Whig tradition – the ability to communicate and explore clearly – need to lift their eyes from the stream of analysis governed by outdated deployment of terms and address in a foxlike way the background to and the experience of living in the contemporary world.

Notes

1   Clive Ponting, *Broach of Promise: Labour in Power, 1964–70* (1987).
2   M. Bentley, 'What is political history?', *Durham University Journal*, XXVI, 1983, p. 469.
3   P. F. Clarke, 'Political history in the 1980s', *Journal of Interdisciplinary History*, XII (1), 1981, pp. 45–67.
4   Richard Brent, 'Butterfield's Tories: "high politics" and the writing of modern British history', *Historical Journal*, 30 (4), 1987, p. 944.
5   Gareth Stedman-Jones, *Language of Class: Studies in English Working-Class History, 1832–1982*, second edition (1984).
6   David Mayfield and Susan Thorne, 'Social and its discontents: Gareth Stedman Hones and the politics of language', *Social History*, 17 (2), 1992, pp. 165–88.
7   Adrian Wilson (ed.), *Rethinking Social History: English Society and its Interpretation* (1993), p. 2.
8   Keith Wrightson, 'The enclosure of English social history', in Adrian Wilson (ed.), *Rethinking Social History* (1993), p. 73.
9   Steven Fielding, Peter Thompson and Nick Tiratsoo, *England Arise! The Labour Party and Popular Politics in the 1940s* (1995).
10 Brent, 'Butterfield's Tories', p. 944.
11 Brent, 'Butterfield's Tories', pp. 944–5.
12 Brent, 'Butterfield's Tories', p. 947.
13 Brent, 'Butterfield's Tories', p. 949.
14 M. J. Cowling, *The Nature and Limits of Political Science* (1963), p. 1, quoted by Brent, 'Butterfield's Tories', p. 949.
15 Brent, 'Butterfield's Tories', pp. 950–1.
16 Cowling, *The Nature and Limits*, p. 22, quoted by Brent, 'Butterfield's Tories', p. 951.
17 Brent, 'Butterfield's Tories', p. 953.
18 Brent, 'Butterfield's Tories', pp. 944–50.
19 Richard Davenport-Hines, *The Macmillans* (1992), a strange hybrid which combines some of the methodology of 'high politics' writing with a brave attempt at psychological profiling of an entire family.
20 John Clive, *Not by Fact Alone: Essays on the Writing and Reading of History* (1989), pp. 34–47.
21 Clive, *Not by Fact Alone*, p. 35.
22 Anthony Gorst, Lewis Johnman and W. S. Lucas (eds), *Post-war Britain*,

1945–64: Themes and Perspectives (1989); *id.* (eds), *Contemporary British History, 1931–61: Politics and the Limits of Policy* (1991); Brian Brivati and Harriet Jones (eds), *What Difference did the War make?* (1993); *id.* (eds), *From Reconstruction to Integration: Britain and Europe since 1945* (1993).

23 This is the end of an exchange which although rather obscure in places contains the heart of the linguistic debate between the modernists and the postmodernists. See F. R. Ankersmit, 'Historiography and postmodernism', *History and Theory*, XXVIII, 1989, pp. 137–53; Perez Zagorin, 'Historiography and postmodernism: reconsiderations', *History and Theory*, XXIX, 1990, pp. 263–74; F. R. Ankersmit, 'Reply to Professor Zagorin', *History and Theory*, XXIX, 1990, pp. 275–96. The quotations are from the latter, p. 296.

24 Isaiah Berlin, *The Hedgehog and the Fox: an Essay on Tolstoy's View of History* (1992 edition), p. 3.

25 Zygmunt Bauman, 'Violence, Modern and Postmodern', the Jon Loptagui memorial lecture, Kingston University, May 1995.

Further reading

There is a growing literature on historiography in contemporary history and on postmodernism. Chapter 3 lists a good range of book-length studies. A large number of articles debate the relevance of the postmodernist approach, evoking a number of important and well argued responses. Readers interested in following the argument further should also consult recent issues of journals such as *History and Theory*, the *Journal of Contemporary History*, *New Formations* and others in which lively debates have been going on for the past decade. The following list is very much a sample of the kinds of question that have been raised and the strong responses that have emerged. It includes the classic defences of traditional approaches to history which answer much of the postmodernist critique. It is important to understand fully the sophistication of traditional historiography in assessing the extent to which some of the wilder postmodernist ideas have long since been dealt with.

D. Attridge, *Post-structuralism and the Question of History* (1987).

J. Barzun, *Clio and the Doctors* (1974).

M. Bevir, 'Objectivity in history', *History and Theory*, 33 (3), 1994, pp. 330–44.

M. Block, *The Historian's Craft* (1954).

G. Eley and K. Nield, 'Why does social history ignore politics?' *Social History*, 5 (2), 1980, pp. 249–71.

P. Geyl, *Debates with Historians* (1962).

I. Hassan, 'The culture of postmodernism', *Theory, Culture and Society*, 2 (3), 1985, pp. 119–32.

E. Hobsbawn, 'The revival of narrative: some comments', *Past and Present*, 120, 1980, pp. 3–8.

M. Howard, *The Lessons of History* (1981).

K. Jenkins, *Rethinking History* (1991).

H. A. Lloyd, *The Relevance of History* (1972).

C. Lorenz, 'Historical knowledge and historical reality: a plea for "internal realism"', *History and Theory*, 33 (3), 1994, pp. 297–327.

D. Lowenthal, *The Past is another Country* (1985).

T. Patterson, 'Poststructuralism, postmodernism: implications for historians', *Social History*, 14 (1), 1989, pp. 83–7.

L. Stone, 'History and postmodernism', *Past and Present*, 131, 1991, pp. 217–18, and the reply from Catriona Kelly, 'History and postmodernism', *Past and Present*, 133, 1991, pp. 204–13.

R. Rorty, *Consequences of Pragmatism* (1982).

R. Rorty, Contingency, *Irony and Solidarity* (1989).

H. White, *Metahistory: the Historical Imagination in Nineteenth Century Europe* (1973).

H. White, *Tropics of Discourse* (1978).

E. Wolfe, *Europe and the People without History* (1982).

Part II
International perspectives

Chapter 11

The European scramble from Africa

Michael Twaddle

Since the Second World War over fifty African states have been freed from European colonial control.[1] This European scramble out of Africa historians have tended to analyse within four sometimes competing analytical frameworks – in the very first years, and in the most recent ones, a constitutional and (in strictly British terms) a 'Commonwealth' paradigm; secondly, a political economy framework; thirdly, the 'British world system' approach; and, fourthly, an African nationalist paradigm.

The constitutionalist approach

To start with, and most recently with the establishment of a transitional government in South Africa and post-military regimes elsewhere, constitutionalist concerns have been paramount. In the British empire during the nineteenth and earlier twentieth centuries power was devolved on the whole peacefully to former colonies. Canada, Australia, New Zealand and white South Africa were all freed before the Second World War; India, Pakistan and Sri Lanka shortly after it. This led to what Kenneth Robinson has characterised as 'a pervasive conviction' that the 'representatives of British democracy would not ... persist in a policy of repression' where continuance of British colonial rule was threatened seriously by local opposition'.[2] The tradition of granting dominion status made it easier to concede territorial independence, and with less loss of metropolitan face even after such embarrassments as the Boer War. Indeed, some scholars have even argued that subsequent African decolonisation was actually planned from within the British government shortly after World War II by Sir Andrew Cohen.[3]

Within this constitutionalist approach, the principal arguments are almost always over personalities and timing, because the basic framework of devolution of power within the Commonwealth tradition makes long-term decolonisation itself unproblematic. Flint has suggested that planning for African decolonisation within the Colonial Office effectively began even before World War II.[4] Ronald Robinson's writings on Sir Andrew Cohen suggest that planning for post-war reconstruction in Britain's African colonies, through staged devolution of power and economic development, was further enormously and unexpectedly speeded up by British overreaction to the Accra riots of 1948 in West Africa. The subsequent acceleration of the decolonisation process in East and Central Africa in 1959-61 is also a prime concern for this particular paradigm, with considerable attention focused by commentators upon ministers such as Harold Macmillan, Iain Macleod and Rab Butler.[5] Nevertheless, there has also been the contemporary historian to argue that:

> speeding-up seems ... to have been primarily dictated, as elsewhere, by events to which Macleod and Butler and local colonial governments had to react, the principal event being the transfer of a radical nationalist sentiment from West to East and Central Africa. There is no strong evidence for schemes of reform in the sense of a prescient, preemptive policy in London.[6]

'Radical nationalist sentiment' first became apparent in British-ruled Africa in the activities of Kwame Nkrumah and his allies. Although the Accra riots of 1948 were not especially noteworthy in themselves, the onset of the Cold War and Nkrumah's appeals for outside help combined to force British constitutional concessions. Why, in retrospect, did the Accra riots prove so significant for the subsequent independence of Ghana? Was it principally British miscalculation locally,[7] or overreaction in Whitehall[8] that caused them to get out of hand, or was it the relentless operation of 'radical nationalist sentiment' in Africa itself? And, if it was at least in part the latter, precisely wherein lay the springs of anti-colonial action? In addressing these matters Richard Rathbone has examined the Ghanaian nationalist movement in some detail.[9]

He begins by noting that many scholars have been unhappy about assuming the imperative of 'political liberation' to explain why so many Ghanaians became engaged in nationalist politics after 1945. But why did those groups who became active 'do so while others, no less oppressed, remain less involved'? Rathbone rejects as too simplistic arguments that an emergent petty bourgeoisie constituted the backbone of anti-colonial nationalism because it alone 'bore the brunt of colonial restriction, shared few of the limited privileges brought by colonialism and, at the same time through its limited literacy and location in 'modern' occupational strata, was most likely to be receptive to the sophisticated ideological and organizational creations of nationalist leaders'. The reality was that there was not just one dynamic anti-colonial movement in Ghana but two. Far from dismissing the National Liberation Movement as simply backward-looking and tribalistic, Rathbone maintains that it was composed of an 'entirely new generation of [business] aspirants, no different in many respects from their counterparts in the Convention People's Party five or six years previously', and a new generation of businessmen moreover which 'found such support for the NLM their own means of entering the gainful sectors of the economy'.[10]

Rathbone's work here may be seen as a bridge between a predominantly constitutionalist paradigm of decolonisation and the political economy approach, particularly in his stress upon 'the "referee function" of the British government and public opinion' regarding political competition in Ghana during the 1950s.

The political economy paradigm

At the heart of most demands for independence from European colonial rule in Africa lay the question: independence for whom? During actual struggles for independence this was a question very rarely posed formally because at the time the answer seemed so patently obvious, and nowhere more so than in colonial Kenya. There, in the early decades of this century, white settlers on the temperate western highlands had established farms whose affluence contrasted starkly with black squalor. After independence many of these farms were taken over by local people, bulldozers were sent into the shanty towns, and Kenya as a whole enjoyed a rate of economic development unmatched by its immediate neighbours in East Africa until the onset of structural adjustment programmes in the 1980s. But independence from Britain in the 1960s did not benefit all Kenyans equally. Colin Leys in particular has been concerned to attack earlier analyses of African independence movements which concentrated upon issues of national integration as perceived by ruling elites rather than upon the difficulties experienced by oppressed and exploited groups. In particular, earlier analyses were taken to task for exhibiting 'extraordinary resistance to the idea that there are classes and class struggles in Africa, let alone that they may be of central importance'.[11] Leys's arguments concentrated upon the successive stages by which Kenya was incorporated into the expanding world capitalist economy during the period of formal empire, and upon how certain social strata ('*comprador* elements') were brought into existence whose presence would ultimately make direct rule by the metropolitan power in his view unnecessary. Leys also stressed the peripheral character of capitalism in Kenya. Economic cleavages existed within both the capitalist and the peasant sectors of the economy, but they did not solidify into cohesive classes; instead government survived by force and by playing populist tricks with ethnic rhetoric.

Much of this argument, informed as it was by earlier perspectives on underdevelopment theory imported from Latin America, has been repudiated subsequently by its author in the light of more recent research into the evolution of a national petty bourgeoisie in colonial Kenya.[12] But stress upon the farsightedness of metropolitan decision-makers, which characterised much of the earlier political economy literature, seems both excessive and ahistorical nowadays, the transfer of power at the time being actually far more muddled and uncertain.[13] Nowhere does the picture appear more muddled and uncertain than in late colonial Kenya. Current research into the Mau Mau emergency of the 1950s presents a complex picture of disparate social movements, sometimes overlapping, at other times going off in completely different directions: a squatters' revolt, resistance against enforced agricultural improvement schemes, a cultural revival, an internal civil war, and an anti-colonial movement echoing earlier primary resistance against the initial imposition of British colonial rule.[14]

A. G. Hopkins's *An Economic History of West Africa* must also be considered within the political economy paradigm for reasons other than its title. For its later chapters courageously offer 'an economic interpretation of the rise of African nationalism that also runs counter to some well known, if simplistic, beliefs'.[15] Hopkins's principal targets here were evidently both the older constitutionalist and the newer African nationalist paradigms of decolonisation:

> Opposition to colonialism was based on an imperfect alliance of three major interest groups of farmers, traders and wage-earners, all of whom shared a degree of commitment to the exchange economy which distinguished them from the bulk of the population ... By taking a disaggregated view of what is often regarded simply as African opposition to colonialism, it becomes possible to relate the evolution of nationalism to the performance of the open economy. ... Nationalism, in its modern forms, had its origins in the period 1930-1945, when a serious downturn in real and anticipated living standards occurred, following a phase of sustained, if modest, advance.[16]

The argument is nicely put but remains as disdainful of politics as any account of decolonisation from an earlier political economy point of view. It also neatly sidesteps the crucial question of why opposition to colonialism by such disparate interests took the form of 'radical *nationalist* sentiment' (my italics).

The British world system paradigm

If Hopkins's 'economic interpretation' was concerned among other things to counter both perceived constitutionalist and nationalist simplicities, the originally Cambridge-based architects of the 'British world system' paradigm were initially more irritated by Commonwealth ideology at Oxford. Ronald Robinson furthermore tells us that he found his period of employment in the Colonial Office immediately after World War II suggestive as regards 'witnessing the new terms of African collaboration in the transition from "indirect rule" to "Democratisation" while local crises detonated in colony after colony'.[17] It was perhaps only to be expected that, after his work with Gallagher on the 'imperialism of free trade', and *Africa and the Victorians* (1961) had been published, they should move on from studying the onset of colonialism in Africa to interpreting its demise.

Ronald Robinson published a 'sketch for a theory of imperialism', embracing decolonisation as well as colonisation, in which he argued that 'at every stage from external imperialism to decolonisation, the working of imperialism was determined by the indigenous collaborative systems connecting its European and Afro-Asian components'.[18] He also suggested that

> when the colonial rulers had run out of indigenous collaborators, they either chose to leave or were compelled to go. Their nationalist opponents in the modern elite sooner or later succeeded in detaching the indigenous political elements from the colonial regime until they eventually formed a united front of non-collaboration against it. Hence the inversion of collaboration into non-cooperation largely determined the timing of decolonisation.[19]

This negative model of anti-colonial nationalism has proved popular with a number of historians of decolonisation in Africa. But it fell to Gallagher and his students to work out the theory of anti-colonial nationalism more fully as 'a ramshackle coalition' mirroring the structures and defects of British colonialism and eventually overcoming it in the context of Indian history,[20] whence it has returned to more recent African historical writing as 'the Indian model'.

If the resulting image of British colonialism in Africa has not been heroic, the picture of anti-colonial nationalism presented by the Cambridge school was hardly flattering either. But among contemporary historians of Africa it has proved extremely popular. For example, of four studies of decolonisation in a *Festschrift* for Frederick Madden,[21] three contemporary historians followed the ramshackle line and only Kenneth Robinson retained a more respectful attitude towards the corrosive effect of African nationalism in undermining both British and French rule as well as a stress upon 'habits of mind' more characteristic of the older constitutionalist tradition.

The popularity of the ramshackle view of African nationalism was not weakened by the shortage of funds in Mrs Thatcher's Britain for historical research in Africa itself, nor was it undermined by the seemingly ever-increasing amounts of archival information becoming available about British policy in the terminal colonial period. Viewed from almost any vantage point within this growing mountain of metropolitan records, British policy on decolonisation does appear to be more easily and persuasively understood in terms of either justificatory rhetoric regarding the importance of individual British Cabinet Ministers in decision-making, or as a part of the desperate quest by the British power elite to retain whatever power possible through NATO, the nuclear deterrent and informal influence now that formal empire again seemed on the way out. The case for serious reappraisal of the role of anti-colonial nationalism in undermining

European empires in Africa therefore went increasingly by default among contemporary historians of Africa, especially when colleagues in economic history of both Marxist and non-Marxist persuasions wrote disparagingly about it. When historians of Africa noted the importance of anti-colonial nationalism they appeared more concerned with the timing of its significance in accelerating the European scramble out of Africa after the Second World War than with its actual ingredients. This point was underlined by W. Roger Louis in introducing the accounts of British- and French-ruled Africa by Anthony Low and Keith Panter-Brick included in a symposium which he edited with Prosser Gifford in 1988 on *Decolonisation and African Independence*.[22] However, in the present economic circumstances of Africa it seems unlikely that the local intricacies of anti-colonial nationalism in the terminal colonial period will be studied intensively by African historians themselves. Overall disparagement of African anti-colonial movements is therefore likely to remain substantially unchalleneged from within Africa, except by the romantic nationalist interpretations of history so favoured by African governments and taught so frequently as official orthodoxies in African schools and universities.

Gallagher's posthumously published Ford lectures possibly demonstrated disdain for African nationalism at its deepest within the British world system paradigm:

> In West Africa, just as in India before it, mass parties were the sum of a series of local political situations converted by government machinery into the apparent expression of nationalist demands. In a word, government needed economic growth in West Africa. It suspected that this would have to be paid for by political concessions. And so it turned out ... But where in all this are the freedom fighters? Not in West Africa, that is clear, for there was nothing to fight over except a timetable. But the places to look for them are in East and Central Africa. And there they were the white settlers.[23]

Nonetheless, the disdain here for African anti-colonial nationalism may be more apparent than real, for just a few pages later Gallagher writes, 'In practice, political developments in the colonies tended to take the game out of the croupier's hands. These colonial political developments are the one constant factor in decolonisation.'[24]

For what was anti-colonial nationalism within an African colony if it was not principally a matter of 'colonial political developments' from both African and colonial points of view? Here, surely, is the black box left behind by Gallagher. What we need is a revised historiographical paradigm within which the complexities of African nationalism may be studied as closely as the struggles to retain their respective 'world systems' by the British, the French, the Portuguese and white South Africans up to 1994 – and, most important of all, the dialectical relations that developed between the constituent elements of the various 'African' nationalist movements and their respective 'white' rulers.

A new African nationalist paradigm?

Certainly, the romantic paradigm of nationalist activity as developed by much Africanist historiography in the 1960s can no longer be accepted without major qualification. It is not so much, as A. G. Hopkins has remarked, that 'African nationalism was not simply a spontaneous, mass movement of the downtrodden, directed against sun-helmeted, exploiting masters and led by men whose readiness for self-sacrifice was matched only by their determination to survive long enough to improve the living standards of their fellow countrymen'.[25] The irony of the second part of this comment is understandable, but it is misleading. West Africa was not the first part of the world where political crusaders very quickly became mere spoilsmen upon actually attaining power. More seriously, the first part of the comment may also be wrong, in the sense that there does seem to have been 'a spontaneous, mass movement of the downtrodden' taking place in association with the massive urbanisation that occurred in several parts of Africa as a result of World War II and its aftermath. This urbanisation seems to have introduced new elements of uncertainty into the African political game, in the shape of mass involvement in politics from which some African nationalist leaders clearly benefited. Proponents of the political economy approach also err when they treat African anti-colonialism as reducible to economic interest without reference to political context.

And that, let it be admitted, was not something the pioneers of African nationalist historiography wholly ignored. At the start of his seminal study *Nationalism in Colonial Africa*, for example, Thomas Hodgkin included a separate section on the 'Policies of the [European] Powers' because he considered them to have been important influences upon African nationalism.[26] Shepperson also remarked that:

> All nationalism is the product of a reaction against external forces. But in Africa, whose partition and introduction to the apparatus of the modern state came at a time when Europe was throwing up chaotically those processes for which the terms 'nationalism', 'imperialism', 'racialism' and 'socialism' are inadequate but necessary labels, external labels have a peculiar force.[27]

Subsequently, historical study of African nationalism, particularly in East and Central Africa, concentrated upon the African side of the story, stressing the origins of nationalism and proto-nationalism, debating the comparative importance of elite leadership and mass support, and identifying connections between primary resistance movements in the early colonial period and later political parties.[28]. In retrospect, it is perhaps unsurprising that subsequent scholars, disillusioned on discovering that many nationalist leaders had not behaved as earlier rhetoric promised they would, 'unmasked' anti-colonial nationalism as in fact economic interest in political disguise. But this reductionist (and anachronistic) mistake would not have been made so frequently if the fascination with the genealogy of African nationalism on the part of a Hodgkin or a Shepperson had been developed with a more effectively counterbalancing interest in the dialectical political relationships which developed over time between nationalist movements and differing European colonial powers. This is particularly the case for the period immediately following the Second World War. Then, as Anthony Low and John Lonsdale pointed out twenty years ago, a 'second colonial occupation' occurred in East and Central Africa,[29] but its implications for, and interconnections with, many individual nationalist movements in the region remain to be investigated. With the continuing difficulties of research in Africa, and the even greater accessibility of archival evidence in the Public Record Office by publication of key 'British Documents on the End of Empire',[30] there is likely to be an even greater bias of evidence in favour of paradigms stressing constitutional conferences in the Commonwealth tradition and attempts to retain world influence through strategy and sway. Anti-colonial nationalism, on the other hand, is likely to continue to go by default as a serious contributor to the processes of decolonisation (other than as its beneficiary or victim, depending on your point of view) unless a much more conscious effort to allow for it is made by contemporary historians.

How is this to be done? Lionel Cliffe suggests that Zimbabwe, 'with three-quarters [of the population] having a common language and culture and a "minority" making up the rest, might best be analysed in terms of "nationalities" rather than "tribes" ',[31] and that much more research is needed into the critical moments during the preceding thirty or forty years – these 'critical moments' sound very comparable to the 'events' of Austin.[32] Other kinds of study are suggested by two other studies of anti-colonial nationalism. One is by Benedict Anderson and is a seminal study of how, first in Europe and the Americas, and more recently in Asia and Africa,

> under the impact of economic change, 'discoveries' (social and scientific) and the development of increasingly rapid communications ... a harsh wedge [was driven] between cosmology and history. No surprise then that the search was on, so to speak, for a new way of linking fraternity, power and time meaningfully together. Nothing perhaps more precipitated this search, nor made it possible for rapidly growing numbers of people to think about themselves, and to relate themselves to others, in profoundly new ways.[33]

This search, which ultimately led to the nation being 'imagined' in new ways in colonial Africa as well as in other parts of the world, of course lies at the heart of many studies of the transition from oral to literary and post-literary cultures undertaken by many contemporary students of Africa. But

116

before nationalism, however 'imagined' in newly literate circles, could become politically important, another transition had to take place. Here the work of John Breuilly seems helpful,[34] stressing 'the way in which the political and institutional structures of the state against which individual nationalisms react conditions their form and ultimate possibility of success'.[35] Nationalism becomes politically important when it attempts to seize political power by forming a social movement. Ideology is therefore important, but in a secondary sense, as a means by which a nationalist leader seeks to obtain mass support, not as a guide to what it is actually doing: Why nationalism should have been more effective than other ideologies in obtaining such support is explained by its ability to transform sentiments or practices habitually accepted as belonging to the 'private sphere' (family, community, solidarity, etc.) into public values, as symbols and ceremonies particularly fitted to the situation and social groups for which they are intended. There is a clear overlap here with Benedict Anderson's suggestive analysis of the impact of 'print capitalism' upon differing oral cultures outside Europe. There is also an enormous amount of research still to be done in Africa into those 'subaltern cultures' upon which Indian historians have written so illuminatingly, as Frederick Cooper remarks,[36] as well as upon newly literate elite ones.

Additionally, many structural adjustment policies imposed upon Africa in the economic sphere during the last ten to fifteen years have already had important implications both for nationalist movements and for African states. Political conditionalities, frequently assumed by international donors to be likely to weaken nationalist particularisms and to strengthen central state authorities, sometimes have the opposite effect to that expected by external agencies. In Uganda, for example, popular consultations for a new constitution in 1989–93 in a part of the country where an ancient kingdom had existed for several centuries but had been dismantled in 1967 elicited the widespread view in both opinion polls and written memoranda that the single most important demand was for the kingdom to be restored. And restored it was in 1993.[37] 1993 was also the year in which UNESCO finally published volume eight of its *General History of Africa*.[38] In it, a halftone photograph of the new monarch's late father appears above the now clearly erroneous description: 'King Mutesa II, the last Kabaka of Buganda'. Contemporary historians need to be as careful not to write off Africa's cultural leaders in the era of structural adjustment as in the terminal years of European colonialism.

Notes

1 Ethiopia and Liberia have also experienced 'revolutions' in their political arrangements, in 1974 and 1984 respectively, not to mention more recent economic upheavals caused in all African countries by externally imposed

structural adjustment programmes.

2 Kenneth Robinson, *The Dilemmas of Trusteeship* (1995), p. 129.

3 Ronald Robinson, 'Andrew Cohen and the transfer of power in tropical Africa, 1940–57', in W. H. Morris-Jones and G. Fischer (eds), *Decolonisation and Africa: the British and French Experience* (1980); R. D. Pearce, *The Turning Point in Africa* (1982).

4 John Flint, 'Planned decolonisation and its failure in Africa', *African Affairs*, 82, pp. 389–411.

5 See David Goldsworth, 'Conservatives and decolonisation', *African Affairs*, 69, pp. 278–81; *Colonial Issues in British Politics, 1945–61* (1971); *id.* (ed.), *The Conservative Government and the End of Empire, 1951–57* (1994); Prosser Gifford and William R. Louis (eds), *The Transfer of Power in Africa: Decolonization, 1940–60* (1982); *id.*, *Decolonisation and African Independence* (1988).

6 Dennis Austin, 'The transfer of power: why and how', in W. H. Morris-Jones and G. Fischer (eds), *Decolonisation and After* (1980), p. 25.

7 J. D. Hargreaves, 'Toward the transfer of power in British West Africa', in P. Gifford and W. R. Louis (eds), *The Transfer of Power* (1982), pp. 135–6.

8 Ronald Robinson, 'Andrew Cohen', pp. 65–6.

9 Richard Rathbone, 'Businessmen in politics: party struggles in Ghana, 1949–57', *Journal of Development Studies*, 9, pp. 391–401; 'Parties' socio-economic bases and regional differentiation in the rate of change in Ghana', in P. Lyon and J. Manor (eds), *Transfer and Transformation* (1983); Richard Rathbone (ed.), *Ghana* (1992).

10 Rathbone, 'Businessmen in politics', but see also Jean Marie Allman, *The Quills of the Porcupine: Asante Nationalism in an Emergent Ghana* (1993), for further data on the National Liberation Movement.

11 Colin Leys, *Underdevelopment in Kenya* (1975).

12 Michael Cohen, 'Differentiation in a Kenya Location', paper presented to the East Africa University Social Science Council conference, Nairobi, 1972; 'Capital and Household Production: the Case of Wattle in Kenya's Central Province, 1903–64', Cambridge University Ph.D. thesis, 1979; 'The British state and agrarian accumulation in Kenya', in Martin Fransman (ed.), *Industry and Accumulation in Africa* (1982); Gavin Kitching, *Class and Economic Change in Kenya* (1980); T. Swainson, *The Development of Corporate Capitalism in Kenya, 1918–77* (1980), noted in Colin Leys, 'Accumulation, class formation and dependence, Kenya', in Martin Fransman (ed.), *Industry and Accumulation in Kenya* (1982).

13 Richard Jeffries, 'Beyond the crisis in African studies', *West Africa*, 16 May 1983, pp. 1178–80, for a critique of earlier political economy literature dealing with Africa.

14 See Rob Buijtenhuis, *Essays on Mau Mau* (1982), for a useful summary of approaches to Mau Mau, and Bruce Berman and John Lonsdale, *Unhappy Valley* (1992), for brilliant critiques of recent Kenyan history.

15 A. G. Hopkins, *An Economic History of West Africa* (1973), p. 289.

16 Hopkins, *An Economic History*, p. 291.

17 Ronald Robinson and Anil Seal, 'Professor John Gallagher, 1919–80', *Journal of Imperial and Commonwealth History*, 9, 1981, p. 122.

18 Ronald Robinson, 'Non-European foundations of European imperialism: sketch for a theory of collaboration', in Roger Owen and Bob Sutcliffe (eds), *Studies in*

the Theory of Imperialism (1972); reprinted in William R. Louis (ed.), *Imperialism: the Robinson and Gallagher Controversy* (1976), p. 147.

19 Ronald Robinson, 'Non-European foundations', p. 147.

20 Robinson and Seal, 'Professor John Gallagher', pp. 123–4.

21 Robert Holland and Gowher Rizvi (eds), *Perspectives on Imperialism and Decolonisation* (1984).

22 Prosser Gifford and W. Roger Louis (eds), *Decolonisation and African Independence*, (1988). Incidentally, the bibliographical essays by Tony Kirk-Greene and David Gardinier in this work are invaluable.

23 John Gallagher, *The Decline, Revival and Fall of the British Empire* (1982), p. 148.

24 Gallagher, *The Decline*, p. 153.

25 Hopkins, *An Economic History*, p. 291.

26 Thomas Hodgkin, *Nationalism in Colonial Africa* (1956).

27 George Shepperson, 'External factors in the development of African nationalism, with particular reference to British Central Africa', in T. O. Ranger (ed.), *Historians in Tropical Africa* (1961), p. 317.

28 T. O. Ranger, 'Connections between "primary resistance" movements and modern mass nationalism in East and Central Africa', *Journal of African History*, 9, 1968, pp. 437–53, 631–41; 'African reactions to the imposition of colonial rule in East and Central Africa', in L. H. Gann and P. Duignan (eds), *Colonialism in Africa*, I (1969).

29 Anthony Low and John Lonsdale, 'Introduction; towards the new order, 1945–62', in D. A. Low and Alison Smith (eds), *History of East Africa*, III (1976).

30 Ronald Hyam (ed.), *The Labour Government and the End of Empire, 1945–51* (1992); Rathbone, *Ghana*; Goldsworthy, *The Conservative Government*, etc.

31 Lionel Cliffe, 'Zimbabwe: Political Economy and the Contemporary Scene in Southern Africa', proceedings of a seminar, Centre of African Studies, Edinburgh, 30 May–1 June 1983, pp. 125–7.

32 Dennis Austin, *Politics in Ghana, 1946–60* (1964); 'The transfer of power'.

33 Benedict Anderson, *Imagined Communities: Reflections on the Origin and Spread of Nationalism* (1983, enlarged 1991), p. 40.

34 John Breuilly, *Nationalism and the State* (1982).

35 S. J. Woolf, 'Appealing to the masses', *Times Literary Supplement*, 19 November 1982, p. 1281.

36 Frederick Cooper, 'Conflict and connection: rethinking colonial African history', *American Historical Review*, 99, 1994, p. 1519.

37 H. B. Hansen and M. Twaddle, *From Chaos to Order: the Politics of Constitution Making in Uganda* (1994).

38 Ali Mazrui (ed.), UNESCO *General History of Africa*, VIII (1993), p. 437.

Further reading

Jean-François Bayart, *The State in Africa: the Politics of the Belly* (1993), translation of *L'Etat en Afrique: la politique du ventre* (1989).

Frederick Cooper, 'Conflict and connection: rethinking colonial African history',

American Historical Review, 99, 1994, pp. 1516–45.

John Darwin, 'British decolonisation since 1945: pattern or puzzle?' *Journal of Imperial and Commonwealth History*, 12, 1984, pp. 187–209.

Bernt Holger Hansen and Michael Twaddle (eds), *Changing Uganda: the Dilemmas of Structural Adjustment and Revolutionary Change* (1991).

J. D. Hargreaves, *Decolonisation in Africa* (1988).

J. D. Hargreaves, 'Habits of mind and forces of history: France, Britain and the decolonisation of Africa', in Michael Twaddle (ed.), *Imperialism and the State in the Third World* (1992).

John Kent, 'The Ewe question, 1945–55': French and British reactions to "nationalism" in West Africa', in Michael Twaddle (ed.), *Imperialism in the Third World* (1992).

Jaques Marseille, *Empire colonial et capitalisme français: histoire d'une divorce* (1984).

Kenneth Robinson, 'Colonialism French style, 1945–55: a backward glance', *Journal of Imperial and Commonwealth History*, 12, 1984, pp. 24–41.

Michael Twaddle, 'Decolonization in Africa: a new British historiographical debate', in B. Jewsiewicki and D. Newbury (eds), *African Historiographies: what History for which Africa?* (1986).

Michael Twaddle (ed.), *Imperialism and the State in the Third World* (1992).

Acknowledgements

An earlier and longer version of this chapter appeared in B. Jewsiewicki and D. Newbury (eds), *African Historiographies: what History for which Africa?* (1986). I am grateful to colleagues and students at Copenhagen, London and Makerere Universities for further revisions.

Chapter 12

Continuities in state policy: a case study of Ethiopia

Karen Wells

Introduction: the state and development in Africa

Perceptions of the developmental role of the African state have changed dramatically within Africa and internationally since independence from colonial rule. In the first two decades after independence it was generally accepted that the state should intervene directly in the production process, chiefly through import substitution strategies (ISI) and in the structuring of society. This model of the state as the principal agent for development was informed by three aspects of African history: the overdeveloped nature of the colonial state; the struggle for national liberation; the role of African states in the international economy.

The expanding state

Colonial state formation was a process of creating or refining the state as a repressive, undemocratic, authoritarian instrument of resource extraction. At independence the successor states to colonial rule inherited a state apparatus which was overdeveloped in relation to society.[1] The colonial era did nothing to create, and much to retard, the conditions for the development of a local bourgeoisie. In the absence of a vigorous bourgeoisie or proletariat both capitalist and socialist regimes in Africa looked to the state as the agent of economic development. This internal dominance of the state has been reinforced by the intersection of African states in the international economy. The dependence of African states on external finance necessarily implies negotiations on the conditions for the approval of loans and grants. Any alliance in economic development is necessarily dominated by this alliance between international capital and the domestic state. The local bourgeoisie may enter as a crucial third player in the alliance[2] or may be so unviable as an independent class that it merges inseparably with the state.[3]

Withdrawing the state: problems and contradictions

State-led development strategies are no longer fashionable.[4] In Africa the capitulation of states to the development strategies of the IMF and the World Bank reflected the combined impact of poor economic performance and loss of bargaining power in the international arena with the ending of the Cold War. It is now argued that the market is capable of enabling the rational and fair (or at least rational and fair relative to state monopolies) allocation of resources, will strengthen civil society, decentralise economic decision-making and guarantee civil liberties.

There are a number of contradictions inherent in this new strategy for development. Since the state is the only agent in society capable of enacting this strategy, it is to be charged with the responsibility for implementing reforms designed to restrict its own capacity. Secondly, given the dependence of developing states on international aid finance, the state will necessarily remain the most significant actor in the domestic economy. Furthermore, certain tasks remain beyond the capacity of the market. Principally, protecting the state's territory against external force, maintaining internal order, public works, the provision of public goods, the protection of infant industries, the control of private monopoly power, and measures to offset the tendency to concentration and to protect employment and welfare.[5] The principal contradiction, however, is that a class has not emerged in Africa which can relieve the state of its developmental role.

The state and development in Ethiopia

Ethiopia successfully resisted the imposition of colonial rule. For this reason it is often excluded from discussions of the state in sub-Saharan Africa. The 1974 revolution in Ethiopia was widely perceived to be qualitatively different from other revolutions on the continent, which had been essentially concerned with securing national independence. The Ethiopian revolution was perceived to be more comparable with France in 1789 or Russia in 1917 than with to the wave of post-1945 national liberation revolutions.[6]

These differences in the trajectory of Ethiopian history, as compared with the broad similarities in the history of the rest of sub-Saharan Africa from the colonial period (with the exception of Liberia), should not blind us to the essential similarities. Ethiopia can be characterised as a neo-colonial social formation, highly vulnerable to changes in the international system. In common with other peripheral states, Ethiopia is characterised by low levels of GDP, a highly undifferentiated economy with low levels of market integration, low levels of industrialisation, urbanisation, education and literacy and high levels of dependence on agricultural production and primary goods export markets. Domestic class formation is correspondingly weak.

Foundation of the Ethiopian nation-state

Although Ethiopia as a territory and polity can be traced back some 2,000 years, the current borders were fixed in a series of treaties in the early twentieth century by the emperor Menelik II with Britain, France and Italy. Haile Selassie was crowned in 1928, having been Prince Regent since 1916. Ethiopia joined the League of Nations in 1923. A written constitution was introduced, and Parliament convened in 1931. Italy invaded Ethiopia in 1935 and occupied it until liberation in 1941. Haile Selassie's rule was fatally weakened by his attempts to enhance central state power without forcefully confronting the regional nobility and by his failure to resolve the problems underlying the agricultural crisis. In 1974 the military seized power and enacted a series of radical reforms including the nationalisation of banks and industry and sweeping land reform. In 1977 the military administration, known as the Derg, from the Amharic for 'committee', aligned Ethiopia with the Soviet Union. The military held power until 1991, when the forces of the Tigrean People's Liberation Front (TPLF), which had been fighting for the autonomy of Tigre region, in the north-east, marched into Addis Ababa and took over the government. The coalition government, the Ethiopian People's Revolutionary Democratic Front (EPRDF), in which the TPLF is the major force, has adopted a programme of political and economic reform which is broadly congruent with the World Bank's strategy. Ethiopia has now joined the other states on the continent whose development policy agenda is being managed, if not set, by external agencies.

Continuities in Ethiopian state strategies for development

The hypothesis which this chapter is concerned with is that state dominance in development is not a voluntary enterprise but follows from structural conditions. The continuities in the effect, if not always the letter, of policy implementation across the three models of government which Ethiopia has seen – modernising autocracy, revolutionary and social democratic – serve to underline the material constraints on policy change.

This section examines the record of the Ethiopian state in four key areas: land reform, the nationalities question, economic policy and foreign policy. In order to highlight the continuities in state policy the discussion is ordered thematically rather than sequentially. In this way I hope to underline the structural conditions which prevent political actors from radically altering the political and economic context in which they find themselves.

Agricultural policy

Prior to the 1974 revolution there was general agreement that the under-productivity of the rural economy demanded land reform. The rural economy was dominated by subsistence farming. Farmers worked small-holdings which did not allow economies of scale or the use of technical inputs. Land tenure before the 1975 land reform was staggeringly complex. Although its diversity makes generalisation difficult, it is useful to note that, regardless of which type of tenure farmers were operating under, some form of sharecropping or tribute would be used by landowners, the local nobility or the Church to divest farmers of a substantial part of their surplus. This acted as a further brake on agricultural development, since any increase in productivity implied a comparable increase in tribute.

Under Haile Selassie's rule few state resources were allocated to agricultural development, despite the dominant role which agriculture played in the economy. In the third five-year plan (1968–73), for example, peasant agriculture was allocated 1 per cent of total investment. Government attempts at initiating land reform began with the 1961 committee on land reform and ended with a 1973 Ministry of Land Reform and Agriculture proposal for the expropriation and redistribution of holdings. This proposal, like those that had preceded it, was blocked by Parliament and not supported by Haile Selassie. Tax reform fared little better. These reforms failed because they sought to break the power of the landed aristocracy, attacking them direct through proposals for the expropriation of large holdings and indirectly by attacking their financial base through tax reform.

Foreign investment

Haile Selassie's government was more successful in attracting foreign investors to the Awash valley development. The Awash valley, which was nominally government land, was chosen as the site for developing large-scale commercial agriculture in partnership with foreign investors, who were given exemption from paying tax and import duties for the first five years of operation. Nearly 40 per cent of the area was controlled and managed by two firms, HVA (Handels Vereniging Amsterdam) Ethiopia and the Tendaho Plantations Share Company. Profits in the Awash valley region were impressive in 1971, reporting net commercial profits of Eth$2 million, 20 per cent of the value of production. By 1973 production per hectare had more than doubled, as had the price of cotton per kilogram. In 1973 the total value of output had increased from Eth$9 million to Eth$29 million and pre-tax profits were 67 per cent of the value of production.[7]

The Awash valley development transformed class relations in the area.[8] Land prices rose in response to the increased demand. Pastoralists and peasant farmers were increasingly drawn into capitalist relations of production and the coercive relationship between landlord and peasant was increasingly stripped of any veneer of reciprocity. These developments contributed to the grievances which eventually culminated in the 'creeping *coup*' of 1974 and the eventual seizure of state power by the Derg.

The agricultural policies of the Derg

The critical issue facing the new regime in 1974 was therefore how to increase agricultural productivity. The March 1975 land reform proclamation was intended to resolve the problem by breaking the power of the landlord class. The surpluses derived from peasant production would remain under the control of the peasant producer. The proclamation abolished private ownership of rural land and limited holdings to 10 ha per family. It allowed for periodic redistribution of land to prevent the concentration of holdings. The use of hired labour was prohibited. Commercial farms were taken over by the state.

Land reform as an instrument for increasing agricultural productivity was far from effective. In practice it entrenched peasants in their existing mode of production.[9] Their surplus was simply redirected. Where before it had been taken by landlords and the rural nobility, through sharecropping or tribute, it was now taken by the state for the payment of direct and indirect taxes. However, as an instrument for altering the structure of class relations by effectively destroying the landlord class, and as an instrument through which the new regime bought the goodwill of the peasantry, at least in the south, it was very effective.

The Derg's subsequent strategy on the agricultural question would suggest that it was aware of the limitations of land reform as an instrument for developing the rural economy. None of the strategies adopted was particularly successful. The structural food deficit (a shortfall even in average harvest years) is some 400,000 tons of grain, in addition to which productivity must be increased by some 320,000 tons per year, simply to keep up with population growth.[11]

Post-military developments

The new government has left the 1975 land reform basically intact: ownership of land continues to reside with the state. In December 1993 a law on the attribution of urban land leaseholds was promulgated and has met with opposition from urban households and international donor agencies.[12] Rural land policy has generated much less debate in the capital's press, despite the fact that ninety per cent of Ethiopians are smallholder farmers and only 1 per cent work in manufacturing. Rural land leasing will probably be implemented, although how much the leases will cost, and how payments will be structured, is still unclear. Farmers have complained that farmland is being distributed on the basis of political loyalty and that the fourteen ethno-linguistically based regional governments tend to discriminate against non-indigenes in land allocation.

In an interview with the EU ACP newsletter, *The Courier*, President Meles Zenawi was asked why ownership of land would continue to reside with the state, despite the government's commitment to establishing a free market economy. His reply clearly highlights the role of land reform as a political rather than an economic instrument:

> The land reform [of 1975] was extremely popular in the south in 1974 and
> people have to differentiate between the land reform and the policy of collec-
> tivisation and so on that followed it. These people still remember the past and
> they feel that if people were allowed to sell and buy land they would soon be
> dispossessed and they would soon go back, in effect, to the pre-1974 situation.
> So anybody who wants to allow land to be sold and bought ... must be pre-
> pared to suppress that big majority of the population ... [which would be] ...
> neither possible nor desirable.[13]

The government's intention is to develop large commercial farms under
the direction of private farmers by breaking new land. 'So we can also satisfy our economic requirements by allowing the commercial farms to break
new land and the peasants to be fully attached to their own land ...'[14]

Agricultural reform: continuity in perspective
The above discussion points to a number of continuities in agricultural
policy. In particular both the Mengistu regime and the current government
have courted the political goodwill of the peasantry through the enactment
and maintenance of land reform. The distribution of state farm land to peasants after 1991 essentially represents an extension rather than a retraction
of the 1975 Land Reform. In this respect it is likely to exasperate rather
than resolve the problem of the underproductivity of the rural sector, once
again entrenching farmers in their existing mode of production. If the government is successful in attracting foreign investment into agro-industry it
may find that, as with the Awash valley development, the transformation
of class relations will increase political and economic grievances, with
harmful consequences for political stability. The breaking of new land is not
just a question of land use, it is also a question of restructuring labour. The
major problems in the agricultural sector continue to be dependence on
rain-fed agriculture, the dominance of subsistence farming and an underdeveloped infrastructure. The government may find problems of infrastructural development exasperated by the policy of regionalisation. The
emphasis in the government's programme on some devolution of power to
the regions is an attempt to resolve the nationalities question, and it is to
this issue that I now turn.

The nationalities question
Until 1991 the national question in Ethiopia was dominated by the war
with Eritrea province, as it then was. Lack of space precludes any detailed
consideration of the sources and outcome of the conflict. In brief, Eritrea
had been federated to Ethiopia in a UN post-war settlement. In 1962 Haile
Selassie annexed the territory and Eritrea became the fifteenth province of
Ethiopia. In the lengthy negotiations leading up to the 1952 settlement con-

fessional differences became politicised. In the period to 1974 the Eritrean Liberation Front was a Muslim-dominated body which saw political liberation in an alliance with the Middle East states. The incorporation of the Christian majority into the national struggle appears to have been a direct response to the brutality with which the war was prosecuted by the Ethiopian side.

In any event, the 1974 revolution coincided with a dramatic upsurge in Eritrean nationalist activity. Notwithstanding a number of attempts at a political solution to the conflict, the Derg pursued a military solution. The civil war contributed substantially to the inability of the Ethiopian state to overcome the endemic problems of its political economy and was a major factor contributing to regime collapse in 1991.

Eritrean independence

The question of Eritrea's position *vis-à-vis* Ethiopia can now be considered settled. In April 1993 Eritreans voted in a referendum for independence, which was declared on 24 May 1993. Whether some sort of realignment becomes expedient in view of the political and economic ties between the two countries remains to be seen. The associated struggle of Tigray province for autonomy which was led by the TPLF can also be presumed resolved: the TPLF armed forces took state power when the Mengistu regime collapsed and the TPLF is the major party in the coalition of forces which make up the ruling party, the EPRDF.

The satisfaction of Eritrean demands for secession and Tigrean demands for regional autonomy by no means exhausts the full play of the national question in Ethiopia. As with Eritrea and Tigray, claims by non-Amhara nationalities to regional autonomy and or secession intensified after the 1974 revolution. This was a response to two contradictory tendencies: on the one hand, the Derg's attempts to increase state centralisation and, on the other, the expectations of a significant role in exercising state power for non-Amhara nationalities which the revolutionary conjuncture had provoked.

Nationalities policy in historical perspective

Prior to 1974 the country was organised into fifteen administrative districts under governors-general, with eighty-seven sub-provinces administered by governors and 391 districts. The 1977 war with Somalia for control of the Ogaden region checked the centrifugal tendencies of the revolution.[16] The Derg's project was essentially one of national integration, conceived in part to remedy the problems of economic development which the previous administrative structure embodied. Nevertheless the Derg was 'prepared to go a surprisingly long way towards conceding Ethiopia's ethnic differences'.[17] This was reflected in the PDRE's constitutional commitment to autonomous regions and the April 1976 Programme of the National Democratic Revolution.

The 1987 reorganisation of the administrative structure ostensibly returned Ethiopia to civilian rule with the founding of the People's Democratic Republic of Ethiopia (PDRE). The reorganisation divided the country into twenty-four administrative regions and five autonomous regions. Eritrea was given the status of an autonomous region with three administrative regions. Each region had its own assembly and the power to elect its own executive body. Devolved powers varied but, in general, included some control over culture, health, education, development and local taxation. Eritrea was given considerably more freedom to act than other autonomous regions. The intention was that each administrative region should consist largely of one ethnic group. However, no attempt was made to ensure that all the members of an ethnic group lived in one region. Indeed, in the case of the larger groups, such as Tigreans, Somalis, Oromos and Amharas, this seems to have been deliberately avoided.

The ambiguities of this somewhat contradictory policy of state centralisation with regional autonomy, which clearly borrowed heavily from Soviet nationalities policy, are suggested by this contemporaneous comment on the 1987 reorganisation:

> With its distrust of government and its cynicism towards an already cumbersome bureaucracy, the wider population has greeted the proposals with a marked lack of enthusiasm. Excitement is largely restricted to local politicians. The verdict is that, while the proposals may signify a loosening of the leash, the government in Addis Ababa will still retain tight control.[18]

The continuity between the pre- and post-1991 governments' approach to the national question is striking. In the transitional charter the EPRDF flagged its intention of transforming Ethiopia into a federal state with autonomous regions in which different 'nationalities' would be represented. The apparent willingness of the new government to resolve the national question by political means may make the commitment to regional autonomy more meaningful than it has been in the past. Nevertheless, the competition for state power between the centre and the regions which arose in the uncertain period of 1974–77 has been re-enacted since 1991. It is for this reason that one of the two issues which dominated the June 1994 elections was whether or not the draft constitution should include the right to regional self-determination and secession. (The other issue was whether property should be privatised or state-controlled.) The signs are that the same organisations which contested the legitimacy of the Derg on the grounds that it represented an Amhara constituency are opposing the EPRDF on the grounds that it represents the interests of the north.[19] The constitution commits the government to self-determination up to and including secession. It remains to be seen what the outcome will be if President Meles Zenawi is not correct in his view that the regions will not secede, since: 'When you start talking about development, you start talking about a wider economy, a bigger market and you cannot have bigger markets by dividing up states. That, we believe, even the peasant will understand'[20]

Economic policy

In the areas of economic policy and foreign policy the government has made its clearest break with the Mengistu regime. In economic policy this break is mainly represented by the apparent commitment to the privatisation of parastatals and the removal of price controls in agricultural and industrial markets. Nevertheless, it is still unclear in which direction the economy is moving; in human terms the economy is mired in crisis. It is locked in an awkward transition from a state-owned commandist system (a legacy of both Emperor Haile Selassie and Mengistu) to a market-oriented one (about which most of the government is deeply sceptical).[21]

The state will retain control of electricity and water supplies, telecommunications and certain large-scale engineering, iron and steel and chemical plants, and industries of strategic importance. Mineral resources will remain state property. Movement on privatisation has been slow. Donor uncertainties about the veracity of the government's commitment to reform led to the temporary suspension of projects financed by the African Development Bank. At the World Bank's consultative group on Ethiopia, held in Paris in March 1994, several strong recommendations were made, including that the government must reinforce the efficacy of productive investment, mark up 'significant progress' on privatisation and liberalise and restructure its financial sector.[22]

Notwithstanding the reservations of donor agencies, the IMF's July 1994 mission to Ethiopia reporting on the year 1993–94 was favourable. The budget deficit had been halved as a result of the slow-down in government expenditure. Currency reserves were equal to about twenty-four weeks' imports, the balance of payments was in surplus and the offical exchange rate had come close to the open (parallel) market rate, at US$1 = Birr 5·58. Growth for 1992–93 was valued at 12·3 per cent although it had collapsed in 1993–94 to 1·2 per cent (against a projected 2·2 per cent), principally as a result of a 5·3 per cent fall in the agricultural sector following a drought which hit the cereal harvest. The IMF claims inflation was virtually zero from July 1993 to June 1994. Yet many prices continue to show sharp rises.[23]

The budget for the fiscal year 1994/95 agreed by the Council of Representatives on 26 August (the year starts on 8 July) puts overall government expenditure at Birr 9·9 billion (US$1·83 billion), an 18 per cent increase on 1993's total. (It should be noted that decreases in government expenditure reflect the 'peace dividend' at the end of the civil war.) This is split roughly 50:50 on revenue and capital projects and 1:2 regional and central expenditure. Of the capital budget, more than 25 per cent is marked for the construction of new roads; 11·3 per cent for investment in state-owned industries and 9·4 per cent on energy development. Fiscal 1992/93 registered significant growth for the first time in six years, provisionally 7·6 per cent as compared with the estimated 9.6 per cent collapse in 1991/92. However, the improvement was due above all to agricultural recovery as a result of improved rains. Confirmation, if any were needed, that 'the dependence on rain-fed agriculture remains the economy's main structural weakness'. Agriculture accounted for 50·3 per cent of GDP in 1991/92, an increase of 7·7 per cent over 1986/87, mainly due to the contraction of the industrial manufacturing sector in 1990–92. Urban unemployment and underemployment are high. In 1993 the Addis-based UN Economic Commission for Africa estimated that 30 per cent of the Ethiopian work force was unemployed, although the parallel economy provides some compensation. Over 200,000 largely unskilled young men have been demobilised, many state corporations are to be disbanded or pruned and the government is relying on the private sector to create new posts.[24]

The role of coffee
Coffee remains the key export product. The dependence of the economy on single crop exports or the direction of exports to Western hard-currency markets was not changed in the period 1974–91. Throughout, coffee production has remained largely in the hands of small-holders. Contraband trade is still significant. Together with high domestic consumption this significantly reduces production for the export market.

The above discussion suggests that asking whether or not the government is committed to 'rolling back' the state is asking the wrong question. As with agricultural and national policy certain structural conditions prevent the minimalising of the state's role in the economy – in particular, dependence on a single export crop, the share of agriculture in GDP, the dominance of the rural economy by subsistence farming, and the need to develop the country's infrastructure extensively. Perhaps most significantly, and a consequence of these factors, the state is compelled to intervene in the economy because of the absence of a bourgeoisie with capital. Dismantling the public sector, far from stimulating production, could be to dismantle the only potential instrument of accumulation.[25]

External relations and foreign policy
However expedient the government's commitment to limiting the state's role in the economy may be, its repudiation of Marxist Leninism has earned it conditional support from international aid agencies. In October 1992 the IMF approved a Structural Adjustment Facility of SDR49·4 million (approximately $US75 million). That said, once again differences between the pre-

and post-1991 governments should not be overstated. Despite the Derg's alignment with the USSR and a certain tension in US–Ethiopian relations, Ethiopia has been the largest recipient of EC aid since 1973, ahead of any other ACP state. Ethiopia was a signatory to Lomé I, II, and III, receiving ECU 120 million, ECU 141 million and ECU 210 million respectively.

One significant difference in external relations, although it shows continuity with Haile Selassie's foreign policy, is Ethiopia's courting of America. Ethiopia was a rear base for US army forces in Somalia in 1992–93 and joint defence exercises were held in early 1994. Addis Ababa's independent press has recently reported unconfirmed rumours that the United States is planning a military base in Ethiopia.[26]

Conclusion: limitations on state transformation

This chapter has placed the particularities of Ethiopian state development in the general field of the African state. The central role which the state has played in African development has been a product of weak class formation, in particular the absence of a vigorous bourgeoisie or working class with the capacity to realise its own objectives independently of the state. This is not to suggest that the state is independent of class forces, or that it acts in the general interest. It is to suggest that the central role which the African state occupies in development cannot simply be abandoned in favour of a new model.

Whether or not the current Ethiopian government's commitment to rolling back the state is sincere is beside the point. The continuities in the problems which successive regimes have faced in Ethiopia, as well as in their strategies for resolving those problems, should alert us to the limitations of state transformation. Important as agency is, it does not write on a *tabula rasa* but is forced to make a compromise with history.

Notes

1 H. Alavi, 'The state in post-colonial societies: Pakistan and Bangladesh', *New Left Review*, 74, 1972, pp. 59–82.

2 P. Evans, 'Reinventing the bourgeoisie: state entrepreneurship and class formation in dependent capitalist development', in Michael Burawoy and Freda Skocpol (eds), *Marxist Inquiries* (1982).

3 R. Fatton, *Predatory Rule: state and Civil Society in Africa* (1992).

4 D. Booth, 'Alternatives in the restructuring of state-society relations: research issues for tropical Africa', *IDS Bulletin*, 18 (4), 1987, pp. 23–30.

5 A. Stepan, *The State and Society: Peru in Comparative Perspective* (1978); E. A. Brett, 'States, markets and private power in the developing world: problems and possibilities', *IDS Bulletin*, 18 (3), 1987, pp. 31–7; J. La Fontaine, 'Evolving economic policies and disinvolving states: notes in an African context', *IDS Bulletin*, 18 (4), 1987, pp. 17–24.

6 F. Halliday and M. Molyneux, *The Ethiopian Revolution* (1981).

7   L. Bondestam, 'People and capitalism in the north-eastern lowlands of Ethiopia', *Journal of Modern African Studies*, 12 (4), 1974, pp. 435–6.
8   Bondestam, 'People and capitalism', p. 437.
9   C. Clapham, *Transformation and Continuity in Revolutionary Ethiopia* (1988).
10 Andargachew Tiruneh, *The Ethiopian Revolution, 1974–87: a Transformation from an Aristocratic to a Totalitarian Autocracy* (1993).
11 *Economist Country Report*, fourth quarter (1994), p. 21.
12 *Indian Ocean Newsletter* (Paris), 639, 24 September 1994, p. 1.
13 Meles Zenawi, interview in the *Courier* (Brussels), 145, May–June 1994, p. 25.
14 *Ibid.*
15 H. Erlich, *The Struggle over Eritrea, 1962–78: War and Revolution in the Horn of Africa* (1983), p. 16.
16 Clapham, *Transformation and continuity*, p. 62; M. Chege, 'the revolution betrayed', *Journal of Modern African Studies*, 17 (3), 1979, pp. 359–80.
17 Clapham, *Transformation and Continuity*, p. 199.
18 *Africa Confidential*, 18 November 1987, p. 7.
19 *Africa Confidential*, 1 July 1994, p. 4.
20 Meles Zenawi, interview, p. 26.
21 *Africa Confidential*, 21 January 1994, p. 4.
22 *Indian Ocean Newsletter*, 12 March 1994.
23 *Indian Ocean Newsletter*, 24 September 1994, p. 1.
24 *Economist Country Profile*, 1994, pp. 14–16.
26 La Fontaine, 'Evolving economic policies', p. 21.
26 *Economist Country Report*, fourth quarter, 1994, p. 13.

Further reading

Bahru Zewde, *A History of Modern Ethiopia, 1855–1974* (1991).
A. Bequele and E. Chole, *A Profile of the Ethiopian Economy* (1969).
Christopher Clapham, *Haile Selassie's Government* (1969).
A. Cohen and D. Weintraub, *Land and Peasants in Imperial Ethiopia: the Social Background to Revolution* (1975).
Z. Ergas (ed.), *The African State in Transition* (1987).
P. Evans *et al.*, *Bringing the State back in* (1992).
Makonnen Getu, *Socialism, Participation and Agricultural Development in Post-revolutionary Ethiopia: a Study of Constraints* (1987).
P. Gilkes, *The Dying Lion: Feudalism and Modernisation in Ethiopia* (1975).
R. Greenfield, *Ethiopia: a new Political History* (1965).
Bereket Haile Selassie, *Conflict and Intervention in the Horn of Africa* (1980).
J. Harbeson, *The Ethiopian Transformation: the Quest for the Post-imperial State* (1988).
G. Kebbede, *The State and Development in Ethiopia* (1992).
Y. Okbazghi, *Eritrea: a Pawn in World Politics* (1991).
M. and D. Ottaway, *Ethiopia: Empire in Revolution* (1978).
D. Rothchild and N. Chazan (eds), *The Precarious Balance: State and Society in Africa* (1988).
R. Sandbrook, *The Politics of Africa's Economic Recovery* (1993).
J. Wunsch and D. Oluwu (eds), *The failure of the Centralised State* (1990).

Chapter 13

Democratisation and economic change in Latin America

George Philip

Latin America consists of twenty republics, each of which has its own history and current concerns. This chapter will focus principally on two questions, out of many that could be the subject of discussion. One is democratisation. This topic is particularly relevant because so much of the region was under authoritarian military rule as recently as the beginning of the 1980s. Today almost all the region (with the noteworthy exception of Castro's Cuba) has some form of elective government. Because of tragic previous experiences of democratic breakdown, the issue of democratisation is of particular salience.

The second issue relates to the politics of economic policy. Latin America is today generally considered part of the Third World, although it can reasonably be said that Argentina and Uruguay no longer fit into that category. It is, however, also a region in which there has been considerable economic volatility. Huge booms, and apparent 'miracles', have been followed by severe slumps. The 1990s have on the whole told a happier story, although the dramatic Mexican devaluation of December 1994 raises the question of how firmly founded the recent economic recovery actually is.

Democracy and democratisation

Rueschemeyer, Stephens and Stephens's recent study *Capitalist Development and Democracy* should be a point of departure for studies of democratic change in the region. This work is one of the outstanding contributions to comparative politics anywhere within the past decade. It contains major chapters on both South and Central America and an overall comparative context which is also of relevance to the region.

Rueschemeyer *et al.* begin by pointing out that there exists a gap between cross-sectional studies of democratisation (such as those of Lipset) and comparative historical sociology as written by figures such as Barrington Moore. Cross-sectional analysis points to fairly robust positive correlations between economic development and democracy. However, comparative historical work often sees democracy as almost an accidental outcome of conflicting forces, and comparative historical sociologists have spent much time identifying and examining cases where economic development did not immediately lead to democracy at all. Obvious examples are pre-1917 Russia and pre-1914 Germany.

Rueschemeyer *et al.* argue that there is simply too much evidence for the hypothesis that development tends to lead to democracy for any alternative conclusion to be sustained. To that extent, the heavily criticised 'modernisation theorists' of 1960s fame turned out to be right after all – at any rate for the most part. However, modernisation theories are problematic at best and seriously flawed at worst. Democracy is rarely a gift, handed down from above to a grateful population. It is usually achieved as the result of a long period of political struggle and often setback. What is it about the processes of economic development that increases the probability of democracy?

Rueschemeyer *et al.* bring out a series of factors, the relative importance of which varies by region. In a European context, the key development is the rise of the democractically led working class – whose nature is defined culturally by the authors rather than according to pure socio-economy. In Latin America the situation has been significantly different. Here the organised working class has been historically weak. This is partly because late developing countries do not have so large a working class, owing to the greater capital-intensity of most manufacturing production. A further factor, important in the regional context, is that the capture of the region's two most powerful working classes (in Argentina and Mexico) by different kinds of authoritarian corporatists set back the process of democratisation.

Rueschemeyer *et al.* also identify some interests as inherently anti-democratic. These include large landowners. In the Latin American context, the key factor during past generations has been the gradual decline of the landowner class. This has been the result of urbanisation and, in some cases, agrarian reforms. However, this decline is still not fully evident in several Central American countries. Other important factors in a Latin American context have been the variable strength of political parties, and the sometimes insufficiently autonomous and sometimes overbearing role of the state.

The Rueschemeyer arguments need not be accepted in their totality. However, the question has surely been posed correctly, and the willingness of the authors to look at a range of variables is also a strength. Earlier historical sociologists (such as Moore) tended to start out with a few relatively simple ideas. This made them vulnerable to the criticism that they were determined to find a place for everything within their limited conceptual frameworks, whether the facts fitted properly or not. Studies of Latin American politics, and political economy, have frequently suffered at the hands of writers attempting to 'prove' too much with some simplistic ideas.

Rueschemeyer *et al.* essentially use the variables commonly studied by political sociology. Their work may be usefully supplemented by two other approaches, one of which focuses largely on international factors and the other on political economy.

External developments and political change

The kinds of international factor which I have in mind are those discussed in Huntington's sketchy but interesting work, *The Third Wave*. During this century, at least, democratic ideas have had to struggle against those of fascism and communism. Democracy was mainly extended at the end of the Second World War with the defeat of fascism and at the end of the Cold War with the downfall of communism. Earlier in the century the growing prestige of fascism brought about setbacks for democracy in both continental Europe and Latin America, where the 1920s and 1930s saw multiple cases in which democratic – or at any rate elective – government broke down. The defeat of fascist ideas was never as complete in Latin America as it was in Europe, and some of them lingered on into the authoritarian regimes of the 1960s and 1970s. General Pinochet, who led the 1973 *coup* in Chile, was trained as an officer by the German-influenced Chilean army of the 1930s. He has never hidden his admiration for the German militarism of that time. However, the defeat of communism at the end of the 1980s was also a powerful setback for authoritarian anti-communism within the region, since there was no longer a plausible international enemy.

It is clear that there have been internationally determined turning points in the strengthening and weakening of democratisation within the region. The influence of US policy at particular times has also been clear. There is now virtually no dispute that the United States played a part in bringing down some democracies in Latin America and in helping to establish dictatorships. Since the end of the Cold War, Washington has become markedly pro-democratic – even invading Haiti in 1994 in order to restore an elected government which was overthrown by force. Lowenthal's recently published compilation *Exporting Democracy* looks at the historical record of Washington's efforts to bring about political change in Latin America. The tone of the essays is mainly sceptical, perhaps too much so, but the questions which they raise are topical.

Political and economic change

Political economy is generally understood to refer to the relationship between particular economic junctures and political change. J. Friedan's discussion of democratisation in Brazil (though not Chile) during the early 1980s is an example of the kind of work referred to. Political economy therefore includes, but is not limited to, works within the broad framework of public choice theory. In fact almost any political economy approach to the issue of democratisation is likely to be more cautious about the prospects facing the region than the optimism of approaches which focus on the end of the Cold War (which has, after all, ended) or those which focus on political organisation.

One reason for this is that the region has not successfully 'developed' in the manner of western Europe or even parts of Asia. This is not to deny that there has been a general (though uneven) trend towards better living standards, improved life expectancy, more extensive literacy, etc. The point is rather that Latin American economies are (for some rather complex reasons) more dependent on other parts of the world than is generally the case in Europe or Asia. The consequence is a greater degree of insecurity, vulnerability to development 'traps' such as over-dependence on a particular commodity for export or on short-term capital flows. Economic weakness clearly does transform itself into political change, and sometimes to threats to democracy. For example, in Venezuela two *coup* attempts took place in 1992. While it is true that they were not successful, they came quite close to overthrowing the government. Neither international politics nor internal political organisation offers much of an explanation as to why there should have been so much unrest in Venezuela. A political economy approach (based on Venezuela's over-dependence on oil and economic decline since 1980) explains more.[1]

A second reason why political economists are less than euphoric about the region's prospects is that governments in the region, even democratic ones, have not found a way of counteracting the social effects of an unequal distribution of income which is far more pronounced than in Europe. This inequality is not specifically the result of the recent introduction of market-oriented reforms. Its historical roots go back to highly concentrated patterns of land tenure and (in some countries) a pattern of racial discrimination against indigenous or black citizens. Whatever the causes may be, questions may be asked about the prospects for democracy in Latin America if one allows that democratic stability in Europe cannot be fully understood without reference to the existence of welfare states, old age pensions and free compulsory education.

Looking to the future: grounds for optimism

It would be wrong to write off Latin America's development experiences as a complete failure. Most writers tend to emphasise the region's failures rather than its successes, though this may not be an entirely fair reflection of some rather complex economic history. It is true that most Latin American countries are officially classified as Less Developed Countries (LDCs). Argentina rejects this classification, and Uruguay does not really fit the picture either. The Chilean economy also looks very strong today. However, most countries of the region, considered according to pure 'GDP per head' criteria, are not merely lagging behind the 'old' developed world but are now being overtaken by such Asian countries as South Korea and Malaysia.

It is, however, important also to give due weight to the question 'What went right?' Most (though not all) Latin American countries are now democracies, and few of them seem likely to suffer democratic breakdown in the near future. Most Latin Americans, however poor, are at least literate and enjoy life expectancies which are not significantly worse than in the developed world. Furthermore the region has coped with huge increases in population without any major 'Malthusian' crises. It did not have the opportunities enjoyed by European countries a century ago to build empires for the benefit of European migrants. Nor has there been any resort to some of the more drastic family planning policies adopted in parts of Asia. Inevitably rapid population growth and concomitant social change created problems for the region's economy and political institutions. Nevertheless birth rates are now falling across Latin American and the average age of most populations is increasing. The area can now be seen to have an urban majority. Manufactured goods make up the vast majority of the exports of both Brazil and Mexico, and are significant elsewhere.

... and pessimism

When we look at the pattern of income distribution the picture is more unequivocally depressing. Clearly the rate of population growth does not help here, but it is far from being the whole story. There are a litany of problems facing reforming governments. Castaneda's recent study of the left, *Utopia Unarmed*, makes many of the key points. The wealthy tend to export their savings and resent paying taxes. Robots and micro-chips have reduced the demand for manual labour in countries where employment is already scarce enough. Moreover Latin American governments are, by European standards, severely under-resourced. Furthermore state bureaucracies do not work well. They are often corrupt, and poor public-sector pay does little for morale or discipline. As a result poor people tend to face a state that just does not work in practice as it should on paper. The police and judiciary are not to be trusted. Hospitals kill as many poor people as they cure. Educational provision is unsatisfactory, owing, in part, to large-scale absenteeism among teachers. Some public-sector workers do not work at all, but merely turn up to collect their salaries. There is little effective public scrutiny of these problems, though most observers know them to be real and serious enough.

While looking at the (sometimes) dismal reality, some scholars have doubted whether Latin American democracy is meaningful at all. Is it just, some have wondered, 'democracy by default' or 'low-intensity democracy'?[2] Critics claim that Latin American elites now prefer democracy because it confers electoral respectability, and because they do not find it threatening, since it holds out little prospect of real change.

Other observers (including the author) consider that the existence of democratic institutions is important, but readily agree that they need strengthening in most cases by policies of institutional and social reform. The issue of social reform and, more particularly, effective means of relieving poverty is now very much alive and at last being considered seriously by mainstream local and international institutions.

Dependency and development

An important question which arises in this context is whether elected governments have enough freedom of manoeuvre to bring about social change, or whether they are constrained by economic factors. If there is one distinctively Latin American contribution to the social sciences it has been 'dependency analysis' which precisely raises the question of how much internal autonomy any poor country can enjoy in the context of a global capitalist economy.

This is not a new idea in a Latin American context. In the mid-1960s dependency theorists were beginning to evince profound scepticism as to whether any part of the Third World, including but not limited to Latin America, could ever achieve sufficient economic progress to catch up with the First World. A. G. Frank was the most uncompromising exponent of dependency theory; Cardoso and Faletto among the most sophisticated.

Despite fears expressed by dependency writers, economic growth in the region continued to be fairly rapid until the debt crisis of 1982. However, during the 1970s a number of countries, often under the control of military governments, adopted interventionist policies of state-fomented capitalism. Cardoso and other writers such as Evans (on Brazil) and Becker (on Peru) explored the conditions necessary for the continuation of this form of economic growth. They accepted that the Latin American state and private sector could under some circumstances co-operate with foreign capital in order to promote industrial development. However, there were constraints on this alliance, and limits as to what could be achieved. One of the problems was that the industrial growth achieved tended to be very capital-intensive, with the result that poorer Latin Americans tended to be left behind.

The 1982 debt crisis changed perspectives again. The root cause of the problem was not so much micro-economic or 'structural' as global macro-economic imbalances with catastrophic consequences for much of Latin America. During the 1960s and 1970s, particularly, First World governments and bankers were increasingly willing to lend to Latin American governments in order to find a home for international capital flows and, later, petro-dollar surpluses. Unfortunately nobody was able to prevent this lending boom leading to over-indebtedness and subsequent default when international interest rates increased and commodity prices fell. Debt crises are not unknown in capitalist economies anywhere, but the absence of any means of legitimate default or other way of resolving bankruptcy problems which involved sovereign governments ensured that the social cost of the 1982 crisis was extremely high. A decade of growth was lost, and by 1990 only Colombia and Chile had fully recovered from the setback caused by the crisis.

It is mildly ironic that dependency theory had been developed and largely abandoned before the 1982 crisis, which might otherwise have appeared to vindicate some of its essential tenets. However, the intellectual climate of the 1980s was quite different from what it had been a generation earlier. Public choice theory tended to take over from the dependency approach. Any idea that there was a socialist alternative with anything to offer Latin America was already largely discredited, and there were also clearly formulated doubts as to whether the moderate economic nationalism characteristic of many governments in the region was feasible either.[3] Elite scepticism became transformed into a more popular consensus when hyperinflation took place in Argentina in 1989, Peru in 1990 and Bolivia in 1984 (some would also add Brazil in 1993). These developments decisively changed the political preferences of voters in those countries and made them very sceptical of big-spending government. By the end of the decade free-market liberals were claiming intellectual as well as political victory in most countries of the region.

From populism to neo-liberalism – the new policy agenda

Over the last few years Latin America has had some of the most radically pro-capitalist governments of the entire century. The governments of Menem in Argentina and of Fujimori in Peru have privatised more aggressively even than the Chile of General Pinochet, once held up as the extreme example of an economically liberal government. In retrospect it may be that these privatising governments took advantage of a window of opportunity afforded by low US interest rates to sell state assets at relatively high prices. In any event the role of the public sector has been permanently altered in several important countries of the region.

These experiments in democratic free-market economics have clearly proved controversial; the jury is still out on their ultimate impact. Some authors (including this one) are cautiously sympathetic to policies of market-oriented reform. There are dangers in such policies, but there are opportunities as well, as long as economic growth is not treated purely as an end in itself but is also seen as a means of facilitating policies of social and institutional reform.

Another significant recent change, which has been more unequivocally welcomed, has been the great improvement in trade and other relations between the various Latin American countries. Until fairly recently South American countries tended to view their neighbours with suspicion and even hostility. Today Brazil, Argentina, Uruguay and Paraguay have formed a free-trade area (Mercosur) while there have been other trade agreements involving the Andean countries and Colombia, Mexico and Venezuela.

Rather more controversial has been the free-trade agreement between Mexico, Canada and the United States. Mexico entered NAFTA in January 1994. The year was in many ways a difficult one for that country, but NAFTA membership will be of long-term significance. The US government is also seeking closer trade links with other Latin American countries. The main problem here lies not with the Latin American governments but with the US Congress, which as always has some protectionist representatives.

The economic power of the United States is plainly an overwhelming influence in the Caribbean area (including Mexico in this context). It is significant, but not quite overwhelming, south of the Panama Canal. There has not been the space in this account to discuss the whole issue of US relations with the Central American area. The ending of the Cold War has changed a number of realities in any case. What is clear, however, is that the economic integration of the North American region is increasingly a fact. In 1993 over 90 per cent of Mexico's exports went to the United States, and capital and migration flows were also highly significant. By the same token Mexico is the third largest market for US exports. Before the devaluation Mexico had briefly overtaken Japan to become the second largest market for US exports after Canada – whose own trade with Mexico is also increasing rapidly.

Clearly a number of hugely significant historical events in the region – for example, the direction taken by the Cuban revolution – can be seen convincingly as a reaction against US hegemony. Nevertheless recent years have seen a considerable diminution in tension between the United States and the more nationalistic Latin Americans. The US invasion of Haiti in 1994, for example, was supported by many people who might once have been relied upon to oppose any US intervention in the region. Furthermore the predicted backlash in Mexico against the United States following the NAFTA agreement has not happened. Such unpopularity as there has been – especially after the devaluation of December 1994 – was directed mainly at the Mexican authorities themselves.

It may well be, then, that 'Latin America' is increasingly bifurcating into two regions. The area north of the Panama Canal is increasingly caught up in the overall political economy of North America. South of the Panama Canal there is clearly an independent region which is slowly integrating economically. Argentinians and others would clearly object to any idea that it was doing so under the leadership of Brazil, but the Brazilian economic influence is nevertheless of primary importance. Future researchers into the political economy of Latin America will have to weigh the process of globalisation alongside that of regional integration. If one is an optimist, one might conclude that regional integration could hold out a possible counterweight to that of dependent globalisation.

Notes

1 G. Philip, 'The Venezuelan *coup* attempt of February 1992', *Government and Opposition*, 27 (4), autumn 1992, pp. 455–69; *The Political Economy of International Oil* (1994).

2 B. Gills and J. Rocamora, 'Low intensity democracy', *Third World Quarterly*, 13 (3), 1992, pp. 501–23; L. A. Whitehead, 'Democracy in Latin America', *Third World Quarterly*, special issue ed. D. Held (1992).

3 F. Larrain and M. Selowsky (eds), *The Public Sector and the Latin American Crisis* (1991).

Further reading

Students of Latin America often have much to learn from works which do not ignore the region but place their questions in comparative context. On democratisation, the key recent work is D. Rueschemeyer, E. Stephens and J. Stephens, *Capitalist Development and Democracy* (1992). These authors refer back to the path-breaking, but flawed, work of Barrington Moore, *The Social Origins of Dictatorship and Democracy* (1966). Also relevant is S. M. Lipset, *Political Man: the Social Bases of Politics* (1980). Within the specifically Latin American context there is the work of G. O'Donnell and P. Schmitter, *Transitions from Authoritarian Rule: Tentative Conclusions about Uncertain Democracies* (1986).

The same strategy, of consulting both comparative works and works on Latin America itself, should lead a student interested in the impact of post-Cold War international politics first to S. P. Huntington, *The Third Wave* (1993), and thence to A. Lowenthal (ed.), *Exporting Democracy* (1991).

However, by the early 1990s Latin Americanists had generally come to accept that democratisation had definitively occurred in the region, and they have since tended to move on to attempts to characterise the new democracies themselves and to evaluate their ability to cope with complex policy issues. Jorge Castaneda, *Utopia Unarmed* (1991), is an extremely interesting work from a Mexican closely involved in left-wing politics in his own country. A relatively optimistic perspective on the current Latin American situation is provided by G. Philip, 'New economic liberalism and democracy in South America', *Government and Opposition*, 29 (3) 1994. More sceptical, if not actually dismissive, treatments appear in B. Gills and J. Rocamora, 'Low intensity democracy', *Third World Quarterly*, 13 (3) 1992, pp. 501–23, and L. A. Whitehead, 'Alternatives to "liberal democracy": a Latin American perspective', in D. Held, *Prospects for Democracy: North, South, East, West*, Cambridge, Polity Press, 1993, pp. 312–30.

When looking at the making of economic policy, a longer-term view is generally helpful. It is interesting that left-of-centre observers have tended to focus mainly on the problems facing the region's policy-makers when operating in a global economy, whereas more conservative writers have often considered, as primary variable, characteristics of the region itself. D. North, *Institutions, Institutional Change and Economic Performance* (1990), does not focus specifically on Latin America but does demonstrate that the behaviour of public institutions is a key variable from the viewpoint of economic development. There have also been relatively recent, and very critical, discussions of the role of the public sector in Latin America. A discussion of the role of the public sector precipitating the debt crisis is F. Larrain and M. Selowksy (eds), *The Public Sector and the Latin American Crisis* (1991). A very critical discussion of the impact of the legal system on small business in the region is H. de Soto, *The Other Path* (1989).

Other writers have concentrated more on Latin America's traditional (though now declining) dependence on commodity (raw material) exports as an explanation for subsequent structural problems. G. Philip, *The Political Economy of International Oil* (1994), is a comparative study which focuses on the problems facing a particular set of commodity exporters seeking to achieve economic development. The importance of commodity dependence would seem to be borne out by the fact that Venezuela is on a very different trajectory from most other Latin American countries. The first of the 1992 *coup* attempts in that country is discussed in G. Philip 'The Venezuelan *coup* attempt of February 1992', *Government and Opposition*, 27 (4),autumn 1992 pp. 455–69. A more optimistic discussion of the possibilities of commodity-led development is D. Becker, *The New Bourgeoisie and the Limits of Dependency: Mining, Class and Power in 'Revolutionary' Peru* (1983).

Students interested in the longer-term debate about the relationship between globalisation and economic development may start with the classic (though flawed) work of A. G. Frank, *Capitalism and Underdevelopment in Latin America* (1966), and compare it with F. H. Cardoso and E. Faletto, *Dependency and Development in Latin America*. (The English language version was published in 1979). Cardoso is now President of Brazil, and has become somewhat more conservative than he was when author of the book. Later works focusing on the issue of globalisation include P. Evans, *Dependent Development: the Alliance of Multinational, State and Local Capital in Brazil* (1979), and R. Thorp and G. Bertram, *Peru 1890–1977: Growth and Policy in an Export Economy* (1978) A recent work within a recognisably similar tradition, not focused purely on Latin America, is L. Sklair, *Sociology of the Global System* (1991).

An important work on the politics of the debt crisis, from what is loosely speaking a public choice perspective, is J. Friedan, *Debt, Development and Democracy* (1991). A work written from a similar perspective is A. Przeworski, *Democracy and the Market: Political and Economic Reforms in Eastern Europe and Latin America* (1991). An explanation of why Przeworski's scepticism about the prospects of democractically led, market-oriented reform may be misplaced appears in G. Philip, 'The new economic liberalism and democracy in Latin America: friends or enemies?', *Third World Quarterly, 14 (3), 1993*.

Chapter 14

Japan and the Pacific

Ian Neary

In 1964 Japan was formally admitted to membership of the OECD; the first, and so far only, non-white member. By the end of the 1960s Japan's GDP was larger than that of any country in the world except the two 'super-powers' but there was still some reluctance to take Japan seriously. At best the study of Japan's contemporary history was a 'How did they do it?' exercise; at worst, under the influence of the 'modernisation school' it was assumed that the larger their GDP grew the more like 'us' (i.e. North Americans) the Japanese would become. Only following (though not necessarily because of) the publication of Herman Khan's *The Emerging Japanese Superstate* in 1970[1] was there an attempt to re-evaluate Japan's more recent history by American academic historians.

Americans, of course, have a special relationship with Japan. They defeated the imperial army in the Pacific War, they acted as mentors during the occupation, they guided Japan through the process of democratisation and they stood as guarantors of Japan's sovereignty, underwriting the defence of Japan in a way that enabled her to direct resources to the task of rebuilding the economy. The United States did not, in fact, carry out all these tasks alone but there has been reluctance to recognise the role of other powers in these processes and most Japanese are unaware of the non-American contributions. Japan re-emerged, almost unnoticed at first, as a world power in the early 1970s at the same time as US self-confidence was being shaken by the country's inability to impose its preferred solution on the people of Vietnam. Meanwhile Japan was able to demonstrate its economic strength by effectively shrugging off the effects of the 'dollar shock' of 1971, and the 'oil crises' of 1973 and 1979. Impressive economic growth continued into the 1980s as many industries which had previously been competing with US exports in third markets began to control significant sectors of the US domestic market. Further challenges to US prowess seemed to come from the second wave of economic growth which was taking place in the four 'little tigers' of South Korea, Taiwan, Singapore and Hong Kong.

And, in the 1990s, there was yet a further wave of growth in a 'third tier' of countries; Malaysia, Thailand and parts of China were poised to break into the world economic system. It was, then, not just the rise of Japan as an economic power, but the growth of several east Asian economies to international significance which could be said to mark 'the end of the long era of Western domination of world history'.[2]

This brief account of contemporary history in Japan and Asia Pacific must necessarily be incomplete. Firstly, I shall refer only briefly to the concerns of contemporary Japanese historians and hardly at all to the vernacular writings of the post-war histories of east Asian states. Secondly, more space will be devoted to Japan than might be justified from the point of view of population size, partly because of Japan's economic significance and partly because there is more written about Japan than any east Asian society except China. Finally we will consider the recent literature that asks whether Asia Pacific, or the Pacific rim, has any meaning other than as a geographical category.

Occupation and reconstruction

Any discussion of the nature of contemporary Japan must inevitably take account of the impact of the occupation. Were the reforms tantamount to a 'social democratic revolution'?[3] Were they imposed by a Western state on one which was powerless to resist them despite there being no cultural foundations for them? Or were they ultimately significant only in areas where they built on an indigenous desire for reform which was manifest before the occupation and the moves towards total war that began in 1931. Progress towards land reform, changes in the legal status of women, the creation of a union movement and demands for the decentralisation of the education system had all been made in the 1920s. Did the US reforms simply release this hitherto suppressed potential? In this interpretation the war years were an unfortunate interlude which interrupted Japan's advance from the pre-modern to the modern. However, another reading of the same period sees the state domination of society 1930–45 as creating the central institutions which were to be the foundations of the political and economic structures of the post-war world. As Sheldon Garon has pointed out, 'Historians and political scientists are only now beginning to demonstrate the impressive continuities in politics and policies between pre-1945 and post-war Japan.'[4] Either these structures were untouched by the occupation reforms or such reforms as were introduced were implemented with little enthusiasm after the first 'New Deal' phase. For example, the purges which were supposed to transform the country's leadership left the bureaucracy virtually untouched.[5] The attempts to break up the conglomerates on the grounds that they were monopolistic and militaristic originally produced a list of 1,200 firms, which was whittled down to nineteen, and

finally only nine were actually dealt with.[6] As Halliday notes, in one of the
few of the leftist readings of contemporary Japanese history to acquire a
wide readership, most Western sources tend to concentrate on US policies,
ignoring what the Japanese rulers were doing, and place their emphasis on
fluctuations in US policy in the early years of the occupation, obscuring its
'structural unity', which, he argues, was a process 'of America's attempted
integration of Japan into its new empire.'[7]

That which remains unchanged from the occupation period is the constitution, and there has been a large literature on its origins, its impact on
post-war Japan and the prospects of reform, especially in Japanese but also
in English. Many on the right of the political spectrum have argued that
Japan will not be completely free from the occupation until the constitution
is revised to remove Article 9, which precludes the use of war by the Japanese state and seems to make even the existence of military forces illegal if
not unconstitutional. For some time the fiction was maintained that the
constitution was Japanese in origin, but this became impossible to sustain
in the 1950s. Now it is widely accepted that it was rather hastily drafted
by Americans based in Tokyo, translated into Japanese and forced on the
Japanese as the price of keeping the emperor. In a similar way, in 1952
Japan was virtually forced into a security treaty with the United States as
the price of an early end to the occupation. The circumstances surrounding the adoption of the constitution, the negotiation of the Security Treaty
in 1951 and its re-negotiation in 1960 and 1970 have been fertile ground
for historical debate between conservatives, liberals and Marxists. While
some argue that 'Japan cannot be a normal state as long as the Socialists,
the constitution and the security treaty remain',[8] others stress that pacifism
has permeated deeply into Japanese society; 'the significance of Article 9 is
duly appreciated not only by those who suffered the disasters of war, but
also by those who are sensitive enough to regard the experience of those
touched by war as their own experience'.[9] As Japanese politics enters a
period of radical reform, this debate on the constitution will continue.

The State and economic development

Explaining the 'Japanese miracle' was something that was left mainly to
economists until the 1980s. The seminal work on Japan's industrial policy
is Chalmers Johnson's *MITI and the Japanese Miracle*, which was published
in 1982.[10] He emphasises the differences that exist between capitalist states,
in particular the radically different priorities of public policy in Japan and
the United States since 1868. Japan has been guided by a 'developmental
state' which has sought to manipulate capitalism to secure national autonomy and bureaucratically defined goals. He seeks to demonstrate how the
Ministry of International Trade and Industry (MITI) acted as a 'pilot organisation', guiding industry in general and some industries in particular

through the pre-war and post-war eras. Okimoto followed up Johnson's work with a study of telecommunications policy and explicitly makes the point that MITI believes that the 'market mechanism cannot be expected to generate economic outcomes that are always in the nation's interest.'[11] Since then a number of American and British authors have written on other industrial sectors: Richard Samuels has written on energy market policy;[12] David Friedman has examined the machine tool industry.[13] Howells and Neary's work on the pharmaceutical industries in the United Kingdom and Japan is one of a series of ESRC-funded research projects on a variety of industrial sectors co-ordinated by Stephen Wilks and Maurice Wright, who themselves have written on aspects of government–industry relations in Japan.[14] Most of the authors of these studies would regard themselves as political scientists rather than historians but each of the studies is concerned with the development of policy over the last fifty years or so. The key debate is over the role of the state in the process of development. What role did it play? How did it interact with industry? What, if anything, can we (Europeans, Americans, non-Japanese) learn from it?

The cultural context

Perhaps not surprisingly, there has been substantially less written in English about the post-war history of the union movement in Japan. An important study of the militant industrial unionism of the first years of the occupation period suggests that Japanese workers have not always been as passive as may often appear from work on post-war industrial relations.[15] However, most of the studies which have paid any attention to the union movement have done so in the context of the study of industrial relations. The earliest studies built up a picture of labour–management relations centred on the concept of 'lifetime commitment' both of the worker to his employer and vice versa, at least for those employed in the elite section of the dual structure of the Japanese system.[16] These studies noted how the union tended to be organised within the structure of the company rather than on the basis of a trade or an industry as in the United States or western Europe. Western commentators assumed and Japanese activists hoped that this was an aspect of Japan's backwardness and that it would change as Japan 'modernised'. As Japan moved down the pathway to advanced capitalism it would inevitably take on the political and social structures which all such advanced systems had in common. Ronald Dore was one of the first to suggest that convergence, at least as usually conceived, was unlikely.[17] Indeed, rather than industrial systems in Japan becoming more like those in the United States or Europe, he suggested, companies in those countries might come to resemble the Japanese, and some recent studies suggest that he was right.

Woodiwiss considers not so much the labour movement as labour law and demonstrates the way in which the interpretation of a law which was explicitly copied from US statutes early in the occupation has evolved into something quite different in the Japanese cultural climate. He shows how the 'revolution' in Japanese industrial relations which was made possible by changes in the labour law which culminated in the 1949 Trade Unions Act has been reversed, particularly since 1972, by the reinvention of 'a largely secular and sociologically ideological formation which I have termed "enterprise-ism" which continues to show 'hostility towards fully autonomous and assertive trade unions'.[18]

Nine hundred people died from Minamata disease, over 2,000 patients have been certified and another 300 await certification.[19] Minamata was one of the four cases of industrially generated environmental pollution which slowly worked their way through the legal system during the 1960s. Success in the courts led to legislation in the 1960s and 1970s aimed at preventing the re-emergence of similar tragedies – and, indeed, no similar cases have occurred. Moreover it did stimulate some to re-examine the era of rapid industrial growth to enquire how it was that so many people had been caused to suffer. One of the first English was Reich *et al.*, who surveyed the main areas of policy.[20] It was followed a little later by studies of the process of citizen protest against instances of industrial pollution and the process that led to the adoption of environmental legislation.[21] More recently there has been the translation of Japanese material into English making it clear that critics within Japan were well aware of the problems and how they have been campaigning to change attitudes towards them.[22]

The 'discovery' by Western scholars of industrially generated pollution in Japan coincided with a move away from the 'Japan as model' approach which emphasised harmony, consensus and loyalty. Historians and sociologists began to explore the role played by conflict in modern Japan's history and to demonstrate that the fruits of economic growth have not been evenly distributed, such that many lost more than they gained in the process of industrialisation.[23] A recent collection of essays, mainly by historians, has attempted to re-examine the period 1945–90 as history. They too are interested in the 'contested character' of the post-war decades, during which a variety of outcomes were always possible, at the same time as they analyse the development and domination of the conservative hegemony which even now is unlikely to be disturbed.[24]

Within Japan the achievements of economic growth were critically examined by Marxist scholars across the spectrum of disciplines but particularly by economic historians. The central debate among Marxists for much of the post-war period has been an extension of that which dominated the 1930s. In the view of one faction, the Ronoha (Worker Peasant Faction), the emergence of Japanese capitalism had its roots in the Tokugawa period, resulting in a Japan in the 1920s which was essentially capitalist. Meanwhile the Koza-ha argued that the Japanese economy was characterised by semi-feudalism and militarism. The Koza-ha welcomed the occupation as an opportunity to eliminate all remaining traces of feudalism, but they continued to emphasise the subordination of Japan to the US-led 'world imperialist camp' while the Ronoha stressed Japan's relative economic independence.[25] Rapid economic growth in the 1960s challenged many of these Marxist conclusions but Marxist scholarship in Japan has shown considerable flexibility in developing a critical analysis of contemporary Japanese capitalism. Dower commented in the 1970s that 'much of American scholarship on Japan has tended to be congruent with the objectives of the American government ...'.[26] As writing on contemporary Japanese history is scrutinised for signs of bias, be it 'Japan bashing' or whatever, it is increasingly important to be better informed about the writings of those Japanese who are critical of Japan's economic and political structure.

Korea and Taiwan

Until recently just about the only aspect of post-war Korean history which attracted any attention was the Korean War, and most writing concentrated on the military engagements. Bruce Cumings changed all this with a massive two-volume study of the origins of the Korean War which placed the military action clearly in its social and political context.[27] It was extremely controversial when first published, as it portrayed Korea after 1945 as divided between numerous rival groups in which the governments in Seoul and Pyongyang were able to exert control only by the violent suppression of dissent. It did not subscribe to the official view of the outbreak of the war and thus was not welcomed either by the South Korean government or by the small Korean studies community of the time. However, the extent of the detailed research contained in the two massive volumes plus the more relaxed post-Cold War environment has ensured that it is now recognised as the most important single piece of writing about post-war Korea.

The 28 February 1947 (28/2) massacre was not as significant in terms of world history as the occupation of Japan or the Korean War but it was just as important in the development of the foundation of the modern Taiwanese state. Those who sympathise with the opposition parties such as the Democratic Progressive Party (DPP) would argue that the deaths of 8,000 protesters in an island-wide uprising that lasted over two weeks typified the mainlanders' attitude to the residents of Taiwan in particular and to notions of human rights and democracy in general. More particularly it destroyed the already weak indigenous elite which was struggling to assert control following the withdrawal of the Japanese colonial administrators. This prepared the way for KMT refugees and then the refugee KMT to establish its authoritarian regime with relative ease in the period 1947–49. Until the more relaxed political climate of the late 1980s research into this period was not permitted. However, in 1991 the first monograph in English on the incident by Lai *et al.* showed that the KMT repression turned the population against the Chiang Kai Shek regime and generated the first Taiwan Independence Movement. A similarly anodyne official report on the same incident was produced by the government in 1992. We may expect that as opposition groups are able to act free of repression there will be more uninhibited research into the events which immediately preceded and followed this incident.[28]

As in the case of Japan, most recent writing about both Korea and Taiwan has been concerned with how they have managed to engineer such rapid economic growth, and the discussion has largely followed on from the debates on Japan's industrial policy. Development economists such as Wade have argued that in the Taiwanese case 'the role of government has gone well beyond the practice of Anglo-American and the principles of classical economics, while at the same time resources allocation has occurred primarily through vigorous functioning markets',[29] meanwhile political scientists such as Lucian Pye have placed more emphasis on a 'sense of dependency which makes the Confucian tradition of paternalistic authority so effective in working for the collective goal of economic development.'[30]

The human rights record of east Asian states has come under increasing scrutiny since the collapse of communism in Europe. During the Cold War human rights issues played a key role in the dialogue between the United States and the Soviet Union, with Americans castigating the Russians for their lack of respect for political and civil rights while the Russians claimed a superior record in guaranteeing social and economic rights. The United States continues to champion human rights but the main butt of criticism has now become China and the countries of East Asia. Lee Kwan Yew, acting almost as a surrogate for the PRC, has argued that democracy and human rights have no place in east Asian societies. The argument is that the US strategy in the area is 'an aggressive effort to export Western values to the non-West',[31] and has even hinted that the attempt to do so amounts to a strategy to restrict the rate of economic growth in the region so as to maintain the domination of the West. This has prompted scholars in the West and within the region to put forward a counter-argument that there are within Asia many democratic traditions and that an examination of the post-war record shows how, 'In Asia, democracy can encourage greater self-reliance while respecting cultural values'.[32] We can expect this theme to reverberate in the writing on post-1945 Asia for many years to come.

The challenge of the Pacific rim

For some years now it has been fashionable to talk about a shift in the balance of world history towards the Pacific. Such predictions are nothing new. Two writers in the mid-nineteenth century argued that 'the Pacific

Ocean will have the same role as the Atlantic has now and the Mediterranean had in Antiquity and the Middle Ages – that of the great water highway of world commerce; and the Atlantic will decline to the status of an inland sea, like the Mediterranean'.[33] This proved rather premature but in June 1969 the Japanese Prime Minister, Sato Eisaku, was perhaps the first to use the term 'Asia Pacific' and there are many who now talk of the forthcoming 'Pacific century'. A substantial literature is building up as authors examine the post-war record of the region to discover trends in that direction. Curiously, one of the most influential and early examples concludes that 'thinking of the Pacific as a separate region has never made much sense and will increasingly make less sense ...'.[34] Others are happier with the idea that 'the "Pacific century" has meaning '... in terms of the emergence of a twin core within the Pacific itself and the relationships between its American and Asian arms, between the US and Japan in particular.'[35] Over the past five years at least eight books have been written on the theme of developments in Pacific Asia as historians and others try to place contemporary events in an historical context. At the Asia Pacific Economic Co-operation summit held in November 1994 agreements were reached that promise to strengthen the ties between its members. If and when these agreements are put into operation there will be increased interest in the way trans-Pacific interaction has developed and we can expect to see further writing in this area.

Few, if any, Asian societies feel comfortable with their post-war histories. The occupation of Japan, the Korean War, the 28/2 massacre in Taiwan and the experience of decolonisation were crucial moments in the formation of the modern state. This makes the analysis of these periods by historians all the more important to an understanding of the modern world but also more dangerous, sometimes literally where authoritarian regimes still rule. The death of the Showa emperor prompted a number of re-assessments of post-war Japan. The fiftieth anniversary of the end of the Pacific war will undoubtedly encourage historians throughout east Asia to reassess their contemporary history and the relations that have built up in the Pacific region. There are encouraging signs that the democratisation process at work in many of these societies is making the task of the contemporary historian now possible in a way it formerly was not. The role of the contemporary historian in explaining the position of these countries in the world will become increasingly important to those societies; and it is important for their non-Asian colleagues to keep abreast of these developments.

Notes

1 London, 1971.
2 D. Williams, *Japan: Beyond the End of History* (1993), p. 4.
3 R. P. Dore, *British Factory – Japanese Factory* (1973), p. 115.

4   S. Garon, *The State and Labor in Modern Japan* (1987), p. 229.
5   H. H. Baerwald, *The Purge of Japanese Leaders under the Occupation* (1959), p. 83.
6   K. Kawai, *Japan's American Interlude* (1960), p. 147.
7   J. Halliday, *A Political History of Japanese Capitalism* (1975), p. 163.
8   T. Kataoka, *The Price of a Constitution* (1991), p. 219.
9   Norimoto Tsuneoka *et al.* (eds), *The Constitution of Japan* (1993), p. 150.
10 C. Johnson, *MITI and the Japanese Miracle: the Growth of Industrial Policy, 1925–75* (1982).
11 D. I. Okimoto, *Between MITI and the Market: Japanese Industrial Policy for High Technology* (1989), p. 2.
12 R. J. Samuels, *The Business of the Japanese State: Energy Markets in Comparative and Historical Perspective* (1987).
13 D. Friedman, *The Misunderstood Miracle: Industrial Development and Political Change in Japan* (1988).
14 S. Wilks and M. Wright, (eds), *The Promotion and Regulation of Industry in Japan* (1991); J. Howells and I. Neary, *Intervention and Technological Innovation: Government and the Pharmaceutical Industry in the UK and Japan* (1995).
15 J. Moore, *Japanese Workers and the Struggle for Power, 1945–47* (1983).
16 J. Abbeglen, *The Japanese Factory: Aspects of its Social Organisation* (1958).
17 Dore, *British Factory*.
18 A. Woodiwiss, 'A revolution in trade union law?' in Ian Neary (ed.), *War, Revolution and Japan* (1993), p. 116.
19 A. Mishima, *Bitter Sea: the Human Cost of Minimata Disease* (1992), p. 7.
20 M. Reich *et al.* (eds), *Island of Dreams* (1975).
21 M. A. McKean, *Environmental Protest and Citizen Politics in Japan* (1981); J. Gresser, *Environmental Law in Japan* (1981).
22 Mishima, *Bitter Sea*; Ui Jun (ed.), *Industrial Pollution in Japan*, (1992).
23 T. Najita and Koschmann (eds), *Conflict in Modern Japanese History* (1982); E. S. Krauss, T. P. Rohlen and P. G. Steinhoff (eds), *Conflict in Japan* (1984).
24 A. Gordon (ed.), *Post-war Japan as History* (1993).
25 T. Morris-Suzuki and T. Seiyama, *Japanese Capitalism since 1945* (1989).
26 J. Dower, *Origins of the Modern Japanese State* (1975), p. 33.
27 B. Cumings, *The Origins of the Korean War*, I, *Liberation and the Emergence of Separate Regimes, 1945–47* (1981), II, *The Roaring of the Cataract, 1947–50* (1990).
28 T. H. Lai, R. Myers and W. Wei, *The Taiwan Uprising of February 28, 1947* (1991).
29 R. Wade, *Governing the Market: Economic Theory and the Role of Government in East Asian Industrialisation* (1990), p. 8.
30 L. Pye, 'The new Asian capitalism: a political portrait', in *In Search of an East Asian Development Model* (1988), p. 97.
31 K. Mabhubani, 'The West and the rest', *National Interest*, summer 1992, p. 3.
32 Kim Dae Jung, 'Is culture destiny?' *Foreign Affairs*, November–December 1994, pp. 189–94.
33 K. Marx and F. Engels, *Collected Works*, 10 (19), p. 266.
34 G. Segal, *Rethinking the Pacific* (1990).
35 E. L. Jones, *Coming Full Circle* (1993).

Chapter 15

China:
a state in search of a civilisation

Chris Hughes

In 1990 China was described by Lucian Pye, the pioneer of research into the cultural dimensions of Chinese politics, as a civilisation pretending to be a state.[1] Such a statement reflects much about the condition of research in Chinese studies following the decade of radical economic reform. In particular, the eruption of the demonstrations which swept China in 1989, culminating in the 4 June bloodshed in Tiananmen Square, drew attention to the fact that the growing values of consumerism, entrepreneurship and democratic government which developed with economic liberalisation and integration into the global economy had rendered the Marxist–Leninist theory of the dictatorship of the Chinese Communist Party (CCP) somewhat anachronistic. Such processes brought into sharp focus the necessity for deepening the analysis of the relationship between economic reform, social change, and the viability of the PRC party state.

If exploration of the relationship between Chinese party state and Chinese society had become central to the field of Chinese studies by 1990, subsequent research in this area has since arrived at a rather different perspective on the problem from that indicated by Pye's remark. Particularly influential has been that the crisis of confidence in CCP leadership climaxed at the same time as the disintegration of the Soviet Union, the end of the Cold War, and the subsequent rise of nationalist forces working to redraw the world map. In this context, new attention has naturally been paid to discerning and understanding centrifugal forces within the People's Republic of China (PRC) that might contribute to the development of similar processes of disintegration.

A state in search of a civilisation

If the collapse of communism has had a heavy influence on studies of China, though, the direction of research had in fact already been moving towards a better understanding of the complex heterogeneity of Chinese society before the events of 1989. In many respects this was due to the availability of new sources of evidence and new research methods. Whereas, during the Mao period, it had been difficult for scholars even to visit China, let alone carry out fieldwork, this situation changed dramatically during the 1980s. Not only have travel in China and scholarly exchange become relatively easy, but new archives have also been made available for research by both central and local government authorities. In addition, the generally more open social climate of the 1980s allowed writers, artists and key political figures an unprecedented degree of freedom of expression, resulting in an explosion of literature, fine art and cinema.

The ultimate effect of this plethora of new material on the research agenda is impossible to predict. At the very least, the increasing feasibility of undertaking micro-historical research has accelerated a growing awareness of the degree of regional diversity that exists within what has too often tended to be seen as a monolithic Chinese nation. Combined with the collapse of communist states, this has led to a new direction of research for the 1990s which is increasingly described as deconstructing China. What is novel about this agenda is that China ceases to be a given identity, setting the margins within which research should take place. Instead, the identity of China itself becomes the central topic of research. In this context, and given the great diversity that exists within the society over which the Chinese state must exert its control, it may actually be better to adjust Pye's description and view China more as a state in search of a civilisation.

If what has tended to be taken as a homogeneous Chinese national identity is to be deconstructed, this presents the researcher with a host of interesting questions. The political scientist Elizabeth Perry has gone so far as to suggest that applying categories such as state and civil society to China at all, which have after all been developed out of attempts to analyse European historical processes, may be misplaced. It may be better to try to develop new categories of analysis which derive from the study of Chinese society itself, allowing Chinese studies to make a contribution to the wider field of social science theory for the first time. Whether or not researchers in the field will be able to live up to this task, it certainly constitutes a significant challenge for the future.

Chinese national identity: dynamics and developments

At present, however, the ways in which the dynamics of Chinese national identity can be analysed remain limited to the application of more familiar approaches. One such method is to try to apply wider theories of nationalism to the study of China. This is particularly interesting because such theories tend to agree that nationalism is a doctrine which emerged in Europe in relatively recent times. Yet, if we are to accept that nations should be understood as a product of the age of nationalism, how can such a view fit with the claim that China is a nation with several millennia of history to boast of? A new understanding of the relationship between tradition and modernity in China is thus required. At the very least, such an approach must call into question the tendency to divide Chinese history into traditional and modern periods and then to search for links between the two. Instead, the significance of history itself in China must be understood as a product of the unfinished revolution that began with attempts to replace the imperial culture of the Qing dynasty (1644-1911) with an exclusive national tradition designed to articulate what Benedict Anderson might call China's 'imagined community'. In this respect, historical enquiry can no longer be concerned with tracing the history of a given Chinese entity as such, but must rather confront the task of understanding how a Chinese tradition has been articulated as an ideological construct in the service of Chinese nationalism.

If, then, deconstructing Chinese identity is the way forward, it has already begun to yield interesting results in a number of areas. Anthropological research, for example, has begun to disclose how concepts such as race and nation in China should be understood not as objective elements of the natural order but as ideas with their own history and political significance. This is particularly evident in studies which look at areas where the political ramifications of ethnic identity are especially salient, such as the border areas of the autonomous regions of Tibet and Muslim-populated Xinjiang. But the politicisation of ethnicity has also been shown to be active right down to the identification of small groups of individuals in urban centres such as Shanghai.

Bridging the external nation: Hong Kong and Taiwan

Another interesting development that is initiated by a better awareness of the political dynamics of Chinese identity is the possibility of arriving at a new understanding of the external relations of the Chinese state. These relations can be studied on at least three different levels of analysis: relations with communities of people identified as Chinese who live outside the PRC, regional relations within east Asia, and the global international relations of the PRC. Concerning the first of these levels, if the CCP claims legitimacy to rule in terms of the nationalist principle that, as Ernest Gellner puts it, the political and the national unit should be congruent, there arises the problem of the relationship between the PRC state and other territories occupied by individuals defined by that state as Chinese. This applies most immediately to the crises of identity in Hong Kong and Taiwan, over which the PRC claims sovereignty. In Hong Kong this crisis of identity has landed the British government with a dilemma, split between Beijing's demands that sovereignty should be located in the will of the Chinese nation as expressed through CCP dictatorship and the demands of many of the colony's residents that sovereignty should be expressed at the local level through a system of democratic politics.

Yet it is on the island of Taiwan that conditions have sparked off the most heated debate over the relationship between nation and state in Chinese politics. Politically divided from the Chinese mainland in 1949 by the Chinese civil war, Taiwan's long period of separation has left many of the island's 21 million people questioning the nature of their links with the Chinese nation. A process of democratisation which began in the mid-1980s has resulted in the formation of a secessionist opposition party with a manifesto to declare Taiwan an independent republic, an eventuality that Beijing has threatened to use force to prevent. A process of searching for a new definition of Chinese identity in terms that can at least loosen the political bond between Chinese nation and Taiwanese state has been the result. Whether or not the regime in Taiwan can succeed in developing economic and cultural links with a supra-state Chinese community, while maintaining political independence from the PRC, will be one of the main subjects for research during the 1990s.

The international implications of the principle of Chinese nationalism do not stop with the issues of Taiwan and Hong Kong, but apply somewhat less directly, although no less interestingly, to relations between the PRC, Singapore and some 35 million overseas Chinese scattered throughout the world. When this wide diaspora is taken into account, the fact that China indicates much more than just the people living within the territory controlled by the PRC state provides a rich area of research in terms of attempts to understand the nature of what is increasingly called Greater China. How this trans-state identity develops can only have a deep impact on the international politics and economics not only of east Asia but of the whole world. On the one hand, optimists view the PRC's staggering rates of economic growth as acting like a magnet that will lead to new economic formations in the Asia Pacific around a Chinese economy that will be the world's largest at some time in the first quarter of the next century. On the other hand, pessimists claim that the peripheral economies of Greater China may act as a centrifugal force to further erode the control of the central state, already considerably weakened by the process of economic liberalisation. Whatever the outcome, there is much scope for exploring the links not only between nationalist ideology and the right to self-determination, but also the impact of factors such as global economic integration and media links on the formation of national identity.

South-east Asian linkages: the centrality of China

Concerning the relations of the PRC with other east Asian states, China can be seen to be no exception to the general need to reinterpret the international relations of this region in terms of its post-colonial history. As with

China itself, pioneering work has been carried out into how nations and identities have arisen out of the nationalism bred by the impact of imperialism on east Asian cultures. What still needs to be achieved, however, is a comprehensive match between these understandings of the domestic politics of east Asian nationalisms and their implications for inter-state relations. China's central position and massive size must accord its history a central role in determining the evolution of a new order. That the PRC is willing to play the role of a great power is increasingly evident not only from its arms build-up but also from its active diplomatic manoeuvring over issues such as the withdrawal of Vietnamese forces from Kampuchea and influencing an easing of tensions in the Korean peninsula. As with other states in east Asia, the PRC has emerged from the pressures of imperialism clinging to a hard conception of its own sovereignty. But with the historical legacy of imperialism having left many borders uncertain, a dangerous recipe can result from the conflation of territorial disputes with nationalist imperatives. When claims such as that made by Beijing over the South China Sea and its islands are contested by surrounding states, major security threats for the region will arise from the high stakes at risk for regimes eager not only to have access to natural resources but also to enhance their legitimacy in the eyes of their respective populations.

Faced by the challenge of reinterpreting China's international relations, Samuel S. Kim, an eminent scholar of PRC foreign policy, has called for efforts to be made to overcome the dialogue of the deaf that exists between China specialists and international relations theorists. This remains a major task for both disciplines. For International Relations, hopefully China specialists can contribute to wider theoretical debates by suggesting new concepts and tools for understanding the role of national identity and nationalist imperatives in the foreign relations of post-imperial states. Conversely, for Chinese studies, not only is there a need to develop an understanding of the relationship between nationalism and foreign policy, but theories of hegemony and the balance of power should be useful in understanding the effects of the diminishing of Russian and American power in east Asia and how the PRC sees its future role in the area.

Quite how far the PRC can develop a leadership role for the region can only become a matter of increasing concern to students of international relations. The only other candidate for the position is Japan. However, with Japanese imperialism having left deep scars in the Chinese imagination, Japan retains an ambiguous status as both looming threat and model for development. With Japan's post-war economic growth having again provided that country with immense economic power over east Asia, and with recent moves to allow Japan's armed forces to serve overseas, old fears have not been diminished. This has resulted in the continuation of China's uncertain relationship with Japan, on the one hand cultivating good relations through economic and diplomatic activity, while on the other expressing doubts about Japanese intentions when issues such as compensation for women forced into wartime prostitution and the teaching of Japan's wartime history have come to the fore. Again, understanding the condition of Sino-Japanese relations requires a careful weighing of contending nationalist forces, on the one hand, against incentives to regional economic integration, probably under the umbrella of the Asia Pacific Economic Co-operation forum (APEC), on the other.

Regime legitimacy and international integration

Finally, this brings us on to the global international relations of the PRC, where a number of long-standing issues have taken on new immediacy in the light of deconstructing China. As has been mentioned above, the impact on Chinese national identity of integration into both the global economy and the society of states is still uncertain and remains a rich and important area of research. With nationalist imperatives playing such a crucial role in the legitimation of the Chinese state, demands for the PRC to co-operate with international norms in the fields of trade, the environment and human rights tend to be seen as threats to national integrity and raise fears of a return to neo-colonialism. It is in this light that problems such as the PRC's membership of the World Trade Organisation, trade conflicts with the United States, and the export of products produced by prison labour, take on a new political significance that is seen to erode the very legitimacy of the PRC regime itself. Analysis of such issues is interesting not only in the degree to which they may further erode central government control, but also for the wider questions that are raised about the future of sovereignty in a changing world order.

Like the problems consequent upon the collapse of communist states, the relationship between state sovereignty and inter-state economic integration for the PRC provides the possibility of locating Chinese studies within a wider debate and of breaking out of what has been a degree of past academic isolation. Yet what seems certain to force contemporary Chinese studies further up the general academic agenda in the near future is the problem of political stability in the world's fastest growing and largest market following the death of Deng Xiaoping. It is in the context of a generational transfer of power that the forces for integration must be weighed against the forces for disintegration in the PRC. It is also in the context of legitimating future state power that the nature and function of nationalist ideology in Chinese political culture must be understood. Only then will it be possible to understand the true significance of actions taken towards China's own people, towards Greater China and East Asia, and to gain some insight into how emerging leaders see China's place in the world.

Note

1 Lucian Pye, 'China: erratic state, frustrated society', *Australian Journal of Chinese Affairs*, 29, 1993, pp. 107–34.

Further reading

This sketch of the current state of Chinese studies has attempted to reflect the results of a number of pioneering works which are most likely to shape the future of academic research in the context of the momentous changes ahead. Among recent works which directly address the issue of China's national identity is *China's Quest for National Identity*, edited by Lowell Dittmer and Samuel S.Kim (1993), which marks a tentative first step towards analysing this subject from various angles and in various periods. Extremely useful has been a series of penetrating articles on the meanings and ramifications of Chinese nationalism carried by recent issues of the *Australian Journal of Chinese Affairs* (starting with No. 23), from which the Lucian Pye quote above is taken (issue 29). An interesting discussion of ideological continuity between the nationalist and communist regimes in China is Robert E. Bedeski's *State Building in Modern China: the Kuomintang in the Prewar Period*, China Research Monograph 18 (1981). A more recent historical overview of the historical relationship between state ideology and national identity can be found in Germaine A. Hoston's extensive monograph, *The State, Identity, and the National Question in China and Japan*, (1994).

From a more anthropological perspective, Leo J. Moser's *The Chinese Mosaic: the Peoples and Provinces of China*, (1985), is a landmark portrait of the scale of regional diversity that exists among the Chinese nation. More recent pioneering studies of China's ethnic minorities have been Dru C. Gladney's *Muslim Chinese: Ethnic Nationalism in the People's Republic of China*, (1991), and Thomas Heberer's *China and Its National Minorities: Autonomy or Assimilation?* (1989). Both these works draw attention to the politicisation of ethnicity by the PRC party state, which is further explored in the context of China's largest metropolis by Emily Honig's *Creating Chinese Ethnicity: Subei People in Shanghai, 1850-1980*, (1992). Adopting a longer historical perspective, Frank Dikotter has attempted to understand ethnic identification in China in terms of discourse theory in *The Discourse of Race in Modern China*, (1992). For some interesting insights into the relationship between the crisis of regime legitimacy and the impact of global integration on Chinese culture and identity, *Popular Protest and Political Culture in Modern China*, edited by Jeffery N. Wasserstrom and ELizabeth J. Perry, provides probably the most recent account, which benefits from adopting an interdisciplinary approach.

Concerning the emergence of a Greater China, the best starting point is provided by the December 1993 (No. 136) special issue of T*he China Quarterly* on this subject. In *Taiwan: National Identity and Democratization*, (1994), Alan Wachman provides an up-to-date survey of the debates over national identity in the Republic of China. A comparable work on Hong Kong is still lacking, although something of the debate can be discerned from the numerous works that have been produced in the run-up to the transfer of Hong Kong to PRC sovereignty in 1997. A comparatively pessimistic prognosis of the impact of economic reform on China's future domestic and foreign relations is Gerald Segal's *China Changes Shape: Regionalism and Foreign Policy*, (Adelphi Paper 287, 1994). This theme is followed up more comprehensively by a number of contributors to the debate in *China Deconstructs: Politics, Trade and Regionalism*, edited by David Goodman and Gerald Segal, (1994).

A longer-term perspective on the role of nationalism in Chinese foreign policy is John W. Garver's *Chinese Soviet Relations, 1937–45: the Diplomacy of Chinese Nationalism* (1985). The theoretical problems of analysing China's foreign relations are addressed by Samuel S. Kim's 'China and the World in Theory and Practice', in Samuel S. Kim (ed.), *China and the World: Chinese Foreign Relations in the Post Cold War Era* (1994). The same writer has also provided a seminal sketch of the PRC's view of its place in the post-Cold War order in 'Mainland China and a New World Order', in Bih Jaw Lin and James T. Myers (eds) *Forces for Change in Contemporary China* (1993).

Finally, a word must be said concerning the impact of newly available Soviet sources on our understanding of modern Chinese history. Collaborative works between scholars of different nationalities have already begun to appear, most notable of which is the new insight into Sino-Soviet relations provided by S. N. Goncharov, J. W. Lewis and L. Xue in *Uncertain Partners: Stalin, Mao and the Korean War* (1993), which hopefully points the way forwards for another revolution in Chinese historiography.

Further information

In relationship to the size and future importance of China, Chinese studies in Britain are still relatively undeveloped, which presents a challenge in terms of resources but a bonus when it comes to developing original research projects. Although the number of places where research can be undertaken has been growing in recent years, as departments in the social sciences and humanities develop a knowledge of China, access to resources and expertise can still be a problem. The main Chinese collections are to be found at the School of Oriental and African Studies and the British Library, both in London. Outside London, the Oriental Institute in Oxford has a Chinese collection which should soon be moving to the new Contemporary China Institute. Other universities having departments with a proven speciality in Chinese studies include Leeds, Durham and Edinburgh. An optimistic sign of things to come has been the launching of no fewer than nineteen research projects by the ESRC under a Pacific–Asia Programme, several of which specialise in China, while most have a substantial Chinese content. It is too early to predict what the long-term effects of this scheme will be, but information can be obtained from the Project Director, Gerald Segal, at the International Institute of Strategic Studies.

Something that should also be borne in mind is that some command of the Chinese language is increasingly the mark of serious scholarship in the field. This should not daunt prospective researchers, however, because there are exciting opportunities for study in Chinese-speaking territories. The British Council runs an exchange scheme with the PRC for this purpose, while many individuals learn the language while teaching English in the PRC for a year. A different approach is to work your way through one of the excellent language courses run by Taiwan's universities. For more information about such schemes contact: Education Section, Embassy of the People's Republic of China, 11 West Heath Road, Hampstead, London NW3 7UX; British-Taiwan Cultural Institute, 44 Davies Street, London W1Y 2BL.

Chapter 16

The turbulent decade: Soviet and Russian politics, 1985–95

Philip Boobbyer

There is an old Oxford anecdote which says that if you want to create a beautiful college lawn, you have to plant the grass seed and then water and cut it for about 500 years. Perhaps the same kind of story could be applied to the development of democratic political systems. After all, British democracy has roots which go back centuries. Such a leisured approach to time is typical of a conservatism which is never in a hurry to see social and political change. It has its weaknesses in that it can be cynically manipulated to justify any kind of *status quo*; on the other hand, its advantage is that it does not seek to impose solutions on societies which are not yet ready for them. The liberal alternative also has its pros and cons. Its impatience with injustice and inequality and its defence of individual liberty are vital components of a healthy society; at the same time, the very impatience can also lead to the introduction of abstract systems of good government which are entirely alien to the traditional culture of the country.

These kinds of general dilemma about how quickly societies can and should change are typical of those faced by both Gorbachev and Yeltsin as they have sought to transform Soviet and Russian politics and society. Their dilemmas have been made much more difficult because the Soviet Union was no ordinary polity. Most, if not all, scholars would agree that the Stalinist political system was totalitarian, meaning that it attempted a form of total control which was something much more sinister and all-embracing than in traditional authoritarian societies. To a considerable extent that system had changed by the time Gorbachev came to power. Indeed, the USSR's literacy rates, education system and levels of urbanisation suggested that it was very much a modern industrialised society. The political system, however, had not caught up with the process. Although decision-making was more consultative than under Stalin, the system was still unaccountable, the Communist Party continued to vet all important appointments, the economy remained highly centralised and the KGB retained its dominant guardian role in society.

As important, however, as the structures of Soviet society was the fact that a totalitarian mentality had been internalised by much of the population. One reason for this was that the KGB, through its network of informers had created an atmosphere of fear and suspicion. People's private thoughts were given little public space for expression. To use an Orwellian phrase, doublethink – the enormous gulf between public and private thoughts and lives – had become endemic. The economic system was also a factor. Apart from people's right in the countryside to use their own agricultural plots, there was no private property to look after, and no private business to be responsible for. The capacity to take initiative was severely affected. In 1983 a top Soviet sociologist, Tatiana Zaslavskaia, published what has come to be known as the 'Novosibirsk Report' in which she stated that the Soviet crisis had its roots in the 'human factor': the fact that the mass of the Soviet population felt unengaged in Soviet economic life. The system of incentives had completely failed. Indeed, a 'you pretend to pay us and we pretend to work' mentality was widespread, as indeed was a high level of alcoholism which was rooted in the subsequent cynicism. These, then, were some of the factors which contributed to a kind of victim mentality. And these features were accentuated by the fact that the bulk of the Soviet population had been born since the revolution and had no experience of any other system.

Gorbachev and the problem of reform

To say these things is not to say that Western liberal democracies have discovered all the answers or do not express any of the same features. Far from it. But it is important to appreciate the nature and depth of the crisis faced by Gorbachev when he came to power in March 1985. The Soviet Union remained on the surface a super-power, but to maintain that position in the world it would have to undergo serious reform. Gorbachev, who had travelled in the West and had many friends who belonged to the reformist 'men of the 1960s' generation, was well aware of this. What is less clear is whether he had a real strategy to address the situation. The likelihood is that he wanted to improve the Soviet system radically but not to transform it altogether. He was still a communist, his life had been spent serving the Communist Party, and he did not knowingly question the legacy of the Bolshevik revolution itself. Indeed, his book of 1987, *Perestroika*, was full of phrases demanding a return to traditional Leninist principles.

What were Gorbachev's options? In theory, he could have adopted a Chinese-style approach to reform, introducing market mechanisms but maintaining tight control over the political process. His problem was that his own communist bureaucracy was basically against radical economic reform and was stuffed with hangovers from the Brezhnev era of stagnation. Thus, starting with the plenum of the party's Central Committee of January 1987, he was forced to go down the road of political reform in order to introduce a younger, more reform-oriented generation into the leadership. While attempting to keep the Communist Party's leading role in society, he introduced various democratic mechanisms into the political process which culminated in mass, nationwide elections in March 1989 to a new Soviet Congress of People's Deputies. In 1987 he also introduced a Law on State Enterprises, which aimed to introduce certain market mechanisms into the economy. In effect, he thus embarked on a programme of radical political and economic reform at the same time.

The result was a veritable revolution. In itself the formation of the Soviet Congress of People's Deputies, and its proceedings, which were televised across the country, was something completely new in Soviet political life. For the first time since 1917 open debate became possible. Very briefly, Gorbachev looked like the herald of a new order, and he was championed both at home and abroad. Unfortunately for him, the democratic process got out of hand. Free discussion of issues, permitted by the policy of *glasnost* (openness), was designed to engage the Soviet population in the reform process. However, open discussion soon went beyond that, to open up the underbelly of Soviet history for inspection. Openness about the nature of Stalinism led on to a reassessment of Leninism itself. Some began to question the right of the Communist Party to maintain its leading role in society. Others, from the non-Russian republics of the USSR, began to demand greater autonomy, and the leaders of the Baltic states, in questioning the validity of the Nazi–Soviet pact of 1939, when they had been forcibly annexed into the USSR, cast doubt on the legitimacy of the Soviet Union itself.

The nationalist question

The rise of nationalism was, in fact, crucial to the Soviet Union's demise. The USSR was in theory a federal state, constructed on the basis of a free agreement of fifteen republics to cede power to the centre, from which they could secede at any time. Each republic had its own institutions and language. At the same time, the system of decision-making was rigidly hierarchical. Party and governmental institutions in those republics were subordinate to all-union institutions at the centre. The mixture of a federal and a highly centralised state was well summed up in Stalin's original description of the Soviet state: 'national in form, socialist in content'. However, by tying nationalities to specific territories, giving them their own institutions – however small the scope of their decision-making – creating something of a modern urban culture in these republics, and formally giving them the right to secede, Soviet federalism created the basis for the emergence of new nation states. When Moscow's control started to weaken, when Gorbachev started to dismantle aspects of the command system of the economy, when the full story of Soviet oppression in the

Ukraine, the Baltics and Central Asia was told, the unity of the Soviet Union itself came into question. A crucial event here was the elections to the new republican parliaments in the spring of 1990. The new leaders of the republics suddenly had a democratic mandate, something which Gorbachev himself, who never stood in nationwide elections, lacked.

By spring 1990 power had started to slip from Gorbachev's hands. Reform from above had become reform from below. Where Gorbachev had been the initiator of change, it suddenly seemed that he was reacting to events and issues. The Communist Party began to split. A coherent democratic political opposition began to emerge. Huge demonstrations in early 1990 forced Gorbachev to accept the abandonment of Article 6 of the Soviet constitution which guaranteed the Communist Party's leading role in society. The democrats moved to the left and demanded a move towards a liberal democratic state. The communists and Soviet nationalists moved to the right, calling for a slowdown in the reform process. In the summer of 1990 different plans for economic reform were offered: one by the Soviet Prime Minister, Nikolai Ryzhkov, offered a gradualist vision of change which was tentative about a radical move to the market; another, the 500-day Shatalin plan suggested a Polish-style shock-therapy approach to economic reform. Gorbachev found himself in the centre of these competing visions, but lacking either a clear perspective of what policy to follow or, perhaps, even the power to carry it through. And into the emerging void stepped Boris Yeltsin and the Russian republic.

It is easy to see all these things with hindsight. It is easy to be critical of Gorbachev's politics because they led to the collapse of his regime. At the same time, hardly anyone, from Russian dissident to Western sovietologist, really believed that the Soviet system was reformable at all in such a radical way, or considered that the Soviet Union would turn out to be so fragile. Gorbachev can hardly be criticised for not seeing what no one else could see. His greatest quality, although ironically it was also a cause of his fall from power, was his reluctance to use force to preserve the old system. Values, as well as power, were important to him, and he paved the way for a relatively peaceful transition from Soviet rule in a way which would have been almost unthinkable a few years before. With all that, with hindsight, much of his political strategy does appear a muddle. He wanted to involve the population in policy-making but to keep control at the same time. He wanted openness in order to support his policies, but was less enthusiastic when it turned against him. He attempted to set up a socialist legal state with its checks and balances, but only reluctantly conceded the idea of a multi-party system. Gorbachev's policies can easily be compared, for example, to the ambiguous reformism of Tsar Alexander II in the nineteenth century. The motive behind them was a desire, as it was for Alexander II, to preserve the power and influence of the regime. Reforms were seen to be needed, but the ultimate ends were ambiguous. Gorbachev was undoubtedly a great reformer, but one about whose intentions there will always be some uncertainty.

The Yeltsin factor

Yeltsin was party secretary in Sverdlovsk (now Ekaterinburg) before Gorbachev called him to Moscow in 1985, where he took over as First Secretary of the Moscow Party. In 1987 he clashed with Gorbachev and the conservative Yegor Ligachev and was forced out of the Politburo in humiliating circumstances. He re-emerged as a deputy for the Moscow region at the 1989 congress. The secret of his rapid rise to power was that he came to represent certain new interests. In the first place he ostentatiously left the Communist Party in the summer of 1990 and found himself a co-leader of the emerging camp of committed democrats. Secondly, however, he became in June 1990 the first speaker of the newly created Russian parliament. The parliament, which immediately declared its sovereignty over the territory of the Russian Federation within the USSR, offered an alternative power base to Soviet institutions. The result was that Yeltsin also won the loyalty of an emerging Russian nationalist opinion.

Events came to a head in the famous August *coup* of 1991 when opponents of the reform process attempted to seize power. The immediate cause of the *coup* attempt was dissatisfaction among conservatives with the forthcoming revised Union Treaty that Gorbachev was about to sign with some of the republics. At the same time, conservative forces had been increasing their pressure on Gorbachev since the end of 1990. Yeltsin's vigorous denunciation of the attempted *coup* immediately drew the support of the Moscow democratic intelligentsia. The armed forces were divided: many of their younger members were attracted by the strong leadership of Yeltsin and tired of the old communist establishment. Gorbachev's leadership suddenly appeared weak and indecisive, especially when, on returning to Moscow after his seclusion in the Crimea, he continued to declare his commitment to the cause of socialism. The result was that the centre of power moved from Gorbachev to Yeltsin and from Soviet to Russian institutions. It was the Russian rather than the Soviet government which was now taking the decisions. When Gorbachev was unable to conclude yet another revised Union Treaty in the months that followed, the Soviet Union found itself without its constituent parts. At the end of December it ceased to exist.

At the end of 1991 Gorbachev and Yeltsin presided over different institutions, Soviet and Russian, which had different strategies for the future. A similar split occurred in the first years of the Yeltsin era. Yeltsin was elected President of the Russian Federation in a nationwide vote in June 1991. He was backed by the Russian Congress of People's Deputies during the *coup*, and in November 1991 they gave him emergency powers to proceed with radical reforms. Yeltsin immediately introduced a number of ministers into the government who had a commitment to radical political and economic reform. They included the economist Yegor Gaidar, who became the architect of the rapid programme of privatisation which was launched from January 1992 onwards. However, the Russian Congress, which had been elected in early 1990, was actually full of conservatives, who became very anxious about the direction of change. So from April 1992 onwards there started to occur a backlash against Yeltsin's programme of radical economic reform. Gaidar and his 'Chicago boys', as they were sometimes called, were accused of importing Western economic ideas and forcing them on to a Russian body politic which traditionally had been built on collectivist values.

A new Russian identity

During the nineteenth century there had been a major debate among Russian intellectuals about Russia's role and destiny in the world. Two camps – Slavophiles and Westernisers – argued for different visions, the former arguing that Russia had its own unique traditions and beliefs, different from those of western Europe, the latter that Russia should become more rational and Western in its mode of development. This discussion was intertwined with debates about modernisation, and about whether Russia needed to pass through a capitalist stage of development. These nineteenth-century debates were, in a way, repeated in the early 1990s. Russia had to address the question of her identity in a post-imperial and post-Soviet world. Already in the 1970s the Russian dissidents, Alexander Solzhenitsyn and Andrei Sakharov had suggested very different visions of the future: the former arguing for a combination of liberal principles with Russian national and Orthodox values, the latter calling for a more secular, rational, liberal democratic approach. Similar discussions in the early 1990s were given added immediacy by the rapid economic reform programme. Gaidar's reforms, which have been broadly pursued by his successors were defended by some as the best chance of moving out of a disastrous economic decline and rescuing the country from corruption, centrism and autocracy. Others, the more extreme of whom also called for the restoration of the former USSR, were fiercely critical of what they perceived to be the artificial introduction of Western techniques of government and management. These criticised the social dislocation caused by radical reform, the loss of identity and security felt by many as one system of values was swept away.

This debate came to be focused on Yeltsin's struggle with the Russian Congress of People's Deputies, led by its speaker, Ruslan Khasbulatov. The immediate reason for the struggle was this battle over differing visions of the speed of economic reform. The situation was worsened by the fact that the Russian constitution was ambiguous about whether the President or the congress had the ultimate authority. So the conflict also became a struggle over the constitution, and beyond that over the kind of state Russia should become. What kind of constitution would be best for Russia? Would a presidential system be better suited to Russia's autocratic traditions, and more effective at a time of transition? Russia, formally entitled the Russian Federation, is a multi-ethnic state. How much power, then, should Moscow give her autonomous republics, such as Chechnya and Tatarstan, and her wealthy regions? How indeed could Moscow hold together the many forces which could easily pull Russia apart? Both Yeltsin and parliament came up with their own alternative constitutions. Not surprisingly, they both favoured solutions which would enhance their own power.

The political struggle for Russia

Initially the struggle came to a head in spring 1993, when the congress narrowly failed to impeach the President, and when the country, in a national referendum, voted its confidence in Yeltsin and his economic reforms. However, Yeltsin still proved unable to push his own constitution through. In September he suspended the parliament, and the result was a two-week showdown which resulted in an attempt to seize control of Moscow by Khasbulatov and other parliamentary hard-liners. Yeltsin survived with the backing of the military, and pushed through new elections to the Russian parliament in December as well as a plebiscite to introduce a new presidential-style constitution. Thus, on the face of it, Yeltsin won his struggle against the parliament. At the same time, the success of the ultra-nationalist Vladimir Zhirinovsky in the elections in December 1993 pointed to the fact that the Russian electorate itself was and remains very volatile. The presidential constitution, which puts so much power in the hands of one man, could be misused if an extreme nationalist or communist leader came to power.

The constitution which was passed in December 1993 is heavily weighted in favour of the President. Indeed, it has been likened to the constitution of France's Fifth Republic, introduced by de Gaulle in 1958. The Russian President is commander-in-chief, as well as head of state, nominates his own Prime Ministers, makes appointments to the Supreme Court, can suspend the constitution in times of national emergency, and can be impeached only with great difficulty. The parliament is divided into two houses: the Upper House, called the Council of the Federation, which has 178 seats, and which represents Russia's eighty-nine regions and republics, and the Lower House, the State Duma, which has 450 deputies, half of whom are elected by a Westminster-style 'first past the post' system, and the other half by proportional representation. Although the parliament's power is limited, it does provide a forum for public opposition to the government, a framework for the development of Russia's new political parties, many of which are still vehicles for powerful personalities, and for the development of a committee system. And in these matters it has been moderately successful. Time alone will tell whether the constitution will manage to keep the Russian Federation together. However, at least the formal struggle for power between President and parliament has been resolved.

The fact that the institutional framework of democracy is in place should not obscure the fact that no radical change of outlook, either in the new political elites or among the population at large, has actually occurred. The Soviet mentality will take a long time to change. This is important for the West to bear in mind. It can export any amount of technical aid, but to export the moral underpinnings of trust and responsibility which make democracy healthy and stable is of a different order altogether. The Russians have two words for freedom: *volia* and *swoboda*. The first of them implies anarchic freedom; the second assumes that freedom goes along with duties and responsibilities. To know the balance between freedom and responsibility is the sign, surely, of a healthy mind. It is that balance which Russia most needs.

An attempt to offer the second kind of freedom is one of the greatest challenges presented to the Russian media. The emergence of independent newspapers, such as *Segodniia* (Today) and *Nezavisimaia Gazeta* (The Independent), and television stations, such as NTV, suggests that a robust intellectual class which will not be intimidated by government is genuinely in the making. Indeed, in regard to the invasion of Chechnya and the subsequent war there, the media proved themselves very resilient in the face of government intimidation. At the same time, recent attempts to ban the advertising of alcohol and cigarettes indicates concern that the media could easily become the channel through which certain commercial interests could try to force themselves on a population which has lived for years under communism and perhaps does not yet know how to defend itself against them. For many, access to Western life styles and the immediate consumer happiness it is associated with has meant a profound culture shock. There is a deep underlying need in modern Russia for the recreation of the responsible individual – in a way, the recreation of a self: neither a victim of Soviet communism, nor a sponge of the worst aspects of the consumer society.

The challenge, then, is the creation of democratic minds as well as institutions. The values of the new political elites will be important in this regard. In his memoirs, *The View from the Kremlin*, Yeltsin criticises one of the architects of the democratic reform process, Gennady Burbulis. He suggests that Burbulis was the first of the new Russian elite to be corrupted by the privileges of high office, and that his ability to carry through his reform programme was impaired by jealousy and ambition.[1] He couldn't work with other people. Unfortunately, both Yeltsin himself and his administration have also become tarred by the atmosphere of corruption and self-seeking – which plays directly into the hands of those who seek for a return to the old regime. Corruption is perhaps inevitable at times of rapid transition, but it still remains an important issue. It is part of the Soviet legacy that people learned to give and take orders but not to be ultimately responsible. And democracy and a healthy civil society depend finally on the internalisation of an attitude of responsibility. It is true that the purpose of democratic institutions is to manage conflict: they provide a framework for controlling the worst in human nature. However, without a new sense of responsibility, the Russian institutions of today could easily become a framework for the domination of mafia or military interests. The freedom not to be bought is a priceless quality in a democracy, and it will depend on the existence of enough people who will put principle above ambition. Machiavelli, writing on the 'Transition from servitude to freedom' in *The Discourses*, notes the disastrous influence of corrupt leaders on public life and liberty.[2] Corrupt leaders, he suggests, create corrupt nations. So Russia needs political leaders with real moral stature, as well as stable and working democratic institutions. A stable polity and a healthy civil society depend on the quality of the people who are responsible for it.

How far has Russia come? Can a corrupt semi-democratic country with decades of tyranny behind it turn into a healthy polity in just a few years? Surely not. Nevertheless, during the process of state-building of the 1990s, Russia has laid the groundwork for democratic government, a system of private property defended by the rule of law and a functioning market. For all her problems, Russia, a decade since Gorbachev came to power, has come a remarkably long way.

Notes

1   *The View from the Kremlin*, Boris Yeltsin (1994), p. 158.
2   N. Machiavelli, *The Discourses*, (ed.) B. Crick (1983), p. 158.

Further reading

G. Hosking, *A History of the Soviet Union* (1990).
G. Lapidus, (ed.), *The New Russia: Troubled Transformation* (1995).
D. Remnick, *Lenin's Tomb* (1993).
A. Roxburgh, *The Second Russian Revolution* (1991).
A. Sakharov, *Memoirs* (1990).
R. Sakwa, *Russian Politics and Society* (1993).
A. Solzhenitsyn, *Rebuilding Russia* (1991).
A. Stanger, 'Refounding by referendum: De Gaulle and Yeltsin', *Oxford International Review*, winter 1994, pp. 71–4.

Chapter 17

Forward into history:
the liberalisation of eastern Europe

Julia Buxton

The swift and dramatic collapse of the communist regimes in eastern Europe was heralded as the 'End of History',[1] the final victory of capitalism over the socialist model. It was a development of profound political and historical significance, the global assertion of democratic hegemony and the end of the bipolar configuration that shaped the twentieth century. For the victorious opposition movements it was a return to western Europe, a liberation from the alien bondage of the Soviet Union.

Far from inaugurating a period of democratic evolution and political stability, events in the region during the 'transition' phase have forced a re-examination of previously held assumptions and paradigms. The civil war in the former Yugoslavia, the division of Czechoslovakia, the recent electoral success of the reformed communists, and popular disaffection with the political systems, have exposed the fallacious assumption that the democratisation of the region would be a simple, linear movement towards Western constitutional and economic forms. Fundamental to the contemporary problems of democratisation is the legacy of the region's historic evolution, both prior to and during the communist period. This chapter will offer an overview of east Europe's history and the social and political configurations it has shaped.

Nationalism and new states: a difficult birth

Poland, Hungary, Czechoslovakia, Romania, Bulgaria, Albania and Yugoslavia were reconstituted or founded following the collapse of the Austro-Hungarian and Ottoman empires in 1918. Established on Wilson's Principles of National Self-determination, the formation of the states was a victory for the nationalist movements that had campaigned for independence in the region throughout the nineteenth century. Although inspired by Western nationalism, the ideology was involuted by the east European elites, forging an exclusivist basis for the new nation states.

This was related to the divergent social and historical evolution of the East and West. In the Western experience, nationalism was a democratic ideology, formulated as a repudiation of oppressive absolute government. Significantly, the existing Western states were ethnically homogenous and economically advanced. Eastern Europe provided a divergent context for the development of the nationalist movements. They were primarily elite-led, representing disaffection with the prevailing distribution of power within the empires. The region was ethnically heterogeneous and economically retarded and the focus of the campaign was the creation of a new state. This underlies the chauvinistic element of east European nationalism, which mobilised putatively rooted ethnic identities for elite ends.[2]

Nationalism played a role in cementing popular loyalties to the new states, to the detriment of the sizeable ethnic minorities. Racism and discrimination undermined loyalty to the regimes, generating powerful secessionist movements. In Czechoslovakia the Germans and Slovaks became increasingly disaffected by the centralising tendencies of Prague, a situation paralleled in Yugoslavia, where the Croat Peasant Party bitterly opposed Serbian domination. The nationalist problem was compounded by the economic weakness of the new states, a result of the breakdown of traditional empire markets and the impact of the Depression in the mid-1930s. A more fundamental dilemma was the absence of a bourgeoisie capable of playing a leading role in the modernisation of the region. Potential entrepreneurs were absorbed into the state bureaucracy, which dominated the political and economic system.

With the exception of Czechoslovakia, none of the new states established legitimate and functioning democratic institutions. Although copying the Western constitutional framework, political parties were elite friendship circles, lacking a wider constituency and devoid of ideology. Elections were subject to fraud, parties were frequently banned and electors intimidated. Again, apart from in Czechoslovakia, the communist parties were illegal, representing a pervasive fear of Bolshevik influence. The main beneficiary of the political elites' failure to develop effective institutions and arrest economic decline was the far right. The Arrow Cross in Hungary and the Iron Guard in Romania mobilised popular antipathy to the traditional elite. Ultimately, the veneer of democracy was replaced by outright authoritarian government, either monarchical or civil, as in Poland with Pilsudski, in Bulgaria with King Boris and in Romania with King Carol.[3] The nationalist foundations of the state and the lack of an integrated civil society in this period are fundamental to understanding the problematic nature of contemporary democratisation. In effect the communists 'froze' (or, in the case of nationalism, exacerbated) the historical experience, only for it to thaw following the collapse of 1989.

The communist take-over

After 1943 the Red Army swept through eastern Europe, liberating the region from German occupation. Apart from Yugoslavia and Albania, where Tito and Hoxha were victorious without Soviet assistance, this gave Stalin a commanding position in the area's reconstruction. The communist take-over was rapid, aided by the absence of coherent opposition, which had either been discredited, as in the case of the right, or annihilated by the German forces, as in the case of the social democratic left. The communists also garnered significant popular support, principally because of their role in the resistance and the ideological appeal of a modernising and egalitarian state following the devastation of the war.

The take-over can be sequenced as in Seton Watson's model.[4] Initially the communists formed part of a genuine coalition with opposition forces. Having consolidated their position in key Ministries and at local government level, the communists forced their socialist allies into a bogus coalition, finally advancing to the monolithic bloc stage during which the pretence of a national democratic orientation was subsumed by overt pro-Sovietism and the duplication of the Stalinist model. This latter stage was controlled and centrally directed by Moscow.

The Stalinist experience, 1949–53

The Stalinist system was exported in its entirety to eastern Europe, with the exception of Yugoslavia, where Tito had sufficient domestic legitimacy to develop an indigenous socialist model. The east European economies were modelled on the Soviet command system, characterised by the elimination of market relations. These were replaced by central planning, formulated and administered by the expanding bureaucratic apparatus. Agriculture was collectivised and priority was placed on the development of labour-intensive heavy industry at the expense of light industry and consumer durables. The model enabled rapid initial growth, whilst locking the economies into the same structural inefficiencies and irrationalities that had developed in the Soviet system.

The political equivalent of the monopolistic role of the state in the economy was the monolithic position of the party in society. The parties claimed that their legitimating ideology, Marxism-Leninism, was the embodiment of rationality and truth was used as a pretext to eliminate alternative organisations, values and ideologies. This gave the communists a monopoly of power, organisation and initiative. To acculturalise the population to the communists' value system, the cult of Stalin, ritual glorification of the Soviet Union and the 'terror' were transplanted to eastern Europe. Show trials and the purging of 'Titoist' elements reinforced the political message that the absolute domination of the Communist Party could not be resisted. The system was 'totalising' in that both the public and the private spheres were controlled, thereby atomising society.

The 'mini-Stalins' – Rakosi in Hungary, Gottwald in Czechoslovakia, Beirut in Poland, Gheorghiu Dej in Romania, Chervenkov in Bulgaria and Ulbricht in East Germany – enforced an alien model and ideology, regard-less of their economic appropriateness or long-term political consequences.

Destalinisation and the failure of reform

The death of Stalin in 1953 was not only symbolic, it removed the central pillar around which the entire political system had been constructed. More fundamentally his death indicated the potential for change and reform. These were necessary, as both the terror and the heavy industrialisation strategy had become manifestly dysfunctional. Stalin's successor, Khrushchev, launched a series of strategic initiatives at the Twentieth and Twenty-second Congresses of 1956 and 1961. They were designed to sta-bilise the system and generate popular consent. Termed the 'new course', the destalinisation process included a reduction of the terror, economic reform and the endorsement of collective leadership.

In 1955 there was a *rapprochement* with the 'deviant' Yugoslav model, indicated by Khrushchev's visit to Belgrade. This legitimised national paths to communism, as opposed to the duplication of the Soviet experience. Whilst signalling a tactical reorientation of party operations in the Soviet Union, the manoeuvre had profoundly destabilising consequences for the eastern bloc. The series of reactions that followed reduced the homogene-ity of the region. It was replaced with greater diversification as the com-munists launched defensive reactions to maintain their authoritative position. In the case of Albania the destalinisation was rebuked, with Hoxha leaving the Soviet sphere of influence and allying his country more closely with China.

The New Course expanded the latitude of party initiative, a recognition that criticism of the system was both possible and necessary. This was widely welcomed by reform communists and the technocratic elite. It appeared to indicate a shift away from the application of dogmatic Stalin-ism. Marxism was to be subjected to scientific rationality in a return to sources which would engender broader social support through its applica-tion in a national context. A deeper contradiction lay at the heart of the destalinisation process. Economic reform required the loosening up of the system of control and central domination. This had to be paralleled by rational and flexible planning, marked by a change of investment priorities. To anti-reform elements this seemed a dangerous policy, as the rudiments of the control system would be negated and the vested interests of the pow-erful heavy industrial lobby undermined.

Ideology was a further obstacle to economic reform as elements of the free-market economy could not be legitimately or feasibly integrated into the command model. As a result, the capacity of the state to recognise consumer requirements was arrested owing to the lack of basic supply and demand mechanisms. Political reform was equally problematic. Although recognising that diverse interests existed in society, no changes could be introduced which would undermine the leading role of the communist parties. Events in Czechoslovakia and Hungary demonstrated the inability of the monopolistic structure to act as a mechanism for recognising and integrating complex demands without generating alternative and uncontrollable political organisations.

East European responses: reform and repression

Not all parties in the region moved forward when the green light was shown in Moscow. Change occurred only where divisions in the party emerged between reformist and pro-Stalinist factions, with the former supported by the intelligentsia and wider population. In Hungary, Czechoslovakia and Poland this confluence of interests propelled the reform process. In Germany, Romania and Bulgaria the regime remained united and moves towards economic and political reform were curtailed.[5]

The repression of the Hungarian and Czech reform movements in 1956 and 1968 demonstrated the limits of Soviet tolerance of national communist models. In both cases, the reformist initiatives of Imre Nagy and Alexander Dubček generated multiple groupings in civil society and the democratisation of social and political life. For Moscow, this posed a perilous threat to the leading role of the communists and the security of the Soviet sphere of influence. The Czech 'Action Programme' emphasised that the party had to earn its leading role in society. The Soviets drew their own conclusion about the consequences of the party failing in its attempts at self-legitimation. The invasion of the two countries arrested all attempts at reform from within the party. This blocked any progress towards national acceptance of the regimes, which were clearly maintained purely by demonstrations of physical force. Although Kadar and Husak, the successors of Nagy and Dubček, launched a consumerist-oriented economic programme to placate society (the so-called social contract), this became increasingly unsustainable in the absence of fundamental economic liberalisation.

The opposition movements

The Czech invasion marked a profound alteration in the nature and tactics of the opposition. It was concluded by Marxist intellectuals and the intelligentsia that the party itself was unreformable and the entire system had to be removed. This ended attempts to reform the regimes from within, signalling a move away from dialogue with the state and towards the mobilisation and development of civil society. Political change was now seen to be a long-term evolutionary process made possible by expanding the spheres of self-directed individual action. Through this process, social forces would be empowered, forcing concessions from the state, culminating in democratisation.

A second lesson drawn from the Czech and Hungarian experience was that physical resistance to the party or the Soviets was untenable. This led to a tactical shift in strategy. Motivated by the signing of the Helsinki Agreements by all east European states in 1975, opponents of the regime prioritised human rights and governmental recognition of constitutional commitments to the rule of law. This was the founding basis of Charter 77 in Czechoslovakia and the KOR in Poland, which defended the rights of workers arrested in the 1976 strikes. The decay of the regimes stood in contradistinction to the expansion of action within civil society throughout the 1980s. Ecology groups, religious organisations and peace movements gradually expanded the spheres of autonomous action and initiative. The parties' monopoly of information and censorship was eroded by the distribution of *samizdat* and the founding of independent publishing houses and covert educational forums.[6] The deveopment of the opposition movements occurred most prominently in Poland, with the Hungarian opposition forces acting as a 'para-opposition',[7] tolerated by the relatively liberal Kadar regime. In contrast, the dearth of opposition organisations in East Germany, Bulgaria and Romania is testimony to the repressive nature of the Honnecker, Zhivkov and Ceaucescu regimes respectively.

Polish Solidarity

The strategy of non-violent and evolutionary change was endorsed by Solidarity, which emerged in August 1980. The movement built on the experience of strike action in Poland in 1953, 1956, 1971 and 1976. The catalyst for the movement's emergence was an ill conceived economic policy which created major economic instability and generated a US$20 billion debt. Following negotiations in December 1980, the PUWP[8] was the first communist party in the bloc to accept the existence of an autonomous and independent grouping in society. Despite the overwhelming strength of Solidarity it was not until September 1981 that the organisation ratified demands for an 'independent self-governing republic'. This challenge to the authority of the party was motivated by the failure of the Gierek and Kania regimes to operationalise earlier concessions. Despite the repression of Solidarity and the declaration of martial law in December 1981, the movement survived underground, finally re-emerging to lead sustained strike action throughout 1987 and 1988. This indicated that, in the absence of major economic and political reform, the regimes across eastern Europe would be incapable of stabilising themselves in the short term. It was not until Gorbachev's accession to power in 1985 that Moscow's hostility to national solutions was lifted and domestic solutions could be sought.

The varied strength of the opposition movements provides an insight into the transition process that occurred in 1989 and the subsequent evolution of the party system. In Poland, Czechoslovakia and Hungary the emergent umbrella organisations acted as a focal point for the campaign for political change and as a conduit for social participation. The absence of similar groupings in Romania accounts for the anarchic nature of the December 1989 upheaval. In both Bulgaria and Romania it was the reformed communist parties that came to power in the 'open' elections of 1990, indicating a lack of mobilisational organisation in society. The contemporary party system has been largely shaped by the process of breakdown and differentiation within the united umbrella organisations.

Towards democratisation

The speed with which the communist administrations collapsed indicated the inability of each of the countries to insulate itself from developments within the bloc and the underlying similarities in root causes. The rapidity of the change ruled out an incremental 'opening' as in the Latin American transitions and the lack of defensive rearguard actions on the part of the regimes contributed to the bloodless nature of the upheavals. Crucial to the whole process was the timing of negotiations between the government and the opposition forces.

It was the Jaruzelski government in Poland which initiated the liberalisation process. The round-table discussions with Solidarity ended in the semi-free elections of June 1989, in which the organisation was allowed to contest 35 per cent of the seats in the Sejm. The overwhelming demonstration of support for Solidarity impelled Jaruzelski to accept the Solidarity candidate, T. Mazowiecki, as Prime Minister.[9] The success of the movement influenced the Hungarian opposition to push for unfettered elections during the round-table negotiations in June 1989. The political liberalisation in Poland and Hungary, in conjunction with the opening of Hungary's borders with Austria, provided a major incentive for the weaker opponents of the regimes in Czechoslovakia, East Germany, Bulgaria and Romania. The replacement of the neo-Stalinist leadership in the first three provided the opportunity for their successors to offer concessions to society. These were inherently insubstantial, as indicated by the continued demonstrations of mass opposition throughout October and November, which culminated in the opening of the Berlin Wall. As a result the Czech, Bulgarian and East German regimes invited leading opponents to participate in Governments of National Understanding, leading to the free elections of 1990.

The fundamental dilemma: a twofold transition

Unlike the redemocratisation of Latin America, the problematic process of regime change has been compounded by the transition to a free market. Since the transition occurred during a period of profound political disorientation, the economic model makes the creation of capable and functioning institutions vital. The perception that the command economy failed absolutely led to a broad rejection of the state's role in economic development. The influence of Western governments and international financial institutions weighed heavily in the reorientation of economic policy. Pronounced emphasis on 'shock therapy' and aversion to 'gradualism' are a result of both Western pressure and the domestic belief that structural adjustment programmes would generate economic stability and growth. It appeared that the Western historical experience could be grafted on to the east European tradition. This failed to recognise that the requisite social and economic configurations were absent.

Primarily, the homogenisation of society under communism in conjunction with the inter-war experience stifled the development of a native bourgeoisie. The lack of private capital and entrepreneurial initiative has left the economy open to foreign ownership of strategic and lucrative privatised industries. In conjunction with growing unemployment and a decline in wages, this has led to union opposition and a growing nationalist backlash.

A second structural weakness is the uncompetitive nature of the region's industry and manufacturing, a product of the heavy-industry bias of the command system. Adding to this problem is the protection of west European markets, which has undermined the integration and acceleration of the east European economies. This would appear to indicate that, far from being replaced by the hidden hand of the market, the state has a key role in promoting selected exports, as in the south east Asian development model. An interrelated aspect is the provision of welfare. The communist period was pronounced in expanding the role of the welfare state, despite the increasing incapacity to provide basic services in the 1970s. The egalitarian nature of these provisions has had a profound influence on society's perception of the role of the state. The cutbacks resulting from the adoption of stabilisation and structural adjustment programmes removed a vital safety net in a period of economic and political turmoil. The consequent division between those with marketable skills and the portion of society reliant on welfare has exacerbated social polarisation. This has not only led to a favourable reassessment of the old system, it has also contributed to political alienation, expressed through declining rates of participation. This development makes the consolidation of democracy more problematic.

The Polish and Czech governments have taken the lead in the application of free-market policies. In Hungary, Bulgaria and Romania the administrations have moved towards a more gradualist approach, fearing the political ramifications of economic decline, inevitable in the initial phases of structural adjustment and economic stabilisation.

The political dilemma

Not only is the dual nature of the transition unprecedented and inherently more complicated, it is occurring within the framework of the communist and nationalist experience. It is these latter aspects which have impeded the development of the fundamental requirements of a democratic polity: an active, participant civil society in conjunction with representative and responsible institutions.

The euphoria following the removal of the communist regimes has been replaced by widespread scepticism and pronounced anti-political attitudes. Opinion polls and the high rates of abstention in both national and local elections are indicative of this development, which has two underlying causes.[10] Firstly, the communist experience of ritual participation has negated the value of political interaction and devalued the pluralist terminology. The absence of intermediary mechanisms such as autonomous organisations has weakened individual participatory experience. Furthermore it has undermined the linkages between the contemporary state and society. As a result, government is still seen as operating beyond the will of the individual, deepening the predisposition to see the political process as remote and abstract.

This development is not solely a residual effect of the communist experience, it has been perpetuated under the post-communist regimes. The transitions were elite-led, forged by the interactions of the intellectuals subsumed within the umbrella organisations. These groups, such as Solidarity and Civic Forum, perpetuated the communist homogenisation of interests, subordinating differentiation in the course of the struggle. Unity was unsustainable following the formation of the post-communist governments, leading to the splintering of the umbrella movements. This occurred predominantly on the basis of personal animosity. Besides making the formation of government majorities exceedingly problematic, as in the case of Poland, fragmentation has not resulted in the diversification of political agendas or platforms. The lack of ideological diversity within the new party systems is related to the dominant support for the free-market economy and the initial discrediting of the left. This operates to the detriment of broader representation and articulation of social interests, compounding political alienation.

The absence of identifiable grass-roots constituencies is a product of the lack of interaction with society. Interest groups remain weak and inchoate, the parties have no local or national organisational structures and policy formation occurs only within the top circle of the party elite. Diminished accountability and participation have undermined the emergence of a pluralist society committed to the expression of interests through democratic and legitimate mechanisms. Interacting with this development is the historical preference for strong leadership. All the east European countries have opted for presidential forms of government, which have provided a platform for prominent individuals. As the new political actors work to define the parameters of their authority, conflict has emerged between President and government. Indicative of this phenomenem is the elevation and increasingly dominant political position of the Polish President, Lęch Walesa. His hostile criticism of the past five administrations in conjunction with his continued interference in the formation of policy has undermined successive governments as the economic situation continues to deteriorate.[11] Similar but less pronounced divisions emerged between the Hungarian HDF administration and the former President Arpad Goncz during the Hungarian taxi drivers' strike in 1991. Both Presidents emerged as forceful national figures arbitrating between the state and society. These actions afforded them supra-political status, a wide perception that both Presidents were above politics, a Bonapartist predisposition that Walesa has been the most keen to exploit. This has not only added to institutional paralysis and instability, it further demonstrates the lack of clearly defined constitutional roles.[12]

The party system

The party system has not evolved on the same left–right spectrum as in the West, or with parallel mechanisms of interest articulation. The absence of a bourgeoisie has undermined the development of a class-based system and the dearth of economic debate has perpetuated the significance of non-material issues such as ethnic rights and abortion. This stands in contradistinction to the multiple, cross-cutting cleavages that characterise Western voting alignments.[13]

Voting patterns have remained volatile, representing the slow institutionalisation of the parties and the weakness of clearly defined partisan interests. The ideological spectrum diverges significantly from that in the West. The nationalist parties have increased their levels of support across the region and the reformed communist parties have made electoral advances.

Initially the left wing of the political spectrum was poorly represented. This was an innevitable result of widespread hostility to both the terminology and the historical experience of 'socialism'. In conjunction with electoral thresholds for party representation, it worked against the social democrats, shifting the entire political system over to the right. The recent re-emergence of the 'left' is due to its emphasis on a more gradual transition to the free market, a sentiment widely supported as the stabilisation programmes began to impact on the population. It seems ironic that the former communists have gained support not only in the Balkan areas but also in Poland and Hungary. Western observers severely underestimated the depth of popular commitment to equality and full employment, which are widely seen as inalienable rights.

The emergence of ethnically based parties is a disturbing yet significant development. In the former republics of Yugoslavia and Czechoslovakia the lack of cross-national parties prevented the party system from generating nationally legitimate administrations, culminating in the disintegration of the two states. The potency of ethnic sentiments in the region, in conjunction with political alienation and economic hardship, has generated a high degree of sympathy for nationalist parties. Inevitably this has contributed to an overriding refusal to acknowledge social differentiation or human rights, particularly those of the sizeable ethnic minorities. This situation is most pronounced in Slovakia and Romania, where the Hungarian minorities continue to face discrimination.

The post-communist regimes have sought to duplicate the Western political and economic model without recognising the long-term evolution that led to the formation of nationally distinct class systems and political institutions. The historically unprecedented nature of the transition, reinforced by the political legacy from which it emerged, makes it difficult to predict the final characteristics of the new states. The overriding lesson of the east European experience is that domestic history and not international pressure has the greatest role in shaping the final contours.

Notes

1 F. Fukuyama, *The End of History and the Last Man* (1994).
2 P. Sugar and I. Lederer, *Nationalism in Eastern Europe* (1969).
3 G. Schöpflin, *Politics in Eastern Europe: the Communist Takeover* (1993).
4 H. Seton Watson, *The East European Revolution* (1956).
5 Schöpflin *Politics in Eastern Europe*.
6 For example, Nowa and Padlock Press in Poland and Czechoslovakia and the Hungarian 'Flying Kindergarten'.
7 Schöpflin in R. Tökés (eds), *Opposition in Easter Europe* (1979).
8 The Polish United Workers Party, the Communist Party.
9 see Paul Lewis, 'Non-competitive elections and regime change: Poland 1989', *Parliamentary Affairs*, 43 (1), January 1990, pp. 90–107.
10 See S. Wolchik 'The repluralisation of politics in Czechoslovakia' *Communist and Post-Communist Studies*, 26 (4), December 1993, pp. 412–31.
11 See V. Zubek 'Walesa's leadership and Poland's transition', *Problems of Communism*, 40 (1–2), January–April 1991, pp. 69–83.
12 See R. Taras, 'Leaderships and executives', in S. White, J. Batt and P. G. Lewis (eds), *Developments in East European Politics* (1993).
13 A. Evans and S. Whitefield, 'Identifying the bases of party competition in eastern Europe', *British Journal of Political Science*, 23 (4), October 1993, pp. 521–48.

Further reading

The inter-war period
J. Bell, *The Bulgarian Communist Party* (1985).
Z. Brzezinski, *The Soviet Bloc* (1967).
T. Hammond, *The Anatomy of Communist Takeovers* (1975).
R. King, *A History of the Romanian Communist Party* (1980).
W. Kolarz, *Myths and Realities in Eastern Europe* (1972).
B. Kovrig, *Communism in Hungary from Kun to Kadar* (1977).
M. McCauley, *Communist Power in Europe, 1944–49* (1977).
M. McCauley, *Marxism Leninism in the G.D.R.* (1979).
J. Rothschild, *Return to Diversity* (1989).
G. Schöpflin, 'The political traditions of eastern Europe', *Daedalus*, 119, 1990, pp. 55–90.
G. Schöpflin, *Politics in Eastern Europe, 1945–92: the Communist Takeover* (1993).
H. Seton Watson, *The East European Revolution* (1985).
J. Szucs, 'The three historical regions of Europe', in J. Keane (ed.), *Civil Society and the State* (1988).
J. de Weydenthal, *The Communists of Poland* (1986).
Z. Zeman, *The Making of Communist Europe* (1991).

The Stalinist period, the command economy and the terror
M. Djilas, *Conversations with Stalin* (1962).
H. Gordon Skilling, *The Czechoslovak Political Trials, 1950–54* (1971).
C. Milosz, *The Captive Minds* (1981).
A. Nove, *The Economics of Feasible Socialism Revisited* (1991).
A. Smith, *The Planned Economies of Eastern Europe* (1983).
A. Szczypiorski, *The Polish Ordeal: the View from Within* (1982).
R. Tucker, *Stalinism: Essays in Historical Interpretation* (1977).
T. Von Laue, 'Stalin in Focus', *Slavic Review*, 42 (3), 1983, pp. 373–89.

Nationalism in eastern Europe
W. Connor, *The National Question in Marxist Leninist Theory* (1984).
I. Deak, 'Uncovering eastern Europe's dark history', *Orbis*, 34 (1), winter 1990, pp. 51–65.
G. Klein and M. Rabin, *Politics of Ethnicity in Eastern Europe* (1981).
J. Rothschild, *Ethnopolitics* (1981).
G. Schöpflin, 'The ideology of Croatian nationalism', *Survey*, 19 (1), 86, 1973, pp. 123–46.
G. Schöpflin, 'The ideology of Romanian nationalism', *Suvey*, 20 (1), 912, spring–summer 1975, pp. 77–104.
P. Sugar and I. Lederer, *Nationalism in Eastern Europe* (1969).

The problems of reform, Hungary and Czechoslovakia
J. Batt, *Economic Reform and Political Change in Communist States* (1988).
S. Bialer, *Stalin's Successors* (1980).
F. Fetjo, *A History of the People's Democracies* (1974).

S. Fischer Galati, *Twentieth Century Romania* (1991).
C. Gati, *Hungary and the Soviet Bloc* (1974).
H. Gordon Skilling, *Czechoslovakia's Interrupted Revolution* (1976).
V. Kusin, *The Intellectual Origins of the Prague Spring* (1971).
P. Lendvai, *Eagles in Cobwebs.* (1970).
O. Sik, 'Prague Spring, roots and reasons: the economic Impact of Stalinism', *Problems of Communism*, 20, 1971, pp. 1–10.

The Hungarian economic model, 'goulash communism'
T. Bauer, 'The Hungarian alternative to Soviet-type planning', *Journal of Comparative Economics*, 7 (3), September 1993.
I. Berend, *The Hungarian Economic Reforms, 1953–88* (1990).
R. Tökés, 'Hungarian reform imperatives', *Problems of Communism*, 39 (6), November–December 1990, pp. 44–65.

The 1970s, decline, decay and the opposition movements
A. Arato and F. Feher, *Crisis and Reform in Eastern Europe* (1991).
J. Batt, *East Central Europe from Reform to Transformation* (1991).
A. Bromke, *Gierek's Poland* (1973).
T. Garton Ash, *The Polish Revolution: Solidarity* (1991).
T. Gilberg, 'Ceaucescu's Romania', *Problems of Communism*, 23, (4), 1974, pp. 29–43.
H. Gordon Skilling, *Charter 77 and Human Rights in Czechoslovakia* (1981).
V. Havel, *The Power of the Powerless* (1985).
V. Kusin, 'Husak's Czechoslovakia and economic slowdown', *Problems of Communism*, 31 (3), May–June 1982, pp. 24–37.
A. Michnik, *Letters from Prison* (1985).
D. Paul and A. Simon, 'Poland today and Czechoslovakia in 1968', *Problems of Communism*, 30 (5), September–October 1981, pp. 25–39.
A. Pravda, 'Poland 1980: from premature consumerism to labour solidarity', *Soviet Studies*, 34 (2), April 1982, pp. 167–99.
V. Sobell, 'Czechoslovakia: the legacy of normalisation', *East European Politics and Society*, 2 (1) winter 1988.
J. Staniszkis, 'On some contradictions in socialist society: the case of Poland', *Soviet Studies*, 31 (2), April 1979, pp. 167–87.
V. Tismaneanu 'Ceaucescu's socialism', *Problems of Communism*, 34, January 1985, pp. 50–66.
P. Tokes, *Opposition in Eastern Europe* (1979).
A. Touraine, *Solidarity: Analysis of a Social Movement* (1983).
J. Vanous, 'East Europe's economic slowdown', *Problems of Communism*, 31 (4), July–August 1982, pp. 1–19.

The collapse of communism
M. Almond, 'Romania since the revolution', *Government and Opposition*, 25 (4), 1990, pp. 489–96.
C. Biberaj, 'Albania at the crossroads', *Problems of Communism*, 40 (5), September–October 1991, pp. 1–16.

A. Brumberg, 'Poland: the demise of communism', *Foreign Affairs*, 69 (1), 1989–90, pp. 70–80.

L. Bruszt, '1989: the negotiated revolution in Hungary', *Social Research*, 57 (2), summer 1990, pp. 365–87.

V. Bunce, 'Decline of a regional hegemony: the Gorbachev regime in eastern Europe', *East European Politics and Societies*, 3 (2), spring 1989.

M. Calinescu, 'The 1989 revolution', *Problems of Communism*, 41 (1–1), January–April 1991, pp. 42–59.

K. Dawisha, *Eastern Europe, Gorbachev and Reform* (1990).

G. Ekiert, 'Democratisation processes in east central Europe', *Britsh Journal of Political Science*, 21 (3) July 1991, pp. 285–313.

D. Friedham, 'Bringing society back into democratic transition theory after 1989', *East European Politics and Society*, 7 (3) autumn 1990.

T. Gallagher, 'The disputed elections of 1990', *Parliamentary Affairs*, 44 (1), January 1991, pp. 79–93.

C. Gati, *The Bloc that Failed* (1990).

Z. Gitelman, 'The roots of east Europe's revolutions', *Problems of Communism*, 39 (3), May 1990, pp. 89–94.

H. Hodgkinson, 'Albania: Hoxha and after', *Political Quarterly*, 56 (3), July–September 1985, pp. 285–90.

A. James-McAdams, 'Towards a new Germany and problems of unification', *Government and Opposition*, 25 (3), summer 1990, pp. 304–16.

A. Karosenyi, 'Post-communist politics in Hungary', *Political Quarterly*, 62 (1), January–April 1991, p. 52.

R. Levgold, 'The revolution in Soviet foreign policy', *Foreign Affairs*, 68 (1), 1989, pp. 82–98.

P. Lewis, 'Non-competitive elections and regime change: Poland 1989', *Parliamentary Affairs*, 43 (1), January 1990, pp. 90–107.

A. Michnik, 'Towards a new democratic compromise', *East European Reporter*, 3 (4) spring–summer 1989.

G. Prins, *Spring in Winter* (1990).

G. Schöpflin, 'Why communism collapsed', *International Affairs*, 67 (2), April 1991, pp. 235–50.

O. Ulc, 'The bumpy road of Czechoslovakia's velvet revolution', *Problems of Communism*, 41 (3), May–June 1992, pp. 19–33.

G. Wightman, 'The collapse of communist rule in Czechoslovakia and the 1990 parliamentary elections', *Parliamentary Affairs*, 44 (1), pp. 94–113.

The problems of post-communist reconstruction

J. Batt, *Czecho-Slovakia: from Federation to Seperation* (1993).

A. Evans and S. Whitefield, 'Identifying the bases of party competition in eastern Europe', *British Journal of Political Science*, 23 (4), October 1993, pp. 521–48.

J. Keane, 'The Polish laboratory', *New Left Review*, 179, January–February 1990, pp. 103–10.

Y. Kiss, 'Privatisation in Hungary', *Soviet Studies*, 44 (6), pp. 1015–38.

J. Kornai, 'Socialist transformation and privatisation: shifting from a socialist system', *East European Politics and Societies*, 4 (2), spring 1990, pp. 255–304.

P. Murrell, 'What is shock therapy? What did it do in Poland and Russia?' *Post-Soviet Affairs*, 9 (2), April–June 1993, pp. 11–140.

D. Olson, 'Dissolution of the State: political parties and the 1992 election in Czechoslovakia', *Communist and Post-communist Studies*, 26 (3), September 1993, pp. 301–14.

P. O'Neil, 'Presidential power in post-communist Europe: the Hungarian case in comparative perspective', *Journal of Communist Studies and Transition*, 9 (3), September 1993, pp. 177–201.

R. Portes, *Economic Transformation in Central Europe: a Progress Report* (1993).

H. Poulton, *The Balkans: Minorities and States in Conflict* (1991).

J. Sachs and D. Lipton, 'Poland's economic reform', *Foreign Affairs*, 69 (3), summer 1989–90, pp. 47–66.

C. Skalnik Leff, *National Conflict in Czechoslovakia: the Making and Remaking of a State, 1918–87* (1988).

S. White, J. Batt and P. G. Lewis, *Developments in East European Politics* (1993).

S. Wolchik, 'The repluralisation of politics in Czechoslovakia', *Communist and Post-communist Studies*, 26 (4), December 1993, pp. 412–31.

V. Zaslavsky, 'Nationalism and democratic transition in post-communist societies', *Daedalus*, 121 (2) spring 1992.

V. Zubek, 'Walesa's leadership and Poland's transition', *Problems of Communism*, 40 (1–2) January–April 1991, pp. 69–83.

Chapter 18

Contemporary conservatism and contemporary history in the United States

Gerard Alexander

The United States has generated one of the Western world's strongest literatures on contemporary history, made up of thousands of well researched, ably written, and memorable texts. This inventory may not be an entirely expected product of the post-war American scene: Americans are often understood to have mastered political middle-of-the-roadism, prosperity, and suburban life at the expense of turmoil, invasions, and other forms of drama susceptible to ambitious projects of individual research and national recollection. This gap between historical appearances and historiographical reality may stem in part from the partially hidden nature of the wealth of America's post-war record. The modern history of the United States is short on Europe's epic experiences of decolonisation, transnational integration, and the occasional *coup* but is, in fact, rich even by European standards, in other ways. Its own epics range from the human dramas derived from the intensely personal nature of the American presidency, to the most nettlesome racial issues in the developed world, which served as the background for the tragedies and triumphs of the civil rights movement, and to a long and painful experience of international war and the domestic discontent with which it was associated, rivalled in the post-war West only by France's own involvement in Vietnam and later Algeria. These and a very wide variety of other events have inspired hundreds of historians to extensive and respectable scholarly efforts.

The middle of the road

And yet, as one peruses the major monographs on leaders, parties, every aspect of government, the economy, the fifty states, changing popular culture, social mores, and daily life, the university, foreign policy, communications, the effects of technology and science, and dozens of other topics, a student not of America's contemporary history but of its contemporary historiography would be right to arrive at a set of critical (and admittedly somewhat exaggerated) observations: these texts are rich in footnotes but short on controversy; empirical findings are lengthy but conclusions are lean; minor disputes between authors are plentiful but real debates are rare; most of these majestic books lack an edge. Arguably, the blandness of much of contemporary American historiography can be traced to the absence from the American intellectual scene of sharp differences between clearly defined schools of thought. In this sense, middle-of-the-roadism is as much a feature of American historians as it is of the American people as a whole, and perhaps more of one. What is missing in this mass of literature is the clashes between left and right interpretations that have often characterised debates between historians in France, Spain, Germany, and elsewhere over the past two centuries. Such clashes may have threatened national historiographical traditions with the spectre of systematic bias, but they also inspired ambitious projects of research and reinterpretation as authors marshalled facts in the course of sometimes intense interpretative competition, often driven as much by an author's desire to set the historical record straight, in the face of an opponent's book, as by the desire to establish the record to begin with. It is, in this sense, no coincidence that in many national historiographical traditions there are at least two 'leading' and opposing texts on each major subject, neither of which is accepted as authoritative by both sides.

The dominant ethos

In the United States, in contrast, a centre-left 'liberal' (in the diluted social democratic sense in which the term is used in America) viewpoint is hegemonic within post-war historiography, and adjectives such as 'authoritative' and 'definitive' routinely appear in the discourse (and book reviews) devoted to the subject. If one of the compelling questions in the study of twentieth-century American history is 'Why is there no socialism in the United States?'[1], one of the most important issues in the study of the contemporary historiography should be 'Why is there no conservatism in the United States?' (again, in the American sense). For most of the post-war period, only a minority of the most prominent works in contemporary history depart from the dominant establishment-liberal view, and even these challenged that standard from the vantage point of radicalism on the left, particularly regarding events in the first half of the post-war period. In contrast, the voice of the right has been largely absent from the public discourse. That has only begun to change, and promises to invigorate this field of study in the United States in the process.

The contemporary history literature can be broken up into large chunks:

External relations

US relations with other countries constitute not a marginal issue but a central one within the field, largely because of the importance of the confrontation between the Western and Eastern blocs from 1945 until the 1990s. The Cold War was not only one of the dominant concerns facing America in the initial years after World War II, but also the country's paramount security concern: for the first time in US history, another nation – a Russia equipped with the atomic and then with the hydrogen bomb – possessed the capacity directly to threaten US survival. Moreover, the framework of East-West hostility and rivalry, and the burdens and opportunities with which America was thereby presented, finally framed much of the overall US experience in those five decades, including Americans' sense of their place and role in the world. Relations with regions other than the Soviet bloc, particularly Latin America and the Middle East, were also important, simply not to the same extent.[2]

The dominant historiographical treatment of both the causes and the evolution of the Cold War is accomplished from the etablishment-liberal view suggested above: most authors have squarely placed the blame for the initiation of the Cold War on Soviet expansionism, but typically did not critique the peoples' republics in the systematic terms later outlined by conservatives. Most prominent scholarly discussions of the 'shattered peace,' including for instance Fleming's, Gaddis's, Yergin's, and Hinds's recent innovative studies, represent varying strands of the same liberal view.[3] The limited range of opinion among the majority of historians concerning the Cold War is exemplified by the comparatively narrow 'debate' over the origins of confrontation between Gardner, Schlesinger, and Morgenthau.[4] In so far as the liberal interpretation of the causes of inter-bloc hostility was challenged, it was by the 'revisionists' of the left, associated most famously perhaps with Gar Alperovitz's *Atomic Diplomacy: Hiroshima, Potsdam, the Use of the Atomic Bomb, and the American Confrontation with Soviet Power*, which portrays Russian build-ups and strategems as defensive responses to American provocation and puissance.[5] The debate over the Cold War clearly demonstrates the value of even this modest clash of ideas between historians: the revisionist challenge to the liberal interpretation of the origins of the Cold War inflamed historiographical energies enough to provoke not only the occasional loss of courtesy (Adam Ulam, immersing his readers in revisionist theorising, concluded, 'We are in the realm of sheer fanstasy'[6]) but also to generate one of the few vigorous debates in post-war American historiography. Most prominent texts which consider the evolution of America's strategy *vis-à-vis* the Soviet Union, including Ulam, Ambrose, Weisberger and Walker, arrive at establishmentarian conclusions comparable to those presented by Gaddis in one portion of his impressive research effort on the question. For him, from the vantage point of 1982, the policy of containment appeared as 'a surprisingly successful strategy: historians looking back on the post-World War II era are likely to rate it as one of the more stable and orderly of modern times, and to give the architects of containment no little credit.'[7]

Containment and Vietnam

The consensus among the liberal historians regarding the efficacy and morality of containment is at its most feeble – as it was among Americans in general – when it comes to that strategy's most sanguinary expression: America's intervention in Vietnam. The dominant liberal historiographical view of the war in Vietnam, like most contemporary analyses of US policy toward other specific regions, stands a full notch to the left of general interpretations of US global strategy toward Soviet power. In the case of the discussion of policy in south-east Asia in the 1960s, this means a movement of liberal historiographical thinking well to the Left of the liberal policy-makers who led the war effort itself: if it was easy at the time to distinguish between liberal hawks like Kennedy, Johnson, and Humphrey, and their radical critics on the anti-war left, twenty years later, it is not as easy to distinguish liberal from radical historians. In almost all texts which have appeared since the end of the war, establishment-liberal historians like Buttinger, Karnow, Sheehan, and Moss essentially echo the radical interpretation of decades earlier, in viewing the US intervention in the on-going Vietnam conflict as a fundamental error, American conduct there not only as professionally inadequate but morally sub-par, and the entire episode as regrettable: in Buttinger's terms it was 'an unforgettable tragedy', in Karnow's 'the war nobody won'.[8] The fusing of liberal and radical interpretations is visible in 'reconsiderations' of the war, such as Salisbury's edited volume, as well as in numerous treatments of the domestic aspects of the war, whether in Foner's discussion of labour, Taylor's of race relations, or MacPherson's and Kattenburg's of the unhappy affairs of the 'haunted' youth at the time and traumatised policy-makers ever since.[9]

If we limit ourselves to prominent works in contemporary history, the response from the conservative scholarly viewpoint to the liberal view of the Vietnam War has been quite limited. The two main dissenting exceptions highlight the ways that opposition can inspire useful research efforts: Podhoretz carefully reviewed the decision-making process and national debate at the onset of war and at various points in its escalation, to argue that the reasons Why We Were In Vietnam were fundamentally idealistic rather than cynical. Guenter Lewy, motivated to respond to persistent, wildly exaggerated, and widely repeated estimates of US atrocities in south-east Asia, has produced one of most thorough pictures of casualties, deaths, and assassinations in the war.[10]

Presidential studies

The domestic discontent spurred by the war helped inform a corresponding crisis of national political institutions, particularly regarding excessive executive power. These concerns inspired Schlesinger to trace the evolution and concentration of that power and sharply to criticise the 'imperial presidency' which was its product.[11] The study of individual Presidents did not, as a result, become less popular. Such studies, indeed, stand at centre stage in post-war US historiography. Much as with biographers of British Prime Ministers, leading biographers of American Presidents are treated as the deans of contemporary historiography, as if the importance of the subjects had rubbed off on their students: the roles filled in Britain by Alistair Horne, Martin Gilbert, and Kenneth Harris are in the US played by Arthur Schlesinger, Stephen Ambrose, and David McCullough. In part because American historians have produced few 'biographies' of administrations or Congresses in the style of Kenneth O. Morgan's study of the 1945–51 Labour governments,[12] it is often the case that the best discussions of national policy and performance in the 1950s, 1960s, and the first half of the 1970s appear in the course of biographies of individual executives.

If these studies of Presidents serve as among the foremost vehicles for examination of the post-war US experience, this literature also exemplifies the central weakness of contemporary American historiography. Many of the prominent texts – each President from 1945 to 1975 is accorded at least one biography that is widely considered authoritative – are written from a liberal perspective, and while rival books differ in their interpretation of minor or even medium-range empirical points, the narrow range of existing disputes is highlighted when we consider the absent debater: we are in possession of no prominent, scholarly, systematic critique of the Truman, Kennedy, or Johnson administrations from a conservative standpoint, despite the crucial role those Presidents played in the successive waves of expansion of bureaucratic power and welfare-state policies in the post-war period. Truman's enduring down-home popularity has attracted considerable scholarly attention. Older volumes include Hamby's *Beyond the New Deal*, Donovan's *Tumultuous Years*, and Ferrell's *Harry S Truman and the Modern American Presidency*. McCullough's massive and recent *Truman* is likely to remain for some time the central study of this President's life and tenure.[13] Ambrose has contributed a similarly authoritative biography of Truman's successor: *Eisenhower*.[14] The abbreviated nature of Kennedy's administration, and the distracting prominence of his death, have led to a relative paucity of studies of American policy from 1961 to 1963. One of the best texts remains Schlesinger's 1965 *A Thousand Days: John F. Kennedy in the White House*, which is equal parts history, memoir, and hagiography. Later studies include Parmet's *JFK*. (Most recent books

examine Kennedy's family, youth, and death rather than his political contributions.)[15]

A number of serious studies exist of two of the most important but most
unromantic post-war Presidents: Johnson and Nixon. Many of these texts
consider ethical questions relating to each politician, but none systematically assesses or critiques the important domestic policy legacies of these
executives from a clear ideological standpoint other than the establishment-
liberal one. The personal and professional histories of both men, more
coloured than colourful, are ably, if at times unkindly, rendered by a 'leading' biography. The most prominent discussions of Johnson career are
Robert Caro's *Path to Power* and *Means of Ascent* and Robert Dallek's *Lone
Star Rising*; neither arrives with Johnson at the White House, and further
volumes are awaited.[16] Biographies of Richard Nixon include Ambrose's
enormous *Nixon*, the studies of Parmet and Morris, and the Strobers' recent
oral history of the administration.[17] For the period after Nixon's 1974 resignation, one of the largest (and presumably temporary) gaps in contemporary American historiography opens. In the absence of prominent
scholarly biographies of Gerald Ford (1974–77), Jimmy Carter (1977–81),
Ronald Reagan (1981–89), and George Bush (1989–93), we must rely for
the moment on autobiographies and briefer accounts.[18] The role which
biographies play as a vehicle for the study of post-war America extends to
other spheres of national politics. To rival existing and forthcoming biographies of national British figures who failed to become Prime Minister, one
may consult important studies, for instance, of Thomas Dewey, Strom Thurmond, Robert Taft, Adlai Stevenson, Hubert Humphrey, George Wallace,
and Robert and Edward Kennedy, as well as biographies of strictly regional
figures such as Robert Moses, whose political engineering profoundly
altered New York's modern infrastructural life.[19]

The civil rights movement

The importance of biographies in contemporary American historiography is
nearly as evident in the recent study of the civil rights movement, perhaps
owing to its highly personalistic nature. Early civil rights leaders are the
focus of two effective biographies: Pfeffer relates the underappreciated efforts
of the labour leader Philip Randolph, and Hamilton has produced an ele-
gant biography of Adam Clayton Powell, Jr – 'Mr Civil Rights' – which manages to be alternately admiring and damning of its bold but troubled
subject. Pearson's recent biography of Huey Newton is one of few extensive
and balanced studies of a Black Panther leader. Given the seminal importance of Martin Luther King, Jr, to the movement, the limited nature of biographical work on him is surprising, although several useful studies exist of
his life and career, including Lewis, Hanigan, Colaiaco, and Fairclough.[20] A
number of other aspects of the civil rights movement have also been treated.

Myrdal's classic 1944 'outsider's' view of race relations in the United States serves as a backdrop. The contemporary historical literature includes general histories of the civil rights 'quest,' including Taylor Branch's acclaimed *Parting the Waters: America in the King Years*, and texts by Cashman and Sitkoff;[21] and more specialised studies of the period in which state intervention in these conflicts crystallised: Burk on uncertain policy during the Eisenhower years, and Stern on the to-and-finally-fro of the Kennedy and Johnson administrations.[22] We have several useful histories of the largest rights movements, including Record's and Kellogg's of the National Association for the Advancement of Colored People (NAACP), Meier and Rudwick's of the Congress of Racial Equality (CORE.), and Zinn's and Carson's of the Student Non-violent Coordinating Committee (SNCC), as well as Van Deburg's consideration of 'the Black power movement', but we are in possession of few satisfying monographs on the dozens of other significant organisations that made up the infrastructure of mobilisation of the highly decentralised civil rights movement.[23] (On the experience of the largest linguistic sub-group in the United States, see for instance Skerry's *Mexican-Americans: the Ambivalent Minority* and Rodriguez's *Puerto Ricans*.)[24]

Considering post-1945 American history in periodised terms, the high civil rights era – dating from World War II and ending perhaps with the 1968 assassination of Martin Luther King, Jr, as he prepared to move his campaign northward and against non-legal forms of racial discrimination – may be the last of the major post-war episodes discussed historiographically almost entirely in establishment-liberal terms. Within a decade, developing experience of America's contemporary history would continue to be interpreted by scholars operating within the liberal framework, but, for the first time in the post-war period, events – and those liberal views – would be subjected to sustained and systematic reinterpretation from a conservative perspective. The cultural and institutional origins of this new critique suggest that the new voices within modern historiography are for all practical purposes a permanent addition to the American scholarly scene, representing a major development within the public discourse over the nation's recent history and the possibility of vigorous and enduring debate over its meaning and direction.

The welfare state

This is exemplified by an important shift in the debate over the welfare state, much of whose contemporary form was assembled in the second half of the 1960s and whose great fiscal expansion occurred in the 1970s and 1980s. The view of most historical discussions of the post-war welfare state, including Burke, Gronbjerg, Wilson, Marmor, Mashaw, and Harvey, and Berkowitz, even at their most critical of the welfare state, is distinctly benign; in their more generous moments, they attempt to spotweld the notion of the gradual expansion of welfare spending to the very conception of the evolution of history.[25] Traditionally, what opposition has arisen in scholarly circles was from the left, criticising welfare-state managers for stinginess and possibly even suspect intentions.[26] Extensive political concerns arose, however, in large part from the fact that the 'misunderstood' American welfare state, while modest by northern European standards, has been associated with the most visibly persistent communities of poor, communities, moreover – and more troubling – whose size and misery have expanded and deepened, rather than reduced, in the decades during which these federal and state programmes augmented and matured. The heated exchanges and marginal reforms of the Reagan era which resulted from this conservative reconsideration in turn provoked strenuous defences of the post-war record by liberal scholars, in the form for instance of Piven and Cloward's *The New Class War*, and Block *et al.*'s *The Mean Season*.[27]

But by the 1980s, a conservative voice was being generated in scholarly commentary on America's contemporary history. Five serious texts of national prominence emerged which subjected post-war welfare programmes to systematic criticism based on a reading of their empirical record since the 1960s: Gilder's pathbreaking *Wealth and Poverty*; Thomas Sowell's study of the divergent experiences of groups whose pattern of national integration with and without the welfare state, *Ethnic America*; Murray's *Losing Ground: American Social Policy, 1950–1980* – without doubt the most influential; Glazer's *The Limits of Social Policy*; and Magnet's recent *The Dream and the Nightmare: the Sixties' Legacy to the Underclass*.[28] At their most generous, these studies concluded with Glazer that policy-makers and experts were 'becoming more uncertain about what measures will be most effective, if effective at all, in ameliorating pressing problems'.[29] In their more ambitious forms, nearly all of these scholars argued that the post-war record demonstrated that welfare subsidies actually constituted important incentives to counterproductive behaviour.

The ideas of Gilder, Murray, and other conservative scholars clearly formed a part of the broader conservative cultural revival in the United States in the 1970s and 1980s, and the physical points from which their work emanated is notable: just as conservative political commentary created spaces alternative to the mainstream (and liberal) print media, largely in radio, so conservative scholarship tended (and tends) to be located outside predominantly liberal universities, largely in think-tanks such as the Manhattan Institute, with which Murray was initially associated. Much of the early work emerging from these institutes concerned contemporary public policy issues too narrow to enter this discussion, but in an expanding number of cases the narrow policy interests of these scholars developed into broader enquiries, were researched in the context of the recent (typically post-war) historical record, and appeared in the public arena not as briefing papers but rather as scholarly monographs. The fact that conservative historiography originated not in random incidents of independent scholarship or precarious journals of opinion, but rather in self-sustaining institutions suggests that its appearance is unlikely to be temporary.

The conservative reinterpretation of the history of the American welfare state is only one of the most prominent examples of the right's emergence into scholarly discussion. Its effects demonstrate the contribution which intellectual competition can make: the recent and on-going policy discussion over the record and direction of welfare, both on the left and on the right, is vigorous, energetically researched, and passionate in a way that much of the literature reviewed above is not. The clear lines of interaction, moreover, between the left–right debate over welfare between scholars and the deepening debate over welfare among policy-makers suggests that the research and opinions of scholars are most useful to their fellow citizens when they are both vigorously advocated and avidly contested. The emergence of a conservative alternative to liberal historiography is by no means limited to welfare issues. General critiques of the Keynesian economy policy which predominated for most of the post-war period did exist, in such classic texts as Friedman's *Monetary History* (which covered the period until 1960), but also in studies by Wanniski, Gilder, Roberts and dozens of others.[30]

The opening of this alternative scholarly viewpoint, and the debates it has helped generate, are very visible in non-economic arenas as well. One recent example is the often strident debate over multiculturalism in the academy, to which Schlesinger, Bernstein, and others responded with substantial reconsiderations of patterns of ethnic and cultural integration in the United States and the dangers both of censorship and of 'disuniting' of the country.[31] The rapidly unfolding national discussion over affirmative action – or preferential treatment for women and members of ethnic or racial minority groups in education, employment, and advancement, long a sacred cow within the boundaries of polite discussion— has come under the critical scrutiny of conservative studies, including Williams, Sowell, and D'Souza (as well as the forthcoming study by Roberts and Stratton).[32]

The new conservative literature suffers a central handicap. It remains not simply primarily but almost wholly concerned with policy-making: scholars of the right tend to research the past so as to nourish debate on the present and future. This is useful, and perhaps a more legitimate, use of scholars' time than studying history for the sake of the past alone. In doing so, they stand in contrast to historians who continue to rage over whether Napoleon or Peter the Great was rapacious or in fact great, who may be seen to be drawing on the politics of the present to infuse and guide their study of the past, rather than the other way around. Because conservative scholarship in America has hardly begun the set of sidelong glances and over-the-shoulder piques of distracting interest that motivate such historical work, they have produced, for instance, no thoroughgoing

193

and nationally prominent reinterpretations of most post-war presidencies (or that of Franklin Roosevelt, for that matter), or of many other aspects of the post-1945 era. Areas of contemporary history on which they have trained their historiographical guns have emerged as among the most energetically debated episodes in our record, as they have thrown fresh ideas into the discussion and inspired many liberals to respond with renewed effort and more creative research techniques. The further that debate expands, the better contemporary historiography in the United States promises to be.

Notes

1 E.g. Werner Sombart, *Why is there no Socialism in the United States?* (1976).
2 The American experience with other regions has generated a substantial literature. See for instance, Ivan Musicant, *Banana Wars: a History of United States Military Intervention in Latin America from the Spanish-American War to the Invasion of Panama* (1990); Tom H. Carothers, *In the Name of Democracy: US Policy toward Latin America in the Reagan Years* (1991); Walter LaFeber, *Inevitable Revolutions: the United States in Central America* (1983); Peter Wyden, *The Bay of Pigs: the Untold Story* (1979); Daniel Yergin, *The Prize: the Epic Quest for Oil, Money, and Power* (1991); H. W. Brand, *Into the Labyrinth: the United States and the Middle East, 1945–93* (1994); Warren I. Cohen, *America's Response to China: a History of Sino-American Relations* (third edition, 1990); Thomas Noer, *Cold War and Black Liberation: the United States and White Rule in Africa, 1948–68* (1985);
3 Denna Frank Fleming, *The Cold War and its Origins, 1917–60* (1961); John Lewis Gaddis, *The United States and the Origins of the Cold War, 1941–47* (1972); Daniel Yergin, *Shattered Peace: the Origins of the Cold War and the National Security State* (1977); Lynn Boyd Hinds, *The Cold War as Rhethoric: the Beginnings, 1945–50* (1991).
4 Lloyd C. Gardner, Arthur Schlesinger and Hans J. Morgenthau, *The Origins of the Cold War* (1970).
5 1965; reprinted, 1985.
6 *The Rivals: America and Russia since World War II* (1971), p. 96.
7 John Lewis Gaddis, *Strategies of Containment: a Critical Appraisal of Postwar American National Security Policy* (1982), p. 357; also, Gaddis, *Long Peace: Inquiries into the History of the Cold War* (1987); Stephen E. Ambrose, *The Rise to Globalism: American Foreign Policy since 1938* (1971); Bernard A. Weisberger, *Cold War, Cold Peace: The United States and Russia since 1945* (1984); and Martin Walker, *The Cold War: a History* (1994)
8 Joseph Buttinger, *Vietnam* (1977); Stanley Karnow, *Vietnam: a History* (1983; revised edition, 1991); Neil Sheehan, *A Bright Shining Lie: John Paul Vann and America in Vietnam* (1988); George Moss, *Vietnam: an American Ordeal* (1990).
9 Harrison E. Salisbury (ed.), *Vietnam Reconsidered: Lessons from a War* (1984); Philip S. Foner, *US Labor and the Vietnam War* (1989); Clyde Taylor, ed., *Vietnam and Black America* (1973); Myra MacPherson, *Long Time Passing: Vietnam and the Haunted Generation* (1984); and Paul M. Kattenburg, *The Vietnam*

Trauma in American Foreign Policy, 1945–75 (1980). See also a journalistic biography of the late anti-war senator from Arkansas: Haynes Johnson and Bernard M. Gwertzman, *Fulbright: The Dissenter* (1968).

10 Norman Podhoretz, *Why we were in Vietnam* (1982); Guenter Lewy, *America in Vietnam* (1978).

11 Arthur M. Schlesinger, *The Imperial Presidency* (1973).

12 One well organised exception is Susan Hartmann's mixture of the two: *Truman and the 80th Congress* (1971).

13 Alonzo L. Hamby, *Beyond the New Deal: Harry S. Truman and American Liberalism* (1973); Robert J. Donovan, *Tumultuous Years: the Presidency of Harry S. Truman, 1949–53* (1982); Robert Ferrell, *Harry S. Truman and the Modern American Presidency* (1983); and David McCullough, *Truman* (1992).

14 Stephen E. Ambrose, *Eisenhower* (2 vols., 1983–84).

15 Arthur M. Schlesinger, *A Thousand Days: John F. Kennedy in the White House* (1965); Herbert S. Parmet, *JFK: the Presidency of John F. Kennedy* (1984); on the family's history see also Peter Collier and David Horowitz, *The Kennedys: an American Drama* (1984).

16 Robert Caro, *The Path to Power and Means of Ascent* (2 vols, 1983, 1990); Robert Dallek, *Lone Star Rising: Lyndon Johnson and his Times, 1908–60* (1991); also Vaughn Davis Bornet, *The Presidency of Lyndon B. Johnson* (1983); and the useful essays in Robert A. Divine (ed.), *Exploring the Johnson Years* (1981).

17 Stephen E. Ambrose, *Nixon* (3 vols., 1987–91); Herbert S. Parmet, *Richard Nixon and his America* (1990); Roger Morris, *Richard Milhous Nixon: the Rise of an American Politician* (1990); and Gerald S. and Deborah H. Strober, *Nixon: an Oral History of his Presidency* (1994).

18 See, for instance, Gerald R. Ford, *A Time to Heal: the Autobiography of Gerald R. Ford* (1979); Jimmy Carter, *Keeping Faith: Memoirs of a President* (1982); Ronald Reagan, *An American Life* (1990); also, Erwin C. Hargrove, *Jimmy Carter as President: Leadership and the Politics of the Public Good* (1988); and John Dumbrell, *The Carter Presidency: a Re-evaluation* (1993).

19 Richard Norton Smith, *Thomas E. Dewey and his Times* (1982); Nadine Cohodas, *Strom Thurmond and the Politics of Southern Change* (1993); James T. Patterson, *Mr. Republican: a Biography of Robert A. Taft* (1972); John Bartlow Martin, *Adlai Stevenson of Illinois* (1976); Porter McKeever, *Adlai Stevenson: his Life and Legacy* (1989); Carl Solberg, *Hubert Humphrey: a Biography* (1984); Stephan Lesher, *George Wallace: American Populist* (1994); Arthur M. Schlesinger, *Robert Kennedy and his Times* (1978); Joe McGinniss's controversial treatment of *Edward M. Kennedy: the Last Brother* (1993); Robert Caro, *Power Broker: Robert Moses and the Fall of New York* (1974).

20 Paula F. Pfeffer, *Philip Randolph: Pioneer of the Civil Rights Movement* (1990); Charles V. Hamilton, *Adam Clayton Powell, Jr.: the Political Biography of an American Dilemma* (1991); Hugh Pearson, *The Shadow of the Black Panther: Huey Newton and the Price of Black Power in America* (1994); David L. Lewis, *King: a Critical Biography* (1970; second edition, 1978); James P. Hanigan, *Martin Luther King, Jr., and the Foundations of Nonviolence* (1984); James A. Colaiaco, *Martin Luther King, Jr.: Apostle of Militant Nonviolence* (1988); and Adam Fairclough, Martin Luther King, Jr. (1995).

21 Gunnar Myrdal, *American Dilemma: the Negro Problem and Modern Democracy*

(1944); Taylor Branch, *Parting the Waters* (1988); Sean Dennis Cashman, *African-Americans and the Quest for Civil Rights, 1900–90* (1991); and Harvard Sitkoff, *The Struggle for Black Equality, 1954–92* (1993).

22 Robert Frederick Burk, *The Eisenhower Administration and Black Civil Rights* (1984); Charles and Barbara Whalen, *The Longest Debate: a Legislative History of the 1964 Civil Rights Act* (1985); and Mark Stern, *Calculation Visions: Kennedy, Johnson, and Civil Rights* (1992).

23 Wilson Record, *Race and Radicalism: the NAACP and the Communist Party in Conflict* (1964); Charles Flint Kellogg, *NAACP: a History of the National Association for the Advancement of Colored People* (1967); August Meier and Elliott Rudwick, *CORE: a Study in the Civil Rights Movement, 1942–68* (1973); Howard Zinn, *SNCC: the New Abolitionists* (1964); Clayborne Carson, *In Struggle: SNCC and the Black Awakening of the 1960's* (1981); and William L. Van Deburg, *New Day in Babylon: the Black Power Movement and American Culture, 1965–75* (1992).

24 Peter Skerry, *Mexican-Americans* (1993); and Clara E. Rodriguez, *Puerto Ricans: Born in the USA.* (1989).

25 Vincent J. Burke, *Nixon's Good Deed: Welfare Reform* (1974); Kirsten A. Gronbjerg, *Mass Society and the Extension of Welfare, 1960–70* (1977); William Julius Wilson, *The Truly Disadvantaged: the Inner City, the Underclass, and Public Policy* (1987); Theodore R. Marmor, Jerry L. Mashaw, and Philip L. Harvey, *America's Misunderstood Welfare State: Persistent Myths, Enduring Realities* (1990); and Edward D. Berkowitz, *America's Welfare State: from Roosevelt to Reagan* (1991).

26 Among the prominent radical critiques are Frances Fox Piven and Richard Cloward, *Regulating the Poor: the Functions of Public Welfare* (1971); Ruth Sidel, *Women and Children Last: the Plight of Poor Women in Affluent America* (1986); and recently, Jill S. Quadagno, *The Color of Welfare: how Racism Undermined the War on Poverty* (1994).

27 Frances Fox Piven and Richard Cloward, *The New Class War: Reagan's Attack on the Welfare State* (1982); and Fred Block, Richard Cloward, Barbara Ehrenreich, and Frances Fox Piven, *The Mean Season: the Attack on the Welfare State* (1987).

28 George Gilder, *Wealth and Poverty* (1980), especially pp. 114–69; Thomas Sowell *Ethnic America: a History* (1981); Charles Murray, *Losing Ground* (1984); Nathan Glazer, *The Limits of Social Policy* (1988); and Myron Magnet, *The Dream and the Nightmare* (1993).

29 Glazer, *Limits of Social Poverty*, p. 6.

30 Also Milton Friedman, *The Tyranny of the Status Quo* (1984); Jude Wanniski, *The Way the World Works* (1978; revised edn, 1983); Gilder, *Wealth and Poverty*; and Paul Craig Roberts, *The Supply-side Revolution* (1984).

31 Arthur Schlesinger, *The Disuniting of America* (1992); Richard Bernstein, *Dictatorship of Virtue: Multiculturalism and the Battle for America's Future* (1994); on a vigorously contested portion of this debate, see James Crawford, *Bilingual Education: History, Politics, Theory, and Practice* (1989).

32 Walter Williams, *The State against Blacks* (1982); Thomas Sowell, *Preferential Politics: an International Perspective* (1990); Dinesh D'Souza, *Illiberal Education: the Politics of Race and Sex on Campus* (1991); the book by Paul Craig Roberts and Lawrence M Stratton, Jr, is being published by Regnery. Alan H. Goldman's *Justice and Reverse Discrimination* (1979) is more philosophical and middle-of-the-road. See also Hugh Davis Graham, *The Civil Rights Era: Origins and Devel-*

opment of National Policy, 1960–72 (1990); and Shelby Steele, *The Content of our Character* (1990).

Further reading

Guides to Archives and Manuscript collections in the United States: an Annotated Bibliography, complied by Donald L. DeWitt, 1994 is the latest and fairly comprehensive guide to manuscript collections, although the number of contemporary political sources is strictly limited. *The Directory of Archives and Manuscript Repositories in the United States,* 1988 is also invaluable. The full guide builds cumulatively from 1959 with a name index for the period 1959–84. It is in annual volumes with good indices, *Library of Congress National Union Catalog of Manuscript Collections* – descriptions of contents are minimal.

Chapter 19

India

Tom Nossiter

On 9 March 1966 the then British Prime Minister, Harold Wilson, announced the reduction of the fifty-year embargo on government records to thirty years and an expansion of official histories beyond the two world wars. One result was ten volumes of the least adulterated records ever published by a government, the history of *The Transfer of Power, 1942–47*, ed. N. Mansergh and E. W. R. Lumby. The volume in front of me, II, *Quit India, 30 April–21 September 1942*, runs to 1,044 pages – and costs £9.[1]

The records of the Raj are prodigious, paralleled by extensive but uneven documents of the nationalist movement and a vigorous though preponderantly urban press. Private papers of both British and Indian actors are copious (India's National Archives in New Delhi, the India Office Library, London, and the South Asia Institute in Cambridge, for example). Out of them has emerged a considerable and often distinguished literature but except in the sense that the past is the present it is not of course 'contemporary history'.

By contrast the serious output on post-Independence history is modest. Paul Brass in *The Politics of India since Independence*[2] lists only some 300 books and articles. Though the listing of significant contributions may not be complete, the order of magnitude is indicative. Two of the classic studies of modern India – Rajni Kothari's *Politics of India* (1970) and Morris-Jones's *Government and Politics of India* (1964) are still widely used in their reprints while Granville Austin, *The Indian Constitution* (1966) remains the basic text on its subject long after the subtitle *Cornerstone of a Nation* seems increasingly inappropriate. All three are major works but they would now need to be supplemented for an introduction to India by Robert Hardgrave and Stanley Kochanek's *India: Government and Politics in a Developing Nation*[3] as well as by Paul Brass. Both are excellent syntheses but also show how much there is to be done to understand the most remarkable political system in the modern world. India is counterfactual to all our assumptions about the conditions for liberal democracy and social stability. Its current population is approaching one billion; there are one million more mouths to feed every month; officially defined poverty is around 40 per cent and life chances are essentially defined by caste facts of birth. The diversity of language and culture is at least as great as that between Britain and Turkey and, though 80 per cent Hindu in religion, it is the third largest Muslim country in the world.

Yet with the exception of two years, 1975–77, when Mrs Gandhi declared a state of emergency, national elections have been held on or before schedule. Turnout has paralleled that in the United States and electoral malpractice has never been such as to vitiate the people's verdict at all-India level. There has been no attempted *coup* and no possibility of revolution. Two Prime Ministers have indeed been assassinated but their deaths were exceptional. Only one other Cabinet Minister has been killed. India has survived what Selig Harrison called 'its most dangerous decades'.

The shortfall in scholarly explanations of why India is a political success story is different from Indian and Western academics. In general contemporary history is a poor relation in Indian universities. Historians have little private practice, unlike medics, lawyers and scientists and the public resources available to them in terms of libraries – outside Delhi – are meagre. Scholarships are few and far between, especially for study and training overseas. West Bengal with its intellectual traditions is brave enough to offer three for doctoral research at selected institutions but the problem is summarised by the fact that the state's population is roughly that of Britain. Nationally there are a handful of prestige fellowships, and overseas agencies play a modest part but in the arts and social sciences India is no longer in general a part of the international community of scholarship, which makes the achievements of individuals the more remarkable.

In funding research government and its academic quangos are reluctant to fund inquiries into the problems or processes of the body politic. India's mandarinate, the Indian Administrative Service, for instance, whose 5,000 men and women manage India, is off-limits as much as are the threats to India's unity in separatism or communalism. It also has to be admitted that in a very hierarchical society the doctoral student or young academic has little chance to arrange interviews with senior politicians or officials, and even professors are often given just courtesy time.

The Western problem is not unrelated. Until the 1990s India had modest strategic and minimal economic significance to the major countries. Now that India is seen as an emerging market this may change, although careful studies of the governance and governability of India will need to be 'marketed'. The decline in the resourcing of language acquisition in Britain illustrates the point.

In the 1950s the servants of the Raj, those who had been in the subcontinent during the Second World War – Paul Scott as a novelist, Harry (A. H.) Hanson on planning or Morris-Jones – and descendants enthused by *Plain Tales from the Raj*[4] wrote extensively on India but that link has been lost. Those who might have replaced them, the children of Asian migrants, typically opt at university for vocational subjects, accounting, law and business. In fact very few universities in Britain offer an option on the government and politics or modern history of India or the subcontinent, and the British Association for South Asian Studies was founded ten years ago precisely to reverse the decline. The recent publication of *India and Britain*, ed. K. N. Malik and Peter Robb,[5] is a good example of the success of this academic activism.

Now that India has gained recognition from the paymasters of research as both the 'last great economic frontier' (Manmohan Singh, India's Finance Minister) and a democracy whose nature and persistence cannot be taken for granted as it was when the Old Harrovian Nehru was its Pandit, the fascination of the world's greatest democracy coincides with career possibilities.

Assuming an interest in some readers, what are the sources for the contemporary history of India and what problems do they raise? One is tempted to say simply that the sources are the problem: too many and too diverse. Taking official publications first, the Government of India and the provincial governments produce copious documentation. In addition non-governmental organisations (NGOs) publish on a major scale. In India the term increasingly refers to social action groups as much as interest or pressure groups. Political parties are less prolific, with the notable exceptions of the communist parties and the Hindu nationalist BJP (Bharatiya Janata Party) and its affiliates. Diversity is expressed not only in the types of records but in language and script. There are nineteen major languages in India – in the north primarily Indo-Aryan and in the south Dravidian. Kashmiri, is neither, and the language of 'my' state of Kerala, Malayalam, has over 450 separate symbols. In practice all governmental records of any significance will appear in either English or Hindi (often both) as well as the originating provincial language if it is not Hindi. English was given a finite life span at independence but then in the mid-1960s was granted an indefinite stay of execution in response to the southern states' refusal to accept Hindi – the language of the north – as *the* national language. In senior administration, business beyond the local level, the professions and much of academic life English is the *lingua indica*. A curious illustration in my own research occurred when I had Malayalam-language press accounts of meetings translated into English to discover that they tallied very closely. The reason was simply that the Malalam journalist took his shorthand notes in English which were then converted into Malayalam in the paper's office. With all those symbols the English typewriter and Pitman's was the answer.

Of course fluency in English is only exceptionally enough for serious research and a second language selected on the basis of the work to be done is normal. However, many projects may require more, in which case interpreters and translators are necessary, but such research services are readily available at distressingly low rates and in my experience are discharged with commitment and skill. High-profile documentation is what readily survives although it is not always easy to find other than in the National Archives. It is also carefully composed in bureaucratic or political code. The dictum that the first question to ask when reading a document is who was writing it, for whom, in what circumstances, definitely applies. Taking the communist movement as an example, national statements are opaque at best and banally obtuse at worst. The 'real story' – a common Indian usage – appears ever more clearly in proportion to the obscurity of the party organ, but finding such documents can be tantalising: the security agencies, the paper salvage man or simply indifference have destroyed far more than inner party sensitivities. Guharpal Singh's *Communism in Punjab* (1994) and Harihar Bhattacharryya's 'Communism in Tripura'[6] show how much is 'lying around' somewhere.

Official government documents are now covered by a thirty-year rule but the transfer of the material to national or state archives is not a major priority and cataloguing is slow and haphazard. It cannot be too strongly emphasised that as so often in India personal contacts or connections are much more efficacious than formal procedures. But beware the phrase 'Come back tomorrow,' which all too often means 'I can't be bothered.' Newspapers and magazines are legion. The major publishers have files and will grant access. Files of cuttings in major houses are usually excellent and older hacks are generous with their expert advice. The Indian press is changing as journalism becomes more of a career and less of a profession and proprietors businessmen rather than fighters for a cause. Nevertheless there is an old-fashioned feel to much of the press, with some very well informed political reporting, many column inches of factual material and a better distinction between 'op ed' and 'straight' reporting than in the United Kingdom. Rival partisan positions are represented but seldom as shamelessly confused with propaganda as now in Britain. Libel law is not such an 'iffy' business, either, so that financial scandal is more fully exposed than sexual peccadilloes. Essentially political magazines are a growth area, glossy in style but revealing: *India Today* or *Frontline*. What is, or has been until very recently, missing is the informational or investigative functions of television or radio. The Indian equivalent of the BBC. Doodarshan, is politically emasculated and in so far as there is any political content it is determined by the government of the day.

Contemporary history owes much to the oral interview technique in the United Kingdom. Potentially this is still more important in India. Memoirs and autobiographies can be illuminating but there is nothing to compare with Benn's or Castle's diaries. Private papers are rarely systematically preserved. James Manor's study of Chief Ministers – the Prime Ministers of the provincial states – is an example of what can be done but it is a rich seam barely prospected so far.[7]

In addition to the advice given elsewhere in this volume, two culturally specific points should be made. First, the distinction in Indian politics and government between the individual and the group is not so clear-cut in Indian life as in much of the West. Ireland is the nearest Western country I know where this fusion (and sometimes confusion) operates. Second, the exclusiveness of categories of political action is frequently blurred, not out of professional necessity to build as wide a support base as possible – America? – but because moral understanding is more embracing than liberal democratic traditions easily countenance. Interviews deal with such questions as the role of the individual great (wo)man, the parameters of political action in a specific arena or how public choices are made.

Since there were giants in the land – the Nehrus and Gandhis – there have been relatively few biographies. The big players operate at provincial level, so reducing the incentive to explore their life and times but expressing the cultural point made above. It may be that the political process is an aggregative activity in which few individuals play a decisive role. As Manor has shown there is a strong case for collective biographies of classes of political actors. Vir Chopra's forthcoming comparative analysis of provincial legislators in five states is another instance.[8] The Indian house of commons (Lok Sabha) has 530 MPs. They represent 930 million people, performing, at least in theory, similar functions to the British MP but so far as I know they have not been systematically studied. The turnover of MPs in India, where there are far fewer 'safe seats' and the sheer difficulty of articulating the interests of constituencies of 2 million to 3 million electors may, however, mean that it is more meaningful to look at the 5,000 Members of Legislative Assemblies. These MLAs are generally more constant political actors and much closer to their constituents. Chopra's work produces several intriguing conclusions from his lengthy interviews: in predicting political outlook, state of origin matters much more than party; MLAs spend much time every day meeting electors but seldom about great matters of state. The request is for help with pensions, jobs and the like but the suppliant knows as well as the MLA that there will be no outcome. Last, MLAs are politically bilingual. They articulate demands from the base and translate the decisions of the top into the idiom of the street and field.

Other excellent illustrations of this approach to the Indian governmental and political process are Sangeeta Ahuja's examination of judicial activism[9] and Apurba Kundu's work on civil–military relations – why there has not been thought of a *coup*.[10] Both are largely based on interviews in their respective arenas.

There remain many other inviting opportunities: the mandarins, for one. Under the Raj they were the 'steel frame of India' (Viceroy Curzon). Established in the wake of the Indian Mutiny (and in the UK by the Crimean disaster) the Indian Civil Service, 1,000 British civilians, backed by 2,500

British army officers, leading a sepoy (Indian) army one-seventh the size of today's Indian forces, controlled a country of some 300 million. By the time Taub published his *Bureaucrats under Stress* in 1969[11] the successor Indian Administrative Service was torn between its historic role as custodian of law, order and tax collection, responsible only to the foreign power, and development functions under the direction of an elected Indian government. Potter expands and extends the analysis, using some splendid interview material.[12] Still further changes have taken place in recruitment patterns, socialisation and training and job specifications but these 5,000 men and women – saints, timeservers and trimmers, and just a few crooks – keep the show on the road. An Indian Hennessy,[13] however, would be faced with not one Whitehall but thirty-three. North and South Block in Delhi, headquarters of the union government, through Uttar Pradesh, with a population of over 140 million, to micro-states of one or two million. Each has its own distinctive political system and bureaucratic personality.

It has to be admitted that the government of India is (unduly) sensitive to attempts to unlock the mysteries of the Block but at provincial level at least the attitude to honest enquiry is more relaxed. Among the issues that attract are the process of planning (Hanson[14]) and the politics of economic liberalisation from 1991.[15] Contemporary economic historians please note: the statistics available[16] and the readiness of senior Indians to respond to intelligent scrutiny offer great opportunities.

Left-wing historians in India and Britain have demonstrated that, even before (qualified) suffrage, the people had their say: in India through peasant movements, in Britain through class struggle. In India since independence there has been a competitive struggle for control of government and the consequent allocation of resources through universal suffrage. In Britain we may argue whether this shift should be dated to 1929 or 1945 but the time period is roughly the same. Likewise the basis of electoral choice has parallels: in India caste and community, in the United Kingdom class shifting over time to informed dealignment. Much money and effort has been expended in Britain on the study of voting behaviour, but in India little, and this is another promising area of investigation.

Surveys of the attitudes of the electorate enjoyed some interest among (American) behaviourally influenced academics in the 1960s and 1970s. The technical problems of sampling and executing interviews were severe but in this author's view the work suffered from insufficient attention to the modalities of Indian society, culture and predicaments. Since the late 1980s political parties have increasingly made use of opinion polling organisations. The press has commissioned 'horse race' polls as Congress's historic dominance of the political system has faded, the BJP Hindu revivalist party has risen as a conceivable national alternative, and most recently the Dalit (the majority poor) movement has challenged both.

Theoretically driven research is almost non-existent, notwithstanding the massive social and economic change of the last decade or so. It could be that conventional survey research even with a theoretical base may not be the immediate way forward. Group discussions, semi-structured interviews and anthropological methods may illuminate more the interaction between caste, community and clientelism on the one hand and the 'feel good, feel bad, feel threatened' factors on the other. At its simplest we have no idea how far, if at all, the appeal of the BJP is atavistic rather than materialistic. Are the 110 million Muslims whom it claims are not truly Indians the moral enemy or the economic scapegoat?

Linked with this but better served in the literature are the political parties competing for the vote. Brass and Robinson in the centenary volume for the Indian National Congress give a sampler as well as an extensive bibliography.[17] Also recommended are Graham,[18] Jaffrelot[19] and Tapan Basu[20] on Hindu nationalism, Nossiter on Indian communism[21] and Kohli with the broad enquiry into how well the party systems, national and provincial, articulate priorities and discontents.[22] Kohli in particular tackles questions of India's fundamental governability, echoing Selig Harrison's 1960 *Dangerous Decades*.[23]

The most recent issue (15 August 1995) of the influential weekly *India Today* offers the cover story 'Preparing for the polls: shifting alliances is the new name of the game as major political parties scramble cynically for electoral partners in the hope of gaining a ruling majority in what could be a hopelessly hung parliament following the 1996 general elections'.

The study of parties in India is certainly as well pursued through the concepts of factionalism, clientelism and (primitive) social movements as programmes, organisation and mass membership but my sense is that whatever the qualities of party leaders and activists one should not be cynical about the electorate, for all the comparatively low levels of literacy. Mass mobilisation melds traditions of real or imagined communities, often layered: the extended family, the sub-caste, through the 'ethnic' group and on to India as an entity of unity in both diversity and conflict. Reference was made earlier to the political irrelevance of Doodarshan (Indian TV) and All India Radio (All Indira Radio) but loyalty to ancient traditions is subtly exploited in electoral campaigning through myth and modern technology: the film stars enter politics – particularly in the south – battling as mythic figures to restore the Golden Age and in the 1990s using VOWS, Videos on Wheels – Japanese vans with state-of-the-art rear projection – to narrowcast their political message in the villages and slums. India's most recent Reagan is N. T. Rama Rao of the Middle Indian state of Andhra Pradesh; its Hollywood is Bollywood. The Cowboys and Indians/Russians of Good and Evil line up in the mythological Battle of Kurukshetra but Middle India is no less sophisticated than Middle America or Middle England. If the god does not deliver – and the Hindu pantheon is considerable – then there is electoral retribution. Mixing metaphors, Middle England was sufficiently fat to take a second opinion within the same practice when Mrs Thatcher's medicine became unpalatable but in Bombay, where 51 per cent of the population are official estimated to sleep on the pavement, the state's 'natural party of government', Congress, was thrown out by Shiv Sena in elections in 1995.

However, the new generation of historians of contemporary India approach their task, exploiting the vast array of statistical information freely available, generating their own data through elite or mass interviews, or culling the primary and secondary records. There is a career ahead and a lifetime of fascination, frustration and above all friendship ahead.

Notes

1 N. Mansergh and E. W. R. Lumby (eds), *The Transfer of Power, 1942–47*, II, *Quit India, 30 April–21 September 1942* (1971).

2 Paul Brass, *The Politics of India since Independence*, The New Cambridge History of India, second edition (1994).

3 Fourth edition (1986).

4 Charles Allen, *Plain Tales from the Raj: Images of British India in the Twentieth Century* (1975).

5 K. N. Malik and Peter Robb (eds), *India and Britain: Recent Past and Present Challenges* (1994).

6 Harihar Bhattacharyya, 'Communism in Tripura', University of London Ph.D. thesis (1991); Harihar Bhattacharyya and T. J. Nossiter, 'Communism in a micro-state: Tripura and the nationalities question', in T. J. Nossiter (ed.), *Marxist State Governments in India* (1988).

7 James Manor, *Nehru to the Nineties: the Changing Office of the Prime Minister* (1994).

8 Vir Chopra, *Provincial Parliamentarians in India* (1996).

9 Sangeeta Ahuja, 'Public Interest Litigation in India: a Socio-legal Study', University of London Ph.D. thesis (1995); *Public Interest Litigation in India: a Casebook* (forthcoming).

10 Apurba Kundu, 'The Indian armed forces: Sikh and non-Sikh officers' opinions of Operation Blue Star' (the Indian government's assault on the Sikh holy places), *Pacific Affairs*, 67 (1), spring 1994, pp. 46–69; 'Civil–Military Relations in British and Independent India, 1918–62, and Coup Prediction Theory', University of London Ph.D. thesis (1995).

11 Richard P. Taub, *Bureaucrats under Stress: Administrators and Administration in an Indian State* (1996).

12 David C. Potter, *India's Political Administrators, 1919–83* (1986).

13 Peter Hennessy, *Whitehall* (1989).

14 A. H. Hanson, *The Process of Planning: a Study of India's Five Year Plans, 1950–64* (1968).

15 R. N. Malhotra, 'Recent policy change in India', in K. N. Malik and Peter Robb, *India and Britain* (1994).

16 *Economic Review* (annual).
17 Paul R. Brass and Robinson.
18 Bruce D. Graham, *Hindu Nationalism and Indian Politics* (1990).
19 Christophe Jaffrelot, *Nationalists hindous* (1993), translated as *The Hindu Nationalist Movement and Indian Politics, 1925–94* (1995).
20 Tapan Basu *et al.*, *Khaki Shorts and Saffron Flags* (1993).
21 T. J. Nossiter, *Communism in Kerala: a Study in Political Adaptation* (1982); (ed.), *Marxist State Governments in India* (1988).
22 Atul Kohli, *India's Democracy: an Analysis of Changing State-Society Relations* (1988); *Democracy and Discontent: India's Growing Crisis of Governability* (1991).
23 Selig S. Harrison, *India: the Most Dangerous Decades* (1960).

Further reading

Stephen P. Cohen, *The Indian Army: its Contribution to the Development of a Nation* (1990).
Economic and Political Weekly (Bombay).
India Today (New Delhi, fortnightly).
Subrata K. Mitra, 'State power in India', in Mitra K. Subrata (ed.), *The Post-colonial State* (1990).
Vikram Seth, *A Suitable Boy* (1993), a fine novel which says more than one dare say in non-fiction.
Mark Tully, *No Full Stops in India* (1991).

Chapter 20

Britain and 'Europe':
the shape of the historiographical debate

John W. Young

One of the most significant debates for historians of post-war Britain concerns the country's relationship with its European neighbours in the European Union or, as it used to be known, the European Economic Community (EEC). A considerable amount of work has already been produced in this area by historians working on the early post-war years when, in reaction to the Schuman Plan in 1950 and the EEC in 1957, British governments are said to have 'missed the European bus';[1] work is now under-way on the early 1960s, when Harold Macmillan's government decided to apply for EEC membership, only to have the door closed by France's Charles de Gaulle. In the 1950s, it can be argued, Britain, despite its world trading role, its reliance on the US alliance for security and its hopes for the success of the Commonwealth, should have recognised that its future lay in an increasingly European focus. For historians of British foreign policy, who look beyond 1961, right down to the present day, relations with the EEC are likely to loom as the most important issue. Yet, obviously, the EEC did not only affect foreign policy considerations: membership impacted upon party politics (cutting across party loyalties), the constitution, economic and social policy, defence and the structure of government. Certainly by the mid-1980s it was as if domestic and foreign policy had blended into one on this issue, an embodiment of the argument that no individual or government could escape the growth of global economic 'interdependence', which the EEC was an attempt to manage. Political, constitutional and economic historians, as well as those working in the international field, should be interested in this area and, as research proceeds, it may be necessary to have a grasp of all these areas if one is to understand the issues which shaped policy in any one. It is also, of course, important to consider evidence from beyond Britain on this question, the attitudes and policies not only of other EEC states, such as de Gaulle's France, but also of the European Commission (with its role as the central EEC bureaucracy); of Britain's partners in the Commonwealth and, between 1959 and 1972, in the European Free Trade Area; and of the United States, which did much to foster European integration in the first place and which encouraged British membership in the 1960s. The scope for researchers on the European issue is therefore wide but the problems facing them are also formidable if a balanced and comprehensive view is to be achieved.

The growing preoccupation with European issues among British decision-makers since the Victorian era is well brought out in the most recent history of twentieth-century British foreign policy by David Reynolds.[2] At least two general texts exist which try to survey the general development of British policy towards European integration since the war, and there is a well established work by Stephen George which looks at the narrower field of British policy since joining the EEC in 1973.[3] George is very much identified with the 'awkward partner' thesis, which sees Britain as somehow unique in being out of step with other West European States. There is certainly much to be said for such an argument. Britain was the most important democratic European power not to participate in the EEC at the outset – West Germany, France and Italy all did so – and, once inside the EEC, frequently seemed at odds with its neighbours. There is a catalogue of post-entry developments which demonstrate this: the renegotiation of entry terms and holding of a referendum in 1974–75; the delays caused by the House of Commons to the first European elections in 1978–79; the failure, at that same time, to become a founder member of the Exchange Rate Mechanism; Margaret Thatcher's long-running crusade against the British net budgetary contribution in 1979–84, her Bruges speech of September 1988 and opposition to the Delors Plan for monetary union (EMU); and, of course, John Major's 'opt-outs' on EMU and the social chapter of the Maastricht Treaty in 1991. Yet it is possible to argue too that other states have been out of step with the rest of the EEC at times (de Gaulle in the 1960s being the prime example) and that Britain has been far from unique in seeking to use European institutions to achieve national aims. Nor did the country delay too long, after the initial creation of the EEC, before seeking entry; and exclusion in 1963 and 1967 was due to de Gaulle's two vetoes. All historians who take up the subject of British policy towards the EEC need to keep in mind a number of long-term questions. Has Britain been 'unique' in its attitude towards the EEC, owing perhaps to its position as an island, its slowly evolving, unwritten constitution, its belief in a global free trade policy or its winner-takes-all political system? Or rather, has the country been no more than a 'normal' actor in the European environment, with some unique national elements perhaps, but essentially no different from other members of the EEC in trying to strike a balance between a national agenda and the need (itself in the national interest) to work through European institutions? It was Britain after all which encouraged the creation, in 1975, of the European Regional Development Fund, a central institution of enormous potential for redistributing wealth in the EEC, from which it was

believed Britain would gain. And in the mid-1980s the Thatcher government was ready to back the creation of a 'single market' enthusiastically,
since it was consistent with London's own free-enterprise policies.

Another interesting question is how far British policies changed when
the country entered the Community. It is possible to argue that membership was a 'profound revolution in British foreign policy' yet also to say that
there 'was no conversion to the idea of European union ...'.[4] Entry did make
a difference to British commercial policy, the operation of government, agricultural policy and Parliament's oversight of legislation, to name but a few
areas. Yet in many ways British attitudes towards European co-operation
were the same in 1990, when Thatcher fell from office, as they had been
in 1950, when the Schuman Plan was launched: aversion to 'federalism'
and any loss of British 'sovereignty'; belief that Britain should play a world
role and welcome global attempts (through GATT) to reduce trade barriers;
a belief that the country was separate from the 'Continent', which should
be treated as a subject of 'foreign' policy; a desire to remain close to the
United States and to base defence plans on an 'Atlantic' alliance. Indeed, it
is clear that such considerations ran as threads through Britain's European
policy even before the Schuman plan. The first occasion on which a federal
Europe was first seriously suggested was in 1929 by the French Foreign
Minister, Aristide Briand. At that time too the British preferred a global,
laissez-faire trade policy to regional blocs, they had little liking for any loss
of sovereignty, they wished to preserve the preferential trade system with
the Commonwealth and they were reluctant to separate themselves from
the United States.[5] Those who study the three applications, of 1961–63,
1967 and 1970–71, need to look carefully at how far the British planned
to change existing policies when they entered the Community, at how far
they aimed to 'convert' Europeans to a British agenda and at how far they
believed membership would give Britain the power to limit further supranational developments in the EEC. Certainly, a recent analysis of the policy
of Edward Heath's government argues that, whatever Heath's own commitment to a European future, there was no real mental adaptation by
people, Parliament or government to that idea. Instead it was hoped that,
once inside the Community, Britain would be able to veto any unwelcome
developments, and entry was seen not as an idealistic adventure but as a
pragmatic step, designed to stimulate greater economic growth and even
as a way to improve the country's ability to play a world role.[6]

In reviewing the debate among historians on British policy before
Macmillan's application, it is clear that the story has not all been negative.
In the late 1930s a number of eminent Britons had already created the Federal Union movement[7] and in June 1940 Winston Churchill desperately
tried to keep France in the Second World War by offering her an 'indissol-
uble union', which would have included a single government and common
citizenship.[8] It was Churchill too who, as wartime Prime Minister, took an

interest in forming a new regional organisation, to be called the 'Council of Europe', and in September1946, as leader of the opposition, he made his famous appeal in Zurich for a European union, after which he formed his own United Europe movement. Churchill's views were clearly complex, for during this same period he opposed the creation of a British-led military alliance in Western Europe (the so called 'Western bloc'), because of the likely cost to the exchequer, and even in the Zurich speech he saw Britain only as the 'sponsor' of European unity, alongside the other great powers, America and Russia. Also, although Churchill gave support to the Council of Europe, when it was finally created in 1949[9] he was quite clear, on returning to the premiership in 1951, that he never saw Britain as a member of a European federation.[10] Furthermore, although he made the first serious proposal for a European army in the autumn of 1950, he became a bitter critic of the European Defence Community, which was negotiated by West European states but not Britain in 1952 and which collapsed two years later.[11] A single, comprehensive study of his attitude towards European co-operation has yet to be written.

Turning to the Labour Party in the first post-war decade, it is clear that it too was not without its 'pro-European' inclinations, and a group of historians have argued that there was far more to the Labour government of 1945–51 than the error of 'missing the European bus'. In 1944 the consensus in the Foreign Office, as well as among the Chiefs of Staff, already favoured the creation of the 'Western bloc' and in 1945 the Labour Foreign Secretary, Ernest Bevin, was very sympathetic to the idea. He was not only interested in creating a military alliance with France and other West European countries but even, in 1946 and 1947, established study groups to look at the idea of a customs union. Co-operation with Western Europe, in addition to co-operation with the Empire and Commonwealth, was seen as a way for Britain to balance the power of the United States and Soviet Union.[12] In the summer of 1947 Bevin led west European nations in taking up the Marshall aid programme, through which the Americans hoped to create a thriving anti-Soviet economic bloc in Europe.[13] When a diplomatic breakdown with the USSR finally occurred, Bevin, in January 1948, revealed to the world his vision of a Western Union and, two months later, helped form the Brussels Pact organisation. Mainly intended as a military alliance, the Brussels Pact was extended in 1954 to become the Western European Union, now seen as a potential security wing of the European Union. One historian, John Kent, has even seen the signing of the North Atlantic Treaty in April 1949, not as the triumph for Bevin's diplomacy which it is usually portrayed as being, but as a defeat for Bevin's earlier hopes of building a European imperial group as a way to maintain British equality with the United States.[14]

As with Churchill's European policy, a full analysis is still required of the failure of the original Western Union concept in 1948–9. However, a number of reasons why Britain was unable to achieve the leadership of a Western European group seem clear. One was that Britain lacked the material resources to maintain a strong military alliance in the face of the USSR.[15] Another was that the British disliked any idea of forming central institutions in western Europe with supranational powers. Such a development would have restricted Britain's independence and compromised its position as a great power: in London's eyes European integration was designed to bolster Britain's independence, not compromise it.[16] Nor could the British successfully co-operate with other European colonial powers on imperial policies, despite Bevin's idea of a 'Euro-African' bloc.[17] Finally, there was a series of economic factors which made an Anglo-European customs union extremely complicated. Even without the preference of the Treasury and Board of Trade for a global trade system, the British and European economies were felt to be too competitive to combine easily, and half of British trade was still with the Commonwealth. These economic factors have been analysed best by Alan Milward.[18] All in all, it seems clear that British policy was set on a different course from the Continentals' well before the Schuman Plan for a coal steel community was launched, and it can be argued that the French government initiated that particular project with little hope of British membership. In particular the British reluctance to accept the principle of supranationality was very strong in the spring of 1950, Britain's economy was still far larger than those of its Continental neighbours and the prediction in London was that the Schuman Plan would not succeed. It is notable that Whitehall officials did spend considerable time drawing up their own version of a European coal and steel authority, but they wanted the authority to make decisions on a unanimous basis. As seen in the creation of the Organisation of European Economic Co-operation (which managed the Marshall aid programme), the Brussels Pact and the Council of Europe, the British preference was for 'intergovernmental co-operation'.[19] And given the failure to enter the Schuman Plan it was never likely that the Labour government would compromise its military independence by taking up the idea of a European army when it was suggested a few months later. Whereas the post-war decade has now been the subject of considerable analysis by historians, the early years of the European Community are only just becoming part of historical debate. The standard account of British policy in the period 1955–63 is still the dated, but thorough and remarkably well informed, study by Miriam Camps.[20] There are a number of obvious questions in this period but the lines of debate surrounding each are yet to be established. Why did the British fail to become founder members of the EEC in 1957 despite initially being invited to take part in the negotiations, when the Schuman Plan states held their fateful meeting in Messina in June 1955? Why, in late 1956, did the British launch an alternative proposal for a European industrial free-trade area, talks on which ran into the sand two years later? In view of the failure of the free-trade area talks, it was logical perhaps to lead non-EEC states in creating a European Free Trade Association in 1959 but why, only two years after that, did Macmillan's government decide to change tack and apply for Community membership? The decision was obviously highly complex, involving political, economic and security issues, and has been seen as part of a general reconsideration of the whole of government policy by the Conservative government, which was only too aware of Britain's failure to match the economic growth rates of other European powers.[21] However, it was always clear that the application could be vetoed by de Gaulle (who had already done much to kill off the industrial free-trade area) and it will be interesting to discover how, on the British side, Macmillan felt he could win de Gaulle over and whether, on the French side, there was ever much chance that de Gaulle would allow the British into the Community. Although a few items have appeared on this period based on original sources,[22] the subject is still in the world of just-to-be-completed doctoral theses.

The next major area to be opened up to such investigation will of course be the Labour governments of Harold Wilson, which submitted a second membership application to the EEC in 1967. Those who take up this subject at least have a good range of published primary sources in the form of diaries and memoirs. The former include the three volumes by Richard Crossman, as well as two volumes by Tony Benn and one by Barbara Castle;[23] the latter include accounts by the Prime Minister himself, two of his Foreign Secretaries (Michael Stewart and George Brown), and other Ministers and officials.[24] Apart from a collection of documents by Uwe Kitzinger,[25] little has been written by political scientists on European policy between 1964 and 1970, but there are, once again, a number of important questions to answer. Not least, how and why did Wilson, never an enthusiast about Europe, persuade his equally unenthusiastic (and divided) party to apply for entry to the EEC? In what way was the decision linked with Britain's continuing economic problems, division in the Commonwealth over Rhodesia's Unilateral Declaration of Independence and the decision, also taken in 1967, to withdraw from military bases East of Suez? There is also a perplexing problem with the Wilson period which is similar to that surrounding Macmillan: why did Downing Street pursue EEC membership in the face of almost certain defeat at the hands of de Gaulle? The answer may be that in 1967, as in 1961, many British leaders simply concluded that, given the disappearance of empire, the declining value of the US alliance and the relative underperformance of the British economy, there was simply 'no alternative' to entering the EEC. Even if entry proved impossible to achieve, it had to be attempted. The fact that such a course was adopted almost in a sense of resignation and defeat, may also help to explain for why, when Britain did finally join in 1973, it was without eagerness for the task in hand.

Notes

1   On the 'missing the bus' thesis see especially A. Nutting, *Europe will not Wait* (1960); N. Beloff, *The General says No* (1963), and M. Charlton, *The Price of Victory* (1983).

2   D. Reynolds, *Britannia Overruled* (1991). Other general surveys pay less attention to the European Community and its impact: P. Kennedy, *The Realities behind Diplomacy* (1981); B. Porter, *Britain, Europe and the World, 1850–1982* (1983); R. Holland, *The Pursuit of Greatness: Britain and the World Role* (1992).

3   S. Greenwood, *Britain and European Co-operation since 1945* (1992); J. W. Young, *Britain and European Unity, 1945–92* (1993); S. George, *An Awkward Partner* (1990); and see also the last's *Britain and European Integration since 1945* (1991).

4   Reynolds, *Britannia*, p. 238; George, *Awkward Partner*, p. 40.

5   R. W. D. Boyce, 'Britain's first "no" to Europe: Britain and the Briand Plan, 1929–30', *European Studies Review*, 10, 1980, pp. 17–45; P. J. V. Rollo, *Britain and the Briand Plan: the Common Market that never was* (1972); R. White, 'Cordial caution: the British response to the French proposal for European Federal Union', in A. Bosco (ed.), *The Federal Idea: the History of Federalism from Enlightenment in 1945* (1991), pp. 237–62.

6   C. Lord, *British Entry to the European Community under the Heath Government* (1993).

7   R. A. Wilford, 'The Federal Union campaign', *European Studies Review*, 10, 1980, pp. 102–14.

8   A. Shlaim, 'Prelude to downfall: the British offer of union to France, June 1940', *Journal of Contemporary History*, 9, 1972, pp. 27–63.

9   Young, *European Unity*, 7, 19–20, 24.

10 On the debate in the Conservative Cabinet in 1951–52 see J. W. Young, 'Churchill's "no" to Europe', *Historical Journal*, 28, 1985, pp. 923–37.

11 S. Dockrill, *Britain's Policy for West German Rearmament, 1951–5 5* (1991).

12 Works which see a positive policy by Bevin towards Europe include G. Warner, 'The Labour governments and the unity of Europe', in R. Ovendale (ed.), *The Foreign Policy of the Labour Governments* (1984), pp. 61–82; J. W. Young, *Britain, France and the Unity of Europe, 1945–51* (1984); S. Greenwood, 'Ernest Bevin, France and Western Union, 1945–56', *European History Quarterly*, 14,1984, pp. 312–26.

13 On the importance of Marshall aid to European integration see M. Hogan, *The Marshall Plan* (1987).

14 J. Kent, *British Imperial Strategy and the Origins of the Cold War* (1993).

15 J. Kent and J. W. Young, 'The Western Union concept and British defence policy, 1947–48', in R. Aldrich (ed.), *British Intelligence, Strategy and the Cold War* (1992), pp. 166–92.

16 This is argued most forcefully in A. Shlaim, *Britain and the Origins of European Unity* (1977).

17 J. Kent, 'The British Empire and the origins of the Cold War', in A. Deighton (ed.), *Britain and the First Cold War* (1990), pp. 165–83.

18 A. Milward, *The Reconstruction of Western Europe, 1945–51* (1984) and see *The European Rescue of the Nation State* (1992), chapter 7.

19 Two studies on Britain and the Schuman Plan are forthcoming at the time of writing, one, by Edmund Dell, from Oxford University Press; the other, by Christopher Lord, from Dartmouth Publishers.

20 M. Camps, *Britain and the European Community, 1955–63* (1964).

21 K. Middlemas, *Power, Competition and the State*, II, *1961–74* (1990), pp. 89, 16, 334.

22 Young, *European Unity*, ch.3.

23 T. Benn, *Out of the Wilderness: Diaries, 1963–67* (1987), and *Office without Power: Diaries, 1968–72* (1988); B. Castle, *The Castle Diaries, 1964–70* (1984); R. Crossman, *Dairies of a Cabinet Minister*, I, *1964–6*; II *1966–8*, III *1968–70*, (1975–7).

24 G. Brown, *In my Way* (1971); M. Stewart, *Life and Labour* (1980), H. Wilson, *The Labour Government, 1964–70* (1971).

25 U. Kitzinger, *The Second Try* (1968).

Appendix to Part II

Bibliographical sources

For all countries covered, consult the excellent and up-to-date World Bibliographic Series (Clio Press), which covers bibliographical resources in separate volumes for 110 countries.

Africa

Africa Bibliography
C. H. Allen
Guide to Research and Reference Works on sub-Saharan Africa
P. Duignan
Africa: a Directory of Resources (1987)
T. Fenton
Index Africanus
Hoover Institution Bibliography
Africa, a Guide to Reference Material (1993)
J. McIlwaine
Modern History of Ethopia and the Horn of Africa
H. Marcus
International African Bibliography
School of Oriental and African Studies
African Resources and Collections (1989)
J. Witherell

Latin America

Handbook of Political Science Research on Latin America (1990)
D. Dent
Latin American Studies: a Basic Guide to Sources (1990)
R. McNeil and B. Valle

Handbook of Latin American Studies (1993)
D. Moyano Martin
Latin American Politics: a Historical Bibliography (1984)
Research Guide to Andean History (1981)

Soviet Union and eastern Europe

Stalin: an Annotated Guide to Books in English (1993)
M. Bloomberg and B. Barret
Rise and Fall of the Soviet Union: a Selected Bibliography (1992)
A. and H. Edelheit
European Bibliography of Soviet, East European and Slavonic Studies
Editions de l'Ecole des hautes études en sciences sociales
V. I. Lenin: an Annotated Bibliography of English Language Sources (1982)
D. and M. Egan
The Soviet Union and Eastern Europe: a Bibliographical Guide (1985)
Guide to the Collections in the Hoover Institution's Archives relating to Imperial Russia, the Russian Revolution and Civil War (1986)
C. Leadenham
Library Resources in Britain for the Study of Eastern Europe and the former Soviet Union (1992)
G. Walker and J. Johnson

China

Contemporary China: a Research Guide (1967)
P. Berton and E. Wu
Mao Zedong: a Bibliography
A. Lawrence
Bibliographies of World Leaders No. 7
China in Western Literature (1958)
Tung-Li Yuan
Documentation on China, 1963–65 (1977)
Vimla Saran
The Cultural Revolution in China: an Annotated Bibliography (1976)
J. Wang

Part III
Archival sources and debates

Chapter 21

Private papers

Angela Raspin

This chapter aims to show in outline what researchers can expect from the private papers of politicians and of other figures of interest to the contemporary historian, and to provide some basic advice on their use. Attention is drawn to the obstacles that the researcher may encounter, as well as to the natural limitations of the material. Provided such limitations are borne in mind, private papers can offer the contemporary historian remarkable advantages in the form of 'unofficial' information. Since there is little agreement about archive terminology among archivists themselves and none between archivists and historians, I begin with some definitions. In what follows, 'private papers' and 'personal' papers are interchangeable terms signifying 'the private documents accumulated by, belonging to, and subject to the disposition of, an individual person';[1] 'repository' is the normal, neutral term for a manuscript-collecting and holding institution, and 'depositor' for the person who donates or loans a collection to a repository. For brevity, I have used 'originator' to denote the person who originated a set of papers of interest to historians.

What do private papers contain?

Personal papers are the physical survivals of a life. A politician's papers may contain correspondence with family, personal friends and political colleagues, minutes, notes on informal meetings, drafts of policy papers, formal correspondence, and official papers retained from periods of office. Unless the originator kept copies of his letters or asked for the originals back, his papers will contain only letters written to him.

All these kinds of record are a by-product of activity or a means of carrying it out, not produced for their own sake. The information content of a collection of private papers depends on a number of factors independent of the importance or interest of the originator. The major one is the degree to which he used writing as a means of clarifying his thoughts or communicating with others. Labour politicians of the old school, such as Ernest Bevin or Emanuel Shinwell,[2] clearly preferred speech as a means of doing business, so their papers tend to be very thin.

Technological change has had its effects. Much important business is now carried on by telephone and is very sparsely recorded. Letters dictated to a secretary and typed tend, whoever the recipient, to be more impersonal than those written by hand. People's paper-keeping habits vary: some keep almost everything, as did Sir Winston Churchill and Sir William Beveridge;[3] some, like R. H. Tawney,[4] keep nothing of consequence; some discard their papers when they move house or retire; and some sort and, one suspects, edit them when they come to write their memoirs, as with Hugh Dalton and the first Earl of Swinton.[5] Memoir writing is often the crucial stage in the originator's realisation that a mass of old letters is in fact an archive of some general interest.

Most twentieth-century collections of private papers consist of fascinating fragments. It is very unlikely that they will give a complete picture of the originator's activities. Even in cases where papers have survived in fair abundance, there will almost certainly have been a degree of editing, conscious or unconscious. The parts of the life which were particularly unhappy, unsuccessful or just boring for the person who lived it are likely to be documented less fully. So, on the other hand, is carefree youth. The paper-keeping habits of small organisations are very similar. Their active lives are often longer, but their officers and thus the place where the papers are kept may change at intervals of a few years. The result is that records which are felt to reflect the corporate existence of the organisation – minutes especially – will survive, while material felt to be of only temporary importance will not. It frequently happens that, by the time the archivist or historian examines the records, all the correspondence and reports which actually explain the minutes have gone.

So far conventional manuscripts have been considered. There may also be Hansards, election leaflets, broadsheets, sound records, pieces of film. Sound recordings, where the originator has taped meetings or conversations, are likely to become more common and offer peculiar problems as regards both conservation and consultation. It is relatively easy to skim a written text by programming the eye to pick out certain text combinations; skimming a recording is slower and inherently less accurate, since it can only be done by listening to a series of short samples.

One special kind of record found in private papers poses particular problems of interpretation. Personal diaries are not kept as an essential part of normal business. The diarist has to decide to keep a diary and to go on keeping it. A detailed political diary represents a considerable expenditure of time and mental effort, and its character will depend on the diarist's motives for keeping it: it may be a deadpan record of events for reference like Sir Walter Citrine's;[6] or, like James Meade's,[7] it may be confined to a particularly stimulating or unusual part of the diarist's life; or it may serve, like Sir Alexander Cadogan's,[8] as a safe vent for frustrations and subjects which could not be discussed elsewhere.

The reader, in evaluating the information in a diary and in accounting for omissions, should always attempt to gain some idea of the diarist's intentions. This entails reading a substantial amount of the text, not just consulting an index. He should also consider the mechanical aspects of diary-keeping. Was the record a set of instant shorthand notes, written every day, or at intervals by the diarist? Was it dictated to a tape recorder or at intervals to a typist from notes or from memory? Answers to such questions will help to establish to what extent the record has been subjected to subsequent analysis or to conscious or unconscious editing. Diarists of today and tomorrow may well use word processors to keep their diaries. Such techniques are seductive but make editing, without leaving traces, alarmingly easy. The distinction between diary and memoir, between what a person thought at the time and what that same person says in retrospect, becomes ever slighter.

Because private papers are so fragmented, and because of problems of incomplete knowledge and conscious and unconscious bias on the part of their originators, it is impossible to write more than the most limited study from one collection. The historian should be prepared to undertake a kind of mosaic work with incompatible scraps of information from a great variety of sources and to spend a good deal of time and heart-searching evaluating their relative unreliability as well as their meaning. He may indeed find that the narrative framework comes from the public record and from printed sources and that private papers provide the occasional but essential moments of illumination.

The 'archivisation' of private papers

One of the defining characteristics of private papers is that they are at the free disposition of their owners. No legislation directly applies to them (with the partial exception of some controls on the export of material of national importance). They are usually held by the originators or their heirs, by manuscript-collecting institutions or by third parties, biographers or research institutes. As with government records, but for different reasons, private papers do not usually become available to the historian until long after the events they record. Politicians rarely allow outsiders any kind of access to their papers until their active career is drawing to a close and the papers rarely become available to all comers in public institutions until the originator has died or has wholly withdrawn from public life.

Where the owner still holds the papers, the user has no right of access, moral or legal. The owner may agree to show his papers, or a section of them, as an act of generosity. This is probably the only way of consulting very recent material and has the advantage that the originator may be available to give explanations. The disadvantages are that it may be very difficult to gain an accurate idea of the extent or contents of the archive, and that the time available for consultation is likely to be very short. Users under these circumstances should do their best not to annoy or inconvenience the originator in any way. They should take particular care to leave papers in the state in which they found them, to remove nothing, and to resist the temptation to rearrange them. To do so may suit their own research but destroy underlying relationships to the detriment of future researchers. The same absence of rights of access applies to papers held by third parties, though here the potential user's moral position is stronger if the papers are already in use for research purposes.

The position is radically different when the papers are held by an institution. In the United Kingdom institutions fall into three main groups: those funded by central government, including the Public Record Office, the national libraries and the major museums; institutions funded by local government, in this context primarily the local record offices; and educational establishments, mainly universities.

In the United Kingdom there is a marked absence of central direction, central funding and legislation controlling the administration of private papers. With the exception of the national and county record offices, manuscript departments form part of larger institutions, usually libraries or museums. This fact has important consequences for funding. Most manuscript departments are funded out of their institution's block grant. This is usually inelastic and some of the most active institutions rely on grants from private sources. Such grants are usually earmarked for specific projects, not for general administration, acquisition and cataloguing. The system has, in the past, proved highly flexible in adapting to new research trends, but has serious deficiencies. The low level of long-term funding available to most institutions has meant that few have been able to grow sufficiently to make economies of scale in the balance between professional and non-professional staff, and that it has often been easier to set up a new repository to deal with a new branch of research than to provide extra staff and space for an existing one. There are, in consequence, a large number of small repositories, and standards of provision vary considerably.

From the researcher's point of view however, the situation is less chaotic than this outline may suggest. The demands of institutional prestige, the existence of influential professional organisations and of a common curriculum for the training of archivists, and the co-ordinating role of the Royal Commission on Historical Manuscripts (HMC) have meant that the is a fair degree of agreement about basic standards. There are, however marked differences between institutions on matters of principle, in relation to access to material and to reprographic facilities, and in matters of practice, as in the running of search rooms.

Manuscript collections may come into the custody of archives by a number of different methods. With recent political papers of importance purchase by auction or through a dealer is uncommon and acquisition is usually by negotiation with the originator or his heirs. These negotiations are generally confidential and may involve direct purchase or an element of indirect purchase – for example, if the collection is set against inheritance tax. Even in the case of an outright gift, the archive will probably accept certain conditions as the price of receiving the collection. The degree to which the repository agrees to accept such conditions depends on the importance of the collection, the policy of the institution and the perceptions of the negotiator. If the collection is thought to be exceptional it is easier to accept conditions which will be expensive to operate. There may be an element of quiet competition for such papers and some depositors may shop around for the best package.

The conditions of deposit which are most likely to affect users are restrictions on access to the collection and on the publication of information Such restrictions may be imposed for one or a combination of reasons. They may be to comply with the Official Secrets Act and other legislation controlling the availability of information. Institutional policies differ considerably on the degree to which it is necessary and politic to co-operate with the authorities on matters of official secrecy. Some repositories prefer the evasive, some the compliant stance. Restrictions may be imposed at the instance of the depositor. He may wish to protect his own reputation or his privacy or to prevent his friends from discovering what he said about them in his diary. He may require the repository to accept the obligations of confidentiality which he assumed towards his informants. Such obligations are frequently accepted by a member of Parliament towards his constituents in trouble, by a politician towards a civil servant who tells him about malpractice in his department, by an anthropologist towards the people he interviews, or by a university teacher towards his students. Restrictions may also be intended to protect third parties. Information which they did not know was recorded may embarrass or harm them. The final reason for restrictions is to protect the repository and its parent institution. A reputation for reckless indiscretion does not help an acquisition programme. The purist argument is that everything which is in a manuscript collection should be open to inspection and that material which cannot be inspected should not be acquired. In the long run this is a truism. Private papers are collected for use and one of the essential points in negotiation is to set a time after which all restrictions are lifted. In the short run the negotiator is frequently faced with the choice between acquiring the whole archive with restrictions or rejecting material of real historical value in the knowledge that it may be lost or even deliberately destroyed. The three principal methods of restriction are as follows

1. *Absolute closure.* The collection is placed under seal. This is the pre-

ferred method of dealing with highly confidential papers or those closed under the Official Secrets Act.

2. *Restrictions on access.* The papers are closed but a procedure is set up whereby the potential user may apply for permission to consult them, from the original depositor or his representative, from a special committee or from the governing body of the repository. Some institutions accept this system as a matter of course, others only as a last resort. It is often useful as a means of reassuring a nervous donor. Some collections appear to be hedged around by the most obstructive conditions and yet permission to see them has never been refused.

3. *Restrictions on publication.* This method is usually combined with restrictions on access. The user undertakes, in return for permission to consult the papers, that he will not attempt to publish any information from them without permission. The user is in any case prevented from publishing actual text by the law of copyright. Always take care to keep a record of your acceptance of such conditions. Infringement may prevent your use, on a later occasion, of material in the same institution.

Political historians, partly because of the nature of their subject, partly because of the importance to them of the closed periods for official records, are particularly sensitive to restrictions on access. My own experience suggests that the problems are usually easier to surmount for politicians' papers than for some other kinds of material. Records of interest to social historians and anthropologists' field records can cause agonising moral dilemmas over the scientific value of the material and the rights of those who supplied that material in confidence. It is worth noting, too, that business firms tend to be far more protective of the inviolability of their records than most politicians are.

How to locate private papers

The historian who proposes to use private papers should draw up two lists of names: names of those whose private papers are known to exist and must be consulted, and names of those whose papers may not have been kept or be accessible but whose activities were relevant to the subject. Even if the papers of the second group cannot be found, useful letters by them are likely to turn up in other collections. These lists will be constantly added to in the course of research. New collections are constantly being acquired or freed for research and the historian must be flexible in revising his research plans.

The master indices to manuscript holdings in the British Isles (primarily the United Kingdom, but also including some information on the Republic of Ireland) are compiled by the National Registry of Archives (NRA) at the Royal Commission on Historical Manuscripts (HMC).[9] These are arranged by name, place and subject. For the present purpose, the name indices are the most useful. They also include entries for important runs of correspondence by one person in the papers of another. The indices are based on annual returns to the HMC by collecting repositories, on the detailed lists of the contents of collections supplied by those repositories, and on information collected by the HMC itself. Inevitably there are gaps, owing to incomplete or delayed reporting, but the indices are the most up-to-date source outside the repositories themselves. They may be consulted together with the lists on which they are based at the HMC search room. The NRA indices will be available to remote users via the internet some time later in the year 1995/96. Staff at the NRA will also answer limited and specific enquiries by post or e-mail.

The most useful printed guides for the contemporary historian are *Sources in British Political History 1900–51* and *Sources in Contemporary British History* for the period after 1945 edited by Chris Cook and *British Archives* edited by Janet Foster and Julia Shepherd. Cook's volumes cover the papers of organisations and individuals, give a summary description of each collection and its location and include many sets of papers particularly of organisations still in private hands.[10] *British Archives* is arranged by town and archive and gives a brief summary of collecting policy and major holdings for each. It covers the entire period of British history and includes information about many institutions which run their own archives. It also includes a subject classification.[11]

Apart from the general guides noted above, many repositories publish overall guides to their holdings and there are a number of special guides to particular subject areas. The HMC and the Institute of Historical Research[12] have good coverage of these. Some archives are about to make their catalogues available over JANET, the British Joint Academic Network, for remote searching.

A number of important manuscript collections, including the archives of the Conservative and Labour parties, are becoming available on microform. These are published in very small editions and are not reliably listed in *Books in Print*. The best guide is Donald Munro's *Microforms for Historians: a Finding-list of Research Collections in London Libraries*,[13] which provides information about many commercial packages which can also be found in libraries outside London.

How to approach the repository

This section is expressed as a series of instructions. Many of them will be obvious to most readers, but all are essential. It is advisable to write to archivists in advance. Explain the subject of your research. Ask whether the repository holds the collection in which you are interested; whether it holds similar material which you should consult, and whether there are any special conditions attached to consultation; what the opening hours are and whether you need to make an appointment for your first and subsequent visits. It is wise, if you want a prompt reply, to keep your questions brief and to include a stamped addressed envelope. It is useful to be able to produce a general letter of introduction from a person in a position of responsibility; if you are a research student it should be your director of studies. If you wish to consult restricted access collections, be prepared to produce a *curriculum vitae*, a full statement of your research project and a specific letter of recommendation. When you first arrive at the repository you will probably be asked to fill in a record card and to sign an undertaking to observe the rules of the repository as a condition of being allowed to consult the manuscript collections.

The usual sources of information about a repository's contents are the overall guides to its holdings and the detailed catalogues. Guides consist of a list of collections, arranged alphabetically, by dates covered, by subject, or by order of acquisition. Their object is to give the user a quick overview of what is available. They normally give, for each collection, its name, a brief indication of subject and date coverage, the size of the collection and information about catalogues.

The usual practice is for repositories to prepare a separate catalogue for each collection of reasonable size, often in the form of a bound volume. The basic rules in cataloguing manuscript collections are (1) to observe the principle of provenance – that is, to keep all material from the same source together and to introduce nothing extraneous; (2) to retain the original order of the collection as far as possible; and (3) to lay out the material in such a way that the user can see what is there, how it fits together, and, equally important, what is not there. The amount of detail given by catalogues varies. The collections most likely to be described item by item are very important collections, very small collections (where the contents are so disparate that they cannot be summarised) and collections received in a very chaotic state – i.e. collections that can be sorted into a comprehensible state only by writing a description of every separate item and playing happy families with the slips of paper on which the descriptions are written. If the collection was already divided into files, the catalogue description may be limited to a general summary of the contents of each file with perhaps a note on any particularly significant document. Very detailed listing is expensive, and difficult to justify when there is a backlog of unlisted collections. It is often wiser to use the resources needed for one detailed catalogue on listing four summary ones.

The repository may also have indices which cover all collections and are particularly useful for locating interesting material in collections which may appear irrelevant to the research in hand. Subject indices, which raise severe methodological problems, are uncommon. How does one predict the future subjects of research? Name indices are easier to produce and can form excellent pointers to information. Their coverage may, however, be patchy and they are usually in arrears. A number of repositories now have computerised catalogues. These are often constructed on full text databases, which means that one can search for a name or any word which appears in the description of the file or document; they allow compound searches, for instance for 'Dalton and Poland and 1940–46' and bring up the complete text of the catalogue entry. In the long run, computerised databases offer one of the best solutions to the indexing problem. Getting the information into machine readable form is, however, slow and few repositories have anything near full coverage of their holdings.

It is worth spending time and care on a repository's finding aids and drawing up a list of material for examination. It is important to note the exact call mark on every item you wish to consult so that you can order it for inspection and so that you identify it clearly and accurately when you come to write up your research. Archive repositories permit the consultation of manuscripts only in a closely supervised reading room. The material you wish to consult is fetched for you and you will probably be required to use a pencil for making notes. Some repositories now also allow the use of portable computers. You should take great care in handling original documents. Modern paper is of poor quality and easily damaged. Do not rearrange files, and, if you find any discrepancies, report them to the person in charge of the reading room. Find out what the arrangements are for fetching; they vary according to the layout and staffing of the repository. Documents may be fetched on demand or at fixed intervals. For example, there may be no fetching in the middle of the day or after a certain time in the afternoon. The time taken to deliver orders will depend on the distance between the reading room and the storeroom. Some material may be kept in another building. You may be able to order in advance: establish the correct method, because it will save you a considerable wait on your next visit. You will probably be allowed to consult only a few items at a time in order to minimise the dangers of misplacing, but you may be able to ask for additional items to be kept ready for you.

Reproduction and copyright

The contemporary historian should assume that the text he wishes to quote is in copyright and that a large proportion of the copyrights in any given collection never belonged to the originator of that collection. If A. writes a letter to B., the letter belongs to B. but the copyright remains with A., the author, and his heirs. Many repositories require readers to sign some kind of undertaking to clear copyright. In cases where it is intended to publish large quantities of copyright text – an edition of a diary, for instance, or a book with an extensive documentary appendix – outline copyright permission should be sought at the start of the project. If the project is likely to make money, the copyright holder may require a special fee or a share of the royalties.

The law of copyright relates only to actual quotations, not to the transmission of information. If you have not undertaken to seek permission before publication, you may freely paraphrase, while avoiding plagiarism, but should take care to identify the source you have used. Give the name or number which the repository uses to identify the collection, instead of, or as well as, any pet name in common use; the section- and item-numbering system used by the repository; and a brief summary of the contents. The British Standard *Recommendations for Citation of Unpublished Documents* is a useful guide.[14]

There is a marked divergence of opinion among British archivists about photocopying. Some take the view that nothing may be photocopied without the permission of the copyright owner if it is less than 100 years old; others that the difference between permitting someone to copy a document by hand and selling him a photocopy is not great enough to justify a ban. Those offices which do photocopy insist on the work being done by their own staff and charge a price which covers labour costs and overheads. They also reserve the right to refuse to photocopy material which may be damaged or about which there are special problems of copyright or confidentiality. Expect long delays over photocopying, especially during the long vacation. Do not assume that the provision of photocopies implies the right to publish. Some repositories can also provide microfilm. However, the potential problems over copyright are here much more severe, because of the larger quantity of material involved (it is usually not worth ordering less than 200 pages to be filmed) and because it is so easy to make subsequent copies illicitly.

Principal repositories

The main repositories where valuable material on contemporary British history may be found are the British Library and the British Library of Political and Economic Science, London; the Bodleian Library, Oxford; Churchill College, Cambridge; the Cambridge University Library; the Brynmor Jones Library at the University of Hull; the Modern Records Centre at the University of Warwick; the National Library of Scotland; the National Library of Wales; and University College, London. The Conservative Party's papers are housed at the Bodleian Library, Oxford, and are open up to 1964. Access to subsequent material is by prior arrangement. The Labour Party's papers are at the National Museum of Labour History in Manchester. In the case of both parties, files which are obviously 'personal' are closed. Some Liberal Party archives are held at Bristol University Library and the British Library of Political and Economic Science. The Social Democratic Party's archives are at the University of Essex.

Notes

1 Definition of 'personal papers' in Peter Walne (ed.), *Dictionary of Archival Terminology*, International Council on Archives, Handbook No. 3 (1984).

2 Ernest Bevin (1881–1951), papers at Churchill College, Cambridge; Emanuel Shinwell (1884–1986), papers at British Library of Political and Economic Science (BLPES), London School of Economics.

3 Sir Winston Churchill (1874–1965), papers at Churchill College; Sir William Beveridge (1879–1963), papers at BLPES.

4 R. H. Tawney (1880–1962), papers at BLPES.

5 Hugh Dalton (1887–1962), papers at BLPES; Sir Philip Cunliffe-Lister, first Earl of Swinton (1884–1972), papers at Churchill College.

6 Walter McLennan Citrine (1887–1985), diary at BLPES.

7 James Meade (1907–), diary at BLPES. An academic economist, Meade was Director of the Economic Section of the Cabinet Office, 1946–47.

8 Sir Alexander Cadogan (1884–1968), diary at Churchill College.

9 The Royal Commission on Historical Manuscripts, Quality House, Quality Court, Chancery Lane, London WC2A I HP. Telephone number 0171 242 1198, Internet address: http://www.hmc.gov.uk/.

10 'Studies in British Political History, 1900–51', compiled by Chris Cook *et al.*, I, *A Guide to Archives of Selected Organisations and Societies* (1975); II, *A Guide to the Papers of Selected Public Servants* (1975); III-IV, *A Guide to the Private Papers of Members of Parliament* (1977); V, *A Guide to the Private Papers of Selected Writers, Intellectuals and Publicists* (1978); VI, *First Consolidated Supplement* (1985). *The Longman Guide to Sources in Contemporary British History*, ed. Chris Cook *et al.*, I, *Organisations and Societies*; II, *Individuals* (1994).

11 *British Archives*, ed. Janet Foster and Julia Sheppard (1995).

12 Institute of Historical Research, Senate House, University of London, London WC1E 7HU.

13 *Microforms for Historians: a Finding-list of Research Collections in London Libraries*, compiled by D. J. Munro, London: Institute of Historical Research (1991).

14 British Standards Institution *Recommendations for Citation of Unpublished Documents*, BS 6371 (1983).

Chapter 22

Parliamentary sources

Dermot Englefield

'The functions of the Parliament of the United Kingdom may be broadly described as legislative, financial, representational and judicial.'[1] Parliament is, therefore, concerned with passing legislation, with debate in both Houses on government policy and adminstration and in the House of Commons with consent to taxation and control of expenditure. There is also the role of the House of Lords with regard to appellate jurisdiction, which is not considered in this chapter.

As we enter either of the small chambers used by the Lords or the Commons, or one of the two dozen or so even smaller committee rooms, we find ourselves listening to a series of voices: the voice of government policy and its administration delivered through a hundred or more Ministers; the voice of backbench members expressing constituents' views through their own particular political filter; increasingly the voice of lobbies and special groups seeking to show how the shoe of current policies pinches them; and finally the voice of experienced citizens – though it might be argued that with the advent of life peers this experience may be richer and more varied in the House of Lords. These chambers, unlike the hemicycle opera house of many foreign parliaments designed for *ex cathedra* speeches, are built for argument and the clash of ideas.

Westminster then, as the media still recognise, remains very much the sounding board of contemporary society, and it would be surprising if the information submitted to Parliament and the information generated by it, nearly all of which is published, were not essential to the understanding of the society which is speaking, first for immediate commentators, and subsequently for contemporary historians. This chapter discusses first the main areas of Parliament's work and the documents they produce and then the mechanics of reaching that material.

Parliament's legislative work

Before a new Parliament meets, the different political parties will have set down their policies in election manifestoes for the judgement of the electors, who decide on society's contemporary priorities at the polling booth.[2] These manifestoes are an essential part of the election system but they also reveal the current needs of society as well as submitting proposals to meet them. They are published by the individual political parties but are also included in *The Times Guide to the House of Commons*, published after each election, and collected in *British General Election Manifestos 1900–74*.[3]

The Queen's Speech, delivered at the opening of Parliament before both Houses and outlining the programme of work during the coming session, derives, at least to some degree, from the government's election manifesto.[4] Although carefully structured to reflect the different elements of the British constitution, the Queen's Speeches, examined over a period, give an idea of the problems on the mind of the government of the day, and the general debates which follow during the first six days of the session – technically the debate on the Address – offer a chance for backbenchers to test Ministers on their policies and for Parliament to indulge in a *tour d'horizon*, a luxury which seldom comes its way. But the session is only a few days old when the government begins to introduce its programme of legislation. Parliament takes up its first role. (Private members' Bills are limited to a few each session, often quite important but normally concerned with less political issues. Procedurally their history is similar to that of government Bills.)

By the time a Bill is introduced and receives its first reading, and the House where it is introduced orders it to be printed for all to know the text, it is already late in the cycle of its preparation. Civil servants and Ministers, often consulting lobbies and specialists, will already have spent weeks, maybe months, modifying drafts. Parliamentary counsel have clothed the resulting compromises in a legally acceptable draft Bill. This Bill is published with a Long Title defining its scope, and – of increasing importance – an explanatory and financial memorandum is often attached which has been written by the responsible department to help explain the background to the proposed legislation. The second reading gives the Minister in charge of the Bill, the opposition shadow spokesman and an assorted number of interested and sometimes knowledgeable backbenchers the chance to discuss the principles of the Bill. The vote at the end of this debate is of key importance; if there is not a majority in favour, the Bill will be withdrawn.

Very occasionally, following this second reading in the House of Commons, a new procedure introduced in 1980 is used. Before the Bill is considered in standing committee a special standing committee, moved for by a Minister, takes evidence on the Bill in the same manner as is done by a select committee. The maximum period for which it can take evidence, which is of course published, is three two-and-a-half-hour sessions. This procedure is sparingly used and only when Bills are not politically controversial, but it does enable the House to secure more information on a Bill at an early stage of its journey through Parliament.

The standing committee stage is of course a detailed examination, when amendments and new clauses are proposed; as academic studies have often shown, however, the number of amendments accepted is not great. But the government listens and may introduce amendments itself when later the Bill reaches the House of Lords. Further stages of passing legislation are the report stage, when the standing committee reports back to the House and amendments can still be made, and the third and final reading, when amendments are accepted only in the House of Lords. The royal assent is given in the House of Lords.

Many Acts empower Ministers to issue Statutory Instruments and the important ones are published with an explanatory note and are laid before Parliament. If they require an *affirmative* resolution of the House of Commons, this will be moved by the Minister of the department responsible and debated for up to an hour and a half. If, however, they come into effect unless there is a motion to *annul* them within a certain time (i.e. a 'prayer'), then the initiative of tabling such a motion rests with members.

As law establishes the framework of society and attempts to ease the tensions within it, Parliament's legislative proceedings offer many insights into the society of the day. Above all, legislation reflects the country's changing needs, whether major, as with the European Communities Act 1972, or a matter of a specific urgent problem, as in the case of some swiftly enacted legislation on immigration. Bills may be introduced to tidy up administration, for purely political reasons or to meet a moral dilemma.

In studying Parliament's work on legislation it is necessary to consider several printed sources. The first printing of the Bill is cited, if introduced into the House of Commons, as [session, Bill number], or, if introduced into the House of Lords, as [session, (number)]. The explanatory memorandum may refer back to earlier statements of government policy on the subject which have been published as Command Papers [prefix followed by running number 1–9999]. The relevant Hansards for the second reading, report stage, third reading and consideration of amendments of the other House are cited [HC Deb., volume, or HL Deb., volume]. The text of the marshalled list of amendments and new clauses to the Bill is published [HC Supplement to the Votes and Proceedings, or HL a separate paper with session number and letter]. The Commons standing committee debate is a separate part of the Official Report [HC Deb. SC]. Indexes to these papers are considered later in the chapter.

Following royal assent the Bill is published as an individual Act, later in the annual volumes of *Public General Acts* and often in the loose-leaf series of volumes called *Statutes in Force*, a subject arrangement of major current legislation which has an alphabetical list of statutes included. More up-to-date than these printed sources is the computer-based database LEXIS. Work is also progressing on the preparation of a computer-based Statute Law Database. Statutory Instruments are published individually and later by serial number in a series of volumes each year. They number 2,000 or more a year, while statutes normally number fewer than 100 a year. The *Index to the Statutes* (a subject index) appears every two years, and so does the *Chronological Table of the Statutes*, which includes Acts which have been repealed. The equivalents for Statutory Instruments are the *Index to Government Orders* and the *Table of Government Orders*. The full text of Statutory Instruments from 1 January 1987 is now available on CD-ROM and also on CD-ROM is a catalogue of Statutory Instruments from 1 January 1980.

Parliament's financial work

The second main area of House of Commons work concerns taxation and control of expenditure. The financial procedures of the House of Commons are often regarded as recondite, but if the student of history sets out to look at the broad structure of parliamentary responsibility regarding financial matters it is possible to see a clear pattern of information.

The House is always interested in the country's economic situation. There are two particular interests, namely future expenditure plans and raising the necessary taxation – the Budget. Until the 1960s both of these areas were brought to the attention of the House of Commons at Budget time, normally in March. Following the Plowden report in 1961, and the introduction of the annual Public Expenditure White Paper, it became clear that it was more efficient to announce future expenditure plans not immediately before the financial year starting in April but some months in advance. Between 1982 and 1992 this was formalised into the Autumn Statement in November, when economic forecasts and departmental expenditure plans for the future were announced. The paper was examined by the Treasury and Civil Service Select Committee, which reported to the House so that the subject could be debated before Christmas. The Budget continued to be introduced in the spring. In 1992 the government decided to move the Budget, together with publication of its important background paper the Financial Statement and the Budget Report (the Red Book), back to November, thus drawing together publication of expenditure plans and taxation plans forming the so-called 'Unified Budget'. That is why in 1993 there were the last spring Budget and the first November Budget, which covered 1994–95. The Treasury and Civil Service Select Committee examines the Budget in the same way as before, reporting back to the House of Commons before the second reading of the Finance Bill. Although this change has inevitably led to some timing problems, reaction is generally favourable. The government has proposed making what might be called a Summer Statement to keep Parliament informed on economic matters between November Budgets.

A further development over this period has been the introduction of annual departmental reports linked with the government's expenditure plans for each major department over the coming three years. These reports started in session 1990–91 and are published as a series of twenty Command Papers with sequential numbering which can be purchased as a group. They are used in particular by the departmental select committee which examines the plans and estimates of the department under its purview. Starting in session 1994–95 more details concerning departmental estimates are to be included in these annual reports, an idea which, if acceptable to the House of Commons, will lead to a reduction in the size of the published estimates and the Treasury's burden in compiling them.

A second feature of this House of Commons financial work is that various Estimates, Supplementary Estimates and Votes on Account are laid before Parliament during the year. They give a great deal of information under about twenty main classes, subdivided into nearly 200 votes, which cover the whole range of government expenditure. This service to Parliament is of great importance in understanding the allocation of central government funds. The expenditure is authorised by Consolidated Fund Bills, which are taken formally.

Finally, at the end of the financial year, lines need to be ruled, columns totalled and the accounts audited by the National Audit Office. They are then laid before the House as the Appropriation Accounts. It is the Public Accounts Committee which examines them, takes evidence from accounting officers (civil servants) and reports to the House. It is not policy that concerns the committee but the administration of policy – 'efficiently, effectively and economically'.

A small library results from this House of Commons interest in economic affairs and its work concerning taxation and control of expenditure. The debates in the House include a day on the Autumn Statement, a day on the government's expenditure plans, and the four or five days on the Budget. There is a day's debate on the second reading of the Finance Bill and then there are the debates during subsequent stages. There are three days of debate on the Estimates, with the subjects chosen by the Liaison Committee (a select committee including all the chairmen of the departmental select committees) after it has examined the work of the Public Accounts Committee and the departmental select committees. There is also a day spent debating the reports of the Public Accounts Committee itself. All these are to be found in Hansard [HC Deb., volume]. The Autumn Statement, the Financial Statement and Budget Report, the reports of the Treasury Committee, the Estimates and related material, and the reports of the Public Accounts Committee, together with the government replies to those reports called Treasury Minutes, are published as House of Commons Papers [session, HC number]. Finally, the government's expenditure plans are published as Command Papers.

Parliament's oversight work

The third main area of parliamentary work consists mostly of debate on government policy and scrutiny of government administration. Debates on policy may be based on a government motion seeking approval, or, if conducted on one of the twenty days available to the opposition each session, will normally be a motion of criticism. Debates may also be a private member's motion on Wednesdays, 9.35 a.m. to 2.30 p.m., or a short, half-hour adjournment debate at the end of the day's proceedings. Whichever type of debate is used, some aspect of proposed policy is probed, new ideas are floated or the administration of agreed policy is challenged. In the last case the debates may be concerned with problems at constituency level. All this work is to be found published in Hansard [HC Deb., volume]. The House of Lords, which does not need to spend its time either on constituency matters or on financial ones, has more time for considering wide-ranging subjects such as 'the arts' or 'conservation', and contributions to such debates are often very well prepared by a range of speakers with impressive credentials. The House of Lords also devotes more time to European Union matters than the House of Commons is able to do. Its work is to be found in Hansard [HL Deb., volume].

The consideration of government policy and the scrutiny of administration is also the focus of select committee work. Select committee inquiries on behalf of each House of Parliament have for centuries been the traditional means whereby Parliament gathers information. In the nineteenth century a highly developed select committee system not only provided an archive of published information superior to that found in any other country at the time but, Whitehall being then only a small dot on the political–administrative landscape, was often the seedbed of legislation, initiated by committee members on the basis of their findings in committee. Today, as we have seen, most Bills are introduced by the government. During much of the first half of the twentieth century, in the face of growing government powers stimulated by wartime conditions, regular select committee work was on a very modest scale, but in recent decades and especially since 1979 a much more co-ordinated approach to committee work has been adopted.[5] The seventeen House of Commons departmental select committees and the House of Lords European Communities' Committee with its six sub-committees do set out to examine more systematically than hitherto the government's policy concerning, and administration of, domestic matters, foreign affairs and some aspects of British membership of the European Union.

The traditional method of work is to take written and oral evidence from the relevant government department (both the Minister and his civil servants), to invite written evidence more generally and then maybe to select a number of specialist witnesses to give oral evidence. The oral evidence is normally published, sometimes on a sitting-by-sitting basis. The written evidence is also published but sometimes selectively. Written evidence from government departments would always be printed, and, with the committee's permission, witnesses may publish their own evidence. Written evidence reported by the committee but not ordered to be printed may be consulted in the House of Lords Record Office, which is mentioned later in this chapter. People take great pains in preparing evidence for select committees – they are a very good public platform – and for this reason all types of researchers find the evidence of interest. But these days it is very rare for reports and certainly for evidence to be indexed, which means that both have to be examined very systematically. They are published as House of Commons Papers or House of Lords Papers.

If evidence is published on a sitting-by-sitting basis it will have a roman sub-number for each sitting – for example, 1982–3 HC 285 i–v, indicating the publication of oral evidence taken on five occasions. For the most part, these House of Commons departmental committees are concerned with the domestic scene, though the Foreign Affairs Committee is one of the most active and prolific. The House of Lords European Communities Committee publishes the most far-ranging reports on EC matters, and they are more widely read in Europe than the reports of any other member parliament. In conclusion, it should not be forgotten that the committees may order evidence submitted to them to be printed even if they do not choose to issue a report.

There are two further methods whereby Parliament can scrutinise the government's performance and draw out information. One is the use of parliamentary questions tabled by individual members. In recent sessions the number of these probes has exploded. Oral questions for answer by Ministers in the House remain at 6,000–7,000 a session, because the time devoted to them has not increased, but questions for written answer have more than doubled, from under 20,000 to more than 40,000 a session. All are indexed in the computer-based index POLIS (see below). From the viewpoint of researchers the written answers to questions which are concerned far more with facts than with politics are especially important. Indeed, information is sometimes set down in such convenient form that one wonders whether it has been presented in that way specifically to help researchers. Ministers will, however, be told by their civil servants if the cost of answering a question is more than £450 and may sometimes decline to answer on the grounds of cost. Equally, Ministers sometimes use written answers to release quite important information. Oral questions and answers are in the main text of Hansard. Written questions and answers are in a separately numbered sequence at the back of Hansard, and sometimes in their own issue called 'Part II' of a particular date. Starting in October 1992, where a member has tabled a question to a Minister on operational matters which have been delegated to an agency chief executive, it is the chief executive's reply which appears in Hansard under the sequence of written answers. It takes the form of the text of a letter from the chief executive to the Minister responsible.

The government is also subject to scrutiny through the work of the Parliamentary Commissioner. Since 1967 members have been able to pass on to him complaints which they have received concerning maladministration by government. About 800 cases a year are examined. About a quarter of this number are pursued and the complainant has been upheld on about half these occasions. The commissioner works directly to a select committee of the House of Commons. He issues annual reports, a quarterly selection (about one-third) of his case reports, and occasionally a report on a specially important case. With his high-level access to files, his probing can often be highly effective, his reports sometimes entertaining. Civil servants and Ministers may be called to give evidence to the select committee, and that can be quite revealing of how policy decisions are arrived at and especially of how they are carried out.

How to find material

The published record of Parliament's work fills five to ten metres of shelving every session and is not the most straightforward of research material. It can be divided into three main groups. The first consists of the working papers – covering the record of what has taken place together with the programme of future work. Some of the former material ends up in the Journal of each House, which is the permanent and legal record. The second group is the record of what was said. The third group consists of the papers laid before or created by Parliament. The following tabulation summarises the material in each group.

1 *The record of what takes place*
   HOUSE OF COMMONS
   . ·'Vote bundle'
   (a) Votes and Proceedings: minutes of the previous sitting; a list of papers laid before the House
   (b) Order Paper: agenda for the day's sitting
   (c) Notice Paper: motions to be moved, parliamentary questions to be asked in the future
   (d) Public Bill List: indicates the stage reached by public Bills
   (e) Supplement to the Vote: list of amendments to public Bills

HOUSE OF LORDS
Minutes
(a) Minutes of the previous sitting; a list of papers laid before the House
(b) Notice of business for the next sitting day
(c) Notice of business for the next month
(d) Parliamentary questions for written answer
(e) List of public Bills
(f) List of future committee meetings

2 *The record of what is said*

	Frequency	Indexes
HOUSE OF COMMONS		
Official Report	Daily; weekly; fortnightly (volume)	Fortnightly; volume; session
Official Report, Standing Committees	Each sitting	None
HOUSE OF LORDS		
Official Report	Daily; volume	Cumulating by volume; session

3 *Papers*

	No. each session	Indexes
HOUSE OF COMMONS		
Public Bills	About 150	Sessional
House of Commons Papers	400–600	Sessional
Command Papers	About 350	Sessional
HOUSE OF LORDS		
Public Bills and Papers	200–300	None

(From 1987/88 these have been published as two series: (1) Bills, (2) House of Lords Papers)

These papers are all published by HMSO. Group 1 can be purchased or part-purchased only by subscription. In group 2, House of Commons debates are also available on microform from Pergamon Press. Starting with session 1988–89 the full text of Hansard is available on CD-ROM. It is cumulated three times a year at the Christmas, Easter and summer recesses and finally in one CD-ROM at the end of the session. Forthcoming on CD-ROM it is proposed to publish Hansard indexes of the period 1803–1941. In group 3, House of Commons papers can also be bought on microform. Although groups 2 and 3 mostly have published indexes, the ability to retrieve information from these documents has recently been transformed by the introduction by the House of Commons Library of POLIS (Parliamentary On-line Information System). Started in 1980, this computer-based index, compiled in the House of Commons Library, adds some 60,000 to

70,000 parliamentary references a session to the main database. From the general election of 1992 it has been run by Data Sciences with Information Dimensions BASIS + software. It is available on-line through a number of larger public and university libraries and is a very comprehensive index to all Parliament's proceedings and papers. POLIS is also available on one CD-ROM covering the two Parliaments 1979–87, a further CD-ROM covering the Parliament 1987–92 and a third CD-ROM from 1992 and cumulating twice a year at the Easter recess and at the end of the session. These CD-ROMs dovetail into the on-line service, which is updated daily, and make consultation of POLIS much less expensive. In addition, POLIS is used by the library to prepare the indexes to the House of Commons Hansard and the sessional indexes to House of Commons Bills, Papers and Command Papers. This means that the subject terms used in the reports of the spoken word and in the parliamentary papers are being aligned, to the benefit of those seeking information. The full implications of this powerful information-retrieval system have yet to be realised by commentators, researchers and historians.

The following tabulation summarises the coverage of parliamentary material by POLIS.

Parliamentary material	*Abbreviation*	*Starting date*
Proceedings		
Commons Hansard	CH	4 November 1981
Commons Hansard (Legis)	CH	3 November 1982
Lords Hansard	LH	4 November 1981
Lords Hansard (Legis)	LH	3 November 1982
Commons standing committees	SC	3 November 1982
Early day motions	EDM	4 November 1981
Questions		
Commons questions	PQ	27 October 1980
Lords questions	LPQ	4 October 1981
Legislation		
Public and general Acts	PGA	9 May 1979
Local and personal Acts	LPA	3 November 1982
Laid Statutory Instruments	SI	3 November 1982
Papers		
Commons public Bills	Bill	9 May 1979
Command Papers	Cmnd, Cm	9 May 1979
Commons Papers	HC	9 May 1979
Lords Papers and Bills	HL	4 November 1981

(From 1987/8 House of Lords Bills are abbreviated as HL Bill. House of Lords Papers continue as HL)

Collections of these papers are available in a number of places throughout the country. The HMSO catalogue *Government Publications* includes a list of those libraries, in addition to copyright libraries, that subscribe to official publications, and most of them hold a collection of parliamentary material. The catalogue advises a telephone call to ensure availability and gives the telephone numbers. The Public Information Office of the House of Commons Library, which is always ready to respond to letters and telephone calls, has prepared *Access to Parliamentary Resources and Information in London Libraries* (APRILL), a detailed union list of those public libraries in London and the south-east which hold collections of parliamentary papers. A fourth edition was produced by the Library in 1991. The House of Commons library has also published *Parliamentary Holdings in Libraries, 1993* (PHIL) which covers collections of parliamentary debates, papers, journals, statutes and bulletins held by over 250 national, university, college, government departmental, private and public libraries throughout the United Kingdom and Ireland.

Finally, Parliament has its own record office for the public, the House of Lords Record Office, situated in the Victoria Tower in the Palace of Westminster. Apart from manuscripts dating back to 1497, it holds comprehensive collections of the printed sources mentioned in this chapter and has a public reading room open Monday to Friday, from 9.30 a.m. to 5.00 p.m. The staff have specialist knowledge not only of the bibliographical background but also, most important, of the historical and procedural background of Parliament's work. There is a *Guide to the Records of Parliament*[6] which lists and explains the various collections, and the Record Office publishes an annual list of new accessions as well as a number of memoranda on special aspects of the collection, which numbers some 3 million items.

When the sound broadcasting of Parliament started in 1978 it was decided after a couple of sessions that tapes would be passed over to the National Sound Archive, which is part of the British Library. Today all the sound tapes of parliamentary debates 1978–89 are kept in the National Sound Archive.

Experiments in televising the House of Lords from January 1985 followed and in televising the House of Commons from 21 November 1989. When these trials were judged a success, a Parliamentary Broadcasting Unit was established to cover the televised proceedings from both Houses of Parliament and on occasion from their committees. Anyone wishing to consult these tapes from the 1980s onwards, for research purposes, is asked to approach the Parliamentary Broadcasting Unit, which is at 7 Millbank, London SW1A 0AA, in the first instance, as the tapes are held there. In due course older tapes will be passed for permanent archiving to the National Film and Television Archive, which is part of the British Film Institute.

Conclusion

This chapter in some respects complements Chapter 24, on public records. Parliament and government have been entwined for centuries, although their cultures are rather different. Government, like law, is sharply concerned with precedent and is conceived in privacy – hence the twenty-five years before the final government departmental selection of documents to be passed to the Public Record Office and the thirty-year rule governing access. Parliament, on the other hand, has changed from being a privileged, rather private club (it was only in this century that it offered the vote to all and took responsibility for reporting its own debates) to being an advocate of openness.[7] Democracy today means access to your constituency member, to the Palace of Westminster, to information. Though its means are procedures leaning on precedents, Parliament's end is public debate and a search for greater accountability. In the background the communications revolution of telephone, air travel, television, computers, and so forth, has virtually eliminated time and space and has transformed the scale and tempo of Parliament's work. The resulting accumulation of first-hand evidence offered by Minister, civil servant, backbencher, specialist and citizen and made available in Parliament's published records is, not surprisingly, a vital resource for the contemporary historian.

The workings of Parliament have been transformed during the last generation. Consider a random list. The House of Commons has, by statute, separated itself completely from executive control. It has greatly increased its staff, over eightfold in the information field. It has introduced significant allowances for members to pay for secretaries and personal research assistants. It has established a Public Information Office to help anyone who wishes to know of its work. By telephone, by letter, by publications such as the *Weekly Information Bulletin* and the *Sessional Information Digest*[8] it is, today, very easy for everyone to learn about its past and present proceedings. It has modernised and set in order its Record Office and added to that archive its broadcast and televised proceedings. It has gathered together references to its work (1980–) in a computer-based indexing system, POLIS. It has introduced a positive and comprehensive select committee system and given members the opportunity to probe administration through the services of the Parliamentary Commissioner. The catalogue of change could be lengthened but suggests that those shelves of parliamentary debates, annual reports, accounts, committee reports, evidence, and so forth, which attempt to lay bare the way we are, are part of today's democratic accountability and as such are important contemporary evidence for the writing of history.

The words 'democratic accountability' have a fine ring; what do they really mean? One straw in the wind: a generation ago it would have been unthinkable for a Minister to come and explain his policy to a select committee. Today it is commonplace and is often broadcast too!

Appendix: official publications

While Parliament's papers are all published by Her Majesty's Stationary Office, the situation is less clear-cut with regard to other official publications. In recent years, although more material has been issued by government, its bibliographical control has become far less assured. Some of this material is closely related to the role of Parliament. The result is a grey area in official publishing which is a matter of concern to librarians, researchers and academic writers. Government departments are encouragted to apply their initiative in getting material published, with the result that today HMSO is publishing only a proportion of papers coming from the departments. Where HMSO is the publisher, details of the material will be found in the HMSO *Daily List*, the *Monthly Catalogue of Government Publications*, and *Government Publications*, the annual catalogue. If HMSO is not used, details will probably be found in the *Catalogue of British Official Publications not Published by HMSO* (1980–), which appears six times a year, followed by an annual catalogue.

Below are some alphabetically arranged notes aimed at elucidating some of these areas.

Command Papers

Command Papers are presented to Parliament by a Minister. They cover either a statement of policy (a White Paper or Blue Book) or information generally – for example, an annual report which has been submitted to a Minister and then laid before Parliament. But they also include, for instance, Treasury minutes where the government replies to reports of the Public Accounts Committee or reports of the Review Body concerning salaries of doctors, dentists, the armed services, senior civil servants, etc. Command Papers have a prefix followed by a serial number between 1 and 9999. They were first numbered in 1836, and appear in the following series.

Nos	*Dates*
[1–4222]	1836–68/9
C 1–9550	1870–99
Cd 1–9239	1900–18
Cmd 1–9889	1919–55/6
Cmdn 1–9927	1956/7–85/6
Cm 1–	1986/7–

Departmental inquiries

Internal departmental inquiries are set up by civil servants or Ministers. To what extent they 'go public' is a matter for the Minister. Sometimes a report may be laid before Parliament. The evidence is not published. Researchers should approach the department direct. In time most of the papers should be found in the Public Record Office (see Chapter 24). Chairmen may be traced in *British Government Publications: an Index of Chairmen and Authors, 1800–1982* (4 vols, 1974–84). The House of Commons Library compiles a Chairmen's Index which covers these enquiries and is available through the scope notes applied to entries in the POLIS database. Unlike other compilations, it is based not on published reports but on earlier information in parliamentary questions, press notices, and so forth.

Green Papers

These consultation documents are government proposals for policy inviting comment from anyone interested. The early ones, which first appeared from April 1967, were published in green covers as Command Papers. Today there appears to be no consistency in the way they are published. They are occasionally Command Papers but also appear as HMSO departmental publications, non-HMSO departmental publications or even restricted-circulation publications. The *House of Commons Weekly Information Bulletin* lists all those sent to Parliament, together with the department issuing it and the closing date for comment. This is bibliographically a very untidy area.

Parliamentary or sessional papers

The usual definition covers Public Bills, House of Commons Papers and Command Papers and House of Lords Public Bills and Papers. The House of Commons Papers were arranged from 1800 to 1968/69 as Public Bills, Reports of Committees, Reports of Commissioners, and Accounts and Papers; from 1969/70 to 1979/80 as Public Bills, and Reports, Accounts and Papers; and from 1980/81 as Public Bills, House of Commons Papers and Command Papers, in these three sequences, arranged numerically. House of Lords Public Bills and Papers were in one sequence until the end of 1986/87. From 1987/88 they are in two sequences, Public Bills and House of Lords Papers. There are no Command Papers in the House of Lords set. Published indexes to these papers exist for each session (the index is a House of Commons Paper) and cumulated 1800–50, 1851–99, 1900–48/49, 1950–58/59, 1959/60–68/69. A cumulated index covering 1969/70–1978/79 was published in 1995. House of Lords Papers have cumulated indexes 1801–59, 1859–70, 1871–84/85 but none during the twentieth century.

Reports and accounts

A number of annual reports and annual accounts of bodies in the public sector must be laid before Parliament as required by statute. In addition major government departments must produce reports in connection with their forward plans. These are mostly published by HMSO and are then given a House of Commons Paper number or a Command Paper number. They will all be included in the HMSO catalogue *Government Publications*. If the organisation publishes through another method the reports should appear in the *Catalogue of British Official Publications not Published by HMSO*. All papers laid before the House of Commons are listed in POLIS and the *Journal of the House of Commons*.

Royal Commissions

These are set up by the government by royal warrant. There are a number of standing Royal Commissions – for example, Ancient and Historical Monuments. Other Royal Commissions are set up to examine a specific topic, although the Conservative government of 1979–87 did not make use of them. To date, thirty-two have been appointed since 1945 – the last, on Criminal Procedures, being set up in December 1977 and reporting in January 1981. Royal Commission reports are published as Command Papers, but the evidence is not a parliamentary paper, though published by HMSO. The Stationary Office Sectional List No. 59 lists Royal Commissions from 1937 to 1981. *British Government Publications: an Index of Chairmen and Authors, 1900–40* (1974), pp. 168–74, includes a list of Royal Commissions from 1900 to 1940.

Treaty Series

Agreements with foreign countries or concerning commodities, and the like, are ratified by the government after the text has been published for twenty-one days. After ratification they are published in the Treaty Series, in different languages if appropriate, as Command Papers. Lists of ratifications, accessions, and so on, are published every few months as Command Papers and an annual index is produced. A general index to the Treaty Series 1101–1968 was published in 1970. It was prepared in the University of Nottingham Treaty Centre and published by HMSO. In 1992 the series was continued in Volume 4 of the *Index of British Treaties*, which covers the period 1969–88 and was also prepared in the University of Nottingham and published by HMSO.

White Papers

These are statements of government policy published as Command Papers. The term 'Blue Book' was used when they were big enough to merit a blue cover. It is used less frequently today. See the section above on Command Papers.

Notes

1 Erskine May, *Treatise on the Law, Privileges, Proceedings and Usage of Parliament*,

twentieth edition, ed. Charles Gordon (1983), p. 3.

2 *Conservative and Labour Party Conference Decisions, 1945–81*, compiled and ed. F. W. S. Craig (1982).

3 *British General Election Manifestos 1900–74*, compiled and ed. F. W. S. Craig (1975).

4 *The Most Gracious Speeches to Parliament, 1900–74: Statements of Government Policy and Achievements*, compiled and ed. F. W. S. Craig (1975).

5 See Dermot Englefield (ed.), *Commons Select Committees: Catalysts for Progress?* (1984). This includes (pp. 136–278) a comprehensive list of the work of the committees from 1979 to 1983, prepared with the aid of POLIS. A supplement listing the membership and reports of departmental select committees 1983–87 is available gratis from the publisher. See also Gavin Drewry, *The New Select Committees: a Study of the 1979 Reforms* (1985; paperback edition with updating chapter, 1988).

6 Maurice F. Bond, *Guide to the Records of Parliament* (1971).

7 See the Croham Directive (1977) on Disclosures of Official Information, and the Memorandum of Guidance for Government Officials appearing before Parliamentary Select Committees (1980). These are published as appendix 3 and appendix 2 of Dermot Englefield, *Whitehall and Westminster: Government informs Parliament: the Changing Scene* (1985).

8 The House of Commons *Weekly Information Bulletin* is published each Saturday during the session. It includes not only parliamentary work of the past and of the next week but also comprehensive listing of the papers issued during the past week, including public and private Bills, Select Committee Reports and Evidence, White and Green Papers, European Communities documents and Compliance Costs Assessments for Bills without Explanatory Memoranda.

The *Sessional Information Digest* is published a few weeks after the end of the session. It includes not only statistics about parliamentary work during the session but also comprehensive sessional lists of House of Commons Select Committee Reports and Special Reports, National Audit Office and Northern Ireland Audit Office Reports, European documents considered in standing committee, public and private Bills, Northern Ireland legislation, public general Acts, local and personal Acts and, together with a subject index, White and Green Papers. Both the *Bulletin* and the *Digest* are published by HMSO.

Chapter 23

National archives in the United States: the case of intelligence history

Bradley F. Smith

For more than one hundred years the government of the United States has stood in the forefront of openness regarding the records of its activities, both routine and sensitive. As early as the 1870s, the State Department began yearly publication of the *Foreign Relations of the United States*, which contained documents much more delicate and secret than European governments would allow to appear publicly even a century later. For example, included in the *FRUS* volume for 1879 was the text of a secret intelligence report chronicling Sitting Bull's activities after he had fled across the border into Canada in the wake of the battle of the Little Big Horn.[1]

During the 1920s and 1930s, when the major European belligerents attempted to win the *post hoc* battle over World War I war guilt by publishing carefully selected items from their diplomatic archives, the US government expanded its *FRUS* series. Thereafter Washington made public a broad range of materials about diplomatic events within ten years of their occurrence.

Even today, the *FRUS* series remains a highly useful tool for the intelligence researcher, for although it seldom contains highly sensitive intelligence documents, it does continue to reproduce important, and sometimes highly revealing, policy papers which can provide great benefit to those studying the secret world. Even more important, nearly every document appearing in a *FRUS* volume bears a decimal filing number, and such numbers provide the best possible indicator a researcher can acquire regarding which State Department files in the National Archives may contain secret papers related to intelligence.

With the opening in the early 1930s of a new National Archives building on Washington's Pennsylvania Avenue, the US government again led the way in lessening the secrecy of governmental records. Researchers were soon allowed access to many military and naval records as well as those of the State Department (and various civil domestic departments). All this availability was however, limited by the so-called twenty-five year rule, which did not obligate government departments to release to the public any records until at least a quarter-century had passed.

In the post-World War II era, additional moves were made in the American march toward greater openness. A series of presidential libraries was established, run by the National Archives, which more effectively met researchers' requests for access to recent high-level historical documentation. The 1960s and 1970s saw the passing of the Freedom of Information Act, with various amendments, which simultaneously provided individuals with broader rights to know what information government departments might be holding about them as individuals, and gave scholars some legal instruments to compel the government to release sensitive information for public use.

These American moves to lessen secrecy regarding historical records did not make the records of the US government an open book. Rather than send sensitive materials to the archives, some departments simply retained 'operationally necessary' documents in their own files and employed various security blocking devices to make many files which were sent to the archives inaccessible to researchers. Furthermore, non-US citizens are not covered by some of the appeal provisions of the Freedom of Information Acts, even though foreign governments were, and are, able on some occasions to restrict access to their materials in US governmental archives.

Despite these secrecy measures, the government of the United States remains unusually openhanded regarding government documentation, and at this moment, when another huge National Archives building is under construction in College Park, Md., the central National Archives system remains the last best hope for those doing research on intelligence, as well as most other aspects of American national policy. The new building in College Park will solve one of the main problems which have long frustrated researchers working on the history of intelligence as well as other sensitive subjects. The main policy files of the State and service departments will no longer be divided between two locations, because the Suitland, Md., research centre will soon give up its high-level documents to the College Park facility, and the same fate will fall to most of the documents now being held on Pennsylvania Avenue.

The general move to College Park will not eliminate other peculiar, and often frustrating, features of the National Archives system, however. Computer ordering of documents will not be employed at College Park, nor will there be comprehensive and detailed guides available comparable to those in the British Public Record Office. The latter deficiency will in part be rectified by the scheduled appearance in the mid-1990s of a new survey guide to the military/naval holdings prepared by a skilled senior archivist, Dr Timothy Mulligan, of the Military Reference and Captured Enemy Records Branches.

Dr Mulligan's guide notwithstanding, the National Archives will remain a confusing and frustrating institution for many researchers, especially those pursuing such arcane subjects as the history of intelligence. Although in recent years American intelligence agencies have shown greater willingness to transfer some of their historical records to the National Archives, and even opened them to public scrutiny, not all of these materials have been placed in distinct and clearly defined collections. The National Security Agency has provided the National Archives with some signals intelligence documents, including a bloc of Vichy French decrypts, but much of the cryptanalytic material in RG 457 has been pulled out of its original context and turned over to the National Archives in the form of individual xerox copies, which makes evaluation of context, as well as the importance of the material, difficult to assess. The Central Intelligence Agency has, however, transferred to the archives the bulk of the documentary records of its predecessor organisation, William Donovan's World War II intelligence unit, the Office of Strategic Services, and these may be found clearly and systematically arranged (RG 226) in the Military Reference Branch under the care of John Taylor and Lawrence MacDonald.

In addition, as Richard Aldrich has emphasised,[2] since the end of the Cold War, nearly all US intelligence agencies have shown more willingness to open up their historical records to researchers. Large quantities of CIA, NSA, and military intelligence records are now being transferred to the National Archives, although much of the material will require extensive processing time before it can be opened to the public.

Even before these materials are organised and released, other disembowelled but coherent groups of open intelligence records have been scattered around the main National Archives, including some FBI material on counter-intelligence in the Diplomatic Branch and subversive control documents originating with the Shanghai police in the Military Reference Branch (RG 263). One will not be able to count on the RG number or long-term location of such truncated groups of records, however, because they can easily be transferred to other branches, or combined with other record groups, in the near future.

By and large, however, the National Archives staff have recognised that the original context and organisation of blocs of records should be preserved, and except for a few sections of records such as those just mentioned, the context of nearly all the intelligence documents open to research has been conscientiously preserved. No special, or artificial, organisation has been impressed on most record groups. Documents have simply been placed within the large departmental record group to which they originally belonged. All Joint Chiefs of Staff records from World War II went into RG 218, army staff records into RG 165 and RG 319, and all three of these record groups passed along with other military materials into the custody of the Military Reference Branch. Similarly, the general correspondence records of the State Department were placed in RG 59, and assigned to the

Diplomatic Branch.

Nor were blocs of records simply thrown helter-skelter into a record group. Each group of records received its own identifying 'Entry Number'. For example, the reports of the US Army Attaché in Moscow during World War II are designated Entry 47, and are filed in Record Group 319, while reports made by American officials dealing with Soviet military attachés in Washington in this period, although also part of RG 319, have a sub-group designation of their own, Entry 57.

Even the records of huge offices of the US government have been held within the entry number system. Every section of the World War II War Department, from the Operations Division to the offices of the Chief of Staff, G-2, and the Secretary of War, has its own entry number inside RG 165 and RG 319. Therefore researchers working on nearly any subject, even one as obscure and arcane as intelligence history, can fairly easily isolate appropriate groups in the National Archives.

Even so, the formidable fact remains that some entry groups, such as that used for the World War II Operations Division of the War Department (in RG 165), contain thousands, perhaps even tens of thousands of document boxes, and only a final set of clues will make it possible accurately to pinpoint the records one is seeking. This is the main subject filing system employed by offices or departments of the US government. The common filing system for most US departments concerned with intelligence in the mid-twentieth century was a five or six-digit decimal number. So, for example, a filing number frequently employed by the State Department for OSS material was 103.918, while a good G-2 (Intelligence Branch of the War Department) number for intelligence liaison relations was 350.05. No series of decimal numbers is good for all times and places, simply because filing clerks change their minds, and events alter the way departments view subjects, thereby forcing them to alter file designations.

Consequently, along with seeking all possible assistance from other scholars in tracking down records, researchers should carefully search for citation clues in existing works (especially decimal and entry numbers as well as record group designations). As indicated above, the *Foreign Relations of the United States* volumes are particularly rich sources for such designations within the Diplomatic Branch.

In addition, letters should be written in advance of any research trip to the various branches of the National Archives (and if possible directed to specific archivists) setting out the subject to be researched and listing out tentatively inviting decimal numbers in order to give the archivist time to think about the possibilities, explore a bit, and consider whether the suggested record group and decimal numbers are the best way into the documents.

This prospect may seem daunting but it is self-evident that, with hundreds of record groups, thousands of entry numbers, and hundreds of thousands of decimal file number combinations in the National Archives, there is usually no easy path through the central holdings of the archives in Washington.

Fortunately, however, the National Archives system is not only made up of many departments and divisions in Washington and College Park, it also has a series of other archives spread across the United States. Regional archives, such as the west-coast centre at San Bruno, Ca. (south of San Francisco), hold both military and civil records of the US government applicable to a particular region. These are smaller institutions, and generally easier to use than the huge central holdings in Washington/College Park, but they too hold materials relevant to national and international subjects, as well as regional matters. Civil defence and Japanese internment materials in the San Bruno centre, for example, can throw valuable light on the actions and attitudes of American officials at the time of the great Japanese invasion scare of 1941/42.

A more broadly useful portion of the National Archives system, at least for scholars researching intelligence history, is the presidential libraries. Every American President from Herbert Hoover to Ronald Reagan has had established in his honour a presidential library, usually located in his birthplace. Owing to security restrictions and other considerations such as fundraising and construction schedules, the libraries of the most recent US Presidents such as Gerald Ford and Ronald Reagan are more theoretical than actual. But those for Presidents Hoover to Eisenhower are extremely useful, and those for Kennedy and Johnson are very valuable despite a high incidence of withheld documentation.

Each of the presidential libraries contains an extensive array of the working papers of the particular Chief Executive to whom it is dedicated. The papers are usually arranged according to the filing system which was used for them in the White House. In consequence the structure of the collections varies rather widely from one presidential library to another. All, however, have the common characteristic that, since most of the papers which they hold were produced by people in US government employment, they are public, not private, papers, which means there are few copyright restrictions on their use. Unfortunately, however, all security and declassification requirements apply to them just as they do to collections in Washington and College Park. Documents are withheld under the regular twenty-five year rule, as well as other special security withholding regulations. It appears, however, that in some of the older presidential libraries security restrictions have on occasion been applied somewhat less rigorously than in Washington.

Clustered around the Chief Executive's papers in each presidential library are the records of many of his most important aides and associates. Although most of the materials in these collections date from the period of the particular President's administration, some documents come from earlier or later periods, such as Walter Bedell Smith's very valuable collection of World War II material, dating from his service as Eisenhower's wartime chief of staff (1942–45), which is deposited in the presidential library in Abilene, Ks.

Estimating what one is likely to find in a specific presidential library regarding intelligence history or any other sensitive subject, is, however, often a matter of uneasy conjecture. While the cost of organising, weeding, and maintaining the records in these institutions is carried by the federal budget, and the libraries are administered by the National Archives, the cost of some of their features, including portions of their decoration, part of their reference library costs, travel grants, etc., are usually borne by citizen groups or committees of friends of the former President. Some presidential libraries, such as that for Dwight D. Eisenhower, therefore excel in decoration and formality, while others, such as the Harry S. Truman Library, have used much of the local money they have acquired for reference library resources and travel grants for researchers.

Obviously researchers must accept the special characteristics of the presidential libraries as they find them, but useful preparatory and precautionary steps may be taken before one departs on an odyssey to West Branch, Johnson City, or Independence. Each presidential library produces its own extensive guide to its manuscript holdings, including indications of the time period covered and the overall size of each sub-section of its collection. Special lists providing details of large sub-sections of the overall collection have also been prepared, and may be supplied in advance if requested.

It is therefore essential that those desiring to do research at a particular presidential library should request manuscript guides well in advance of travel, so that sufficient time remains to request supplementary guides to promising collections, as well as information on housing and means of travel. Once one has established the general range of documentary materials in a particular presidential library, it is wise to enquire whether the library holds copies of the reference books, memoirs, etc., essential to effective use of those records for a subject like intelligence history. Central Kansas is not the place to discover that an indispensable book or article is not available.

This hazardous feature of peripatetic documentary research in America also applies to another main segment of the US archive system, the plethora of manuscript collections held by universities, historical associations, and other public institutions. At first glance such archives may not seem to fall within the boundaries of institutions likely to hold documents related to intelligence history. In fact, however, extensive collections of such documentation built up by individuals during their years of government service are frequently turned over to such libraries and archives after retirement, or through family bequests following an ex-intelligence man or woman's death. Like the collections maintained by the presidential libraries, these independent manuscript collections vary greatly in size and quality, and they are scattered even more widely across the United States. Compounding the difficulties they pose for the researcher is the fact that a substantial number of these collections have been built up with more regard for honouring the individual in question than assisting scholarly use of the materials the collection contains.

To gain maximum benefit from this category of archive materials, the researcher from abroad should therefore make careful preparations. Fortunately, much of this effort can be carried out relatively easily in the United Kingdom owing to the existence of the Library of Congress guide to manuscript collections of the United States. The *National Union Catalogue of Manuscripts* includes not only a name index of manuscript collections but a subject index with headings such as 'intelligence', 'spies', and 'espionage'. It also provides a summary of each collection, its size, the address of the repository, access rules, etc. To top off its virtues, *NUCM* publishes supplemental volumes which keep this index of available American collections as current as possible, and are readily available in the British Library and major scholarly institutions in Britain.

Of course, even this worthy series does not provide a researcher with a magic carpet to archival success in the United States. Letters and telephone calls to archives are still essential to determine the quality and range of individual collections, as well as current restrictions on use. Vast distances and frequent deficiencies in reference materials are at least as serious an obstacle in using such collections as they are for the presidential libraries. But with careful overall planning and sensible recognition that such research takes considerable time and effort, and that intelligence material is not ladled out freely in any country, research on intelligence history can be a highly rewarding experience in the central National Archives of the United States, in the presidential libraries, and in the manuscript collections of public institutions.

Notes

1 *Foreign Relations of the United States* (1879), pp. 217 and 496–508.
2 Richard Aldrich, 'Never Never Land and Wonderland? British and American policy on intelligence archives', *Contemporary Record*, 8 (1), summer 1994, pp. 133–52.

Chapter 24

National British archives:
public records

Nicholas Cox

The letter had been brought in at twenty minutes to nine. It was just on ten minutes to nine when I left him, the letter still unread. I hesitated with my hand on the door handle, looking back and wondering if there was anything I had left undone. I could think of nothing. [Dr Sheppard, in Agatha Christie, *The Murder of Roger Ackroyd*, chapter 6]

A fictional snippet of autobiography. Whether or not we care who killed Roger Ackroyd, readers to the end of the story discover that the village doctor's bland account had concealed the purpose of his visit, accomplished in those blank ten minutes, which was murder by stabbing.

This is an extreme example of deliberately misleading testimony. Contemporary historians have access to new techniques, such as tape-recording of oral evidence, and much more in published form, through newspapers, broadcasts, film, parliamentary debates and memoirs, than existed for earlier periods. Although they neglect these secondary sources at their peril,[1] the quotation may explain why they are likely, for the foreseeable future, to pursue investigations behind the outwardly more appealing faces of public personalities by stepping into the dry world of official archives.

Using archives, and in particular those of central government, presents historians with difficulties which do not exist for users of books, of documents published in editions, or of private manuscript collections. They arise largely from the special nature of archives as a source, from the circumstances of their creation, from the consequential way in which they are arranged and made available for research when they come to be transferred to a record office, and from the fact that there are usually restrictions on their availability. Additional difficulties are caused by the fact that the quantities of material generated by modern central governments are so vast that what is preserved can usually be only a selection from what was originally brought into being.

What are archives?

'Archives' and 'manuscripts' tend to be used interchangeably as terms to describe collections and accumulations of papers and records. But in fact they are not the same thing at all. What are archives, then? They are not like manuscripts, accumulated by libraries or private collectors, or kept by individuals, because they are not artificially gathered collections of items. They consist of the papers (or, usually, a selection from the papers) which official authorities (in the case of the archives of the state, the central government) drew up for the purposes of the conduct of their affairs, or which they used in conducting them. They are papers which themselves *formed an actual part of that conduct of affairs*. They may not even be 'papers' at all, but may consist of any objects conveying information in the administrative context in which they were created or used. They will have been preserved afterwards by those responsible for the transactions in question, or by their legitimate successors, in their own custody and for their own reference.[2] Above all it is their *official* character which defines them.[3]

Archives have particular and significant characteristics which follow from this definition. First, as what has been called 'the secretions of an organism' they form a natural accumulation in government departments or other official bodies, because documents, as objects, form a real part of the administrative actions which produce them. Indeed, they may now be the only physical residue of those actions. Secondly, their natural 'secretion' by the administrative process means that they form an organic whole, in the same way that the organisation that created them formed one, and so any item among them is likely to be closely related to other items, both within and outside the series of records in which it exists. It is on these relationships that very much of the significance of archives depends. Lastly, archives, as a natural secretion, are historically impartial: that is to say that (with some very significant exceptions), they were not drawn up for the benefit of historians – or, for that matter, of anyone else outside the administrative process.

For researchers in libraries, used to author, title and subject catalogues, the move into a record office can be bewildering and exasperating. Because books are deliberately manufactured articles, they can be equipped with an identification, and with internal means of reference, such as a contents list and index, when they are published, and they nearly always are. Because they are individual, discrete items, each with its own separate significance and title, and normally with an identifiable author, they can be acquired and then catalogued individually. Because they tend to exist in multiple copies, possessed by many different owners, the librarians who care for them have long since been able to develop shared standards for describing them and providing means of reference to them – in fact they have had to do so – and researchers who have used one library will usually have no difficulty in finding their way round another library's catalogue, whether in the same country or not. Furthermore, depending on its specific acquisitions policy and the funds at its disposal, a library can decline to acquire any particular item, because the librarians know that another major library, such as one of the British copyright libraries, is bound to possess a copy, and that the item will therefore be available elsewhere. Similar considerations apply to newspapers and other publications.

Because archives are the incidental by-products of official actions, they usually have no obvious 'author', and very often not even a declared title. Because they consist not of discrete items but of selections from accumulated *series* of records produced by official activities, they have to be described largely by reference to the administrative activities which created them. Because the archives in any one record office are likely by definition to be unique, archivists have been much slower than libraries in establishing principles and in developing common standards for arranging and describing what has been transferred into their custody. In countries such as the Netherlands, with a centrally organised system of record offices, national principles and standards were developed relatively early on,[4] but in countries such as Britain or the United States, without a centrally controlled archive network, each record office may have its own, slightly different, methods, and some may present the researcher with the need to learn a whole new system from scratch. This may apply too in moving from record offices in one country to those in another one.

Last, when selecting or handling archives, archivists know that what they have before them is unique, and that its destruction, or any step which makes it unavailable, will almost certainly obscure the particular information that it contains. However, they will be aware that its underlying organic interrelations with other archives may mean that the information is indirectly recoverable elsewhere, and that awareness is likely to affect their approach in deciding whether to preserve it or not. What the researcher finds is the result not of a purchasing or acquisitions policy based on the availability of funds for buying, but of archivists' selection policy based on appraisal of the informational value of the material.

This excursion into archival theory may seem a little arcane to prospective users of archives, but it is worth putting what follows into context. Setting out the underlying reasons for the peculiarities of research in archives may help to explain some of them. It is unfortunate, perhaps, that nearly all the explanatory literature on the way to use archives has been produced by the archivists, who keep them, and hardly any by the historians, who use them, even though there has always been a two-way traffic in careers between the two professions. The resulting slant in approach has often given archivists the appearance of being obsessed by the world they inhabit and by their own problems and procedures, to the cost of their relations with researchers. Anyone who knows Michael Frayn's play *Alphabetical*

Order,[5] in which an earnest newcomer is inducted into the ludicrously idio-syncratic filing system of a newspaper-cuttings library, will understand what is meant. This chapter is probably no different, and its readers ought to bear in mind (but maybe it will be only too apparent) that it has been written by an official archivist.[6] It is also written by one who works in the Public Record Office in London, and a great deal of what follows is partic-ularly related to the history of the PRO and its records.

How are archives created and how are they arranged?

Archives were created by official activities in the past. By now they may well be the only evidence of them. But, since they are not simply a retro-spective account of those activities, but the documents which played an actual role in them, they are not merely evidence for the facts. They are part of the facts.

Most researchers, other than historians of administration, are only inci-dentally interested in what officials were doing in the past. They are more likely to be concerned with a wider subject of investigation, on which offi-cial activities had some bearing. But, if you are working on archives, you have in front of you records which exist because they played a part in what officials were doing in the past. You are using the written transactions, the part of the facts which has come down to us in tangible form, to reconstruct the activities, or to throw light on the wider topic of research. To say that archives are part of the facts is not to say that what is written in them is, or was, the 'truth'. It is to say that what they contain had a particular sig-nificance at the time it was written, and in the circumstances of the time. So, if you are to make right use of the written transactions, you need to understand the reasons that the officials who created them had for being involved in the subject we are concerned with, and for writing or doing what they did. You have to know how they worked in their particular organisations, and also – this is important – how they used and created the documents we are looking at. That is why record offices' guides to their con-tents tend to describe them in terms of administrative background and record-keeping practices, rather than by subject matter. If you are more interested in a subject than in what clerks in an office or court were doing, or in how papers were being arranged, these guides can make for dry read-ing. After all, it is not so long since interest in good filing systems was seen by Anthony Crosland as going hand in hand with advocacy of total absti-nence as a mark of an over-austere approach to life.[7]

All this may appear obvious: master the sources. It may seem arid advice too, until you order up a bundle or file of documents, which for all you know may never have been read by anyone in the record office before, and find a paper which you do not understand. Then it is worth recalling. Each piece of paper, however enigmatic it may appear, is there for a reason, even if you cannot at first understand what that reason is. It was not placed there as a conundrum. Someone in the past wrote it, and had a reason for writing it. Someone was intended to read it – maybe the writer, if it was written as a reminder; maybe someone else. Unless you can understand what the writer was engaged on, what part he (until the twentieth century, almost certainly *he*) was playing in the office that produced the records you are looking at, you may not be able to fathom the writer's purpose. To understand the part he was playing, you will need to understand how his office worked, and the kinds of document that its workings might have produced. Above all, to understand why he might have written what you have in front of you, and to be able to use the information it may convey, you have to put yourself in the writer's position and achieve a realisation of the circumstances in which he was working. This calls for a leap of imagination, whether you are dealing with records of the thirteenth century or of the twentieth. Of course, the ability to make this leap is a matter of historical training and experience. But it is more likely to be made in the right direction if it is based on a full understanding of the nature of the records being used, and of the whole range of related records available for use.

But users of archives in a record office face a further complication. Not only do they have to understand the workings of the original creators of their sources. They have also to cope with the way in which archivists themselves have, maybe imperfectly, tried to understand those workings in retrospect, and to present the resulting archives accordingly.

Although this chapter has been written with contemporary historians in mind, a little delving into the past is needed to explain the rationale behind the organisation of the papers they may want to see. The archival arrangement of papers goes back to medieval times, but a brief account of what was done during the nineteenth century may show how the present system emerged, and also show how work on papers by the departments which created them affected the subsequent approach of the Public Record Office, once it had come into existence.

The Treasury had begun to number incoming papers and to keep systematic annual registers of them in 1782. It was not long before it employed a succession of members of its staff to investigate and sort into some sort of order its older unregistered papers. The Foreign Office had appointed a librarian in 1801, and had begun to keep registers of its despatches and papers in country series and to index them. In 1811 the Admiralty had begun an even more elaborate scheme for sorting and indexing its correspondence, and for making a subject-arranged summary of the papers, the 'Digest', and also carried out some retrospective 'digesting' of its correspondence back to 1793. Soon after the PRO was set up in 1838,[8] officially to deal with the records of the courts of law and to provide them with a single home, its staff were being called on by departments to provide assistance in working through, reporting on and arranging their accumulations of non-current records. It began to accept deposits of these records, and from that point onwards its archivists began to become much more closely involved not only with older records but also with arrangements for the way in which records were handled in their originating departments, a process which was accelerated by an order-in-council in 1852 which brought all departmental records under the 'charge and superintendence' on the Master of the Rolls, the senior Chancery judge who was then also Keeper of Public Records. The process was taken further in 1854 by the incorporation into the PRO of the State Paper Office, which by then held records of the Home, Foreign and Colonial Offices down to 1830, and some even later material. The Treasury, exercising its growing powers over other departments' organisation and methods, and taking advantage of the existence of the PRO and the extension of its area of responsibility, set about a series of investigations into government records, and began to interest itself in departments' arrangements for handling papers, and in ways in which their records could be transferred systematically to the PRO for safe keeping.

The great change in current record-keeping which came about in this process was the development of the registered file. Instead of simply numbering papers in order as they came in, or as they were generated in the office, and keeping registers of those numbers, departments began to organise their papers by subject, keeping incoming letters, internal minutes, drafts of replies and any other related material together from the start, in a cover with a reference and, usually, a title. Twentieth-century researchers are so used to using registered files that it is often hard for them to remember how recently they appeared on the scene. Departments which were new, or which had had only loose control over their correspondence and papers, tended to be the earliest to move over to this new system. The War Office began to keep structured subject files in 1855, and the Home Office in 1871. Departments which already had a highly developed system of keeping and registering numbered series of papers were usually the slowest to reform. The Treasury did not completely abandon the system it had set up in 1782 until 1920, although from the 1850s it began to formalise methods of bringing numbered papers on one topic together, and storing them out of their original numerical order, recording their movements and their final physical locations in a separate series of registers. This was the pattern followed by most departments. They retained annual numbered series of papers, but devised ways, which were usually cumbersome, either of keeping correspondence on the same subject together, as those working on new incoming papers called for any earlier related papers, or of cross-referencing papers on similar topics. Relatively homogeneous departments, such as the Home Office or Treasury, maintained office-wide registration systems for the whole of their correspondence. Departments broken down into distinct divisions, with markedly different areas of responsibility, decentralised their systems. The Board of Trade, for instance, initiated separate series of numbered papers for its Commercial, Marine, Railway, Finance, Harbour, Establishment, Companies and Bankruptcy Departments as they were set up.

As archivists came into contact with other departments and had to take in orderly transfers of usually already arranged papers from them, their growing understanding of departmental registration systems rapidly led to a realisation of the basic principles of the arrangement of archives. They were realised more quickly abroad, and in a more systematic form, than in Britain. In 1841 the French Ministry of the Interior, which was responsible for the Archives Nationales, developed the principle of *respect des fonds*, according to which the records of any particular institution were to be grouped together as that institution's *fonds* (there is no adequate English translation) *and not arranged together with records from other fonds* on the basis of any similarity in subject matter or format. Archives should be classified so that the organisation and functions that produced them would be clearly reflected by them. In 1881 the Prussian State Archives reformulated this principle, in the German guise of a *Provenienzprinzip*, or principle of provenance, and developed it further by establishing as well a *Registraturprinzip*, or principle of original order. According to this, the records within each institution's *fonds* were to be arranged, or maintained, when transferred to the archives, in the order in which the original institutional registry had arranged them.[9] If the records had become disordered, it was the foremost duty of the archivist to discover and restore the original order. These principles aimed, as far as humanly possible, to preserve the impartiality of the archives, and to leave the facts that they represented undisturbed. They were set out, and argued for, at length in 1898, in the Dutch *Manual*,[10] and have been the basis of all archivists' operations ever since.

In the Public Record Office these principles have led to the arrangement of the records in *groups*, each of which consists of the archives resulting from the work of an administrative unit of government which was an organic whole, complete in itself, capable of dealing independently with every side of its business – i.e. what most people would recognise as a separate government department or court. Within each group are *classes*, each of which represents an original series of records (in most other English-speaking countries what the PRO calls classes are called *series*), all resulting from the same accumulation or filing or recording process, and all of similar physical nature and information content. Within each class are the individual *pieces* (or items), which are the single files, bundles of papers, maps or volumes which made up the original series.

The record groups in the PRO were originally all given mnemonic letter codes, representing the courts or departments of government which created, or transferred, the records in them. So, records of the Treasury are in the T group, those of the Cabinet Office in CAB, those of the Court of King's

Bench in KB, and so on. Within each group the classes are arbitrarily assigned numbers, simply in the order in which the decision to transfer them was taken; the numbers have no other significance. Each piece or item within the class is separately numbered, so that, in theory, every item can be referred to, or ordered up, using a simple three-part reference.

This system worked well for 'dead' archives, and for those created during a period when administrative structures were stable and relatively uncomplicated. It would still work well in an archival institution which had the ability directly to control records in other departments, and to classify them, from the point of their original creation or from very soon after it. In Britain, the PRO has no direct executive control over other departments' filing systems, although it can advise on them, and does not have the opportunity to classify or arrange archives until the point at which they are due to be transferred, usually after they are twenty-five years old. During that time span, administrative changes, and transfers of administrative functions from one department to another, usually involving the physical transfer of the related working papers as well, have often made strict adherence to traditional principles impossible.[11]

Getting the records into the record office

In the United Kingdom the general process of selecting, transferring and giving public access to the state's archives is governed by the Public Records Act of 1958. But most of the detailed processes are not statutory. They are controlled by principles laid down in the 1954 report of the Committee on Departmental Records, usually known by the name of its chairman, Sir James Grigg.[12]

The committee's aim was to devise arrangements which would ensure that records that had a permanent historical or administrative value would be selected for transfer to the PRO, to be made available in due course; that material which was clearly identifiable as having no permanent use would be got rid of as quickly as possible, so as to simplify the job of selection from the rest; and that these two aims would be achieved without a huge increase in the numbers of the staff of the PRO, and of those who were responsible for records in government departments.

Briefly, the committee recommended that departments should prepare schedules of standard series of routine records, according to their own arrangements for categorising papers in use, which they would have discretion to dispose of automatically after fixed, probably short, periods of time, without going through them paper by paper. Other standard series might be marked at that stage as automatic candidates for permanent preservation. All other papers, those which could not be dealt with at the series level, should be reviewed by their departments, file by file, five years after they had passed out of active use. The departments should destroy the ones which they did not need to keep any further for their own use. At that stage the staff reviewing papers should exercise their judgement according to the criteria that they understood best, by putting the question, 'Is my department likely to require this paper any longer for its own purposes?' The committee believed that, if the question was properly answered, taking account of papers which were still related to current business, and of the department's need to document its own activities in similar circumstances, the papers which survived this first review would include those which had material historical significance.

However, some of the papers which survived this first review would not be worth keeping permanently. So the committee recommended that, when the papers which had survived were twenty-five years old, they should be reviewed again, on this occasion directly using the criterion of permanent historical value in the perspective brought about by the intervening lapse of time. In general, the committee believed that the responsibility for these selection procedures would have to rest on the departments, with the PRO acting as co-ordinator and supervisor, but that decisions about what to keep or destroy after twenty-five years should be taken jointly by the department and a representative of the PRO. The records selected after this second review should be transferred to the PRO, unless they still needed to be kept in their department for administrative use.[13]

When the Grigg committee reported, there was no legal right of public access to British government records at all. Most departments which had transferred records to the PRO had agreed dates down to which researchers could see their papers. But those dates were at the departments' discretion and the dates differed from department to department. The committee recommended that a period of fifty years should be fixed, after which records should become accessible automatically, unless notice was given by a department that it did not want particular records to be made available.[14]

As a result of these recommendations the Public Records Act was passed in 1958. It did not provide for the details of the reviewing procedures outlined above, but it did provide an administrative framework in which they could be carried out. And it provided the fixed period of fifty years after which records would become accessible, as recommended. But it gave the Lord Chancellor, the Minister now responsible for public records, the power to prescribe an increase or decrease in this period for particular records, if he saw fit. The Act is the basis on which the PRO operates today, and the only major amendment to it has been the reduction of the fixed period for access to records to thirty years. That change was brought about by a second Act in 1967.

These arrangements for selecting records differ from those in many other countries in that such very large numbers of files are examined individually during the process of review.[15] In Australia, for instance, although the archives legislation is much more detailed in its provisions for the review process, selection is carried out almost entirely at the class level, and it is the whole run of files in any particular series that will be either kept or destroyed. But in the process of review in the United Kingdom sight is not lost of the principles of archival arrangement described earlier. Files are reviewed individually within their file series. At the point at which a new series is due for its final review, arrangements are made within the PRO for a new *class*, with its own appropriate letter code and an individual class number, and a title, to be assigned to the records which will be transferred after the review has taken place. Once that has happened, the records, although they have been reviewed individually, will be kept together in their series, and will appear within the appointed period, as pieces in the assigned *class*.

The statutory provisions for access also differ from those in countries which have freedom-of-information legislation, as Australia, Canada, Sweden and the United States do, although it is possible for countries to operate simultaneously under a Freedom of Information Act, giving a right of access to categories of current government papers, and archival legislation as well, which provides for general access to records in the archives after a longer fixed period. Australia does just that. The UK legislation is also different in that its access provisions are expressed negatively, rather than positively: 'Public records in the Public Record Office ... shall not be available for public inspection until the expiration of the period of thirty years. ...'[16] There is a presumption against disclosure before the prescribed period is over. But the period is calculated for each single file or item separately. The calculation is made so that an item is available at the beginning of the year following the year in which the latest paper in the item is thirty years old. Thus 1964 papers, so long as they were not included in files or volumes running on beyond 1964, were opened to the public at the beginning of 1995.

As mentioned earlier, there can be exceptions to the thirty-year access provision, and under section 5(1) of the Public Records Act the Lord Chancellor can approve a longer or shorter period. Under the terms of the government's White Paper on Open Government, published in July 1993 (Cm 2290), extended closure is approved for exceptionally sensitive records containing information the disclosure of which would not be in the public interest in that it would harm the defence, international relations, national security, including the maintenance of law and order, or the economic interests of the United Kingdom and its overseas territories; for records whose release would or might constitute a breach of confidence; and for records containing information about individuals the disclosure of which would cause either substantial distress, or endangerment from a third party, to persons affected by disclosure or their descendants.

The Act also prohibits the release of records which contain information that government has obtained under statutes which themselves prohibit its disclosure. For instance, returns made by farmers under the 1979 Agricultural Statistics Act and its predecessors, and by businesses under the 1947 Statistics of Trade Act, are permanently withheld under those Acts. There is also provision in section 3(4) for departments to retain records with the Lord Chancellor's approval, and under this section 'blanket' approvals have been given for the retention of records concerned with intelligence and security and with civil and home defence planning, and of those dealing with atomic energy. Some records are retained for continuing administrative use, and are accessible in their departments, although most retained records are simply unavailable. The approvals for retention are subject to reconsideration after stated periods.[17]

The fact that nearly all records transferred to the PRO are examined individually as part of the selection process, and also as part of the process of declassification which has to be carried out before transfer, means that there is an opportunity at the same time for each item to be described separately as well. Where records are handled at the series level, as in some other countries, the means of reference provided for them on transfer is likely to be simply a description of the series rather than a detailed list of its contents, or, at best, to consist merely of the original departmental file docket book. This may be rudimentary, and even misleading, since the file titles shown in it will probably be those that were given when the files were first brought into use – as a mark of intent, as it were, rather than as a description of the business which was actually transacted on the files after they had begun to be used. The detailed listing of files by departmental staff, in a specified standard form, after the final selection is made and before they come to the PRO, has now become part of the Office's regular procedure for transfer. The legal arrangements for access mean that each item needs also to be dated, and appropriately marked as well if any variation from the thirty-year 'rule' has been prescribed by the Lord Chancellor. And so the dates of each item, and a note of any variation from the normal access arrangements, can also be included in the descriptive list.

In most record offices the greater part of the staff's time may be spent in sorting and describing accumulations of records after transfer or deposit. Individual members of staff who have worked in this way on particular bodies of records will usually have acquired very detailed knowledge of their contents, and so be able to advise prospective researchers about them – if necessary, before any detailed inventory of the records has been completed. In some archives – and the National Archives of the United States are a particular example – the whole process of making more modern records available to the researcher depends on having members of staff available to discuss with them the topic of research, and to identify for them series of records, or items from series, on which they can work, rather than on the provision of pre-prepared detailed item-by-item listings.

The arrangements for transferring records to the PRO mean than, at the point at which any class of papers arrives, there is a detailed inventory of its contents already in existence, which can be made *immediately* available for use by researchers. There has to be, if the papers are to be effectively prepared for access in the fairly short time between the process of their final selection and the point at which the thirty-year period runs out. But there is a consequential disadvantage, in that the PRO's own reader services staff have usually not worked on the papers themselves and so built up prior knowledge of their contents. Or, at least, that knowledge will have been acquired by the relatively small group of PRO staff who are involved in the process of selection and description, and who are therefore away working in other departments and not readily available to advise prospective users. So researchers need to acquaint themselves with the very detailed, but at first mystifying, means of reference that are provided. Because the archives themselves are so extensive and complex, reflecting the complex administrative activities which produced them, the means of reference are bound to be complex too, but in theory the PRO's system provides the means for researchers to find their way through to the records that will provide the material for their investigations.

Up to this point, in discussing general aspects of archival arrangements, comparisons with the situations in other countries and other record offices have been made. What follows relates entirely to what the user of the records in the Public Record Office in London will find.

Finding what you want

In a letter to *The Times* on 7 May 1977 Lord Greenhill of Harrow, former Permanent Under Secretary of State at the Foreign and Commonwealth Office, wrote,

> I think all my colleagues would agree that it will be in the future quite impossible for anyone to unravel with any accuracy from the archives the detailed history of events. The sheer volume of documents, the inevitable decline in the standards of filing, the mass of unrecorded telephone conversations, all contribute to the fact that the course of events can no longer be followed from the original documents, and individual documents of special interest may well be overlooked.

Lord Greenhill's words are discouraging, unless seen as a challenge to the contemporary historian, but they do at least point out some of the problems posed by modern archives. The complexity and extensiveness of the records have just been referred to. It has been estimated that contemporary British government produces around 100 miles of paper every year. Of this, usually, a little under one mile eventually comes to the PRO, after the reviewing procedures described earlier. That mile probably consists of around 50,000 files, volumes or bundles of papers.

The complexity of the records was just as much a problem for their creators and filers as it is for their users nowadays. Civil servants who put papers in the wrong file, or kept them on their desk because they could not find the right file, were not just making it difficult for their colleagues to trace them. They were making the task of the future historian that much more complicated.

The last problem is probably the most important to bear in mind. We can find on a file only what was put there at the time. If an official transacted a piece of business on the telephone, or by walking down the corridor to speak to a colleague, and then saw no reason, or did not take the trouble, to note what had been said, then we shall have no record of it. Parts of discussion at meetings which were deliberately not minuted will in the same way not be available to us. The missing piece of business, or the unminuted statement at the meeting, may well be implicit in what follows in the papers, but it will be left to historians to understand what really happened through their handling of the evidence. They need to remember what was said earlier about realising the circumstances in which the writers of the papers were working.

The problem of unrecorded pieces of business is one we can now do nothing about. It is a fact about the nature of the records. It will affect the way we use the records, once we have found what we want. But the problems of the bulk and complexity of the records are ones which it is the archivist's job to help the researcher overcome, by providing guidance through the apparent maze.

Researchers planning to visit a record office usually try to find first a published description and analysis of the records that it holds, so that they can be fairly sure that they are visiting the right institution, and so that they have some notion of the area in the archives that they ought to be investigating. In 1963 the PRO published a two-volume *Guide* to the whole of its contents, which was up to date down to the middle of 1960. In 1968 a third volume was added, completing the coverage to 1966.[18]But, with almost a mile of new records, consisting of around 1,000 new classes, or additions to old classes, coming into the Office every year, there is now no hope of keeping researchers who are interested in the most modern records fully up to date by means of a traditionally produced printed publication. It would always be too far in arrears to be fully of use to them.

The *Current Guide to the Contents of the Public Record office*, which has superseded the whole of the published *Guide*, is a loose-leaf production (for ease of content updating) which is available in 'hard copy' form in the PRO, and is also being made available for sale on microfiche. Although it contains all the information that was available in the old published *Guide*, but in a much more up-to-date form, it is arranged quite differently. It is in three parts. Part I contains detailed administrative histories of the departments, courts of law and other organisations which have transferred records to the PRO, and follows each section of the administrative history with a series of cross-references to the classes of records in the Office which contain material produced by the various departments and organisational subdivisions just described, giving the letter and number code assigned to them. Part II consists of a description of the classes of records, arranged alphabetically and then numerically, by their class codes, giving their titles, the date range of the records so far transferred into them, the number of items transferred and their general form, and, more important, a general description of the records that makes up each class. If the class represents one original file series of a department's records, as most recently transferred classes do, or possibly a number of such series, the description will explain the purpose for which the original file series was created for use in the department. Failing such a correspondence, it will explain the nature of the class. If some basis for selection of the records other than the one which has already been described has been adopted, that also will be explained. Part III is a persons, places and subject index to parts I and II. It is not an index to the records themselves.

From the descriptions of the classes in the *Current Guide*, part II, it is possible to move straight to the descriptive list of the contents of any class described there.The lists are arranged on the shelves in the same way as the descriptions of classes in part II, in alphabetical and then numerical order. Most modern lists are preceded by an introductory note, which sets out the same sort of background information provided in the *Guide*, though in greater detail; explains the arrangement of the list, if it needs explanation; point out the existence of any indexes or registers of the papers in the class and of any related series of papers in other classes; and also explains why any records which you might expect to be in the class are absent, either because they did not survive at the point at which the class was transferred, or because they exist elsewhere.

In using the *Guide* researchers will notice that many of the letter codes now used to designate classes are not obviously meaningful. Those who are used to finding Cabinet Office records in CAB classes, or War Office files in WO classes, are likely to be confused at first to find classes of records of the United Kingdom Atomic Energy Authority with AB codes, and Department of the Environment classes with AT code. These codes are without any significance of their own – AB does not 'stand for' some descriptive title, such as 'atomic bomb'.

As explained earlier, frequent transfers of functions between departments, with consequential transfers of series of files as well, mean that most modern departments' records contain quantities of files inherited from their predecessors in exercising their functions, and worked on by them. Some very short-lived departments, such as the Ministry of Land and Natural Resources (1964–67), while it existed, held in its records a great preponderance of material taken over from other departments. The inherited files continued to be worked on in the new department, and were reregistered. But, when the new department ceased to exist, these inherited records together with newly created records were taken over and reregistered again by their successors for their own use. There may well now be hardly any records which are clearly identifiable from their file covers or their registered references as having been used in the Ministry. In most cases, then, their existence would be revealed only by an investigation of the relevant files' contents. In such circumstances the use of meaningful letter codes, although helpful in that they are easy to remember, would actually be misleading, because it would suggest something which is not actually true – i.e. that records with a particular PRO letter code are records of the department that the letters supposedly stand for, when they may in fact consist in large part of papers inherited from other departments.

To take another example, the Ministry of Supply, while it existed from 1939 to 1959, incorporated into its records considerable quantities of material from the Ordnance Office, which it superseded. Its own records were in their turn later incorporated in large measure into the records of its successors, and in particular into the records of the Atomic Energy Authority and of the Ministry of Aviation, which itself took over records created within the Ministry of Aircraft Production. At first sight, a researcher who finds classes with SUPP and AVIA letter codes would expect that those codes 'meant' that the classes must contain records originally created by the departments that the codes suggest, and perhaps that they contain all such records. From what has just been said, the reader can see that this may be very far from being so, although I should add that there are many identifiable Ministry of Supply files in existence, because the Ministry existed long enough for files which it created to have passed out of active use during its own lifetime. So the use of unsuggestive letter codes for the records of new departments is a way of avoiding misleading impressions. But their use means that researchers will have to rely on the administrative analyses and on the class description in the *Guide*, rather than on the suggestions offered by the letter codes themselves, to pick out the records of the department whose records they are interested in investigating.

Once a class has been identified, and its class list found, the researcher is faced, at last, with the description of its contents. The standard form of an entry in a list provides not only a description of the contents of each item, but also its date range and its original departmental reference, together with the modern number within the class by which it can be referred to or ordered up. The date range is important, because the final date determines when the item first becomes available.

Most classes are arranged as far as is possible in the order in which the papers were arranged in their original registration system. Because of the way the access date is calculated, and because only a few departments (the

Foreign Office was one) organised their papers so that no file extended over several years, and sometimes files ran over a very long period indeed), the individual files in any class may become available at a wide variety of dates.

If research is being conducted into records of the 1960s, or even of the 1950s, it is common to find that the papers of interest are on files which extend beyond the latest date to which records are generally available, and are therefore not yet accessible. For instance, the records of the Cabinet Ministerial Committee on Future Legislation for late 1964 (CAB 134/1927) are bound together with records of the committee for the first half of 1965. Thus at the time of writing (1995) the volume is not due to be open until 1996. In the past, departments sometimes ran files for very long periods. Treasury papers of 1916 on accommodation for the Post Office Savings Bank may be found in a file which ran on until 1952 (T 219/199) and so was unavailable until 1983.

If the original series of files being worked on was a long-lasting one, the contents of the class to which they now belong may be very extensive. For instance, the series of General Correspondence, Political, which the Foreign Office began to use in 1906 continued beyond the date at which records are now available, and the class in which the papers are now to be found, FO 371, already contains nearly 179,140 items and is still growing. It must be admitted that, however good the means of reference to an accumulation of papers of this size – and there are very detailed indexes to most of FO 371 – it is very daunting to be faced with a list of such length. Most classes are nothing like FO 371 in size, but the advantage of an all-inclusive class of this sort is that it is at least fairly obvious in which class to look for a particular category of material (in this case, records of diplomatic activities transacted by the political departments of the Foreign Office). The more decentralised and subdivided a department's filing system was, the more difficult it may be to find the particular series in which the papers produced by any specific area of activity were originally filed.

These 'nut and bolts' suggestions of the way to find particular series of records are probably useful only if the researcher already has a clear idea of the departments responsible for the areas of activity that are being researched. The index to the *Guide* will help in giving ideas, but, like all subject indexes, the references it gives for very broad subjects, such as economic policy, are likely to be so numerous as to be unhelpful, and the broadest subjects may, for that reason, not appear at all. In its *Handbook* and *Readers' Guide* series the PRO publishes analytical guides to the records relating to particular areas. Where no published analytical guides exist, the records created in this century by the machinery for the co-ordination of government policy can satisfy the need for them.

The records of the Prime Minister's Office, and in particular PREM 3 and PREM 4 (1940–45), PREM 8 (1945–51), PREM 11 (1951–64) and PREM 13 (1964–), can give a particular insight into the way successive Prime

Ministers initiated or co-ordinated policy and handled Cabinet and government business. What is there depends a great deal on the 'style' of the Prime Minister in question. But, because of these differences in style, the PREM records, invaluable as they are for policy studies, are not likely to give as complete a conspectus of the whole range of government activities at any time as those of the Cabinet.

From 1916, when the Cabinet Office first came into existence, the records of the Cabinet and its committees, and the working files of the Cabinet Office staff themselves, provide an invaluable guide to the Ministers and departments who had responsibility, or were made responsible, for particular areas of policy or activity.[19] They 'comprise the most valuable single collection of modern material for historical purposes that can be obtained from official sources'.[20] Working through the minutes of Cabinet meetings and the memoranda prepared for them, and the parallel records of the complex structure of committees which has grown up below the full Cabinet, particularly since 1945, can provide an insight into the structure of modern British government that can hardly be obtained elsewhere.

But there are pitfalls in this approach. Memoranda put up to the Cabinet and its committees, and the recorded minutes of decisions taken on them, are highly refined documents. They are the result of meticulous processes of drafting and of interdepartmental diplomacy. So they often lack the quality of unself-consciousness that the working papers of the departments themselves possess. Precisely because the Cabinet Office records are so structured and ordered, it is very tempting to concentrate on them and to fight shy of grappling with the great mass of records produced by the working of government in the departments, where policy was initiated and executed.

No one in his right mind – and perhaps least of all the archivist, who has had to try to reduce it to usable order – would suggest that dealing with this mass of records is a simple matter. The temptation is to be, like Lord Greenhill, too discouraging to the researcher. But the very extent of the archives of the modern state means that the researcher who makes the attempt, and takes account of the complicated relations between the various organs of government when pursuing investigations, and is not content to pursue obvious and well trodden paths through the records, can hardly ever fail to find undiscovered material. Perhaps it is not as inappropriate as it may have seemed at first that this chapter began with a quotation from a detective story.

Access to the Public Record Office

Most modern departmental records are held at the PRO's building at Kew. The reading rooms at Kew and in the original building in Chancery Lane are currently open from Monday to Friday from 9.30 a.m. to 5.00 p.m.

(census microfilms are available also on Saturdays). No records can be ordered up for the same day after 4.00 p.m., although until 4.15 p.m. orders can be accepted for records to be available the following day. It usually takes about half an hour for a record to arrive after being ordered, and, to enable this 'production time' to be kept to, the number of items which can be ordered at any one time is limited to three. Like nearly all record offices, the PRO allows only pencils and typewriters to be used in the reading rooms, in order to minimise danger to the records from ink. Full details of the Office's public services can be found in its leaflet *Information for Readers*.

Once the new building at Kew is completed, towards the end of 1995, all original records regularly used by readers will be transferred to Kew. The target date for consolidation at Kew is December 1996. Extended opening hours are planned thereafter.

Notes

1 See Patrick Cosgrave, 'Can we believe these papers?', *The Times*, 2 January 1987, p. 12.

2 Cf. Hilary Jenkinson, *Guide to the Public Records: introductory* (1949), p. 2, and *A Manual of Archive Administration* (1937), pp. 11–13. Sir Hilary instanced a difficulty in dealing with objects, which he described as a *reductio ad absurdum*: 'Supposing, for example, that a Viceroy sends to the Secretary of State in England an elephant, with a suitable covering note or label; or supposing, to take a more actual example, that the Governor of a Colony presents to the First Commissioner of Works a two hundred foot spar of Douglas Pine: the question may be imagined to arise: Is the spar "annexed" to correspondence with the Governor of British Columbia? Is the elephant attached to the label or the label to the elephant?' (*Manual*, p. 7.)

3 It is often thought that the term indicates some quality of antiquity, as if it were comparable with words in English beginning with 'archaeo-', derived from the Greek *archaios*, 'ancient'. It is not: it derives from the Greek word *archeion*, 'a public office'.

4 Cf. S. Muller, J. A. Feith and R. Fruin, *Handleiding voor het Ordenen en Beschrijven van Archieven* ('Manual for the arrangement and description of archives') (1898).

5 Michael Frayn, *Alphabetical Order* (1977).

6 However, the chapter is written personally, not officially.

7 C. A. R. Crosland, *The Future of Socialism* (1956), p. 524.

8 By the Public Record Office Act, 1 and 2 Vic. cap. 94.

9 See R. R. Schellenberg, *Modern Archives: Principles and Techniques* (1956), pp. 174–5.

10 It was translated into German in 1905, into Italian in 1908, and into French in 1910, but did not appear in English until 1940, in the United States. There has never been a British edition.

11 See Michael Roper, 'Modern departmental records and the record office', *Jour-*

nal of the Society of Archivists, 4, 1972, pp. 402–3.

12 *Report of the Committee on Departmental Records*, Cmd 9163 (1954). The records of the committee, which carried out its functions administratively, rather than as an inquiry hearing evidence and then reporting on it, are available among the files of the Treasury's Organisation and Methods Division (T 222/606–15).

13 *Report of the Committee on Departmental Records*, paras 57–71, 78–87, 240–1.

14 *Ibid.*, paras 153–5, 240–1.

15 In 1990/91 just under 155,000 ft of records were reviewed when they were five years old, and 23,100 ft of twenty-five-year-old records underwent the final review. That adds up to almost thirty-four shelf miles of records reviewed file by file in a year. The year 1990/91 was not untypical. See *The Thirty-third Annual Report of the Keeper of Public Records on the Work of the Public Record Office, 1991* (1992), p. 8.

16 Public Records Act 1958, section 5(1), as amended by the Public Records Act 1967.

17 A leaflet, *Access to Public Records*, gives fuller details.

18 *Guide to the Contents of the Public Record Office*, 3 vols (1963, 1963, 1968).

19 A handbook, *The Cabinet Office to 1945*, was published by HMSO in 1975.

20 *Report of the Committee on Departmental Records*, para. 147.

Chapter 25

National archives in the United Kingdom: a case study of the Waldegrave initiative on Public Record Office releases

Anthony Gorst and Brian Brivati

> I would like to invite serious historians to write to me ... those who want to write serious historical works will know, probably better than we do, of blocks of papers that could be of help to them that we could consider releasing. [William Waldegrave, June 1992[

With this announcement the then Chancellor of the Duchy of Lancaster and Minister with responsibility for open government, William Waldegrave, made public a change in the culture of government that had been developing within Whitehall for at least a year. This change involved a move towards greater openness in the availability of government information to the individual citizen and therefore of the release of official documents to the Public Record Office (PRO) at Kew: according to the Cabinet Office over the last two years some 25,000 previously retained records have been released.[1] The PRO with its vast holdings of government papers is the first port of call for anyone interested in the policies of the British state and their impact on society, therefore any change in the policy covering release has profound implications for the writing of the history of contemporary Britain.

Since the Second World War there has been an explosion in the amount of information produced in the everyday actions of the state and this in turn increases the amount of evidence potentially available to the historian. The control of this evidence by the state through release mechanisms is a unique problem for historians working on the twentieth century, who are therefore vitally concerned with the manner in which the historical record is created, maintained and made available. Once a 'record' has been created it is by no means certain that it will find its way into the PRO: a system of five-year reviews evaluates whether it is worthy of preservation. Even at the twenty-five-year mark the 'weeders' in each department of state can decide what is to be passed over to the national depository of government documents, the PRO, and what is to be retained. Estimates vary but only about 5 per cent of all government documents created by departments are released into the

272

public domain after thirty years. In addition to those which are released a proportion are subject to extended closure under section 5(1) of the Public Records Act of 1958 and a further proportion are retained for an unspecified period under section 3(4).[2]

The apparently increasing number of closures and retentions for the 1950s and 1960s as well as the number of areas deemed to be sensitive have caused concern amongst historians of the post-1945 period: therefore when Mr Waldegrave's announcement was made the historical profession was quick to respond by organising two conferences which highlighted their concern.[3] The worries included, for example, the fact that no reasons have to be given for the retention or closure of records, and the diversity of subjects felt to justify of retention has suggested little apparent consistency in policy: records have been retained in the past which concerned such miscellaneous subjects as the international whaling agreement of 1939, Aberystwyth hospitals and civil defence planning, black-market activity in World War II, private housing in Crawley in the 1950s, the operation of the Poor Law in the 1930s, Anglo-Swedish relations in 1941, food production in World War II and relations between Turkey and South Korea in 1957. Moreover, retaining documents leaves gaps in the evidence relating to important or controversial issues: for instance, files were closed relating to the abdication crisis of 1936, wartime Cabinet minutes were closed, probably relating to the Nazis sympathies of the Duke of Windsor, material relating to Nazi subversive operations in Britain in World War II, pre-war Nazi sympathisers in high places in Britain, British army action during the Easter rising of 1916, British irregular forces in Ireland 1919–21, Sudeten Germans in Czechoslovakia in 1938, Anglo-Iranian relations in 1953, and the July plot against Hitler. Any changes in the mechanisms of retention or release would have wide-ranging significance for the historian.

The first conference, while constructing a list of individual records requested by historians, also began to consider the wider context and evolved a series of general recommendations, which constituted the historians' response to the government's initiative.[4] The full recommendations are contained in the appendix to this chapter; in summary the conference was concerned to maximise the volume of material available to the historian at the PRO, and the recommendations included, *inter alia*:

1   More consistent application of the procedures of the existing thirty-year rule.
2   A re-examination of the criertia for closures and retentions of records.
3   A fundamental review of the existing retained files and the use of selective blacking out of sensistive sections to allow the release of the remainder.

At the second conference further issues were raised in the light of one year's operation of the new regime: one of the most interesting ideas aired was the creation of a rolling index of closed or retained documents. This would address one of the fundamental problems facing the historian, that of not having an exact picture of what is withheld, as well as allowing the profession to monitor the operation of the 'open government' initiative. There was also a lengthy discussion of the criteria for closure. Under the White Paper on Open Government published in July 1993[5] the government would in future have to give a reason for the closure or retention of a record. It could be on broad grounds of, for example, national security, material given in confidence or that which might jeopardise an individual's personal security.

The second conference also explored the more general theme of who will write the history of Britain in the second half of the twentieth century. Will it be British historians working from what the state chooses to release or will it be historians from other countries, writing histories based on more open archives? For example, so long as there are significant retentions in the area of the intelligence and security services the Russians and the Americans will be free to write the history of the Cold War while British historians can only speculate. Moreover, former KGB agents can make allegations in the press about individuals' and institutions' role in the Cold War which the historian cannot challenge or validate from British sources. The case of Gordievsky's allegations in the *Sunday Times* about Labour politicians in February 1995 clearly illustrates the potential problems.

There are two types of debate highlighted in the discussion of the conferences above. A technical debate about how records are released into the public domain and the operation of the thirty-year rule and a general debate about the relative merits in principle and in practice of a full freedom of information environment as against the more limited open government initiative. The case for comprehensive freedom of information legislation on the American model is based on the right of citizens in a democracy to have access to information held by the state that directly affects them and the right of voters to hold their elected representatives and non-elected officials accountable. The merits or otherwise of this argument are essentially political; the argument is not directly related to the practice of writing history but the establishment of a system of freedom of information does have certain impacts on historical writing. Historians may benefit indirectly from the release of information, and those who are interested in security or controversial issues will in theory be able to get the information they require. Freeing historical records from the control of the state represents a step towards a more mature democracy and provides more raw data for the historian. Moreover, a request system by which the historian specifically asks for the declassification of a particular record establishes a 'market' in historical records that reduces the number of documents that are handled to those that are actually wanted and used.

The case against freedom of information as a matter of principle are again essentially political, but there are arguments against its operation in terms of its impact on the writing of history and on the historical record. The existing thirty-year rule guarantees the systematic release of records; the historian knows that in any one specific year the records of government thirty-one years ago will become available. This is crucially important for the vast majority of historical subjects and is in contrast to freedom of information, which encourages a fragmented pattern of release with the focus on certain areas, for example, espionage, UFOs, scandals and past malpractice. In addition there is the very real fear that the potentially large volume of freedom of information requests may slow down the overall release programme. If and when freedom of information is seriously considered in Britain these concerns will no doubt form part of that debate. For the moment the present reforms represent an adaptation of the existing release mechanisms.

One of the most pressing concerns for historians in the 1980s was the unavailability of material relating to intelligence operations, which were governed by a simple blanket retention. This left the field open for the conspiracy theorist and the thriller writer to hypothesise freely on the presumed role of the government's security services. Therefore the release of this material makes a good test case for the operation of the open government initiative.

In the last two years previously retained Joint Intelligence Committee papers of the Second World War have been made freely available to the historian for the first time. One of the first historians to examine these papers was Richard Aldrich of the University of Nottingham. A debate that they have shed light on, which Dr Aldrich has examined in some depth, is the revisionist allegation that Churchill had prior knowledge, derived from Japanese signals traffic, of the attack on Pearl Harbour on 7 December 1941. If it were proved that Churchill knew about the impending attack and chose not to inform the United States, in order to drag Washington into the war, it would have profound consequences for both the historiography of the Second World War and for the continuing 'special relationship' with the United States. In fact, as Richard Aldrich has shown, from June 1941 all signals traffic intercepted by the Far Eastern stations of British intelligence was routinely shared with the Amercians:

[The Minutes of the JIC] show that American personnel had already been attached to the Far Eastern Combined bureau, which presided over the 'collection, collation and dissemination' of all British intelligence in that region, including signals intelligence ... One particular revisionist account of Pearl Harbour had gone so far as to suggest that on the 5 December 1941, Britain's JIC met and discussed the impending Japanese attack on Pearl Harbour at length. This author, Constantine Fitzgibbon, writing in 1976, claimed to base these assertions on a letter received from none other than Victor Cavendish-Bentick. wartime chairman of the JIC. How do these claims compare with the JIC minutes for the fateful week prior to Pearl Harbour? The minutes, which are entirely extant for this period, reveal that the JIC did not even meet on 5 December. It met on the 3 December and on the 9 December and did not mention Pearl Harbour at either meeting.

This particular example shows that the conspiracy theorists, in this case at least, were wrong and could have been shown to be wrong much earlier, say in 1972, when the bulk of the British records relating to the Second World War were released. At the very least it shows the potential strengths of a consistent application of the thirty-year rule: as the departments of state work through their backlog of retained materials it will be intriguing to see how many other 'sensational' conspiracy theories are consigned to the dustbin of history.

There may also be more general implications in the changes currently taking place. What at first glance appears to be a technical debate about access to historical records is ultimately concerned with the ownership of information in a democracy. That the state decides which records are to be released and which are to be retained is based on the presumption that we are subjects of the state. Records are the possession of the Crown and it is for the government of the day to decide the terms of access to those records. However, as the culture of the control of the records moves towads more open access may we not also be seeing increasing recognition of the rights of the citizen not only in terms of present govenrment documents that contain information about them as individuals but also in terms of the decisions made by past governments that have shaped contemporary society?

Appendix 1 General recommendations of the first ICBH conference

1 *The application of the thirty-year rule*
The conference had a full discussion on the principles that underlay the statement by Mr Waldegrave. It was felt that the Waldegrave initiative was a separate issue from 'freedom of information' in general. The conference expressed differing opinions on the value of 'freedom of information' to historians but it was agreed that the terms of reference of this report should be confined to consideration of more consistent application of the existing procedures of the thirty year rule. However, it would be desirable to see a wider release of non-policy papers in advance of the thirty-year period in line with the Croham directive: this would be especially welcome in the case of material relating to non-controverial domestic social policy issues such as health, housing, education and nutrition. In this connection increased use of section 5(1) of the Public Records Act of 1958 which allows release in advance of thirty years should be made.

This recommendation is in line with stated government intentions on 'open government'. If good history is to be written by British historians, they need access to British records, otherwise our history will be written predominantly from overseas records. Moreover the need for a rational release policy goes beyond the realm of politics or the needs of historians. It is about maturing as a democracy and having the self-confidence to allow the existing rules to operate as they should. A climate of secrecy and retention serves only thriller writers and conspiracy theorists.

2 *Reviewing retention policy*

The problem of retention is much worse for the historian of the post-Second World War period than for those working on early periods and it is particularly unfavourable for those working on the 1950s and 1960s, as the number of files subject to retentions and closures has increased year on year. Moreover, because of the security constraints imposed by the Cold War the historian of external policy suffers comparatively greater problems of access than historians of internal policy. As a matter of urgency therefore the criteria for retentions and closures should be reconsidered, particularly in the light of the ending of the Cold War. While the acceptance of new criteria may cause some delay in processing the large accumulation of documents hitherto withheld from the years prior to 1962, this should in no way be permitted to affect the release of material for 1963 and succeeding years, which ought promptly to be made available under the new criteria at the normal time.

Concern was also registered by many historians at the difficulties caused by two practices. Firstly, closing files or classes for fifty years and then retaining them under section 3(4) on the expiry of the closure period. Secondly, opening classes as normal after thirty years and then either closing or retaining them after they have been released. These practices reinforce the necessity of a review of the policy on retention.

3 *Release of retained documents*

Following this review procedure, previously retained documents should be released as soon as possible. In this connection the repercussions of the ending of the Cold War on retention policy was emphasised. In general, historians would like access to government papers over thirty years old but they acknowledge that exceptions may have to be made, especially in the external policy area, to protect intelligence sources and methods that may still be current. However, official, political or personal 'embarrassment' should not in itself be grounds for closure. Where appropriate, the conference felt that censoring documents to remove sensitive material was preferable to the closure of whole files; this would be a particular way of protecting the identity and privacy of individuals. This is established practice in the United States, and indeed in the minutes of the UK Chiefs of Staff.

The conference recognised the practical difficulties in following its recommendations through. To overcome the worst of these the following priorities with regard to the release of material could be observed. The least sensitive and oldest, i.e. pre-1914, material should be released first. In all releases coherent sequences of material should be opened together.

4 *Retained material available elsewhere*

Concern was expressed over of certain anomalies. Material originating from the British government is available in the archives of other countries and in non-governmental British archives. There are also instances of material retained as a class at the PRO being open in other files. A procedure should be established where material available elsewhere is placed in the Public Record Office.

Concern was also expressed over material originating from non-government sources and held in non-official archives (for example, at the BBC) being retained at the request of government departments.

5 *The role of the historian*

The conference felt that the possibility should be explored of including historians in the release process. An enhanced role should be developed for the Lord Chancellor's Advisory Council on the Public Records: it should be able directly to inspect retained material. In addition, the conference concluded that historians could be seconded to departments to advise on what documents should be preserved and what documents should be released.

6 *Initial steps*

The conference suggested that closed or retained Cabinet minutes and papers should be reviewed as a matter of urgency, and internal 'official' histories, some of which are retained, should be released in advance of the classes to which they refer. While it was recognised that issues of confidentiality might require the retention of a few records, on the whole everything before 1914 could be released.

While acknowledging the problem of resources the conference felt that there were a number of practices that needed to be reviewed as part of the initial programme. Firstly, the destruction of and/or delay in releasing files wrongly assumed to be unimportant or to contain only duplicate material – such as Foreign Office embassy and consular files – should cease. Secondly, all files that have reached the thirty-year deadline but have not yet reached the PRO should be transferred as soon as possible. Thirdly, from the point of view of historians the practice of creating and maintaining files that cover long time periods should be avoided, as it results in the effective closure of the earlier material in the file for longer than thirty years: for example, a file created in 1946 that contained material up to 1964 would not be opened till 1995. This reinforces the need for historians to become involved in the review procedure.

Notes

1 'Records' is a generic term which could cover whole files, or individual telegrams or sections of papers.
2 For a full discussion of the workings of the PRO see Chapter 24.
3 The first conference was held on 25 November 1992 at the University of Westminster and the second was held at the Institute of Historical Research on 24 November 1993. Both were organised under the auspices of the Institute of Contemporary British History.
4 The purpose of the first conference, held in 1992, was to draw up a collective reponse to the Minister. The second, held in 1993, was to review progress. Observers were present from the Public Record Office and historical sections of departments of state. These officials were extremely helpful in clarifying technical points and made a valuable contribution in the course of the day.
5 Cmd 2290.

Chapter 26

The case for preserving our contemporary communications heritage

Philip M. Taylor

Because by definition most historians tend to be preoccupied with the past, issues of contemporary and future significance rarely excite their academic concern. Such is the case with the preservation of new kinds of contemporary record material which are likely to prove of enormous benefit to future generations of historians. In the past century the enormous technological advances in what Asa Briggs termed in the 1960s the 'communications revolution' have transformed our lives and the way we see the world around us. The pace of this transformation has been even more rapid in the past decade. It is sobering to think back to the Falklands War of 1982, which today seems even more like a nineteenth-century type of conflict than it did at the time, fought as it was in an age before accessible domestic video-cassette recorders, multi-channel satellite television, portable camcorders and satphones, laptop computers, fax machines and modems, let alone before most of us had heard of the like of 'CNN', 'Microsoft', the 'Internet' and 'information superhighways', digital data transmission or the Global Information Infrastructure. Anglo-US deregulation in the area of communications and the media in the 1980s, coupled with the end of the Cold War, has encouraged technological trends which finally perhaps make the concept of a 'global village' realisable. During the abortive Moscow *coup* of 1991 an interned Mikhail Gorbachev in the Crimea could learn of events in Moscow by the BBC World Service while Boris Yeltsin at the White House could chart the progress of his supporters in the streets around him by tuning in to Atlanta-based CNN. By contrast with the Falklands, the Persian Gulf War, less than a decade later, in 1991, could be fought out on real-time live global television, viewed by professors and printers from Vancouver to Vladivostock at the same time as Presidents and Prime Ministers on both sides of the conflict. Converted American EC130 aircraft were capable of transmitting multi-standard and multi-frequency radio and television pictures into the battle zones of occupied Kuwait while messages from one side to the other could be sent instantaneously via electronic mail (e-mail).

This indeed is the New World Information and Communications Order where the media act not simply as observers of events but also as participants and sometimes even as catalysts, as in the case of television pictures of the Kurds prompting John Major to suggest Operation Provide Comfort to the Americans in 1991 or to Bill Clinton's reversal of American policy in Somalia after watching pictures of a butchered American airman being dragged through General Aideed's camp.

All this has happened at such breathtaking speed that contemporary historians have inevitably struggled to grapple with its consequences. In Britain, at least, historians tend by nature to be a conservative profession – although this is changing because we have to a large extent had change imposed upon us – and the study of 'contemporary history' has always been hamstrung by the thirty-year rule. Yet despite changing academic fashions, and despite trends towards more 'open government', we remain extremely cautious about encouraging our research students to tackle issues more recent than a generation before because 'the evidence' is not yet available at the Public Record Office. Yet our undergraduates cry out for courses which address the confusing and momentous period through which they have lived and are living, becoming less and less interested in far away time periods such as the First and Second World Wars. They are, of course, the first generation of young people weaned wholly on colour television and for whom the world wars are 'black and white' wars; anyone who has used the admittedly rare colour footage of the Nazi period in teaching will know of the shock which it induces, finally bringing home the immediacy of a period they had previously considered remote.

The history of the mass media is barely a century old – as indeed is the profession of the modern historian. Yet despite the progress made, in the past ten years especially, in teaching and in research, and even in film archive policy, can we as a profession really be said to have done justice to the history of a century which is unique from all others by virtue of the existence of the mass media? When modern twentieth-century history text-books mention the mass media they do so almost as if they were a sideshow – with the press still taken the most seriously (because it is printed in the familiar and hallowed written word), but with radio relegated to the ephemeral and cinema to the trivial. And as for television, we have barely begun to regard that as a phenomenon worthy of serious consideration. Yet in 2095, when history students look back to our century as we now look back to the nineteenth, they will read that the twentieth century was indeed different from all that went before it by virtue of the enormous explosion in media and communications technologies. Mass media. Mass communications. But when they come to examine the primary sources for the period they will find, alas, only a ramshackle patchwork of surviving evidence because *we* lack the foresight, let alone the imagination, to preserve our contemporary media and communications heritage. By not addressing this issue now we are reducing our history to relative obscurity and future historians to sampling and guesswork.

If this may seem extreme in a century that already provides too much evidence for any one historian to master in a lifetime, let us just recall that only about 50 per cent of the films ever made since 1896 have survived. There is no radio or television archive anywhere in the world which contains a complete archive of the material transmitted since the inception of those media. We have in other words already lost a great deal of our twentieth-century heritage. There are perfectly understandable reasons for this, especially when one remembers, for example, that only a fraction of material which our government departments produce on an annual basis reaches the PRO for our perusal 30 years later. The argument is that there is simply too much paper to preserve it all; there simply isn't the space. Regardless of long-standing concerns over archival policies – Who decides to keep what? What is the process of selection and elimination? etc. – historians as users of evidence are bound to clash with archivists as storers or custodians of records. In an ideal world the former would have everything preserved so that *they* or their successors could decide what was or was not significant. The latter, however, argue that it is not an ideal world and that some things have to go for sheer pragmatic reasons of cost and storage, so they decide which piece of evidence is significant. Both, however, need to recognise that they have a symbiotic relationship and that they need to work together to resolve the problems. Moreover, with media archives, there are even greater problems. Prior to 1951, for example, film was produced on perishable (and highly inflammable) nitrate stock and before such organisations as the Imperial War Museum or the National Film (and, since 1993, Television) Archive could do what they could, with limited resources, to convert those which had survived into a more durable (and safer) format of acetate, much had already be lost for ever. Even the newer post-nitrate acetate stock is subject to a form of deterioration known as the 'vinegar syndrome'. Preservation is an expensive and time-consuming business, while restoration creates even greater problems, as anyone will know who has watched with admiration the kind of restoration work which film historians like David Brownlow have undertaken. The logic should thus be that it is better – and more economical – to preserve and conserve before the need for restoration becomes imperative.

The problems are even further compounded when one realises that a cinematic production is an end-product of a commercial exercise. An individual film will contain but a fraction of the footage taken, because it has been edited to meet the commercial imperative of making a profit. This may seem less significant to those growing hordes of cultural studies scholars who use films as semiotic texts that encode some ideological purpose, but historians can only lament the loss of unused footage to the cutting-room floors of history, especially on their more familiar ground of 'factual' films as evidence (documentaries and newsreels or, today, current affairs programmes or investigative journalism reports).

Herein lies another clue to the difficulties faced. Mass media products, such as films, radio and television programmes, are invariably produced by commercial organisations whose purpose is primarily to entertain people with a product that invariably has a limited life cycle. There are notable exceptions, such as *The World at War*. Yet such organisations do not foster an institutional culture which sees their products as potential historical artefacts that need preserving for future historical analysis. If the product survives at all, it is only because it may serve some future recycling for commercial purposes, such as selling *I Love Lucy* programmes to Third World countries or to nostalgic cable channels. Many news organisations wipe their tapes after a given period of time so that they can be reused to save costs. Even public service broadcasting organisations such as the BBC, whose purpose is supposedly to inform, instruct and entertain, have not in the past decided to keep everything. Moreover the BBC archives of broadcasting output that do survive (beyond the splendid and under-used Written Archives Centre at Caversham) are organised not on an academic archival basis but on a commercial one which permits outside researchers to scrutinise their material only at commercial rates that are prohibitive to most academic researchers. This means that, for the most part, historians who wish to write about, say, the BBC and the Suez crisis, are able to do so only from conventional written archives rather than to see or hear the actual radio and television broadcasts themselves, with a corresponding loss of appreciation of those special characteristic nuances carried by the audio and audio-visual media.

There are, of course, problems with such forms as evidence, both in terms of the methodologies for dealing with them and in terms of evaluating their impact. Their ethereal nature need no longer be a deterring factor now that we have the technological capacity to record them for posterity, in the form of audio- and video-cassette, let alone newer digital technologies. These are very small formats – a VHS cassette is the size of a paperback book – and we may again face problems of deterioration with formats that are themselves made of comparatively new materials. If the history of film archives can teach us any lesson, it is that planning for likely future conversion on to newer formats must always be incorporated into preservation policy. There may still be some purists who argue that it is better to look at, even *feel*, the original parchment than scrutinise a photocopy or a facsimile reproduction, but there is no room in the preservation of communications archives for such attitudes. That is because the communications media are themselves invariably copies – whether they be newspapers, film prints or television programmes. Of the three boxes which one needs to fill in for addressing e-mail, the third in most software packages is 'c.c.'.

But questions remain as to how much one needs to preserve. The evening news broadcasts? Documentaries? Soap operas? Surely not the adverts as well? Ceefax and Oracle? E-mail press releases from the White House, NATO, the UN and the WEU possibly, but surely not the more bizarre examples of cybercasting on the Internet, as in the Usenet group 'alt.sex.fetishes.feet'? Well, frankly, yes. It is for future generations to decide the significance of material which many of us still don't see as important. Ceefax, for example, was the first BBC service to report the resignation of Margaret Thatcher.

But it is not just the speed at which the medium reports the message which needs to be borne in mind – although the breaking of live stories before they have been fully verified is becoming a phenomenon which our decision-makers are increasingly have to take on board. Hence the growth in 'spin doctors', public relations activity, even in public diplomacy. Yet television viewing, for example, is rarely something someone does just for one programme. Viewing habits indicate that people do sit down for an evening's television and even daytime viewing is done in blocks of time. Channel hopping is normal, and the *cumulative* effect of all this activity, especially when combined with newspaper reading and radio listening habits, does help to shape the way in which we see the world. So we need to record all four British domestic terrestrial television channels twenty-four hours a day to stand a chance of understanding what that cumulative effect may be. After all, that means three four-hour tapes (slow speed) per station per day, a total of twelve tapes to secure a day in the life of terrestrial television output in the United Kingdom. Seven days a week, 365 days per year – which is almost 5,000 tapes per year, requiring about 417 ft of shelving. It could be far less if preserved in newer formats such as optical disc or CDI, especially as the technology shifts from analogue to digital. Logging of such material is as simple as preserving the *Radio Times*, an obvious index of such output. However, this permanent recording operation would need to secure copyright waivers from the broadcasting authorities. The costs could not be borne by one individual; it would need to be a national archive. The tragic loss in 1994 from these shores to the United States of Barry Hill's unique archive of radio broadcasts is a salutary reminder that, had it not been for the messianic enthusiasm of one individual who took it upon himself to record every radio broadcast he could receive over the past twenty years from his house in Leeds, much of our radio heritage would have been lost. Mr Hill frequently despaired of the lack of vision in this country, especially when professional radio broadcasters asked *him* for material which they no longer possessed. Surely this is a damning indictment on the inability of government, communications industries, archives and academia to get together to preserve our heritage?

In terms of the reception of such material, we already possess public opinion polling and broadcasting research data, with such organisations as MORI, NOP and others. However, once again, there are commercial organisations whose day-to-day research for contractors rarely sees the public light of day. Historians of public opinion in the 1930s and 1940s thank God for Mass-Observation or the American Institute of Public Opinion Research, but to my knowledge few approaches have been made to their present-day equivalents in order to secure comparative data. How they would respond, therefore, remains to be seen, but the value of such material to scholars not just in history but in sociology and the other social sciences is inestimable. Again the costs of public opinion polling and surveys are too high for an academic institution to carry out on anything but a random basis, but, given that much invaluable data already exist, the costs of archiving them are already reduced considerably.

The arrival of global media services such as trans-border satellite television raises a further problem that needs to be overcome. Given that many people in, say, Europe can all watch the same programmes, we need to consider the recording and preservation of the proliferating number of international television, radio and other services if we are to begin understanding the international impact of such issues as 'Americanisation' or 'Coca-Colonialism', let alone the role of international communications in the ending of the Cold War. The political obstacles are undoubtedly immense, as reflected in the 1993 GATT negotiations that were almost scuppered by Franco-American disagreements over the transfer of media products. Yet the very centrality of that issue in the GATT negotiations underlines the need to preserve the products for posterity.

These are not essentially new arguments; Sir Arthur Elton made a similar plea for film back in the mid-1950s and a growing number of individuals since then are now more sensitive to the issue. But the historical profession as a whole has been slow to respond, almost to the point of irresponsibility. Teachers see the student interest in courses offered by the occasional colleague who does take an interest in such evidence, but they regard it as a still somewhat 'cranky' activity in which showing films is a substitute for 'real teaching' by scholars who are not really taken seriously. How many of those historians can really own up to considering film seriously as a source for their research when they are considering their somehow more respectable topic? Rarely do major international conferences dealing with a central topic consider putting on a film programme – the 1994 Leeds International First World War Commemoration Week was a rare if encouraging exception which attracted many converts from the distinguished gathering of 'the great and the good'. Even there, however, this participant was struck by the level of indignation combined with ignorance as to how the media world actually operates when several historians, after viewing extracts, discovered that the BBC TV series *The Great War* would not be shown again. No amount of explanation concerning copyright, the different uses to which film evidence is now used in the post-*World at War* era of television historical documentaries, and so on, could shift the indignation of people who admitted that their interest in the First World War had been first sparked by that series.

The massive proliferation of communications and media in recent years does require new thinking and new solutions. Much, of course, has already been done with the oldest of the new media, especially with film, where the door was left ajar. But the history of cinema was marked by the kind of random preservation policies we are already beginning to witness with the newer media. The problem of accessing scattered film archives – whether they be at the Science Museum, the National Film and Television Archive or BFI, the Imperial War Museum, the East Anglian Film Archive, the Yorkshire Film Archive or other regional collections – may one day be overcome by the new communications technologies currently being vaunted in the form of multi-media information superhighways. Communication technology has always been about the conquest of time and space, and there is no reason to believe that in the next century such technology will not allow researchers to access multi-media archives anywhere they exist – provided they are wired. The gradual convergence of communications and computing offers genuine opportunities of access on a worldwide scale. But the archives themselves must first exist. Temporal and spatial matters concerning storage and preservation are likely to be overcome but *only* if we address the questions which have always lain at the heart of archival policy: costs, copyright and comprehensiveness. Even the National Film and Television Archive was able to preserve only just over 25 per cent of the total broadcast output of ITV and Channel 4 in 1993–94. That means 75 per cent lost for posterity – lower than the annual amount of Whitehall material denied to the PRO, but still only a fragment of our contemporary record. Admittedly, communications media contain only part of that record anyway; with film 'evidence', for example, we are seeing only what lay within the camera's angle of vision, not that which went on behind the cameraman's back. But no individual form of historical evidence can provide us with a complete picture anyway. Historians piece together different types of evidence rather like a jigsaw; pieces will always be missing, but they or their successors have no chance even to begin understanding our audio-visual century, our information and communications age, without access to the very media which have made it thus. There is therefore an urgent need for the Institute of Contemporary British History, as the most dynamic body of recent years dealing with and co-ordinating different approaches to the study of our present century, to bring together the interested parties – from the communications industries, the archivists and the academics – to act now before it is too late.

Part IV
Printed sources

Chapter 27

Using contemporary written sources: three case studies

Brian Brivati

This chapter examines the problems and possibilities of contemporary written sources. In addition to the textual, physical and visual sources that we have for every period of history – in varying amounts and in varying quality – we have a startling range of sources that are unique to the last century or so. In other chapters in this book we discuss witnesses, radio, film, television, newsreel and computers as contemporary sources. Each of these sources has problems unique to itself. Some of the problems are general to all sources and to the study of history at any level and any period. This chapter concerns some of the general and the specific problems associated with dealing with contemporary written sources and offers some guidance for thinking about approaches to their use.

The retreat from the word?

When music hall developed in the late nineteenth century and became one of the most popular forms of entertainment, vicars denounced the development as the end of the written word, the end of books. When radio and cinema developed, H.G. Wells postulated that they would be the end of books. When television started many worried that it would end reading. And now computers, multi-media workstations and CD-ROMs are supposed to be threatening the buying and reading of books. Each of the developments just mentioned actually resulted in the sale of more books – even if they were only computer manuals. Television and radio espeically increased the sale of books; the BBC alone encouraged the sale of millions of books. In the UK in 1993 79,000 new titles were published, 80 per cent of the population purchased a book and the publishing industry had sales valued at £30 million. The largest grosser of the year was the book of the film *Juassic Park*. According to market research the average amount of time people claimed to devote to reading was five hours a week. But then people always lie to pollsters. Whether or not the books are all read, the written word is alive and well, and reports of its death have been greatly exaggerated.

Written words are the stable currency of historical work. They enable the work of the historian to take place. Without the documentary record of previous times our historical understanding of the world would be bare, broken and fragmentary. Without the documentary record of individuals our understanding of their motivation, feelings and actions would be one-dimensional. We might know that a battle took place at a certain time and in a certain place from the physical remains. We would not know, could not know, the feelings, plans, orders and so on of the generals involved unless they had written them down. The process of creating a document is one of the central processes in the creation of the evidence of which history is made. There are a number of different ways of approaching a document. But in all cases it is essential to 'contextualise' all that you encounter. Contextualise is a fancy way of saying that you have to know where a text is coming from.

The historian and the text

The job of an historian, as far as texts and other forms of evidence are concerned, is to be a detective, to discover the context of the document and suck the information out of it. When you approach a text you have to keep a number of different things in mind. Indeed, you have to read the text through these questions, as though the questions were a filter. There are different filters through which a document should pass and different historians develop filters of their own. Tables 27.1 and 27.2 are examples.

Table 27.1 Contextualising a document

Reader

Filter
Who wrote the document?
When and how did we gain access to it?
Why was it written?
What sort of document is it?
What other information do we need to make sense of it?

Text

> **Analysis**
> What does the text tell us?
> What does it say about those who wrote it?
> What are the messages the writer wanted to convey?
> Why was this medium chosen to convey the ideas?

Table 27.2 Types of Written Record: examples of particular problems

Diaries and Autobiographies
When and why written – for private use or for publication?

Private Papers
When written, and who by? During the subject's career, or after? By a friend of by an enemy?

Local Records
What sort of document is it – parish, local government?

Newspapers
Why was this medium chosen? Political bias? The notion of a newspaper of record? Other periodical literature?

Diplomatic documents
What does it say about those who wrote them? What messages did the writers want to convey? Within governments, between governments? Selectivity of publication. Self-justification.

Government documents
All other types. Freedom of information, access and control. How did we gain access to them?

Secondary sources
Textbooks, monographs, polemic, times and purposes of authors, sources used.

The problem of selectivity

Before examining the problems and possibilities of the documentary record, there is one point that should be made about the existence of writing itself. The first selection that takes place, and therefore the first subjectivity in the creation of the historical record, is by the person recording the past in written form. For earlier times this selection process can be critical when the only written record that survives is that of an individual scribe, or a particular fragment. For later periods the process of selection has come to be increasingly understood and the writers themselves are aware of the power they have of defining perceptions in the future. How do the filter and the problem of selectvity work in practice? Some examples follow.

The memoir as testimony

Primo Levi was an Italian Jew and partisan captured by the Italian fascists in late 1943 and deported to the concentration camp at Auschwitz. He survived because he was made a special worker and, as a chemist, was given some special privileges. He was ill when the Russian advance reached Auschwitz, so he did not join the 20,000 fit prisoners who left the camp on a forced march and were never seen again. After many adventures, recounted in *The Truce*, he returned to his home in northern Italy and wrote *If this is a Man*, his testimony. The book was first published in 1947 and did not sell. It was reissued in 1957, has been in print ever since and has been translated into a dozen languages.[1]

In Primo Levi's work there is an acute sense of the importance of recording and remembering events in the concentration camps that the Nazis had established.

> The need to tell our story to 'the rest', to make 'the rest' participate in it, had taken for us, before liberation and after, the character of an immediate and violent impulse, to the point of competing with our other elementary needs. The book has been written to satisfy this need, first and foremost, therefore, as an interior liberation.[2]

Levi stresses over and over again the need to remember, in the face of the Nazi attitude that people would never believe any of the survivors that such a place as Auschwitz could have existed. Indeed, the organisation of the camp was such that no one was supposed to see more than they had to. Levi, along with many other survivors, wrote first to tell the world what had happened, and then as the years went by, to remind the world what had happened.

Words in this instance as a historical source are not simply the instrument through which facts are recalled, they are, in some cases, the only way in which memories and testimony can survive. In the case of the Holocaust we should be grateful that the Nazis were so methodical in recording the process of annihilation. From their own hands they have provided layer upon layer of irrefutable proof of their crimes, before we even consider the oral and other forms of physical evidence. So words, written and spoken, have power, and the selection and control of those words can profoundly influence the way in which history is written.

The diary as a window on to the political world

In understanding the contemporary world we are often at the mercy of politicians and their biographers. The politicians can provide the diaries and the memoirs on which the history of a government will be based. Sometimes these records can be honest, open and frank. The Labour governments of the 1960s and 1970s produced a number of excellent diarists. Richard Crossman is perhaps the most famous and the most indiscreet. The memoirs of Tom Driberg, a promiscuous homosexual throughout his political career, show another kind of honesty and courage. The problem with all such works is the purpose for which they are written. The place of the Alan Clark *Diaries* in this field is a little problematic.[3] Alan Clark was a Minister devoted to Mrs Thatcher and also a sometime military historian, castle owner and son of the art historian Kenneth Clark. Here is a typical entry, a few days before Michael Heseltine's challenge to Margaret Thatcher for the leadership of the Conservative Party in November 1990:

I thought I'd have a talk to Peter. [Peter Morrison was in charge of the Thatcher campaign.]

I listened outside the door. Silence. I knocked softly, then tried the handle. He was asleep, snoring lightly, in the leather armchair, with his feet resting on the desk.

Drake playing bowls before the Armada and all that, but I didn't like it. This was ten minutes past three in the afternoon of the most critical day of the whole election. I spoke sharply to him. 'Peter.'

He was bleary.

'I'm sorry to butt in, but I'm really getting a bit worried about the way things are going.'

'Quite all right, old boy, relax.'

'I'm just hearing bad reactions around the place from people where I wouldn't expect it.'

'Look, do you think I'd be like this if I wasn't entirely confident?'

'What's the arithmetic look like?'

'Tight-ish, but OK'.

'Well, what?'

'I've got Michael on 115. It could be 124, at the worst.'

'Look, Peter, I don't think people are being straight with you.'

'I have my ways of checking.'

'Paul?'

'I know about Paul.'

'The Wintertons?'

'The Wintertons, funnily enough, I've got down as "Don't Know's"'

'What the fuck do you mean, "*Don't Know*"? This isn't a fucking street canvass. It's a two-horse race, and each vote affects the relative score by two, unless it's an abstention.'

'Actually, I think there could be quite a few abstentions.'
'Don't you think we should be out there twisting arms?'
'No point. In fact it could be counter-productive'[4]

As we now know, Thatcher won, but she withdrew after seeing all her Cabinet individually. Clark told her to fight to the end because her place in history was assured and that she would lose to Michael, who was a nonentity. Later he offered to write her memoirs for her. They certainly would have been lively. What are we to make of a source like Clark, the candid diaries, written in longhand at the end of a day or a week; written by a one-time historian with more than a passing concern with going down in history, although claiming that he never had any intention of publishing the diaries. They are the dialogue of politics, and as such they are a window into the political world, in a similar way that Levi is a window into the world of the camp. They have a humanity about them which breaks down the divide between the historian and the past. Clark is an historical actor, describing history. We know he is sexist, right-wing, patriotic, fiercely loyal to Mrs Thatcher and her beliefs but to little else in life or politics. We know he knows the great diarists of the past, like Crossman, and wonders whether his diaries will equal those of Chips Channon, an earlier Conservative diarist. We know all this because he tells us is in the pages of his diaries. In fact he is most honest and open. He also speaks in the language of the period in which he lives.

The written word as a living document

It is difficult to overestimate the importance of a document and the correct interpretation of it. Examples abound in history of the precise meaning of words being crucial to understanding the intentions of diplomats, the truth of the actions of politicians, or indeed, to the defence of individuals against injustice. However, when something is loosely worded it can be just as significant. Moreover when the different sides in a dispute or argument view the use of language differently the fact can be equally important.

Simply reviewing the role of words since 1945 in the shaping of the modern Europe emphasises their central importance. Consider the Treaty of Rome, signed in 1957 following the long and complex conference in Messina. At the end of the Second World War most European political leaders wanted above all to prevent another Europe-wide conflict. The need to prevent such a conflict was felt most acutely by the French. The French response was to plan the European Coal and Steel Community to tie the French and German economies so closely together that the two countries could never go to war again. These events and developments are discussed in Chapter 20.

The other motivation for the increasing unity of Europe was the division of the continent by the expansion westwards of Russia into eastern Europe. By the early 1950s it was clear that Europe was to be divided between East and West. The western part of Europe then began to move quickly towards greater unity. Between May 1950 and April 1951 the European Coal and Steel Community and the European Defence Community were established. Britain was invited to join both, but declined. The EDC was eventually rejected by the French. In parallel the Western European Union was founded, with its secretary Duncan Sandys, the son-in-law of Churchill. Thus before the Messina conference of 1955 there were a number European organisations, some with Britain in, some not, some economic, some political, but most cultural, all designed to prevent war and to build Western solidarity in the face of the Iron Curtain and the division of Europe.

It was Jean Monnet, the Frenchmen who played such an extraordinary role in the creation of the EEC, who described the process that was set in train at the Messina conference as a 'journey to an unknown destination'. For the six who gathered in Messina and together formed Euroatom and the European Economic Community, the treaty of Rome was a declaration of faith in the European idea. The text of the treaty is one of the most critically important documents in post-war European history, particularly the preamble, which declares faith in the creation of a United States of Europe.

The British governments of the time did not feel able to have faith in the idea of European integration. The text of the Treaty of Rome promised the eventual creation of a united Europe. It did not specify how this was to come about, it did not state that it would involve a surrender of sovereignty, it did not question the nature of the EEC as an economic association of powers at intergovernmental level. It did say that directives issued by the Commission in Brussels would pass into the law of the member states. And it did say that some powers would be exercised by a commission based in Brussels and by a parliament which would eventually be directly elected. The fathers of the European Community, Alcide De Gasperi, Italian Prime Minister at the time, and the French economist, Jean Monnet, envisaged the Treaty of Rome as the founding document of a United States of Europe. This union would not perhaps be seen in one generation, or even in two. It would arise not from the precise words of the Treaty of Rome, but from the intention they contained.

So from the basis of a document signed in Rome in 1957, by six countries, the European Union has developed. Each stage – indeed, everything the Community does – is based on the written word. It is a highly legalistic organisation, but it is also a visionary one. The meaning of words can evolve. So in 1965, after years in which the French had blocked any further progress towards union, the Luxembourg compromise abolishing majority voting in the European Council of Ministers, and establishing the principle that Community institutions could raise their own resources, was achieved. It was from this compromise that Lord Cockfield devised and Mrs

Thatcher approved the Single European Act and it was from the Single European Act that the Maastricht Treaty came about. So the Treaty of Rome begot the EEC, the EEC begot the Council of Ministers, the Council of Ministers begot the Luxembourg compromise, the Luxembourg compromise begot the EC and the Single European Act, the Single European Act begot the Maastricht Treaty and the European Union. In another generation perhaps we shall see a United States of Europe. We shall truly be citizens of the ideas of Monnet and De Gasperi, written down in the Treaty of Rome, in such a way that the process of integration could develop.

These are three simple examples of ways in which the written word is a challenge to the contemporary historian. The first, brief example gave a glimpse of the vitality and importance of testimony, of writing down an individual's experience of a time and place. In the second there is the subjective, arrogant testimony of Alan Clark's ego, an open window on the way politics actually is. In the third, the various ways in which a particular public document can be interpreted differently and mean very different things to different people at different times is explored.

Putting the written word to work

So what use are Clark and Levi, as against the Treaty of Rome? How are we to understand the difference between these documents and the role they play in understanding the contemporary world? We have to place the people who wrote the documents in relation to the events they are describing. We can place Levi and Clark inside the historical events they describe, and we can picture them speaking out to us as contemporary historians. In contrast, the secondary sources, the books and articles, are outside the historical event, and they are talking back to it. In the case of the Treaty of Rome, it is a document whose meaning has evolved through time. It is in motion historically; it speaks to us from the past, from 1957, when it was written, and it speaks to us from the present as part of the continuing political process. Its meaning, the meaning of its words, is not fixed but develops with changes in the institutions and organisations of the European Community which it established.

The experience of the Alan Clark *Diaries* and the experience of the Primo Levi book are different. The events which they describe have taken place. Each individual and each generation will bring new meanings to their words, but the facts they relate of their own experience are fixed. Other kinds of documents have different fates. Some speak to us from the past, and the meaning of their words can change and play different roles in political discourse as time goes by: it is a great mistake to see language as something that is fixed and static. Others are from a particular time and place, and their importance is directly related to that time and place: they change because we who analyse them change.

There is a hierarchy of sources in the historical profession, which is perhaps the exact opposite of the hierarchy of priorities in the political world and for most people. For the historian the document is the most important piece of evidence, particularly if it was written close to or as part of the event, and if we have full information about the circumstances of its creation. Within the category of the written document the greater the supposed subjectivity of the author the greater the kudos of the document, but documents serve so many different purposes in history that it is difficult to quantify this factor. Second to the written word comes oral evidence, whether written down at the time or soon after the event, or recorded subsequently and analysed. Finally come the visual images of television and film.

For the politician communicating his or her ideas, the order in a late twentieth-century democracy is reversed. Television is king, radio and the print media are second and third. They may compete. For most people in contemporary society the order is the same. Television and film are of the first importance, music is second and the written word last.

These challenges to the written word in the contemporary world are profound. There will never be a time when society will function without words written on paper in some form. The real challenge is that those whom we need to read and understand are increasingly communicating in a visual manner. Images, since the 1930s, have become increasingly important as the words which accompany them decline in importance. The written word will remain, however, a central part of the process of understanding the contemporary period.

Notes

1 Primo Levi, *La tregua* (1963), translated as *The Truce* (1965); id., *Se questo è un uomo* (1947), translated as *If this is a Man* (1960).
2 *If this is a Man* (Pengin edition, 1987), p. 15.
3 Alan Clark, *Diaries*, (1993).
4 Clark, *Diaries*, p. 354.

Chapter 28

The press

Chandrika Kaul

Whoever seeks to write the history of a period close to their own must, by the nature of things, be something of a pioneer. There will, as a rule, be no established body of secondary work, no sifted chronology of 'key' facts, no generally accepted interpretation of events. In this context is the importance of the daily press for the contemporary historian best appreciated. For in its pages can be found what is usually the only available connected and structured narrative of events, a narrative, moreover, supplemented by the on-going analysis of informed commentators. Thus does Eric Hobsbawm observe in the preface to his recent book, *Age of Extremes*, 'As the historian of the twentieth century draws closer to the present he or she becomes increasingly dependent on two types of sources: the daily or periodical press and ... publications by national governments and international institutions.' 'My debt,' he adds, 'to such papers as the London *Guardian*, the *Financial Times* and the *New York Times* should be obvious.'[1]

That British historians have consistently used the press as a source should therefore not surprise us. It is, indeed, almost natural for them to have done so. Viscount Camrose, proprietor of the *Daily Telegraph*, described the British in the first quarter of this century as 'a newspaper-ridden people', and this characterisation retains contemporary relevance – notwithstanding intense competition from other media forms. Britain has enjoyed a long and distinguished press ancestry. Newsbooks appeared in the early seventeenth century, and London's first daily newspaper dates from 1702. The nineteenth century saw the leading national dailies consolidate their position as the Fourth Estate of the realm, while throughout this century Britain has had a press of unrivalled diversity and vigour. Behind the evolution of newspaper journalism lies a complex web of change, reflecting developments in society and culture, as well as altering conditions of ownership, technology and competition within the industry itself – all of which it is important to appreciate when using newspapers as source.

'The only true history of a country is to be found in its newspapers'
[Macaulay]

The press as a collective noun covers a wide variety of publications, at national, provincial and local levels, each with its own distinctive characteristics. It is most commonly understood to refer to the national (and provincial) dailies, as well as the weekly magazines of current and political affairs. For historians, the case for utilising these publications ultimately resides in a truth expressed by the first Royal Commission on the Press in 1947–49: 'The Press may be judged, first, as the chief agency for instructing the public on the main issues of the day. The importance of this function needs no emphasis.' Given the absence, or paucity, of other kinds of connected narrative for the most recent decades, newspapers make a crucial contribution to our perception of the past, as much as the present. A comparison with countries in eastern Europe, where traditions of press and reporting have been either absent or subverted, makes the advantage we enjoy transparent. As a first record of contemporary events, newspapers offer an almost indispensable service to the historian.

This contemporaneity of the press is itself an important asset. It provides a window on to the past, a witness of the times, conveying something of the intangible 'atmosphere' which surrounds events. In leading articles and on the letters page the ebb and flow of opinion may be traced. Consider the mid-1990s wrangle between the *Guardian*'s editor Peter Preston and Conservative MPs over the matter of parliamentary privilege. There is, in all such controversies, a hothouse atmosphere, inevitably reflected in the writings of contemporaries, which cannot be altogether superseded by the calmer and subsequent accounts of historians.

It is thus possible to recover some of the animation which inheres in an event by the very fact that it is *new*. This is of great value for, in seeking to understand the past behaviour of men and women, it is necessary to remember that they were reacting to events which were unique, unprecedented – often unexpected. J. H. Clapham, in his *Economic History of Modern Britain*, acknowledged his debt to Alfred Marshall, who had entrusted to him the bound files of the *Economist* from the 1840s to the 1870s. 'It is,' said Clapham, 'an uncommon privilege to stroll about the business world of the 'sixties and 'seventies with Walter Bagehot, the editor of those years, literally at one's elbow. He is more vivacious than most economists, trade historians, or secretaries of Commissions; and wiser too.'[2] By capturing some of the 'spirit of the times', a newspaper account is frequently more interesting to the historian than the carefully documented 'truth'. As Marshall McLuhan, guru of the 1960s communication studies revolution, wrote, 'The press is a group confessional form that provides communal participation. It can "color" events by using them or by not using them at all. But, it is the daily communal exposure of multiple items in juxtaposition that gives the press its complex dimension of human interest.'[3] The 'collective mosaic form' of the press preserves an image of the character, interests and concerns of Britons in years past.

Being a product of society, newspapers reflect and are moulded by public opinion. Much may consequently be gleaned from their pages concerning contemporary politics and economy. In democracies the press is especially valuable as the forum within which debate is undertaken and opinion formed.[4] A newspaper is in this sense a peculiarly reactive source – its existence defined and constituted by immediate engagement with contemporary events. Historians of social history will benefit from the tendency of postwar newspapers to move away from exclusive coverage of 'high' Westminster-based politics, giving greater emphasis to wider aspects of national life. Special supplements have become more common, and the number of daily sections has almost doubled in the two decades since 1969.[5] With the growing interest in cultural history, the tabloid press assumes increasing importance for the insights it gives into mass culture. Consider the value of popular papers in chronicling the career of a band like the Beatles or a prominent footballer such as Gary Lineker.[6] Indeed, to the historian of sport the coverage of the dailies as well as magazines offers the most comprehensive of all sources. For writing the history of an industry or profession, specialist reviews provide often the only consistent historical reference. Examples abound of such publications: *The Shoe and Leather News*, *Cotton and General Economic Review*, *Coal News*, *Consulting Engineer*, *The Legal Diary*, *Dental Practice*, etc. Bertrand Russell even argued that without a vocational press a vocational organisation itself could not live, as its ideas would not be explained by the popular press, nor its work reported and made interesting.[7]

Party journals provide valuable insights into the process of debate and policy formation. Indeed, Lenin's advice to revolutionaries was to organise around a newspaper, and the radical press often provides the basic source for the study of its attendant organisations. Examples include *The Daily Worker* and *Morning Star* for the Communist Party, *Militant* for the Militant group within the Labour Party, *Socialist Worker*, the weekly paper of the Socialist Workers' Party, and *The Socialist Standard*, since 1904 the official organ of the Socialist Party of Great Britain.

Provincial and local newspapers too have a distinguished ancestry. By 1760, says Cranfield, 'the local newspaper had established itself firmly as an essential part of country life'.[8] The following two centuries saw the relative fortunes of provincial and national papers fluctuate. During the industrial revolution the position of local papers strengthened as there developed important centres of economic, commercial and political life significantly removed in distance and culture from the traditional sphere of the London papers. In 1863 Richard Cobden could point to 'half a score of men, the conductors of journals in Leeds, Edinburgh, Liverpool, Manchester, Norwich, Etc.', who by leading public opinion had done as much as the great inventors to bring about the industrial transformation of British sociéty.[9] In 1920 provincial daily newspapers outsold the Fleet Street national mornings, while the years 1950–75 were among the more prosperous experienced by the provincial press in Britain.[10] Tunstall, however, reminds us that 'the "local" media tend in fact to be city media', and the same is true of the 'regional' media. 'Very few papers have a real regional spread.'

Whatever the accuracy and balance of newspaper reporting, it may be accepted that the press testifies to the sort of things that interested or worried people at any given time. It is, for instance, probable that the growth in crime reporting reflects as much the developing fear of crime in society as its increasing prevalence. Yet there can be no doubt that fear of crime is an important fact in our society, appreciation of which is necessary for understanding many aspects of government policy, as well as such changes in individual conduct as parents' unwillingness to let their children walk to school. On the other hand, it is undoubtedly true that certain categories of the press thrive on the commercial exploitation of such fears. Philip Jenkins argues that the media have distorted the nation's image of itself, contributing to a perception of social menace and 'moral panic' during the 1980s.[11]

Features and exposés are an important dimension of the modern press and form the source for another kind of contemporary historical endeavour – the event-based analysis of the past. This in turn can be traced back at least to the late nineteenth century, being graphically evidenced in W. T. Stead's 'The Maiden Tribute of Modern Babylon' campaign of 1885 in the *Pall Mall Gazette*. Stead, seeking to expose the horrors of the white slave traffic in London, 'procured' a girl of fifteen so as to shock the government into raising the age of consent, then only thirteen. Though the campaign landed him in prison for three months, it helped to alter the law.

Egon Larsen's *First with the Truth* chronicles case studies of campaigning journalists, including those centred in the emerging *Sunday Times* Insight Team during the 1960s.[12] A range of investigative reports have been produced by the latter – *The Thalidomide Children and the Law* (1973), *Suffer the Children: the Story of Thalidomide* (1979), *Ulster* (1972), *Insight on the Middle East War* (1974) and *Seige!* (1980). These have coloured aspects of British press history, as well as collective attitudes towards the role of the press in society, in ways similar to the *Washington Post*'s exposure in the early 1970s of the Watergate scandal. Demonstrating the ability of the medium to uncover, investigate and report on various aspects of politics, society and business, such stories serve as benchmarks of the use to which historians can put information gleaned from the papers.

Certain tendencies within the culture of journalism itself have favoured an historical perspective upon events. Over the century newspapermen have generally become more highly educated, with an increasing overlap between the journalistic and historical professions. Combined with greater specialisation, this has ensured that, of those in the privileged position of watching history being made, a larger number have taken to historical writing. Accounts of warfare are more and more being written by journalists – for instance, Max Hastings and Simon Jenkins on the Falklands War.[13] Two journalists who have made a special study of national politics during the 1980s, and have published books based on their knowledge, are Hugo Young and Peter Riddell. The former has written the well known biography of Margaret Thatcher, *One of Us*, while the latter has produced informative accounts on *The Thatcher Government* and *The Thatcher Era and its Legacy*.[14]

This leads us to another sphere in which press men have the advantage over specialist historians. Journalists are much closer to the leading actors and thus often have a shrewder understanding of the game being played than can be acquired from a distance through the sanitised medium of political memoirs and government papers. There is a sense in which journalists are 'of' the world they describe. Apart from being noteworthy editors, men such as C. P. Scott of the *Manchester Guardian* and J. A. Spender of the *Westminster Gazette* were eminent figures in the world of Liberal politics in the first quarter of this century, interacting daily with leading politicians. Their writings not only reflect the on-going process of policy formation but capture some of the controversies and tensions within the party. Familiarity of contact has been institutionalised in more recent times in the Westminster lobby – an inner core of journalists given access to confidential sources and the candid opinions of those in authority. In existence since at least the late nineteenth century, and having precursors in Macaulay's Fourth Estate parliamentary reporters, by the 1930s lobby correspondents were receiving frequent collective briefings at 10 Downing Street. However, these relations were placed on a regular daily basis only with the post-war Labour government, and till about 1960 the lobby mechanism remained 'shrouded in almost complete secrecy'.[15] Often, of course, these correspondents are unable to utilise their information directly, but there is no gainsaying the insights to be derived from a careful reading of the pieces of an established commentator on the 'hidden agendas' of the political elite.

Several further tendencies have improved the quality of the newspapers' political analysis. Information is far more readily available than it was in earlier decades. There has been, also, what Francis Williams describes as a 'swelling tide' of editorial freedom. By the end of the Second World War the party attachments of newspapers, as they had been understood to operate since the mid-nineteenth century, had generally been abandoned.[16] Whilst the social distance, in terms of income, education and status, separating politicians and press men has largely been eroded. Even the Prince of Wales, heir to the throne, has taken into his confidence Jonathan Dimbleby, one of the heirs to the Dimbleby journalistic dynasty.[17]

One paradoxical development should, however, be noted. With the massive increase in the scale of journalistic enquiry, individual journalists have perhaps enjoyed rather less personal access to the upper reaches of power than before. The image of the renowned *Times* correspondent W. H. Russell sitting on the Secretary of State's desk and filing his reports on the battle of Bull Run during the American Civil War has today, even to the most privileged of press men, something of the surreal about it.

'Freedom of the press in Britain means freedom to print such of the proprietor's prejudices as the advertisers don't object to' [Hannen Swaffer]

Whilst the press deserves a central place amongst the historian's sources, any enumeration of its advantages should yet be qualified. The researcher needs always to bear in mind the nature of the source and the caution necessary in interpreting its coverage. The underlying truth about 'news' and the 'newspaper' lies in the fact that what is represented is not the newsworthy event itself, but rather a 'report' or 'account' of an event. A newspaper selects, arranges and reformulates the information, passing to it through a variety of channels.[18] News gains much of its shape from the nature of the medium in which it appears. Second, newspapers are a commercial business. The need to pay their way has, in fact, become more stringent in recent decades. Whatever high purposes journalists may claim, a newspaper is ultimately a commercial venture, selling the written word on a day-to-day basis.

The perspective of the daily press is generally myopic, lacking that most valuable of assets: hindsight. Pressure of time and space, and the nature of news reporting, conspire to make the journalist's style different from that associated with the historian's considered judgement. The axiom 'Yesterday's news is no news' runs counter to the very nature of what we regard as history. In addition, press sources should be viewed with a degree of scepticism. Most journalists work in the context of imperfect knowledge. Access to information is usually restricted and frequently denied. Inflexible deadlines preclude deep and extensive investigation, enhancing the possibility of inaccurate coverage. The very fact of immediacy, whose benefits we commented upon earlier, has also its disadvantages. Further, the phenomenon of a 'good news' day and a 'bad news' day introduces an arbitrary bias into the newspaper's coverage. The amount of space that a paper gives to a story can thus be a poor guide to the historian.

Interpreting the meaning and importance of news stories is itself problematic. Newspapers are in a sophisticated relationship with their readers, and well established practice defines for each title what constitutes 'news' and how it should be presented. A *Times* 'scoop' is not necessarily the same as a 'scoop' for the *Mail*. It should always be enquired 'when dealing with so complex a process as historical and social change, what available stock of meanings was brought to bear by the newspaper so as to make that process intelligible to its readers'.[19]

Beyond these biases intrinsic to the medium, the press is subject to various external pressures and influences.[20] We have already noted the claims of profitability. Other potential sources of distortion include the political allegiances of journalists and proprietors. Those reading the *Daily Express* on the first post-war elections will be struck by the consistent championing of Churchill and the simultaneous vilification of Harold Laski, and will need to turn to the autobiography of the editor, Arthur Christiansen, to realise just how far a proprietor like Beaverbrook would go in using the paper to promote his political ends.[21] 'Newspapers,' said the PEP *Report on the British Press* in 1938, 'naturally reproduce the propaganda of the parties they support, and this in many cases strongly favours their treatment of the news.'[22] Political bias amongst the nationals has weighed in favour of the Conservative Party for most of this century – even at the time of the Liberal landslide victory in 1906. Margaret Thatcher announced a general election in 1983 enjoying the support of daily papers with circulations totally 11,400,000, as opposed to the combined circulation of 3,650,000 of newspapers favouring opposition parties.[23] Henry Porter claims that during the Thatcher years the consensus of opinion among newspapers was greater than at any time since Attlee's post-war government, and that there was an increase in politically opinionated news stories.[24]

There is also systematic manipulation by government and its agencies. All governments wish to shape the reporting of newspapers and the media in general. It is in their nature as political organisations to want to do so. Concern with the power and influence of the press is evidenced by the succession of Royal Commissions on the Press instituted since the war – 1947–49 (Ross Commission), 1961–62 (Shawcross Commission) and 1974–75 (McGregor Commission). Government can always favour a newspaper by advance information, as well as exercise a direct influence in times of national crisis. When Britain abandoned the gold standard in 1931 the government summoned a conference of leading editors to explain the decision.

To secure favourable coverage administrations have employed both the carrot and the stick. Legal action and punitive sanctions have been threatened, whilst at the same time honours for favoured press men, inaugurated on an extensive scale by Lloyd George, continued to be bestowed through into the Thatcher era. There has been, all the while, an on-going development in the techniques of press cultivation available to the political elite. The extent of media management in the past largely reflected the personality of the Premier. While Clement Attlee, it is said, picked up a newspaper only to glance at the headlines and read the cricket scores, and even a politician as sensitive to public opinion as Macmillan met the Westminster lobby only a couple of times a year, leaving regular contact to his press secretary, Harold Wilson 'saw the lobby frequently, attended press parties, dispensed drinks, "called everyone by his Christian name and flattered with amazing skill" '.[25] However from the 1980s political parties have come increasingly to value the deliberate presentation of policy and initiatives, with consequent expansion of specialist staffs to oversee government–press relations on a continuous basis. Mrs Thatcher's particular attention to securing the support of the popular press, together with Bernard Ingham's skilful handling of the lobby, coloured much contemporary newspaper comment – a fact which anybody tracing the history of the period must take into account. A minor episode during the Falklands War is instructive. The Royal Navy's quota of six journalists to accompany the task force was more than doubled at the last minute, the 'decisive intervention' coming from the Downing Street press office. Viewing the matter as of political as opposed to military importance, Ingham (without consulting the PM) instructed the Ministry of Defence to 'ensure not only that more reporters went but also that they comprised a more representative group'. 'The mere flourishing of Mrs Thatcher's name,' says Robert Harris, 'was enough. The Royal Navy gave in.'[26] Nevertheless the Falklands campaign has come to be called 'the worst reported war since the Crimea', as government successfully prevented a quick and full picture of the situation from emerging.[27]

Approaching the press

Newspapers are seductive. They are intended to be. The quantity of material placed before the reader, the careful regard to layout and style, the deft mixture of serious and lightweight items, the conscious manipulation of hopes and fears – all are purposely designed to hold the reader's attention, to give him a sense of being well informed, of excitement without danger – all within the context of his own home. To this process of seduction the historian is equally exposed. It is consequently essential for him to retain a sense of perspective in the face of the plethora of information available.

I have personally discovered the value of approaching the medium indirectly through a variety of avenues. Before using the press in the writing of history, it is first of all necessary to familiarise oneself with the history of the press itself. Consulting secondary literature throws light upon such matters as a paper's origin and development, its commercial history, the personalities and objectives of its proprietors, the nature and size of its readership, its political allegiance and the biographies of its journalists. John Grigg's recent *History of The Times* reveals how, for example, under Rees-Mogg, critical coverage of the Wilson administration not only reflected the editor's conservative politics but was 'strongly reinforced' by his personal antipathy towards the Prime Minister.[28] By means of such information a more sophisticated evaluation may be attempted of the nature of a newspaper's reporting and the opinions expressed therein.

In this respect the contemporary historian is well served, since recent decades have seen a burgeoning literature testifying to the interest in this field. Numerous books have focused upon the press – its personalities, methods and power, whilst a series of up-to-date press histories have appeared, including those of *The Times, Financial Times, Guardian, Economist, Daily Telegraph, Independent* and the *Independent on Sunday*. Recollections and autobiographies of press men offer a fascinating insight into newspaper culture. A particularly good account of the world of London journalism is to be found in *Fleet Street*, a book published in 1966 to raise money for the reconstruction of the Press Club, with contributions by over fifty people associated with newspapers in various capacities. The move to Wapping saw an outpouring of tributes to Fleet Street – with evocative titles like *Goodbye Fleet Street, A Farewell to Fleet Street, The End of the Street*, and so on.[29] Such secondary literature provides a valuable starting point when critically examining the contents of a newspaper.

Day-to-day political events are admirably catalogued in the official index to *The Times*, which has existed in its present form for most of this century. Unfortunately *The Times* has been, in this respect, something of an exception, with most newspapers lacking a publicly available index until recent times. (Colindale houses the (*Manchester*) *Guardian* index 1929–55 and 1986 to date, the *Financial Times* 1981 to date and the *Independent* 1992 to date – see the next section.) Generally the researcher has little alternative but to look up select dates and turn over page after page of newsprint. *Keesing's Contemporary Archives* have provided, since 1931, a concise summary of news reported in the national press. Background information as regards circulation, political allegiances and ownership can be garnered from press directories such as *Willing's Press Guide* (1928–) and *Mitchell's Newspaper Press Directory*, first appearing in 1846 and published since 1978 successively as *Benn's Press Directory* and *Benn's Media Directory*.[30]

Contemporary historians additionally have access to more thorough means of understanding the nature of the press and the society in which it operates. Opinion poll data help us chart contemporary political attitudes and the social structure of newspaper readership. 'In total,' summarises MORI chairman Robert Worcester,

> 51 per cent of the public in 1993 read a 'popular' daily newspaper regularly, while 15 per cent read a national 'quality' daily. Hardly anything so divides the British by class as do their newspaper reading habits. ... It is fair to say that newspaper readership is a surrogate for the class composition of the electorate, reflecting as it does such a clear division across the middle-class/working-class division that exists in this country ...[31]

JICNARS – the Joint Industry Committee for National Readership Surveys – can also be profitably utilised by the researcher. Yet such information has to be analysed with caution – consideration being given, for instance, to how useful the population found their newspapers in particular situations.

Data generated by one of the 1992 MORI election polls reflected as much upon a newspaper's readership as on its coverage, with readers of the *People, News of the World* and *Sunday Mirror* claiming that 'they were satisfied about their paper's coverage of the election when there wasn't any, at least on their front pages'.[32]

In the post-war period detailed investigations into the nature of press and other media coverage have been undertaken by a series of media study groups. Amongst the best known are the Glasgow Media Group, Action Press Group, Birmingham Cultural Studies Centre, the Communications Research Centre at Loughborough University and the European Institute for the Media in Manchester (from 1992 in Düsseldorf). Their reports, in conjunction with *Admap* – the British magazine devoted to the study of media behaviour – ensure that the writer of recent British history is far better served with the means to contextualise and interpret press reporting than his counterpart working on the early twentieth century.

He or she enjoys, besides, another unique advantage: the facility of personally interviewing press men so as to ascertain their opinions, their motives, and the pressures to which they were subject. Working, as I do, on the early inter-war period, this enormous resource is one of which I continually feel the lack, especially since so little 'behind the scenes' information has survived the ravages of time and the deliberate policy of destruction.

Some major press sources for the researcher

Of the historian's primary sources, newspapers are probably the most accessible. Besides taking the main national dailies, nearly all university libraries, and some public libraries as well, stock post-war copies of at least *The Times*. Historians of town or village are well served by Britain's especially rich provincial press, issues of which may often be consulted in local or university libraries.[33] The Bodleian Library (Oxford) and the British Library of Political and Economic Science (London) hold useful collections. For instance, the Bodleian stocks not just the main national newspapers and reviews but also an array of local papers like the *Oxford Mail* and the *Oxford Times*, and titles from the nearby towns of Abingdon, Bicester, Wantage, Witney, Didcot and Wallingford.

However, the serious contemporary researcher will soon find himself making the journey to the British Library's Newspaper Library at Colindale, north London. First opened in 1932, all British and Irish daily, weekly and fortnightly papers are there collected by legal deposit. It is thus not simply the national press which is catered for but the whole range of provincial, trade and specialist publications. There exists a *Catalogue of the Newspaper Library* in eight volumes, published by the British Library (1975), which is widely available. Two titles per country is the allocation for overseas newspapers, though in practice many more are taken from English-speaking countries – the United States heading the list with around fifty. Comparative national studies based on the press are thus feasible. Colindale also houses an extensive array of press bibliographies, from, among others, Great Britain, Europe, the Commonwealth, the United States, Latin America and Japan. Invaluable for the researcher are the indexes of select British and overseas titles (varying dates), including, for instance, the complete set from 1851 of the *New York Times*. General indexes for Britain held by the Newspaper Library include the *British Humanities Index*, *Clover Newspaper Index*, *Chester Newspaper Index* and *Subject Index to Periodicals*. In addition to indexes of select individual titles, both regional and local, Colindale holdings include other useful bibliographies such as *Glasgow Newspapers 1715–1979*, *Northern Ireland Newspapers 1737–1987*, *South Yorkshire Newspapers 1754–1976* and *Guide to Local Newspapers in Dyfed*. In this connection, mention must also be made of two indispensable works of reference for the historian: the annotated bibliographies on *The Newspaper Press in Britain*, a survey of published works on the press in general, and *The Twentieth Century Newspaper Press In Britain*.[34]

A reader ticket survey for 1990–91 at Colindale revealed that, of the nationals, *The Times* was the most heavily used, accounting for over 20 per cent of the total use of national newspapers, followed by the *Daily Telegraph* (9 per cent), *Guardian* and *Daily Mirror* at 8 per cent each, and the *Daily Mail* (7 per cent). For the nationals the most popular period was 1950 to date, with a third of all use being of items published from 1980 onwards.[35]

In November 1994 the *Daily Telegraph*'s *Electric Telegraph* (ET) was launched on the Internet, described by the paper's editor-in-chief, Max Hastings, as a 'pontoon bridge into the future'. Users with a home PC (and modem) can key into ET at http://www.telegraph.co.uk.[36] It was reported by *The Times* in May 1995 that during 'the past four months the number of newspapers around the world offering on-line services has doubled to 240, with 136 magazines and 180 commercial and college newspapers also on the Internet'.[37] With the advance of technology newspapers also increasingly appear on CD-ROM; the first to do so was the *Northern Echo*, and from the early 1990s nearly all national broadsheets are available in that medium. The *British Newspaper Index* (BNI) is now available on CD-ROM as a single disc containing five years of information (1990–94), providing a cumulative electronic index to eight quality newspapers, *The Times*, *Financial Times*, *Sunday Times*, *Independent*, *Independent on Sunday*, the *Times Literary Supplement*, the *Times Educational Supplement* and the *Times Higher Educational Supplement*. General information regarding the availability and cost of CD-ROMs is contained in such directories as *CD-ROM Directory 1994*, *CD-ROMs in Print 1994*, and from individual publishers and distributors like the British Library, Research Publications International, Microinfo Ltd, etc. CD-ROMs are, however, relatively expensive. For instance, the BNI cumulative disc is priced at £2,750 and often major libraries will be the only stockists.[38] One of the most comprehensive and specialised of these is, of course, the national newspaper library and, as no inter-library loan is possible, a visit to Colindale remains a must. See you on the Northern Line!

Notes

1 Eric Hobsbawn, *The Age of Extremes* (1994), p. xi.

2 Sir John Clapham, *The Economic History of Modern Britain* (1967), p. vi.

3 Marshall McLuhan, *Understanding Media: the Extensions of Man* (1967 edition), p. 218.

4 See Peter Dahlgren, *Journalism and Popular Culture* (1992).

5 JICNARS, *The Estimation of Newspaper Section Readership* (June 1990), p. 5.

6 Colin Malam, *Gary Lineker: Strikingly Different* (1993). For a mainly photographic account see Bob Thomas and Rob Hughes, *Lineker: Golden Boot* (1987).

7 Bertrand and Dora Russell, *The Prospects of Industrial Civilization* (1923).

8 G. A. Cranfield, *The Development of the Provincial Newspapers, 1700–60* (1962), preface, p. v.

9 G. A. Cranfield, *The Press and Society* (1978), p. 203.

10 J. Tunstall, *The Media in Britain* (1983), p. 220.

11 Philip Jenkins, *Intimate Enemies: Moral Panics in Contemporary Great Britain* (1992).

12 Egon Larsen, *First with the Truth: Newspapermen in Action* (1968).

13 Max Hastings and Simon Jenkins, *The Battle for the Falklands* (1983).

14 Hugo Young, *One of Us* (1993 edition); Peter Riddell, *The Thatcher Government* (1983) and *The Thatcher Era: and its Legacy* (revised edition 1991; first edition *How Britain has Changed during the 1980s* (1989).

15 Jeremy Tunstall, *The Westminster Lobby Correspondents* (1970), pp. 3, 5. See also Colin Seymour-Ure, *The Press, Politics and the Public* (1968).

16 Francis Williams, *The Right to Know* (1969). A prominent exception being the pro-Labour *Herald*, the most conventionally partisan paper in Fleet Street till its demise in 1964.

17 Jonathan Dimbleby, *The Prince of Wales: a Biography* (1994).

18 Anthony Smith, *The Politics of Information* (1978), p. 209.

19 A. C. H. Smith, *Paper Voices* (1975), p. 12.

20 See Charles Wintour, *Pressures on the Press* (1972); James Margach's penetrating studies *The Abuse of Power* and *The Anatomy of Power* (1978 and 1979 respectively); also the books by Seymour-Ure and Tunstall cited earlier.

21 Arthur Christiansen, *Headlines all my Life* (1961).

22 PEP (Political and Economic Planning), *Report on the British Press* (1938), p. 125.

23 Henry Porter, *Lies, Damned Lies* (1985 edition), p. 53.

24 *Ibid.*, pp. 54–67.

25 Ben Pimlott, *Harold Wilson* (1992), p. 443. See also Philip Ziegler, *Wilson* (1993), pp. 266–9.

26 Robert Harris, *Gotcha!* (1983), pp. 19–21.

27 *Ibid.*, p. 56. See Derrik Mercer, *The Fog of War* (1987); Valerie Adams, *The*

Media and the Falklands Campaign (1986).

28 John Grigg, *The History of The Times*, VI (1993), pp. 47–9.

29 Robert Edwards, *Goodbye Fleet Street* (1988); Susie Barson and Andrew Saint, *A Farewell to Fleet Street* (1988); Linda Melvern, *The End of the Street* (1986); Michael Leapman, *Treacherous Estate* (1992); Tony Gray, *Fleet Street Remembered* (1990); Charles Wintour, *The Rise and Fall of Fleet Street* (1989).

30 It is now published by M-G Information Services Ltd, Tonbridge.

31 Robert M. Worcester, 'Demographics and Values: What the British Public Read and what they Think about their Newspapers', paper presented at City University, London, 5 February 1994, p. 5.

32 *Ibid.*, p. 17.

33 See Ian Jackson, *The Provincial Press and the Community* (1971); Harvey Cox and David Morgan, *City Politics and the Press* (1973); David Murphy, *The Silent Watchdog* (1976); D. H. Simpson, *Commercialisation of the Regional Press* 1981).

34 David Linton and Ray Boston, *The Newspaper Press in Britain* (1987); David Linton, *The Twentieth Century Newspaper Press in Britain* (1994).

35 Newspaper Library *Newsletter*, No. 13 (autumn/winter 1991), p. 12.

36 *Daily Telegraph* Arts Section, 19 November 1994, p. 15.

37 *The Times*, 17 May 1995, p. 2.

38 *International Newspapers and Periodicals* (1995), *Research Publications International* catalogue, p. 4.

Acknowledgements

The author would like to acknowledge the assistance she has received from Godfrey Hodgson, Martin Linton, Brian Jones and David Linton in writing this chapter.

Chapter 29

Books and journals[1]

Michael David Kandiah

For the use of those studying, researching or simply wishing to further an interest in contemporary British history the printed resources available for consultation and reference have improved tremendously as the century draws to a close. Increasingly historical works have pushed their analyses right up to current times, and the trend seems certain to continue. No doubt this is a reflection of demand: there is a popular desire for a better under-standing of the recent past, undergraduate university courses on contemporary history are often oversubscribed and master's-level courses have been introduced at a number of institutions. Additionally, historians have been willing to adapt and borrow from other disciplines, particularly political science and sociology, and to develop new methodological techniques – by using oral testimony, for instance. They have thus expanded the boundaries of their analysis, and that has made the study of contemporary history more viable than before.

Bibliographies

Peter Catterall's *British History, 1945–87* is a comprehensive bibliography that covers all aspects of historical research. It includes more than 8,600 entries and lists over 20,000 works – books, journal articles, pamphlets, theses and dissertations.[2] It is conveniently divided into fifteen main sections: general; political and constitutional history; external relations; defence; the legal system; religion; economic history; environmental history; social history; education; intellectual and cultural history; local history; Wales; Scotland; and Northern Ireland. These sections are further divided into sub-sections that facilitate searching ease, and cross-referencing has been provided whenever possible. This is an invaluable reference work: it supersedes such works as A. J. Walford's *Guide to Reference Material*, but it should be used in conjunction with the *British Humanities Index*, which indexes periodicals and the quality press. It will also be necessary to consult the various editions of the Institute of Historical Research's *Writing on British History*, which lists publications on post-war history until 1974,[3] and from 1975 onwards the Royal Historical Society's *Annual Bibliography of British and Irish History*.[4] Also of use is the *International Bibliography of Historical Sciences*.[5]

Reference guides and dictionaries

Longman have published a two-volume *Sources in Contemporary British History* that is an essential guide to archives. The first volume, compiled by Chris Cook and David Waller, locates and describes the records and archives of over 1,000 different organisations, institutions and societies – from the major political parties to pressure groups; the second, by Chris Cook, Jane Leonard and Peter Leese, identifies the papers of more than 1,200 individuals who have led active and prominent public lives in the post-war period. For individuals principally active in the pre-war period Chris Cook's six-volume *Sources in British Political History, 1900–51* should be consulted, as should Cameron Hazelhurst and Christine Woodland, *A Guide to the Papers of British Cabinet Ministers, 1900–51*.[6]

There are a number of reference works and dictionaries which identify eminent individuals and include brief biographies. The most obvious sources are *Who's Who*[7] and *Distinguished People of Today*.[8] The *Blackwell Biographical Dictionary of British Political Life in the Twentieth Century*, edited by Keith Robbins, provides an authoritative list of prominent political figures for the first eight decades of this century.[9] After each general election *The Times* publishes a *Guide to the House of Commons*, which provides basic biographical information on MPs. All active politicians and government Ministers are listed in the annual editions of the *Whitehall Companion* (first publication 1992), *Keesing's UK Record* (between 1931 and 1988 entitled *Keesing's Contemporary Archives*), *Dods's Parliamentary Companion* and *BBC-Vacher's Parliamentary Companion*. Each of these works contain considerable information about government departments and personnel. Further details about government personnel may be found in the *Civil Service Yearbook* and *Diplomatic List*, which replaced the *Imperial Calendar and Civil Service List* in 1973. Business leaders have been detailed in a six-volume reference work, *Dictionary of Business Biography*.[10] *Burke's Peerage*, *Burke's New Extinct Peerage, 1884–1971*, *Debrett's* and L. G. Pine's *New Extinct Peerage* provide information about those who have been ennobled and their families. The *Dictionary of National Biography*, the *New Dictionary of National Biography* and *Who Was Who* publish details of prominent persons recently deceased.

In a class of its own is *British Political Facts*, edited by David and Gareth Butler (published by Macmillan), now in its seventh edition and updated to cover the period 1900–94. This work is a mine of information and a required tool. It has no fewer than twenty-two chapters: Ministries; political parties; Parliament; elections; political allusions; Royal Commissions; committees of inquiry and tribunals; justice and law enforcement; social conditions; employment and trade unions; the economy; the public sector; royalty; British Isles; local government; the Commonwealth; international relations; Britain and Europe; the armed forces; the press; the broadcasting authorities; and religion. Each chapter contains a plethora of useful information, gleaned from a wide variety of sources.

Almanacs, annuals and surveys

To ascertain the sequence of a year's events a variety of publications may be consulted. G. Foote's *A Chronology of British Post-war Politics, 1945–87* is a quick reference guide.[11] *Whitaker's Almanack* and *Pears' Cyclopaedia* have sections that chronicle British and world events during a year. *Annual Register: a Record of World Events, The Statesman's Year Book, The Times Yearbook of World Affairs* and, until the year 1963, the *Royal Institute of International Affairs' Survey* are devoted to describing and analysing world events in a particular year. HMSO publishes monthly the *Survey of Current Affairs* that details developments in government, external affairs, defence, the economy, science and culture. More detailed and considered analysis of a year's events may be found in various annuals like *Britain: an Official Handbook* (from 1947 onwards), and *Contemporary Britain: an Annual Review.* The latter, published by the Institute of Contemporary British History since 1990 and edited by Peter Catterall and Virginia Preston, has an impressive collection of essays from leading academics – Peter Hennessy on the machinery of government, Philip Norton on Parliament, David Butler on elections – and provides a considered analysis of the year in question.

Official publications and histories

Most government departments issue regular statistical bulletins which may be mined for data and statistics. For instance, the Commissioners of Customs and Excise, the Commissioners of Inland Revenue, the Registrars General for England and Wales and for Scotland, the Ministry of Labour/Department of Employment all produce either monthly or annual reports. HMSO publishes the *Annual Abstract of Statistics, Social Trends* and the *General Household Survey*, from which considerable information may be gathered. The texts of Acts of Parliament and measures of the Church of England's General Synod which have received the royal assent are published each year under the title *Public and General Acts and Measures.* Similarly *Statutes in Force* gives detailed notes on Acts commonly in effective use.[12] Hansard remains the principal written record of parliamentary debates in the House of Lords and the House of Commons and for that reason is an important source.

To help track down government publications there is a regularly updated list published by HMSO – variously entitled *Government Publications: Monthly and Consolidates Lists* (between 1936 and 1953), *Government Publications* (until 1984) and at present *Annual Catalogue*. Since 1981 there has been the *Catalogue of British Official Publications not Published by HMSO* (published by Chadwyck-Healey) – these are mostly press releases.

In the past official histories were the first comprehensive treatment of government activities, of an important historical theme or of a period. There are fewer works for the post-war period. Margaret Gowing has written with Lorna Arnold two important volumes relating to the development of Britain's nuclear policy in the immediate post-war period entitled *Independence and Deterrence*.[13] Norman Chester's *The Nationalisation of British Industry*, however, is undistinguished in the sense that it does not extend the debates surrounding the issue of nationalisation.[14] Donald Cameron Watt is reportedly still working on his Defence Organisation since 1945. There are also a number of documentary series to appear over the years: for instance, *The Transfer of Power in India, 1942–47*, *British Documents on the End of Empire* and *Documents in British Policy Overseas*.[15] It would seem that official histories have gone out of fashion, as only a few new projects have been announced in the recent past. Indeed, given the fact that only a handful of the projects undertaken thus far have had access to documents in advance of the thirty-year rule, or have appeared since the thirty-year rule became effective, there is little reason why they should continue to be commissioned.

General histories

There are now a number of general histories covering the post-war period. Always worth consulting is Alan Sked and Chris Cook's *Post-war Britain: a Political History*, first published in 1979 but now updated to 1992.[16] Another work by Chris Cook is *British History and Society since 1945*, written in collaboration with John Stevenson.[17] Covering a similar period is Kenneth O. Morgan's *The People's Peace: British History, 1945–90*.[18] Arthur Marwick's *British Society since 1945* surveys culture since the Second World War. Keith Middlemas's three-volume *Power, Competition and the State* examines the relationship between the government, employers and the trade unions since 1940.[19] The last three authors accept the notion that a post-war consensus defined British politics and it underpins their analysis. Morgan's book is divided into three evocative sections: 'The era of advance, 1945–61', 'The years of retreat, 1961-79' and 'Storm and stress, 1979–89'. Marwick extends the idea of consensus to society and he defines it as a kind of 'secular Anglicanism'. It is always worth remembering that certain ideas are implicit in works of history – general history included – and that they will affect the periodisation, construction and presentation of the argument, and the interpretation of events.

The Institute of Contemporary British History's *Making Contemporary Britain* series (general editor Anthony Seldon) provides an overview of specific themes in post-war history. Each volume in the series is written by an acknowledged expert in the field. The titles of published and forthcoming volumes suggest the variety of the topics covered: *Britain and European Integration since 1945* by Stephen George; *Women in Britain since 1945* by Jane Lewis; *British Public Opinion* by Robert M. Worcester – to name just three out of the present thirty-plus published and forthcoming titles. The Historical Association Studies series has a much wider remit than Making Contemporary Britain but it includes a few general studies of interest to contemporary historians: for instance, *British Politics since 1945: the Rise and Fall of Consensus* by David Dutton and *Britain's Decline: Problems and Perspectives* by Alan Sked.[20]

There are also a number of works which survey modern British history from an extended time span, notably the following: *The Longman Handbook of Modern British History, 1714-1987* by Chris Cook and John Stevenson;[21] Glyn Williams and John Ramsden's *Ruling Britannia: a Political History of Britain, 1688–1988*;[22] Robert Blake's *The Decline of Power, 1915–64*;[23] and T. O. Lloyd's *Empire to Welfare State: English History, 1906–85*.[24] Such works have certain advantages as far as analysis is concerned, as their perspective is wider, and many trends in British history are better examined in the longer term. Nevertheless the breath of their analysis can make aspects of their discussion superficial and therefore they cannot replace monographs that examine particular topics in detail.

Monographs

For historians the thirty-year rule covering the release of government documents has tended to act as a deterrent to the production of monographs, which are the culmination of intensive and extensive research in archives. Using a variety of archival resources, Kenneth O. Morgan has focused on the Attlee governments in *Labour in Power, 1945–51*.[25] Kevin Jefferys is working on the Conservative government, 1951-64. Nevertheless, not all historians have been so reticent, and this has provided some remarkable results: for instance, Martin Holmes's three-volume examination of the performance of British governments between 1970 and 1983 is a landmark.[26] Even so, the methodology employed by such works to construct an argument in the absence of official documents leaves them open to revision as new archival sources become available and as official papers are released. Other fields of history besides political history also need to be explored. Rodney Lowe has written a masterly *Welfare State since 1945* and Jim Tomlinson has written an important book on British economic policy, *British Macroeconomic Policy since 1940*.[27]

It is the task of political scientists to study current political developments and their analysis may be of considerable use to contemporary historians. The evolution of British politics may be traced in the changes noted by political scientists over a period of time: for instance, *New Trends in British Politics* and its successor, the 1984 and 1988 editions of *Developments in British Politics*.[28] The work of academics in fields such as sociology and medicine may be used as source material. Those wishing to explore further afield will find it worth while consulting the most recent editions of the *British National Bibliography*, the *Cumulative Book Index*, the *London Bibliography of the Social Sciences*, the *International Bibliography of the Social Sciences* and *International Political Science Abstracts*.

Instant histories

Contemporary historians may find their starting place in so-called 'instant histories'. Obviously some of these are better than others, and many are written by accomplished political scientists or journalists of note. Each of the Nuffield studies of general elections since 1945 are important and are now more or less standard works of reference. The Thatcher governments had the effect of upsetting, perplexing and exciting commentators (scholarly and otherwise), as is reflected in the unusual number of works attempting to explain the nature of Thatcherism and the politics of the late 1970s and 1980s. Hugo Young and Anne Sloman sought to find answers in *The Thatcher Phenomenon*,[29] and Dennis Kavanagh and Anthony Seldon have attempted to grapple with the complexities of the Thatcher and Major governments in their edited volumes *The Thatcher Effect* and *The Major Effect*[30]. Such works provide valuable early analysis and thus provide the basis upon which future historians can build. Stephen Fay and Hugo Young's *The Day the Pound nearly Died* provides a journalistic account of the 1976 IMF crisis.[31] While their account is now certainly superseded by the more substantial and analytical work by Kathleen Burk and Alec Cairncross, *Goodbye, Great Britain*,[32] it retains its usefulness as a contemporary account and will always be worth consulting for that reason.

Collected essays

Challenging interpretations of contemporary history are often found in edited collections of essays, sometimes containing the early work of younger scholars. For example, *The Attlee Years*, edited by Nick Tiratsoo,[33] questions the traditional interpretations of the political scene in the immediate postwar period, as does *Post-war Britain, 1945–65: Themes and Perspectives* and *Contemporary History, 1931–61: Politics and the Limits of Policy*, both edited by Anthony Gorst, Lewis Johnman and W. Scott Lucas,[34] and *What Difference did the War Make?*, edited by Brian Brivati and Harriet Jones.[35] Edited collections of essays may provide the arena for seminal scholarly discussion to occur. For example, Peter Hennessy and Anthony Seldon's *Ruling Performance* is an important preliminary examination of post-war administrations;[36] Peter Catterall and Jim Obelkevich's *Understanding Post-war British Society* is an attempt to examine trends in British history since 1945 by a mixture of sociologists and social historians;[37] and Anthony Seldon and Stuart Ball's *Conservative Century: the Conservative Party since 1900* examines the Conservative Party's record this century.[38]

Autobiographies, memoirs and diaries

In the absence of other primary sources autobiographies, memoirs and diaries are likely to be important reference points for contemporary historians. Nearly all post-war Prime Ministers have decided to commit their version of political events to print: Anthony Eden,[39] Harold Macmillan (six volumes),[40] Lord Home,[41] Harold Wilson (two volumes),[42] James Callaghan[43] and Margaret Thatcher.[44] Churchill was probably too old to write about his post-war premiership and Edward Heath has to date preferred to reminisce about his favourite pastimes of sailing, music and travel[45] – although it has now been confirmed that at some point in the near future he is planning to publish his political memoirs. Many senior government Ministers have also felt similarly inclined, with former Foreign Secretaries more likely to publish than Chancellors of the Exchequer. There are also seemingly legions of lesser politicians who have recorded their activities for posterity. A few civil servants have been tempted to write memoirs – for example Alix Meynell,[46] Antony Part[47] and Lord Redcliffe-Maude,[48] the only head of the home civil service to have written an autobiography. Diplomats have been only slightly more inclined to do so: Nicholas Henderson's *The Private Office*,[49] for instance. That an autobiography or memoir exists does not necessarily make it useful or revealing. Certainly Lord Home's effort leaves one wondering why he bothered. Some useful autobiographies and memoirs are never printed. For instance, the Churchill Archive Centre, cambridge University, contains the most interesting autobiography of Henry Willink, Minister of Health during the Second World War, which is informative on Conservative attitudes to the provision of national health care before the NHS was established. Publishers have in the past been reluctant to accept manuscripts which they believed were too controversial. For instance, Cassell informed Lord Woolton that a denunciation of Churchill in his memoirs would not go down well with the reading public and, to ensure its publication, Woolton duly cut the offending passages.[50]

The best autobiographies and memoirs are those which, firstly, are written without excessive discretion and, secondly, are not solely reliant on memory. There are notable achievements – Edmund Dell's *A Hard Pounding* is a detailed account of the IMF crisis.[51] Dell was at the time Paymaster General and Deputy to the Chancellor of the Exchequer and then Secretary of State for Trade. His account is a view from the inside, and he was in a position to consult new primary material and his own diaries for the period. The result is an important interpretive memoir until official documents are released and it is a valuable counterbalance to Bernard Donoughue's *Prime Ministers*.[52] For a similar reason Jock Bruce-Gardyne's *Ministers and Mandarins*, a useful account of his time as a Treasury Minister in the first Thatcher government, is of use.[53] Autobiographies and memoirs are also helpful, as they can sometimes conjure up what documentary evidence cannot – 'atmosphere'. Some authors have chosen to destroy their personal papers following publication (for instance, David Maxwell Fyfe after he had written *Political Adventure*[54]), and this may mean that their autobiographies or memoirs remain an important source of information on their opinions and their career.

However, there are several reasons why autobiographies and memoirs should be approached with some circumspection. Firstly, memory is nearly always inaccurate – events may be conflated or distorted beyond all recognition. Even though an author may use a private diary, personal correspondence, press cuttings, and so forth, around which he constructs his narrative, errors will occur. For instance, the account by the journalist James Cameron of Macmillan's meeting with Khrushchev in mid-May 1960 is inaccurate and probably a conflation of different events.[55] Hearsay and second-hand information may be related as fact. Authors may use researchers to help them write their autobiographies or memoirs, and that may make the work unreliable and problematic, as the distinction between an author's memory and the researcher's framework of events can become blurred – what then is the value of a memoir or autobiography? Secondly, authors are prone to emphasise their role in events and are likely to over-stress events they believe to be important. Thirdly, the reason why an author decides to publish his autobiography or memoir and the timing of publication also need to be kept in mind. The publication in quick succession of the memoirs of Nigel Lawson,[56] Margaret Thatcher and Geoffrey Howe[57] makes one suspect that self-explanation and self-justification were primary concerns for the authors. The long-term value of such works is therefore not ensured.

Caution is also urged in utilising published diaries as sources. Diarists are likely to record what they believe to be important and exaggagerate its significance. For instance, Cecil King's diaries overstate the extent of political machinations and use of influence during the first Wilson government.[58] A good editor will excise irrelevant material, but that in turn brings attendant problems because the determination of what is valuable and what is not may, in places, be dangerously subjective.[59] Establishing how and with what frequency a diarist has recorded his material is crucial. Recollections set down soon after an event are preferable to those recorded after the leisurely passage of time. Even so, there may be notable distortions if, for instance, there is a tendency on the part of the diarist to vent a day's spleen – John Reith was quite prone to use his diary in this way[60] – or if the author is self-consciously attempting to explain his actions to a future readership. The latter point suggests the important issue of the diarist's motives for keeping a record. Some people keep a diary as a matter of course: they, however, would appear to be a minority – Cuthbert Headlam appears to be the only example that comes readily to mind.[61] Others may wish to keep some sort of record for their own use or for the use of their immediate circle: Alan Clark's effort[62] would appear to fall into this category. Most diarists are recording for posterity. The diary of Lord Moran, Churchill's private physician, was kept principally for that reason, and it is almost solely devoted to describing visits to his patient.[63] His diary gives a misleading picture of Churchill's post-war premiership, however, because he generally got to see Churchill only during bouts of ill-health. Churchill was probably a more able Prime Minister than Moran's account would suggest.[64]

Nevertheless, despite their shortcomings, diaries are an important resource for contemporary historians. This is partly because diaries may give an indication of how important decisions are made prior to the official release of government records and before other archives are trawled. Indeed, in some cases diaries may be the most accessible source, for example *Patrick Gordon Walker: Political Diaries, 1932–71* on the Wilson government's foreign policy. Diaries also may be able to convey what scholarship cannot – the contemporary feel of events. Barbara Castle's diary is more evocative of what it must have been like to serve in the Wilson governments than any scholarly monograph.[65]

Biographies

Biographies may be a helpful resource if used with care and discretion. Most major political figures have had their biographies written: all post-war Prime Ministers, and most Chancellors of the Exchequer and Foreign Secretaries. Indeed, there is a veritable biographical industry connected with Churchill, with several volumes of official biography and with periodic 'reinterpretations' of his record. Biographies are undoubtedly popular with the reading public. However, many historians are sceptical of the value of biography as a genre and do not believe that it is good history. They argue that focusing on a single individual leads the picture of the social and political matrix of which the individual is a part to become distorted and misleading.[66] Indeed, this criticism should be kept in mind when reading any biography. Additionally some biographies are hagiographic – Michael Foot's *Aneurin Bevan*, for instance, scarcely acknowledges his subject had any faults.[67] Although some biographers may be accused of prurience, others may be obliged to be reticent, particularly in deference to members of the family still alive. This has been a criticism levelled at Robert Rhodes

James's biography of Bob Boothby.[68] Some biographers write with the intention of being controversial and, in their determination to find controversy, the soundness of their analysis may fall by the wayside. Clive Ponting stated in the introduction to his biography of Churchill that he was going to show his subject's life 'in a wider and different context' and would thus construct a reappraisal.[69] However, while it is true that some of his analysis was stimulating, little of value was added to the understanding of Churchill. Although ideally a biography should be written from a variety of sources, many are written about individuals still alive and are heavily reliant on newspapers, other published sources and oral testimony. In such cases separating fact and myth may be difficult. However, biographies of contemporary figures are often early detailed treatments of episodes of historical interest and will therefore be an important source until archival material is open to research. For that reason John Campbell's biography of Edward Heath will remain of use for many years to come.[70] Some biographies are written with the co-operation of the subject, who furnishes the author with private papers and agrees to give tape-recorded interviews. Such authorised works may be very informative if used with prudence and discretion – like Patrick Cosgrave's *The Lives of Enoch Powell*, for example.[71]

Party publications

All political parties publish material on policy and for publicity. Such material will outline the development of policy, which voting groups the parties wish to address specifically, and which issues are contentious for all political parties. For similar reasons campaign guides, manifestoes and annual party conference records are important. If there is an important political point to be made at a particular time, then a party publication will make it. Political publications may also provide information about the party's organisation and structure. Since 1951 all major political parties must publish their accounts, and although these are more opaque than they should be ideally, such accounts do give a some idea of the party's fund-raising activities and sources of finance.

Documentary collections

There are now a quite a few documentary collections on the market. Lawrence Butler and Harriet Jones have edited a two-volume documentary reader on twentieth-century British history which has brought into print a wealth of primary material.[72] Manchester University Press is publishing a series called Documents in Contemporary History. The first was on *War and Reform: British Politics during the Second World War*, edited by Kevin Jefferys (who is also the series' general editor) and many more titles have been commissioned.[73] Such documentary collections can only be good news. However, it should be always kept in mind that a selection process has occurred and that such collections represents authors' interpretation of events. Moreover, there is no replacement for original research and these documentary collections are designed to meet the needs of sixth-formers and undergraduates.

Journals

Articles in scholarly journals are sometimes precursors of more substantial seminal work in progress and many are substantial and important pieces in their own right. Most journal articles establish their argument by outlining and encapsulating the literature on the topic concerned, and this may be a quick and useful introduction to the historical discourse on the subject. Certain periodicals deal largely with issues relevant to contemporary history. The vast bulk of (though by no means all) articles in *Contemporary Record* are devoted to examining developments in post-war history and the journal regularly includes 'witness seminars'. These witness seminars recount, through the views of those involved, important events in recent British history. Similarly, *Contemporary European History* and *Journal of Contemporary History* frequently contain useful articles on Britain. *Twentieth Century British History* bears investigation, as does the *English Historical Review*, the *Historical Journal*, *History*, the *Journal of Social History* and *Transactions of the Royal Historical Society*. Additionally, economic history is an area of fruitful investigation, particularly the *Economic History Review*. Periodicals in other academic fields will also contain articles of interest. Political science journals are bound to contain useful material – particularly the *British Journal of Political Science*, *Political Quarterly*, *Political Studies*, *Parliamentary Affairs*, *Public Administration* and the *American Political Science Review*. Less obviously, periodicals in such fields as sociology (notably the *British Journal of Sociology* and *Sociological Review*), administration, industrial relations and statistics (particularly recommended is the *Journal of the Royal Statistical Society*) are useful. Similarly periodicals devoted to specialist subjects occasionally contain articles of interest to contemporary historians: for instance, *Local Government Studies* and *Public Opinion Quarterly*. Semi-academic journals such as *History Today* contain useful review articles.

Part B of the ABC-Clio Information Service's *Historical Abstracts* series lists a selection of books and articles published worldwide dealing with history since 1914 – this is a better source for finding journal articles than the *Guide to Current British Periodicals in the Humanities and Social Sciences*. Lists of scholarly articles published in important academic journals are to be found in issues of the *English Historical Review* and the *Scottish Historical Review* and on particular subjects in other specialist journals.

Fiction

Novels and published scripts of television series and films may give a view of the social setting of a particular period and provide some political commentary as well. Jonathan Lynn and Antony Jay adapted for publication their screenplays of *Yes, Minister* and *Yes, Prime Minister*, and both the television programmes and the books are a delight to read.[74] Martin Amis's novels – *London Fields* and *Money*, to name just two – are penetrating views of certain aspects of modern British society. James Kelman's work, particularly *Not Not Now the Giro*, illustrates the lives of the poor in recent times. Bill Naughton's short stories evoke contemporary life in the north of England. However, fiction is fundamentally the result of imagination and, additionally, the picture being presented to the reader may not be as representative as the author believes it to be. All writers of fiction (and indeed all writers of history) have their own political agenda, which always needs to be taken into account. This is not to say that as a source fiction is negligible or should not be used at all, only that it should be treated with the greatest prudence. There should be no compromises while undertaking serious academic research.

Notes

1 This chapter is an update of John Barnes's 'Books and sources' in Anthony Seldon (ed.), *Contemporary History Practice and Method* (1988). For a different approach see Peter Catterall, 'The state of the literature on post-war British history', in Anthony Gorst, Lewis Johnman and W. Scott Lucas (eds), *Postwar Britain, 1945–64: Themes and Perspectives* (1989).

2 Peter Catterall, *British History, 1945–87: an Annotated Bibliography* (1990).

3 D. J. Munro (ed.), *Writing on British History, 1946–48* (1973); D. J. Munro (ed.), *1949–51* (1975); J. M. Sims (ed.), *1952–54* (1975); J. M. Sims and P. M. Jacobs (eds), *1955–57* (1977); Heather J. Creaton (ed.), *1958–59* (1977); C. H. E. Philpin and Heather J. Creaton (ed.), *1960–61* (1978); Heather J. Creaton (ed.), *1962–64* (1979); *1965–66* (1981); *1967–68* (1982); *1969–70* (1984); *1971–72* (1985) and *1973–74* (1986).

4 *Annual Bibliography of British and Irish History* (1976–).

5 *International Bibliography of Historical Sciences* (1956–).

6 *Longman Guide to Sources in Contemporary History, I, Organisations and Societies*, ed. Chris Cook and David Waller, and *II, Individuals*, by Chris Cook, Jane Leonard and Peter Leese (1993 and 1994). *Sources in British Political History: 1900–51*, compiled for the British Library of Political and Economic Science by Chris Cook, six volumes (1975–85). Cameron Hazelhurst and Christine Woodland, *A Guide to the Papers of British Cabinet Ministers, 1900–51*, first published in 1975, being revised.

7 *Who's Who* (1897–).

8 *Distinguished People of Today* (1988–).

9 *The Blackwell Biographical Dictionary of British Political Life in the Twentieth Cen-*

tury, ed. by Keith Robbins (1990).

10 *Dictionary of Business Biography: a Biographical Dictionary of Business Leaders active in Britain in the Period 1860–1980*, compiled by David Jeremy (deputy editor Christine Shaw), six volumes (1984).

11 G. Foote, *A Chronology of British Post-war Politics, 1945–87* (1988).

12 *Public General Acts and Measures* published since 1945, and *Statutes in Force*, published since 1972.

13 Margaret Gowing and Lorna Arnold, *Independence and Deterrence*, two volumes (1974).

14 Sir Norman Chester, *The Nationalisation of British Industry* (1975).

15 Nicholas Mansergh, *The Transfer of Power in India, 1942–74* (1970-83); *British Documents on the End of Empire* (1992–), and *Documents on British Policy Overseas* (1985–).

16 Alan Sked and Chris Cook, *Post-war Britain: a Political History*, second edition (1992).

17 Chris Cook and John Stevenson, *Longman Companion to Contemporary Britain: British History and Politics since 1945* (1995).

18 Kenneth O. Morgan, *The People's Peace* (1992). The hardback edition ends 1989; the paperback edition is updated to include the events leading to the resignation of Margaret Thatcher in 1990.

19 Keith Middlemas, *Power, Competition and the State, 1, Britain in Search of Balance, 1940–61* (1986); 2, *Threats to the Post-war Settlement: Britain, 1961–74* (1990); 3, *The End of the Post-war Era* (1991).

20 Both the Making Contemporary Britain Series and the Historical Association Studies are published by Blackwell.

21 *The Longman Handbook of Modern British History, 1714–1987* by Chris Cook and John Stevenson (1995).

22 Glyn Williams and John Ramsden, *Ruling Britannia: a Political History of Britain, 1688–88* (1990).

23 Robert Blake, *The Decline of Power, 1915–64* (1984).

24 T. O. Lloyd, *Empire to Welfare State, English History, 1906–85* (1986).

25 Kenneth O. Morgan, *Labour in Power, 1945–51* (1984).

26 Martin Holmes, *Political Pressure and Economic Policy* (1982), *The Labour Government, 1974–79* (1985) and *The First Thatcher Government* (1985).

27 Jim Tomlinson, *British Macroeconomic Policy since 1940* (1990).

28 Dennis Kavanagh and Richard Rose (eds), *New Trends in British Politics* (1977); Henry Drucker, Patrick Dunleavy, Andrew Gamble and Gillian Peele (eds), *Developments in British Politics* revised edition (1984); *Developments in British Politics*, second edition (1988).

29 Hugo Young and Anne Sloman (eds), *The Thatcher Phenomenon* (1986).

30 Dennis Kavanagh and Anthony Seldon (eds), *The Thatcher Effect* (1989) and *The Major Effect* (1994).

31 Stephen Fay and Hugo Young, *The Day the Pound nearly Died* (1978).

32 Kathleen Burk and Sir Alec Cairncross, *'Goodbye Great Britain': the 1976 IMF Crisis* (1992).

33 Nick Tiratsoo (ed.), *The Attlee Years* (1991).

34 Anthony Gorst, Lewis Johnman and W. Scott Lucas (eds), *Contemporary British History, 1931–61: Politics and the Limits of Policy* (1991).

35 Brian Brivati and Harriet Jones (eds), *What Difference did the War Make?* (1992).
36 Peter Hennessy and Anthony Seldon (eds), *Ruling Performance: British Governments from Attlee to Thatcher* (1987).
37 Peter Catterall and Jim Obelkevich (eds), *Understanding Post-war British Society* (1994).
38 Anthony Seldon and Stuart Ball (eds), *Conservative Century: the Conservative Party since 1900* (1994).
39 Anthony Eden, *Full Circle* (1960).
40 Harold Macmillan, *Winds of Change, 1914–39* (1966); *The Blast of War, 1939–45* (1967); *Tides of Fortune, 1945–55* (1969); *Riding the Storm, 1956–59* (1971); *Pointing the Way, 1959–61* (1972); *At the End of the Day, 1961–63* (1963).
41 Lord Home of the Hirsel, *The Way the Wind Blows* (1976).
42 Harold Wilson, *The Labour Government, 1964–70* (1971); *Final Term* (1979).
43 James Callaghan, *Time and Chances* (1987).
44 Margaret Thatcher, *The Downing Street Years* (1993).
45 Edward Heath, *Sailing: a Course of my Life* (1975); *Music: a Joy for Life* (1976); *Travels: People and Places in my Life* (1977); *Carols: the Joy of Christmas* (1977).
46 Alix Meynell, *Public Servant, Private Woman* (1988).
47 Sir Antony Part, *The Making of a Mandarin* (1990).
48 Lord Redcliffe-Maud, *Experiences of an Optimist* (1981).
49 Sir Nicholas Henderson, *The Private Office: a Personal View of Five Foreign Secretaries and of Government from the Inside* (1984).
50 Earl of Woolton, *Memoirs of the Rt Hon. the Earl of Woolton* (1959). The author of this chapter is engaged in writing Woolton's biography.
51 Edmund Dell, *A Hard Pounding: Politics and Economic Crisis, 1974–76* (1991).
52 Bernard Donoughue, *Prime Ministers: the Conduct of Policy under Harold Wilson and James Callaghan* (1987).
53 Jock Bruce-Gardyne, *Ministers and Mandarins: Inside the Whitehall Village* (1986).
54 David Maxwell-Fyfe, *Political Adventure: the Memoirs of the Earl of Kilmuir* (1964).
55 James Cameron, *Point of Departure: Experiment in Biography* (1969), p. 211. This error was pointed out in John Turner's biography *Macmillan* (1993), p. 152.
56 Nigel Lawson, *The View from No. 11: Memoirs of a Tory Radical* (1992).
57 Geoffrey Howe, *Conflict of Loyalty* (1994).
58 *The Cecil King Diary, 1965–70* (1972), *1970–74* (1975).
59 For the editors' side of the debate see 'Editing diaries: witness seminar', *Contemporary Record*, 7, (1), summer 1993, pp. 103–31.
60 Charles Stuart (ed.), *The Reith Diaries* (1975).
61 Stuart Ball (ed.), *The Headlam Diaries, 1935–51* (forthcoming).
62 Alan Clark, *Diaries* (1993).
63 Lord Moran, *Churchill: the Struggle for Survival* (1966).
64 A point cogently made in Anthony Seldon, *Churchill's Indian Summer* (1981).
65 Barbara Castle, *The Castle Diaries, 1965–70* (1984).
66 D. C. Watt, *Personalities and Policies* (1965), and Maurice Cowling, *The Impact of Labour* (1971), p. 6.
67 Michael Foot, *Aneurin Bevan*, 2 vols (1962, 1973).

68 Robert Rhodes James, *Bob Boothby: a Portrait* (1991).

69 Clive Ponting, *Churchill* (1993).

70 John Campbell, *Edward Heath: a Biography* (1993).

71 Patrick Cosgrave, *The Lives of Enoch Powell* (1989).

72 Lawrence Butler and Harriet Jones, *Twentieth Century Britain: a Documentary Reader*, 2 vols (1994, and 1995).

73 Kevin Jefferys (ed.), *War and Reform: British Politics during the Second World War* (1994).

74 See M. D. Kandiah, 'Writing *Yes Minister*' (1) 'Sir Antony Jay, CVO', and 'Writing *Yes Minister*' (2) 'Jonathan Lynn', interviews, *Contemporary Record*, 8 (3), winter 1994, pp. 506–34.

Chapter 30

Survey and opinion polls

Tom Nossiter

Political historians too often adopt an atheistical, or at best agnostic, stance towards numerical data, allowing the political scientist (frequently a lapsed 'historian') to queer the pitch. It is hard to see any justification for this attitude. The primary business of the historian is to explain how the particular occurred, and to deny the use of statistics in this quest is to dismiss a useful explanatory tool. Why James Callaghan decided not to go to the country in the autumn of 1978 may be a question for his biographer; but when in June 1979 'Labour's Baldwin' lost to the less popular figure of Mrs Thatcher the outcome was influenced by a number of factors – the 'winter of discontent', the radical right thrust, sociological change and the campaign itself – all in part susceptible to quantitative evaluation, which is to say that the statistician can supply evidence of their relative importance. If sources exist which shed light on what may turn out with the benefit of hindsight to have been the most profound change in the direction of British history since the supplanting of the Liberals as HM opposition by the Labour Party, what self-respecting historian would ignore the data merely because they were statistical? By their training historians have honed one skill to a fine edge: the ability to examine the nature of a source of information. The need now is to encompass statistical data in the range of evidence deemed worthy of study.

This chapter is concerned with the nature of the numerical sources relevant to the concerns of the contemporary political historian, and will draw attention to their pitfalls as well as their potential. Space does not permit a detailed explanation of statistical and computational techniques, but recourse may be had to one of the several excellent 'cookbooks' on the subject,[1] as well as to specialist colleagues. Bear in mind that the statistician is best able to help if he or she knows what hypothesis one wishes to test. The more precisely specified the problem the better. The statistician is also sure to underline that all the available techniques rest on particular assumptions which need to be understood if proper conclusions or inferences are to be drawn from the analysis of the data. Statistics, it cannot be said too often, are no more able to speak for themselves than a written document is. They too need to be interpreted, and with the same caution.

Some problems with survey data

Before turning to the range of sources available, some general comments are necessary. First, the historian will ordinarily be relying on data collected by others – government, commercial agencies, fellow academics – and collected for purposes quite different from his or her own. The opinion pollster, for instance, is primarily interested in the temperature of bodies politic as measured by answers to the question 'If there was a general election tomorrow, how would you vote?' The fact is that the respondent knows that there is not going to be an election tomorrow. The results can make good copy on the front page of a newspaper but it would be rash to assume that at mid-term the electors are genuinely expressing a considered view of what they would do in an impossible contingency. More likely they are sending a message to Downing Street about how well, or badly, they think the government is doing, which may be a reason why 'electoral' volatility half-way through a Parliament is not matched when it comes to making real choices on polling day. Beyond the temperature, opinion polls normally take a few other measurements – leader ratings and ranking of issues especially – but the sort of data which might permit diagnosis of the reason for shifts in opinion are usually insufficient.

Second, data sets fall into two distinct categories: aggregate and individual-level data. Aggregate data will typically be returns of comprehensive information for a territorial unit, possibly a constituency; individual-level data will usually be based upon some sampling procedure. The former, while complete, suffer from the problem that there are many variables but insufficient cases – for example, 650 parliamentary constituencies – to enable even powerful statistical tools to shed much light on political dynamics. There is also the danger of the ecological fallacy, the 'storks and babies' syndrome: correlations are not causalities. Individual-level data sets, on the other hand, suffer because the expense involved in conducting interviews mean that rarely will there be more than 2,000 respondents, and normally they will not be more than 1,000. If the selection of the individuals has been random in the strict statistical sense, then it is possible to calculate the margin of error for any size of sample in relation to the total population from which they were selected. However, the largest data sets we typcially have – opinion polls – are usually based on quota sampling. For example, interviewers seek so many young working-class males, and the final figures are subjected to correction (weighting) on the basis of census and similar information to ensure that the sample contains the proper proportion of that category relative to others. Quota sampling is often treated as if it were random in character and, to the degree that any opinion polling organisation produces meaningful and consistent patterns over time, there are some commonsense grounds for the assumption if what we are concerned with is overall measures of political popularity. However, the non-random character of such surveys undermines their utility when we proceed to analyse the shifts of opinion in the light of the demographic, sociological or political variable, because the numbers in each category are small enough for distortions to matter. The phrase used to describe where electors were interviewed – 'sampling points' – may well mean supermarkets, and it is human for interviewers subconsciously to select the more congenial faces to approach for answers. It is also salutary to note the impact of the poll tax on the official population of Britain.

Third, the vast majority of data on individuals are cross-sectional in nature. We may interview 1,000 individuals this month and 1,000 next month, but they will be different individuals. If in the 1959 general election one-third of the working class interviewed voted Conservative, and the same was true in the 1964 election, it would seem to follow that there had been little change in the composition of the Conservative working class. But the fact that the net figures are the same may mask considerable gross changes. More generally, and seriously, the political stability of a class-aligned electorate has been contrasted with the recent volatility of a class-dealigned electorate. Since, prior to the early 1960s, we have almost no information on the political behaviour of individual electors over two elections or more, we cannot actually be sure that the gross figures do not hide significant real shifts of opinion. There is suggestive evidence that such may indeed be the case.[2]

Longitudinal or panel designs are preferable but are disproportionately expensive, since individuals interviewed in the first round have to be chased and cajoled into a second interview, and so on. Unsurprisingly, the drop-out rate is high, and, even though it is possible to test whether there is demographic bias in the falling sample, more subtle biases may still exist. For example, in their remarkable study *How Voters Decide* (second edition 1985), covering fifteen years and six general elections, Hilde Himmelweit and her colleagues were open to the criticism that those patient enough to accommodate their interviews so many times would end up particularly politically conscious, and so may have become untypical.

Last, it is crucial to remember that all statistics are founded on the concept of covariance or correlation. However, the fact that two variables – the dependent variable of political opinion, and the independent or predictor variable of, say, class – correlate with each other positively or negatively does not establish a causal link between them. What significant correlations do is merely alert us to the *possibilities* of causal explanation.

The observation that the height of a person – controlled by sex – correlates well with voting preference in Britain does not mean that *because* people are taller they vote Conservative. Large correlations are in fact few and far between, and, conversely, there is some truth in the old adage that everything correlates with everything else at a level of ±0.3, or 9 per cent of the total variation. Such levels normally become interesting only when they persist with all other sources of variation 'controlled' out and when there is a theoretical model which suggests a meaningful connection. Reverting to our sample of tall Tories, it is obvious that nutrition in childhood will influence final height and that income, social class and education will condition nutrition. Without a plausible hypothesis the observed correlation is meaningless.

Electorally relevant data

Election data are probably the principal kind of statistical material that the contemporary political historian will wish to use. Ironically, the historian of Britain before 1872 is a great deal better placed in this regard than a colleague studying much of the twentieth century. He or she can consult records of how individuals voted and the original census returns.[3] Although the first opinion poll was conducted in Britain in 1937, it was not until the 1950s that statistics enabling us to chart the flows of opinion in the mass electorate with any degree of accuracy became available.

The 1950s, then, mark the electoral 'enlightenment': in quick succession we had the 1950, 1951 and 1955 studies of Bristol by R. S. Milne and H. C. Mackenzie,[4] Gallup and National Opinion Polls; the Labour Party controversy on the marketing of politics like a consumer product and the consequent argument about the embourgeoisement of the electorate in Richard Rose and Mark Abrams's *Must Labour Lose?* (1959). Then, with the 1959 general election, came the acceptance of (campaign) political argument as a proper function of public service broadcasting on television and radio. The effects of television on politics were immediately tested in Joseph Trenaman and Denis McQuail's *Television and the Political Image* (1961), Jay Blumler and Denis McQuail's *TV and Politics* (1968) and the neglected but challenging article by A. H. Birch and colleagues, 'The floating voter and the Liberal view of representation' (1969)[5] – challenging because it can be read with hindsight as suggesting that the class-polarised Red (Labour) and Blue (Tory) Monkey theory of post-war electoral stability may be an artefact of available research designs. By 1963 David Butler and Donald Stokes had embarked on the panel study of electors which led to the first edition of *Political Change in Britain* (1969). Likewise the opinion polls had become an established part of the electoral landscape, not withstanding Aneurin Bevan's complaint that they took the poetry out of politics.

The electoral rolls are updated annually; constituency boundaries are revised at best decennially, owing to administrative delays in census work and sometimes to the political turpitude of governments. Returning officers responsible for the preparation of the electoral registers offer the contemporary historian a little known bonus. For six months after an election anyone may see (or purchase a copy of) the 'marked up' register, so affording an opportunity, in conjunction with other sources such as census data, to investigate the demography of electoral turnout. Turnout itself is another concept which is frequently treated as far more solid fact than it really is. The register, even when fresh (collated in October/November, published in February) is by no means a complete record of all those entitled to vote, as the head of household may not have entered all relevant names. The young and the old are underrepresented, as are certain ethnic groups.

More important is the degree to which the register deteriorates in accuracy through population movement at an average of approximately 1 per cent a month. Were it not for postal votes on the one hand, and deaths on the other, the turn out, as a percentage of all registered voters, would need to be 5 per cent higher in a spring election than in an autumn one on the same register to give the same effective percentage turnout in terms of the number of registered voters still living in the constituency where they are registered. The 1 per cent per month formula provides a rough estimate. But how misleading it is can be illustrated by considering the 1950 and 1951 general elections, when turn out was a democratically impressive 80 per cent plus. Indeed, it is often assumed that familiarity with, or cynicism about, politicians and political parties has contributed to a secular downward trend in turnout in Britain since the war. However, if we consider the housing shortage of the immediate post-war period, and the attendant geographical immobility of a youthful population, and contrast them with the in the 1970s situation, on the one hand, where some 10 per cent of the population moved house annually and, on the other, with the 1980s and 1990s, where the proportion of the (very) elderly is growing fast, then it is far from obvious that the average citizen is less mindful of his democratic duty than Tommy Atkins who had just returned from a war fought in defence of democracy.

Population movement from the inner cities to the suburbs is the fundamental reason for the revision of constituency boundaries, only partially compensated for by immigration into some urban areas from the 1960s onwards. In the ten to fifteen years between one boundary revision and the next, not only do imbalances in the size of constituencies occur but, more interestingly, so too do changes in the make-up of the constituency. One is reminded of the character in N. F. Simpson's *One Way Pendulum* who pleaded not guilty to the crime he was accused of committing in Chester le Street six months previously on the philosophically ingenuous grounds that he was no longer the same person. Constituencies too may alter significantly, even profoundly, over a decade: the swift gentrification of Islington helped the SDP just as the ageing of Bermondsey (and the old are overwhelmingly female) contributed to the success of the distasteful campaign against Peter Tatchell, the gay Labour candidate there, in 1983.

Since 1966 census information has been officially published by parliamentary constituency. Prior to that, demographic and sociological data on constituencies were a rough-and-ready approximation from census units which bore only an adventitious relationship to constituency boundaries. In 1983, which witnessed the most radical changes in parliamentary boundaries since 1885, and possibly since 1832, a different problem arose. The census has not caught up with the new boundaries, and so for data on the revised constituencies we have to rely on the psephological paratroops of the BBC and Independent Television News, Robert Waller's *Almanac of British Politics* (latest edition) and Ivor Crewe and Anthony Fox's *British Parliamentary Constituencies: a Statistical Compendium* (latest edition). Together these sources give insights which not only raise the issue of the 'Political Geography of Britain', as Ian McAllister and Richard Rose call it,[6] but also provoke the question of how far – if the relevant quantitative and qualitative data were available – a political geology of contemporary Britain might be discerned. The geographically inclined may find Henry Pelling's *The Social Geography of British Elections, 1885–1910* (1967), Michael Kinnear's *Atlas of British Politics* (1982), Robert Waller's *Atlas of the 1983 General Election* (1987), P. J. Taylor and R. J. Johnston, *Geography of Elections* (1979), and my own *Influence, Opinion and Political Idioms in Reformed England* (1976) stimulating. Fascination with that early tool of mass political arithmetic, Robert McKenzie's 'swingometer', has led to some exaggeration of the degree to which post-war British politics has exhibited a nationwide movement of opinion. Even in 1945 there was intriguing regional variation, which would be hard to explain away on grounds of the old psephological warhorse of class.

Opinion polls

The biggest single source of politically relevant data for the contemporary historian is the opinion poll; at the same time it is the most problematic. Regular opinion polling has been a feature of election campaigns since 1959. Between election periods, Gallup and National Opinion Polls have produced soundings of the state of political opinion and (reported) behaviour on slightly different but fairly consistent technical bases. Other pollsters – Marplan (from 1959), Harris (from 1965) and Mori (from 1969) – have broadened the field. By the late 1960s opinion polling was an established part of the political scene, publicly sometimes impugned by politicians when the results did not suit their interests but avidly consumed and privately commissioned. The 1970 general election, however, challenged the pollsters' credibility. Four out of five opinion polls incorrectly predicted a Labour victory and even the one which got the result right underestimated the Conservative lead. During the 1970s the technical problems which had led to the disaster appeared to have been ironed out and opinion polls were so far rehabilitated that by 1983 Ivor Crewe could talk of 'saturation polling'. 'Polltalk' has become part of the tactics of campaigning itself: selective release of privately commissioned polls by political parties is common, and so is the less than impartial presentation of results by some of the newspapers that are the major patrons of opinion polling: results supportive of their partisan line make front-page leads, while less comfortable findings tend to be tucked away on one of the inner pages. By 1987 newspapers had begun to have recourse to the 'poll of polls', so many being on offer. In 1992 the polls met what David Butler and Denis Kavanagh in The British General Election of 1992 (1992) called their Waterloo. The final four polls published on polling day gave Labour a lead of 0·9 per cent. In fact the Conservatives won by 7·6 per cent. John Birt, Director General of the BBC, who had instructed his staff not to lead on opinion polls, was vindicated. The relevant chapter is both instructive and entertaining. Murdoch's Sun claimed credit for the 'late swing' but Curtice and Semetko deny this on the basis of careful research in A. Heath *et al., Labour's Last Chance* (1994).

The integrity of the polling organisations themselves is not in doubt: at the very least it would be commercial suicide to fiddle polls when predicting election results, the most visible of all their activities. For the historian such embarrassments as the pollsters' failure to get the result right in 1970 or 1992 are essentially trivial. His or her interest is not in the perverse electoral geography of Britain under a simple plurality system or the technicalities of allowing for a lower turnout in the holiday month of June, or whatever other special factors may have thrown the pollsters off the scent, but trends over time. Exact representativeness is marginal. What the contemporary historian is concerned with is movements of opinion and how they may be explained. Let us consider an example. Table 30.1 charts the rise, retreat and recovery of the SDP, Liberals and SDP Liberal Alliance in the context of Conservative and Labour fortunes from the creation of the SDP in March 1981 to the general election of 1983. A preliminary inspection draws attention to some intriguing features: how little Labour's support varies through the series; the marked jump of Conservative support with the onset of the Falklands crisis in April 1982; the way that support for the Alliance tends to fluctuate in line with support for the SDP rather than the Liberals; the downward trend of SDP (and Liberal) support from the peaks at the end of 1981, well before the 'Falklands factor' took effect; and the awesome contrast between the 50·5 per cent of those polled in December 1981 who would have opted for the Alliance parties if the hypothetical general election had been imminent and the 26 per cent who actually did vote Alliance in June 1983. Awareness of the political events of the period would suggest hypotheses transcending notions of the SDP as a creation of the media, and of the Falklands War as the parting of the ways between the electorate and the Alliance, to be tested against the detailed analyses of the Gallup polling.

Table 30.1 SDP, Liberal and Alliance support compared with Conservative and Labour support as measured by Gallup's unprompted question on voting intentions[a]

Date	SDP	Liberal	Alliance	Alliance total	Conservative	Labour
1981						
March	14	18	–	32	30	34
April	19	14	–	33	30	34·5
May	11	18	–	29	32	35·5
June	12·5	18	–	30·5	29·5	37·5
July	12	14·5	–	26·5	30	40·5
August	19	13	–	32	28	38·5
September	17·5	11·5	–	29	32	36·5
October	26·5	13·5	–	42	26·5	28
November	27	15	–	42	26·5	29
December	36	14·5	–	50·5	23	23·5
1982						
January	26·5	13	–	39·5	27·5	29·5
February	21·5	14·5	–	36	27·5	34
March	19·5	11·5	2	33	31·5	33
April	20·5	11	5·5	37	31·5	29
May	13·5	9·5	6	29	41·5	28
June	15	10	3·5	28·5	45	25
July	13	7·5	3·5	24	46·5	27·5
August	13·5	10·5	3·5	27·5	44·5	26·5
September	12	8·5	2·5	23	44	30·5
October	11·5	12	3·5	27	40·5	29
Noovember	11·5	8	2	21·5	42	34·5
December	10·5	9	2·5	22	41	34·5
1983						
January	9	11·5	22·5	44	31·1	
February	8	10·5	3·5	22	43·5	32·5
March	13·5	10·5	5	29	39·5	28·5
April	7·5	10	5	22·5	40·5	35
12 May[b]	6	7·5	4	17·5	49	31·5
19 May[b]	6	9	4	19	46	33
25 May[b]	6	7	5	18	48	33
29 May[b]	6	6	6	18	49	31·5
3 June[b]	8·5	9	5·5	23	47·5	28
5 June[b]	7·5	7·5	7	22	45·5	31·5
9 June (election result, GB)				26	43·55	28

[a] The 'prompted' question naming the Alliance as a choice sometimes indicated a significantly greater amount of support for the Alliance, particularly during the

SDP's first year. The total Alliance support as measured by the prompted question for each of the ten months in 1981 was: March 46%, April 45%, May 40%, June 37·5%, July 39%, August 41·5%, September 39·5%, October 46·5%, November 43%, December 51%.
[b] Poll during election campaign; date is that of publication in the *Daily Telegraph.*
Source: Gallup Political Index.

Academic survey data

While academic surveys of political attitudes and behaviour are not as common in Britain as in the United States, they are sufficiently common to be a major source for the contemporary political historian. In contrast to opinion polls, their objective is to offer a theoretical insight into the political process: the number of questions asked is usually larger; the background variables are more searching and numerous; and the processing is more sophisticated. However, they are by nature anything but instant and are normally geared to predictable 'events' in the political life cycle of a democracy. Many, but not all, of the more recent studies involve a panel design, whereby the same respondents are interviewed more than once. Yet it cannot be said that such surveys achieve anything of the unanimity that opinion polls do. Although a large slice of Social Science (now Economic and Social) Research Council budgets was spent on the study of British voting behaviour, we still do not know how or why the voter decides. It may be that smaller, more tightly controlled surveys specifically designed to test one hypothesis to destruction will be the way forward.

For the contemporary historian there are two ways to utilise the findings of such surveys: simply to cull the published work for relevant tabulations; or to engage in the time-consuming work of secondary analysis, by subjecting the data set to further processing. The Essex Data Archive has collected some of the best surveys of the last twenty years, 'cleaned' the data, and made the package available in standard form. The historian exploiting this rich resource would undoubtedly be wise to examine the nature of the sample, the quality of the questionnaire and the logic of the argument. Survey work is littered with battered reputations.

Official statistics

The serious historian will doubtless be stimulated by the findings of pollsters and psephologists but it is very likely that he or she will soon have recourse to the less glamorous, indeed often pedestrian, outpourings of the government machine for 'hard facts'on the trends of the economy, on the state of law and order, even on how many people saw an allegedly opinion-forming current affairs programme on television. Official and semi-official statistics – literally facts and figures for the use of the state (sometimes confused with the governing party of the day) – are our biggest source of numerical data.

Surprisingly, however, though censuses have been compiled since 1801, the British Government Statistical Service was not established until 1941. Its wartime origin and its subsequent expansion under Harold Wilson's premiership in the 1960s underline the point that governments do not collect statistics for the benefit of historians or social scientists. Nonetheless, official figures are a mine of information as well as a minefield for the unwary. The returns are only as sound as the quality of reporting and processing. Mistakes are made. Two that did come to light were an apparent balance of payments crisis stemming from the accidental omission of a zero by the employee of a major firm reporting its exports, and the publication, undetected for several months, of a nonsensical set of trade figures, for the simple reason that a clerk had transposed two lines of figures on the coding sheet.[7] We may assume other errors have passed undetected into 'history' to bemuse the doctoral student.

British government statistics emanate from three main sources: the Office of Population Censuses and Surveys, the Business Statistics Office, and the statistical units of the main government departments, the whole co-ordinated by the Central Statistical Office. The greatest undertaking of all is the decenuial census, costing roughly £1 per head of the population. By international standards it is comparatively limited in scope – for example, ethnic origin was still not directly included in 1981 – but undoubtedly highly professional. England and Wales are divided into just over 100,000 enumeration districts, some 180 households per district, and data for this level are available in machine-readable form.

The censuses are supplemented and updated by a number of official sample surveys. These include the Family Expenditure Survey, which began in the 1950s, and charts the income and spending of households; the General Household Survey, dating from 1971, which deals with population, housing, employment, education and health; the Labour Force Survey, begun in 1973; and the National Readership Survey, started in 1956. There are more specific surveys and it is fair to work on the presumption that some government department has collected the information you are interested in, even if, as happens on occasion, it was politically too sensitive to be published immediately, if at all. Catherine Hakim's *Secondary Analysis in Social Research* (1982) is an excellent overview of official governments statistics; the Central Statistical Office's annual *Guide to Official Statistics* is definitive; and the Royal Statistical Society's periodical *Review of UK Statistical Sources*, edited by W. F. Maunder, is invaluable. On the census, David Rhind's *A Census User's Handbook* (1983) is well worth reading.

The most obvious and readily accessible sources for the historian are the *Annual Abstract of Statistics*, which dates from the last century, and the

Monthly Abstract, from which it is aggregated; *Social Trends*, a 'good read', which may be the place to begin; *Economic Trends*, also accessible; the more intimidating *British Business*, on which *Economic Trends* is based; and *Regional Trends*, providing a provincial breakdown of the national information in the parent *Social Trends*. Other important sources are *Population Trends*, *Criminal Statistics* and the *Employment Gazette*, a monthly publication which records figures for the unemployed as well as for those in work.

This last publication provides a salutary illustration of how careful one must be in using and interpreting official (and other) statistics. As Martin Slattery has written,

> by excluding or ignoring certain groups the [Conservative] government has managed to stabilise unemployment at about 3.3 million over the [1982–86] period. In 1982 Norman Tebbit, the then Minister of Employment, changed the counting rules to exclude from the official figures those who did not register for unemployment benefit. This alone cut 264,000 people from the dole queue. In 1983 men over 60 on higher long-term rates of supplementary benefit did not have to sign on at an unemployment office, thus removing a further 162,000.[8]

No party has a monopoly in such administrative 'adjustments', and the moral is to look carefully at the explanatory notes, mindful of Disraeli's aphorism about 'lies, damned lies and statistics'.

Official statistics deal with facts, even if they are not necessarily the facts in which historians, sociologists or political scientists devil. What is missing from the official record is systematic data on opinions and attitudes. However, in 1983 the Department of Employment and the Department of the Environment agreed to co-sponsor a national survey of social attitudes, based on a sample survey which echoes the invaluable American General Social Survey. *The British Social Attitudes Survey*[9] has already established itself as a major source of reference and deserves to be a protected species of socio-political inquiry.

Content analysis

One other kind of quantification which the contemporary historian may occasionally find useful is content analysis of the mass media. Political information and political messages assail the democratic citizen through television, radio and the press. Only rarely is there reason to suppose that a particular headline, article or party political broadcast could have swung opinion as the Zinoviev letter is alleged to have done in 1924. More plausible, given the volume of propaganda, and the low level of attention of a family audience to a tabloid press or a news bulletin, is the dripping tap effect.[10] Here a distinction should be made between the daily press, which in its mass circulation popular form is unashamedly partisan, and the terrestial broadcasting organisations, which are bound by public service requirements to be fair, impartial and accurate in their treatment of news and current affairs. In practice, the balance between political parties on television is measured by ratio of air time, usually known as the 'tot' (total), although in the 1992 campaign ITN abandoned this straitjacket in favour of commercially driven news values.

The Committee on Political Broadcasting, an *ad hoc* and unofficial group composed of representatives of the political parties, the BBC and the Independent Broadcasting Authority, under the chairmanship of the Leader of the House of Commons, have met at least annually to agree a ratio for party election (or, between election campaigns, for party political) broadcasts, which then, unofficially, determines the ratio of news coverage during the election period. Note, however, that out of campaign periods no such convention exists for news coverage. In 1983 the ratio for the Conservatives, Labour and the Alliance was 5:5:4, in 1987 it was 5:5:5. By contrast, without such informal regulation the popular press coverage in terms of column inches in 1983 was in a ratio of 5:5:2. Seconds or column inches, of course, tell us nothing of the direction of the coverage. Measuring the coverage of particular issues, as in Paul Hartman and Charles Husband's study of the treatment of race in the British press from 1963 to 1970 (*Racism and the Mass Media*), can offer background to the development of public attitudes.[11]

As content analysis passes from basic categorisation into such refinements as coding for positive and negative statements and context, the work becomes enormously time-consuming and it is unlikely that the contemporary historian will lightly undertake such investigation him or herself. Especially difficult is the content analysis of television, which, to be convincing, requires analysis of the visual as well as the verbal dimension, and where, as in the case of news programmes, one has to reckon with a large number of brief items. The controversy over the Glasgow University Media Group's *Bad News* (see, for instance, Martin Harrison's *Whose Bias?*), illustrates the problem.[12] Harrison criticised the Glasgow group's work but did not have access to most of the videos of the material on which the group based its analysis. For those with the inclination, an increasing amount of news and current affairs programming is available as script or videotape.[13] Party political broadcasts and election programmes of all kinds from 1974 onwards are on tape at the University of Leeds, as are the programmes made for the EEC referendum campaign of 1975. Much else of a political nature has been recorded in various social science departments, especially in media studies, but there is no central record. Broadcaster invariably charge market rates for past programme tapes.

Even when scrupulously conducted, content analysis invites almost as many questions as it answers. How far does 'biased' coverage reinforce attitudes, as opposed to creating them? Do newspaper readers read the *Sun* because of its Conservative line or are they Conservatives because they have been exposed to the *Sun*? A Mori poll in 1979 found that only 28 per cent of its readers thought that the Sun was biased towards the Conservatives, while in 1983, despite such headlines as the notorious 'GOTCHA!' when the *General Belgrano* was sunk in 1982, the Sun reader was only 6 per cent more likely to have voted Conservative than the average voter was.[14] As for television, the consensus amongst researchers suggests that any effects it may have are complex, are strongly influenced by viewers' prior disposition, and are far less than commonly supposed by some politicians. Party political broadcasts, like commercial advertising, tend to be more defensive than proselytising: they remind the faithful that their party is still in the field. Whatever the technical objections to the Glasgow University Media Group's work on preferred readings of industrial relations or on the problems of the British economy in the 1970s, the alleged bombardment with the notion that strikes were a fundamental cause of the country's difficulties did not avert the 'winter of discontent' in 1978–79, i.e. the alleged bias seems to have had little or no effect on events.

Preparing your own survey

Despite the mass of underused data available, it may still be that the historian has no choice but to embark on his or her own survey. Without going into the techniques involved,[15] it is worth stating here a number of principles that should be borne in mind if the time and effort, which are always considerable, are to be well spent.

First, once your questionnaire has gone out, there is no going back because you forgot to include something. In any sample of ordinary citizens, there are likely to be a goodly number that you will never find again, let alone persuade to give more of their precious time; and a sample of, say, lobby correspondents will be far too busy to answer further enquiries. Remember too that, unlike the unchanging archive, people change their views over time as they respond to experience.

Second, and clearly linked with this admonition, it is imperative to define your purpose clearly if the enquiry is to be intellectually worth while. The carpet sweeper is no use. Where the investigation is designed to test a hypothesis it must be rigorous and capable of falsification from the information gathered. Such an approach will impose its own discipline: do I need this question and why?

Third, a hypothesis is about the relationship between concepts, but those concepts need to be operationalised into measures and indicators which can be understood in the same way by all members of the sample. A simple example will illustrate the point. Take the question usually rendered as 'Do you think you have a duty to vote, or do you think you should vote only if you want to?' On the face of it this question, familiar enough in political science surveys and designed to tap the citizen's internalisation of democratic norms, is straightforward. Unfortunately, young voters asked the question in the early 1970s, by me, had a quite different perception of the term 'duty' from their parents. Had 'responsibility' been substituted for 'duty' the findings might have been more satisfactory.

Fourth, it is better to have fewer but more reliable data. In the world at large, attention spans are not geared to the fifty-minute lecture or the 4,000 word article. The number of questions must take into account the staying power of the least attentive respondent; like a good lecture, the questionnaire should begin by gaining attention, raise the crucial issues a few minutes into the encounter and devote the last few minutes to bread-and-butter matters as the audience loses concentration.

Fifth, never put words into your respondent's mouth, as it is so easy to do. Questions such as 'What class would you say you belong to?' where it has not been established that the respondent construes his or her world along class lines, are very misleading and so inadmissible.

Finally, when the questionnaires have been returned, do remember that analysis of the data is at least as demanding as their collection. The phrase 'number crunching' is quite misleading. The possible permutations of tables of this variable against that, controlling for some other variable, are endless; and, for reasons which will be clear from even the above short list of pitfalls, the best organised surveys rarely offer neat, consistent and incontrovertible conclusions. The analysis of a survey is something of a military operation where a strategy is essential if one is not to become bogged down in the trenches hoping vainly for some new statistical weaponry to come to the rescue. If nothing else, conducting a survey teaches humility.

Conclusions

The attentive reader will have noticed that it appears to be the masses who are recounted, not their governors. This is not far wide of the mark, even though one might instance exceptions such as studies of elite recruitment or of legislative behaviour – from W. O. Aydelotte's classic enquiry into the ideological dimensions of the House of Commons in the 1840s to Hugh Berrington's studies of backbench opinion through 'early day' motions in the 1950s and 1960s,[16] to Vir Chopra's major study of Indian MLAs.

From quite another perspective, however, political marketing experts share the belief that political communications are influential. To the extent that 'sources close to the party leaders' believe things to be real to the masses, they are real in their consequences. Even the political historian who takes the high politics view of decision-making must now take into account the statistical reports on mass politics, sound or not, which modern Tadpoles and Tapers lay before their leaders. The long forgotten Sir William Petty, who wrote his *Political Arithmetick* as long as ago as 1691, has his contemporary equivalents in Bob Franlin, *Packaging Politics* (1994), Dennis Kavanagh, *Political Marketing* (1995), Margaret Scammell, *Designer Politics* (1995) and R. H. Worcester, *British Politicial Opinion* (1991), and much else besides.

However, the good historian will use his or her forensic skills: who wrote for what purpose to whom? Bernard Ingham could well have figured in Maitland's famous cartoon of how 'history' was recorded in the Middle Ages. But, imperfect though quantitative data are, they offer a sub-alternative view of history – the worm's eye view of the world of property, power and occasionally patriarchy. The Cambridge School of Population Studies has shown how much can be done with unpromising data. In due course Essex man and woman, Middle England, and the modern Boadicea, Mrs Thatcher, will be explained without excessive emphasis on the Leader Syndrome – by exploration of the mine shaft of high and low grade ores readily available to the historical geologist willing to pan for gold.

Notes

1   See, for example, Roger Jowell, Gerald Hoinville *et al.*, *Survey Research Practice* (1986).

2   A. H. Birch, R. Benewick, Jay G. Blunder and A. Ewbank, 'The floating voter and the Liberal view of representation', *Political Studies*, 17 (2), June 1969; T. J. Nossiter, 'Working class Tories', *Socialist Commentary*, February 1974.

3   See, for example, J. A. Phillips, *Electoral Behaviour in Unreformed England* (1982); T. J. Nossiter, *Influence, Opinion and Political Idioms in Reformed England* (1976); R. J. Olney, *Lincolnshire Politics 1832–85* (1973).

4   R. S. Milne and H. C. Mackenzie, *Straight Fight and Marginal Seat, 1955* (1954, 1958); M. Berney, A. P. Gray and R. H. Pear, *How People Vote* (1956).

5   See note 2 above.

6   See Ian McAllister and Richard Rose, *The Nationwide Competition for Votes: the 1983 General Election* (1984).

7   Irvine I. Miles and J. Evans, 'Demystifying social statistics, 1979', quoted in Martin Slattery, *Official Statistics* (1986) p. 130.

8   Slattery, *Official Statistics*, p. 83

9   Roger Jowell and Colin Airey, *British Social Attitudes Survey* (1984–).

10 See Jay G. Blumler and Michael Gurevitch, 'The political effects of mass communication', in Michael Gurevitch, Tony Bennett, James Curran and Janet Woollacott (eds), *Culture, Society and the Media* (1982); G. J. Goodhart, A. S. C. Ehrenberg, M. A. Collins and Aske Research Ltd, *The Television Audience: an Update*, second edition (1987).

11 P. Hartmann and C. Husband, *Racism and the Mass Media* (1974).

12 Glasgow University Media group, *Bad News* (1976), *More Bad News* (1980); Martin Harrison, *Whose Bias?* (n.d.).

13 The British Film Institute is perhaps the largest public source. The broadcasters can assist on a modest scale.

14 Michael Bilton and S. Himelfarb, 'Fleet Street', in D. E. Butler and D. Kavanagh

(eds), *The British General Election of 1979* (1980), table 5.16, p. 113; P. Dunleavy and C. Husbands, *British Democracy at the Crossroads* (1985).

15 See Russell Langley, *Practical Statistics for Non-Mathematical People* (1986).

16 W. O. Aydelotte, 'The House of Commons in the 1840s', *History*, XXXIX (137), October 1954, pp. 249–62; Hugh Berrington, *Backbench Opinion in the House of Commons, 1945–55* (1973).

Part V
Oral and audio sources

Chapter 31

Oral history

Michael Roper

History and definitions

Oral history is the recording and analysis of spoken testimonies about the past. It refers both to a process of research in which the act of remembering is prompted by an interviewer, and to genres of writing – usually but not exclusively historical – based on the interpretation of oral sources. Oral history is sometimes distinguished from oral tradition. Whilst the former is principally a narrative of events within an individual's lifetime, oral tradition is shared knowledge of the past, passed on between generations.[1]

The spoken word is perhaps the most well-established of all sources. It is one of the main ways of transmitting knowledge of the past in non-literate societies.[2] In European societies its use was widespread until the mid-nineteenth century. The French historian Jules Michelet used what he called 'living documents' for his *History of the French Revolution*, on the grounds that official sources needed to be counterbalanced by popular accounts.[3]

Oral history as we now know it – involving the systematic recording of life histories – developed only after the Second World War. It was partly due to the spread of the portable tape-recorder. In 1947 Alan Nevins at Columbia University completed perhaps the first modern 'oral history': a project of taped interviews with industrial and political elites.[4] By contrast, however, the subsequent post-war expansion of oral history was driven by a desire to broaden the range of historical sources beyond the records of elites. A key factor in this was the growing influence of the new social history, or 'history from below', during the 1960s, with its emphasis upon reconstructing the daily lives and experiences of ordinary people.

Its most radical incarnation was 'the oral history movement' of the late 1960s and '70s, in which young historians, writers and community activists claimed a special role for the method as a humanistic enterprise.[5] Oral history enabled the lived experience to be recorded of those who lacked the education, leisure and influence to write, and whose accounts were perhaps not congruent with those of literary and official elites.[6] The very act of interviewing was seen as empowering because it brought historians into the community and gave a voice to socially and historically marginalised groups. As Paul Thompson explained, 'the academic is prised out of the closet and into the outside world. The hierarchy of higher and lower institutions, of teachers and taught, breaks down in joint research'.[7]

The commitment to documenting hitherto hidden histories characterises the 'reconstructive mode' of oral history. This type of oral history is widely used in academic studies and in the many innovative public oral history projects which have flourished since the 1960s (see below). From its initial foundation in local studies, however, oral history has become increasingly international and multidisciplinary. This has encouraged epistemological debate about the use of retrospective testimonies, a debate which has centred on the distinction between historical reconstruction and the interpretation of meaning. The implications will be explored below.

Oral history in the reconstructive mode

The achievements of oral history in the reconstructive mode of the new social history are considerable. A comprehensive survey can be found in chapter 3 of Thompson's *The Voice of the Past*. Occupational studies range from coal mining,[8] fishing,[9] agriculture,[10] and assembly line work[11] to midwifery[12] and domestic service.[13] Local and community studies have used oral sources for regions as diverse as a single street in the East End of London,[14] a Suffolk farming village,[15] and a black community in San Francisco.[16]

Women's history has relied heavily upon oral sources because of the paucity of official information about women. For example, British census material has generally under-represented the extent of women's paid work because the enumerators based their assessment on the occupation of the head of the household. Research into women using oral sources has helped to rectify gaps such as this, demonstrating the diversity of women's employment during the late nineteenth and early twentieth centuries.[17] Such research has also generated new questions, concerning issues such as the different patterns of labour-market participation of women and men through the life cycle, or the fluidity of boundaries in industrial societies between women's paid and unpaid employment.[18]

Yet other studies have used oral sources to explore the individual and generational experience of social change. This is the focus of the 'Edwardians project', perhaps the most ambitious UK oral history study to have been completed.[19] Over 500 women and men born between 1870 and 1900 were interviewed for the project, which covered such issues as the experience of childhood, class, crime and deviance, education, work and social mobility. As Paul Thompson has explained, the aim of the project was to highlight the experiences of 'ordinary people' and their perceptions of social change:

I wanted to know what it was like to be a child or a parent at that time; how young people met and courted; how they lived together as husbands and wives; how they found jobs, moved between them; how they felt about work; how they saw their employers and fellow workers; how they survived and felt when out of work; how class-consciousness varied between city, country and occupations.[20]

The scepticism of some document-based historians towards oral sources undoubtedly influenced the methodological approach developed by historians working in the reconstructive mode. Critics have claimed that oral history presents too individual a picture of the past, as such data cannot easily be applied in the analysis of wider economic, demographic or social change.[21] Its chronological reach is limited to living memory. Furthermore, because oral sources lack the chronological precision of documentary sources they cannot readily be used to study change over time. The most often cited argument against oral history concerns its retrospective nature and the inherent unreliability of memory.[22]

The early generation of post-war oral historians responded to these criticisms by seeking to establish an equal footing for oral and written sources. They argued that oral sources are no less or more accurate than written sources. Newspapers, diaries or court records may appear at first sight to be eye-witness accounts, but are often written after the event, and are subject to the same mediating processes of memory and subjective selection as oral sources.[23]

Its supporters have even argued that reliability is a strength of oral history because researchers are able to cross-question their informants.[24] Moreover psychological tests suggest that the majority of memory loss occurs in the short term and that long-term memory remains consistent.[25] This is particularly true of repeated activities such as domestic or occupational routines, which are precisely the kind of everyday activities that social historians have been concerned with.

Oral historians working in the reconstructive mode have answered their critics by developing criteria of accuracy and representativeness to help overcome problems of bias. Interviewees for the Edwardians project were chosen according to a 'quota sample' based on the 1911 census. This ensured a representative balance of rural and urban dwellers, women and men, and occupational and class backgrounds.[26] Accuracy is often sought through 'triangulation', or cross-referencing within and between oral and other sources.

Representing the past: oral history in the interpretive mode

The development of new forms of oral history, influenced by disciplines such as women's studies, anthropology and interpretive sociology, has brought some of the methodological standpoints of the reconstructive mode into question. These more 'interpretive' approaches are concerned with how the past is represented in oral testimonies. Anthropologists working with oral sources have focused upon the linguistic resources that a narrator (or community of narrators) draws upon to construct a version of the past.[27] Here the primary objective is to identify genres of discourse about the past rather than to reconstruct the past experience of social change. Indeed, such work exhibits a suspicion of 'correspondence theories' which seek to extract knowledge of past realities from oral accounts as if such knowledge was analytically separable from conventions of discourse. Thus Elizabeth Tonkin warns that 'historians who use the recollections of others cannot just scan them for useful facts to pick out, like currants from a cake'.[28]

A further development concerns the study of 'social memory'. This entails analysis of the cultural processes through which, from the mass of accumulated past experience, individuals compose and transmit meaningful accounts of their past. Rather than defending oral accounts against accusations of retrospective bias, such studies treat errors of fact as interpretive resources. As James Fentress and Chris Wickham put it in an edited collection entitled *Social Memory*, 'the issue of whether or not a given memory is true is interesting only in so far as it sheds light on how memory itself works'.[29]

The study of the social shaping of memory has been central to the work of the Italian oral historian Allesandro Portelli. Turning the argument about oral history's innacuracy on its head, he has asserted that the special strength of oral history is its ability to give access to 'the cultural forms and processes by which individuals express their sense of themselves in history'.[30] Oral history in this interpretive mode tends to assert the 'different credibility' of oral and written sources rather than seeking factual consistency between them. Misremembering, silences or the elision of dates separate in time furnish the starting point for an analysis of 'subjective truths'.[31]

Portelli gives an example of his method in *The Death of Luigi Trastulli and other Stories*.[32] Trastulli was killed by the police in Terni, an industrial town in northern Italy, during a relatively peaceful demonstration against NATO in 1947. Yet when Portelli interviewed Terni's ex-communist leaders some thirty years on, they dated the event to 1953, when mass protests against the police accompanied the sacking of 2,000 workers from the town's steelworks. Where the oral informants recalled Trastulli dying in a hail of machine-gun bullets with his back to the factory wall, newspaper accounts (whilst not entirely consistent) claimed that he had died in the street. Factual errors in the oral testimonies, Portelli explains, alerted him to the existence of a 'communal mode' of remembering in which state brutality and worker resistance were key themes.[33] Terni's workers had turned Trastulli into a political martyr, repositioning his death from a relatively unimportant protest in 1947 to a more significant moment in local labour politics.

The effect of Portelli's approach is to reinstate a degree of scepticism as to the truth claims of oral sources in matters of 'exact knowledge' about the past. Whilst subjectively 'true', memories do not give unmediated access to the past as it was lived. Other emerging fields of oral history share this emphasis. There is a growing body of research on historical consciousness and the interaction between 'public' and 'private' memory.[34] In an oral history of Australian First World War veterans, Alistair Thomson has shown how returnees struggled to square their often painful memories with a public legend of the war as the nascence of the Australian nation.[35] In Thomson's account oral testimony is used less to explore the experiences of soldiers during the war than to analyse public and private conflicts about how it should be remembered.

A further development within oral history is the study of community and family myths, and of the means through which they are transmitted across generations.[36] This approach has been used in studies of social mobility to obtain information about how familial values affect occupational choices.[37] The effect of this stress upon intergenerational transmission has been to blur the orthodox distinction between 'oral history', defined as an account of events within living memory, and 'oral tradition'.

Subjectivity and ethical problems

In the initial post-war expansion of oral history its practitioners tended to understate the inter-subjective nature of their method. This was partly because of their desire to emphasise the reliability of information gained from oral sources. Equally, the belief in oral history as an experiment in equality sometimes discouraged analysis of how informants perceived, and constructed their accounts according to, the interviewer's background.

The development of oral history in the interpretive mode has brought greater awareness of how differences in background between interviewer and interviewee influence the nature of the testimony. For, as Sherna Gluck and Daphne Patai explain, oral history involves 'at least two subjectivities, that of the narrator and that of the interviewer'.[38] When Portelli began recording Italian folk singers during the 1970s he was intrigued to find that even men who he knew were communists would sing fascist-inspired songs to him. Their surprising selection, he concluded, was based upon assumptions about his class background and semi-official capacity as a university researcher. A lifetime of discriminatory treatment had taught them to conceal their politics from those in authority.[39]

In many recent oral histories, how differences of age, sex, class, ethnicity and race are manifested in the interview, or the impact of location (whether the interview takes place at work or at home, whether in the interviewee's social space or the interviewer's) are considered as starting points for interpretation. 'Reflexivity' is thus a resource which can stimulate new research questions and insights. In my research into masculinity and managerial culture in British industry, interactions in the interviews provided many clues about the nature and wider significance of men's networks.[40] I was puzzled by the preoccupation of my interviewees – senior managers in their sixties – with stories of older men and mentors. In part it could be explained as the product of their identification with me. My status as a young researcher reminded them of their early career, whilst the interview situation reproduced emotional relations which were resonant of a mentor relationship.[41] This kind of oral history does not deny that testimonies contain knowledge about the past that is objectively true. However, its focus is on how the past acts as a resource for stories which are, as Tonkin puts it, 'identity constitutive'.[42]

It is within feminist oral history that the awareness of inter-subjectivity is perhaps most fully developed.[43] With the interest in documenting the 'personal' has come increased concern with ethical issues. Initially the aim of feminist historians was a history by, about and for women.[44] It would be a history that validated the importance of women's shared experiences. However, interviewing not only revealed the ways in which gender united women; it also exposed the central role which race, class and age play in differentiating women's identities. And as feminist oral historians have realised, the power of the oral history method to ameliorate these inequalities is limited, at the very best.[45]

Tensions such as these between the needs of public advocacy and private academic research have characterised the practice of oral history since its post-war revival. How to 'give back' to the community what is taken for the purpose of academic research will always be a pressing issue, because the oral historian's sources are living women and men. One outcome of this problem has been the development of entirely new forms of public history over the past two decades, in which academics have at most a consultative role. These include local oral history societies, 'do it yourself' community publishing groups, reminiscence therapy within social work, and the use of oral history in television and radio programme-making.[46] From its post-war incarnation as a source which was used principally to 'fill the gaps' in documentary evidence, oral history at the end of century is changing the culture of public and academic history.

Notes

1 D. Henige, *Oral Historiograph* (1982), pp. 2–4.

2 Henige, *Oral Historiography*; J. Vansina, *Oral Tradition as History* (1985).

3 J. Michelet, *Histoire de la Révolution française* (1980); P. Thompson, *The Voice of the Past: Oral History*, second edition (1988), pp. 23–45.

4 Henige, *Oral Historiography*, p. 107; V. R. Yow, *Recording Oral History: a Practical Guide for Social Scientists* (1994), pp. 2–3.

5   Thompson, *Voice of the Past*, chapter 1.
6   Yow, *Recording Oral History*, pp. 11–12.
7   Thompson, *Voice of the Past*, p. 265.
8   R. Moore, *Pitmen, Preachers and Politics* (1974).
9   P. Thompson, J. Waley and T. Lummis, *Living the Fishing* (1983).
10 George Evans, *Ask the fellows who cut the hay: on life in the Suffolk village of Blaxham* (1956).
11 M. Clucksmann, *Women Assemble: Women Workers in the new Industries in Interwar Britain* (1991).
12 N. Leap and B. Hunter, *The Midwife's Tale: an Oral History of Midwifery, from Handywoman to Professional Midwife* (1993).
13 E. Roberts, *A Woman's Place: an Oral History of Working Class Women, 1890–1940* (1984).
14 J. White, *Rothschild Buildings: Life in an East London Tenement Block, 1887–1920* (1980).
15 Evans, *Ask the fellows*.
16 A. Broussard, 'Oral recollection and the historical reconstruction of black San Francisco, 1915–40', *Oral History Review*, 8, p. 12.
17 L. Davidoff and B. Westover (eds), *Our Work, our Lives: Women's History and Women's Work* (1986); Roberts, *A Woman's Place*.
18 T. Hareven, *Family time and Industrial Time* (1982); Roberts, *A Woman's Place*.
19 P. Thompson, *The Edwardians: the Remaking of British Society*, second edition (1993).
20 *The Voice of the Past*, p. 86.
21 Yow, *Recording Oral History*, pp. 15–22.
22 Henige, *Oral Historiography*, pp. 109–17.
23 Thompson, *Voice of the Past*, pp. 101–7.
24 T. Lummis, *Listening to History: the Authenticity of Oral Evidence* (1987), p. 12.
25 Thompson, *Voice of the Past*, pp. 111–12.
26 *Ibid.*, pp. 125–8.
27 E. Tonkin, *Narrating our Pasts: the Social Construction of Oral History* (1992).
28 'History and the myth of realism', in R. Samuel and P. Thompson (eds), *The Myths we Live by* (1990), p. 27.
29 J. Fentress and C. Wickham, *Social Memory* (1992), p. xi.
30 A. Portelli, *The Death of Luigi Trasulli and other Stories: Form and Meaning in Oral History* (1991), p. ix.
31 *Ibid.*,
32 Portelli, *Luigi Trastulli*, chapter 1.
33 Portelli, *Luigi Trastulli*, p. 24.
34 Popular Memory Group, 'Popular memory: theory, politics, method', in r. Johnson (ed.), *Making Histories: Studies in History Writing and Politics* (1982); M. Frisch, *A Shared Authority: Essays on the Craft and Meaning of Oral and Public History* (1990).
35 A. Thomson, *Anzac Memories: Living with the Legend* (1994).
36 J. Byng-Hall, 'The power of family myths', in R. Samuel and P. Thompson (eds), *The Myths we Live by* (1990).
37 D. Bertaux and P. Thompson, introduction, in *id.* (eds), *International Year Book of Oral History – and Life Stories: Between Generations* (1993).

38 S. B. Gluck and D. Patai (eds), *Women's Words: the Feminist Practice of Oral History* (1991), p. 2.

39 *Luigi Trastulli*, p. 30.

40 M. Roper, *Masculinity and the British Organisation Man since 1945* (1994), pp. 37–40, chapter 3.

41 See K. Figlio, 'Oral history and the unconscious', *History Workshop Journal*, 1988, 26, pp. 120–32.

42 Tonkin, *Narrating our Pasts*, p. 135.

43 Gluck and Patai, *Women's Words*.

44 Gluck and Patai, *Women's Words*, p. 2.

45 J. Stacey, 'Can there be a feminist ethnography?' in S. B. Gluck and D. Patai (eds), *Women's Words* (1991).

46 R. Samuel, *Theatres of Memory*, I, *Past and Present in Contemporary Culture* (1995), pp. 191, 351.

Further reading

G. Ewart-Evans, *Where Beards Wag All: the Days that we have Seen* (1975).

L. Passerini, *Fascism in Popular Memory: the Cultural Experience of the Turin Working Class* (1987).

R. Samuel, 'Quarry roughs: life and labour in Headingham quarry, 1860–1920', in *id.* (ed.), Village Life and Labour (1975).

R. Samuel and P. Thompson (eds), *The Myths we Live by* (1990).

Chapter 32

Elite interviews

Anthony Seldon

Elite interviewing is the black sheep among the contemporary historian's sources. Many are inclined to agree with A. J. P. Taylor that all it gives us is 'old men drooling about their youth'.[1] Yet Taylor conducted few interviews when writing his many books, and many other critics of interviewing have surprisingly little experience of it, either. To be provocative at the outset of this chapter, contemporary historians who are critical of the value of elite interviews are often either too busy to conduct them or lack the confidence or imagination to grasp their function and potential. Blanket condemnation of interviews is evidence of shallow comprehension.

This chapter will discuss those occasions when researchers may find elite interviews a valuable adjunct to their other sources; the likely problems and benefits of elite interviewing; methodology; and, finally, how to evaluate reliability and how to use elite interviews in written work. The term 'interview' will be adhered to throughout, although 'oral history' or 'oral evidence' could have been used in its place. 'Elite' interviews can be defined as those conducted with individuals selected because of who they are or what they did, but there is considerable overlap in methodology with interviews conducted with 'ordinary people', discussed in Chapter 31.

When interviews may help

Interviews are almost always an inferior source of information to documents written at the time. But, because neither state nor private institutions nor individuals immediately release their papers for general inspection, interviews can be an essential stop-gap which allows contemporary history to be written. In Britain scholars must usually wait until thirty years after the event to see the state papers at the Public Record Office at Kew, and even then some material, especially relating to intelligence matters, is held back, Waldegrave initiative notwithstanding.

Interviews have thus allowed numerous highly informative books to be written before the release of official papers. To take two episodes from recent British history, the Suez crisis of 1956 and the Falklands War of 1982, without interviews we should have had to wait until 1987 and 2013 respectively for the inside stories to be made known. But, thanks to works such as Paul Johnson's *The Suez War* (1957) and Hugh Thomas's *Suez Affair* (1967), the inner history of aspects of the Suez crisis such as the secret Anglo-French collusion with Israel and divisions of opinion among ministerial and official ranks became generally known much earlier.[2] When the relevant documents (or most of them) became available in January 1987, surprisingly few 'secrets' remained. Detailed chapter and verse could be added, but the broad story as reconstructed by earlier historians was verified. Much as authors, and rather more their publishers, might claim that post-1987 books relating to Suez were offering, at last, the true story, such statements had a hollow ring, at least to those in the know. Likewise, the spate of books on the Falklands War that have appeared following that episode, in particular Max Hastings and Simon Jenkins's *The Battle for the Falklands* (1983) and Lawrence Freedman's *Britain and the Falklands War* (1988), have probably left few secrets for future revelation.[3] Much the same is true of Britain's role in the Gulf War of 1991.

But, even if the researcher has some or most of the documents at his – or her – disposal (it would be foolhardy to claim one had access to all extant documentation), there may still be gaps that interviewing can help fill. Martin Gilbert, for example, when conducting research for the volume of his Churchill biography covering the years 1914–16 (published in 1971), found that by 'conversation and correspondence with those who knew Churchill during this period ... I have been able to include reminiscences of Churchill's moods, and of the atmosphere of events not always obvious from the documents, and have been able to describe several incidents not recorded in any contemporary source'.[4] Interviews can be particularly helpful in fleshing out documents when it comes to reconstructing the roles and methods of personalities, and their relations with others. As the historian of the Royal Air Force, Denis Richards, has commented, information on relationships often 'does not get into the official records'.[5] Such relationships may not only be complex, but may also be veiled from contemporaries. To take an example: a Secretary of State may not be very close to his Permanent Secretary, and may rely far more heavily on advice from more junior civil servants; he may be scornful of Deputy Secretary A but intimate with Deputy Secretary B. Such relationships can critically affect the unravelling of the history, and but for interviews we might never know of them.

Interviews can also be valuable in helping researchers gain an overall grasp of available documentation. The American author David J. Mitchell has written, 'the oppressive weight of the himalayas of paper found in modern archives can be the greatest obstacle to the biographer interested in encapsulating the experiences and expression of his subject in a single book'.[6] Interviews can help identify which documents are important, which were read and acted upon. 'Records have a history of their own,' writes John Barnes trenchantly. Some papers are ignored, others widely read and discussed; the historian without recollections to aid him may not know which are which[7] Lewis Namier noted in the preface to his *Diplomatic Prelude, 1938–39* (1948), 'Even more important than direct information has been ... guidance [from interviews]. ... A great many profound secrets are somewhere in print, but are more easily detected when one knows what to see.'[8] Interviews can help the researcher order seemingly confusing documents. 'It may be,' Martin Gilbert has said, 'that in a crisis there is no way that an historian can reconstruct the sequence of events from documents alone.'[9]

Interviews can fill gaps in documentation. Regarding scientific history, Nicholas Kurti has observed that 'in scientific research the false starts are very often not recorded in contemporary documentation'.[10] Biographers are another group to find frequent gaps in documents. Roger Berthoud estimates that between 20 and 25 per cent of the material for his biography of the artist Graham Sutherland came from interviews, including many with the subject himself (who died before the research was complete).[11] The decline in letter writing (and possibly diary keeping) has played a role, if one that has been exaggerated, in creating gaps in contemporary documentation.

Interviews can also assist by revealing the assumptions and motives lying behind documents. Reports of meetings often fail to reveal the full picture: convenient rather than real reasons may be given, or underlying philosophies and approaches may have been so taken for granted by participants that no need was felt to elucidate them in the written record. Interviews can 'make positive what was latent', as Michael Holroyd has put it.[12]

Potential problems

All research requires careful evaluation of evidence. There has been a tendency for some to regard some types of evidence, notably material in the Public Record Office, as above suspicion, and for interviews to be treated as uniquely unreliable. Interviews do certainly require very careful treatment, and the problems associated with them can be divided into three main categories.

The first, and perhaps the most significant, relates to the interviewee's own limitations, and especially those of memory. Almost all who have conducted interviews would agree with Roy Jenkins that 'If detailed work on the events of a period a number of decades ago is followed by the opportunity to talk to someone who was there at the time, the only too common result is that his recollections, not only of the dates, but of the sequence of events, do not fit the framework of the firmly established written facts.'[13] Anthony Howard in his life of R. A. Butler (1987) is another who has found interviews highly misleading, especially with regard to sequence.[14] A common finding is that the older the witness, and the more distant the events under discussion, the less valuable his evidence. David Marquand, in interviews for his biography of Ramsay MacDonald, found 'memories amazingly short and amazingly fallible', which he suggested may have been because 'most of the people whom I interviewed were elderly and many were very old indeed'.[15] Robert Rhodes James, however, suggests that there are equal difficulties in interviewing people soon after events: recollections of busy younger witnesses can be 'clouded by personal impressions and, oddly enough, by the very *recentness* of the episode'. He continues, 'It seems to be the case that it is only after a period of time that the mind can put matters in perspective and differentiate between similar occasions which, in the aftermath, tend to merge into one.'[16]

Anxieties about memory are not eased by the mystery that attaches to its workings. Stuart Sutherland, the experimental psychologist, wrote in 1983, 'the relation between short-term and long-term memory remains obscure. Nor do we know with any certainty what causes forgetting ... Above all, we do not understand how memories are indexed.'[17]

The interviewee may, of course, deliberately set out to falsify or mislead, but that difficulty can be exaggerated. More worrying is *unintentional* inaccuracy. Excessive discretion can be a problem, not least in the time it wastes, and is usually encountered where the interviewee is suspicious of the use to which the interviewer will put the material. Thus, before entering on an interview, one should do everything possible to establish one's credentials and integrity. Account needs also to be taken of other possible distortions in an interviewee's evidence: oversimplification of events; exaggeration of his own or his organisation's role and importance; a partisan perspective; and the influence of hindsight. Philip Williams has noted that 'Politicians subconsciously adapt their views about the past to fit a stance they adopted later.'[18] Beware too of interviewees who let their personal likings (as opposed to animosities) colour their evidence: for example, an interviewee asked about his friends' actions is likely to be charitable, even if he remembers feeling rather differently at the time.

The interviewer can do more to guard against the second category of problems associated with interviewing: those deriving from his own methodology. Unrepresentative sampling is an obvious error that can be avoided by drawing up systematic lists of potential interviewees from a wide variety of different organisations, backgrounds, sympathies, or whatever distinctions may be relevant. Surprisingly, few experienced authors appear to seek a representative sample when preparing interview lists. Biographers, for example, do not always interview enemies as well as friends of their subject, in some cases because those antipathetic to the subject are unwilling to discuss him or her. The Great Reaper may make unrepresentative sampling inevitable to some extent by gathering up certain partisans and leaving others free to roam the stage to guide (or mislead) historians. Loaded questioning is another avoidable error. It is all too easy to leave an interview having heard exactly what one wanted to hear, because one has asked only certain questions, or phrased them in a certain way. This subtle point requires particular attention, and is a trap into which many of the most experienced contemporary historians have sometimes fallen.

Younger researchers are particularly vulnerable to the danger of being too deferential to interviewees. The risks have been well described by Donald C. Watt:

> It has seduced some of the best-known historians of our day, Sir Lewis Namier being the outstanding example and John Wheeler-Bennett running him a close second. The seduction of being placed on the inside track, being made accessory to the non-written history, is extraordinarily difficult for anyone to resist and I must say most of all for the young researcher, fired as he is with the hope of discovering something sensationally new.[19]

It can indeed be very awkward to be unpleasant about or critical of someone at whose hands one has received kindness and hospitality. Getting to know someone can be extraordinarily unbalancing if one is trying to write dispassionate history.

The final category of problems has to do with the nature of the interviewing exercise itself. A whole day can be spent preparing for an interview, travelling, being entertained, conducting the interview, and writing or typing it up afterwards. The same time might well have been better spent reading books, newspapers or documents. Interviews are also expensive in financial terms: the cost of travelling, subsistence, tapes and typing can be heavy. Grant-giving bodies have not, in the past, proved especially friendly to applications to help defray such expenditure.

Where interviewing is considered, a host of unpredictable factors combine to put off many researchers used to the hard certainty of documents. No piece of written evidence will change between visits to archives, but interviewees asked about the same event can and do say different things at different interviews. Worse, they can even change their mind in the course of a single interview. What they say in the morning may be at variance with what they say in the afternoon, and they change again after a drink in the evening. Interviewees may be much more forthcoming in their own home than in a neutral meeting place, and may be far more open to a female interviewer than a male, or *vice versa*. Which is the individual's *real* testimony? One often doesn't know and is forced to rely on one's own judgement.

Other inherently unsatisfactory aspects of interviews are the fact that some individuals do not communicate well in such exchanges, and the difficulty of representing exactly what the interviewee said, or meant, including the *way* he said it. Francis King has written, 'As every journalist, psychiatrist and detective knows, what people say is often less revealing than the manner in which they say it. ... This is the drawback of interviews. ... The final product is a wholly accurate record of what has been in the speaker's tongue but rarely in his mind or heart.'[20]

With all these snags of interviewing – and there are many more that could have been mentioned – one could be forgiven for wondering whether it would not be better to dispense with it altogether. To do so, however, would be an error, for it would deprive one of much insight and information, as well as sheer enjoyment.

Potential benefits

Some benefits of interviewing have already been alluded to earlier in the chapter, and can be dealt with briefly. The range of benefits can be divided into four main categories.

First, one can gain information not recorded in documents. It may be about events, but is more likely to be about individuals, and organisational and personal relationships. J. A. G. Griffith found when writing his study (with T. C. Hartley) of central–local government relations that 'we were engaged on a highly *political* exercise – trying to find out the nature of the relationship in practice. There was no other way of doing it but to conduct interviews. The information we sought was nowhere written down. It was a matter of personalities and relationships.'[21]

Secondly, interviews may help one interpret personalities and events. Here the aim is not objective fact but gaining the interviewee's perspective on people, events and processes. Ben Pimlott wrote that interviews gave him 'a series of free tutorials or seminars in which I could begin to understand a particular area that was puzzling me'.[22] (It is indicative of a changing climate that Pimlott, author of *Hugh Dalton*, one of the most distinguished recent British political biographies, is one of many younger historians who are enthusiastic supporters of the interview.) Obtaining an interviewee's comments can thus help clarify and explain areas that might otherwise remain baffling.

Thirdly, interviews can help one interpret documents, by providing an overview that explains underlying motives and assumptions, or by filling gaps, or by helping to clear up confusion over facts. Finally, there are what one might term the incidental benefits of interviews, a random but significant array of gains. Interviewees may well produce documents to be inspected, although one had no thought of seeing any such material when requesting an interview. Martin Gilbert finds that at least one-third of those he interviews produce documents for him to see[23] – although it would be an error to bank on such windfalls. Interviews can open the door to a fruitful relationship with someone personally connected with the subject of one's research: one can go back to that person for further material, or send them drafts for comment. Someone whom one may have found unforthcoming or awkward in interview may turn out to be an admirable source of information when reading and commenting upon one's written work in the seclusion of his own home. Even very senior people, especially if retired, are often more than willing to read and comment on passages of text.

'The atmosphere of the time often does not appear in the documents,' says Norman Chester.[24] Chandrika Kaul describes in Chapter 28 how the press can be a fertile source of mood and contemporary colour; so too can interviews. Nigel Nicolson found when writing his biography of Alexander of Tunis that interviews gave him insight into 'the atmosphere of a headquarters, what Alex talked about in his mess', as well as 'how he arrived at decisions, his relations with Monty and Patton etc.'[25] This gain is all the more important because, as David J. Mitchell has observed, 'increasingly large volumes of papers found in archives, official or otherwise, can be colourless and impersonal collections of documents'.[26] Insight into a subject's personality and thought processes, and enrichment of one's own experience and understanding through *meeting*, instead of just reading about, living people who made or witnessed great events, are further benefits. Warm, vivid contemporary history has almost always been written by authors who have conducted interviews; dull, clinical history is often produced by those who have buried themselves in libraries and archives.

Conducting interviews

The advice that follows, based upon my own experience and that of other practitioners, may appear unnecessarily rigid, but space precludes a full explanation of the rationale behind each of the steps suggested here. I am not, moreover, recommending that one should slavishly follow the advice, but rather am offering food for thought: each researcher will discover in practice how to modify the process to suit his or her own style and needs.

The first question to tackle is *when* to interview. The advantages of interviewing early in one's research are that profitable avenues of discovery are opened up and an overview of one's subject is obtained. There is also less chance that key witnesses will die or become too ill to see strangers before one can visit them. Asa Briggs has said, 'In my experience, you have to watch age above all: I've lost some notable people through not seeking them in time.'[27] On the other hand, if one conducts interviews in mid-research, or towards the end, one knows much better what questions to ask, and how far to trust the answers one receives. Much depends on the judgement of the researcher, who must consider questions of timing and availability in the context of a research programme. Time permitting, major figures can be seen twice, at the beginning and near the end of research.

At an early stage one needs to draw up lists of potential interviewees. The latest volume of David and Gareth Butler's *British Political Facts* can be useful for uncovering names of Ministers, and the *Imperial Calendar and Civil Service List* for civil servants, or *Vacher's* or the *PMS Parliamentary Companion* for civil servants and others from more recent years. If organisations other than central government are being researched, they will usually have produced magazines, reports or catalogues which can be consulted for names. Biographers have no short cut, and must proceed piecemeal, asking family, friends and commentators for suggestions of people to see. Acknowledgement sections of earlier or related biographies can be a good guide. Usually, once lists have been drawn up, some selection has to be made: it is rare for authors to exceed 200 interviews for a book, and twenty-five to 100 is common. Who then to leave out? Surprisingly, those at the very top – who may well have published their memoirs – may be less helpful than those more junior. 'It is almost axiomatic,' Beatrice Webb wrote in her classic brief text on interviewing, 'that the mind of the subordinate in any organisation will yield richer deposits of fact than the mind of the principal.' John Campbell, a seasoned political biographer, makes a similar point: he finds most useful 'the recollections of civil servants and second-rank figures who may not have written memoirs, and whose evidence may be less distorted by the urge to self-gratification'.[28]

Some groups, then, may prove better than others. Nikolai Tolstoi finds that 'soldiers are very good interviewees'[29] and H. Montgomery Hyde that 'lawyers were the most reliable [witnesses] because their memories of facts and cases are so good'.[30] There is broad agreement that the least satisfactory class of interviewees is current or retired politicians, who often encounter pathological difficulty in distinguishing the truth, so set have their minds become by long experience of partisan thought. Conversely, civil servants can be the best interviewees, with former principal private secretaries perhaps the best of all. Civil servants tend to be dispassionate creatures by nature and profession: cat-like, they observe action, storing the information in mental boxes that can yield a rich harvest to those who take the trouble to prise them open, or who can instil the trust required to allow the contents to pour forth.

Having drawn up one's lists of targets, the next stage is the approach. Letters are the best method, setting out clearly one's status, the nature of one's research, and the likely end product. Letters should sound enthusiastic about the possibility of seeing the interviewee: 'Flattery is at the root of most successful interviews,' writes Paul Ferris.[31] It can be helpful to send out letters in 'batches' of ten or twenty, to avoid being swamped. If uncertain how to address 'top people', consult the latest edition of *Titles and Forms of Address*. One's chance of a favourable response is much higher if one is an established author rather than a doctoral student or unknown journalist. Mention in a letter of a supervisor or other mentor may help, but never offer money as an incentive. Remember that no one does anything for nothing, so if you can subtly suggest that remarks made in an interview will see the light of day in print, that could be a carrot (although, equally, it could deter the fainthearted). It is a problematic business, interviewing.

Seeing a subject in his home environment is usually an advantage: he will be more relaxed, with fewer likely distractions, and his papers will be at hand. Not that everyone would agree with even that statement. Bernard Crick, for example, found interviewees 'much more discursive and difficult to keep to the point' in their own home.[32] Wherever the interview takes place, it is essential for it to be thoroughly prepared. Interviewees, especially if they are still working, tire very easily of those who have not done their homework. Their frustation, which is fully justified, has been admirably articulated by Quentin Bell:

> I am frequently interviewed by complete strangers; they tend to ask for infor-mation I have already supplied, and they talk so much that I barely have a chance to answer them. They do not have enough background information to use any material that I do supply. I usually ask interviewers to list informa-tion they seek in advance. They then discover that the information is already available in printed form or that they have no notion of what it is they want to discover. This saves us all from wasting our time.[33]

The least one can do, where relevant, is to consult entries in the latest edition of *Who's Who*. Sending questions in advance can be helpful in preparing the ground and allowing the interviewee the opportunity to reflect and dredge up memories, where relevant consulting his or her papers. (Beware, though, if he has read up *other people's* books, or has been concocting elaborate defences or smokescreens!)

So to the interview itself. Three main methods exist of storing the infor-mation: memory, notes and tape recorder. It is common to hear authors decry two of the systems as ineffective, and say only one, their favoured method, is reliable. In reality, they are commenting less on interview meth-ods than on themselves. All the methods have benefits and drawbacks: no one way is foolproof or 'correct'. The advantages of using memory are that the conversation can flow swiftly, even over a meal, and the interviewee is not distracted by recording devices. The main disadvantage is that one can forget exactly what was said, and consequently write incorrect notes. Method two, taking notes, improves accuracy and gives a fuller record, but can be distracting and slow (unless one has shorthand). 'Hang on a minute' (or some politer variant) can be a disconcerting interruption to any inter-viewee exploring the deeper reaches of his memory. The third method is the tape recorder. The bonus is its accuracy and relative invisibility: the snags are that it may put people off, especially the elderly (although this drawback can be exaggerated), and it can take a long time to transcribe tape into a form that one can readily use. If using tape, employ a lapel microphone, and take batteries in case there is no convenient power point. In general, the researcher would be wise to experiment with all three methods, and then settle on the one he or she finds most helpful.

Practitioners also have strong feelings about the best way to structure questions. Some favour a rigid questionnaire approach, others a play-it-by-ear or lucky-dip style. The best advice here is to come to an interview with a list of questions carefully prepared (preferably one that has been sent to the interviewee beforehand) but to allow for flexibility. What interviewees have to say unprompted, the way and the order in which they say what they say, can all be enlightening. David Marquand found that:

> for political biography interviewing, a highly structured interview would have been disastrous. ... I had a general idea of the things I wanted to talk about before I started the interview, but it often happened that my original inclinations turned out to be wrong, and that the person I was interviewing led me into quite different areas, to my immense profit.[34]

The conduct of the interview very much depends upon individual circumstances. If the interviewee is very elderly, get the main questions in early, because he may well tire after thirty minutes or so. Interviews should seldom last longer than two hours – at least, not without a break. Generally, the older the subject the longer will need to be spent with him before and after the interview. Margaret Morris found, when interviewing for *The General Strike* (1976), that 'usually I spent at least half a day and frequently a whole day with the subjects. I do not think this could have been shortened. The whole process of achieving a relaxed and friendly atmosphere and sparking off reminiscences among elderly people cannot be rushed.'[35] Clearly, the younger the interviewee, especially if he is still in harness, the less the time required and likely to be available. Also, the crisper will need to be the style in which questions are put.

Now for some controversial advice: before you leave the interview, or by post subsequently, ask the interviewee to sign a form governing access to the interview record: this will not only guard your own security but also benefit other researchers in the future. If you reach no agreement, your records will join the countless others which researchers have collected in the course of their work, with no idea what to do with them after their books or studies have been written. If they deposit the records in libraries for others to see, they could be breaching confidentiality; if they destroy them, priceless historical records could be lost. So, awkward though it may be, ask the interviewee to sign a form permitting the use of the record under specified conditions. The most convenient method is to ask the interviewee to select from a series of options such as the following, which may be listed on the one form.

1 Record freely available for interviewer and for others to use without further permission.
2 Available to all, but permission for researchers other than the interviewer required before citing or quoting.
3 Available to the interviewer only, and permission required before citing or quoting.
4 Available to others only with the prior written appproval of the interviewee. After death, the record to be generally available.

One can play around with the categories, but to miss the opportunity of clarifying the basis of the interview can only lead to problems in the future.

If you have relied on memory or taken notes, set to work as soon as possible after leaving the interviewee at making a record or fleshing it out. Also write a thank-you letter, however the interview went, since such courtesy should at least make the subject more willing to see others in the future. If possible, interview records should be typed, clearly headed with details of who the interview was with, where it took place, how it was recorded, and how long the session lasted. Listing a precise record of your questions, together with the answers, rather than trying to convert the interviewee's comments into a consecutive whole, may also be helpful. Overall, maximum professionalism and fidelity should be the rule: one can never know how important historically your interview records may prove to be.

Evaluation and use of interview records

How far should one trust interview records? To begin with, one should recognise them for what they are: the memories or impressions of *individuals*, often many years after the events discussed. One must ask why the interviewee has said what he has, whether he was an eye witness or a participant or is repeating hearsay, what his precise position was at the time and what access to information he had. Junior figures tend to glorify and glamorise; senior people to be cynical and egocentric. Consider subsequent careers and predispositions. Christopher Thorne has written:

> No matter how self-critical and objective witnesses may be (and obviously they vary enormously in these respects) they cannot 'unlearn' what they've come to know subsequently of what came after the moment or period about which they're being questioned. Their evidence may be first-hand, but it isn't contemporary.[36]

In order to assess reliability during an interview, it may be found useful to ask, where appropriate, 'Is that what you thought at the time?' (or some suitable variant); to prepare in advance some specific factual questions – for example, on dates and names – to gain an overall idea of the witness's reliability; and to return to the same issue from different angles in the course of the interview. After the interview, it is vital to check the information remorselessly against other sources; and when there is no other source one should say so in any published account using the evidence.

Whenever interview evidence is employed in published work, it should be acknowledged as meticulously as other sources, giving the name of the interviewee, the date of the interview, and possibly also the place. If the interview has been located in an archive, the source note should state which. If alluding to information obtained in an interview that one has not received permission to cite, one should be as discreet as possible and give the source as 'private information'.

The more rigorous the interviewer's procedures, and the more discriminating his use of oral evidence, the sounder will be the conclusions drawn from it. Only in that way can the residual antipathy to such evidence be reduced, and its rightful status as a valuable, if problematic, source of information be recognised.

Notes

1 A. J. P. Taylor, quoted in Brian Harrison's valuable article 'Oral history and recent political history', *Oral History*, 3, 1972, p. 46.

2 Paul Johnson, *The Suez War* (1957); Hugh Thomas, *The Suez Affair* (1967).

3 Simon Jenkins and Max Hastings, *The Battle for the Falklands* (1983); Lawrence Freedman, *Britain and the Falklands War* (1988). See also review article by Freedman on the Falklands literature in *Contemporary Record*, 1 (2), 1987, pp. 34–5.

4 Martin Gilbert, *Winston S. Churchill*, III, *1914–16* (1971), p. xxvi.

5 Denis Richards, responses to oral history questionnaire (see 'Acknowledgements' below), quoted in Seldon and Pappworth, *By Word of Mouth*, p. 40.

6 David J. Mitchell, 'Living documents: oral history and biography', *Biography*, 3, winter 1980, p. 284.

7 John Barnes, 'Teaching and research in contemporary British history', in Donald C. Watt (ed.), *Contemporary History in Europe* (1969), pp. 41–2.

8 L. A. Namier, *Diplomatic Prelude, 1938–39* (1948), p. v.

9 Interview with Martin Gilbert, 5 November 1981, quoted in Seldon and Pappworth, *By Word of Mouth*, p. 44.

10 Interview with Professor Nicholas Kurti, 4 December 1981, quoted *ibid.*, p. 38.

11 Interview with Roger Berthoud, 17 September 1981, cited *ibid.*, p. 45.

12 Interview with Michael Holroyd, 11 September 1981, quoted *ibid.*, p. 45.

13 Roy Jenkins, *The Development of Modern Political Biography 1945–70*, Don Carlos Coloma Memorial Lecture, 1971.

14 Anthony Howard, *Rab: the Life of R. A. Butler* (1987). Also interview with Howard in *Contemporary Record*, 1 (1), 1987, pp. 31–5. Subsequent issues of *Contemporary Record* contain many interviews by Anthony Seldon with leading contemporary historians, including John Campbell, Ben Pimlott, Philip Ziegler and David Butler.

15 Letter from David Marquand to the author, 9 November 1981, cited in Seldon

and Pappworth, *By Word of Mouth*, p. 17.

16 Robert Rhodes James, quoted by Harrison, 'Oral history', p. 34.

17 Stuart Sutherland, 'All in the mind', *Sunday Telegraph*, 2 January 1983.

18 Philip Williams, 'Interviewing politicians', *Political Quarterly*, 51 (3), 1980, p. 311.

19 Donald C. Watt, quoted by Harrison, 'Oral history', p. 37.

20 Francis King, *Sunday Telegraph*, 3 January 1982.

21 Interview with J. A. G. Griffith, 3 November 1981.

22 Ben Pimlott, responses to oral history questionnaire, September 1981. See also interview with Pimlott in *Contemporary Record*, 1 (3), 1987, pp. 56–7.

23 Interview with Martin Gilbert, 3 November 1981.

24 Interview with Sir Norman Chester, 28 November 1981.

25 Nigel Nicolson, responses to oral history questionnaire, August 1981.

26 Mitchell, 'Living documents', p. 284.

27 Interview with Lord Briggs, 27 November 1981.

28 'The method of the interview', a four-page appendix in Beatrice Webb's *My Apprenticeship* (1926), pp. 423–6; interview with John Campbell, *Contemporary Record*, 1 (2), 1987, pp. 42–6.

29 Nikolai Tolstoi, responses to oral history questionnaire, October 1981.

30 H. Montgomery Hyde, responses to oral history questionnaire, September 1981.

31 Paul Ferris, responses to oral history questionnaire, August 1981.

32 Bernard Crick, responses to oral history questionnaire, December 1981.

33 Quentin Bell, responses to oral history questionnaire, August 1981.

34 Letter from David Marquand to Seldon and Pappworth, 9 September 1981.

35 Margaret Morris, responses to oral history questionnaire, November 1981.

36 Christopher Thorne, 'Talking about Vietnam', BBC Radio 3 broadcast, transmitted 9 January 1987, transcript pp. 10–11.

Acknowledgements

The argument in this chapter is based closely upon Anthony Seldon and Joanna Pappworth, *By Word of Mouth* (Methuen, 1983). The 'oral history questionnaires' referred to belong to the background research material for this book. This chapter is an updated and edited version of one that appeared in Anthony Seldon, ed., *Contemporary History: Practice and Method* (1988).

Chapter 33

Radio

Siân Nicholas

Radio is in many respects the poor relation of media studies. Although the newspaper press is a well documented and widely used source, and film has become a popular field of study in its own right, radio – and, for that matter, television – has been sadly ignored by historians. Yet within ten years of its inception on a nationwide basis the radio was the principal medium of information and entertainment and the dominant focus of home-centred popular culture for the majority of the population, and it maintained that position until at least the 1950s, when television began to take over. Meanwhile the unique institutional function of the BBC, compared with other nations' broadcasting networks, has given the role of broadcasting in Britain an unusual prominence and distinction. The creation through the 1920s and early 1930s of a national wireless broadcasting system represented a revolution in communications whose impact still needs to be assessed, and in comparison with which the advent of television was simply a technological refinement, from sound to vision.

Radio thus offers insights into virtually every sphere of British life over much of the past century. Yet perhaps radio's very ubiquity has obscured its potential contribution to almost every aspect of contemporary historical research; the radio archives remain some of the most wide-ranging but underused resources in the country. The main problem of radio as a source has always been the nature and extent of its influence: to put it at its simplest, how far does broadcasting influence public perceptions and experiences, and how far does it merely register and reflect the public's attitudes and actions? This is in many respects the great imponderable, and the literature on media influence is vast and complex.[1] Nevertheless, whether the researcher considers the broadcast media as a direct force for change or simply as a mirror of society, radio is an invaluable source. This chapter seeks to demonstrate the potential of radio as a field of research, to outline some of the resources available to the interested historian and to assess a few of the difficulties such an essentially ephemeral medium as radio raises for the researcher.

Radio as a subject of primary interest offers an enormous amount to the historian of twentieth-century Britain. The influence of broadcasting has been a topic of intense speculation since even before the founding of the British Broadcasting Company in 1922; by 1939 it was widely accepted that '[n]o innovation since the coming of compulsory education has affected so large a proportion of the working population as the coming of broadcasting'.[2] Radio transcended barriers of region, class and wealth: as George Orwell famously observed in 1937, 'Twenty million people are underfed, but literally everyone has access to a radio.'[3]

However, radio cannot be studied in a vacuum. For example, Asa Briggs's monumental *History of Broadcasting in the United Kingdom* (five volumes, 1969–95, covering the BBC from the creation of the British Broadcasting Company in 1922 to 1974)[4] is not simply an unsurpassed institutional history of the BBC: it assesses the BBC's domestic and overseas broadcasting achievements, presents an astonishing amount of detail about individual programmes as well as policy, and and seeks to place the BBC in the context of twentieth-century politics and society. Mark Pegg's *Broadcasting and Society, 1922–39*, and Paddy Scannell and David Cardiff's *Serving the Nation*, the first volume of their projected *Social History of British Broadcasting*, attempt further to place radio broadcasting in its social context. In the same vein, John Davies's *Broadcasting and the BBC in Wales* considers the importance of broadcasting both to and for Wales.[5] There is no equivalent publication as yet for Scotland or Northern Ireland. The historian of broadcasting must therefore be genuinely interdisciplinary, 'a social and cultural historian interested in other forces in society and how they operate'.[6]

Yet, just as in order to study radio itself it is necessary to set it in a broad and interdisciplinary context, so a study of radio contributes to far wider fields of research. Radio is an essential element in the social history of twentieth-century Britain, whether one considers changing patterns of popular leisure, the informational and entertainment cultures, or contemporary perceptions of the nation and the world outside. In like manner, radio represents a central component of the nation's political culture – both in what it has reported and represented and in what it has not.[7] No discussion of the General Strike can be complete without consideration of the role of the BBC.[8] Our understanding of the impact of unemployment in the 1930s is made far richer by Scannell's work on the inter-war BBC.[9] No discussion of the civilian's experience of the Second World War can leave out the role of the BBC Home Service (and Forces Programme).[10] Meanwhile, virtually every notable figure since the First World War has appeared on or had dealings with the BBC, and the radio archive offers biographers and political historians alike unique insights not only into their subjects' public personas (in broadcasts) but also into their private characters (through correspondence, etc.). Although this last source of material has barely been tapped, recent work on such topics as popular imperialism and wartime policy towards the Soviet Union have demonstrated the value of radio in providing an illuminating perspective on almost any subject.[11]

The state of secondary academic literature on radio is variable. Before the 1960s very little had been written about the broadcasting history of any country, and the historian of British radio owes an immense debt to Briggs's *History*, not only for the achievement it represents in its own right but for being the means by which the BBC Written Archive became available to researchers. The 'discovery' of radio as an historical topic becomes clearly evident in the 1980s, with the publication of important work by, among others, Jean Seaton, Mark Pegg, Paddy Scannell and David Cardiff, and with the establishment of two specialist journals, *Media, Culture and Society* (1979–) and the *Historical Journal of Film, Radio and Television* (1981–). In the 1990s an increasing number of projects have been emerging in print (notably Scannell and Cardiff's *Serving the Nation*), while researchers in a range of disciplines are recognising the usefulness of radio as a source. Yet, while much has been done, much more remains to investigate.

Commencing research into radio

The first thing to consider when embarking on research in this field is that the history of radio broadcasting in Britain has essentially been that of the BBC. Researchers must also bear in mind the popularity of Radios Normandie and Luxembourg in the 1930s, the brief vogue for listening to German propaganda stations during the Second World War, the influence of pirate radio stations, and the rise of local and, recently, national independent radio. However, the BBC remains the most important and the most accessible source of material relating to radio in Britain. As for the research itself, given the interdisciplinary quality of the source, no researcher should embark on the study of radio without a broad understanding of the period under investigation. That said, broadly three areas of research need specific attention: the programmes themselves, how and why they were made, and their reception by the listening public.

The programmes themselves

For the programmes themselves an obvious starting point is the *Radio Times*, which from the BBC's earliest days provided a full weekly listings guide. While serving as the basic record of broadcast output, it also provides the researcher with an overview of scheduling policy, setting any particular programme in the context of the whole 'broadcast day'. It thus provides an invaluable (though not indexed) introduction to the pattern of BBC broadcasting at any particular time. The Newspaper Library at Colindale, the BBC Written Archive and a few other major libraries maintain collections of the national and regional editions.

As Briggs points out, with radio there is unfortunately 'no equivalent to browsing through a newspaper',[12] and to discover what individual programmes were like poses difficulties. Very little recorded material survives from the 1920s, when output was generally broadcast live, and only a limited amount remains from the 1930s. From the 1940s holdings are more extensive – but there remain some arbitrary omissions. The main source of recordings of radio broadcasts is the National Sound Archive in London (part of the British Library). In addition to its own collection of historic recordings, it holds thousands of hours of BBC broadcasts (including Forces' and local radio), and has access to the holdings of the BBC's own Sound Archive.[13] It is especially useful for BBC radio drama, readings and critical discussion, from the 1930s to the present day. The Library and Information Service is free of charge, although consultation and research carry a fee. The Listening Service is open five days a week (by appointment) and is also free. The National Sound Archive maintains listening facilities at Barnstaple, Devon, and Boston Spa, Yorkshire. The National Library of Wales, Aberystwyth, maintains an extensive archive of recorded material with a Welsh connection (in both the English and the Welsh languages) in its Sound and Moving Image Collection. Its holdings of English and Welsh-language broadcasts about Wales date from 1950, and are virtually complete from 1980. The library also holds a collection of radio scripts broadcast in Wales. The listening and viewing services are free of charge; appointments are recommended. There is no equivalent collection in the National Library of Scotland.

Working from the recorded programmes gives one the most vivid picture of the material under consideration. However, although much is inevitably lost by reading rather than listening to programmes, working from scripts has its own advantages, and many programmes are in any case available only in script form. Where programmes are not available for listening, the content, style and impact of radio broadcasts must be pieced together through existing scripts (where available), archive material (departmental memoranda, correspondence, production notes, etc.), contemporary references and reviews, and other written sources. *The Listener* (1929–91) is, aside from its more general interest as a BBC 'house journal', an invaluable source of reprinted radio talks, and has a fascinating review page. It is indexed from 1929. The BBC Written Archive maintains a substantial collection of scripts, including those of news bulletins. Some radio scripts can be found in published form, from drama (*Adolf in Blunderland*, *The Man Born to be King*) to features (*Junction X*), comedy (*The ITMA Years*), and news (*War Report*), and thus the past fame of some long-forgotten programme is often revealed. Likewise, some series of radio talks appear in published collections (e.g. J. B. Priestley's *Postscripts*, George Orwell's wartime broadcasts on the Overseas Service).

However, the programmes themselves represent only part of the picture. The researcher needs to understand the context in which any programme was made: the reasons behind its creation, the constraints (administrative or technical) on its making, the perspectives of contributors and production staff, and the relation of any one programme or series to general policy. For this it is necessary to consult the written archive, and in general it may be more productive to begin one's research there rather than with the finished product.

The written record: the BBC Written Archive

The principal written archive of radio in Britain is the BBC Written Archive Centre, located at Caversham Park, Reading. Its holdings are vast, comprising the working papers of the BBC from 1922 until the early 1970s (some 250,000 files of correspondence, and 20,000 reels of microfilm, spanning an enormous range of material from the minutes of the meetings of the Board of Governors down to individual performers' booking details), several collections of private papers and an unrivalled catalogue of press cuttings. It holds complete sets of the *Radio Times* from 1923 and *The Listener* from 1929, as well as *BBC Handbooks* and *Year Books*, other BBC publications and a number of related works. Access to archive material is at present (1995) permitted only to 1969, although the date is reviewed periodically. Access to all holdings is subject to legal restrictions, including breach of confidence and libel.

The BBC's written records are arranged through a system of centralised filing registries, modelled on those of the civil service. Numerical classification was introduced in the late 1960s.[14] Files were organised in the first instance by department and only secondarily by topic or programme, and their organisation itself reflects the context in which their contents were compiled. For instance, departmental files (e.g. Talks: R34; News: R28) generally begin with policy, but may also include memoranda concerning the evolution and production of particular programmes. As new policy issues or topics of interest arose within the department, new files within the broad departmental classification were created to house the relevant documentation. Similarly, materials relating to important, controversial or long-running programmes were often moved over at some point into files of their own. Thus not every programme has its own separate file, and programme files are rarely complete in themselves. Even when a programme has its own apparently complete file, a certain amount of cross-reference may still be necessary. For instance, memoranda relating to contributors (artists, composers, scriptwriters, etc.), feature in their own class of file: Radio Contributors (RCONT). Although the files themselves are clearly catalogued, and much material is duplicated across relevant files, researchers must at all times bring a flexible mind to bear when working through the archive.

Beyond the correspondence files themselves, four key sections of the BBC Written Archive merit particular mention. 'Programmes as Broadcast' is the daily log of every broadcast on every BBC service as it went out on the air, containing details of timings, contributors and recordings used. It is virtually complete from 1922. It is sometimes advisable to cross-refer Programmes as Broadcast with the *Radio Times*, especially during wartime or any other occasion when programmes may have not gone out as originally scheduled. The archive also holds an extensive collection of programme scripts, the scripts of all radio news bulletins since 1939, and the news bulletins from the General Strike of 1926. The audience research files (R9), dating from the creation of the BBC Listener Research Department in 1936, provide another immensely valuable source of information, detailing listeners' responses to particular programmes and their opinions on matters of more general policy. It was used during the Second World War as an adjunct to Home Intelligence. Finally, the BBC's press cuttings collection is a remarkably impressive resource that covers virtually every aspect of BBC policy and programming from the days of the British Broadcasting Company, drawing its material from the national, regional and trade press. One afternoon with this collection can save weeks of painful research at Colindale.

Unfortunately, access to the BBC Written Archive has been substantially reduced in recent years, and is now normally restricted to accredited academic researchers and writers who have had their project placed for publication. At present the archive is open to researchers Wednesday to Friday only, and places are limited to four, strictly by appointment. Researchers should apply in writing to the archive, giving as much detail as possible of their project; places are generally booked well in advance. Since access is so limited, it is *essential* to have done as much background research and planning as possible before coming to the original files themselves. A photocopying service is, however, available, and the archivists are helpful above and beyond the call of duty.

Outside Caversham, material is scattered. BBC Wales in Llandaff, for instance, holds Wales Region material dating from the 1930s, which is open to researchers on written application. The Public Record Office contains much documentation relating to government policy towards the BBC, and various other items of interest. For instance, the Ministry of Information's Home Intelligence records and the Wartime Social Survey files provide useful information about the wartime BBC, and the Ministry of Food files contain an almost complete set of scripts from the wartime *Kitchen Front* programme.

For more personal accounts of the period, a few collections of private papers, notably those of Lord Reith, are housed at Caversham. There are as yet very few biographies of former BBC personnel (Lord Reith and Richard Dimbleby are the main exceptions), and the broadcasting careers of people celebrated in other fields have generally been neglected by their biographers. However, a substantial literature of memoirs and reminiscences of former BBC staff and contributors exists, which dates from the very first days of broadcasting.[15] They tend to fall into two camps: the sunny and anecdotal, and the more serious and often critical. Inevitably they vary enormously in usefulness and accuracy – and, as is so often the case, the most interesting and lively accounts are not necessarily the most accurate or the most representative. As with all memoirs, they need to be used with care, but they often provide vivid details about particular programmes, policy disputes and personality clashes. It is certainly fascinating to compare their accounts with the file records. In addition, many figures better known in other contexts have had contact with the BBC at various times, and their recollections (or refusal to recollect – see J. B. Priestley, *Margin Released*, 1962) can provide a valuable outsider's perspective. Interviews with former (or indeed current) members of or contributors to the BBC are also a useful source of information (subject to the standard caveats about oral history), but, fewer and fewer members of the early BBC are still alive.

Audience response and opinion

The third necessary area of research is what the audience thinks of the programmes. This is one of the most difficult research challenges posed by broadcasting, and is a peculiarly difficult issue to investigate in the context of the BBC, since part of the 'Reithian' approach to broadcasting in the 1930s was, if not to disregard audience opinion entirely, certainly to relegate it to the deep background as a factor influencing policy. Fortunately a substantial amount of material is available from the late 1930s at least on listeners' responses both to individual programmes and to more general themes in broadcasting policy.

The most important source of audience opinion is the BBC's own Listener Research archive, held at Caversham. The BBC Listener Research Department was set up amid much controversy in 1936, regarded by many within the BBC as a pernicious concession to 'popular taste'. However, during the Second World War it came into its own, both as a test of the popularity of BBC programmes themselves, and as a gauge of public morale. The Listener Research files provide a mass of information not only on listening figures but also on listening patterns and audience satisfaction. The data are usually broken down by age, sex, class or occupational group, and/or region. The Listener Research Department also periodically reported on listening to non-BBC stations (e.g. Radio Hamburg in 1940–43). The department's methodology, a mixture of sampling, self-selected 'listening panels' and Mass-Observation-style 'local correspondents', is clearly open to a number of criticisms. However, the BBC's pioneering Director of Listener Research, R. J. E. Silvey, constantly stressed the department's awareness of the deficiencies of each of these research methods, and his faith that, when taken together, the methods provided as accurate an impression of listener opinion as it was possible to achieve, and there seems no reason generally to doubt this belief.[16] Audience research material is held under its own file classification in the archive, and is often – though not always – duplicated in other relevant files. Departmental files may contain additional information concerning the reception of particular programmes.

In addition to the BBC's own data, the Mass-Observation Archive at the University of Sussex contains investigations into BBC programmes and audience opinions, particularly from the Second World War. A collection of Mass-Observation File Reports is available on microfiche in some libraries. The Mass-Observation Archive also holds several boxes of material concerning investigations into broadcasting and wartime morale. The newspaper press is another important source of information on a programme's contemporary impact. The columns of such radio critics as Grace Wyndham Goldie and W. E. Williams in the *Listener*, Tom Harrisson in the *Observer*, Graham Greene in the *Spectator* and Collie Knox in the *Daily Mail* provide a useful (if highly subjective) commentary on BBC output. Meanwhile, radio has often been news in itself. Both BBC policy and particular programmes have regularly featured as *causes célèbres* in the press (with not always disinterested motives), and these are generally worth following up at Colindale or Caversham. Lastly, memoirs can again also provide useful – if sometimes self-justificatory – assessments of programmes and their impact.

Using radio as an historical source

How should the researcher use these sources? Most of the methodological and interpretive problems arising from them are those one would generally associate with historical research, and are usually a matter of clear thinking and common sense. However, a few specific points should perhaps be borne in mind.

First, the interpretation of the 'finished product'. The assessment of a source on its own terms is a general problem of historical research that is perhaps most acutely felt in the field of 'cultural' history. Broadcasting inevitably prompts a subjective response, and one's own instinctive evaluation of a radio programme, listened to perhaps half a century out of context, requires careful consideration. Much in the broadcast archive can sound artificial, stilted, exclusive or condescending in tone, and the task facing the researcher is to assess how far listeners at the time would have shared this reaction, and how far those tones were in fact generally accepted stylistic conventions of the time. However, while one can go too far in imposing present judgements on past programmes, one can also go too far the other way and accept everything too much at face value. The absence of hindsight can be as dangerous and limiting as too much hindsight. Certainly the immense contemporary popularity of the BBC newsreaders of the 1930s and 1940s belies at least some of the derision aimed at their 'Oxford' accents and formal delivery in more recent times. Yet the BBC's resolutely 'middle-class' tone has been a feature of British broadcasting under concerted attack since its inception.[17]

Second, the archive record. Although any researcher recognises the need for a degree of detachment (or healthy scepticism) when using the archives, access to such a comprehensive and minutely detailed resource as the BBC Written Archive can require particular care. It is deceptively easy to get drawn into the material as one follows a policy evolving or watches as a programme is created from the first idea, through discussion, negotiation and possibly controversy and argument, to the broadcasts themselves, their reception, appraisal and analysis. The attitudes, opinions and even handwriting of BBC personnel become very familiar during a period of close research, and it is surprisingly easy to catch oneself casting particular individuals in the characters of hero and villain. Just as, during the Second World War, Ministry of Information personnel assigned to the BBC were accused of 'going native', so the researcher must take great care not to accept too quickly the point of view represented in what is, in the last resort, only one particular institution's internal archive. Although the BBC Written Archive offers so much to researchers, they must always look beyond the files to assess problems from the other point(s) of view – while always bearing in mind that the alternative perspective is generally no less partial. To take one example from this author's own research, Richard Dimbleby's career as a war correspondent in North Africa takes on a rather different character if one considers it from the point of view not just of Dimbleby himself (beleaguered in the field by petty authority and red tape) but of his news editor back in London (frustrated and ill informed, with a budget to balance and programmes to get out).[18] Above all (for at this level of research there is clearly no single 'BBC point of view'), one tends to identify with the point of view of the production staff, beleaguered on one side by the interference and caution of the institutional hierarchy, on the other by demanding or recalcitrant performers. This may not be altogether a bad thing: in many instances the production staff are the unsung heroes of broadcasting, but it is something to watch closely. Again, critical hindsight and historical empathy need to be finely balanced.

Third, one needs to consider the 'invisible influences' on radio: those criteria which one cannot always immediately identify, but which one must allow for in the overall assessment of the sources. These factors are probably the most significant, and certainly the most fascinating, problems with which the historian must deal. For what is excluded from broadcasting at any particular time is as important a consideration and as legitimate an area of historical enquiry as what is included. For example, notwithstanding the traditional vaunting of the BBC's independence and impartiality, British radio has been controlled and constrained in various respects by governmental restrictions and edicts from the start. The Foreign Office's prohibition of any discussion of appeasement in the 1930s is well known. During the Second World War the Ministry of Information had final veto power over all BBC output. The wartime 'fourteen-day rule', whereby no topic could be discussed on the radio that was due to be debated in Parliament in the next fortnight, was not formally suspended until 1957. Self-censorship and internally imposed constraints can be as important as official controls. BBC policy throughout the history of the corporation has been punctuated by internal restrictions, from the Board of Governors and Director-General down to programme planners or departmental heads, against which individual producers and programme makers may have fought in vain. Some of the constraints are easily identifiable in the public record or the written archive, others less so. Yet together they represent an essential part of the context in which programmes were made.

Last, a practical caution. All output in every medium of communication must, of course, be assessed in the context of the technology of the day. The researcher of radio must at all times bear in mind the simple technological and logistical constraints on broadcasting. To take just one example, the early BBC's often criticised policy of scripting virtually its entire talks output, including interviews and discussion programmes, can substantially (if perhaps not entirely) be attributed as much to practical and technical necessity as to excessive caution or 'censorship'. In the early days of radio, when broadcasting was a strange and intimidating experience, and when programmes were almost universally broadcast live, the fear that a speaker might 'freeze' or that a discussion would collapse, peter out, or fail to come to a natural conclusion at the end of the allotted time, was believed to require first the rehearsal and then the scripting of even the most casual and ostensibly spontaneous exchanges. During the Second World War, although technology had advanced, the problem was compounded by security fears about 'unauthorised' broadcasts, and pre-scripting remained the norm. Not until adequate means were devised of recording and then editing the recordings before transmission could such lively and genuinely spontaneous discussion programmes as the *Brains Trust* be broadcast. Thus technical advances such as sound recording, the development of portable recording equipment, the introduction of tape recording or of the more recent digital technology, all have had a profound effect on the scope and character of radio output, whether studio-based or outside broadcasts, whether news and sport, features and drama, comedy or music. What today may sound artificial or restrictive may have been at the cutting edge of either technology or controversy when it was first broadcast. We cannot criticise without first understanding the complete picture.

Radio, its influence and effects

Most of this discussion has been principally concerned with what one might loosely term radio's *illustrative* function: what particular programmes or policies illustrate and reveal about contemporary concerns and controversies, about contemporary political, social and cultural perceptions. The most difficult part of radio research is, of course, to go beyond the illustrative and consider the *effect* of a broadcast, i.e. the extent to which broadcasting output or policy may have influenced the attitudes, thoughts or actions of individuals, particular groups of people or society as a whole. And, indeed, greater claims have perhaps been made for no other medium of communication, from averting revolution during the General Strike to popularising a new pronunciation of the name of the town of Daventry, and almost everything in between.

Although the importance of radio in British life is unquestionable, the nature of its influence is a matter of much conjecture and debate, and the researcher into radio must be aware of what levels of influence he or she is seeking to investigate. The influence of radio may be narrowly specific; it may be broadly positive or negative (witness the time-honoured complaints about the effects of broadcasting on manners and morals); it may be conceived in the widest possible terms (providing 'an equalising and unifying factor in national life');[19] but to identify the nature and extent of the influence of radio, among all the myriad forces working within British society, is a challenging task. This aspect of research into radio requires the broadest kind of historical analysis, necessitating not only an appreciation of the programmes themselves but a sense of the development of social and political opinion and behaviour over the short and the long term. Above all, one needs a far deeper assessment of audience responses than that which Listener Research and its associated evidence generally provides, and a particularly clear perception of the role of broadcasting in people's lives throughout the century. The context in which the programmes are heard, the degree of attention paid by the listener (do radio programmes function more often than we might like to admit as little more than 'background noise'?), the extent to which audiences are receptive to new ideas and perspectives or, by contrast, look to radio only for reinforcement of their own opinions, and the extent to which people are then prepared to act on those influences – all are immensely difficult issues to evaluate, and all need to be considered. What researchers into radio must have above all, therefore, is a clear conception of what they are seeking to discover or demonstrate, a sound understanding of the difficulties involved, keen awareness of how best to substantiate their conclusions from the historical record – and the recognition that those conclusions will necessarily be impressionistic and open to challenge.

Clearly, the extremely complex network of influences working within the broadcasting medium, whether on policy, the creation and production of programmes, their message, or their reception by the listening public, means that the significance of radio as a source will always be open to controversy. Yet radio provides one of the most rewarding sources in contemporary history, not despite but because of its complexities. It is and will continue to be a valuable field of research in its own right. It constantly provides new dimensions and new insights into other historical issues and debates. Perhaps above all, it conveys an extraordinarily powerful sense of time and place, clarifying as few other sources can do the obvious similarities and the profound differences between the present and the relatively recent past. Without that perspective our understanding of contemporary history cannot be complete.

Notes

1   A useful introduction is D. McQuail, *Mass Communication Theory* (1987) .
2   H. Jennings and W. Gill, *Broadcasting in Everyday Life* (1939), p. 40. See also J. C. W. Reith, *Broadcast over Britain* (1924), R. Knox, *Broadcast Minds* (1932); H. Matheson, *Broadcasting* (1933); P. P. Eckersley, *The Power Behind the Microphone*, (1941), C. Siepmann, *Radio, Television and Society* (1950); A. Clayre, *The Impact of Broadcasting* (1973); A. Smith, *The Shadow in the Cave: the Broadcaster, his Audience, and the State* (1973).
3   G. Orwell, *The Road to Wigan Pier* (1989), pp. 82–3.
4   *The Birth of Broadcasting* (1961), *The Golden Age of Wireless* (1965), *The War of Words* (1970), *Sound and Vision* (1979), *Competition* (1995).
5   M. Pegg, *Broadcasting and Society, 1922–39* (1983); P. Scannell and D. Cardiff, *A Social History of British Broadcasting*, I, *Serving the Nation* (1991); J. Davies, *Broadcasting and the BBC in Wales* (1994).
6   A. Briggs, 'Problems and possibilities in the writing of broadcasting history', *Media, Culture and Society*, 2, 1980, p. 10.
7   See, for instance, J. Seaton, 'Reith and the denial of politics', in J. Curran and J. Seaton, *Power without Responsibility: the Press and Broadcasting in Britain*, fourth edition (1991).
8   See Briggs, *The Birth of Broadcasting*, pp. 360-84; J. Symons, *The General Strike* (1957), pp. 177–82.
9   See Scannell and Cardiff, *Serving the Nation*, chapter 4.
10 See Briggs, *The War of Words*; J. Seaton, 'Broadcasting and the Blitz', in J. Curran and J. Seaton, *Power without Responsibility*; S. Nicholas, *The Echo of War: Home Front Propaganda and the Wartime BBC, 1939–45* (1996).
11 See J. M. MacKenzie (ed.), *Imperialism and Popular Culture* (1986); P. M. H. Bell, *John Bull and the Bear: British Public Opinion, Foreign Policy and the Soviet Union 1941–45* (1990).

12 Briggs, 'Problems and possibilities', p. 7.

13 The BBC Sound Archive is the most extensive collection of recorded radio output in Britain, but is generally open only to BBC staff.

14 The first volumes of Briggs's *History* antedate the opening up to the public of the BBC Written Archive Centre (BBC WAC) – indeed, the BBC began to put its archive in order partly as a consequence of Briggs's undertaking. In consequence his footnotes referring to BBC WAC material do not include file references, and it is not always easy to trace material from his account back to the BBC WAC files.

15 Particularly interesting are R. S. Lambert, *Ariel and all his Quality* (1940); Eckersley, *The Power Behind the Microphone*; M. Gorham, *Sound and Fury* (1948); H. J. G. Grisewood, *One Thing at a Time* (1968); D. G. Bridson, *Prospero and Ariel: the Rise and Fall of Radio* (1971). The earliest is possibly C. A. Graves, *Broadcasting from Within* (1924).

16 See R. J. E. Silvey, 'Methods of Listener Research', n.d. (1944), BBC WAC R9/15/1.

17 See D. Cardiff, 'The serious and the popular: aspects of the evolution of style in the radio talk, 1928–39', *Media, Culture and Society*, 2, 1980, pp. 29–47.

18 Cf. J. Dimbleby, *Richard Dimbleby: a Biography* (1991), and File R28/277, BBC WAC (discussed in Nicholas, *The Echo of War*, chapter 6).

19 Jennings and Gill, *Broadcasting in Everyday Life*, p. 40.

Further reading

P. Black, *The Biggest Aspidistra in the World* (1972).

A. Boyle, *Only the Wind will Listen: Reith of the BBC* (1972).

A. Briggs, *The BBC: the First Fifty Years* (1985).

M. Gorham, *Broadcasting and Television since 1900* (1952).

E. Katz, *Social Research and Broadcasting* (1977).

J. Kavanagh, 'The BBC archives at Caversham', *Contemporary Record*, 6, 1992, pp. 341–9.

T. J. Klapper, *The Effects of Mass Communication* (1960).

I. McIntyre, *The Expense of Glory: a Life of John Reith* (1993).

B. Paulu, *British Broadcasting: Radio and Television in the United Kingdom* (1956).

J. C. W. Reith, *Into the Wind* (1949).

C. Stuart, (ed.), *The Reith Diaries* (1975).

R. Williams, *Communications* (Penguin, 1968).

Archive holdings

BBC Wales Record Centre, c/o Library Services, BBC Broadcasting House, Llandaff, Cardiff CF5 2YQ. Tel: (01222) 572500.

BBC Written Archive Centre, Caversham Park, Reading RG4 8TZ. Tel. (01734) 472742.

British Library National Sound Archive, 29 Exhibition Road, London SW7 2AS. Tel. (0171) 412 7440.

Sound and Moving Image Collection, National Library of Wales, Aberystwyth, Dyfed

SY23 3BU. Tel. (01970) 623816.

Mass-Observation Archive, University Library, University of Sussex, Brighton BN1 9QL. Tel. (01273) 678157.

Part VI

Visual sources

Chapter 34

Photography

Brian Harrison

Historians tend to be coy about visual evidence. They feel more comfortable with written records, especially archival material. If they use illustrations at all, it is usually only to adorn their prose. If they go further, they risk producing a 'coffee-table book'.[1] Yet, even for the eighteenth century, such prose-centredness will not do. As Roy Porter points out, in chapbooks, broadsheet ballads, illustrated novels and biblical texts, trade advertisements, prints and funeral monuments, 'the interleaving of the verbal and visual is quite explicit'. Word and image were then intermingled at all social levels: 'artists habitually gave their paintings titles, mottoes, tags and quotations, and their works abound in literary allusions'.[2] In the age of the camera, visual evidence becomes still more important.

Photography's broadening scope

Photography's evolution is an important historical development in its own right and demands its historian. At the census of 1851 only fifty-one people were described as photographers, yet ten years later there were 2,879.[3] The earliest photographs, which date from the early nineteenth century, cover only a very small range of human behaviour because they required skill, patience and wealth from the photographer. Cameras were first used in wartime during the Crimean War, but they could not yet capture the full horrors of war in the 1850s. Thereafter exposure times fell, tripods were slowly discarded, and by 1881 the *British Journal of Photography* thought photographs would soon be processed so quickly that the reporter-photographer would eventually oust the war artist. Special photographic periodicals were launched in the 1850s and by the 1880s the idea of 'a National Photographic Portrait Gallery' was in the air.

During that decade the *Photographic News* showed an infectious enthusiasm for this vigorous, thrusting new skill. The paper eagerly publicised new inventions and confidently predicted that tomorrow's discoveries would soon see off the problems of today. In 1881 the camera first revealed how birds fly. In the following year the Prince of Wales was present at the Royal Institution with four princesses and a duke when Edward Muybridge used his photographs to show how incorrectly artists had hitherto portrayed the leg movements of a racehorse. The first photo-finish in a race occurred in 1888, when Ernest Marks set up an improvised darkroom at an American racecourse and handed the negative to the judges within three minutes. Flash photography became possible in 1886, and the Prince of Wales set the fashion for night photographs by posing at midnight after the opera.

Always eager to advertise the camera's achievements, the *Photographic News*, discussing in 1882 'What photography does for science', pointed out that photography was nowadays 'a maid-of-all-work, put upon on every occasion, to discharge all sorts of functions, whether menial or high-class'.[4] The camera had been quick to breach the intimacies of research and record-keeping. The Ordnance Survey experimented with photography in map making during the 1850s,[5] and in the same decade prison governors were systematically photographing their prisoners. By the 1880s the case books of asylums and the library of Scotland Yard collected photographs of lunatics and criminals, and by 1885 photographs of MPs were even helping the police to exclude unauthorised people from entering the House of Commons.[6] Amateur photography was by then growing fast, and grew even faster when George Eastman introduced the easily operated Kodak camera in 1888. In 1889 four men appeared in court at Manchester for sending indecent photographs through the post.[7] By 1905 the camera was being used by one in ten of the population.[8] So photographs of growing spontaneity and quality illuminate an ever-widening span of social life.

During our own century, technical progress has enabled the photographer to cross one frontier after another. During the First World War it was recognised within six months how much cameras on planes could contribute to reconnaissance in preparation for an infantry attack.[9] The experience gleaned in war could be put to good peacetime uses. Through air survey photography the camera contributed massively to the inter-war archaeology of all periods from the prehistoric onwards. O. G. S. Crawford's achievement should be noted here, with the publication in 1924 of the Ordnance Survey's *Map of Roman Britain* in its first edition.[10] The Second World War carried the process further when Kenneth St Joseph applied his hawk-like eye to interpreting photographs in the RAF. Thereafter he transferred his skills to Cambridge University's department of aerial photography, and produced all the huge advances in Roman archaeology flowing from that.[11]

In later life Rebecca West recalled how impossible it was for black-and-white photographs to convey the beauty of an Edwardian suffragette such as Christabel Pankhurst: 'she'd this wonderful colouring, marvellous colouring, and this extraordinary grace. Photography just lagged behind.' This problem, too, the twentieth century solved.[12] Colour film and cine-camera eventually enabled the photographer literally to bring home the awfulness of war, whose hazards he must now himself experience. In 1977 the Annan committee, investigating the future of broadcasting, felt that it must reply to complaints against violent films: 'it is often only through the use of pictures that the true horror of wars, violence, natural disasters and human outrages can be brought home to the public ... News cannot be cosy and reassuring if life is harsh and brutal.'[13] But the colour film which exposes the unpleasant can also be used to enhance the enjoyable – nowhere more than in cookery, where television has done much to accelerate improved standards. The historian of diet since 1945 will of course consult the texts of Elizabeth David, but he would also be prudent to watch the televised cooking conducted by Philip Harben, and still more the *Kitchen magic* programmes conducted by the opulently dressed Cradocks, who made such an impact from the mid-1950s. The Cradocks' secret was the way they played up to 'the snobbery and pretension of the times', says Paul Levy; 'in the post-war era they made their hungry, servantless readers and viewers feel they still belonged to an élite.'[14]

Social impact

Technical progress now equips the photographer to breach social convention. The Conservative politician and master of foxhounds Willoughby de Broke, nostalgic in his memoirs (posthumously published in 1924) for the old days, thought that 'perhaps the snapshot has done more to impair the dignity of the English nation than any other recent invention'. A photograph, he said, 'at its best can only reproduce what the sitter happens to be like at a particular second', whereas the portrait painter 'brings his imagination to bear upon all the facets of the sitter'. He preferred to any photographer the portrait painter Sir Francis Grant, a gentleman and fox-hunter as well as president of the Royal Academy. This great painter of the mid-Victorian English gentry knew his subjects, and could capture their world on his canvas: the mood of settled institutions, affluence, leisure, simplicity and tranquillity. 'He was of their class; he knew a well-bred man ought to sit on a well-bred horse, and he put him there, as few other artists ever could, plumb in the middle of the saddle.'[15] The camera has been a democratising influence, and the photographer has much less scope than the painter for perpetuating class myths. How would Willoughby de Broke have viewed what the telephoto lens, reinforced by a certain amount of agility and ruthlessness in the photographer, can now achieve? 'Wherever you are,' the Prince of Wales complained recently, 'there's somebody hiding behind something, somewhere; and with these immense cameras now, with these huge lenses and magnification, you can sit a mile away and photograph through windows and everything else. And they do.'[16] Asked in 1988 what she most disliked in being Prime Minister, Margaret Thatcher replied, 'The fact that you are constantly in the limelight, not only yourself, but your family as well. There is no private life.'[17]

Nonetheless an agile institution can turn intrusion into advertisement. The future Edward VII soon grasped the new medium's potential. When opening Putney bridge in 1886, he and the princess were seen obediently to comply several times with the photographers' command, 'Now then, quite still, if you please.'[18] With the coronation of 1953 television cameras brought the monarchy into every home, and in the television programmes *Royal Family* (1969) and *Elizabeth R* (1992) made it even seem homely. Other public figures showed a similar astuteness with the new medium in the 1880s. Photographs of late Victorian High Church leaders in full canonicals were distributed widely within the local diocese. At the general election of 1880 portraits of the local candidates were projected by magic lantern in at least one London borough, and at the general election of 1886 Gladstone's portrait was given to many constituents. Yet another divergence between Gladstone and Disraeli lies in Gladstone's willingness to be photographed. 'Sat to Walker Photographer,' he wrote in his diary on 22 August 1881. He had been photographed by Samuel Alexander Walker of Regent Street twice before (in 1862 and 1864). When Walker asked for a third sitting he was told that Gladstone would visit him for the purpose on a particular day for fifteen minutes; Gladstone 'was punctual to the minute, and, with his watch on the table, posed for the stipulated quarter of an hour'.[19]

Photographs of Cabinet Ministers were widely exhibited in late Victorian shop windows, so that public celebrities could no longer travel about unobserved. So persistently did photographers pursue the politician Lord Randolph Churchill during his trip abroad in 1886 that the *Daily Telegraph* thought public figures would henceforth 'have to "make up" before they are allowed to drink in peace from any healing spring or lounge at ease in any kursaal or café'.[20] Asquith was one of the last prominent politicians openly to despise the press; when someone at a meeting accused him of murdering the miners at Featherstone in 1892 when Home Secretary, he satisfied himself only with correcting the date.[21] Yet his contempt for the media was well behind the times. For here was a new source of influence over an electorate that could no longer be controlled through bribery and exploiting local self-interest.

Much has yet to be written on the iconography of Stanley Baldwin and Winston Churchill, and much has already been written about how Harold Macmillan exploited the new medium of television to his benefit, especially at the general election of 1959. Yet Macmillan's career illustrates the fickleness of the camera as an ally, for his final election broadcast on television that year was soon turned against him to devastating effect. Neither Peter Cook nor *Beyond the Fringe* features in the index to Harold Macmillan's memoirs; their presence in his six-volume monument would have sullied the self-image he wanted to project to posterity. Less excusably, there is no reference to them in the first worthwhile biography of Macmillan, published by Anthony Sampson in 1967, and only the briefest reference in the second volume of Alastair Horne's more substantial volume published in 1989. Yet Peter Cook's imitation of that broadcast played its part in eroding Conservative influence with public opinion during the run-up to Labour's victory of 1964, and has certainly moulded Macmillan's image since. Seeking to explain Peter Cook's impact, his obituarists have emphasised the deferential way in which the camera treated politicians until the mid-1960s. 'You have to imagine a time when it was indeed a shocking thing to imitate the Prime Minister of the day on stage and with comic intent.' Cook's imitation had a still wider impact, for it 'changed not only his own life, but the next 35 years of British humour'.[22]

For all politicians since Macmillan, prose-dominated treatment will be seriously incomplete. Who could hope to capture the impact made by Margaret Thatcher without access to footage of the televised interviews (lectures would perhaps be the more appropriate term) she gave in the 1980s, to Geoffrey Howe's resignation speech of 13 November 1990 or to that never-to-be-forgotten parliamentary occasion on 22 November when, on the day she was devastated by being forced into resignation, she put up such a magnificent fighting performance in defence of her governments' record in the confidence debate? Who, for that matter, could hope to capture the relative lack of impact made by her successor without familiarising himself with the cartoons in the *Guardian* of Steve Bell? Since 1988, with the televising of the House of Commons, the historian can reinforce Hansard as a source with evidence on the speaking style and reception of the words that appear on its printed page. The interaction between speaker and audience, reader and visual image, can be captured through direct access to the visual evidence.

The camera's influence penetrates well below the surface. We have already seen how it has helped to undermine concepts of privacy, but a related change is the way it has helped to substitute the pursuit of publicity for the cultivation of reticence. Frank Sutcliffe, the well known late Victorian photographer in Whitby, came across many local working people who thought it unlucky to be drawn or photographed in any way, and many of their social superiors would have thought it vulgar to appear in the newspapers. Reticence was then thought integral to femininity at every social level. Such attitudes are now completely foreign to us. Many are eager to pursue their five minutes of fame, as the *Guinness Book of Records* testifies.

Before the advent of television, cinema films were particularly powerful in moulding social conduct and attitudes, partly because going to the cinema was something of an occasion. In her *South Riding* (1936) Winifred Holtby describes a trilingual maid who 'talked B.B.C. English to her employer, cinema American to her companions, and Yorkshire dialect to old milkmen like Eli Dickson'.[23] As a civil service clerk told Rowntree and Lavers in the late 1940s, 'I often adopt phrases used in films when joining in office chatter ... I find that by seeing so many films my vocabulary has increased and I can hold my own in conversation by sometimes unconsciously copying the attitudes and inflexion of the voice of some of the better stars.'[24] The cinema moulded attitudes as well as accent and manners. *Brief Encounter* (1945), for example, illuminates the situation of the suburban housewife, and in turn helped to mould the behaviour for decades afterwards of the many housewives who saw the film. For similar reasons the historian of sexuality in the 1960s will combine the viewing of *A Taste of Honey* (1961) with *This Sporting Life* (1963).

Television was by then beginning to take over from the cinema. If the historian seeks to chart the reaction against the 1960s he will no doubt read the books of Hayek and the speeches of Keith Joseph, but he will also watch television films like *The History Man* (1982) or *Brideshead Revisited* (1981), though if he wishes to chart the effects of that reaction he will turn also to the cinema for Hanif Kureishi's *My Beautiful Laundrette*. Films of this sort are historically important at three levels: they memorably record aspects of society during their time; they are cultural events in their own right; and, as such, they influence the conduct of the population the historian is studying, whether to change or confirm it. But films mould conduct partly because they also reflect it, and here the interests of historian and film connoisseur overlap but do not exactly coincide. For with film as with literature, the historian searches for the descriptive and the representative whereas the connoisseur prizes the imaginative and the original. The historian will often find the highest flights of creative imagination less valuable as evidence than material with a large infusion of the documentary and the 'realistic'. He may prefer Trollope to Jane Austen, Arnold Bennett to Henry James, Paul Nash to Paul Klee.

Drawbacks and dangers

Still, we should not get carried away with enthusiasm for photographic evidence. There are many things the camera still cannot do, and many dangers flow from viewing uncritically what it can do. The unexpected event rarely finds the photographer on the spot – the assassination of Lord Frederick Cavendish in Phoenix Park in 1882, for example, or the INLA's blowing up of Airey Neave in 1979. Neave's death does, however, illustrate how conventions change on what it is legitimate for the photographer to record. Cameramen in 1979 showed no Victorian scruple: during the election campaign they enhanced the cruelty of public life by pursuing Mrs. Thatcher for her instant reaction to the death of a much respected supporter.

A second point: it would be quite wrong to think that the camera immediately banished earlier visual conventions and ways of seeing things. Earlier artistic conventions profoundly influenced the professional and amateur photographer's choice and interpretation of his subject, just as they influenced how photographs were viewed by the general public. Frank Sutcliffe's photographic style, for instance, owes much to the French painter J. F. Millet. Photographs in every period reflect the artistic convention of the day, and this is especially true of nineteenth-century Britain. All the well known Victorian photographers had earlier been artists or had received an artistic training. The debate on whether photography is an art or a science was vigorous throughout the nineteenth century and remains lively today. Some early photographers thought that the noblest outlet for their skill was merely to reproduce works of creative art, and many more viewed their photographs primarily as artistic creations. 'We photographers have no Rembrandts, no Franz Hals, no Constables, no Whistlers,' wrote Sutcliffe in 1916. 'So the student had better not look at photographs after all till his taste is perfectly broken in. It will be safer for him to look at pictures.'[25] Nor is it surprising that early film makers were guided in their subject matter by the concerns of the nineteenth-century theatre and music hall, and displayed a marked taste for the spectacular: for warfare, ceremonial, melodrama and the exotic.[26]

Artistic convention is not the only barrier between the camera and reality. There is also the problem of forgery. The trial of Graham Ovenden in 1980 showed that the rising price fetched by Victorian photographs had brought many forgeries on to the market.[27] Contemporaries practised milder forms of photographic deception: the *Photographic News* claimed in 1886 that photographs of the Queen in state robes were misleading because she was standing on a concealed box. Everyone who knows they are going to be photographed wants to look at their best, and the sort of photograph that tends to survive is the formal record of a special event. People get themselves photographed more as they want to be remembered than as they usually are. They tend only to photograph what is exceptional and therefore striking – not those recurring day-to-day and relatively uninteresting things that mould our lives so much more profoundly. It is no accident that there was an outburst of photography in connection with the jubilee of 1887, just as in 1953 it was the coronation which firmly rooted television into the home. The camera is brought out for staged occasions, especially for those family functions (weddings, christenings, funerals) where people geographically scattered or generationally divided can for a brief moment be captured together. Reinforced by the family album, the camera has helped to infuse history with nostalgia – especially as so many early group photographs could be taken only in fine weather.

The very act of taking a photograph, like the public announcement that one is keeping a diary, alters the conduct of those who know they are being observed. Besides, some aspects of human behaviour are (for reasons quite other than technical) inherently inaccessible to the camera. The mere externals of a university tutorial may be captured for publicity purposes on film, but not its essence: the interaction of personalities and ideas. A Cabinet may be photographed in session, but not the intricacies of the political process that are central to its function. Enoch Powell, countering arguments for open government in 1979, rightly pointed out that 'secrecy of deliberation and internal communication is always of the essence of all government'. The attempt to impede it, he went on, 'is uniformly self-defeating and only results in government erecting new barriers to defend its necessary privacy'.[28] So prominent is the visual image now in the discussion of public affairs that there is a danger of undervaluing the activities that do not make good television or cannot be televised. 'Those in charge of television must restrain themselves from using its power solely to project the visual aspects of world affairs,' Robin Day told Bernard Levin in 1980 after quarter of a century in television, 'because the most important things are not always visual.' He went on to cite reports of scuffles with pickets at factory gates, pointing out that 'a great deal of our presentation of news and events has been affected by television's appetite for violence'.[29]

So the camera is not neutral in recording the past: it is operated by a photographer who is deeply influenced by contemporary ideas about what ought to be photographed and how. The photograph is less a window giving a clear and comprehensive view of past reality than a mirror reflecting forward into the present the long-lost values and inhibitions of the past. Those values and inhibitions are themselves important raw material for the historian who wishes to explain how the past differs from the present, but such influences can be highlighted only by non-photographic types of source. Only the printed or manuscript document, for instance, can tell us that, when Frank Sutcliffe photographed boys bathing nude at Whitby in his famous 'Water rats' of 1886, much local scandal was caused by his choice of subject matter. Nor would visual evidence tell us that he found it difficult to persuade local working people to be photographed while working: 'laundrymaids hanging out sheets, and carrying heavy baskets of clothes', he wrote in 1914, 'would make grand subjects if laundrymaids had not such objections to being photographed in anything but their Sunday garments'.[30]

Furthermore the photographer, however skilful, can illuminate aspects of society that are accessible to only one of our five senses, the eye, and precious little even of that. Photography can tell us nothing about noise, smell, touch and taste. It has marked limitations even in portraiture. 'Photography was always a little unkind to Mrs Langtry's type of beauty,' wrote *Photographic News* in 1885. 'The camera is powerless where fascination of manner and charms of conversation are concerned.'[31] A historian can no more concentrate exclusively on 'visual history' – on a type of history that grows purely out of visual types of evidence – than on 'oral history', 'documentary history' or 'archaeological history'. There is no conflict between different types of historical source. If television documentaries focus primarily on visual material, for example, they reinforce it by gathering interviews and recollections. In the skilful hands of people like Phillip Whitehead and Steve Humphries such programmes also become books.[32] History is, as Isaiah Berlin once said, 'a rich brew', and its full richness will be available only after every relevant type of source has been drawn upon for the task in hand.

Conclusion

Nonetheless the historian of Britain since the 1880s must incorporate the photograph into his raw material. For all the camera's distortions, its power of accurate representation forced it to the forefront, and artists had to respond. High-speed photography demonstrated how the legs of fast-moving animals really move, the portrait painter now required fewer sittings from his subject and aristocratic good looks could no longer survive challenge from below. The camera helped to create a sort of meritocracy of beauty in which 'professional beauties' of humbler birth – Lily Langtry, Mrs Cornwallis-West, Mrs Luke Wheeler – came to the fore. Indeed, so feeble was the artist's power of representation that in the twentieth century he largely vacated the field of representation to the camera, and retreated into the realms of imagination and abstraction: he would in future found his professional status on doing what the camera could not do.

There is one more reason why the historian will embrace the photograph. For him and his readers it can clarify more vividly than any prose and more accurately than any painting or drawing just how the past differs from the present. It is important for the historian not just to explain what the past was like but also to ensure that his explanation makes an impact on hearers and readers. Here the photograph's immediacy and relative authenticity help immensely. The many systematic photographic collections on long-lost buildings more vividly evoke the mood of Victorian city or slum than any other source. There is a note of despair at the very end of Henry-Russell Hitchcock's huge two-volume compendium *Early Victorian Architecture*, when he admits that his pictures 'must say what the author, even at the end of his book, cannot. Almost all he knows about Early Victorian architecture is in them. If the character of the British building production of the years between the mid-30's and the mid-50's cannot be read in the graphic documents, it can hardly be read anywhere. They epitomize the production of the period as only pictures and not written words can ever successfully do.'[33] The historian who studies P. H. Emerson's scenes of country life in late Victorian Norfolk or Henry Taunt's street scenes in early twentieth-century Oxford will describe those two communities with greatly enhanced insight. The photograph stirs the imagination, and rare indeed is the modern, or even ancient, historian who can afford to ignore it.

Where, then, can the contemporary historian who is alert to visual material go for his photographs? John Wall's *Directory of British Photographic Collections* (1977) is invaluable, and has an index to subjects, owners, locations, titles and photographers together with useful information and a bibliography. Aside from Wall's the range of sources for picture research is vast. Perhaps the best starting point is Hilary Evans's guide to the *Art of Picture Research: a Guide to Current Practice, Procedure, Techniques and Resources* (1979) and the *Picture Researcher's Handbook*, which is available from Mary Evans Picture Library. The fourth edition was published in 1989. It contains 500 pages listing collections in over 100 countries; simple to use, but the range of reference tends to limit the amount of detail on any one entry.

There is a useful short bibliography in *World Photography Directories* by David N. Bradshaw and Catherine Hahn (1982) and a more annotated version in Evans. Further up-to-date information on sources can be obtained from the British Association of Picture Libraries and Agencies, PO Box 93, London NW6 5XW; and the Royal Photographic Society (which has an extensive library and collection), 14 South Audley Street, London W1Y 5DP. Other professional bodies are listed in Evans and in Bradshaw. It is also worth checking with the local university and library to see what sort of collections they have – many have slide or photographic collections. There is a full guide to UK slide collections published by the British Library. The material is based on a survey, the national survey of slide collections, and published as *Directory of Slide Collections* by Roy Mckeown. It covers material from the survey of academic institutions, public libraries, local authority museums and galleries, national museums and galleries, government libraries, government departments, research institutions, professional associations, learned societies, teaching hospitals, postgraduate medical centres and schools of nursing. As it was published in 1990, it is now a little out of date but it is a good starting point in a search for material on slide.

Other useful sources include Rosemary Eakins, *Picture Sources UK* (1985), which is divided into general and thematic collections. The guide has separate lists for collections in local, foreign, military, political and natural history. There is also, as mentioned above, David Bradshaw and Catherine Hahn's *World Photography Directories* (1982). This lists 1,728 different collections around the world but seems due for a new edition. A excellent source of a different kind is the *Picture Reference File* (1976), a compendium of 2,228 pictures, all of which are in the public domain.

Notes

1   I plead guilty – see Colin Ford and Brian Harrison, *Hundred Years Ago: Britain in the 1880s in Words and Photographs* (1983; reissued 1994).

2 'Seeing the past', *Past and Present*, February 1988, pp. 188–9.
3 H. and A. Gernsheim, *History of Photography ... up to 1914* (1955), p. 166.
4 *Photographic News*, 3 March 1882, p. 100.
5 W. A. Seymour (ed.), *A History of the Ordnance Survey* (1980), p. 137.
6 *Photographic News*, 12 June 1885, p. 376.
7 *British Journal of Photography*, 25 January 1889, p. 64.
8 Statistics in this paragraph from Gernsheim and Gernsheim, *History of Photography* (1955), pp. 312–13.
9 T. Wilson, *The Myriad Faces of War: Britain and the Great War, 1914–18* (1988), p. 365.
10 For a good account see Seymour, *Ordnance Survey*, pp. 237–9.
11 Obituaries in the *Independent*, 18 March 1994, p. 30; *Times*, 26 March 1994, p. 21.
12 Author's interview with Dame Rebecca West at 48 Kingston House North, Princes' Gate, London S.W.7, on 15 August 1974.
13 Committee on the Future of Broadcasting, *Report*, Cmnd 6753 (1977), p. 282.
14 *Independent*, 29 December 1994, p. 12.
15 Richard Greville Verney, Lord Willoughby de Broke, *The Passing Years* (1924), pp. 10–11, 24.
16 *Guardian*, 30 June 1994, p. 3 (reporting ITV documentary the previous evening).
17 *Guardian*, 4 January 1988, p. 3.
18 *Daily News*, quoted in *Photographic News* 4 June 1886, p. 360.
19 *Photographic News*, 3 March 1882, p. 102; cf. H. C. G. Matthew (ed.), *The Gladstone Diaries*, X (1990), p. 112.
20 *Daily Telegraph*, 29 October 1886, p. 4.
21 J. A. Spender and C. Asquith, *Life of Herbert Henry Asquith, Lord Oxford and Asquith* (1932), I, p. 210, cf. II, pp. 229–32.
22 *Guardian*, 10 January 1995, p. 19.
23 *South Riding: an English Landscape* (Fontana Books edition 1954), p. 35.
24 B. S. Rowntree and G. R. Lavers, *English Life and Leisure: a Social Study* (1951), p. 250.
25 M. Hiley, *Frank Sutcliffe* (1974), p. 87. On the relationship between art and photography see Aaron Scharf's admirable *Art and Photography* (second edition, Penguin, 1974).
26 J. M. MacKenzie, *Propaganda and Empire: the Manipulation of British Public Opinion, 1880–1960* (1984), pp. 68–9.
27 See John Hooper, 'The art of the authentic', *Guardian*, 22 November 1980, p. 17.
28 *H. C. Deb.*, 19 July 1978, c. 539.
29 *Times*, 5 May 1980, p. 3.
30 Hiley, *Sutcliffe*, p. 62.
31 *Photographic News*, 22 May 1885, p. 328.
32 E.g. Phillip Whitehead's *The Writing on the Wall: Britain in the Seventies* (1985) and Steve Humphries's *A Secret World of Sex: Forbidden Fruit: the British Experience, 1900–50* (1988).
33 H-R. Hitchcock, *Early Victorian Architecture in Britain* (1954), I, p. 613.

Chapter 35

Film as an historical source

Jeffrey Richards

As the film historian Raymond Durgnat has memorably written:

> For the masses, the cinema is dreams and nightmares, ... It is an alternative
> life. One's favourite films are one's unlived lives, one's hopes, fears, libido. They
> constitute a magic mirror, their shadowy forms are woven from one's shadowy
> selves, one's limbo loves.[1]

The content of these dreams and nightmares and how they are arrived
at are matters that historians cannot afford to neglect. Yet historians were
for many years reluctant to quarry feature films for evidence of the social
history of this century. The reason was given by the eminent American historian Arthur M. Schlesinger Jr.

> Historians are professionally a conservative lot. Movies have had status prob-
> lems ever since they emerged three-quarters of a century ago as a dubious
> entertainment purveyed by immigrant hustlers to a working-class clientele in
> storefront holes-in-the-wall scattered through the poorer sections of the indus-
> trial city. Conventional history has recorded the motion picture as a phenom-
> enon but ignored it as a source. Social and intellectual historians draw freely
> on fiction, drama, painting, hardly ever on movies. Yet the very nature of film
> as a supremely popular art guarantees that it is the carrier of deep if enigmatic
> truth.[2]

Non-fiction films

The challenge has now been taken up and historians are turning more and
more to the use of film as historical evidence.[3] When in the 1960s historians first began to admit the use of film to their deliberations, it was to newsreel and documentary that they turned. They were reassured by the
presence of real people and real locations that they were somehow viewing
'reality'. But they were mistaken. Newsreels and documentaries no more

presented 'reality' than did feature films, which told stories, used actors and were often made entirely in studios. In the case of the documentary and the newsreel what was seen on the screen was selected, shaped and placed there in pursuit of certain predetermined policies. Newsreel makers and documentarists worked under the same constraints as feature film makers, subject to interference from censors, sponsors and outside pressure groups. Admittedly, such films provide first-hand visual evidence of clothing, housing and transport, just as photographs do. But, beyond that surface 'reality', newsreels and documentaries were far from being objective. They were, in fact, highly selective and strictly controlled. As one newsreel chief put it in 1938, 'the newsreel companies were always ready to give, and in fact frequently gave, assistance to the government in portraying matters which were deemed to be in the public interest.'[4]

The early film pioneers believed that they were creating new sources of objective historical evidence. But almost at once it was demonstrated that this evidence needed just as much stringent scrutiny as any conventional historical source, if not more so. For between 1896 and 1910 the French film maker Georges Méliès concocted a series of theatrical reconstructions of notable events of the day-events such as the coronation of King Edward VII and the assassination of President McKinley. They were recreated in the studio but sometimes deceived an innocent and not yet media-conscious public. Cinematographers regularly faked dramatic episodes from the Boxer Uprising, the Boer War and the First World War, passing them off as authentic footage to meet the growing hunger for photographic news from the battle front. Some of it has deceived experts ever since and the compilers of such television series as *The Great War*, crucially dependent on contemporary newsreel and documentary footage, had their work cut out establishing that all their material had been shot on location and not recreated, as some undoubtedly was, on the South Downs.

By the time the newsreels had grown up and were depicting actuality, what sort of actuality was it? Sir Arthur Elton, himself a distinguished documentary film maker, lamented in 1955:

> For at least the first thirty years the content of the newsreels was determined mainly by the passing fads and fancies of the time. Of scenes of one-legged men pushing turnips with their noses from Paris to Rome there was much; of boat races, crowned heads, bathing belles, railway smashes, the glossier phases of war, fashion parades, fires, murders and dance marathons, more; but of industry, technology, sociology, art, poetry, agriculture, only accidental glimpses ... Taking a parallel from written sources, it is as if the historian of the early twentieth century had little more to guide him than *The Daily Mirror, Old Moore's Almanac* and a run of Nelson's sixpenny novels.[5]

Even if this were so, I would suggest that it is important to the historian. For it shows us what people were being told by a mass medium of communication, and that has important implications for the shaping of their actions and perceptions, their evaluation of news, their sense of priorities and therefore their reactions, and their value systems. But Christopher Roads took issue with Elton and argued that such film, when it has been thoroughly researched and authenticated, can 'record invaluably but uniquely innumerable aspects of the social, economic, administrative, military and political history of this century'.[6] The value of actuality film, as discerned by historians, is that it can show what image is being presented of political leaders, what is the attitude of the people at great public events, and what version of contemporary history is being disseminated by the newsreel companies. But, in order to use newsreels as historical evidence, it is necessary not just to analyse the on-screen images but to go behind the screen, to look at the organisational structure, policies and personnel of the newsreel companies to establish the context and circumstances within which the films were produced.

In an exemplary study of the newsreels and the Spanish Civil War, Anthony Aldgate did just that, examining both imagery and context, and he concluded that the companies tended to follow the government's line on the subject, emphasising the destruction and devastation in Spain as part of a general campaign to show the horrors of modern war, and endorsing the British government's policy of neutrality, with tacit endorsement of Franco. The newsreels' stance tended always to be consensual rather than confrontational. You could say that is what might have been expected. But suspecting something is one thing and demonstrating it is another – it is essentially the difference between being a gossip columnist and being a serious historian.[7]

Perhaps the greatest cinematic mythology has grown up around the British documentary movement of the 1930s, which is often portrayed as the sole repository of realism and radicalism in a predominantly conservative industry. But that view has to be qualified. Documentaries were made for sponsors and designed to promote their products. So a genuinely moving and revealing film like *Housing Problems*, which graphically details living conditions in the slums of London, also contains messages aimed at persuading local authorities to buy the product of its sponsor, the Commercial Gas Council. More seriously, documentaries were not on the whole shown to the mass cinemagoing public. Exhibitors were extremely reluctant to show them, regarding them as 'box office poison'. As W. R. Fuller, General Secretary of the Cinematograph Exhibitors' Association, speaking in 1936 of the exhibitors' failure to interest the public in the Empire Marketing Board's documentaries, said acidly, 'No documentary ... has ever set the Thames afire.'[8] Documentaries, then, can really tell us only about the aims and attitudes of their sponsors and their producers, though that is in itself a valuable contribution to the cultural history of the period. The old idea that the documentary represented a purer, higher truth than the feature film, however, must be rejected. Examined today, 1930s British documentaries give, like newsreels, a selective picture of the past. They concentrate, for instance, on the old heavy industries, going in for an abstract Soviet-influenced heroisation of the proletariat (the miners, shipbuilders and fishermen in particular); and they concentrate on the male worker and on the north, at the expense of the new industrial areas of the midlands and the south and of women workers, who are largely ignored.[9]

Fiction films

If we are to get to grips with that great intangible 'the national mood', to see what subjects were dominating the popular consciousness, what attitudes to issues, problems, social structures were being disseminated, it is to features films that we must turn.

From the 1920s to the 1950s cinema-going was the principal leisure activity of a large proportion of the British people. The cinema attracted members of all classes, though in particular the working class. It appealed to both sexes and to all age groups, though least of all to the elderly. It occupied a place in people's lives which since the 1950s has been taken over by television, though some of the films that draw today's television audience are the ones that were seen and enjoyed by their parents and grandparents on their regular weekly visits to the cinema.

The cinema was an integral and important part of the mass media, closely associated with newspapers, wireless, pulp fiction and, latterly, television. Its influence was fully recognised in its heyday and was reflected in the regular parliamentary debates on matters cinematographic, in the creation of film propaganda organisations, particularly by the Conservative Party, and in the large number of local and national inquiries, conferences, commissions and investigative studies into the effect of cinema on its audience. The prevalent view was succinctly summarised by the 1936 Moyne committee report into the working of the Cinematograph Films Act:

> The cinematograph film is today one of the most widely used means for the amusement of the public at large. It is also undoubtedly a most important factor in the education of all classes of the community, in the spread of national culture and in presenting national ideas and customs to the world. Its potentialities moreover in shaping the idea of the very large numbers to whom it appeals are almost unlimited. The propaganda value of the film cannot be overemphasized.[10]

Broadly speaking, the cinema both fictional and non-fictional operates in two ways – to reflect and highlight popular attitudes, ideas and preoccupations, and to generate and inculcate views and opinions deemed desirable by film makers. Film makers select in the first case material which they know will appeal to their audience and in the second material with which

they can manipulate their audience and shape its perceptions. It may well
be that a film will aim to do both things at once; perhaps the greatest problem with films is to distinguish deliberate propaganda from what Arthur
Marwick has called 'unwitting' testimony, the hidden assumptions and attitudes, rather than the conscious, and often biased, message.[11] Marwick
argues strongly for the particular value of this aspect of feature films to the
historian:

> The more one makes a comparative study of films, the more one becomes
> aware that, however exceptional within the context of its own country, every
> film is in fact a product of its own culture. No film-maker, it becomes clearer
> and clearer, can really go beyond certain assumptions accepted within his own
> country ... Over and over again, it has been pointed out to me at seminars and
> conferences that films are made by members of the upper and more prosper-
> ous segments of society. That I would never deny; but I am far more interested
> in the fact that ... films ... were seen by large audiences. There *is* a law of the
> market; the bigger its commercial success, the more a film is likely to tell us
> about the unvoiced assumptions of the people who watched it. It is the tedious
> documentary, or the film financed by political subscription, which tells us
> least.[12]

But the cinema can also act as a potent means of social control, transmitting the dominant ideology of society and creating for it a consensus of
support. First, films provide images of the lives, attitudes and values of various groups in society, created from recognisable but carefully selected
facets of such groups. This is important because, as the anthropologist Hortense Powdermaker discovered, film audiences have a tendency to accept as
accurate depictions of places, attitudes and life styles of which they themselves have no first-hand knowledge.[13] Thus, for instance, a working-class
audience may well accept as authentic a cinematic depiction of upper-class
life, however inaccurate, while it would reject an inaccurate depiction of its
own circumstances.

Second, films provide images of society as a whole, again constructed of
selected elements and aspects of everyday life, which are organised into a
coherent pattern governed by a set of underlying presuppositions. The
process of selection confers on certain issues, institutions and individuals –
say, for instance, the police or the monarchy – which regularly appear in
a favourable light.

Third, popular film serves as the vehicle by which a community expresses
its beliefs about what is right and wrong and as 'a medium through which
a community repeatedly instructs its members in correct behaviour'.[14] Popular films, and in particular *genre* films such as crime dramas, horror pictures or westerns, which regularly use the same elements, characters and
situations, function as rituals, cementing the beliefs and ideals of society,
enforcing social norms and exposing and isolating deviance.

Last, there is a tendency for the mass media to promote conformity not only of dress, hairstyle and vocabulary but also, and more subtly, of attitudes and world-view. It is therefore of central importance to discover who controls the production of films and what attitudes and ideas they are disseminating through them.

But the relationship between film and audience is reciprocal. An audience does not accept passively every message that is put across in a film. For one thing, it can choose which films to see and which to avoid. Even within films it can accept elements that it likes and reject unpalatable ones. In the last resort it is positive audience approval, expressed via the box office, that ensures whether a film succeeds or fails financially. So producers must always calculate what will appeal to their audiences, and that will inevitably influence what goes into a film. Direct propaganda rarely works, as the Nazis discovered in Germany. Their first three feature-film exercises in promoting the Nazi Party, *S. A. Mann Brand, Hitlerjunge Quex* and *Hans Westmar* were such disasters at the box office that Propaganda Minister Goebbels ordered that direct propaganda should in future be confined to the newsreels, and he sought to work more subtly on audiences by inserting propaganda elements into 'straight' entertainment films. So in order to understand how Nazi ideology was transmitted it is necessary to examine in detail apparently 'innocent' films like musicals and historical romances, locating them securely in their production, artistic and political contexts.[15]

Admittedly, film analysis poses a fundamental problem in that, unlike the painting or the novel, film is a collaborative rather than an individual art. Films are produced by a conveyor-belt, mass-production process. They are the end product of collaboration between director, writer, cameraman, composer and actors and may often represent considered decisions made by men not actually involved in translating the script into visual images. These are the men with the final say, the producers and production supervisors, the men with logistic, financial and sometimes even overall artistic control. In acknowledgement of an understandable desire to confer artistic respectability on the cinema, the *auteur* theory of the 1960s argued for a single artistic vision in film making and assigned it to the director. There can be no denying that the cinema has produced a high proportion of works of art and that a Hitchcock or a Hawks film, a Michael Powell or a David Lean, is as recognisable thematically and stylistically as a Dickens novel or a Velasquez painting. But the bulk of films are not so much personal works of art as, to use the term employed in the television industry, 'product'. They are not art but artefacts for instant consumption and discard. They cannot be understood in terms of artistic vision, but they can be seen as a direct response to the era which produced them. For every Hawks and Hitchcock, for every Ford and Sternberg, there are a dozen Alfred E. Greens and Albert S. Rogells, directors who were merely proficient craftsmen, the servants of mass culture, taking their cue from current preoccupations rather than from timeless individual vision. For historians it is often the work of these journeymen rather than the work of the great artists that is interesting, just as popular novels, picture postcards and wall posters, designed for the moment and reflecting that moment, are interesting. Indeed, as they are collaborative, films are more likely to reflect, and respond to, the market place and thus the audience. The top box-office films have rarely been great works of art. A great work of art anyway usually tells us more about the artist than about the society that produced him. So the films of Gracie Fields, for instance, are likely to be more valuable to the social historian than the poems of W. H. Auden or the novels of Virginia Woolf.

Nothing demonstrates the collaborative nature of film making more clearly than the exemplary Wisconsin series of screenplays of key Warner Brothers films from the heyday of that company. Each script is accompanied by a meticulously documented essay, which traces the film's production, detailing its development stage by stage. To take just one example, Rudy Behlmer's essay on the classic swashbuckler *The Sea Hawk* (1940) begins in 1935, when Warner Brothers decided upon Rafael Sabatini's novel as a follow-up to its successful *Captain Blood*, which had launched Errol Flynn as a major star.[16] Behlmer shows how the book passed through the hands of four successive screenwriters, moving further and further from Sabatini's novel until nothing but the title remained. The film was directed by Michael Curtiz, but it is clear that the Warner production chief, Hal B. Wallis, was deeply involved in every aspect of filming. We see him intervening constantly, ordering the testing of Dennis Morgan for the leading role in case the tempestuous Errol Flynn had to be replaced, seeking to curb Curtiz's desire to alter the script while on the set and insisting that it be shot exactly as written, restraining Curtiz from injecting too much brutality and violence in order to avoid the wrath of the censors, making constructive suggestions about the lighting and staging of individual sequences and tackling the problem of shooting the final duel raised by the total inability of the villain, Henry Daniell, to handle a sword. His mark remains on the finished film, though he actually made none of it himself. Apart from that, there were the contributions of the production designers, costumiers, composers and photographers who gave Warner Brothers films their distinctive look and feel. This kind of documentation is invaluable in assessing the true nature of film making at the height of the great studio era, which coincided with the period of the cinema's greatest popularity.

This can best be called 'contextual cinematic history' and is the most productive approach for the historian, for it places particular emphasis on the exploration of the context within which a film was produced. A fine example of this approach applied to American cinema is Lary May's *Screening out the Past*, subtitled *The Birth of Mass Culture and the Motion Picture Industry*.[17] This bold, absorbing, infectiously readable book takes as its subject the

American cinema's formative period, 1890–1929, and, by examining its development in the context of the age, produces what the French would call *une histoire de mentalité*. May sees the cinema as a key element in the development of a new urban culture, concentrating on the issues at the heart of change and contributing to the transition in America from what, for simplicity's sake, he calls the 'Victorian Age' to the 'Modern Age'. He demonstrates quite convincingly that in the first decades of the twentieth century the film industry was the focal point of a revolution in morals, expectations and attitudes in American society and that the films themselves reflected, highlighted and advanced the change in the relationship between work and leisure, men and women, and in the promotion of a new success ethic and dominant life style.

His method – and the value of his book lies almost as much in that as in its conclusions – is to analyse the content and structure of groups of films, box-office trends, star personalities and their appeal, contemporary reviews and reactions, staging, lighting and action styles, the role of fan magazines, censorship and picture palaces, and to locate all these elements firmly in the political, social and cultural context. In relation to the products of a mass popular culture, that is surely the right way forward, for it extends our understanding and appreciation of films and their world and, above all, illuminates their place in culture and society.

For British cinema, Charles Barr's indispensable *Ealing Studios* provides a notable example of contextual cinematic history. Barr has revealed the multi-layered richness of Ealing's films by relating them to their background. He demonstrates their key role in the dramatisation of World War II as the 'people's war', the struggle to maintain consensus and at the same time to highlight and defuse social discontent during the period of the post-war Labour government and, finally, the drift to Conservatism and the complacency which followed the return to power of the Tories in 1951. He relates the films to the structure and nature of the studio itself, to the character and attitudes of the personnel involved and to the rise of middle-class radicalism among the generation that voted Labour for the first time in 1945 and then retreated towards Conservatism in the 1950s. He uncovers the debates and dichotomies between age and youth, tradition and change, subversion and conformity. This study gives an entirely new range of meaning to films like *Passport to Pimlico*, *Kind Hearts and Coronets* and *The Titfield Thunderbolt*, a depth of interpretation which can be understood only in context.[18] The major continuing journal outlet for historical research into the cinema, as well as radio and television, is the *Historical Journal of Film, Radio and Television*, which first appeared in 1981 and is now published four times a year. A contextual approach has also characterised the volumes published in Routledge's Cinema and Society series and the same publisher's Studies on Film, Television and the Media.

Film as historical evidence

In using film as historical evidence we need to explore three principal areas. The first necessity is to analyse what the film is saying, and that involves looking at the structure and meaning of the film, as conveyed by script, visuals, acting, direction, photography and music. Second, we need to put it in context with respect to both the film industry itself and the political and social situation which produced it. Third, we must find out how the films were received and what audience reaction to them was. To some extent all three strands are interwoven, for popular cinema has an organic relationship with the rest of popular culture, and popular culture as a whole plays a part in the social and political history of its time. Many films were based on books, for instance, and were not so much original cinematic creations as 'cinematisations' (as the industry called them) of literary properties, whose success with the public in their original form led producers to assume a guaranteed audience. Many films were based on plays, and the stage provided (much more in Britain than in America) not only material but also performers – music hall artists, musical comedy stars and dramatic actors – who became film stars.

We must try to elucidate the production histories of the films and the intentions of the film makers to see who was responsible for what is actually on the screen. Occasionally such information can be gleaned from interviews conducted at the time and recorded in magazines and newspapers or in later years. But the oral history method presents grave problems, for, quite apart from faulty memories, some directors may seek to mislead or may revamp facts to fit their legends. John Ford and Josef von Sternberg, for example, took pleasure in mystifying, confusing and sending interviewers up, while others, like Douglas Sirk on his period in Nazi Germany, could be understandably evasive. Autobiographies by retired directors and producers often reconstruct the past to fit their legend and always need to be measured against other sources.

It has already been noted that it may not be the director who is ultimately responsible for what is on the screen. The guiding intelligence behind the productions of London Films, whoever may have been directing officially, was usually that of the producer, Alexander Korda, while Michael Balcon, as production chief at Gaumont British in the 1930s, had the final say on almost every aspect of production. He left people in no doubt as to who was the dominant creative force at GB when he defined the role of the producer in 1933:

> The work of the film producer is to determine the choice of subjects, of directors and of artistes for every picture and to decide the cost to be borne. Under his supervision director, scenario editor and unit executives prepare the script, the plans of sets and the time schedule for each production. When the film is in the making its daily progress is reported to him. He is the sponsor, and the

guide, and the ultimate court of appeal ... the kind of energy which the producer must stimulate and direct is based upon the creative and artistic
impulses of directors, writers, cameramen and artistes. Such impulses are so
personal that they constantly require the close attention of one directing mind
to blend then into the harmonious unity which is essential for any successful
achievement in a form of entertainment which depends upon the specialized
work of many different hands.[19]

Another element which must not be overlooked is the role and iconography of the stars. It was the stars, after all, whom the public went to see:
successive surveys revealed that the stars and the story were what
attracted the mass audience to the cinema. Fan magazines and fan clubs
charted their doings and their life styles. The stars set the fashions in
clothes, hairstyles, speech, deportment, love-making. As Andrew Tudor
observes, 'The basic psychological machinery through which most people
relate to films involves some combination of identification and projection,'[20]
and what audiences identified with and projected themselves on to was the
stars. This inevitably had an influence on films and on the roles that were
chosen and shaped to highlight the qualities and characteristics of a particular star. As Raymond Durgnat notes, 'The star is a reflection in which
the public studies and adjusts its own image of itself ... the social history of
a nation can be written in terms of it film stars.'[21] A new and valuable study
of how British women related to the Hollywood stars of the 1940s and
1950s can be found in Jackie Stacey's *Star Gazing*.[22]

Beyond the immediate production context there are further constraints
to be considered. In wartime propaganda objectives had to be met. In
Britain in World War II the Ministry of Information and in the United
States the Office of War Information set detailed guidelines for the content
of feature films. There is a growing body of authoritative historical work on
the role of cinema in wartime.[23] But in peacetime there was a continuing
framework within which film makers operated – the censorship system. It
is impossible to understand the development and nature of the cinema
without a full appreciation of the work and influence of the censors. Unlike
that of some other countries, censorship in Britain was not state-controlled.
The British Broad of Film Censors was set up by the industry itself as an
act of self-preservation in 1912. The 1909 Cinematograph Act had given
local authorities the right to license buildings used as cinemas. The intention was for them to concern themselves with fire precautions, but the
wording of the Act was loose enough to be interpreted as conferring powers
of censorship. The possibility that the licensing authorities, estimated at
700 in 1932, might pass different verdicts on the suitability of films obviously constituted a threat to the industry's commercial viability, so central
self-censorship by the industry was deemed necessary. Its stated aim was
'to create a purely independent and impartial body whose duty it will be to

induce confidence in the minds of the licensing authorities and of those who will have in their charge the moral welfare of the community generally'.[24] The basic censorship rules were drawn up by the board's second president, T. P. O'Connor, and known as 'O'Connor's Forty-three'. The censors, he said, were 'guided by the main principle that nothing should be passed which is calculated to demoralize an audience, that can teach methods of or extenuate crime, that can undermine the teachings of morality, that tends to bring the institution of marriage into contempt or lower the sacredness of family ties'.[25] In fact their aim was to maintain the moral, political, social and economic *status quo* and to avoid anything that smacked of controversy. The censors' favourite term of approval was 'harmless', which indicated the negative way in which they viewed the cinema. Their hold on the industry grew during the 1930s as the scope of their activities extended from the vetting of completed films to the inspection of scripts prior to shooting. The rules were relaxed over the years, though always in response to perceived changes in public tolerance of matters like sex and violence. This was particularly true in the 1960s, but by then the cinema was ceasing to be a mass entertainment medium and becoming a sectional and minority one.[26]

In an important article Nicholas Pronay stresses the need to provide a properly documented context for film analysis. He lists and describes the various archives, collections and information sources that the historian using films should know about, and he argues for the value of historical work based on such sources:

> So far from research topics relating to 'film' being narrow and specialized subjects which confine the student to film itself and subjective interpretations of speculation about it ... in fact, such topics lead the researcher who does the job properly through an extensive range of government records both central and local, as well as private archives containing the papers of major political figures, party organizations and pressure groups ... such topics could be said in fact to offer an ideal focus for postgraduate research. They offer the chance of learning about records, and therefore the actual working, of many more parts of modern government and politics and international infrastructure than conventional twentieth-century topics tend to offer.[27]

For the historian seeking to locate films for research purposes, the two principal national collections are the National Film Archive, 21 Stephen Street, London W1P 1PL, which contains a wide cross-section of films of historical interest, and the Imperial War Museum Film Department, for filmic material related to war. The British Universities Film and Video Council, 55 Greek Street, London W1V 5LR, issues an invaluable *Researchers' Guide to Film and Television Archives* listing all the other sources of film, many of them regional film archives, in Britain.

The great imponderable in all this is always how the audience reacted.

The old hypodermic idea that the audience as a whole was directly injected with the message of a film has long since been discredited. The idea that the entire film output of a country directly reflects the collective psyche of that country has also been seriously questioned. These approaches, seen now as too mechanistic, underlay the pioneering work of Siegfried Kracauer, who saw the whole of German cinema as foreshadowing the rise of Hitler in his classic but now controversial work *From Caligari to Hitler*.[28] The relationship between film maker, film and audience is seen to be more sophisticated, a two-way process operating in areas of shared experience and shared perception.[29]

It is reasonable to assume that an audience's reaction depends ultimately on the age, sex, class, health, intelligence and preoccupations of that audience, both as individuals and as a group. Some general evidence exists in the form of box-office returns, where available, and in the record of reissues, which usually signalled a film's success at the box office. There are surveys of audience taste and reactions to films, such as the Mass-Observation work of the 1930s and 1940s.[30] The popularity of stars can be gleaned from the polls taken, particularly the influential annual poll in the *Motion Picture Herald*, which lists stars according to their box-office draw. Newspaper reviews are valuable. Allowance has to be made for the attitude and readership of the various newspapers, but the critics were writing with the tastes and interests of their readers in mind. What they wrote was heeded. As Winifred Holmes testified in a contemporary study of film-going in an unnamed southern town in the 1930s, 'Newspaper reviews of films are read with interest and play a large part in influencing people of all classes in an appreciation of the films shown.'[31] Newspaper film reviewing was part of the wider popular culture and is a phenomenon in itself worthy of study. John Ellis's brilliant analysis of 1940s film reviewing in Britain uncovers the critical agenda and criteria to which 'serious' reviewers were working.[32]

When all this evidence has been taken into account, it is possible for historians to use films to extend and deepen their understanding of the twentieth century and in particular of the attitudes of the 'silent majority' to such important issues as masculinity and femininity, peace and war, life and death, love and work.

Notes

1   Raymond Durgnat, *Films and Feelings* (1967), p. 135.
2   Quoted in John E. Connor and Martin A. Jackson (eds), *American History/American Film* (1979), p. ix.
3   For a good introduction to the study of film and history see Paul Smith (ed.), *The Historian and Film* (1976); Nicholas Pronay and D. W. Spring (eds), *Propaganda, Politics and Film, 1918–45* (1982); K. R. M. Short (ed.), *Feature Films as*

History (1981); Pierre Sorlin, *The Film in History: Restaging the Past* (1980); R. C. Raack, 'Historiography as cinematography', *Journal of Contemporary History*, 18, 1983, pp. 411–38.

4 Quoted in Anthony Aldgate, *Cinema and History: British Newsreels and the Spanish Civil War* (1979), p. 193.

5 Quoted in Aldgate, *Cinema and History*, p. 8.

6 Christopher Roads, 'Film as historical evidence', *Journal of the Society of Archivists*, 3, 1966, pp. 183–91.

7 Aldgate, *Cinema and History*. Also on newsreels see Raymond Fielding, *The American Newsreel, 1911–67* (1972); Luke McKernan, *Topical Budget* (1992); Rachael Low, *Films of Comment and Persuasion of the 1930s* (1979).

8 Board of Trade, Minutes of Evidence taken before the Departmental Committee on Cinematograph Films (1936), p. 89.

9 On the documentary movement see in particular Paul Swann, *The British Documentary Film Movement, 1926–45* (1979); Ian Aitken, *Film and Reform: John Grierson and the Documentary Film Movement* (1990); Alan Lovell and Jim Hillier, *Studies in Documentary* (1972); Rachael Low, *Documentary and Educational Films of the 1930s* (1979).

10 *Cinematograph Act, 1927: Report of a Committee appointed by the Board of Trade*, Cmd 5320 (1936), p. 4.

11 Arthur Marwick, *Class: Image and Reality* (1980), p. 22.

12 *Ibid.* On cinema and the mass market see in particular Richard Maltby, *Harmless Entertainment* (1983).

13 Hortense Powdermaker, *Hollywood the Dream Factory* (1951), p. 13.

14 J. S. R. Goodlad, *A Sociology of Popular Drama* (1971), p. 7.

15 For good historical analyses of Nazi propaganda films see Richard Taylor, *Film Propaganda: Soviet Russia and Nazi Germany* (1979); David Welch, *Propaganda and the German Cinema, 1933–45* (1983); Erwin Leiser, *Nazi Cinema* (1974).

16 Rudy Behlmer (ed.), *The Sea Hawk*, Wisconsin/Warner Brothers Screenplay series (1982).

17 Lary May, *Screening out the Past*, 1982. Other American studies taking the same approach include Kevin Brownlow, *Behind the Mask of Innocence* (1990); Nick Roddick, *A New Deal in Entertainment* (1983); Andrew Bergman, *We're in the Money* (1971); Martin A. Jackson and John E. Connor (eds), *American History/American Film* (1979); Peter C. Rollins (ed.), *Hollywood as Historian* (1983); Philip Davies and Brian Neve (eds), *Cinema, Politics and Society in America* (1981).

18 Charles Barr, *Ealing Studios* (1977). Other British cinema studies taking a contextual approach include Jeffrey Richards, *Age of the Dream Palace: Cinema and Society in Britain, 1930–39* (1984); Robert Murphy, *Realism and Tinsel: Cinema and Society in Britain, 1939–48* (1989); John Hill, *Sex, Class and Realism: British Cinema, 1956–63* (1986); Anthony Aldgate and Jeffrey Richards, *Best of British: Cinema and Society, 1930–70* (1983).

19 Michael Balcon, 'The function of the producer', *Cinema Quarterly*, 2, Autumn 1933, pp. 5–7.

20 Andrew Tudor, *Image and Influence* (1974), p. 76.

21 Durgnat, *Films and Feelings*, p. 138. On the phenomenon of stars see Richard Dyer, *Stars* (1979); Edgar Morin, *The Stars* (1960); Alexander Walker, *Stardom*

(1974).

22 Jackie Stacey, *Star Gazing* (1994).

23 On propaganda and the cinema in World War I see Nicholas Reeves, *Official British Film Propaganda during the First World War* (1986); on World War II see Anthony Aldgate and Jeffrey Richards, *Britain can take it* (1994); Philip M. Taylor (ed.), *Britain and the Cinema in the Second World War* (1988), Nicholas Pronay and Frances Thorpe, *British Official Films in the Second World War* (1980), and Antonia Lant, *Blackout: Reinventing Women for Wartime British Cinema* (1991). On the Office of War Information see Clayton R. Koppes and Gregory D. Black, *Hollywood goes to War* (1987).

24 *The Bioscope*, 21 November 1919.

25 *British Board of Film Censors, Annual Report*, 1919, p. 3.

26 On censorship see J. C. Robertson, *The British Board of Film Censors, 1896–1950* (1985); J. C. Robertson, *The Hidden Screen* (1989); Annette Kuhn, *Cinema, Censorship and Sexuality, 1909–25* (1988); Leonard J. Leff and Jerold L. Simmons, *The Dame in the Kimono: Hollywood Censorship and the Production Code from the 1920s to the 1960s* (1990); Gregory D. Black, *Hollywood Censored* (1994).

27 N. Pronay, 'The "moving picture" and historical research', *Journal of Contemporary History*, 18, 1983, p. 388.

28 Siegfried Kracauer, *From Caligari to Hitler* (1947).

29 See, for instance, Andrew Taylor, *Image and Influence* (1974).

30 Jeffrey Richards and Dorothy Sheridan (eds), *Mass-Observation at the Movies* (1987).

31 *World Film News*, December 1936, p. 4.

32 John Ellis, 'Art, culture and quality', *Screen*, 19 (3), autumn 1978, pp. 9–49.

Chapter 36

Television and contemporary history

Margaret Scammell

On the face of it, television offers sparkling source potential for contemporary historians. Television archives would seem to contain a wealth of evidence for the study of post-World War II political, social and economic history. From visual records of specific events to broader testimony of the spirit of the times, the inventory of potentially useful material is impressive. One can think of: news, with its eye-witness cameras, oral testimony from participants and elite political actors; documentaries, often the source of new evidence and important social documents in their own right; dramas, comedies, soap operas as evidence of social concerns and public attitudes; the fiction and non-fiction texts themselves, as reflections of their particular eras; routine coverage of political events, such as speeches, party conferences, debates in the Houses of Parliament and their committees; reconstructions of the recent past and portraits of participants in events through documentary and drama. The list goes on.

Moreover, television's passion for anniversaries has paid recent dividends with a host of programmes, aired or in preparation, commemorating World War II and celebrating the end of the millennium. 'History becomes sexy,' as the television trade weekly, *Broadcast*, put it.[1] Historians, however, seem rather less charmed by television. There is a relatively small, although increasing, academic literature concerned primarily with the history of British television, focusing on its organisation, leading personalities and relations with governments and parties. Outside that, however, television sweeps in and out like a bit-part actor in the main corpus of contemporary history. Its importance is sometimes acknowledged in passing, but it tends not to be cited or referred to in the routine way that the press and literary sources are. A complaint heard over the years from current affairs journalists is that their work, when mentioned at all, tends to be quoted from printed sources rather than from the original programme.[2]

History's relatively modest contribution contrasts with the mass of literature already accumulated and emerging with ever-increasing velocity from academic departments of media, cultural studies and social and political science. New material, on almost every conceivable aspect of television's political, social and cultural significance proliferates faster than even than professional academics can keep up with. Fortunately, there is much that is extremely valuable, and a good deal of the reading recommended here comes from media researchers not primarily recognised as historians.

We suggest (below) some of the reasons why historians have been relatively slow to engage with television. At this point, however, it may be helpful to spell out the purposes and organisation of this chapter. The following pages offer a guide to new researchers, based upon the answers to the following questions. How *is* television currently used by historians? In what ways *might* it be exploited more fully? What are the particular *guidelines* for approaching television evidence? In the process we will point to some key areas of contemporary debate and interest in TV, and will recommend introductory secondary sources and follow-up bibliographies. The chapter ends with a discussion of archives and lists the most accessible and user-friendly libraries. These few pages cannot hope to offer a comprehensive overview of television in all its vastness. This is an introductory piece, and to some extent exploratory, because there is so little written directly on the subject of television (rather than cinema) and historians. With these qualifications in mind, let us begin.

Historians and television: the obstacles

An immediate stumbling block for researchers is accessibility. There is no single central archive which holds all the British television programmes. Catalogues and subject indices even in the best available video libraries are nowhere near as comprehensive as for newspapers. Locating material is often time-consuming and expensive. Even when the researcher knows precisely the name and date of the desired programme, she/he may be forced to rely on the grace and favour of the television companies for a viewing, never mind a copy. A second important practical difficulty is the impossibility (as yet!) of replicating moving pictures and sound on the written page.[3] The act of producing a written text from moving pictures requires translation, from a 'system with several components into a system with only one – language', and, as Pierre Sorlin suggests, that is often unsatisfactory.[4]

A third reason seems superficially plausible. Television is relatively new. Television's emergence as the dominant mass medium dates from around 1960, and thus the television era begins where history ends in many colleges and schools, notwithstanding the reference to television in the national curriculum guidelines. However, as Ken Ward points out, historians are latecomers not just to television but more generally to debates about the role and function of the mass media.[5] Historians, suggests Ward, were reluctant to venture into territory made unfamiliar by frameworks of analysis established by literary critics and social scientists, deterred by the often impenetrable language and wary of the tendency to spin general theory from particular evidence.

A fourth reason concerns the status of visual evidence itself. This issue is far more developed in cinema debates,[6] where a number of historians have struggled to establish the value of film evidence alongside the traditional repertoire of written archives. Sorlin, a vigorous advocate of film,[7] argues that historians must take an interest in audio-visual material if they do not want to become 'rejected by society as the representatives of an outmoded erudition'. Others – for example, Peter Bucher[8] – criticise the limited focus of mainstream political history, fixed on the state and high politics. Thus the most revered sources are official documents, records and other material pertaining to the state. As a consequence, apart from its use as propaganda, film has been 'rejected' as a source of historical evidence. Bucher's critique is directed at Germany and the overlooked significance of cinema for the study of the Nazi period. However, his main point – and his methodical approach to the use of film evidence – have some force also for Britain and television.

Television and its uses to historians

Broadly, television now interests historians in three main ways: first, as a topic and industry worthy of study in its own right; second, as a provider of evidence, particularly for the study of political and social history; third, as a provider of history programmes. There is some overlap between these categories but they nonetheless offer serviceable starting points.

The history of television

The twentieth century has been in a state of near-permanent communications revolution but over the last thirty years television has held the undisputed crown as the dominant mass information and entertainment medium. Watching the box is the single most time-consuming leisure pursuit in Britain, and, indeed, most of the industrialised world.[9] Almost every British home has one television, most have two, and, on average, Britons spend about twenty-four to twenty-five hours a week viewing. The Independent Television Commission's annual audience surveys confirm that television is overwhelmingly the most important media source of national and international news.[10] Television is also, more arguably, the main medium of political communication. Despite the continuing strength of the national press, there can be little doubt that political presentation and election campaigning have been transformed in direct response to the camera's 'hot probing eye', in the memorable description of Harold Macmillan.[11] Politicians have had to come to terms with the new skills of public communication demanded by television and its ability to create at least the illusion of intimacy with leaders. Undeniably, television is one of the most significant aspects of the political and cultural transformations of the post-war era. Colin Seymour-Ure suggests further that the history of this entire period 'could be seen very largely as a process of adjustment by and to television'[12]

The leading historian in the British field is Asa Briggs with his monumental five-volume *History of Broadcasting in the United Kingdom*,[13] which traces the development of broadcasting from its radio origins to the first two decades of television compeition, ending in 1974.[14] Lord Briggs's *The BBC: the First Fifty Years*[15] is more than a one-volume distillation aimed at a less specialist audience, and it contains a useful chronology of BBC milestones and extensive bibliographical notes. Bernard Sendall and Jeremy Potter's four-volume history *Independent Television in Britain*[16] is the major secondary source for commercial television. Paddy Scannell and David Cardiff's excellent *A Social History of British Broadcasting, 1922–39* deals primarily with radio. However, the authors have extended into the television era their general thesis of the BBC as 'social cement', consciously fostering national unity and promoting a common culture.[17]

A number of authors highlight the contrast between the development of the press and television:[18] the press privately owned, partisan, largely unregulated by law and unprotected in the market place; television a state–private duopoly, far more tightly corseted by regulation and funded by protected monopolies of revenue, the licence fee for the BBC and advertising for Independent Television (ITV). Commercial television came on the air in 1955, inheriting by law much the same terms of public service as the BBC had already established, by convention and conviction. It was obliged to be politically impartial and balanced, and commanded to include in its programming schedules a specified and wide range of fare. Channel 4, since its inception in 1981, has been governed by a special remit to innovate and provide for minorities.

The 1980s and early 1990s brought revolutionary challenges to the broadcasting duopoly. The purposes and funding of the BBC were put under sustained scrutiny, from the Peacock committee (1986) to the 1994 White Paper guaranteeing favourable renewal of the corporation's charter.[19] The commercial sector was re-regulated by the Broadcasting Act 1990, facing new competition from satellite and cable channels (and the planned Channel 5) and additional pressures from cross-media mergers and concentration of ownership at both international and national levels. These developments fuelled and refuelled new and old debates about the appropriate role of broadcasting in democratic society.[20] They also provoked debate on such questions as the importance of public service, regulated 'quality' versus free markets and consumer sovereignty, and the likely consequences, good and bad, of the multiplication of niche-targeted cable and satellite channels.[21] For an authoritative starting place see Seymour-Ure's *The British Press and Broadcasting since 1945*. Stephen Barnett and Andrew Curry's *Battle for the BBC*[22] is a well researched account of the tensions within and pressures on the BBC, and includes a useful bibliography for the period.[23] Lady Thatcher's *The Downing Street Years* contains an unmissable statement of her reasons for shaking up the 'cosy duopoly'.[24] A number of journalists have also supplied entertaining and informative accounts of the ITV franchise battle, the growth of satellite television and the emergence of the global media moguls.[25] Additionally, important sources for the entire post-war period are provided by the memoirs and biographies of leading management figures in television.[26]

Television as historical evidence

Politics and persuasion

The strongest branch of historical interest in media concerns political attempts to control the flow of information and shape public opinion. Studies of twentieth-century propaganda have flourished over the last decade, focusing on press, cinema and radio during the two World Wars and the inter-war period. The literature on television and official propaganda is also dominated by military conflict, although with relatively few contributions from professional historians (*pace* Philip Taylor's study of the Gulf War[27]); rather more from social science, media studies and journalists (e.g. Valerie Adams on the media and the Falklands; Liz Curtis and Northern Ireland; Philip Knightley on war correspondents; Robert Harris on the Falklands; the Glasgow University Media Group on television coverage of the Falklands; the Index on Censorship special edition on the Gulf War; Mercer *et al.*'s *Fog of War*; Morrison and Tumber's sociological study of news reporting in the Falklands; Morrison on television and the Gulf; Philip Schlesinger on media–state relations and political violence.[28]

The regular, often fraught, nature of government relations with television is taken up in the orthodox histories mentioned above.[29] Celebrated flashpoints are highlighted in valuable accounts from journalists, sometimes involved as participants (e.g. Leapman's *Last Days of the Beeb*, Cockerell's *Live from Number 10* Roger Bolton's account of the furore in the wake of *Death on the Rock*, and Grace Wyndham Goldie's enduring *Facing the Nation*[30]). Recent years have witnessed increasing interest in government public relations, advertising and news management.[31] The memoirs of No.10 press secretaries, Joe Haines, Sir Bernard Ingham, Harold Evans and, although she was not formally press adviser, Marcia Williams, are also important sources.[32]

Television's transformation of electioneering is well known: the campaign on television is now the national campaign, to borrow the comment which seems to have appeared in every volume of the Nuffield general election series since the 1960s. Both the Nuffield studies and the more recent general election series on political communication offer chapters specifically on broadcasting and its election coverage, insights from the parties' campaign teams and general overviews of the campaigns.[33] For broader perspectives on what has come to be known as political marketing, see Franklin's *Packaging Politics* and Scammell's *Designer Politics*.[34] There are also a number of important books from former party communication managers, mostly (*pace* Des Wilson) from the Conservative camp.[35]

At some point the researcher is sure to ask about media effects: to what extent can television influence behaviour, change attitudes, increase/alter political knowledge or, by setting the agenda, influence what people think about, if not what they think? There is no space here to do justice to these questions, but Denis McQuail's classic *Mass Communication Theory* is the standard starting place and contains an unsurpassed bibliography.[36] McQuail provides an excellent introduction also to the theories of the media's relations with the state, debates which by and large have been bypassed by historians.[37]

Broader views

The propaganda, political marketing and journalistic approaches all fit fairly comfortably into the traditional historical focus on politics. In each there is clear intertwining of television as historical subject and source of historical evidence. However, social and political historians occasionally dip into television for a broader range of supporting material: for information, oral testimony, descriptive colour and historical atmosphere. The first two are straightforward: one may think of any number of examples; Thames Television's *Death on the Rock* springs to mind, with its challenge to the official version of the killing of four IRA terrorists in Gibraltar; or the oral testimony in recent contemporary historical documentaries about Neil Kinnock, Barbara Castle or Margaret Thatcher.[38] The third and fourth categories require more explanation.

A rough sample of contemporary histories suggests *That was the Week that Was* must rank near the top of historians' favourite television references, and Arthur Marwick is typical in his citation of it as an exemplar of the 1960s mood of youthful irrevence towards old-established (Tory) authority.[39] Ben Pimlott capitalises on *TW3*'s reputation to add spice to his description of Harold Wilson: 'both were cheeky, chirpy upstarts who outraged and stimulated by the audacity of their attacks'.[40]

I cite this example not to suggest that Pimlott and Marwick are wrong necessarily, but as a reminder of the ephemeral nature of much television programming. Generations under the age of forty will scarcely remember *TW3*, and its audacity is unlikely to leap self-evidently from today's screens, even were it to be repeated. However, television is clearly important for understanding personality, offering irreplaceable evidence of looks, mannerisms and style. It can supply powerful, perhaps even pivotal, images of personalities and events. Neil Kinnock will forever curse himself for the over-exuberance captured on cameras at the Sheffield rally in the 1992 election.[41] Michael Dobbs claims that a pivotal point in Mrs Thatcher's premiership was the image of her announcing to the cameras, 'We have become a grandmother.' It 'chilled the hearts of many loyal followers' because it brought the shock of recognition that she had become hopelessly remote and out of touch.[42] Most graphically, the unforgettable image of the Vietcong sympathiser being shot through the head has been claimed as a crucial moment in the encouragement and legitimisation of anti-Vietnam War protest.[43]

Less dramatically, television offers a vast reservoir of evidence virtually untapped by historians other than media specialists. Sorlin, talking of cinema, might equally be describing television as a tremendous source of evidence of 'how the society we are dealing with defined itself, how it interpreted its own situation'.[44] British documentary, with its tradition of social enquiry and self-conscious attempt to hold a mirror up to society, is one clearly promising repository. There is also a developing literature on documentary, looking at its history, subject matter and continuing quest for realism.[45] Soap opera, popular sitcom and drama could also perform a similar function. Arthur Marwick cites *Coronation Street* as evidence of the emergence of working-class life into the cultural mainstream.[46] Equally soaps are testimony to social attitudes and concerns of the day: sex equality, teenage sex, homosexuality, unemployment, drug abuse, wife battering, race relations, and so on, emerge as soap topics in a way that is not random. LeMahieu's analysis of popular Edwardian period dramas (*The Forsyte Saga, Upstairs, Downstairs, Testament of Youth, Shoulder to Shoulder*) demonstrates ways in which fiction relates to contemporary concerns.[47]

Television is also an under-exploited source of evidence of public opinion. For example, the popularity of the Alf Garnett character in the enormously successful 1960s comedy series *Till Death us do Part* speaks at least as eloquently as opinion surveys about attitudes towards immigration.[48] Finally, television fiction is thought to contribute significantly to popular understanding and misunderstanding of politics and government, and David Butler claims as much for *Yes, Minister*.[49] Of course, it is not known with any precision what understandings mass audiences take from television. Even when it is clear that programmes are an important source of public information, such as the news, it is difficult to generalise about the kinds of knowledge gleaned, ignored, forgotten or reinterpreted.[50] However, content analysis can illuminate the types of message disseminated in popular programmes, and that in itself may be important information.[51]

This is a mere sampling of historians' uses and potential uses of television. It does not attempt to be a comprehensive list and comes nowhere near to exhausting the possibilities. However, it may trigger the imagination, for fiction as well as non-fiction, and highlight some problem areas for television evidence.

Contemporary history on television

Television is unquestionably the most popular medium for the dissemination of information about the recent past.[52] Yet the point made by Donald Watt in 1976[53] remains valid in 1995: there is a distinct lack of serious criticism of history programmes on television. A debate threatened to ignite in the early 1980s. Watt, himself involved as a consultant on programmes and a supporter of tele-history, pinpointed four fundamental 'curses' of the small screen: the 'amateur' historical views of programme makers, the distortions wrought by the battle for ratings, the desire to entertain mass audiences and 'contempt' for the intelligence of viewers, and the need to spread heavy production costs through international co-production deals and overseas sales.

Colin McArthur located tele-history and, for that matter, television generally among the ideological apparatus of the state.[54] Tele-history was informed by the inadequacies of 'liberal historiography'. Thus television presented history as a series of unique events, emphasised the role of historical accident, concentrated on the political and military concerns of the nation-state, relied heavily on the testimony of individuals, usually drawn from among the great and the good, and was infused with the idea of progress and the inviolability of chronological monism (the splitting of history into periods which may be explained in terms of themselves). Bennett *et al.* also drew attention to the 'structured absences' of television: imperialism, as opposed to colonialism, labour history, and feminist history, for example.[55]

It is high time there was a re-examination of history on television: partly to assess the contribution of BBC2 and Channel 4, which have made efforts to draw on a wider range of subjects and points of view, with feminist, minority group and labour history; partly because Marxist and radical critiques of television have been substantially revised since McArthur's Althusser-inspired critique; and partly because of television's resurgent interest in history with the World War II commemorations and the ambitious social history *The People's Century*.[56] At the time of writing the BBC was in the final stages of preparation for this twenty-six-episode, £10 million epic end to the millennium. In cost and scale only *World at War* can compare.

There are signs that television's attitude towards history has matured since the early 1980s; that it has become more ambitious, more willing to recognise and supplement the inevitable shortcomings of the screen product. Contrast the defensiveness of Jerry (producer, *World at War*) Kuehl's response to Watt[57] with the more relaxed, co-operative manner of Denys

Blakeway (writer/producer, *Thatcher: the Downing Street Years*) in his interview with Anthony Seldon, even though they reach remarkably similar conclusions about the requirements and limitations of good television.[58] Moreover, some omissions from Blakeway's series will be made good, in significant measure, by his donation to the Institute of Contemporary British History of unaired interviews and background material. There would be enormous benefit to historians if that were to become normal procedure. At the time of writing the BBC was also considering ways in which the mass of unused research for *The People's Century* might be made available to schools and universities. There is clearly a golden opportunity for contemporary history.

Using television as historical evidence

Len Masterman wrote more than ten years ago, 'We are fast approaching the time when skills in "reading the media" will be part of the established repertoire of all students and teachers of history.'[59] Yet, Masterman's remains one of the few pieces of work directed at questions of how and why historians may use television as a source. Paul Smith's edited volume *The Historian and Film* and McArthur's *Television and History* both offer valuable discussion of the nature of film evidence, although both concentrate on the inadequacies of 'tele-history'.[60] For guidance on the broader uses of television as historical evidence one can also turn to the literature on newsreels and feature films.

Assume for the moment that the practical problem of accessibility has been overcome: how then should the researcher approach television evidence? The warning which Bucher offers for film, that 'the complete film-making process must be taken into account', applies equally to television. It is a mass medium of entertainment, information, opinion and persuasion. These elements are built into the product and are difficult to separate out, even in respect of news and current affairs with their requirements of balance and impartiality. Television is no different in this regard from other mass media, film, radio and the press.

However, the 'complete process' involves features which are peculiar to television. Jerry Kuehl suggests the uniqueness of television when he explains the knowledge required for good producers:

> The first thing the good learn is that what they make are television programmes; that is to say works which should follow the rules of television – which are not at all the same as those that govern the production of learned articles, or indeed, purely literary works of any sort. The second thing they learn is that their audience is a mass audience ...[61]

For Kuehl, the rules of television require good pictures and pace: 'episode follows upon episode, without respite', leaving the audience 'virtually no

time for reflection'. Hence television is good for telling stories and anec-
dotes, creating mood and offering diffuse impressions. It is not good for
detailed analysis of complex events and 'quite hopeless at portraying
abstract ideas'. One could (Watt does) take issue with Kuehl's presumption
of mass audience (low) intelligence, as also with his total banishment of
complex explanation and abstract ideas. However, it remains a fair description of the producer's approach and, often, the end product.

The researcher will find, as a general rule, that the television evidence
alone is rarely sufficient. Cross-checking of sources and information is part
of the normal process of historical discovery. In addition, however, s/he
may also need to delve into the making of the programme. The guidelines
which Bucher sets out for newsreel are generally applicable to television,[62]
and usefully supplement the five areas of enquiry set out by Seldon in the
Blakeway interview. First, establish the intended audience, and its social
characteristics.[63] Identify the producer, his/her political viewpoint and
objectives for the programme. Establish the context in which it was made,
including the technical and financial constraints, political pressures and
conditions of censorship, whether external, institutional or self-imposed.
Next come the mechanics: the criteria for research, interviews, filming, cutting and editing. Often the researcher may need to undertake a kind of content analysis of the programme itself: the commentary, the use of symbols,
music and background sound, archive footage, camera angles and close-
ups, and so on. Karl Stamm's suggestion for the content analysis of newsreel, broken down into commentary, images and sounds, is equally useful
for television news, documentary and other factual programming.[64]

There are reasonably accessible sources for much of this information,
other than that self-contained in the film. Many television producers and
journalists are more than willing to be interviewed, and the researcher who
is fortunate and quick off the mark may also get access to background
material. Additionally, there are the published sources. Both the BBC and
ITC publish periodocally updated codes and guidelines for producers which
set out the corporate view on, for example, the achievement of accuracy,
the difference between first and second-hand sources, impartiality, coverage of controversial and sensitive issues. The BBC Archives at Caversham
hold written programme files from initial idea to assessments of the finished
programmes until 1969. There is no equivalent for ITV, although the ITC
library has an extensive collection of periodicals and press cuttings and
some programme publicity material. There are also several specialist magazines and journals: the *Historical Journal of Film, Radio and Television* and
Media, Culture and Society are the leading academic journals; *Broadcast*
magazine is useful for information on programme costs, ratings, television
personalities and political pressures; *Index on Censorship* and *British Journalism Review* offer more considered articles; and the *Listener*, *Radio Times*
and *TV Times* provide schedules, programme information and reviews. Lord

Briggs, once again, is an invaluable source, for both information and bibliography.

Into the archives

The British Universities Film and Video Council is the most welcoming, and probably most useful, place to begin a search. It has a reference library, a non-fiction film and television archive, publishes the *Researcher's Guide to British Film and Television Collections*, and produces films made by historians for higher educational use. It also keeps holdings of virtually all BBC1, BBC2, ITV and Channel 4 programmes for up to two months after transmission. The British Film Institute National Film Archive has the most extensive programme collection: all BBC output since August 1990, and since 1985 much peak-time viewing from all four major channels. It is also to inherit collections from ITV from 1965 onwards. Its collection is not subject-indexed, although it will eventually gain access to the BBC computerised catalogue. Viewing at both the NFA and the BUFVC is charged at an hourly or half-hourly rate. Access to the broadcasters' own archives is both limited and extremely expensive, although the video-for-sale catalogues have expanded rapidly in recent years and may be worth checking.

The BBC's Written Archives Centre holds programme and policy files (not publicly available beyond the 1960s), and programme scripts and news bulletins since 1954. Access is by appointment only, and needs to be booked well in advance. The ITC library is more accessible, although with far less valuable holdings.[65]

There are a number of other more specialised collections: Glasgow University Media Group has kept main news bulletins since 1975; Leeds University has extensive general election and party political broadcast holdings; and the TV History Centre keeps popular history videos – for example, the 'Brixton tapes', in which Brixton residents give their own versions of events in the riots. For details and contact numbers of these and all other archives see the *Researcher's Guide to British Film and Television Collections*.

Notes

1 Rachel Murell, 'History becomes sexy', *Broadcast*, 26 February 1993.
2 The former BBC journalist Michael Cockerell, in particular, has argued this.
3 Rapid advances in computers and compression technology mean that multimedia is the foreseeable future, with historians' work published on CD-ROM, for example, complete with moving pictures, sound, endless footnotes and whatever other accompaniments the author desires.
4 Pierre Sorlin, *The Film in History: Restaging the Past* (1980), p. 5.
5 Ken Ward, *Mass Communications and the Modern World* (1989), p. 4
6 See, e.g., Karsten Fledelius *et al.* (eds), *Studies in History, Film and Society*, 1, *His-*

tory and the Audio-visual Media (1979); K. R. M. Short and Karsten Fledelius, *Studies in History, Film and Society, 2, History and Film, Methodology, Research Education* (1980); John E. O'Connor and Martin Jackson, *Discussions on Teaching: Teaching History with Film* (1974); K.R.M. Short, *Feature Films as History* (1981); Pierre Sorlin, *The Film in History*. See also *Historical Journal of Film, Radio and Television*, which regularly features contributions on the problems of historical authenticity in film and television drama.

7   Sorlin, *The Film in History*, pp. 3–5.

8   Peter Bucher 'Film as a source of historical authenticity', in K. R. M. Short and Stephan Dolezel (eds), *Hitler's Fall: the Newsreel Witness* (1988).

9   See Patrick Barwise and Andrew Ehrenberg, *Television and its Audience* (1988), pp. 12–14.

10 Sixty-two per cent cite television as the main source of news, compared with 17 per cent for newspapers. See Barrie Gunter and Paul Winstone, *Attitudes to Broadcasting, 1992*, Independent Television Commission Research Monograph (1993).

11 Quoted in Michael Cockerell, *Live From Number 10: the Inside Story of Prime Ministers and Television* (1988), p. 81.

12 Colin Seymour-Ure, *The British Press and Broadcasting since 1945* (1991), p. 6.

13 Asa Briggs, *The History of Broadcasting in the United Kingdom*, 5 vols (1961, 1965, 1970, 1979, 1995).

14 See also Tom Burns, *The BBC: Public Institution and Private World* (1977); B. Paulu, *British Broadcasting in Transition* (1981); A. Smith, *The Shadow in the Cave* (1976).

15 Asa Briggs, *The BBC: the First Fifty Years* (1985).

16 Bernard Sendall, *Independent Television in Britain, 1, Origin and Foundation, 1946–62* (1982); Bernard Sendall, *Independent Television in Britain, 2, Expansion and Change, 1958–68* (1983); Jeremy Potter, *Independent Television in Britain, 3, Politics and Control, 1968–80* (1989); Jeremy Potter, *Independent Television in Britain, 4, Companies and Programmes, 1968–80* (1990). Two further volumes, written by Paul Bonner, have been commissioned, with delivery due in 1996 and 1998 respectively.

17 Their view of the BBC's historic role as 'social cement' can be found in David Cardiff and Paddy Scannell, 'Broadcasting and national unity', in James Curran, Anthony Smith and Pauline Wingate (eds), *Impacts and Influences: Essays on Media Power in the Twentieth Century* (1987), pp. 157–73.

18 See, e.g., James Curran and Jean Seaton, *Power without Responsibility*, fourth edition (1991); Seymour-Ure, *The British Press*; Jeremy Tunstall, *The Media in Britain* (1983).

19 The White Paper, *The Future of the BBC* (1994), set out terms for the ten-year renewal of the BBC's royal charter. These were generally greeted as a triumph for the BBC: safeguarding existing television and radio services, guaranteeing an index-linked licence fee until the year 2001, and encouraging the corporation to expand commercial services.

20 Peter Dahlgren and Colin Sparks (eds), *Communication and Citizenship: Journalism and the Public Sphere* (1991); Nicholas Garnham, *Capitalism and Communication: Global Culture and the Economics of Information* (1990); John Keane, *Media and Democracy* (1991); Paddy Scannell, 'Public service broadcasting and

modern public life', in Paddy Scannell, Philip Schlesinger and Colin Sparks (eds), *Culture and Power: a Media, Culture and Society Reader* (1992).

21 Jay G. Blumler and T. J. Nossiter, *Broadcasting Finance in Transition: a Comparative Handbook* (1991); Jay G. Blumler (ed.), *Television and the Public Interest: Vulnerable Values in Western European Broadcasting* (1992); Samuel Brittan 'The case for the consumer market', in Cento Veljanovski (ed.), *Freedom in Broadcasting* (1989); Tony Prosser, 'Public service broadcasting and deregulation in the UK', *European Journal of Communication*, 7, 1992, pp. 173–93; Cento Veljanovski (ed.), *Freedom in Broadcasting* (1989).

22 Stephen Barnett and Andrew Curry, *The Battle for the BBC: a British Broadcasting Conspiracy?*(1994).

23 Ian Hargreaves, *Sharper Vision: the BBC and the Communications Revolution* (1993); and Tom O'Malley, *Closedown: the BBC and Government Broadcasting Policy, 1979–92* (1994).

24 Margaret Thatcher, *The Downing Street Years* (1993).

25 See, e.g., Andrew Davidson, *Under the Hammer* (1992); Peter Chippendale and Suzanne Franks, *Dished!* (1991); Christopher Hird, *Murdoch: the Fall of an Empire*, 1991; Chris Horrie and Steve Clarke, *Fuzzy Monsters* (1994); William Shawcross, *Murdoch: Ringmaster of the Information Circus* (1992).

26 See Briggs, *The BBC: The First Fifty Years* for full references.

27 Philip M. Taylor, *War and the Media: Propaganda and Persuasion in the Gulf War* (1992).

28 V. Adams, *The Media and the Falklands Campaign* (1986); Liz Curtis, *Ireland: the Propaganda War* (1984); Robert Harris, *Gotcha! The Media, the Government and the Falklands Crisis* (1983); *Index on Censorship*, 4–5 (1991), see especially John Simpson, 'Free men clamouring for chains', p. 3; Philip Knightley, *The First Casualty: from the Crimea to the Falklands: the War Correspondent as Hero, Propagandist and Myth Maker* (1989); Glasgow University Media Group, *War and Peace News* (1985); Derrik Mercer, Geoff Mungham and Kevin Williams, *The Fog of War* (1987); David Morrison and Howard Tumber, *Journalists at War: the Dynamics of News Reporting during the Falklands Conflict* (1988); David Morrison, *Television and the Gulf War* (1992); Philip Schlesinger, *Media, State and Nation: Political Violence and Collective Identities* (1991).

29 See especially Briggs, *History*, 1–5; Sendall and Potter, *Independent Television*, 14.

30 Roger Bolton, *Death on the Rock* (1990); Michael Cockerell, *Live from Number 10* (1988); Grace Wyndham Goldie, *Facing the Nation: Television and Politics, 1936–76* (1977); Michael Leapman, *The Last Days of the Beeb* (1987).

31 E.g. Michael Cockerell, P. Hennessy and D. Walker, *Sources Close to the Prime Minister* (1984); Bob Franklin, *Packaging Politics: Political Communications in Britain's Media Democracy* (1994); Peter Golding, Graham Murdock and Philip Schlesinger (eds), *Communicating Politics: Mass Communications and the Political Process* (1986); Robert Harris, *Good and Faithful Servant* (1990); Margaret Scammell, *Designer Politics: How Elections are Won* (1995).

32 Harold Evans, *Downing Street Diary* (1981); Joe Haines, *The Politics of Power* (1977); Bernard Ingham, *Kill the Messenger* (1991); Marcia Williams, *Inside No. 10* (1972).

33 David Butler and Dennis Kavanagh, *The British General Election of February*

1974, (1974); *The British General Election of October 1974* (1975); *The British General Election of 1979* (1980); *The British General Election of 1983* (1984); *The British General Election of 1987* (1988); *The British General Election of 1992*; David Butler and Anthony King, *The British General Election of 1964* (1965); David Butler and M. Pinto-Duschinsky, *The British General Election of 1970* (1971); Ivor Crewe and Martin Harrop (eds), *Political Communications: the General Election Campaign of 1983* (1986); Ivor Crewe and Martin Harrop (eds), *Political Communications: the General Election Campaign of 1987* (1989); Robert Worcester and Martin Harrop (eds), *Political Communications: the General Election Campaign of 1979* (1982); Ivor Crewe and Brian Gosschalk (eds), *Political communications: the General Election Campaign of 1992* (1995).

34 See also Dennis Kavanagh, *Election Campaigning* (1995).

35 Brendan Bruce, *Images of Power*, (1992); Harvey Thomas, *Making an Impact* (1989); Des Wilson, *Battle for Power* (1987); Lord Windlesham, *Communication and Political Power* (1966).

36 Denis McQuail, *Mass Communication Theory*, third edition (1994); see also the two seminal studies of the impact of television on voter attitudes and behaviour in Britain: Jay G. Blumler and Denis McQuail, *Television in Politics* (1968); J. Trenaman and Denis McQuail, *Television and the Political Image* (1961).

37 See James Curran, 'The new revisionism in mass communication research: a reappraisal', *European Journal of Communication*, 5 (2–3), June 1990, pp. 135–64.

38 All the interviews, including the unaired ones, conducted for the BBC's *Thatcher: the Downing Street Years* are to be given to the Institute for Contemporary British History.

39 See, e.g., Arthur Marwick, *British Society since 1945* (Penguin, 1990) p. 123.

40 Ben Pimlott, *Harold Wilson* (1992), p. 269.

41 Kinnock has repeated this view, first made public in an interview with David Dimbleby, BBC2, 5 December 1992.

42 Michael Dobbs, 'Can Mrs Thatcher survive?' *Evening Standard*, 27 October 1989.

43 See David Culbert, 'Television's Vietnam and historical revisionism in the United States', *Historical Journal of Film, Radio and Television*, 8 (3), 1988, pp. 253–67.

44 Pierre Sorlin, *The Film in History*, (1980), p. 18.

45 See, e.g., John Corner (ed.), *Documentary and the Mass Media* (1986); *id.*, (ed.), *Popular Television in Britain: Studies in Cultural History* (1991); A. Rosenthal (ed.), *New Challenges for Documentary* (1988); Elizabeth Sussex, *The Rise and Fall of British Documentary* (1976).

46 Marwick, *British Society*, p. 134.

47 D. L. LeMahieu, 'Imagined contemporaries: cinematic and televised dramas about the Edwardians in Great Britain and the United States, 1967–85', *Historical Journal of Film, Radio and Television*, 10 (3), 1990, pp. 243–56.

48 Asa Briggs, *The BBC*, p. 338

49 David Butler, 'British politics, 1945–87: four perspectives', in Peter Hennessy and Anthony Seldon (eds), *Ruling Performance* (1987), p. 327.

50 John Corner, 'Meaning, genre and context: the problematics of public knowledge in the new audience research', in James Curran and Michael Gurevitch

(eds), *Mass Media and Society* (1991).

51 See, for example, Jim Cook (ed.), *Television Sitcom*, BFI Dossier 17 (1982), p. 1.

52 There is not space here to deal with historical dramas, although it should be noted that there is a lively debate among historians about cinema and feature film re-staging of the past. See, e.g., Natalie Zeman Davis, 'Any resemblance to persons living or dead: film and the challenge of authenticity', *Historical Journal of Film, Radio and Television*, 8, (3), 1988, pp. 269–83; Fledelius *et al.*, *History and the Audio-visual Media*; John E. O'Connor and Martin Jackson, *Discussions on Teaching: Teaching History with Film* (1974); Short, *Feature Films as History*; Pierre Sorlin, *The Film in History*.

53 Donald Watt, 'History on the public screen', 1, in Paul Smith (ed.), *The Historian and Film* (1976), pp.169–76; reproduced in Rosenthal, *New Challenges for Documentary*.

54 Colin McArthur, *Television and History* (1980).

55 T. Bennett *et al.* (eds), *Popular Television and Film* (1981).

56 A BBC press officer, interviewed for this chapter, said that the programme would not be about the 'great and the good' but was designed rather to show the consequences for ordinary people ('the likes of thee and me') of momentous events.

57 Jerry Kuehl, 'History on the public screen', II, in Paul Smith (ed.), *The Historian and Film* (1976), also reproduced in Rosenthal, *New Challenges*.

58 Anthony Seldon, 'Making *The Downing Street Years*: an interview with Denys Blakeway', *Contemporary Record*, 8 (1), summer 1994, pp. 84–102.

59 Len Masterman, *Teaching the Media* (1985), p. 256.

60 Paul Smith (ed.), *The Historian and Film* (1976); McArthur, *Television History*.

61 Kuehl, 'History on the public screen', II.

62 Bucher, "Film as a source'.

63 Television, because of the relatively scarcity of channel choice, its permanent residence in nearly all our homes, and the way it is watched, generates a less socially differentiated audience than other media. Producers, even of self-styled minority programmes, must expect a signficant proportion of casual viewers, tuning in because there is nothing better on. In that sense Kuehl is correct to imply that television has a uniquely 'mass' audience.

64 Karl Stamm, 'The problem of authenticity in the German wartime newsreels' in K. R. M Short and Stephen Dolezel (eds), *Hitler's Fall: the Newsreal Witness* (1988).

65 See Jacquie Kavanagh 'BBC Archives at Caversham', *Contemporary Record*, 6 (2), 1992, pp. 341–9.

Chapter 37

British newsreels

Howard Smith

It seems extraordinary now that, only twenty-five years ago, there was little understanding among historians of the enormous importance of cinema newsreels as a source of evidence both about the events of the recent past and about their influence on the cinema-going public.[1] Yet for the whole period between the introduction of the sound newsreel by British Movietone News in June 1929 and the establishment of the mass television audience in the later 1950s, the cinema newsreels were – for the majority of the public – their most important window on the world. Quite apart from the detailed evidence provided by the newsreels of what places *looked like* and of how people *behaved* in the recent past, there is the enormously valuable evidence of how the newsreels *responded* to personalities and events, and of how they chose to *interpret* such people and events to their audience. The nature of this interpretation is all the more significant because of the newsreels' *immediacy*; they were produced at speed, often under enormous pressure, and accordingly provide us with an instant and authentic contemporary response which was shared by a mass audience.

There had, of course, been silent newsreels in the cinema since before the First World War. They were considered important enough by the government for one of the leading companies producing them to have been bought up by the War Office in 1916 to produce an official newsreel.[2] The newsreels appear to have lost a good deal of their popularity in the early 1920s, and it was the development of synchronised sound by Fox News in the United States in 1927 that suddenly revived their fortunes and revolutionised their significance.

The 1930s: audiences

By the early 1930s the cost of introducing sound had reduced the number of newsreel companies in Great Britain to five – Movietone, Pathé, Paramount, Universal and Gaumont British. All, except Gaumont British, were wholly or partly owned by American parent companies, and – apart from Paramount – there were also substantial financial connections between them. This did not mean that their editorial policies were controlled, either wholly or partly, from the United States; each newsreel company in Britain decided editorial policy itself.[3]

It is not posssible to be precise about the exact numbers of people who went to the cinema during the 1930s, but the evidence suggests that by 1939 between a third and half of the population went to the cinema *every week*; the number increased during the Second World War, and did not begin to fall substantially until the late 1950s. The cinema newsreels therefore had a circulation far exceeding that of any of the popular newspapers. More important than the sheer *size* of the audience, however, is the fact that, although by 1939 cinema-going had become (in A. J. P. Taylor's words) 'the dominant social habit of the age', cinema attendance was concentrated, especially in the 1930s, in the working-class areas of cities and in the younger age groups.

For the first time in their lives, ordinary men and women could see faraway places with their own eyes and hear famous men and women – kings, politicians, generals, industrialists – with their own ears; they could see, in other words, what appeared to be going on in the outside world. Today this is a commonplace; in the 1930s it was a truly revolutionary experience. Perhaps the most interesting example of this is the conclusion of a survey carried out amongst primary school children in the summer of 1938, which reported that '88% dislike the dictators and 55% boo when they appear' and that they 'cheer Mr. Chamberlain and President Roosevelt'. Only a generation previously such an experience – or such a reaction – would have been inconceivable.[4]

Though it is not possible to reach a conclusive judgement about the influence of the cinema newsreels on their audience, such surveys as exist – even surveys carried out by those unsympathetic to them – indicate that the cinema audience viewed them favourably. In any case, the effect of regular attendance, in the warmth and darkness of the cinema, looking at a large screen, on people with a strong tradition of communal participation in leisure time activities (which meant that audience response was a recognised feature of the cinema-going experience) and who – in the 1930s at least – were much less sophisticated, without access to radios and not accustomed to reading a broadsheet newspaper, can only have been considerable.[5]

It is important to remember that the newsreels were shown as part of a cinema programme whose primary purpose was to entertain, and that this determined both the style and the content of the newsreels. This does not, however, mean that the newsreel companies saw their function, as some commentators seem to have believed, as providing the audience with a diet of trivia and sensation.[6] The newsreels saw themselves as providing the same kind of service as the popular press, and they certainly believed that, if they wanted to influence the public, they had also – in Addison and Steele's famous phrase – to learn to entertain it. As C. T. Cummins, the editor of Paramount, wrote in 1934, 'The daily life of the whole civilised world is to be told in pictures; nothing must be omitted. But nothing must be included that the average man will not like.'[7] What was to be included and what was to be left out, and how what was included was to be described, was of course decided by the tight little oligarchy which controlled the newsreel companies. In addition the newsreels – which were issued twice weekly and were therefore put together at great speed – had frequently to resort to constructing sequences, or indeed entire stories, from material in their own substantial libraries in order to cover events and personalities in the news – in other words, to fake sequences and stories because there was simply no relevant material available.

Much of the criticism, both contemporary and more recent, of the newsreels has been based on the fact that, pretending impartiality, the companies did all they could to stress consensus, which led them inevitably to support the *status quo*. Certainly the companies, not being subject to the same process of censorship as the feature film industry, were very wary of screening anything that might provoke official displeasure lest this should result in official controls. They were concerned not to offend either local authorities or the large and influential body of independent cinema owners, both of whom frequently complained about the newsreels' content; and they were anxious not to alienate professional bodies like teachers, who were much exercised by what they saw as a potentially bad influence.

The 1930s: content

In spite of these obstacles, however, the companies managed, throughout the later 1930s, to give their audience a remarkably sophisticated picture of the personalities and events of the period. Perhaps the most interesting example, particularly since there has been so much criticism of the newsreels' coverage of the issue, is the way the companies responded to the rise of Hitler.[8] After a somewhat ambiguous response to the events of early 1933 – an ambiguity which was widely shared by the press and the public – the newsreels were quick to establish the potential threat of Nazism as early as the autumn of that year. Drawing on well established visual stereotypes of German militarism, the companies made up their minds, some time before the government or the broadsheet press, about the sinister nature of the new regime in Germany. In spite of government attempts to prevent the newsreels from challenging the official policy of appeasement, they continued – for example in the way they used German propaganda material about Hindenburg's funeral or the Saar plebiscite – to question what was really happening in Germany. When Hitler announced, in March 1935, that conscription would be introduced, the newsreels had little hesitation in presenting it as a sign that we were back on the road which had led to the First World War.

On other issues, however, the newsreel companies were prepared to co-operate closely with the government – most notably in its campaign for rearmament in the later 1930s. In spite of the tremendous hatred of war generated by memories of 1914–18, a hatred reinforced by the newsreels' own sombre celebration of the Remembrance Day ceremony every November, the companies put together a number of stories in 1935 and 1936, first encouraging men to volunteer for the armed forces and then, because of continuing public resistance to this message, attempting to convince people of the need for, and effectiveness of, air raid precautions. Events in Spain[9] and China, as well as in Germany, were also used to reinforce the government's preferred message. Finally, in 1939, when war became inevitable, the newsreels campaigned to reassure the audience that Britain was prepared for it.

Such directly propagandist use of the newsreels may seem, in the circumstances of the time, understandable – and even, with the benefit of hindsight, providential; their co-operation with the National Government for domestic political reasons during the 1930s is less excusable. This was most apparent during the 1935 election campaign when their presentation of the two party leaders was blatantly favourable to Stanley Baldwin. Interestingly it was the Conservative Party which first realised the potential power of the cinema, and Neville Chamberlain whose public reputation, especially at the time of the Munich agreement in September 1938, benefited most from his skilful exploitation of the newsreels' presentation of the issue. Indeed, the now famous newsreel account of Chamberlain's return fom Munich is both the climax of the media campaign and historical evidence of its result.[10]

More significant even than this directly propagandist use of the cinema was the way in which the newsreels saw one of their most important roles as keeping up the nation's morale in a time of great social and economic difficulty. They constantly repeated the message that, given national unity, economic recovery could be achieved without sacrificing either British democracy or traditional values. The companies lost no opportunity of celebrating what they believed these values to be – bravery, technical competence, gentlemanly conduct. Similarly, they continually compared the peace, order and freedom of Britain with the chaos, violence and uncertainty prevailing in the rest of the world.

Newsreels during the Second World War

During the Second World War the newsreels became an integral part of the government's propaganda machine. For many, like Lord Reith, who was –

briefly – Minister of Information in 1940, news was 'the shock troops of propaganda', and for the Ministry of Information the newsreels were the front line – the main weapon in maintaining the people's will to fight. In the early months of the war, when the official view seems to have been that *any* news might be of value to the enemy, the newsreels were unable to give their audience any coherent idea of what was going on; their credibility, as Mass-Observation recorded, suffered accordingly.[11] After a few months this excessively cautious attitude was changed and the Ministry developed a subtle but effective policy well summed up in its motto 'Truth, nothing but the truth, and as near as possible the whole truth'. The newsreels, as everyone in the audience knew, however, were censored, and this inevitably impaired their credibility. Worse still, for the first three years of the war there was little good news to report, and the prevailing message of relentless optimism, laced with the admission of continuing setbacks, naturally affected people's perception of the messenger. The turning of the tide in 1943, and the newsreels' capacity to judge the mood of their audience, led to some recovery of their popularity; the triumphalism of the last months of the war, which sounds strident today, undoubtedly reflected a general feeling of grim satisfaction at the complete defeat of the enemy.

The Ministry of Information also produced its own specialist newsreels, *Warwork News* and *Worker and Warfront*, for showing to people working in war industries. After the war the official view continued to be conveyed in their successor, *Britain can make it*, made by the Central Office of Information.[12]

The most interesting propaganda problems for the authorities were the way in which Britain's two great allies, the United States and the Soviet Union, were to be portrayed. Before the war, as part of their campaign to reassure the public, the newsreels had presented America as Britain's powerful and committed ally, which was simply untrue. American assistance in the first two years of the war, portrayed as an act of immense generosity, completely ignored the extremely harsh terms on which such assistance had been negotiated – terms which permanently harmed British power and influence. Throughout the war the official emphasis was always on the special – almost mystical – relationship between the two countries and on the complete equality of British and American forces. Though there was enough truth in the former proposition to make it plausible, the second became harder and harder to sustain after D Day. Trickier still was the fact that increasing numbers of American servicemen sat in British cinemas, and that any comments which might prejudice good relations between the allies were banned. In spite of all this, the newsreels were remarkably successful in striking a judicious balance between propaganda and the facts.

The Soviet Union was an even trickier subject. The Molotov–Ribbentrop pact of August 1939 seemed to be conclusive proof of the authoritarian nature of the Soviet regime and justification for the official attitude of uncompromising hostility. The initial humiliation of the Red Army by the Finns in the winter of 1940 was therefore a cause for celebration in the newsreels; Russia's victory a few weeks later was, however, passed over in silence. When Germany attacked Russia in June 1941 the line had to change. Now the newsreels had access to the most effective film propaganda in the world and with astonishing speed – and with the full support of the Ministry of Information – adopted a tone of voice almost indistinguishable from Moscow's. This was so successful that by 1943 Churchill was ordering the Ministry of Information 'to consider what action was necessary to counter the tendency of the British public to forget the dangers of Communism in their enthusiasm over the resistance of Russia'.[13] It took some time, even with the officially inspired interpretation of the early events of the Cold War, to dissipate popular feelings about the Soviet Union so carefully nurtured by official propaganda and assiduously disseminated by the newsreels.

The 1950s

Cinema audiences remained large until well into the 1950s. Even in 1956 – the year of Suez and Hungary, and a year after the establishment of commercial television – as many people were going to the pictures every week as in 1939. By 1959, however, attendances had almost halved, whereas in the same period the number of television licences more than doubled. Universal, the smallest newsreel company, had already ceased production in March 1949. Paramount produced its last issue in January 1957 and Gaumont British in January 1959. Pathé struggled on until February 1970 and Movietone survived until April 1979. By 1959, however, the newsreels had effectively ceased to be a significant factor in the formation of public opinion.

The newsreels had been tainted by their involvement in wartime propaganda, and were subjected to continuing government controls until October 1950. They quickly reasserted their independence, however, and with their traditional blend of entertainment and persuasion, continued to have some influence on public opinion in the 1950s. It is often hard to remember that, given the more deferential, still relatively unsophisticated and socially conservative character of the period, this is less surprising than it seems now. The adulatory treatment of the monarchy, the emphasis on the unique significance of the Commonwealth, the celebration of British industrial achievement, the emphasis on shared experience, whether serious – like Remembrance Day, or light-hearted – like the winter sales, echoed the tone of voice which had prevailed in the 1930s, but all these features are replicated in the surviving examples of BBC television coverage of the period. BBC Television also broadly accepted the Cold War context in which much foreign news was presented, and this frame of reference was shared by the newsreels.[14]

Gaumont British, which had probably been the most influential company before 1939, lost E. V. H. Emmett – its editor and commentator – in 1945, and with his departure the newsreel lost much of its distinctive character. Movietone, which had been closely connected with the Conservative Party in the 1930s, continued to express Conservative sympathies after 1945. Pathé, on the other hand, which was the only newsreel to make any serious attempt to adapt its style and content to the post-war situation, was also much more sympathetic to the Labour government of 1945–51. Throughout the post-war period it was much more willing to raise controversial issues like colour prejudice or the death penalty – issues which, if they had been included at all in newsreels of the 1930s, would have been treated in a much more muted way. It also gave much more time to members of the public expressing *their* views, about subjects as diverse as the lack of choice in clothes shops and the effect of the Budget on their family; if anyone in the media can claim to have invented the 'vox pop' it is Pathé News.

BBC Television Newsreel

The newsreels were already conscious of the potential threat from television in the late 1940s, a threat which was increased by the BBC's own *Television Newsreel*. This began in January 1948, and by June 1952 was being transmitted five days a week, regularly getting important stories on the air several days before the newsreels. In July 1954 the operation was taken over by the BBC's News Division and became *Television News and Newsreel*, and in 1957 it became *BBC Television News*.[15] Some commentators have claimed that the *BBC Television Newsreel* was quite different in character from the cinema newsreels, though the claim does not seem to be based on the evidence of the BBC newsreel itself; such evidence suggests that, on the contrary, the similarity between the two was quite marked. On the other hand, the *BBC Television Newsreel* was able to present stories at greater length, gave much more coverage to social issues and treated politics with considerably more seriousness than the cinema newsreels.[16]

Perhaps the most interesting comments on the character of the BBC *Television Newsreel* and its relationship to the cinema newsreels in the early 1950s are those of its head, Philip Dorté, in a letter to BBC Television's Controller of Programmes, Cecil McGivern, in July 1954. This was written just after the News Division's take-over and the first issue of their *News and Newsreel*, memorably criticised in the press as 'about as impressive visually as the fatstock prices'. Dorté had been invited to the annual lunch of the News and Specialised Theatre Group of the Cinema Exhibitors' Association, where – said Dorté – all the heads of the newsreel companies had approached him to say that 'they had not realised that the BBC was such a friend of the film industry as deliberately to prolong the life of the cinema newsreels by putting *Television Newsreel* out of production and introducing the programme now on the air'. 'I did my best,' writes Dorté, 'to make the right kind of reply', though he continues – no doubt with some satisfaction – that he 'was unable to find an adequate reply.' He adds that Howard Thomas, Pathé's producer-in-chief, told him that he had been visited 'this very morning' by Tahu Hole, the head of the BBC's News Division, 'who wished to pick his brains on the production of newsreels'. Thomas suggested, says Dorté, that 'he would do very much better to talk to me, as the speed and technique of the old *Television Newsreel* had been so far in advance of what Pathé or any other commercial reel had ever achieved'.[17] In the end, however, it was not television *news* which replaced the cinema newsreel as people's window on the world, but television *current affairs* programmes – which brought a range and depth to the presentation of social and political issues which neither the cinema newsreels nor television news could attempt, and which not only reflected such issues but raised them as well.

Notes

1 See the following articles and contributions by Nicholas Pronay: 'British newsreels in the 1930s, 1, Audience and producers', *History* 56, October 1971, pp. 411–418; 'British newsreels in the 1930s, 2, Their policies and impact', *History* , 57, February 1972, pp. 63–72; 'The newsreels: the illusion of actuality' in Paul Smith (ed.), *The Historian and Film* (1976) 'The news media at war', in Nicholas Pronay and D. W. Spring (eds), *Propaganda, Politics and Film* (1982); 'Rearmament and the British public: propaganda and policy', in James Curran, Anthony Smith and Pauline Wingate (eds), *Impacts and Influences* (1983); 'Defeated Germany in British newsreels', in K. R. M. Short and Stephen Dolezel (eds), *Hitler's Fall: the Newsreel Witness* (1988). See also J. A. S. Grenville's *Film as History* (1971) and Arthur Marwick's 'Archive film as source material' in the Open University's *Archive Film Compilation Booklet* (1973).

2 See Luke McKernan, *Topical Budget: the Great British News Film* (1992).

3 The *Researcher's Guide to British Newsreels* (1983); volume II (1988) and volume III (1993), edited by James Ballantyne, are all invaluable; they contain a very useful series of abstracts of relevant publications in the field. See also the anecdotal accounts of their careers as newsreel cameramen by Universal's (and later the BBC's) Ronnie Noble in *Shoot First: Assignments of a Newsreel Cameraman* (1955) and by Movietone's Paul Wyand in *Useless if Delayed* (1959); Leslie Mitchell's *Leslie Mitchell Reporting* (1981) includes an account of his time as Movietone's commentator. On pp. 119–47 of his *With an Independent Air: Encounters during a Lifetime of Broadcasting* (1977) Howard Thomas describes his work as producer-in-chief at Pathé between 1944 and 1955. Philip Norman's 'The newsreel boys' in *The Sunday Times Magazine* of 10 January 1971 is a well informed and amusing account of the activities of the newsreel cameramen.

4 *Today's Cinema* (2 November 1938), quoted in Pronay 'British newsreels', 2, note 26, p.72.

5 See Pronay, 'British newsreels', 2.

6　The most striking example of this attitude is on p.140 of the PEP report *The Factual Film* (1947): 'The content of the average British newsreel before the war was trivial, being devoted mostly to sport, society events and the launching of ships. The only exceptions were various sensational happenings, usually disasters, which were for the most part extremely well covered. Controversial subjects were almost entirely avoided.'

7　*Kinematograph Weekly*, 25 October 1934, quoted in Pronay, 'British newsreels', 2, p. 64.

8　See Nicholas Pronay's review (in the *BUFC Newsletter* No. 35, November 1978) of the film *Before Hindsight*, which casts grave doubt on the credentials, historical and professional, of this attempt to examine the 1930s newsreel coverage of Nazi Germany. The film's producer, Jonathan Lewis, writes about his conclusions in *Sight and Sound*, 46 (2), Spring 1977, and responds to criticisms in the *British Film Institute Production Catalogue, 1977–78* (1978).

9　See Anthony Aldgate, *Cinema and History: British Newsreels and the Spanish Civil War* (1979), though Dr Aldgate's conclusions about rearmament have been challenged by Nicholas Pronay, 'Rearmament and the British public', note 73, p. 96. Aldgate pursues the question of pro-rebel bias in the cinema newsreels in articles in *Film and History*, 3 (1), February 1973, and *History*, 58, 1973, pp. 60–3.

10　See Timothy J. Hollins, 'The Conservative Party and film propaganda between the wars', *English Historical Review*, 96 (379), April 1981, pp. 359–69; John Ramsden, 'Baldwin and film', in Nicholas Pronay and D. W. Spring (eds), *Propaganda, Politics and Film* (1982); Anthony Adamthwaite, 'The British government and the media', *Journal of Contemporary History*, 18, 1983, pp. 280–97.

11　See Jeffrey Richards and Dorothy Sheridan, *Mass-Observation at the Movies* (1987).

12　See Frances Thorpe and Nicholas Pronay (with Clive Coultass), *British Official Films and the Second World War* (1980).

13　See P. M. H. Bell, *John Bull and the Bear: British Public Opinion and the Soviet Union, 1941–45* (1990); Churchill's intervention is described on p. 43.

14　See my article 'Something has to be done: a note on research in cinema newsreels', *BUFC Newsletter*, 35, November 1978, which analyses the newsreel coverage of Germany between 1944 and 1949.

15　The story of the take-over is given in Asa Briggs, *History of Broadcasting in the United Kingdom*, IV, *Sound and Vision* (1979), pp. 588–97.

16　See my article 'The BBC Television Newsreel and the Korean War', *Historical Journal of Film, Radio and Television*, 8 (3), 1988, pp. 227–52.

17　The letter is in the BBC Archives T16/123 (TV Policy-Newsreel).

Sources

It is a particular difficulty of this subject that readers cannot, as with written material, come to their own conclusions about the evidence, since much of it is simply not accessible, except on commercial terms which will be beyond the means of academic researchers. The only major exception is that the issues of *Gaumont British News* for the period of the Second World War (and virtually all issues of *Warwork*

News and *Worker and Warfront*) are held by the Imperial War Museum, and they are available for study. The British Film Institute holds some newsreel material, as well as the issues of *Britain can make it*, which are also available for study.

The Inter-Universities History Film Consortium (which consists of eleven university history departments) has produced a series of Historical Studies in Film, which contain a large amount of newsreel material. Each film, fifty to fifty-five minutes in length, is selected, edited and scripted by historians from British universities and has accompanying explanatory notes. The consortium has also produced a number of issues of its Archive Series, which are thirty to forty-five minute compilations of unedited newsreels with the original commentary, each accompanied by a substantial booklet which gives details of the context and source of each item. Both series are available for hire from the Higher Education Film and Video Library, Scottish Central Film Library, Dowanhill, Victoria Crescent Road, Glasgow G12 9JN. They may also be purchased on video from the British Universities Film and Video Council, 55 Greek Street, London W1V 5LR, where the productions may also be previewed free of charge; the BUFVC will be pleased to provide fuller details.

Some extremely valuable compilations of newsreel material and their accompanying printed study material produced by the BBC's Continuing Education Department and by Macmillan Education with the Historical Association are no longer available. BBC Enterprises are currently investigating whether it might be possible to clear the copyright for a reissue of the four BBC series *Film as Evidence*, *Illusions of Reality* (about the 1930s), *Propaganda with Facts* (about the 1940s) and *Visions of Change* (about the 1950s) but one should not be too optimistic.

Pathé have produced a series of sixty-minute videos of each year of their newsreels from 1930 to 1969 called *A Year to Remember*; these are widely available and contain some items of interest to historians. Movietone have made a three hour compilation video, available in W. H. Smith's, of their entire newsreel output called *A Library of Twentieth Century Newsreels*, but it is of limited value. Earlier compilations from Movietone, dealing with *Major Disasters*, *The Triumph of Flight*, *The Challenge of the Sea*, etc., may still be found in some shops, but again they are of limited use to historians. Visnews (now part of Reuter's, at Cumberland Avenue, London NW10 7EH) have a few copies left of their own compilations of Gaumont British newsreels, one for each decade of the reel's existence; all contain items of interest to historians.

The British Universities Film and Television Council has published, on microfiche, *British Newsreels Issue Sheets, 1913–70: the Complete Collection held by the Slade Film History Register* (Graphic Data Publishing in association with the BUFVC, 1984). These give brief details of all the stories from the five main newsreels.

The National Film Archive holds a wide – though not particularly representative – selection of items from the BBC *Television Newsreel*, which is available to researchers. Details of the items available can be found in *Keeping Television Alive* (ed. Paul M. Madden, 1981; the booklet is unfortunately out of print).

Acknowledgements

I am grateful to Professor Nicholas Pronay for his comments on this brief summary. Anyone writing on this subject is heavily indebted to his pioneering work, some of which, sadly, still remains unpublished. I have drawn extensively on Professor Pronay's published and unpublished work, and on many conversations with him during our work between 1976 and 1983 on four BBC television series concerned with the value of cinema newsreels as historical evidence. Any errors and omissions are, of course, entirely my responsibility.

Part VII
Electronic sources

Chapter 38

Opportunities in electronic information

Seamus Ross

The dependence of contemporary society on information in electronic form continues to increase, and this shift is changing the fabric of historical source materials. From credit card data to medical records, from airline databases to tax records, from electronic mail to image and text databases, vast amounts of information about late twentieth-century society exist in electronic form. However, 94 per cent of all business information in Europe and America is on paper and the increasing use of personal computers has continued to foster a dramatic rise in the production of paper-based records.[1] The demands made on electronically stored information by local and national governments, companies, charities, service providers (e.g. medical staff) and individuals generated in 1993 in the United States alone an estimated one trillion sheets of printed matter. It reflects their need to satisfy customers, meet regulatory obligations, market services and make the most advantageous decisions. While paper continues to play a crucial role in the provision and distribution of strategic management or executive information,[2] in many other areas of business and government electronic data have become the driving force.

The capture, use and storage of operational information are already very much electronically based in businesses from banking to transport or retailing. Although paper is a by-product of most transactions involving operational information (e.g. till receipts, credit card vouchers, tickets, prescription forms, invoices and statements), these paper records include only a fragment of the material captured in electronic form during a transaction. The sheer quantity, diversity and rich quality of the electronic information resources from which such records have been derived indicates that their preservation in electronic form could provide historians with a better opportunity to understand our period than the paper records alone could ever do. Just as contemporary workers use operational information as the foundation of paper-based strategic and management reports, historians will want to have the opportunity to analyse the base data for themselves.

They will wish to examine it in ways contemporary users do not need to and to analyse it in the context of other data sets. Electronic information is a cultural product, e-facts, and it forms an essential fragment of the cultural record of contemporary society.

Since the 1960s archivists have been discussing the increasing prevalence of electronic records, and Richard Cox's review of the literature on electronic records up to 1993 is a good starting point.[3] The number of studies is increasing rapidly but the discussion is still very much driven by problems and activities in America, Canada and, more recently, Australia. The focus has been mainly on government records at national level, and the issues have been examined from the vantage of the archivist. Few studies approach the problems from the point of view of the historian; an issue of the journal *History and Computing* and *Electronic Information Resources and Historians* are two notable exceptions.[4] National governments and international organisations (e.g. the United Nations, UNESCO) were among the early users of computers to process large data sets (e.g. census data, tax records).[5] Statutory obligations require they retain their records in accessible form, and they have the financial resources necessary to experiment with such preservation. In attempting to fulfil these duties, archivists have struggled to address such record retention problems as hardware and software obsolescence, media degradation and data documentation.

The work of archivists has established the remarkable size and complexity of the problem for governmental records.[6] By the year 2000 an estimated 75 per cent of all US government transactions will be handled electronically.[7] The precise implications of this statement are not clear. (Will these be transactions of significance in recording activities, processes, and decisions? How are transactions defined? How will they be documented? What manifestation of the transaction will be preserved?) What is evident is that the transition from paper to computer-based information collection and storage is occurring across a spectrum of human activity.

Bank and credit card details, airline reservations, patient records, Inland Revenue data, satellite images, product manuals, and maps, are all examples of the variety of information encoded via a range of input devices from keyboards to scanners on a daily basis. The use of scanners by cashiers at the supermarket to read bar codes improves efficiency at the sales counter. Shop computer systems use the data to locate pricing information, calculate automatically multi-buy discounts, collect data for sales and stock accounting, perform inventory control and automated ordering, produce item-by-item profit and loss analysis, and identify the items that have attracted greatest customer demand. The electronically captured information could be valuable as a source for social history, the history of consumerism, economic history and ethnic/regional history. Robert Morris has pointed out that not only will the transactions themselves provide a remarkable resource, but how they took place (i.e. their context) will have historical significance.[8] In the commercial and the public sectors, and even at a more private level, astonishing amounts of data are being created as word processed documents, some of which are printed out, whilst others, such as e-mail, are sent over the wires and viewed only on-screen by the recipient or data user. There are some forty million users worldwide of the most commonly used electronic network, the Internet, a figure that is growing at a rate of 10 per cent per month. Little of the information available on the network is adequately archived and even less of it is suitably documented.[9]

The quantities of information being created and destroyed are staggering. For example, 'Visa International, the biggest credit-card company, handles over 6 billion electronic transactions a year, a figure that is expected to rise to 15 billion by 2000. To save itself from being swamped in data, Visa dumps its records after only six months'.[10] So far the demographic and market data contained in these records have not been fully extracted before the data are disposed of. If the commercial benefits to Visa of retaining the data do not outweigh the costs there can be little hope that such data will be accessible to historians in the future. Historians would be likely to 'mine' such a resource in different ways, examining it with change over time in mind and linking credit transaction data or travel information with say medical records or socio-economic groups. They would use the information to understand not the individual transactions recorded in the data but the society(ies) that created it.

In the United Kingdom the three large credit reference agencies, Infolink, CCN and Equifax, hold data on 100 million accounts. While much of their data relates to credit requests and fraud, an increasing amount of information details customer transactions. CCN, for instance, has a database of 43 million consumers in the United Kingdom which includes information about an individuals' creditworthiness, life style, gender, age and purchasing habits. While this information has potential for contemporary target marketing campaigns, it would be immensely valuable to historians studying late twentieth-century Britain. This would be especially so if bi-annual or annual 'snapshots' of the information survived in electronic form. The credit agencies' data provide a detailed profile of only the top two-thirds of the social hierarchy. The Department of Social Services, for instance, has a file on almost every person, and its staff and contractors process 15 million transactions every week.[11] The great bulk of these transactions relate to the poorest third of society. The combined picture offered by the credit agency and DSS data sets would provide historians with the chance to examine the full cross-section of the population.

Discussions of electronic information often focus on large numerical data sets and text files but these represent a fraction of the uses and products of electronic information. Many architects use computer-aided design/drafting (CAD/CADD) systems, and an increasing number use virtual reality systems to design and 'test' building schemes. Architectural historians will wish to have access to this material. If the information is preserved, it will be in an effort to guarantee its availability in case of legal dispute. Such preservation will be most likely where particular programs were run to determine the structural stability or the environmental efficiency of a building, or the individual or institution commissioning the structure had been asked to accept a particular design after a 'virtual visit to or walk around' the planned building. Where geographical information systems (GIS) were used to assess proposals and display data in the course of evaluating road or building development plans, not only the data must be preserved but also the software, any specialised graphics hardware, and even the virtual records that were created during the decision-making process. Since a GIS involves the storage and manipulation of spatial data as well as the use of a graphical display system (two or three dimensional data display) it is feasible that the impression conveyed by the same data used in conjunction with a different display system might be distorted and might not permit future users to comprehend the meaning that it originally communicated. It will be crucial to know about the context(s) in which the system had been used. For example, was the end user the decision-maker or not?

The trend towards downsizing is alarming because it has led to the proliferation of an estimated 176 million personal computers worldwide.[12] Although many of them are interconnected, either locally or to wide area networks, many are not, and many of those which are are used for the generation of electronic materials which are held and used locally. These computers have helped accelerate the propensity for independent users to generate text, keep spreadsheets (which may be laden with formulae that control calculations and are themselves based on discrete assumptions) and construct private databases. Increasingly emphasis is being placed on co-operative work and file sharing. The electronic versions of these documents might be crucial if the historian wanted to understand how the documents were developed, especially in those environments where networks and co-operative work software ('groupware') had been used to enhance worker performance. The final records may exist in paper format, but because the sources and the evidence for the process of document development are electronic it will be impossible to understand how the documents evolved. Linked and embedded documents pose problems as a change to one document effects a change in another. If the process of document generation is to be understood, a record of the links must be retained. As document image processing (DIP), involving the use of optical scanners, mass storage devices and networked computers, becomes a more common way to store paper information new problems will arise, because even those strategic documents and the paper products derived from the operational data will exist only in digital form.

Electronic mail is changing how we communicate, who we communicate with, the kinds of material we can exchange as part of a message, and the speed of communication. As a result electronic mail forms an important historical source.[13]. In the United States in the case of Armstrong *v.* Executive Office of the President,[14] the judge ruled that since there was information contained in electronic records (e.g. transmission and receipt data) that print-outs did not include, printed versions were not faithful to the original. He therefore required electronic mail to be preserved in electronic form. The premise underlying this decision could eventually be extended to all US government electronic information/data, either by the courts or by legislation. More private e-mail messages may be the electronic equivalent of the Paston letters that so enliven the social history of fifteenth-century England. In disciplines such as physics electronic mail plays a critical role in how the results of research are exchanged before formal publication. As a result historians of science will need more than the printed journals, they will need access to the electronic messages and data. In addition the retention of environmental data, experimental data and other scientific information will provide valuable benchmarks for future scientists, and useful resources for historians.

What constitutes a record and whether 'electronic records' are subject to the same archival principles as those applied to paper documents are two hotly debated topics.[15] Records are preserved by archivists for their evidential or legal value and not primarily for their information content. To some extent historians are more concerned with the latter. In administrative and political history the evidential value of records is extremely important, whereas for social and economic history the picture of society that the information held in the records can be used to create is more important. But even in the latter case historians still need to understand the record from which the information is derived, if only to verify its authenticity. So such archival questions as 'Where was the document created?' 'How was it created?' 'What processes were involved?' 'What was the purpose of its creation?' 'Who was it created for?' 'Who received it?' 'What effect did its receipt have?' 'Why has it survived?'[16] are equally relevant to historians and archivists.

Since the late nineteenth century archivists have argued that the order of records must reflect the functions and activities of the organisation that created the records.[17] This information is not naturally inherent in the structure of electronic records, and in the case of the records for which it was created it either does not survive or has been separated from the record itself. Is it better to talk about electronic information resources rather than records? If the term 'electronic records' is used does an electronic record consist of the record, the computer system in which it was created, its data structure, a definition of its purpose, associated hardware and software? If for electronic records the 'computer system itself is an integral part of the record'[18] then when the data or information is separated from the system in which it resided those records can be classified only as proto-records.

The definition of a record or 'proto-record' varies, depending upon the kind of 'electronic information set' with which the historian is dealing. Word-processed documents, spreadsheets, multimedia documents and relational databases are four very different kinds of record. Each requires its own definition, each tells the historian something different about the creation and use of records in contemporary society, and each will need to be used in different ways by future historians. Also, unlike paper, where records either exist or not, some electronically stored information includes 'potential records'. In Sweden these potential documents, 'which could be made available by the possibilities of combining and searching through information using computer techniques were official documents'.[19] In the case of potential or virtual records it is difficult to know not just where but even whether a particular manifestation was created, for what purpose, by whom, and when. Essentially these records exist only as a set of 'access and retrieval instructions' that may have been executed against a given data set or information base which was in 'state' x at time y. With the development of end-user computing even the questions of how a manifestation of the data was made, and why, become ever more difficult to answer. Adhering to the principle of provenance, a central tenant of archival theory, is far more complex with electronic records than it is with paper-based records.[20] The provenance of electronic records in government and business must be related to the culture and organisation that created the information. As Simpson explains 'the life cycle of many records will be a patchwork of different units creating, amending, utilising and determining disposition, possibly without knowledge of what has gone before'.[21]

To understand a document it is necessary to have information about the context of its creation and use. Contextual information will help historians answer such questions as 'Who read the document?' and 'What was the effect of its having been read?' To work effectively with electronic resources historians will need information about the form, format, medium, mode, content, context, use, and even information about how it was originally distributed in society should be retained. We have already seen that in ruling on Armstrong *v.* the President the judge stated that if only the message is retained much valuable information is lost. Printed versions of electronic records also are made at the expense of opportunities offered by the records being electronic, such as ease of searching, comparing and integrating with other electronic records. Of course even with records preserved in electronic form a great deal of documentation is essential. Often the task of documentation fails to preserve remarkably important information, such as contextual information, or details of purpose. To understand a system adequately the user requirements, functional specifications and user documentation as well as information about the behaviour of the organisation that created the resource must be retained for as long as the data are kept.

Natural and man-made forces have always played a crucial role in the survival of the historical record. Many records survive more by accident than by design, although some records have been preserved as a result of planning (i.e. for legal or administrative reasons). Electronic resources will survive in accessible form only through organised efforts at preservation.[22] Preservation requires the selection of records for retention. Are contemporary archivists, historians and records managers suitably equipped to select records to be stored for posterity? Or in the records they preserve for future historians will they pass on little more than an indication of their cultural myopia as certain types of records are selected for preservation at the expense of others? The selection criteria of 'administrative, legal, and information value' as well as long-term research potential used by the National Archives and Records Administration in the United States are similar to the appraisal strategies used by other national archives.[23] Technical issues such as quality of data set/resource documentation and the uniqueness of the operating system, software or hardware environment needed to access/use the information should also be considered when selecting records. Magnetic and optical media appear to have a far shorter life than parchment or paper. In the case of magnetic media the signal degrades, and the access mechanisms become obsolete as new standards of storage and access evolve. Access to information on paper tapes, punch cards and magnetic tapes all require the continuing availability of suitable devices, and for some of these media the devices are already no longer available. Magnetic media degrade if not stored properly, tapes stretch, signals are destroyed by contact with magnetic fields, and even optical media can be damaged through poor storage or the breakdown of the dye layer on the disc. Each new medium is likely to have its own built-in obsolescence, whether the deficiencies are inherent or merely the result of replacement by newer and more efficient technologies.

Overcoming the problems of hardware and software obsolescence, media degradation, support and documentation makes the preservation of electronic records expensive. These are not costs which necessarily decrease with time, either. Electronic resources require continual attention; left unattended, they quickly become inaccessible. To assume that material in electronic form will be available for future researchers is to underestimate the economic cost of transferring records from one medium to another, and the problems of suitably documenting them, as well as to overestimate the benefits an organisation will receive from ensuring the continued availability of its records.

Where there is economic advantage in reusing information there will be an easy business case for the preservation of records. Visa credit card records do not yet appear to have long-term reusable value. Few business data are likely to survive, as few of them have a 'value life' to the creating organisation of more than five years. Financial institutions typically save information only where legal or business requirements make it necessary or useful. This is not a trend new to electronically based information: many businesses in the past disposed of paper records when they had served their useful life. Often it is only when disposal did not go as planned that their existence or the fact that they once existed comes to the historian's attention.

Edward Higgs's unpublished survey of efforts by European national archives to preserve electronic information indicates just how limited such efforts are.[24] Whether government departments retain information that exists only in electronic form often depends upon whether electronic documents or information resources are classed as 'official documents'. In Sweden, for example, there is no difference between electronic and paper records, and both must be retained in an accessible form.[25] Where governments retain electronic records it is usually because national legislation requires their preservation. Even then not all records are preserved. In the United States a survey conducted in 1989–90 by the National Academy for Public Administration for the National Archives found more than 9,000 databases in use throughout the agencies of the federal government. Of these some 1,789 were considered major databases, but the NAPA team thought only 919 of them worthy of examination by a panel of experts to determine whether or not they should be preserved. After this examination the panel of experts concluded that only 448 were worth transferring to the National Archives.[26] Legal issues play a role in the preservation and destruction of the contemporary cultural heritage. They include rights of access, rights of privacy, statutory requirements covering record retention, and the need to secure records for use as evidence in the event of a legal dispute. Some laws, such as the United Kingdom's Data Protection Act, which states that data shall not be kept longer than is necessary for the purposes for which they were collected, encourage the destruction of data. Similar laws exist in other countries such as Norway.[27]

Record retention will lead to a skewed vision of the contemporary world. Besides governments, it is likely that only the largest companies will engage in any kind of record retention and archive management. Companies retain records to meet organisational needs, to fulfil statutory requirements, and to provide evidence in case of dispute. Often they discard compromising data and overlook the need to store certain classes of records. For most small firms the preservation of records beyond the periods stipulated by law will be impossible, but some would argue that it will not really matter because if sufficient government records survive in electronic form there will be enough data for historians to build a picture of the economic and social history of small business in general.

The variety of record categories (e.g. environmental records, electronic point of sale (EPOS) data, health records, criminal court records) is quite large. The range of record types (e.g. e-mail, text files, databases, still images moving images, and audio) expands the dimensions of the problem as they increase the spectrum of material that archivists and librarians must preserve. Documentation is essential for those electronic resources that need to preserve the integral relationships within discrete data units. Records may be held in a variety of file formats and encoded using a number of mark-up strategies. While standards are essential in some areas, such as audio, images (e.g. Photo-CD *v.* GIF *v.* TIFF), video, and numerical data, they remain in a state of flux.[28] Another area in need of standardisation is the description standards for archival data exchange.[29] Currently hypermedia and multimedia standards pose seemingly insurmountable difficulties, and this only intensifies the already complex problems involved in archiving multimedia information. Even more seemingly intractable problems will be posed by attempts to store virtual reality. Here the maintenance of the peripheral devices used to access and present the information will be essential.

Even where long-term access to the raw data can be guaranteed such access is unlikely to be made available to future researchers in the same way as it has been to contemporary users.[30] Valuable cultural data are contained in the record structures and the software that is used to access the resources: to sever the message from its medium of provision debases the message. This is particularly the case with virtual records. Without the original software to process the data it will be impossible to determine what kinds of (or specific) virtual records users may have created. A similar state of affairs holds with software-dependent data objects produced by geographical information systems (GIS) and computer-aided design (CAD) tools. Future generations of cultural and social historians will be interested not only in the information held in the records but in working practices and how social behaviour was conditioned by the equipment available and the working environment in which it had been used.

Software is a cultural artefact, and how it changes tells historians as much about the technological developments as it does about the interface between human and machine.[31] Current efforts to empower the end-user are typical of these developments the qualities of current software documents the transition to end-user computing. The growth in end-user computing will transform the way information is created and preserved. While the distribution of the creation and storage of information – whether text, data, or some other form (e.g. images, audio) – complicates the process of preservation the retention of software poses its own museological difficulties, which make the creation of a software archive or museum complex. Huge cost factors would be involved in developing, organising, and running such an archive, and major managerial and curatorial problems would need to be overcome.

Since the 1950s technological advances have become increasingly rapid. Hardware advances, for example, dramatically improve processing speed, storage densities and display quality. Although these advances bring benefits to users they also make earlier machines obsolete and that poses problems for archivists who wish to run hardware specific applications. The difficulties and costs associated with obtaining spare parts and trained staff make the maintaining of older generations of computer hardware in working order an impossible objective. Charles Dollar has argued that technological obsolescence is one of the most important issues archivists must face.[32] One possible way of providing future access involves the simulation of older generations of hardware on newer equipment using emulation software.[33] Simulation of older generations of hardware on newer systems offers not only a mechanism for accessing data in the way it was originally used but also gives researchers an indication as to how information could be handled in its original context.

Contemporary historians using electronic records will find themselves still dependent upon archivists, librarians and records managers when they need specialist support in the use of access mechanisms (software or hardware) as well as metadata about the sources. The need for highly specialised support staff will eventually require interactive on-line support tools so that users at one location and staff at another can support the use of data sets held at still other locations.[34] There will be a need for increased access to IT, better and more diverse 'finding aids', and new kinds of staff if researchers are to take advantage of the new virtual archives and libraries.[35] Some contemporary historians fear that digital archives will make them less independent as their access to information becomes less immediate and their dependence upon archivists and librarians as mediators between the researcher and the information sources increases.[36] Contemporary historians using conventional paper archives are already heavily dependent upon archivists for access to material and guidance in identifying and selecting sources. Digital archives will probably be liberalising by comparison because they will make access possible to a range of sources (both local and distant) simultaneously, and access in ways not possible with conventionally printed records.

Finding electronic documents and resources for contemporary history is not easy. Moissenko has sketched the vast resources which were generated in electronic form during the late Soviet period[37] but in Russia there is a lack of information about what electronic information survives and where it is. No structure is in place for gathering the data, there is no co-operation between government officials, no information exists to assist with access, and there are no statutory bodies or even adequate laws to protect machine-readable records from loss. For the history of the Soviet people during the last twenty or so years machine-readable data files are crucial. It would be foolhardy to believe that the Soviet case is unique. All over eastern Europe similar cases could be found, and a similar state of affairs probably holds elsewhere. The Netherlands, the United Kingdom, even the United States, all offer parallels involving the loss of vast amounts of machine-readable data and the difficulty of identifying what is available. Contemporary historians would also find it extremely difficult to gain access to the vast commercial data sets which hold so much data about our society.

Even once the resources have been identified and access gained concern about their authenticity and accuracy will need to be addressed. Contemporary worries about the dangers posed to the rights of individuals by incorrect information are reflected in the laws and institutions set up at national level to protect individuals against incorrect data and the consequences of errors. There can be little doubt, however, that inaccuracies in the data abound and will prove as problematic to historians as they can to us today. The distinction between privacy and confidentiality and the implications of both these concepts for electronic records must be considered. How long should records be kept confidential? Will we object in seventy-five years if our ancestors' medical records become publicly accessible? Should 'police records' enter the public domain?

What is evident is that the age of electronic records opens numerous possibilities that will enrich the understanding of contemporary culture. But, on current evidence historians of the future will be left with a large number of disconnected e-facts that will prove difficult to use. As Swade noted, historians always work with the 'residue of the past'.[38] Will a single airline reservation transaction have value to a future historian? Would it be practical to retain all airline reservations for posterity? Swamping future historians with vast amounts of digital information may impede their research as they attempt to navigate through it. Zweig has explained that, faced with the vast quantities of surviving documents in conventional archives, few historians can be comprehensive, but with an electronic archive and a toolchest filled with versatile software historians could work with digital information more exhaustively.[39] A combination of data visualisation tools and neural networks is used in the military, insurance and retailing sectors to mine information from data. These and other software tools and information technology methods will eventually be used by historians.

A certain narrowmindedness has pervaded studies of electronic information, as the focus has been predominantly on the preservation by national archives of the records of the national governments themselves. More attention needs to be paid to other records or information resources that document our culture and to a range of other institutions that produce them. Especially important are records that will allow us to give life to the many stories history can tell. Writing the history of the electronic information-rich countries at the end of the millennium could be done with dynamic resources that would offer comprehensive profiles of the political, economic, social and cultural worlds. This information might be examined using an array of software tools. Historians should not be beguiled into believing that the survival of vast quantities of data will alone provide fertile soil for the writing of history. The quality of the data (whether texts, multimedia, databases or audio), the training of historians, and the tools to investigate the data, will each continue to influence the products of research.

Information resources, once composed predominantly of alphanumeric data types, now consist of binary large objects, knowledge-intensive systems and multimedia resources. The growth of networks has made the provision of information on demand, with little regard to distance, viable and commonplace. These developments are resulting in the capture of many records of contemporary culture in an environment that by its very nature militates against the records being adequately documented, maintained and preserved. Yet electronic information offers the illusion of democratic accessibility and the promise of unprecedented opportunities for researchers wishing to work with the material in the future.

Notes

1 'Paper, paper, everywhere', *Network*, May 1993, pp. 73–80, at p. 73.
2 M. Campbell–Kelly, 'Information in the business enterprise', in Seamus Ross and Edward Higgs (eds), *Electronic Information Resources and Historians: European Perspectives* (1993).
3 Richard J. Cox, 'Readings in archives and electronic records: annotated bibliography and analysis of the literature', in Margaret Hedstrom (ed.), *Electronic Records Management Program Strategies*, Archives and Museum Informatics Technical Report 18 (1993). Updates appear at http://www2.lis.pitt.edu/~nhprc/bibtc.html
4 *History and Computing*, 4 (3), 1992; Seamus Ross and Edward Higgs (eds), *Electronic Information Resources and Historians* (1993).
5 UN Advisory Committee on the Co-ordination of Information Systems, *Management of Electronic Records: Issues and Guidelines* (1990).
6 Cf. National Academy of Public Administration, *The Archives of the Future: Archival Strategies for the Treatment of Electronic Databases* (1991); T. K. Bikson and E. J. Frinking, *Preserving the Present: towards Viable Electronic Records* (1993).
7 *Taking a Byte out of History: the Archival Preservation of Federal Computer Records*, US Congress, House of Representatives, Committee on Government Operations, House Report 101–987 (1990), p. 2.
8 R. J. Morris, 'Electronic documents and the history of the late twentieth century: black holes or warehouses – what do historians really want?' in Seamus Ross and Edward Higgs (eds), *Electronic Information Resources and Historians* (1993), pp. 307–8.
9 Seamus Ross, 'Introduction: networking and humanities scholarship', in Stephanie Kenna and Seamus Ross (eds), *Networking in the Humanities* (1995).
10 *The Economist*, 18 September 1993, p. 120.
11 'Welfare well-being', *Computing*, 20 January 1994, p. 28.
12 Bikson and Frinking, *Preserving the Present*, pp. 20–1.

13 T. K. Bikson and S. A. Law, 'Electronic mail use at the World Bank: messages from users', *The Information Society*, 9 (2), 1993, pp. 124–44.

14 1 F. 3d 1274 (D.C. Cir. 1993).

15 E.g. David Bearman, *Electronic Evidence: Strategies for Managing Records in Contemporary Organizations* (1994); Charles M. Dollar, *Archival Theory and Information Technologies: the Impact of Information Technologies on Archival Practice and Methods* (1992).

16 Michael Duchein, *Obstacles to the Access, Use and Transfer of Information from Archives: a RAMP Study* (1983).

17 Peter Horsman, 'Taming the elephant: an orthodox approach to the principle of provenance', in Kerstin Abukhanfusa and Jan Sydbeck (eds), *The Principle of Provenance*, Skrifter utgivna av Svenska Riksarkivet 10 (1994).

18 J. D. Morelli, 'Defining electronic records: a terminology problem ... or something more?' in Seamus Ross and Edward Higgs (eds), *Electronic Information Resources and Historians* (1993), p. 88.

19 C. Gränström, 'Swedish society and electronic data', in Seamus Ross and Edward Higgs (eds), *Electronic Information Resources and Historians* (1993), p. 145.

20 Rosana Andres Díaz, 'The principle of provenance and the problems of authenticity', in Kerstin Abukhanfusa and Jan Sydbeck (eds), *The Principle of Provenance*, Skrifter utgivna av Svenska Riksarkivet 10 (1994); Catherine Bailey, 'Archival theory and electronic records', *Archivaria*, 29, winter 1989–90, pp. 180–96.

21 H. Simpson, 'The management of electronic information resources in a corporate environment', in Seamus Ross and Edward Higgs (eds), *Electronic Information Resources and Historians* (1993), p. 28.

22 B. Reed and D. Roberts (eds), *Keeping Data: Papers from a Workshop on appraising Computer-based Records* (1991).

23 National Archives and Records Administration, 'Information about Electronic Records in the National Archives for Prospective Researchers', NARA General Information Leaflet 37 (1992).

24 Edward Higgs, personal communication.

25 Gränström, 'Swedish Society'.

26 National Academy of Public Administration, *The Archives of the Future*.

27 Gunnar Thorvaldsen, 'The preservation of computer-readable records in Nordic countries', *History and Computing*, 4 (3), 1992, pp. 201–5.

28 See Michael Lesk, *Preservation of New Technology: a Report of the Technology Assessment Advisory Committee to the Commission on Preservation and Access* (1992), pp. 7–9; Peter Robinson, *The Digitization of Primary Textual Sources*, Office for Humanities Communication Publications 4 (1993).

29 Some of the problems are summarised by M. Cook, 'Towards international archival data exchange: description standards', in Romulo Enmark (ed.), *Humanities Information Cultural Heritage and Humanities Research: Problems and Possibilities in the Light of New Technology*, British Library Research Report 6075 (1992).

30 D. Swade, 'Collecting software: preserving information in an object-centred culture', in Seamus Ross and Edward Higgs (eds), *Electronic Information Resources and Historians* (1993); Jeff Rothenberg, 'Ensuring the longevity of digital docu-

449

ments', *Scientific American*, 272 (1), January 1995, pp. 24–9.

31 D. Swade, 'Collecting software', in Ross and Higgs, *Electronic Information Resources* (1993).
32 Charles M. Dollar, 'New developments and the implications on information handling', in Angelika Menne-Haritz (ed.), *Information Handling in Offices and Archives* (1993).
33 But see Seamus Ross, 'Intelligent graphical user interfaces: opportunities for the interface between the historian and the machine', in G. Jaritz, I. H. Kropač and P. Teibenbacher (eds), *The Art of Communication: Proceedings of the VIIIth International Conference of the Association for History and Computing, Graz, 1993* (1995).
35 Ross, 'Introduction' to Kenna and Ross, *Networking in the Humanities*.
36 R. W. Zweig, 'Beyond content: electronic fingerprints and the use of documents', in Seamus Ross and Edward Higgs (eds), *Electronic Information Resources and Historians* (1993).
37 Tatyana Moiseenko, 'The "secondary use" of databases concerning agriculture and peasantry in contemporary Russia', in Seamus Ross and Edward Higgs (eds), *Electronic Information Resources and Historians* (1993).
38 Swade, 'Collecting software', in Ross and Higgs, *Electronic Information Resources*.
39 Zweig, 'Beyond content', p. 256.

Further reading

Kerstin Abukhanfusa and Jan Sydbeck (eds), *The Principle of Provence*, Skrifter utgiuna av Svenska Riksarkivet 10 (1994).

Charles Dollar, *Archival Theory and Information Technologies* (1992).

Margaret Hedstrom, 'Understanding electronic incunabula: a framework for research on electronic records", *American Archivist*, 54, summer 1991, pp. 334–54.

Edward Higgs and Seamus Ross (eds), *Historians and Electronic Artefacts* (forthcoming).

National Historical Publications and Records Commission, *Research Issues in Electronic Records* (1991).

Seamus Ross, 'Introduction: historians, machine-readable information and the past's future', in Seamus Ross and Edward Higgs (eds), *Electronic Information Resources and Historians* (1993).

Seamus Ross and Edward Higgs (eds), *Electronic Information Resources and Historians: European Perspectives* (1993).

Acknowledgements

Some of the arguments presented here were put earlier in Ross, 'Introduction' to Seamus Ross and Edward Higgs (eds), *Electronic Information Resources and Historians* (1993). The volume is now out of print.

Chapter 39

Electronic record keeping in the UK government and the NHS: opportunity, challenge or threat?

Edward Higgs

On the whole historians are not very interested in records in the abstract. They are fascinated by their 'own' records, and those used by their rivals, but the rather mundane world of the archivist and records manager leaves them cold. Contemporary historians take greater interest in the politics of records keeping because of the limitations placed upon them by the 'thirty-year rule' but even they are hardly thrilled by the 'life-cycle management' of files series. This helps to explain why so few historians have noted what may be described as the subdued panic in the archival community over how to handle electronic records.[1] The current access restrictions also place contemporary electronic records outwith the experience of most historians in Britain. This is a great pity, since decisions which are being taken, or shirked, in respect of such material will crucially affect the ability of historians to write the history of the coming millennia.[2]

Computers have, of course, been with us for a long time but the scale and nature of their use in UK government has been radically transformed in the last fifteen years. Confined to the use of mainframes for large-scale batch processing in the 1960s and '70s, information technology (IT) has now burst the bounds of database management and is increasingly being used for communications within and between departments via e-mail and automated office systems.[3] As with the higher education sector, Whitehall has seen the micro and distributed network replace older centralised systems. Such developments have, of course, gone much further in North America, where a study undertaken for the US Congress in 1990 concluded that by the end of the decade 75 per cent of US federal government transactions would be electronic.[4] Although the 'paperless office' has proved an illusion, the 'less-paper office', in which many important official records will be held only in electronic form, is rapidly becoming a reality.[5]

The existence of such records represents a golden opportunity for historians to study the internal workings of government agencies but they present archivists with numerous difficulties. If the latter cannot be overcome, the former will not be realised. The purpose of this chapter is to outline some of the practical and conceptual problems which electronic records pose to archivists and records managers, and what is being done in the United Kingdom and elsewhere to meet the challenges.

The challenge of electronic archives

Before doing so, however, it will be necessary to review the life cycle of a conventional paper document in Whitehall from its departmental birth to its final archival resting place under the provisions of the 1958 and 1967 Public Records Acts.[6] This is hardly an exciting exercise but it is essential if we are to understand the archival implications of the advent of the electronic record.

Government departments have traditionally been extremely hierarchical organisations with well defined internal structures. Internal branches and sub-departments tend to be fairly watertight in terms of staff and information, and often maintain their own files series organised by specialist function. External hard-copy communications or internally generated papers are filed on subject or case files within these series. When they are no longer active, such files remain in the registry and, when five years old, are subjected to a 'first review' by their creators. Essentially this means asking whether the file is needed for continued administrative use. If it is regarded as ephemeral at this point it is destroyed on the principle that it could not have been very important in the first place. A surviving file then remains in the department, or at the Public Record Office's 'limbo repository' at Hayes, Middlesex, until it is twenty-five years old. At that point it undergoes a 'second review' during which the department and the PRO apply various selection criteria to decide whether or not it should be preserved permanently in the central government archives. This two-tier process leads to the destruction of something like 98–99 per cent of all government records. The remaining files are transferred to the PRO, listed and placed in classes of records according to their administrative provenance. That is, all the records in a particular file series, reflecting the administrative structure of the originating department, are held together under a common class code. The impact of electronic record upon such a system can be summed up in terms of media impermanence, hardware and software dependence, and the split between information and functionality.

Information transmitted on good-quality paper, or better still parchment, with decent inks, will last in a readable state for centuries. The life span of electro-magnetic signals generated by computers is measured in fractions of a decade. Once in an archive such material can be preserved by keeping it in a suitable environment and periodically migrating it across storage media but the problem is getting it there. Information in hard copy on a registered file is usually seen as the property of an organisation, and destroying it is a decision which many bureaucrats shirk. Files on microcomputers are seen as personal property and are cleared out when memory is exhausted. The ease of disposal, in terms of deleting, overwriting or simply failing to save files, makes the survival of such records very precarious. Archivists cannot wait for twenty-five years to ensure preservation. This needs to be done at the point of systems design, when decisions can be taken to accommodate archival considerations in databases or e-mail systems. Can the database software output the data in a form suitable for long-term preservation, and will sufficient documentation be produced to make sense of it? Are the users of e-mail packages given convenient utilities for saving messages, and do such systems give sufficient information to allow the senders and receivers of messages to be identified in the future? Are systems set up to preserve and date multiple versions of an evolving text?

The issue here is not technology but organisational power. Archivists have traditionally dealt with dead records of comparatively little interest to the creating organisations, and, in consequence, lack organisational clout. How do they intervene at the cutting edge of corporate information strategy to impose their requirements on IT specialists, even supposing that they have the knowledge and skills necessary to talk to them in a common language? Instead, decisions on the handling of electronic records are increasingly being taken by a new breed of 'information managers' whose remit is solely the timely and efficient delivery of necessary information to organisations. One of their number has recently advocated retaining only 'the official record' from the electronic office, which means destroying all e-mail, voice mail, word-processing files and superseded drafts of correspondence. This is to prevent competitors gaining access to 'unofficial', and possibly incriminating, information which has not been sanitised by the corporate machine.[7]

One suggested solution to these problems is that data/files should be left with the organisations which created them, archives merely providing information about where they can be located.[8] In this sense the PRO's role would be superseded by that of the Historical Manuscripts Commission, which holds information on the whereabouts of paper records. The problem here is that, although one may be able to disperse data over a network, it is far less easy to disperse responsibility. Will creating institutions be willing to preserve 'dead' records over long periods of time for possible future use? Above all, will institutions themselves last long enough to carry out an archival function? In the NHS, for example, the regional tier of organisation provided a pool of computer data for general use. That tier is now being abolished and there is considerable concern that its database function will cease, and that existing data are at risk.

Such issues are complicated by the pace of electronic change and technological redundancy. One can leave a paper document quietly sitting in a filing cabinet for decades and then read it without any difficulty. Such is not the case with electronic records, where one requires hardware and software intermediaries which change every five or six years. It is questionable that commercial or government agencies will willingly hold dead files and migrate them across such systems indefinitely. Many records in the PRO are closed for 100 years because of private, medical or commercial confidentiality, and that may mean, at the current rate of technological obsolescence, migrating data across ten or fifteen different platforms before they will be used by members of the public.

The answer is, of course, to preserve data or text in a standard, software-independent format such as ASCII, but that has its own drawbacks. One can preserve the informational content of records in this manner but not necessarily their evidential value. Thus I can preserve the data in a database but not necessarily the database package which gave that database a particular functionality. How can I determine the impact that data had on decision-making if I cannot reconstruct how that data could be used in the organisation? Similarly, I can archive the text of an e-mail message without the software which delivered the message in a certain manner, and in conjunction with other messages. As software products to handle organisational work flow become more important the archiving of information passing through institutions may give only a very vague idea of organisational dynamics.[9]

Lastly, the widespread use of IT in organisations is changing their very nature. Institutions are becoming 'spaces' within which shifting task groups evolve and decay rather than organisms with obvious, and defined, organs and cells between which information flows in fixed patterns.[10] If the newly emerging 'flat' structures of companies mean that we cannot identify important communications by post holder, organisational structure or lines of responsibility, how will archivists classify and describe records to facilitate access?

The Public Record Office and electronic records

Have the central government archives had any success in meeting these challenges? The answer, regrettably, is not much. It is not for want of long-standing application. As early as the Keeper of Public Records' *Report* for 1968 we find a member of the Office's Records Administration Division 'making preliminary investigations in this field ...',[11] and this resulted in an initial survey of data sets in departments in 1970.[12] By 1974 the PRO had convinced itself that the ICL 2900 range of computers would become standard in government, and was proposing to establish a 'standard Office format' in which data would be archived on the basis of that hardware. Software was to be written to convert 'all other formats' to the PRO standard, and a programmer employed to undertake the task. It is perhaps understandable that some difficulty was experienced in recruiting such an electronic Stakhanovite![13] By 1977, not surprisingly, the Keeper's *Report* laments that 'greater difficulties than were anticipated, predominantly technical, have been encountered'.[14] After this impasse, attention shifted in the 1980s to storage media, with increasing attention being paid to the suitability of optical disk for archival purposes.[15] This led on in the early 1990s to consideration of the use of computer output to laser disk (COLD) as a means of data storage.[16] The project foundered on the difficulty of getting enough information from departments on the structure of their data sets to establish the feasibility of converting them to COLD. Archival considerations are plainly not given a high priority by government IT specialists. After a quarter of a century the PRO has still not established a machine-readable data archive.[17]

A common strand which runs through this story is concentration on IT (information technology) rather than on IM (information management). Like many British institutions, the PRO has been searching for a technological fix rather than thinking strategically about the relationship between the management of information and the archival function within electronic systems. Several very cogent reasons can be put forward for this lack of strategic vision, not least the low penetration of IT into the Office.[18] The PRO was also not well placed to undertake strategic thinking in the 1980s. Its staff and resources were cut heavily at the beginning of the decade, whilst public demand for its services rose continuously. At the same time the Records Administration Division and its successor, the Government Services Department, have had to struggle with the knock-on effects of constant upheavals in Whitehall, which have seen departments disappear, merge and move out into the private sector.[19]

Nor does the nature of archival legislation in the United Kingdom provide a suitable framework for tackling these issues. Legal structures do not guarantee success but they are the essential prerequisite for strategic action. In the United Kingdom we are subjects of the Crown, or consumers of state services at best, rather than citizens. Since the United Kingdom has no written constitution or abstract set of citizens' rights, the law does not set down individual entitlements but dictates how state bodies should act administratively. In consequence there is no freedom of information or right to know legislation, or any institution directing state record keeping as the representative of the public. Instead the PRO works under the 1958 Public Records Act, which places the responsibility for preserving records 'worthy of preservation' with quasi-sovereign departments, leaving the PRO, in practice, to offer guidance. The national archive does not issue directives, it persuades and cajoles, to greater or lesser effect.[20] At the same time, in the absence of a single department with responsibility for the running of a civil service,[21] several other bodies or post holders, such as the Cabinet Office and the 'Minister for Open Government', pursue their own agendas with regard to certain aspects of the management of public records. The overall result is the lack of a clear lead in the archives field.

Alternative forms of access

It would be incorrect to argue, however, that this story of failure has left the United Kingdom without any archiving facilities for electronic records generated by central government. Rather, *ad hoc* systems of preservation have grown up completely outwith the system set up by the 1958 Public Records Act. Some departments, such as the Department for Education, have established their own data archives to store internally produced data sets which may be of continued administrative and research use. The Office of Population Censuses and Surveys, which undertakes surveys for other government departments, holds hundreds of such commissioned data sets in electronic form. Several departments, such as the Foreign and Commonwealth Office and the Treasury, are embedding long-term storage requirements into their office automation systems. Others, such as Employment, Environment and MAFF are at least attempting to take stock of what computer databases their staff maintain. A more problematic trend has been the archiving of government data for the purposes of commercial exploitation. For example, the Ordnance Survey (OS), the state mapping body, has a remit to become self-financing from sales of its services by 1995. As such it is now storing data from other government departments on its geographical information systems (GIS), and selling them to the public on their behalf.[22]

Little of this activity reflects a desire to preserve documents in perpetuity. The 'shelf life' of such data sources is often limited by current administrative purposes, and they are culled at intervals. Much of the data, such as those held on GIS at the OS, is constantly being updated, destroying the 'historical' record. One institution, however, the ESRC Data Archive at Essex University (DA), has developed as a *de facto* place of deposit for the long-term storage of government data sets. This institution was established in 1967 by the precursor of the present Economic and Social Research Council, the government-funded body which supports higher education research in the social sciences. The DA acts as a national resource centre for data from academic, commercial and public-sector sources within the United Kingdom.[23] It currently holds 3,500 data sets, of which 15 per cent have been deposited by government departments, plus a further 4,000 opinion polls.[24] The DA has built up a close working relationship with government statisticians and IT departments, which allows it to appraise and select data sets on the basis of a wealth of experience and sensitivity to departmental needs. It is expanding its remit beyond current social and economic research, collecting, for example, historical data sets produced by historians in the course of their research. The DA is one of a number of similar national electronic research archives which are members of the International Federation of Data Organisations (IFDO) and the Council of European Social Science Data Archives (CESSDA).[25]

Taking advantage of failure?

Given the existence of this well established data archive of government data sets, there is a strong argument for not attempting to duplicate its work within the PRO. A recent consultancy report on the relative cost of using the DA, or a similar archive, as the PRO's agent for the preservation and dissemination of government data sets, as compared with setting up an in-house PRO electronic archive, revealed that considerable cost savings can be achieved through co-operation.[26] This would be analogous to the PRO's existing designation of the National Film and Sound Archives, and of local record offices, as places of deposit for films, sound recordings and public records of specifically local interest.

Even if such a relationship makes sense in financial terms, there are important cultural differences between the two organisations which would have to be overcome. First, institutions such as the DA are interested primarily in the informational, as opposed to evidential, content of data. If the data sets used by departments are inconsistent, contain errors, or are deficient in some other manner, the DA will 'clean up' the data. What is important to them is the secondary use of a data set, rather than its role as evidence of how government departments performed their responsibilities. The PRO would have to insist on having two data sets kept, one clean, the other 'dirty'. Secondly, the DA has historically collected survey-generated data sets, whilst the PRO would also want to maintain databases created in the course of administrative activity. The DA's approach to finding aids is also essentially bibliographical rather than archival. The whole issue of how one places data sets in their administrative context, including relating them to paper files in the PRO, would need to be addressed. Such institutional differences are not insurmountable, however, as can be seen from the situation in Denmark, where the Danish Data Archives recently merged with the national archives, the Statens Arkiver.[27]

A more important unresolved issue is the whole question of the treatment of the products of e-mail and automated office systems. The DA has as little experience of dealing with such material as the PRO, and its expertise in the secondary analysis of structured, sequential data may make it difficult for the institution to address the very different questions posed by automated office systems. On the other hand, hiving databases off to the DA might give the PRO the breathing space necessary to address the difficult conceptual issues associated with these types of systems.[28]

The PRO now appears to be coming to terms with its past failures and, quite sensibly, is heading down the route of establishing formal links with data archives. It has also appointed an expert in electronic information management to begin to tackle the broader issues surrounding the archiving of electronic records.

Are European patterns emerging?

An obvious question is the extent to which the situation in the United Kingdom is typical of Europe as a whole.[29] At least some European archives, including those in Finland, France, Germany, Norway, Russia and Sweden, hold electronic records, although other archives are aware of the issue. The material is almost entirely composed of databases, although the holdings of some of these archives are plainly quite large. The Bundersarchiv in Koblenz holds 737 magnetic tapes and a number of floppy disks containing personal files and social data. The Norwegians hold 900 files on 2,000 tapes, and the French 5,000 files. Perhaps the largest holdings are in Sweden, where the Riksarkivet holds about one tetrabyte of data on 11,000 reels of magnetic tape. This includes statistical and tax information from a number of central government agencies, as well as data from research projects, mainly medical in nature. Of this sub-set of institutions, four (Germany, Norway, Russia and Sweden) make electronic records available to the public. Only the Swedish and Russian archives make data available on-line.

This exercise indicates that the PRO is indeed somewhat laggardly in its approach to the electronic records issue but that no European national archive has got beyond the stage of holding the output of anything other than database systems. Many of the most interesting developments appear to be in the Scandinavian countries, which have, of course, some of the best developed legislative frameworks for information access. As yet there is no European Union-wide framework for co-operation by national archives but moves are afoot to set up a EU initiative, perhaps building on work undertaken in the Scandinavian countries.

Some archives in North America have begun to apply the principles of records management to the disposal of electronic records within government communication systems. Probably the most advanced example of such work can be found amongst the archivists of the National Archives and Records Administration in the United States.[30] Also in North America, the National Archives of Canada have been attempting to design computer software for the management of automated offices which fully meets archival standards. This application by the Canadian National Archives of the insights of information management to the needs of central government, the IMOSA (Information and Management and Office Systems Advancement) initiative, may well provide a model for future developments.

Selection v. access

A final word needs to be said on the relationship between the selection of records and access. At present archivists are still thinking in terms of the need to select electronic records for preservation. The emerging archival orthodoxy envisages the selection of documentary evidence for long-term preservation being based on prior identification by organisations of the functions, activities, and communications that are worth documenting in their own terms rather than on anticipated future demand for records. This, in turn, will reflect the needs of the 'accountable manager' within organisations.[31] Leaving aside the issue of whether this is desirable from the historical point of view, or even practicable, given the changes to organisations noted above, it is perhaps questionable whether it is necessary. With the cost of computer storage coming down, might archivists be better advised to preserve everything which moves within and across the electronic space of organisations, and shift their attention to the means of accessing such information?

It may be in this area of debate that properly informed historians can make the most impact in order to ensure that tomorrow's archives preserve a full record of today's electronic communications within government.

Notes

1 A notable exception has been Ronald Zweig, 'Virtual records and real history', *History and Computing*, 4 (3), 1992, pp. 174–82.

2 Many of the issues discussed in this chapter are dealt with at greater length in Seamus Ross and Edward Higgs (eds), *Electronic Information Resources and Historians: European Perspectives* (1993).

3 The distinction is drawn here between structured, sequential data held on a database system, such as DBase, Oracle or Paradox, and systems used to communicate and store text files via computer networks. In the latter category the MOD, for example, is experimenting with CHOTS (Corporate HQ Office Technology System), the FCO with Aramis (Automated Registry and Multi-user Information Software), and MAFF with a system with the twee acronym of Maiden (MAFF Integrated Desktop Environment for the Nineties). These developments can be followed in the journal *Government Computing*.

4 *Taking a Byte out of History: the Archival Preservation of Federal Computer Records*, Twenty-fifth Report by the Committee on Government Operations (1990), p. 2.

5 Hard-copy records received in departments can now be scanned into electronic systems using digital image processing (DIP).

6 The whole system is described in minute detail in the Public Record Office's *Manual of Records Administration*.

7 Donald S. Skupsky, 'Establishing retention periods for electronic records', *Records Management Quarterly*, April 1993, pp. 40–9.

8 David Bearman, 'An indefensible bastion: archives as a repository in the elec-

tronic age', in David Bearman (ed.), *Archival Management of Electronic Records*, Archives and Informatics Technical Report 13 (1991), pp. 16–20; Charles Dollar, *Archival Theory and Information Technologies: the Impact of Information Technologies on Archival Principles and Methods* (1992).

9 Keith Hales, 'What is production workflow management software?' in Tony Hendley (ed.), *Document Management '93: Proceedings of the Document Management Conference held in London in June 1993* (1993), pp. 190–5; David Saul, 'Going with the flow', *Document Manager*, 2 (2), June 1994, pp. 23–8. One solution here might be to establish a museum of computer software; Doron Swade, 'Collecting software: preserving information in an object-centred culture', in Seamus Ross and Edward Higgs (eds), *Electronic Information Resources and Historians* (1993).

10 Some of these issues are discussed in Helen Simpson, 'The management of electronic information resources in a corporate environment', in Seamus Ross and Edward Higgs (eds), *Electronic Information Resources and Historians* (1993).

11 *The Tenth Annual Report of the Keeper of Public Records on the Work of the Public Record Office, 1968*, p. 7. The Records Administration Division was responsible for liaison with government departments over the transfer of records to the Office.

12 *The Twelfth Annual Report of the Keeper of Public Records on the Work of the Public Record Office, 1970*, p. 9.

13 *The Seventeenth Annual Report of the Keeper of Public Records on the Work of the Public Record Office, 1975*, p. 9.

14 *The Nineteenth Annual Report of the Keeper of Public Records on the Work of the Public Record Office, 1977*, p. 9.

15 *The Twenty-seventh Annual Report of the Keeper of Public Records on the Work of the Public Record Office, 1985*, p. 11.

16 *The Thirty-third Annual Report of the Keeper of Public Records on the Work of the Public Record Office, 1991*, p. 5.

17 Recently the PRO has been co-operating with the Central Computer and Telecommunications Agency to produce some general guidance for departments with regard to the treatment of electronic archives; Andy Carty, *Requirements under the Public Records Acts when using Information Technology* (1994). The Public Record Office of Northern Ireland has issued its own guidelines for the Northern Ireland Civil Service but as yet holds no electronic records.

18 The PRO was slow to get into word-processing and is still in the stand-alone PC phase of development. It has recently established a networked system for records information but has no e-mail facilities.

19 Edward Higgs, 'Historians, archivists and electronic record keeping in UK government', in Seamus Ross and Edward Higgs (eds), *Electronic Information Resources and Historians* (1993).

20 This is in contrast, at least in theory, to the situation in Australia under the 1983 Archives Act, or in European countries such as Sweden, which had its first freedom of information legislation in 1766: Claes Gränström, 'Swedish society and electronic data', in Seamus Ross and Edward Higgs (eds), *Electronic Information Resources and Historians* (1993).

21 The Treasury has responsibility for budgetary control but does not appear very interested in 'office management'. The PRO is an agency of the Lord Chancel-

lor's Department, which is essentially responsible for the running of the courts of law and the legal system.

22   The commercialisation of the Ordnance Survey is graphically illustrated by an interview with its director, Professor David Rhind, in the June 1992 edition of *Government Computing*. Once OS has digitised all its geographical data, it will cease to publish maps in hard copy except on demand, and this has serious implications for the copyright libraries, which will no longer receive free copies as of right. This is a more general problem for libraries; Peter Vickers and John Martyn (eds), *The Impact of Electronic Publishing on Library Services and Resources in the UK* (1994).

23   Its activities are recorded in the *ESRC Data Archive Bulletin*, available from the ESRC Data Archive, University of Essex, Colchester CO4 3SQ. The DA makes data available at cost price to academics in various formats.

24   The DA's catalogue of datasets, Biron (Bibliographical Information Retrieval Online), can be accessed via Internet on biron.essex.ac.uk.

25   Descriptions of the work of such data archives in the United Kingdom, Austria, Denmark and the Netherlands can be found in Seamus Ross and Edward Higgs (eds), *Electronic Information Resources and Historians* (1993).

26   Kevin Schurer and Edward Higgs, *Possible Procedures for Handling Machine-readable Public Records* (1994).

27   Hans-Jorgen Marker, 'Data conversion at a traditional data archive', in Seamus Ross and Edward Higgs (eds), *Electronic Information Resources and Historians* (1993).

28   As far as I am aware there are no archives in the United Kingdom holding these types of administrative record, although there are a number of repositories for texts in electronic form such as the Oxford University Text Archive.

29   The following is based upon the early results of a survey undertaken by the author on behalf of the International Association for History and Computing.

30   See National Archives and Records Administration, *Managing Electronic Records*, National Archives and Records Instructural Guide series (1990); William Cunliffe and Michael Miller, 'Writing a general records schedule for electronic records', *American Archivist*, 52, summer 1989, pp. 350–6.

31   David Bearman, *Archival Methods*, Archives and Museum Informatics Technical Report 9 (1989), pp. 59–67.

Chapter 40

Multimedia, hypertexts and the contemporary historian

Lorna M. Hughes

To the historian, venturing into the realms of hypermedia or multimedia hypertext may appear to be a jargon and acronym-filled minefield. Even the most computer-literate may baulk at the prospect, fearful of wading through large amounts of technical material, talking to computer types, and spending hours of valuable research time in front of a computer learning new systems and software.

It is, however, becoming increasingly apparent that multimedia is a valuable and significant tool for the teaching of and research in almost all humanities subjects. It is also a tool which is increasingly simple to use and to develop, requiring little more than basic word-processing skills to create one's own multimedia presentations which can present historical materials in a new and interesting way.

For contemporary historians, a multimedia presentation could be used to link original materials, such as archive documents, newspapers, newsreels, film and sound archives, to secondary information, interviews, and background and historiographical materials. The intertextuality of historical material becomes apparent when presented in this way, and a source can be seen to be dependent upon other texts and materials for meaning and definition.

I should first set out to explain the terminology I shall be using, and outline the theoretical background. Multimedia is a general term which I will use to describe the associated concepts of hypertext and hypermedia. Generally speaking, hypertext refers only to textual materials; multimedia and hypermedia refer to materials which include images, film or sound.

Hypertext is a term which was first coined in the 1960s by Theodore Nelson,[1] and it means non-sequential writing. In a hypertext a piece of text is presented and stored on a computer in electronic format, having been keyed in or scanned. The text is not presented alone but linked to an associative web of other texts, illustrative materials, sound and video resources, allowing the links between such materials to be presented graphically.[2] The

462

system consists of nodes and links. A node is a unit of information which is widely variable in length or content – a word, a phrase, an image or a sound – and a link is the electronic connection between the nodes. Each node can be linked to one or more other nodes. An analogy which would be of relevance to the historian is boxed card files. Although one may be researching only one manuscript, or a few key texts, it is almost always necessary to have several boxes of cards under a variety of headings – for example, contemporary events, political and social background, translations and glossaries, etc. These all contain a wealth of background and peripheral information which is relevant to the subject, and can be cross-referenced by the linkage of ideas, themes and concepts.

The theory of hypertext has been expanded, most significantly by Landow,[3] who has described hypertext as not merely a presentation device but the use of a computer to transcend the linear, bounded, fixed and defining qualities of a traditional written text. Unlike the static form of the book, a hypertext can be composed and read non-sequentially, so that the text it contains becomes a variable structure of nodes and links. No particular order determines the order in which a text is to be read, in that the hypertext presents different options which the reader can select to follow when working within a text.

The theory is that, when working with a hypertext or a multimedia application, the reader's approach is significantly altered – conventional 'reading' and comprehension patterns apply within each block of text, or while regarding each image or film, or listening to sound, but as the reader starts to follow links from one block of text to another, new rules and experiences of the text apply. The reader is, essentially, faced with a variable text structure which can be represented on screen in different ways, according to the reader's choice of which links to follow.

It is argued that this approach fundamentally changes the experience of reading a text and the organisation of contextual information which can be peripheral to the text. The boundaries of texts become blurred when they can be embedded in peripheral information, and thus the structural constraints of texts can be removed when they are presented in this way. Readers decide which links to follow when browsing or 'navigating' a hypertext, and are therefore empowered to make choices about the way they approach a text. Thus hypertext can be seen as a method of approaching text in a new way, one which has the potential to deconstruct and reorder in a manner which can be interactive, collaborative and non-hierarchical.

A non-electronic comparison would be a footnote, where the reader would follow a clearly marked link, usually a number in superscript format, and read the text of the footnote at the bottom of the page or at the end of the book.[4] These footnote links may take the reader further, in that they may refer to another page of the same work – 'see page 123' – or they may contain a bibliographical reference to another text in the form 'see also

Smith, 1992'.

Such an example would tend to suggest that hypertext is something that most of us have used for most of our lives. The history of non-linear, non-sequential thinking is practically as long as the codex book. Any historical document one would find in a library is a hypertext, in that references have to be checked or verified by looking in dictionaries or other secondary materials. More obviously, primary materials may contain marginalia which are relevant, such as a reference which has been pencilled in as an afterthought. It may contain important information on the provenance or meaning of a document without having any immediate bearing upon the document itself. Such materials were never intended to be entirely sequential, and are always dependent upon a variety of different readings influenced by the peripheral information the reader chooses to select.

What is different about multimedia or hypermedia presentations is that they enable their creator to present all the information relevant to a particular topic in one package. Rather than a footnote telling the reader to see Smith, 1992, the text of Smith 1992 can be contained within the presentation. This can again open up links with another set of materials, which can also be included and which can allow the reader to go off at another tangent. This aspect of hypermedia is important, in that not only can the links go both ways but the link itself can take one to far more abundant and significant material than the point of origin, so that the footnote can be much longer than the thing footnoted.

There are literally hundreds of multimedia and hypertext products on the market, as technology becomes more available to the academic community, as well as easier to use. However, we can discern two general categories of development. Firstly, the hypertext archive project, where information peripheral to the subject is brought in to create a large source for reference. An example would be a multimedia presentation about World War II, containing transcriptions of archive material and perhaps newsreels, linked with historiography and background information. The second general trend of multimedia tools for the humanities is more suited to a research application, and that is the production of an electronic edition, where instead of working with archive materials to produce an edition in standard, conventionally published format a scholar can produce a hypertext. This is simply a representation of original material, such as a memoir, embedded in peripheral information with hypertext links to a full glossary and notes. The edition may contain a selection of translations, analogue material and introductory essays.

For academics looking at multimedia as a teaching tool, the prospect of having such a wealth of material all in one place for students to peruse is appealing, either when looking for new and innovative ways to teach, or when attempting to surmount difficulties encountered in the present teaching environment, such as increased student numbers, insufficient time to explore all aspects of a subject adequately, or shortage of books in the library. The hardware on which these materials can be used is relatively inexpensive, and is generally available at most academic institutions, either in a computing department or, increasingly, in humanities departments which have decided to invest in computer laboratories.

A number of universities and schools now use some multimedia packages for teaching, and they can be extremely useful in the classroom. As a hypertext, by definition, should contain almost all the materials peripheral to a subject, students can quickly be introduced to the interdisciplinary aspects of a particular topic with ease. Exercises which students can conduct in this environment can be structured by the lecturer in such a way that the pedagogical aspects of a subject can be presented within a courseware application. Materials in a hypertext or multimedia application can be linked with material presented in lectures, and represent a focus of debate in the seminar.

Generally, students enjoy using this kind of interactive, learner-centred material. If it is well designed it can be engaging, and students enjoy working in a framework which opens a subject up and enables them to see it in its widest possible context, bringing in additional material from a wide range of sources. Students working with a multimedia application would be exposed to a variety of items they might never see if simply given a bibliography and sent to find the materials in the university library. Convenience and accessibility are generally extremely important to students.

The problem many academics face in adopting this material, however, is that a number of multimedia packages created by commercial software companies have been of poor quality. When assessing such materials for use in teaching, it is important to establish that they are well researched and pedagogically sound. A good many are not, certainly at the advanced level where specialist knowledge is required. This is logical, in that the commercial designers aim at the largest sector of the market, which is the general, introductory level. Whereas there may be great demand for a multimedia presentation on the origins of World War II, a multimedia CD-ROM entitled 'The economic reconstruction of post-World War II western Europe' will have limited appeal. Therefore it becomes necessary for academics who wish to work with the material to produce their own multimedia applications.

This prospect is not as daunting as it sounds. Hypermedia authoring systems have been developed to work on desktop IBM-compatible or Macintosh machines using minimal system requirements. They have also become easier and more intuitive to use, freeing authors from the burden of programming and allowing them to concentrate on the intellectual aims of the links being demonstrated.

Authoring is simply the process of assembling a number of different media into a cohesive package, and putting in links between them. Media are digitised in a number of ways, and the tools to do so are increasingly accessible. Text can be keyed in or scanned, or it can be obtained from on-line archives of electronic texts.[5] Graphics can be scanned, or created using a painting or drawing program. It is also possible to take photographs which can be developed directly to disk or CD-ROM. Sound can be captured by using sound capture and sampling software. Video or film can be acquired by using hardware and software add-ons such as video overlay cards, although using film presents technical difficulties, as a great deal of computer memory is reqired to store film in a digitised format. However, compression techniques can get around the problem to a certain degree.

In terms of hardware platforms required for developing multimedia tools using the above techniques, the Macintosh computer was originally in the forefront owing to its ability to handle graphics and sound with ease. However, with the advent of the multimedia PC (MPC) there has been an equalising of the capacity of each platform. In general, most computer systems purchased today will support the development of multimedia, as long as they have a CD-ROM drive, video capacity, a sound card, a high-resolution colour monitor and as much RAM as possible – 4 MB is really the bare minimum, and at least 8 MB is strongly recommended. Hardware peripherals which are useful include scanners and OCR (optical character recognition) software, for text and image capture.

Authoring systems have become increasingly user-friendly. Some examples which have been used successfully in the development of multimedia packages for the humanities are Authorware Professional (for Macintosh and PC-compatible), HyperCard (for Macintosh), Microcosm, Toolbook and Guide (for PC-compatible machines only).[6] There is wide disparity in the ease of use and learning curve associated with these applications, but they are all capable of producing high-quality multimedia packages. The end product can be stored and used on a CD-ROM, a computer network, or even made available for wider use over the Internet or the World Wide Web.

There are some pitfalls in multimedia development, which are worth considering before embarking on a time-consuming project. Naturally the process calls for a certain degree of technical ability (or at least the ability to explain the idea and scope of the project to someone with the requisite technical expertise) but more important is the ability to plan and design multimedia packages carefully. The process requires a significant investment in terms of time and resources, and so the navigation of the multimedia application requires considerable thought in advance of actually starting the project. This is made more difficult by the fact that the very quality that makes multimedia so appealing, that is, its ability to include a vast number of materials in different formats which do not follow a structure predetermined by the author makes it a challenging environment to design within. The paradox is that, in order for the multimedia *user* to be free to associate creatively and to explore all the links possible in a hypertext framework, the hypertext *designer* has to design the system meticulously in a very ordered fashion, resisting the temptation to put in links between every imaginable topic. Even in the smallest hypertext it is possible to succumb quickly to the phenomenon known as being Lost in Hyperspace.[7] In terms of designing a hypertext for either teaching or research uses, this is best avoided by keeping to a simple structure, studying examples of what has been done before, and taking advice from experts.

Another problem to be considered is that of copyright. As multimedia brings together materials from a large variety of sources, it is important to be aware of the legalities of working with the different media. Different laws affect the copyright of text, music and pictures. The way in which copyright law affects multimedia development is a rather grey area, in that multimedia is a new means of publishing which is entirely different from paper-based publishing. As such, a lot of copyright principles pertinent to multimedia have not been tested in court. The nature of computer-based material, which is stored in electronic format, makes it difficult to prevent unlawful copying. Generally, if a multimedia product is to be used for educational purposes only, at the institution it was created at, without being sold for any kind of profit, copyright is not a problem. However, it is always wise to try ensure either that materials used are in the public domain (all materials in electronic text archives, for example, are in the public domain – but not those on CD-ROM, like newspapers) or that copyright has been cleared officially at the start of the project.

One of the biggest drawbacks, and the one which prevents most academics from engaging in multimedia development, is the time it takes to use the materials, and the time it takes to learn the skills necessary for creating teaching materials. This is a very valid concern, but help is available. There are a number of potential allies on most campuses, in computing services or humanities computing centres, and multimedia development projects are increasing in number at universities.[8] Multimedia is also something which can save time in the long term, by creating a teaching tool that will facilitate effective teaching and possibly improve communication and interaction with students, who are responsive to learning with multimedia. As such, it may turn out to be a positive use of time invested.

A more insidious concern is that this kind of material can be hard to evaluate, both in terms of its success as a teaching tool and as a means of presenting academic research. The critical vocabulary for assessing it has yet to be defined adequately. For example, one must not just assess the extent to which the worth of an edition or presentation of primary source material has increased – in that not just the quality of the transcription or apparatus of commentary or glossaries around the source is now to be taken into account; one must also assess the value added by the electronic presentation of the commentaries and the ease of access to the material. There are a number of issues inherent in electronic outputs, down to simple matters of quoting and reference. There really are no adequate guidelines on how it is to be done when the text is a presented not as a book but as a hypertext edition. This matters a great deal to academics, who see the production of a written article rewarded but not the creation of a hypertext.

Thus far I have referred to multimedia only as something which is created and disseminated on a desktop machine on CD-ROM or disk, or on a local network or in the classroom. However, there is a wealth of multimedia available worldwide, in an easy-to-use format which can be browsed from a desktop machine using very simple software. It is available on the Internet, or World Wide Web (WWW). The World Wide Web is a notional entity, a term which describes a huge amount of material on computers all around the world which have been given addresses in a standard format. The information can be browsed as a hypertext, following links from one document to another, but the difference is that these documents may be on computers at opposite sides of the world.

Until very recently the academic world regarded the Internet with a degree of benign suspicion. It was perceived as the preserve of the world's largest functioning anarchy, of dubious discussion lists and newsgroups. Recently, however, this attitude has begun to change, for two reasons. Browsing tools such as Mosaic and Netscape have been developed which make navigating the huge amount of material available on the Internet a relatively painless task, and also make it possible to integrate sound, image and film into these materials. Secondly, HTML (Hypertext Mark-up Language) has been developed as a very simple means of putting information on the World Wide Web. HTML offers ease of use which allows anyone with no more than the basic computing skills which facilitate word-processing to create hypertext documents and put them up on the World Wide Web. It is becoming increasingly common for academics to develop their own home pages containing information relevant to their specific area of research. These home pages can be created easily, allowing lecturers or teachers to make available materials which can be used by students. Course descriptions, linked with bibliographies and reading lists, are the most obvious materials which can be put on-line for easy access by students, but as the global potential of the Internet becomes apparent, more and more people are creating home pages devoted to their own sphere of interest, putting research materials and articles on the World Wide Web. Multimedia teaching tools created at one institution could easily be mounted on the World Wide Web and used as course materials at another University elsewhere in the world. Multimedia courses can be run globally, with a limitless classroom. The World Wide Web also affords possibilities of instant publishing, using newly available presentation tools.[9] Academics should bear in mind the issue of copyright, but nonetheless, the WWW could be used to make several categories of publication available to a very wide audience.[10] Preprints could be exchanged with colleagues for comment. Paraprints would no longer be a problem, in that illustrations too numerous to include in a printed publication could be included on a Web site, with a footnote in the printed text directing the reader to the home page which contains the images. Out-of-print materials could be reissued on the Internet.

Harnessing the potential of the World Wide Web, multimedia can be seen as something which is simple to use, which integrates certain basic principles common to all academics, and which has benefits for all if used carefully and selectively to open up research to a wider audience.

Notes

1 Nelson wrote extensively on the subject, and his ideas are outlined in his 1980 work, *Replacing the Literary Word: a complete Literary System*. It describes his idea of a universal hypertext repository for everything which ever has been or will be written, enabling the links between all written work to be explored. So far this project is still at the beta stage.

2 See L. M. Hughes and S. D. Lee, *CTI Centre for Textual Studies Resources Guide* (1994), p. 37.

3 See Paul Delaney and George Landow, *Hypermedia and Literary Studies* (1994), p. 3.

4 See M. Deegan, N. Timbrell and L. Warren, *Hypermedia in the Humanities* (1992).

5 Electronic archives are repositories of freely available machine-readable text which has been prepared by other scholars, usually as a spin-off from a research project. As such, they are eclectic in the nature of the texts they contain, and more obscure texts are not usually well represented. Examples include the Oxford Text Archive (for further information, e-mail archive@vax.ox.ac.uk) and the Electronic Text Centre at the University of Virginia (e-mail: etext@virginia.edu). There are also a number of archives devoted to historical data, a full account of which can be found in K. Schurer (ed.), *A Guide to Historical Datafiles in Machine-readable Format* (1992).

6 For a full review of all of these authoring systems see Hughes and Lee, *Resources Guide* pp. 37 ff.

7 See J. Nielson, *Hypertext and Hypermedia* (1990), p. 133.

8 Some examples of externally funded projects which support humanities academics with the use of computers in teaching and research include the Computers in Teaching Initiative Centre for Textual Studies at Oxford University, the CTI Centre for History at Glasgow University, the Ultralab project at Anglia University and the Hypertext Support Unit at the University of Kent.

9 For example, Adobe Acrobat Pro will enable printed materials to be mounted on the WWW in their original format, losing no formating at all.

10 See, for example, the home page of James O'Donnell at the University of Pennsylvania, at http://www.upenn.edu/jod/teachdemo.

Further reading

D. I. Greenstein, *A Historian's Guide to Computing* (1994).

G. Landow (ed.), *Hypertext Theory* (1994).

T. Munck and E. Mawdsley, *Computing for Historians: an Introductory Guide* (1993).

J. Nielson, *Hypertext and Multimedia: the Internet and beyond* (1994).

K. Schurer and S. J. Anderson, *Guide to Datafiles held in Machine-readable Form* (1993).

Chapter 41

CD-ROM and the historian: information technology and the writing of history

Brian Brivati

Any study in any art or science (except computer science) which exalts the computer is a rather self-conscious study, more concerned with admiring its own method than with its discipline. To the extent that the computer is mentioned, it should be discussed only as part of the method used to solve the problem.[1]

Like it or not, the dominant mode of 'doing history' in all its forms has changed, is changing and will change at ever increasing speed. The reason for this change is an historical one, namely a change in the dominant technology of the society in which we work and to which we must as effective historians relate our work.[2]

In fifty years' time I am writing a chapter on the leadership election of the five times Prime Minister Tony Blair, the longest serving PM of the last two centuries. After I have saved all the newspaper articles written on the election on to my workstation at home I tap into the university's CD-ROM archive of British Political Papers. Entering the Blair, Prescott and Beckett collections I select all I need and transfer them across the wires on to my machine. I then search for and download the abstracts of every major academic journal article written on Blair and in turn search these for specific mention of the election. I call up the National Musuem of Labour History electronic warehouse and sort through the copies of the hard disk of the Walworth Road computer. I find a full range of internal NEC minutes and correspondence from the leader's and acting leader's office. I take a quick look through the PREM files at the PRO to see if there any skeletons worth chasing: I copy a couple of PREM files and a couple from Sir Terry Burns, the Cabinet Secretary in the first Blair government. Finally I enter the national life story/ICBH multimedia witness archive and copy all the sections of interviews with the participants that I need, retaining sound and vision for the added flavour of the time. I now have an archive on my computer of the leadership election, comprising text, sound and vision from four different archives. The process has taken a couple of days, cost a couple of thousand pounds for the external archives, and generated many thousands of pages of evidence, all without my having to leave the house.

Each time a new technology comes along people say, 'This is the end of the book,' or the end of good writing. The book, the written word, will never be replaced as the primary medium of historical communication, because the computer is based on communicating the written word. We must therefore be concerned with the general impact of information technology on the written word, in two respects. First the danger that the speed with which information can be accumulated will replace the accumulation of knowledge. Second the danger that the capacity for accumulating facts will eliminate the time for reflection on those facts. In turn, our concern should extend to an acute awareness of the importance of audio, electronic and visual sources in the study of the late twentieth century. The demands of the late twentieth century are such that if we do not maximise the use of technology in the preservation of sources derived from technology, in a coherent way, insisting on the highest standards of editorial and academic control, the historical profession and the archivists of the future will curse us – a case powerfully argued in Chapters 38 and 39. One form of information technology that can usefully work with text, sound and vision is the CD-ROM; it is used here as an illustration of the problems and the possiblitites.

Computerised information

All computer information is stored in the form of bits, binary digits that have two states, 0 or 1 (or on/off). A bit is represented magnetically by a positive or negative charge held on the surface of the storage medium, written and detected by a read head that passes close enough to the surface to detect or change the polarity beneath it. ROM (read-only memory) devices have data permanently inscribed on the surface through a manufacturing process known as mastering.

The basic unit of computer storage is a byte. One byte represents a single character (letter, numeral, symbol). Storage capacity is measured in terms of megabytes (mb). A megabyte is over one million bytes. As an example, one average A4 page of single-spaced typing contains about 2,500 characters or bytes. One megabyte of storage will hold 400 such A4 pages. An average PC has a hard disc of up to 100 megabytes – giving a storage capacity of 40,000 A4 pages. A single CD-ROM has a capacity of 650 mb. That is enough to store 250,000 typed sheets of A4 paper.[3]

Some of the operations described in the flight of fancy about the Blair election, above – the abstracting and the newspapers, for example – are already possible. The ICBH-PRO CD-ROMs are also available. CD-ROM is already opening up many new ways of doing history. However, most of the focus and interest so far have been on images. For instance, from November 1993 the National Gallery has featured the Micro Gallery, a complete illustrated catalogue 'of probably the most comprehensive art collection in the world up to the modern era'- on CD-ROM for £50. And, according to the *Times* report, 'Microsoft is approaching collections in the United States now, but none of them have done the essential work the National had done with its Micro Gallery. The eventual dream, shared by Mr Gates as well many gallery directors and art academics, is of a world-wide database which can be linked to home-based systems to give access to information on millions of works of art around the world.'[4]

To date, there has been less concern or discussion about the implications of this technology for text storage and retrieval. There is still marked reluctance on the part of historians and government departments, despite the work of the PRO, to take electronic and, to a lesser extent, broadcasting archival practice sufficiently seriously, as Edward Higgs has written and argues in this book:

> Historians are used to asking questions about the closure of paper records, and some are actively interested in the preservation of historical data sets. There has been almost no concern expressed, however, about the implications of automated office systems for future research methodologies. This, of course, may be the proverbial 'chicken and egg' situation, in that historians in this country have not had the opportunity to use such electronic text sources, and have therefore failed to address the issues involved. One might be rather less charitable and argue that the lack of interest reflects a general lack of computer awareness.[5]

Once the historians have become aware of the technology, there is often an apprehensive phase when it is first used. That moment of hesitation is natural and important. The feeling generated in that moment recurs quite frequently when working with technology: when the system crashes, when the edits are lost, when you cannot read the file, etc. Moreover, working directly with and through the technology, a point discussed in more detail later, can run counter to the intuition and the training of the historian. Part of what makes an historian – a prerequisite for doing the job – is feeling a thrill at the experience of working in an archive. It is a 'touchy-feely-thing'. Opening a box file, smelling the dust, seeing the exact order the papers were deposited in – assuming, of course, that the archivist was any good – noting the slips of previous researchers amid the papers, opening the wrong file and finding a treasure trove, spending the day reading irrelevant but ultimately revealing family correspondence when you should have been doing something else, playing detective through the index, seeing things on spec, waiting for the files to arrive – are part of the magic of historical research. So long as technology is the tool rather than the source, all these joys and frustrations remain; they also provide thinking time, digesting time, time for reflection and time for connections to be made. The danger, for contemporary historians, is being swamped by the march of data: old ways of running archives ensure that the process is slow, cumbersome, reflective and smells and feels like history.

Technology and the historian

In most conventional instances the technology is between the historian and the evidence: in word-processing or data-base work. The computer is simply a tool. In this case the technology is a glorified pen or abacus; it is designed to help the historian think and calculate; it enters the research process after or during interaction with historical evidence. When we talk of history and computing we do not generally mean this kind of interaction. We generally mean that the PC's intervention in the process is much more intrusive. Perhaps even determining the area and directions of research to an extent, certainly influencing the nature of the findings. This is crucially important: it has not replaced the direct interaction between the historian and the text but the PC has become more intrusive than a simple tool. In the case of CD-ROM the computer and the source are one and the same. The computer is the tool for analysing and the archive itself. The possibility therefore exists that the computer, and what is available to be read and manipulated by the computer, will begin to determine the parameters of a research project. The possibility exists that the highly pressured student or academic will allow their research agendas to be governed by what can be easily accessed through a desk-top computer. A simple example of this danger is the construction of a literature search using the CD-ROM guides to journal abstracts. There is a growing tendency to assume that the abstracts are universal in their coverage when they are in fact selective. There is also very limited guidance offered to students on the construction of meaningful search terms to ensure that all possible articles are listed. Unless and until all journals are abstracted the CD-ROM must be the first but not the only port of call. For contemporary historians, faced with the sheer volume of material to be consulted, the temptation to rely on what can be easily accessed could be overwhelming.

The current generation of historians has been brought up on computers, as future generations will be. The use of on-line/on screen work has also drastically changed, as John Diamond has written in the *Guardian*:

> There used to be two major impediments to reading books on screen: the first was the quality of the screens and the second portability: you couldn't take a computer to bed with you. Nowadays the high-resolution screen is much more common and laptop computers aren't that much bigger than many books ... So I'm starting to wonder whether young people who are used to reading large blocks of print on screen might be less resistant to the idea of the laptop novel after all.[6]

The historians who have thus far been resistant to the use of CD-ROM and other IT in research may well be a dwindling band. However, problems with historical computing persist. As Daniel Greenstein has argued:

> ... despite repeated calls to integrate methodological and technical discussion with consideration of broader historical problems, computer-literate historians have consistently failed to do so. There is a further irony in this. That is, that methodologically sophisticated historians, so conscious of the past, have been so unconscious of the history of ideas which shapes the intellectual environment in which they work and to which they contribute.[7]

He concludes with the hope that this was only a temporary blindness, that the agenda would move back to focus more directly on the questions that needed asking and answering and less on the ways available to answer them. This highlights a central area of debate, and perhaps the real opportunity for a technology like CD-ROM. The main case for the CD-ROM is its use as a text storage and retrieval mechanism that is simple to use, allows non-computer-literate people access to huge quantities of primary material that can be manipulated in simple or in complex ways and is a positive aid to the research process of writing good history – not of developing good software or being concerned only with methodology. This could represent a considerable departure from the way history and computing has developed so far. It could mean information technology firmly embracing those whom Edward Higgs[8] describes as the hermeneutic historians – what we might call the word crafters – as well as those on the social science history side – what we might call the number crunchers.

The CD-ROM

The friendly interface, the textual basis and the accessibility of the CD-ROM could be a central part of this broadening of the community of historical computing. The shift from number crunching/social science history towards word crafting history will be enhanced by the advent of this technology. Once hooked, the word crafters will find new and interesting ways of utilising the technology. Among British political papers, the scope for the creation of electronic forms of the most heavily used collections seems to be vast, possibly cost-effective and certainly desirable. The application of the technology to other fields would be even more desirable – not least, simply to keep the papers in this country.

The scale of the kind of material that might be suitable is huge: the scale of that which would actually be useful to most historians is much narrower. For the historian facing the demands of the research assessment exercise, or the student facing a deadline, not all documents are of equal value, whereas to the archivists all documents must be of equal value because of the intrinsic value of these 'survivals from the past' and because we cannot judge the interests of future historians. This is the central question that the possibility of the creation of electronic archives poses: where should our priorities lie? In the as yet small area of CD-ROM the market currently decides which collections come out on CD-ROM and the extent of editorial/academic control of them. Already some ill considered things have appeared and there are serious questions about editorial control, academic quality and claims of universality that need to be addressed. Part of this highlights the intellectual difference between historians and archivists, and between both those groups and some of the people now becoming involved in electronic publishing. Yet the challenge of CD-ROM technology cannot be ignored.

> Never before have historians been offered the opportunity to control their material, to construct their own rules for manipulating the sources, to concatenate and rearrange the chance survivals of the past, in quite the way we do. Hitherto, the historian has been at the mercy of time and often, too, at the mercy of others whose task it is to collate, select, edit and prepare: the editor, the bibliographer and archivist.[9]

There are clearly two ways of viewing the advent of electronic archives. One sees it as a source of hope, the other as a source of worry.

The hope is that the speed of access, and the power of the search and retrieval techniques, will take a great deal of the drudgery out of research. Already the CD-ROM editions of the major national newspapers have cut down the amount of time the contemporary historian working on the 1990s has to spend wading through mircofilm and old hard copy. Once the heavily used PRO releases have been published on CD-ROM for a few years they will also be a useful source – of even more use would be the indices and the current guide. As the mass of material available develops, so new ways of manipulating the material will develop. New branches and styles of history will open up. Increasingly text and images will be combined and a new kind of historical source will develop. One can envisage a text, audio and visual version of the Thatcher memoirs or the Tony Benn diaries, with a considerable amount of additional reference material. Such developments and more straightforward private paper conversions into electronic format, will influence the nature of historical writing and change the way in which the historical imagination of the future will be formed. However, there will always be sources that are not being heavily used enough to warrant rekeying or scanning; and there will always be a role for a 'classical' training in research techniques. The optimistic view must be that in fifty years' time the use of electronic archives either on-line or from CD-ROMs in the research process will be as accepted as the use of the personal computer for writing is today. Further, that the speed of electronic source gathering will, on balance, free more time for thought and reflection, and will therefore improve the quality of the history that is published – be it social science or hermeneutic history. Perhaps any such divide will wither away.

There is also a deeply pessimistic view of the future. Each of these developments entails worry as well as hope. Empathy is not a popular word among historians today but no one can write history without an element of feeling for the subject and the individuals concerned – a passion about the ideas or an overwhelming sense of curiosity. Empathy is a virtue in historical writing and not a vice. It is built of small things: of handwritten notes, of glimpses of the ordinary humanity behind the historical facade: it is built up in the direct interaction between the evidence and the historian. John Clive defined Macaulay's historical credo as 'interesting the affections and presenting pictures to the imagination'. He wanted the historian to become 'the bard or poet of the age, reconciling reason and imagination. History was a branch of literature. Historians were to learn from novelists'.[10] The fear is that if the technology is used to its fullest capacity, and continues to grow and develop as it has done up to now, we shall see the end of historical writing as an art and the continued expansion of the art of historical train-spotting. That in the very speed of search and retrieval we will see the accumulation of a mass of evidence and a passion for the process of acquiring information, less time for thought and crafting: 'Quantity has been transmuted into quality'.[11]

A further danger is that the process of the technology may replace intelligent thought: there is the possibility that it will reduce rather than enhance the level of care and attention: for checking things quickly it is obviously very good but, as Paul Fisher has said in the *Sunday Times*, the possibility of the train-spotting approach is also very real:

> At Nimbus Records I spent 30 seconds doing the kind of thought-free fact-studded criticism that would once have earned a Mid-West doctorate. With Jane Austen's *Sense and Sensibility* in the CD-ROM drive I typed in four words and got the following scores: Sense 29, Sensibility 9, Elinor (the sensible one) 586, Marianne 449. The statistics prove Austen more concerned with sense than sensibility, a rather obvious conclusion, but the starting point for a good argument.[12]

There are two ways in which CD-ROM technology will be used in the area of historical records: the preservation and dissemination of historical collections already in existence and the preservation and dissemination of historical records that we are currently creating. As the use of CD-ROMs becomes ever more widespread there will be a number of implications: the opening up of historical computing to historians who prefer crafting words to crunching numbers, the effect of the production of huge volumes of information on the quality of the words that are crafted, greater access by institutions of higher education directly to primary material and the potential this has for growth in research. In respect of the research and writing process there is an optimistic view which says that technology will free more of the historian's time for thought and a pessimistic view which says that the contemporary historian, already swamped by information, will be overtaken by it and quantity of output will become the measure of success rather than quality. It is too early yet to choose between fear and hope, but the warning signs of the final demise of history as an art are clear to see.

Notes

1 Marshall Smelser and William I. Davisson, 'The historian and the computer: a simple introduction to complex computation', Essex Institute of Historical Studies, 54 (2), 1968, quoted by Daniel Greenstein, 'A matter of method', *History and Computing*, 2 (3), 1990, p. 210.
2 R. J. Morris, 'Editorial', *History and Computing*, 1 (1), 1989, p. 2.
3 Technical information from Robin Williamson of Context Ltd.
4 *Times*, 19 November 1993.
5 Edward Higgs, 'Historians, archivists and electronic record-keeping in UK government', in Seamus Ross and Edward Higgs (eds), *Electronic Information Resources and Historians: European Perspectives* (1993), p. 46
6 *Guardian*, 4 October 1993.
7 Daniel Greenstein, 'A matter of method', *History and Computing*, 2 (3), 1990, p. 210.
8 Higgs, 'Historians, archivists', p. 38
9 Deian Hopkin, 'The politics of historical computing', *History and Computing*, 1 (1), 1989, p. 45.
10 John Clive, 'Amusement and instruction: Gibbon and Macaulay', in *Not by Fact Alone*, (1990), p. 79.
11 Walter Benjamin, 'The work of art in the Age of Mechanical Reproduction', in *Illuminations* (Fontana, 1973), p. 232.
12 *Sunday Times*, 19 July 1992.

Appendix 1

Useful addresses

British Library National Sound Archive
29 Exhibitions Road
London SW7 2AS

Sound and Image Collection
National Library of Wales
Aberystwyth
Dyfed SY23 3BU

BBC Written Archive Centre
Caversham Park
Reading RG4 8T

Mass-Observation Archive
University Library
University of Sussex
Brighton BN1 9QL

British Film Institute
21 Stephen Street
London W1P 1PL

Public Record Office
Ruskin Avenue
Richmond TW9 4DU

CTI Centre for Textual Studies
Oxford University Computing Service
13 Banbury Road
Oxford

Contemporary Japan Centre
University of Essex
Wivenhoe Park
Colchester CO4 3SQ

Institute of Communication Studies
University of Leeds
Leeds LS2 9JT

Public Policy Research Unit
Queen Mary and Westfield College
University of London
Mile End Road
London E1 4NS

Institute of Contemporary British
History
Room 357, Senate House,
Malet Street,
London WC1E 7HU

British Library of Political and
Economic Science
London School of Economics
Houghton Street
London WC1A 2AE

Royal Commission on Historical
Manuscripts
Quality House
Quality Court
Chancery Lane
London WC2A 1HP

Institute of Historical Research
Senate House
Malet Street
London WC1E 7HU

Education Section
Embassy of the People's Republic of
China
11 West Heath Road
Hampstead
London NW3 7UX

British-Taiwan Cultural Institute
44 Davies Street
London W1Y 2BL

Appendix 2

The Institute of Contemporary British History

The Institute of Contemporary British History was founded in September 1986 to stimulate research into, and historical analysis of, the years since 1945, which will be of value to decision-makers, students and the wider public. Since then the Institute has undertaken an ever-increasing range of activities in furtherance of that aim. In the process the Institute has not only acquired an enviable reputation for the quality of the conferences, publications and research it has promoted but has become a valuable source of advice and information both for researchers and for those with a general interest in post-war British history.

The Institute fills an important gap in British life. Post-war historians, undertaking a careful examination of all available evidence in a variety of important areas, deserve an organisation dedicated to the dissemination of their work and their conclusions. Politicians, civil servants, business people, students and the general public deserve the opportunity to find out about the latest research into the history which has most affected their lives. For the future the Institute is helping in the collection and preservation of evidence. The Institute is strictly non-political and has recruited a balanced and authoritative team of trustees and advisers to guarantee its standards. Being an independent registered charity, the Institute receives no funding from government or university sources. It relies entirely on donations, sponsorship and income generated from its conferences, journals and books.

The on-going activities of the Institute include:

- Research which seeks to illuminate hitherto unexplored aspects of post-war British history.
- Academic conferences including a summer school, a week-long event in which different days are devoted to different aspects of recent British history.
- Academic symposia and witness seminars (which draw on participants' memories to examine a major event or theme in recent history). The

Institute is also the co-organiser of a seminar series on twentieth-century British politics and administration held at the Institute of Historical Research, London, during term time.

- Sixth-form conferences on politics and history.
- *Contemporary Record:* a journal on post-war British politics and history.
- *Modern History Review:* an educational journal for sixth-form and undergraduate historians.
- Making Contemporary Britain, a series of overviews of themes and events in post-war British history published by Basil Blackwell.
- An information service on sources, archives, on-going research and other activities in the field of twentieth-century British history. The Institute is now a centre to which postgraduates are referred by their academic supervisors and to which people seeking publication of their articles turn for guidance. The Institute already plays a valuable role in British academic life which you, as a Friend, could be helping to support.

For further information about the Institute, please write to the Secretary, Institute of Contemporary British History, Institute of Historical Research, Room 357, Senate House, Malet Street, London WC1E 7HU Tel: 0171 436 2478; Fax: 0171 436 2480; e-mail: ICBH@SAS.AC.UK.

Index